THE BFI COMPANION TO HORROR

D1438354

The
BFI Companion
to Horror

Edited by
Kim Newman

Foreword by
Ramsey Campbell

CASSELL

First published in 1996 by
Cassell
Wellington House
125 Strand
London WC2R 0BB
and the
British Film Institute
21 Stephen Street
London W1P 2LN

The British Film Institute exists to promote
appreciation, enjoyment, protection and development of moving image culture in and throughout
the whole of the United Kingdom. Its activities
include the National Film and Television Archive;
the National Film Theatre; the Museum of the
Moving Image; the London Film Festival; the
production and distribution of film and video;
funding and support for regional activities; Library
and Information Services, Stills, Posters and
Designs; Research, Publishing and Education; and
the monthly *Sight and Sound* magazine.

British Library Cataloguing-in-Publication Data
A catalogue record for this book is available from
the British Library.

ISBN   0 304 33213 5
        0 304 33216 X   pbk

Cover design by Jamie Tanner

Design and typesetting by Ronald Clark

Printed and bound in Great Britain by
Butler and Tanner, Frome, Somerset

FRONTISPIECE Bela Lugosi, *Dracula* (1930)

Foreword

'It's what we try to get away from throughout our lives.'

Thus Boris Karloff once defined horror, and one can imagine that mournful voice pronouncing the words from the depths of his grave. How right he was! A history of the horror genre could be written that was nothing but a series of rejections, of films in particular: the mounting media outrage at the early horror films of Karloff and Lugosi, compared in *The Times* to slaughters in the Roman arena; the British ban on imported horror films throughout the Second World War; the revival of disgust at the Hammer horrors, at Michael Powell's richest film, *Peeping Tom*; at *Psycho*; the nastiness which greeted the availability of horror films on video . . . Perhaps it's a matter for regret more than wonder that so many of the people who have contributed to the genre have attempted to deny it. But horror won't allow them to get away. They're in here with the rest of us.

So Anthony Hopkins's Hannibal Lecter is celebrated, though he later expressed his penitence at having portrayed the character so thoroughly. Here are other actors without whom the field would be much poorer, even if they haven't always let themselves admit it: Barbara Steele, who wished for a while that filmgoers would associate her more with Fellini; Christopher Lee, followed by a shadow that resembles a cloak (as the cinema's most authoritative and aristocratic Dracula, he should expect no less). Here's Freddie Francis, and here are his comments to *Sight and Sound* not many years ago: 'The main reasons I got out of the horror genre were first that I never wanted to get into it in the first place . . . and second . . . all these horror film festivals . . . most of these people were only interested in horror – not just horror films, but horror pure and simple. Well, you know, that wasn't for me, I'm not a weirdo at all.'

Nor, I'm sure, are most of our readers or indeed the folk listed herein. Perhaps we may imagine faint cries of surprise from some of those hauled aboard, though the genre has often been well served by artists who rise to it from elsewhere. (Robert Aickman was fond of pointing out how many prolific writers are remembered only for the ghostly tale or handful of such tales they wrote.) They may find themselves sharing a page with specialists in the field, the careers of some of whom display one drawback of specialisation. Lugosi was unable to lose his famous accent in order to gain wider work, and the genre has weighed down others too: Dwight Frye, even Peter Cushing; Lon Chaney Jr, whose career pretty well sums up this tendency. Indeed, however much Clive Barker declares himself *fantastique*, his fantasy aimed at every age of reader goes straight to the horror shelves of bookshops to join his early work. Perhaps that's the way of genres; after all, you'll find P.D. James's science fiction novel nowhere other than on the crime shelves.

Yet would most of our gathering want to be excluded from it? Not the present writer, I assure you. Not from such a varied assembly; not when so much of the material dealt with has enriched my imagination, nor when I've had so much fun with other films that are in. Horror will always be with us, and as long as we are allowed to dream it will be a part of fiction. However much it may be ignored or vilified, the truth is that as a way of seeing it has never been more important than now. It is everywhere in the arts, and no longer capable of being dismissed as a marginal genre. This book not only provides a succinct guide; it demonstrates how considerable the scope of the field has become. You can't get away from that, I'm afraid.

Ramsey Campbell
Wallasey, Merseyside
17 August 1996

This book is dedicated to those unsung many who gave time, information and resources, making it as detailed as it is. Besides the contributors, this list includes but is not exclusive to Mike Ashley, Pete Atkins, Nicholas Barbano, Eugene Byrne, John Charles, Ronald Clark, Jonathan Clements, John Clute, Nancy Kilpatrick, Lisa Morton, Markku Salmi, Millie Simpson, Lance 'Squiddie' Smith and Tise Vahimagi. Most especially, this is for Maitland McDonagh, who was the first to turn in her copy and practically the only contributor (not excluding the editor) to meet the original deadline.

Contributors

MA: Mark Ashworth. Contributor to *Eyeball, Shock Xpress* and *Shivers*. Dragged up as Barbara Steele for an episode of *Clive Barker's A to Z of Horror*.

AB: Anne Billson. Film critic of the *Sunday Telegraph*, former books editor of *Time Out*, contributor to *Monthly Film Bulletin, The New Statesman*, the *Times, Shock Xpress*. Author of *My Name is Michael Caine* and the novels *Suckers* and *Stiff Lips*.

EB: Ed Buscombe. Author of *Making Legend of the Werewolf*, editor of *The BFI Companion to the Western*.

DC/KW: David Carroll and Kyla Ward. Editors and publishers of *Tabula Rasa*.

SB: Steve Bissette. A comic book artist who has worked on *Swamp Thing, Taboo, 1963* and *Tyrant*. Contributor to *Deep Red, Video Watchdog, Ecco, European Trash Cinema, Fangoria, GoreZone*.

RC: Ramsey **Campbell**. (See text entry).

JC: Jeremy Clarke. Contributor to *What's On, Sight and Sound, Samhain*.

LD: Les Daniels. Author of *Living in Fear: A History of Horror in the Mass Media, Marvel: Five Fabulous Decades of the World's Greatest Comics* and *DC Comics: Sixty Years of the World's Favourite Heroes*, and the 'Don Sebastian' cycle of vampire novels, from *The Black Castle* to *White Demon*.

CF: Christopher Frayling. Rector of the Royal College of Art. Author of *Spaghetti Westerns, Vampyres: Lord Byron to Count Dracula, The House That Jack Built*.

NG: Neil Gaiman. Contributor to *Knave, Penthouse, Today, The Truth*. Co-editor of *Ghastly Beyond Belief* and *Now We Are Sick*, co-author of *Good Omens*, author of *Angels and Visitations*, writer of *Neverwhere*. Comics writer: *Violent Cases, Black Orchid, Sandman, Signal to Noise, Miracleman, Mr Punch*.

PHa: Phil Hardy. Editor of *The Aurum Film Encyclopedia* series and *The BFI Companion to Crime*. Author of *Samuel Fuller* and co-author of *The Faber Companion to 20th-Century Popular Music*.

PH: Peter Hutchings. Author of *Hammer and Beyond: The British Horror Film*.

TH: Tom Hutchinson. Contributor to the *Mail on Sunday*, the *Times*, the *Hampstead & Highgate Express*. Author of *Horror & Fantasy in the Cinema*, co-author of *Horrors: A History of Horror Movies*.

AJ: Alan Jones. Contributor to *Starburst, Cinefantastique, Shivers, Shock Xpress*. Co-organiser of the Shock Around the Clock and Fantasm festivals. Film appearances include *Terror* and *The Great Rock n Roll Swindle*.

SJ: Stephen **Jones**. (See text entry).

ML: Mark Kermode. Film critic for Radio 1. Contributor to *Q, Sight and Sound, Video Watchdog.*

SL: Stephen Laws. Author of the novels *Ghost Train, Spectre, The Wyrm, The Frighteners, Darkfall, Gideon, Macabre, Daemonic.*

TL: Tim Lucas. Editor of *Video Watchdog.* Author of *Throat Sprockets.* Contributor to *Cinefantastique, GoreZone, Fangoria, Eyeball.*

MM: Maitland McDonagh. Author of *Broken Mirrors/Broken Minds: The Dark Dreams of Dario Argento* and *Filmmaking on the Fringe: The Good, the Bad, and the Deviant Directors.* Contributor to *Fangoria, Psychotronic Video.*

DM: David **McGillivray**. (See text entry).

MMcH: Maura McHugh. Former research post-graduate student at Trinity College, Dublin. She has a Masters in Irish 19th Century horror fiction.

TM: Tony Mechele. Co-author of *The Saint,* contributor to *Prime Time.*

DP: David Prothero. Publisher of *Bloody Hell,* contributor to *Shivers, The Dark Side, Scapegoat.*

MP: Marcelle Perks. Contributor to *Redeemer, The Dark Side, Video World.*

JP: Julian Petley. Contributor to *Monthly Film Bulletin, Prime Time, Shock Xpress, The Guardian, Vertigo.* Head of Communication and Information Studies at Brunel University.

MS: Mark Salisbury. Editor of *Empire.* Author of *Burton on Burton, Behind the Mask* and *Clive Barker's Nightbreed.* Contributor to *Fear, Fangoria.*

MSc: Michael Scott. Author of novels for adults young and old, *October Moon, Image, Reflection, Imp.*

PS: Philip Strick. Author of *Science Fiction Movies,* editor of *The BFI Companion to Science Fiction.* Contributor to *Monthly Film Bulletin, Sight and Sound.*

PT: Pete Tombs. Co-author of *Immoral Tales: Sex and Horror Cinema in Europe 1956-1984,* English translator of Jean Rollin's *Little Orphan Vampires.*

ST. Steve Thrower. Publisher of *Eyeball.*

CV: Caroline Vié. Contributor to *Fangoria, Gorezone.* Director of a documentary about rollercoasters and author of a book on John Woo. Member of the selection committee for the Critics' Week of the Cannes Film Festival.

CW. Caroline Westbrook. Staff writer at *Empire.*

DW. Douglas Winter. Author of *Faces of Fear, The Art of Darkness.* Editor of *Prime Evil.* Contributor to *Video Watchdog, Fangoria.*

MW. Mike Wathen. Contributor to *Shock Xpress, The Scream Factory.*

LRW. Linda Ruth Williams. Lecturer at the University of Southampton. Author of *Sex in the Head: Visions of Femininity and Film in D.H. Lawrence, Critical Desire, Carnal Crimes.* Contributor to *Sight and Sound.*

All unsigned contributions are by the editor.

Introduction

Like comedy, tragedy and the musical – and unlike the Western, the War Film or the Gangster movie – horror as a genre defies the fencing-in of definition. The centre of the genre can fairly easily be recognised as a developing tradition that branches off from a line beginning with the gothic novels of the 18th and 19th centuries and is epitomised in cinema by the cycles produced by Universal in the 30s and 40s and Hammer Films in the 50s and 60s. This brand of horror, with its castles and crypts and cloaked fiends, is as instantly identifiable as the Western with its horses, cacti and cowboys. However, the further away from such default horrors we travel, the more blurred distinctions become, and horror becomes less like a discrete genre than an effect which can be deployed within any number of settings or narrative patterns, burrowing like a parasite into the thriller (*Kiss Me Deadly*, 1954), the Western (*Curse of the Undead*, 1958) or the War Film (*Apocalypse Now*, 1979). From the gore-drenched cruelties of Jacobean Revenge Tragedy through the psychological anecdotes of Edgar Allan Poe to such spiritually numbed modernists as Kafka and Beckett, horror – like comedy, its closest kin – is essential to the palette of much fiction. It is impossible to subsume *Det sjunde inseglet* (*The Seventh Seal*, 1957) entirely into genre, but it is as impossible to define the horror film to exclude Ingmar Bergman.

Though horror stories have existed as long as the notion of fiction, and we can now identify as central to the tradition such literary cycles as the original gothic novel and the Victorian ghost story, the definition we now accept of the horror genre did not really emerge until the early to mid-30s, and was almost immediately stretched and distorted by such 'is it or not' entries as *King Kong* (1933). The initial cycle of horror films was dominated by Universal's benchmark undertakings of the major sub-genres: Tod Browning's *Dracula* (1930), with Bela Lugosi, James Whale's *Frankenstein* (1931), with Boris Karloff, Karl Freund's *The Mummy* (1932), Edgar G. Ulmer's *The Black Cat* (1934). With the success of these films, other Hollywood studios tried to get in on the act, often borrowing Lugosi or Karloff as a walking embodiment of whatever it was Universal had hit on. Paramount responded with sophisticated literary adaptions spotlighting acting talent (*Dr. Jekyll and Mr. Hyde*, 1932; *Island of Lost Souls*, 1933), MGM dithered about unleashing Irving Thalberg's repressed sadistic streak (*Mask of Fu Manchu*, 1932; *Freaks*, 1932) and Warners mixed mad science and scarred fiends with their usual fast-talking gangsters and reporters (*Dr. X*, 1933; *Mystery of the Wax Museum*, 1933). Only poverty row independents responded by really trying to imitate Universal (*The Vampire Bat*, 1933; *Condemned to Live*, 1933), and even these films dilute the mix subtly, indicating – as do such Universal 'experiments' as *The Invisible Man* (1932) and *The Old Dark House* (1933) – that the formula was not yet set in stone.

King Kong (1932)

11

Boris Karloff, *Bride of Frankenstein*

The sources of this cycle are also vaguely uncomfortable with the notion of genre. Mary Shelley, Poe, J.S. Le Fanu, Robert Louis Stevenson, Bram Stoker, Arthur Conan Doyle, Oscar Wilde and H.G. Wells have tended to be lumped together precisely because they were drawn on by the film-makers who founded the genre, but none of them would have much cared to be included in the roster. Among even the core literary texts of genre is a wide spectrum of manner and intent, ranging from science fiction (only Le Fanu is really committed to the supernatural; even Stoker tries to locate Count Dracula in a real world of railway time-tables and blood transfusions), through abnormal psychology (Poe and Stevenson bequeathed models for conditions their contemporaries barely believed in) to the sly satire of Wilde or Wells (who address morality and society through their Faustian figures). Though all were commercial writers (witness Poe's desperate prolificness), only Stoker and Doyle – like M.R. James – seem to belong to the 'rattling good yarn' school of tale-tellers for the sake of it, and their works seethe with unconscious meaning.

Silent horror, from the magic acts of Georges Méliès to the one-off talkie of Dreyer's *Vampyr* (1932), can be seen as a series of unrelated attempts at dealing with these nineteenth-century literary sources. All had been adapted over and over by the time Universal and their Hollywood imitators made 'definitive' screen versions, and most specific sub-genres of horror from the Jack the Ripper movie to the waxworks film can be traced back to specific silent films. There has been a tendency, fostered perhaps by the dearth until comparatively recently of informed histories, to treat the precursors of the genre as if they were consciously a part of the form. The German expressionist films, the grotesque Lon Chaney melodramas and the Broadway-derived comedy-'chillers' of the 20s provided a lasting inspiration for the horror film, coining many of the iconic images (clutching hands, wavering shadows, haunted eyes) and tackling the themes (the *doppelgänger*, the human fiend, mad science) that would become central to

Conrad Veidt, Werner Krauss,
Das Cabinet des Dr. Caligari

Boris Karloff, *The Mummy* (1932)

horror. But these were not perceived by their makers or audiences as horror films.

Though F.W. Murnau was drawn to major horror themes and Lon Chaney specialised in disfigured characterisations, they were not limited by genre: their careers take in the horrific, but extend to the sentimental or the mainstream in a way that such successors as the sound-era Browning or Lugosi would be unable to manage. Horror fans, raised on *Famous Monsters* or latterly *Fangoria*, find such foundation stones as *Das Cabinet des Dr. Caligari* (1919) and *Vampyr* (1932) – even *Nosferatu: Eine Symphonie das Grauens* (1922) – hard to sit through because they do not conform precisely to the rituals passed down by the mainstream horror films which they influenced. Though the term 'horror film' seems to have been coined in the sense we now understand it around 1931 – ie: too late for *Dracula*, but early enough for *Frankenstein* – it seems a credible argument that the horror film proper did not exist until the genre started concreting in its foundations by imitating itself. By that ruling, *The Mummy* (1932) – a conscious rewrite of *Dracula* built around the star of *Frankenstein* – is the first proper horror film, though that distinction might as easily be bestowed on the first run of horror sequels, *Bride of Frankenstein* (1935), *Dracula's Daughter* (1936). The purist might even consider *Bride* as the last horror film, since it completes the initial cycle by satirising it – far more effectively that Abbott and Costello would in 1948 – and offers both development and closure. All subsequent entries have been post-horror.

Later cycles like the 40s run of Val Lewton 'chillers' (which were much imitated), the 50s reworking of classic mad science or possession themes in science fiction terms or the Hammer Films gothics (many explicit or tacit remakes of Universal properties) can be defined as anti-Universal. All these films are identifiable as horror for what they borrow from Universal, and as radical by the ways they alter the model: *Cat People* (1942) is *The Wolf Man* (1941) set in the real world, *The Thing From Another World* (1951) is *Frankenstein* from the point of view of the American military who fulfil the plot function of a mob of torch-bearing peasants, and *The Curse of Frankenstein* (1957) and *Dracula* (1958) retell the key Universal horror narratives with a distinctly different style which instantly became the format which the next waves of horror would have to kick against. The 60s offered a succession of alternatives to Universal-reincarnated-as-Hammer, all of which are deeply aware of the need to break from the source but still fulfil audience expectations and requirements: Hitchcock set *Psycho* (1960) in a modern motel in the shadow of a Whale-like Old Dark House, Roger Corman seized on Poe and remaining Universal horror stars (Price, Karloff, Lorre), and Riccardo Freda and Mario Bava added Italianate visual excess and a sado-eroticism beyond the grasp of Terence Fisher.

In 1968, Roman Polanski's *Rosemary's Baby* and George Romero's *Night of the Living Dead* – both syntheses of earlier styles, with Polanski borrowing heavily from Lewton and Romero riffing on 50s s-f and *The Birds* (1963) – opened up new avenues for genre horror. Polanski's take on Ira Levin's novel stands at the head of a steady stream of big-budget horrors, often drawn from best-selling novels and promoted as 'mainstream' cinema, and which is as significant for raising Stephen King and others (Anne Rice, Peter Straub, Dean Koontz, Thomas Harris) to a best-seller superstardom

Tippi Hendren, *The Birds*

unattainable by such niche-market pulp fore-runners as H.P. Lovecraft, Robert Bloch and Richard Matheson. In this tradition are *The Exorcist* (1973), *Jaws* (1975), *The Omen* (1976), *Carrie* (1976), *The Shining* (1980), *The Silence of the Lambs* (1992) and *Interview With the Vampire* (1994), and – by association with the s-f and action blockbuster genres – such horror-in-disguise items as *Alien* (1979), *The Thing* (1982) and *Se7en* (1995). These films fulfil the commercial ambitions of all genre film-makers, in that their primary audiences are people who wouldn't consider paying to see a horror movie.

Romero, however, brought horror home to the heartland, and encouraged a flourishing generation of hand-to-mouth horror auteurs in the 70s. Wes Craven, David Cronenberg, John Carpenter, Tobe Hooper and Larry Cohen emerged from the underground with a ferocious attitude but one-upped 60s gore-sloshers like H.G. Lewis by combining genuine film-making skills and a seriousness of purpose to their willingness to indulge in violent or sexual extremes. The politenesses of Universal and Hammer are torn apart by Romero's ravening ghouls, Hooper's chainsaw family and Cronenberg's sex slugs. John Carpenter's *Halloween* (1978), which is a 'fun' scare movie on the model of William Castle's gimmick pictures, inhabits the same terrain as early Romero and Craven but abjures their intensely-motivated brutalities in favour of a fairytale rollercoaster. However, hundreds of imitations from *Friday the 13th* (1980) on drag back in the brutalities albeit without the motivation, creating a Christians-to-the-lions cinema many die-hard defenders of horror have found hard to cope with.

In the 80s and 90s, horror lost its way somewhat, with the auteur-stars of the 70s detouring into the mainstream (Carpenter), suffering career reversals (Romero) or declining drastically (Hooper). Like David Lynch and the Coen Brothers, David Cronenberg has made a niche for himself with films that hark back to the 20s by not being strictly classifiable as horror but which still inform and are shaped by the genre proper. Only Craven,

Anthony Hopkins, *The Silence of the Lambs*

Robert Englund, *A Nightmare on Elm Street,
Part 2: Freddy's Revenge*

with *A Nightmare on Elm Street* (1984), was able to achieve a continuing career and a developing identity, albeit at the cost of a see-sawing of ambition and achievement as remarkable work alternates with hackery. Sam Raimi's *The Evil Dead* (1982), a development of the Romero-Craven style that substitutes knockabout slapstick for social content, did succeed in founding an 80s horror style, prompting such farcical grand guignol entertainments as Stuart Gordon's *Re-Animator* (1986) and Peter Jackson's *Braindead* (1992), not to mention the bottom-feeding of Troma and dozens of skid row DIY video-makers. Raimi, Gordon and Jackson – like Clive Barker or John McNaughton – have found it as difficult as Carpenter or Craven to sustain their careers within the genre.

There have, of course, been thriving horror cinemas outside America, whether sustained by one-man industries like France's Jean Rollin or Spain's Jesús Franco and Paul Naschy or specific cycles like Mexico's monster-wrestlers, Italy's *giallo* or Hong Kong's Chinese ghost stories. Even the UK has managed several distinct pre-, post- or anti-Hammer movements, taking in Tod Slaughter's barnstorming, Anglo-Amalgamated's sadism, Amicus's anthologies and Peter Walker's provincial misery. But only Italy's Mario Bava and Dario Argento have matched the Americans for commitment to and achievement within the strict confines of genre. And the 20th century has produced a vast and complex literature of horror, plus complex clusters of genre material in the theatre, radio, television and, latterly, interactive computer formats. As this book is completed, genre horror – at least in the cinema – seems well into its decadent phase, but a great deal of its history remains underexamined or even unexplored and the appearance of decadence may well be a side-effect of a proliferation and dissemination that seems to colour an enormous proportion of a media output that has mushroomed beyond belief.

*　　*　　*

For the purposes of this Companion, the horror film is defined as including much science fiction (especially if it involves alien invaders or monsters on the rampage) and a great deal of crime material (particularly if the crimes or criminals are depicted in a manner explicitly designed to provoke horror). Comedies with supernatural themes are allowed in selectively, and welcomed if a few moments of horror are included along with the sentiment or slapstick. Some television series (*Doctor Who*, *The Outer Limits*, *The Avengers*) are read as predominantly horror and listed in filmographies even though they produced non-horror episodes; others (*Star Trek*, *The Snoop Sisters*, *Starsky and Hutch*) get a mention only in reference to specific horror episodes. More problematic are those mainstream or art-house figures – Lang, Hitchcock, Bergman, Fellini, Buñuel, even Cronenberg – who seem indebted to or fascinated by horror but never quite make horror films. Like Kafka, Cornell Woolrich, Welles and Wells – but not, sadly, Shakespeare or Goethe – these artists have earned their own entries, which attempt to address the interface between their worlds and that of genre horror.

This Companion includes entries on actors, creative personnel, authors, historical figures, major themes, television series, radio shows, clichés, recurrent characters, sub-genres, properties, ephemera and much else. Unlike other volumes in this series – on the Western, Crime and Science Fiction – it does not include capsule reviews of individual films. A proliferation of guides offer this approach (see **reference books**) and we confidently expect anyone interested enough to purchase this Companion will already own several. It wasn't thought necessary to duplicate their efforts, no matter how much we might disagree with individual judgments found in Phil Hardy's *Aurum Encyclopedia: Horror*.

A **bold** typeface indicates a cross-reference to another entry. Whenever a date has proved impossible to track down – the birthdates of Mexican wrestlers are surprisingly not found in even the most detailed sources – we have reluctantly listed it as 19??. If information is forthcoming, the question marks will be removed in future editions.

Abbreviations are as follows:

a: actor
c: cinematographer
d: director
e: editor
fx: special effects
n: narrator
p: producer
s: short
st: story
u: uncredited
v: voice
w: screenwriter

Films are referred to, wherever possible, by their original language titles (with the English language/British release title, if available, in parentheses). In the video era, retitling has become so common that many films have five or more alternates, and a multi-national co-production may have titles in three or more languages. Space has prevented the inclusion of a comprehensive index of alternate titles (if, as we hope, this book ends up on CD-ROM, that will be the first addition). Our position is that a film's title is what appears on screen, ie: *Se7en* not *Seven*, *Matthew Hopkins Witchfinder General* not *Witchfinder General*. Some of our decisions – using *Flesh for Frankenstein* rather than *Andy Warhol's Frankenstein* or *Il mostro è in tavola, barone . . . Frankenstein* – are frankly arbitrary. The film commonly known as *Abbott and Costello Meet Frankenstein* is listed, usually, as (**Abbott and Costello**) *Meet Frankenstein*. What it actually says on screen is Bud Abbott Lou Costello *Meet Frankenstein*: our interpretation is that names are part of the credits, not the title. Similarly, we assume possessory credits (Stephen King's *Silver Bullet*) are not part of the title, except in the case of *Bram Stoker's Dracula* and *Mary Shelley's Frankenstein* (so called for copyright reasons) and *Wes Craven's New Nightmare* (which is clever). Every effort has been made to be consistent but definitive statements about what a film is actually called or when it was made are no longer possible. A great many of our readers will be incandescent with fury at this paragraph, but, to quote Judge Roy Bean 'that's m'rulin'!'

Kim Newman
31 July 1996

LEFT Shelley Duvall,
The Shining

RIGHT Udo Kier,
Blood for Dracula

ABOVE Linnea Quigley,
Gunnar Hansen,
Michelle Bauer

RIGHT Udo Kier,
*Flesh for
Frankenstein*

ABOVE *The Toxic Avenger, Part III: The Last Temptation of Toxie*

LEFT Sissy Spacek, *Carrie*

ABOVE Vincent Price, *Masque of the Red Death*

BELOW *The Secret Adventures of Tom Thumb*

ABOVE *Bride of Re-Animator*

OVERLEAF Nick Brimble, Catherine Rabbett, *Frankenstein Unbound*

BELOW Mia Farrow, *Rosemary's Baby*

BELOW *Braindead*

A

Abbott, Bud [William Abbott] (1895–1974) and Costello, Lou (1906–59)

Abbott, the thin straight man, and Costello, the whiny chubby comedian ('Ch-ch-ch-ch-ch-i-ck!'), took fast-talking vaudeville routines to Hollywood. For a decade, from the early 40s, they were America's most popular radio and film **comedy** team. In movies, they met classic **monsters**: *Meet Frankenstein* (1948), . . . *Meet the Invisible Man* (1952), *Abbott and Costello Meet Dr. Jekyll and Mr. Hyde* (1953), *Abbott and Costello Meet the Mummy* (1954). SJ

Hold That Ghost/1941 * *Who Done It?*/1942 * *The Time of Their Lives*/1946 * *Meet the Killer*/ 1949

Abbott, John (1905–96)

British actor. Rare Hollywood starring roles: the patriotic killer in *London Blackout Murders* (1942), an unlikely 400-year-old **vampire** in *The Vampire's Ghost* (1945). SJ

Jane Eyre/1943 * *Cry of the Werewolf*/1944 * *Pursuit to Algiers*/1945 * *The Woman in White*/ 1948

TV: *Matinee Theatre*: 'The Tell-Tale Heart'/ 1956; 'The Suicide Club'/1958 * *Shirley Temple Theatre*: 'The House of Seven Gables'/ 1960 * *Thriller*: 'Trio for Terror'/1961 * *Great Ghost Tales*: 'Mr. Arcularis'/1961 * *Alfred Hitchcock Presents*: 'First Class Honeymoon'/ 1962 * *The Munsters*: 'Johan'/1966 * *Wild Wild West*: 'The Night of the Simian Terror'/ 1968 * *The Cat Creature*/1973 * *Sherlock Holmes in New York*/1976

Ace of Wands (UK TV series, 1970–72)

Children's tea-time show created by Trevor

John Abbott, *The Vampire's Ghost*

Bud Abbott and Lou Costello in 1943

Preston. Paisley-tie **magician** Tarot (Michael Mackenzie) investigates bizarre crimes. Telepath Lulli (Judy Loe) and ex-con Sam (Tony Selby), Tarot's sidekicks, give way to Mikki (Petra Markham) and Chas (Roy Holder) in the third season; pet owl Ozymandias rounds out the team. Villains: Emperor of Thieves Tun-Ju (Willoughby Goddard), sorcerer Mr Stabbs (Russell Hunter), glamorous Thalia (Isobel Black), crippled chess master Ceribraun (Oscar Quitak). The magical advisor was Ali Bongo, the psychedelic theme song was by Andrew Brown. TM

Ackerman, Forrest J (b. 1916)

American editor, fan guru, bit-actor. A significant figure in the 60s repopularisation of **monsters** through genial editorship of the influential if childish *Famous Monsters of Filmland*. In books on **Karloff** (*The Frankenscience Monster*, 1969), **Chaney Sr** (*Lon of a 1000 Faces*, 1983) and his collection (*Fantastic Movie Memories*, 1985), a mania for puckish puns (among his pseudonyms is 'Dr. Ackula') sometimes obscures depth of knowledge. He is a character in Philip José Farmer's novel *Blown* (1969) and plays himself in *My Lovely Monster* (1990). A natural ham, Ackerman takes smirking cameos: monster-mangled in *Dracula vs. Frankenstein* (1970), a **zombie** in *Return of the Living Dead, Part II* (1988). Genre godfather to *FM* readers John **Landis** (he is in 'Thriller', 1983) and Joe **Dante**, Ackerman also presides over the fanboy dreck of Jim **Wynorski** and Fred Olen **Ray**.

Mad Monster Party? (w/u)/1966 * *Queen of Blood*/1967 * *Equinox*/1969 * *Schlock*/1972 * *Hollywood Boulevard*/1976 * *The Howling*/1981 * *Scalps*/1982 * *Evil Spawn*/1987 * *My Mom's a Werewolf*/1988 * *Curse of the Queerwolf*/ *Transylvania Twist*/1989 * *Tower of Terror*/

1990 * *Braindead*/*Innocent Blood*/1992 * *Nudist Colony of the Dead*/1994 * *Attack of the 60 Ft Centrefold*/*Frankenstein and Me*/1995

Acquanetta [Burnu Davenport, Mildred Davenport] (b. 1920)

American model. Publicised as a 'Venezuelan Volcano', the exotic beauty was actually Arapaho Indian. After a bit in *Arabian Nights* (1942), she was 'introduced' by Universal as Paula the Gorilla Girl in **Captive Wild Woman** (1943). SJ

Dead Man's Eyes/*Jungle Woman*/1944 * *Tarzan and the Leopard Woman*/1946 * *Lost Continent*/ 1951

Adamson, Al (1929–95)

American director, producer, writer. He collaborated with producer Sam Sherman on low-budget exploitation fodder, often featuring the so-called 'Freak Out Girl', Adamson's wife Regina Carroll. His most distinctive films are the biker epic *Satan's Sadists* (1970) and the gothic **Western** *Five Bloody Graves* (1971). Adamson proved adept at mingling stereotypical plots, left-over footage and aged actors (from Russ Tamblyn to Lon **Chaney Jr**) with enough titillation to bring viewers to the drive-ins of America. Some Adamson works exist in a bewildering

Acquanetta, *Tarzan and the Leopard Woman*

number of variant editions under several titles: *Psycho a Go Go!* (1965), *Fiend With the Elec-tronic Brain* (aka *The Man With the Electronic Brain*, 1966) and *Blood of Ghastly Horror* (1971) are versions of the same film.
DW

Blood of Dracula's Castle/1969 * *Dracula vs. Frankenstein*/*Horror of the Blood Monsters*/1970 * *Brain of Blood*/1972 * *Doctor Dracula* (addit d)/1977 * *Nurse Sherri*/1978

Addams, Charles (1912–88)

American cartoonist. Addams contributed macabre jokes to *The New Yorker* from 1932. In 1938, he introduced a family of grotesques: a cadaverous homemaker, a grinning fiend in pinstripes, a hulking butler, a bald sadist. In a singleton typical of their skewed values, the family pour boiling oil from their gothic battlements onto a merry group of carol-singers. The **situation comedy** *The Addams Family* (1964–6) popularised and named the characters. Collections include *Addams and Evil* (1940), *Monster Rally* (1950) and *Favourite Haunts* (1976).

The Old Dark House (titles)/1962 * *Murder By Death* (titles)/1976

The Addams Family (US TV series, 1964–6)

Developed by David Levy and Nat Perrin, this **situation comedy** turns Charles **Addams**'s cartoon characters into a mock gothic parody of suburban norms. Imitated by *The Munsters* (1964–6), the show makes much of the perverse relationship between Gomez (John **Astin**) and Morticia (Carolyn **Jones**) and such bizarre characters as the hairy Cousin Itt (Felix Silla) and the disembodied **hand**, Thing. Other regulars: Lurch (Ted Cassidy), Uncle Fester (Jackie Coogan), Grandmama (Blossom Rock), Wednesday (Lisa Loring) and Pugsley (Ken Weatherwax).

Cassidy and Coogan (with Jodie Foster as Pugsley) voice a 1973 animated series spun off from a *Scooby-Doo* guest shot; Jones, Astin, Cassidy and Coogan reunite for a TV movie *Halloween With the New Addams Family* (1977); Astin returns for another animated spin-off (1992–3). Barry Sonnenfeld's *The Addams Family* (1991) and *Addams Family Values* (1993) – with Anjelica Huston (Morticia), Raul Julia (Gomez), Christopher Lloyd (Fester) and Carel Struycken (Lurch) – are stolen by Christina Ricci as the frozen-faced child Wednesday. Herschel Savage's porno *The Maddams Family* (1991) has Ona Zee (Horticia), Mike Horner (Cortez), Ron Jeremy (Pester), Jon Dough (Crotch), Kim Alexis (Tuesday) and Charisma (Cousin Tit). Stephen Cox, *The Addams Chronicles* (1991); John Peel, *The Addams Family and The Munsters Programme Guide* (1994)

Ageing Actresses

Established as a subgenre by Robert **Aldrich**'s *What Ever Happened to Baby Jane?* (1962), with Bette **Davis** and Joan **Crawford** torturing each other in an adaption of Henry Farrell's 1960 novel, the 'ageing actress' gothic springs from *Sunset Blvd.* (1950), which makes Gloria Swanson's Norma Desmond monstrous but pathetic. Billy Wilder's film, with monkey funerals and **Old Dark House** trappings, appears constructed on the template of *Dracula's Daughter* (1936). *Baby Jane* and, more particularly, Aldrich's follow-up *Hush . . . Hush, Sweet Charlotte* (1965), which pits Davis against Olivia de Havilland and Mary Astor, stir in elements of *Les diaboliques* (1955), with its it's-all-a-plot plot, and *Psycho* (1960), with its homicidal mummy. Davis and Crawford sprang from *Baby Jane* into second or third careers in exploitation *guignol*, encouraging peers to heft an axe: Barbara Stanwyck (*The Night Walker*, 1964), Tallulah Bankhead (*Fanatic*, 1965), Joan Fontaine (*The Witches*, 1966), Geraldine Page (*What Ever Happened to Aunt Alice?*, 1969), Geraldine Fitzgerald (*The Beguiled*, 1971), Jeanne Crain (*The Night God Screamed*, 1971), Lana Turner (*Persecution*, 1974), Joan Bennett and Alida Valli (*Suspiria*, 1976).

Curtis **Harrington** specialised in the genre, using Simone Signoret (*Games*, 1967), Julie Harris (*How Awful About Allan*, 1970), Shelley Winters (*Whoever Slew Auntie Roo?*, 1971), Debbie Reynolds (the excellent *What's the Matter With Helen?*, 1971), Ann Sothern (*The Killing Kind*, 1973) and Piper Laurie (*Ruby*, 1978). Vanessa and Lynn Redgrave are cleverly cast in a TV remake of *What Ever Happened to Baby Jane?* (1991). Though the cycle depends on gimmick star casting, cruelly exploiting withered beauty, many of horror's wickedest old ladies are less familiar players: Rosemary Murphy (*You'll Like My Mother*, 1972), Sheila **Keith** (*Frightmare*, 1974), Kathy Bates (*Misery*, 1990).

Aguirre, Javier (b. 1935)

Spanish director. As crude and sluggish as

Altogether Ooky, *The Addams Family* (1991)

LEFT Ageing actresses: Joan Crawford, Bette Davis, *What Ever Happened to Baby Jane?*

backgrounds of startlingly matter-of-fact cruelty and corruption: war (*The Dirty Dozen*, 1967), the West (*Ulzana's Raid*, 1972) or the psycho-thriller (*Kiss Me Deadly*, 1955). He refined the **ageing actress** sub-genre in *What Ever Happened to Baby Jane?* (1962), *Hush . . . Hush, Sweet Charlotte* (1965) and *The Killing of Sister George* (1968). PS

M (assistant d)/1950 * *The Legend of Lylah Claire*/1968 * *What Ever Happened to Aunt Alice?* (p)/1969

Edwin T. Arnold, Eugene L. Miller, Jr, *The Films and Career of Robert Aldrich* (1986)

Alfred Hitchcock Presents (US TV series, 1955–65)

Hitchcock jovially introduces nasty little dramas with twist endings: though criminals often appear to escape punishment, closing comments wryly and morally suggest their bad ends. Hitchcock's favourite of his few self-directed episodes was Roald **Dahl**'s 'Lamb to the Slaughter' (1958): Barbara Bel Geddes kills her husband with a frozen leg of lamb, then cooks the evidence. A few episodes are supernatural horror: 'The Case of Mr Pelham' (1955), a *doppelgänger* story later remade as *The Man Who Haunted Himself* (1970); 'Sign of Satan' (1964), written by Barré **Lyndon** from a Robert **Bloch** tale, with horror star Christopher **Lee** persecuted by witches.

most Paul **Naschy** vehicles, Aguirre's horrors are distinguished by lurid melodrama and fitful melancholia. Naschy commented: 'Aguirre was a strange and somewhat aloof person, but very skilled in fantastic cinema; although I think that at heart he despised it'.

El gran amor del Conde Drácula [*Dracula's Great Love*]/*El jorobado del morgue* [*The Hunchback of the Morgue*]/1972

Aickman, Robert (1914–81)

British writer. A typical Aickman protagonist blunders into a **ghost story** at once personal and supernatural. The heroine of 'The Inner Room' finds the original of her childhood doll's house and enters the inner chamber that frightened her to discover her own picture pierced in a hateful ritual. A honeymooning couple in 'Ringing the Changes' – televised on **Late Night Horror** (1968) as 'The Bells of Hell' – realise a pealing of bells is designed to bring the dead to life and break their marriage. Collections: *Sub Rosa* (1968), *Cold Hand in Mine* (1975) and *Painted Devils* (1979).

AIP * See: **Arkoff, Samuel Z.; Nicholson, James H.**

Alcoa Presents: One Step Beyond * See: *One Step Beyond*

Aldrich, Robert (1918–83)

American director, producer. A spiritedly independent professional, Aldrich applies powerful visual panache to often controversial stories of claustrophobic emotional entrapment. His consistent motif, appropriately that of 'the misfit, outside the mainstream of society, who exhibits more sense and humanity than others', is traced against

Alfred Hitchcock Presents

In 1962 the series expanded and changed its title to *The Alfred Hitchcock Hour*; a highlight of this run was Ray **Bradbury**'s 'The Jar' (1964), directed by Norman Lloyd, in which farmer Pat Buttram at a carnival buys a strange jar which brings him respect but eventually turns him into a murderer. *Alfred Hitchcock Presents* (1985–9) colourises Hitchcock's original introductions and wraps them around new episodes, some of which – notably Tim **Burton**'s 'The Jar' (1986) – are remakes. TM

John McCarty and Bruce Kelleher, *Alfred Hitchcock Presents: An Illustrated Guide to the Ten-Year Television Career of the Master of Suspense* (1985)

Alien (1979)

Released during the *Star Wars* (1977) s-f boom, *Alien* is an important horror film. Dan **O'Bannon**'s script blends the 'body count' premise of *It! The Terror From Beyond Space* (1958) with the attitude of his *Dark Star* (1974), depicting the spaceship *Nostromo* as a freighter crewed by inept misfits and owned by a rapacious company. Director Ridley Scott plays up the then-modish use of ballsy **heroine** Sigourney Weaver and the striking bio-mechanics of artist H.R. **Giger**. The insectile-sexual **monster** appears as a vaginal egg, a face-hugger that impregnates John Hurt, a toothed penile larva which explodes from his chest and a double-dentition phallic adult.

Plot, production design and monster rapist are imitated in by Italian pseudo-sequel *Alien 2 sulla terra* (*Alien Terror*, 1980), big-budget carbon *Leviathan* (1989) and dozens of quickies: *Scared to Death* (1980), *Inseminoid* (1980), *Forbidden World* (1981), *Split Second* (1992), *Death Machine* (1994). Weaver and nemesis return in James Cameron's *Aliens* (1986), a successful **war**-action film which emphasises the redemptive power of motherhood, and David Fincher's *Alien³* (1992), a murky **prison** movie with religion. Other spin-offs include comics, original novels and the in-joke placing of a skull in *Predator 2* (1990).

Aliens

When not scouring the planet with heat-rays, aliens in the invasion movies of the 50s, sensitive of their appearance, were heavily into mesmerism. A convenient economy at a time when rubber monsters could seldom avoid ridicule, the custom of conveying alienness by walking stiff-necked and

Sigourney Weaver, Yaphet Kotto, Harry Dean Stanton, *Alien*

glassy-eyed imparted the subtler but remarkably durable message that being an alien was all in the mind. The subsequent growth of alien-spotting, with thousands of contactees claiming experiences like those described in Whitley **Strieber**'s *Communion* (1987), is very much a mental matter, suggesting mass hallucination and instability if not among the victims then certainly on the part of their visitors.

What has intensified in the attitude towards abduction by aliens has been the fear and disgust at physical intrusion by probes, needles and other penetrative instruments, as illustrated in the one scene of genuine menace in *Fire in the Sky* (1993), the much refurbished account of a 1975 UFO encounter. Significantly, when at last a notorious crashlanded saucer story from 1947 reached the screen as *The Roswell Incident* (1994) it was accompanied by purportedly authentic footage of autopsies performed (as if in revenge) on sexless alien corpses, their body cavities explored in gruesome detail. This physicality has unarguably become a special attraction of space-invader melodramas since the face-clutching, chest-rendering, multi-jawed assaults in *Alien* (1979). Reminders of the Xenomorph vary from the body-count of *Galaxy of Terror* (1981) and the cocoons of *Xtro* (1982), to the eggs that unfurl into the whiplashing parasites in *The Puppet Masters* (1994) and the sensuously lethal **Giger**-creature in *Species* (1995). On

the same principle, the Martians of *War of the Worlds* (1953) metamorphised in 1988 for late-night television purposes into homicidal **zombies** gouging out their victim's eyes and tongues with a spare set of talons, collapsing into a toxic puddle when shot down.

Aliens have also acquired complex motivation. In *They Live* (1988), where extraplanetary hordes become mysteriously cadaverous when studied through suitable shades, they are rapacious businessmen depleting Earth's resources before moving on. In *Dark Angel* (1989), the alien entrepreneur siphons a special serum from the brains of heroin addicts for sale at substantial profit back home. In *Predator* (1987), the multi-weaponed, rarely visible killer, stringing up corpses like joints of raw meat, is an interstellar big game hunter. And in near-parodies like *The Hidden* (1988), *The Borrower* (1990) and *Monolith* (1993), the intruders are fugitives, assuming human anonymity in order to avoid retribution from distant star-systems. PS

Allen, Nancy (b. 1953)

American actress. Once Brian **De Palma**'s wife, Allen is his teen bitch (*Carrie*, 1976), call-girl **heroine** (*Dressed to Kill*, 1980) and doomed chippie (*Blow Out*, 1981). Subsequently, Officer Lewis in *RoboCop* (1987).

Forced Entry/1975 * *Strange Invaders*/1983 * *The Philadelphia Experiment*/*Terror in the*

RIGHT Amicus: Vincent Price or Peter Cushing, *Madhouse*

Aisles/1984 * *Poltergeist III*/1988 * *Limit Up*/1989 * *Memories of Murder*/1990

TV: *The Gladiator*/1986 * *The Outer Limits*: 'Valerie 23'/1995

Amazing Stories (US TV series, 1985–7)

Also listed as *Steven Spielberg's Amazing Stories*, this expensive series ranges from fantasy through s-f to horror but suffers from generaly feeble storylines (many devised by executive producer **Spielberg**). In William Dear's 'Mummy Daddy' (1985), a movie actor on location in the swamps is mistaken for a real reanimated **mummy**; more gruesome is Robert **Zemeckis**'s 'Go To the Head of the Class' (1986), an **EC Comic** revenge tale; with Spielberg's 'The Mission' (1985), these episodes were released overseas as a theatrical feature, *Amazing Stories*. Directors: Joe **Dante**, Tobe **Hooper**, Paul **Bartel**, Bob **Clark**, Clint Eastwood, Martin Scorsese; writers: Mick **Garris**, Michael **McDowell**, Richard **Matheson**. TM

American Gothic (US TV series, 1995–)

Created by Shaun Cassidy and executive produced by Sam **Raimi**, *American Gothic* is set in Trinity, South Carolina, a small town beset by evil in the shape of demonic Sheriff Lucas Buck (Gary Cole). Against Buck are out-of-towner Dr Matt Crower (Jake Weber), orphan Caleb Temple (Lucas Black), his sister's ghost (Sarah Paulson) and reporter Gail Emory (Paige Turco); the Devil's minions are schoolteacher Selena Coombs (Brenda Bakke) and Deputy Ben Healy (Nick Searcy). Similar in style to *Twin Peaks* (1990–91), but a more on-the-nose genre piece, with ghostly and infernal goings-on between dark soap operatics.

American Indians

It is neither a surprise that one of America's first horrors (*The Werewolf*, 1913) features a white-hating Navajo lycanthrope, nor that Indians fail, aside from obscurities (*Death Curse of Tartu*, 1966; *The Devil's Mistress*, 1968), to be a concerted genre resource until the disaffected 70s. Protest **Westerns** (*A Man Called Horse*, 1970; *Soldier Blue*, 1971) mix Indian spiritualism with ultra-**violence**, prefiguring a cycle in which tribal spirits furnish both a **monster** and, typically, an excuse to shoot outdoors: *Haunted* (1976), *Shadow of the Hawk* (1976), *The Manitou* (1977), *Shadow*

American Indians: *Death Curse of Tartu*

of Chikara (1978), *Wendigo* (1978), *Ghost Dance* (1982), *The Dark Power* (1985). Amerindian beliefs are naively deployed by **eco-horror**: *Nightwing* (1979), *Prophecy* (1979), *Wolfen* (1980), *Creepshow 2* (1987), *Pet Sematary* (1989), *Grim Prairie Tales* (1990). Hollywood's late-decade interest in Indian affairs yielded Michael Apted's provocative, supernatural *Thunderheart* (1992). Having contributed to the trend in *The Doors* (1991), Oliver **Stone** mocks it with the captioneering shaman of *Natural Born Killers* (1994). DP

Amicus

British production company, formed by Americans Milton **Subotsky** and Max Rosenberg. After pop musicals (*It's Trad, Dad!*, 1962; *Just for Fun*, 1963), they were, for a while, Britain's second most important horror company. Generally steering clear of **Hammer**-style period horror, they concentrated on present-day settings, often employing Robert **Bloch**, a brand-name after *Psycho* (1960). Amicus made psychological or supernatural thrillers (*The Psychopath*, 1965; *The Skull*, 1965), but their significant innovation was the reintroduction of the **anthology** format of *Dead of Night* (1945). *Dr. Terror's House of Horrors* (1964), *Torture Garden* (1967), *The House that Dripped Blood* (1970) and *Asylum* (1972) offer four or five stories housed within a basic master narrative. At their best, these have economy and wit; though, as is often the case with portmanteaux, quality is decidedly variable. Two later omnibuses (*Tales from the Crypt*, 1972; *Vault of Horror*, 1973) adapt **EC Comics** (a cinema first) but sadly miss the iconoclasm of the originals.

Amicus never developed a distinctive personality, possibly because it lacked the repertory company of actors and technicians cultivated by Hammer. The directors most associated with Amicus (Freddie **Francis**, Roy Ward **Baker**) are reliable professionals of the

Margot Kidder, James Brolin, *The Amityville Horror*

old school, capable of effective but quite impersonal projects. Moreover, in the late 60s and early 70s, when Hammer actively sought younger film-makers and embarked on an updating of its conventions, Amicus were reluctant to change, with the exception of Stephen **Weeks**'s unsuccessful *I, Monster* (1970) and Gordon **Hessler**'s extraordinary *Scream and Scream Again* (1969). After Edgar Rice Burroughs adaptations (*The Land That Time Forgot*, 1975), Amicus faded from view; ironically, given their name, the company foundered in acrimony after the levering-out of Subotsky by Rosenberg. PH

The Amityville Horror (1979)

Amityville, incidentally locale of *Jaws* (1975), became a horror franchise when George and Kathy Lutz provided Jay Anson with material for an alleged non-fiction book *The Amityville Horror* (1978), filmed with Margot Kidder and James Brolin as a couple plagued by supernatural phenomena after buying a house where a mass murder took place. Sequels, prequels, spin-offs: *Amityville II: The Possession* (1982), *Amityville 3-D* (1983), *Amityville 4: The Evil Escapes* (1989), *The Amityville Curse* (1990), *Amityville 1992: It's About Time* (1992), *Amityville: A New Generation* (1993), *Amityville: Dollhouse* (1996). There are 'based-on-fact' imitations – the 1987 book and 1991 TV movie *The Haunted* – but the most credible variant is 'The House That Bled to Death' (**Hammer House of Horror**, 1980), in which home-owners fake a haunting to yield profits from the best seller and the movie.

Andrews, V.C. [Virginia] (19??–86)

American writer, posthumous brand name, heiress to the **gothic**. *Flowers in the Attic* (1979), her first best seller, plays up the child

abuse and **incest** implicit in the family curses and unjust imprisonments of **Radcliffe** and **Lewis**. *Petals on the Wind* (1980) and other sequels extend the tale of the Dollenganger children into a dysfunctional **family** saga. She cameos as a maid in Jeffrey Bloom's weak *Flowers in the Attic* (1986). In a development akin to her plots, which turn on disputed fortunes and bizarre wills, her heirs retained Andrew Niederman to write novels under the by-line 'the New Virginia Andrews', commencing with *Dawn* (1991).

Anger, Kenneth (b. 1932)

American avant-garde/underground film-maker, self-proclaimed student of Aleister **Crowley**, author of the notorious *Hollywood Babylon* (1958). Anger's volatile obsessions with 'magick', sexuality and death, and his use of cinema as an alchemical medium earn him a unique position in the genre. Infant Anger appeared as the Changeling in *A Midsummer Night's Dream* (1935), and he soon became the *enfant terrible* of an unusual trinity of post-war Los Angeles avant-garde fantasist film-makers which he formed with Gregory Markopoulos and Curtis **Harrington**. Anger began at age nine with *Prisoner of Mars* (1942), filmed with miniatures, then created the incest melodrama *The Nest* (1943) and the celebrated *Fireworks* (1947), a homoerotic delirium-dream in which aroused sailors eviscerate young Anger and a roman-candle phallus explodes. Kodak Laboratories reportedly sabotaged *The Love That Whirls* (1949) by seizing a staged sequence of an Aztec human sacrifice. Anger's mature works are landmarks of the new American underground, and are, in and of themselves, transformative rituals: the exquisite *Eaux d'Artifice* (1953); the religious motor-cycle-fetish epic *Scorpio Rising* (1962–4); the hallucinogenic, black magickal *Inauguration of the Pleasure Dome* (1954, revised in 1966);

Animation: *The Secret Adventures of Tom Thumb*

Invocation of My Demon Brother (1969); and *Lucifer Rising* (1970–81). SB/DW

Animation

Film executed not shot by shot, as in live action cinematography, but frame by frame. Techniques include the cel process associated with **Disney** (cartoon animation) and flat cut-outs in two dimensions; puppet, model, material and object animation in three. Certain film-makers (Georges **Méliès**, Ladislaw Starewicz, Jan **Švankmajer**, David **Lynch**, Shinya Tsukamoto) combine 2-D and/or 3-D and/or live action.

Animated shorts accompanied American theatrical features from the mid-20s to the mid-60s, not infrequently mixing horror with 'funny animal' comedy. The Fleischer brothers have hooded figures in dark sanctums (*Bimbo's Initiation*, 1931) and prefigure Disney's *Snow White* feature with their jazzier, macabre Betty Boop version (1933). At Warners, Chuck Jones has Daffy Duck struggle against vanishing backgrounds and morphing body parts (*Duck Amuck*, 1953), Friz Freleng turns Sylvester into a monster (*Dr. Jerkyl's Hide*, 1954) and torments him in hell through a demonic bulldog (*Satan's Waitin'*, 1954). Following Hanna-Barbera's violent MGM *Tom and Jerry* series, Chuck Jones's sadistic *Roadrunner* cartoons take the form about as far as it can go. The insane universe of MGM's Tex Avery enlarges cat, mouse and dog to planet-dwarfing proportions (*King Size Canary*, 1947) or drops a battleship on a bulldog (*Bad Luck Blackie*, 1949).

The radical 50s style house UPA (United Productions of America) break the mould with a **Poe** adaptation in **3-D**, *The Tell-Tale Heart* (1953). The legacy of pioneers Méliès and Starewicz bears fruit in Canada's Norman McLaren (*Neighbours*, 1952) and Belgium's Raoul Servais (*Harpya*, 1979). Czech animators, whose traditions include a distinctive folk puppet theatre, tackle a horror at once politically specific and universal: the repressive regime of Jirí Trnka's swan-song *Ruka* (*The Hand*, 1965) collapses in Švankmajer's *Konec stalinismu v Čechàch* (*The Death of Stalinism in Bohemia*, 1990). In Poland, Walerian **Borowczyk**'s cut-outs conjure the hermetically sealed worlds of *Dom* (*Home*, 1958), *Jeux des anges* (*Angel's Games*, 1964) and the bleak feature *Théâtre de Monsieur et Madame Kabal* (1967). Jules Bass's *Mad Monster Party?* (1967) stop-frame spoofs Universal **monsters**, prefiguring the work of Henry Selick, who made *Slow Bob in the Lower Dimensions* (1989) for MTV before

Animation: *Urotsukidoji II: Legend of the Demon Womb*

employing animator Paul Berry (*The Sandman*, 1992) on *The Nightmare Before Christmas* (1993).

British animated features adapt literary texts faithfully (Halas and Batchelor's *Animal Farm*, 1955) or freely (the **Quay Brothers'** *Street of Crocodiles*, 1986, Dave Borthwick's *Secret Adventures of Tom Thumb*, 1993), while rock music spawns George Dunning's blue meanies (*Yellow Submarine*, 1968) and Gerald Scarfe's drug-addled imagery (*The Wall*, 1982). Japanese puppet animator Kihachiro Kawamoto (*Oni/The Demon*, 1972; *Dojoji Temple*, 1976) recalls both Trnka's puppetry and live action Japanese demon movies; stop motion footage in Tsukamoto's *Tetsuo* movies (1989, 1991) echoes Švankmajer; and Japanese tradition feeds back into the splattery finale of Brit Barry Purves's *Screen Play* (1992). 2-D animation (*anime*) constitutes an extraordinary 10 per cent of Japanese film, TV and video production, partly spawned by pervasive, indigenous *manga* (comic) culture, and has yielded horrors like *Vampire Hunter D* (1985), *Warau Hyoteki* (*Laughing Target*, 1987), *Yoju Toshi* (*Wicked City* 1987), *Ningyo No Mori* (*Mermaid Forest*, 1991), *Urotsukidoji* (*Legend of the Overfiend*, 1989), *Ankoku No Judge* (*Judge*, 1991), *Sazan Eyes* (*3x3 Eyes*, 1991–5), *Teito Monogatari* (*Doomed Megalopolis*, 1992). Other significant animated horrors: *Haunted Hotel* (1907), *Krvavá pani* (1980), *The Victor* (1985), *Frankenstein Punk* (1986),

¡Vampiros en la Habana! (*Vampires in Havana*, 1985), *The Golem* (1987), *The Web* (1987), *Toxic* (1990), *h* (1994), *Batman: Mask of the Phantasm* (1993). JC

Ankers, Evelyn (1918–85)

Chilean-born British actress, in Hollywood from 1940. For half a decade, Universal's leading horror **heroine**. SJ

*Hold That Ghost/The Wolf Man/*1941 ∗ *The Ghost of Frankenstein/Sherlock Holmes and the Voice of Terror/*1942 ∗ *Captive Wild Woman/The Mad Ghoul/Son of Dracula/*1943 ∗ *The Pearl of Death/Weird Woman/The Invisible Man's Revenge/Jungle Woman/*1944 ∗ *The Frozen Ghost/*1945

TV: *Your Show Time*: 'The Adventure of the Speckled Band'/1949

Anthologies

There are as many multi-story horror films as multi-story films of all other genres together, perhaps because of the wealth of short stories available for adaptation. Early examples are *Hoffmanns Erzählungen* (1916), *Unheimliche Geschichten* (1919), *Das Wachsfigurenkabinett* (*Waxworks*, 1924) and *Flesh and Fantasy* (1943), but the form reached its apotheosis in Ealing's *Dead of Night* (1945), which pioneers the use of a frame story, multiple directors and a large cast of guest stars.

After *Dr. Terror's House of Horrors* (1964), an imitation of *Dead of Night*, producer Milton **Subotsky** stayed with the format, mining Robert **Bloch** (*Torture Garden*, 1966, *The House That Dripped Blood*, 1971; *Asylum*, 1972), **EC comics** (*Tales From the Crypt*, 1972; *Vault of Horror*, 1973), R. **Chetwynd-Hayes** (*From Beyond the Grave*, 1974; *The Monster Club*, 1980) and **cats** (*The Uncanny*, 1977). Edgar Allan **Poe**, source of *Unheimliche Geschichten*, is used by Roger **Corman** (*Tales of Terror*, 1962), the Argentine *Obras maestras del terror* (1960), the Malle-**Vadim-Fellini** triad (*Histoires extraordinaires*, 1968) and Dario **Argento** and George **Romero** (*Due occhi diabolici/Two Evil Eyes*, 1990). Others to receive such treatment are Nathaniel **Hawthorne** (*Twice-Told Tales*, 1963), Richard **Matheson** (*Trilogy of Terror*, 1975; *Dead of Night*, 1977), Stephen **King** (*Creepshow*, 1982; *Cat's Eye*, 1984) and H.P. **Lovecraft** (*Necronomicon*, 1993).

Anthology spin-offs from, pilots for or repackagings of TV series include: *The Veil* (1958), **Night Gallery** (1969), *Twilight Zone: the Movie* (1983), *Tales From the Crypt* (1989),

LEFT Apes: *The Gorilla* (1930)

Tales From the Darkside: the Movie (1990) and *Body Bags* (1994). Other examples: *Three Cases of Murder* (1955), *The Devil's Messenger* (1962), *Kwaidan* (1965), *Dr. Terror's Gallery of Horrors* (1966), *Tales That Witness Madness* (1972), *Blood Bath* (1975), *Nightmares* (1983), *From a Whisper to a Scream* (1986), *After Midnight* (1989), the **Westerns** *Grim Prairie Tales* (1990) and *Into the Badlands* (1991), the Australian *beDevil* (1993), the black-themed *Tales From the Hood* (1995). The video boom prompted a proliferation of cobbled-together efforts, often repackaging pre-existing shorts: *Screamtime* (1983), *Freaky Fairy Tales* (1986), *Escapes* (1986), *Terror Eyes* (1987), *The Willies* (1990), *Virtual Terror* (1995).

A few films try for an omnibus feel within a continuing storyline, rarely with success: *House of Frankenstein* (1944), *The Company of Wolves* (1984), *Waxwork* (1988). Portmanteau films are rarely popular successes: even the best – *Dead of Night*, the Archers' *Tales of Hoffmann* (1951), Mario **Bava**'s *I tre volti della paura* (*Black Sabbath*, 1963) – suffer unevenness as weaker episodes sandwich outstanding stories and stop-and-start pacing prevents sustained effects.

The Anti-Christ * See: **Apocalypse**; **The Devil**; *The Omen*

Apes

No animals have a longer association with the horror film, and especially the B-movie, than those in the ape family. Almost always portrayed by men in suits, gorillas provide comical scares from the silent days. The play *The Gorilla* (filmed 1927, 1930, 1939), links a gorilla with murders, a theme introduced by **Poe** in his oft-filmed **'The Murders in the Rue Morgue'** (1841). Killer gorillas (or murderers pretending to be thus) also appear in *The Monster Walked* (1931), *The Ape* (1940), *The Monster Walks* (1932) and *Gorilla at Large* (1954). **Mad scientist** experiments with monkey glands or gorilla brains are commonplace: *The Monkey Brain* (1908), *An Apish Trick* (1909), *Balaoo* (1913), *Go and Get It* (1920), *A Blind Bargain* (1922), *The Wizard* (1927), *The Monster and the Girl* (1940), *Dr. Renault's Secret* (1942), **Captive Wild Woman** (1943), *Bride of the Gorilla* (1951), *Bela Lugosi Meets a Brooklyn Gorilla* (1952), *La horripilante bestia humana* (*Night of the Bloody Apes*, 1968), 'The Creeping Man' (*The Casebook of Sherlock Holmes*, 1991). *King Kong* (1933), epitome of the monster ape, is one of the cinema's great icons, disseminated through sequels (*Son of Kong*, 1933), remakes (1976), parodies (*Queen Kong*, 1976) and merchandising. Other deadly monkeys include chimpanzees (*Link*, 1985, *Phenomena*, 1985), a capuchin (*Monkey Shines*, 1988) and a baboon (*Shakma*, 1990). Killer gorillas (and one good one) return in *Congo* (1995). DM

Apocalypse

Foretold in the Book of Revelation, the unleashing of the Four Horsemen (War, Pestilence, Famine, Death) signals the final battle between Good and Evil at Armageddon. Visualising this prompts considerable cinematic enthusiasm, though the Horsemen themselves are seldom glimpsed other than in two versions of *The Four Horsemen of the Apocalypse* (1921, 1962) and as unexpected reinforcement to Mimi Rogers's fundamentalism in *The Rapture* (1991).

Early apocalyptic films show onslaughts from above: *The Comet* (1910), *Verdens undergang* (*The End of the World*, 1916), *La Fin du monde* (*The End of the World*, 1930), *Deluge* (1933). Not until well into the Cold War was nuclear twilight regularly forecast: *The World, the Flesh and the Devil* (1959), *On the Beach* (1959), *The War Game* (1966). In its shadow, barbarism seems to spread like the plagues of **Night of the Living Dead** (1968), *The Ωmega Man* (1971) and *Rabid* (1976). And the ultimate in chaos, substantiated by Vietnam newsreels, is revealed in *Apocalypse Now* (1979).

Survivalist struggles against the forces of Darkness have become standard horror

RIGHT A Pale Rider, *The Four Horsemen of the Apocalypse* (1921)

material: *The Omen* (1976), *Fear No Evil* (1981), *The Seventh Sign* (1988), *Outcast* (1991), *Warlock: The Armageddon* (1993), *In the Mouth of Madness* (1994). However, the Apocalypse is rarely recognised, more accurately, as prelude to the Second Coming. Apart from a radiant blaze eliminating the Anti-Christ in *The Final Conflict* (1981), nothing has yet matched *Intolerance* (1916) where flights of angels at last bring War to an end. PS

The Archers: See: **Powell, Michael**.

Are You Afraid of the Dark? (US TV series, 1993–5)

A **young adult** anthology show, filmed in Canada by Nickelodeon, the teenage members of The Midnight Society tell spooky stories around a campfire. Episodes feature mid-teenage protagonists tangling with ghosts, magic or traditional **monsters**, and usually pay off with a moral lesson. Regular characters: Tucker (Daniel de Santo), Sam (Joanna Garcia), Gary (Ross Hull), Betty Ann (Raine Pare-Coull), Kiki (Jodie Resther), Stig (Codie Wilbee); frame sequence directors: Jacques Payette, Jacques Laberge. SJ

Argento, Dario (b. 1940)

Italian director, writer, composer, producer. Notwithstanding an unwillingness to stray beyond the confines of his genre, Argento is not only the avatar of **violent** modern horror but also a significant auteur. Responsible for a reiterative series that begins with *L'uccello dalle piume di cristallo* (*The Bird with the Crystal Plumage*, 1970), he is lauded for his exploratory camera and choreographic approach but often accused of insubstantiality. In fact, artificial technique combines meaningfully with the content of films which, disguised as detective thrillers, pose troublesome questions of causality and cognition.

Now shy of theory, Argento entered cinema as a critic, switching to screenplays after a controversial tenure on Rome daily *Paese sera*. A collaborative credit (with Bernardo Bertolucci) on Sergio Leone's *C'era una volta il West* (*Once Upon a Time in the West*, 1968) preceded several Western, war and sex titles. *L'uccello*, an unofficial version of Fredric **Brown**'s *The Screaming Mimi* (1949), is crucially endebted to the *gialli* of Mario **Bava**. Sufficiently underestimated that its backers lobbied for Argento's removal, the film proved a surprise international success. *L'uccello*'s mystery is generated by the partial

witness of a journeyman writer; *Il gatto a nove code* (*The Cat O'Nine Tails*, 1971) unfolds from blind ex-journalist Karl Malden's literal inability to see. With a killer who only murders in an attempt to suppress genetic information that suggests he is a **psychopath**, *gatto* is founded on a provoking tautology. *Quattro mosche di velluto grigio* (*Four Flies on Grey Velvet*, 1972) expands on previous frigidities by having its musician protagonist discover his wife (Mimsy **Farmer**) is also his persecutor. As 'God', a jovial vagrant also borrowed from *The Screaming Mimi*, Bud Spencer provides the mockingly literal *deus ex machina*.

Le cinque giornate (1973) is Argento's single digression: chronicling the collapse of Milan's 1848 revolt, the historical **comedy** usefully reveals its maker as a political animal. *La porta sul buio* (1973) was better received: Argento helmed two of the four TV featurettes ('Il tram', 'Testimone oculare') and acted as series host. With David **Hemmings** begging the comparison to Antonioni's *Blowup* (1966), *Profondo rosso* (*Deep Red*, 1975) is a determined improvement: more fundamentally irrational than before, the film pairs a newly circumlocutious plot with a set of foreboding visual rhymes and hides its felon in plain sight. *Profondo* is stranger for the debut of haranguing pomp-rockers **Goblin**.

Unambiguously supernatural, *Suspiria* (1977) is Argento's most profitable work, and his most baroque. Collapsing expectations by opening with an insuperable double homicide, it flaunts a palette perversely derived from *Snow White and the Seven Dwarfs* (1937). Fairy-tale associations are enhanced by a ballet school setting which, courtesy of co-writer/lover Daria **Nicolodi**, also complicates Argento's vaunted misogyny. The narcotic *Inferno* (1980) extends *Suspiria* via Thomas De Quincey's 'Suspiria de Profundis' (1845). Positing three demoniac Mothers prior to the investigation of New York resident Mater Tenebrarum, the sequel climaxes with an audacious disappointment: far from resolving his sister's disappearance, Leigh McCloskey merely discovers the culprit is Death. Discouraging, genuinely oneiric horror, *Inferno* fell victim to a coup at 20th Century-Fox: the balance of Argento's output responds to its failure.

The bitterly involuted *Tenebre* (*Tenebrae*, 1982) has Anthony **Franciosa** take the place of a killer whose crimes mimic those of his

RIGHT Dario Argento

latest novel. Argento conceived the icily dressed *giallo* after death threats from an American fan. ESP story *Phenomena* (1985) no less diaristically casts the estranged Nicolodi as its brutalised villain, but the sum is self-parodically mainstream. Shot in English to a metal hits soundtrack, the film exhibits a much less ironic attitude to its pseudo-science than previously. Produced by Argento in lieu of brother Claudio and/or father Salvatore, *Phenomena* is the closest of his movies to those he has supervised for Lamberto **Bava** and Michele **Soavi**. Likewise sidelined by mawkishness, *Opera* (1987) nevertheless contains the aptest image of Argento's *ouevre*: the **heroine** watching a killer's oblations, eyes forced open with pins. Made in the wake of an unrealised staging of *Rigoletto* (1851), Argento's most solipsistic entry marks both the end of his latest engagement and Salvatore's passing. The **Poe** anthology *Due occhi diabolici* (*Two Evil Eyes*, 1989) preceded cable game-show *Giallo* (1987–8) and, though another commercial disappointment, is the director's happiest compromise. Argento intended the project to team him with at least three major

US horrorists; in the event, his unexpectedly actor-oriented 'The Black Cat' seems the weightier for George **Romero**'s negligent half.

Trauma (1994), the first of Argento's movies to lens entirely in America, is a perfunctory reprise of pediatric themes (despite daughter Asia's central role). Retrenched to Florence, *La sindrome di Stendhal* (*The Stendhal Syndrome*, 1996) characteristically links high art with murder, taking the Uffizi Gallery as a location, and further inconveniences Asia Argento as a cop persecuted by a mad rapist and a bizarre psychiatric condition. Urbano Barberini is an Argento substitute in Luigi **Cozzi**'s *Il gatto nero* (*Edgar Allan Poe's The Black Cat*, 1991), an unwelcome valentine that imagines the making of another Mothers movie. Argento's interest in stylistics has resulted in a Trussardi fashion show (1988) and adverts for Fiat (1987) and Johnson and Johnson (1992). He cameos in Alberto Sordi's *Scusi, lei è favorevole o contrario?* (1966), *Innocent Blood* (1992) and *Il cielo sempre più blu* (1996), exists as a cartoon in *Profondo Rosso* comic, contributes a voice-over to the Asia-directed segment of *Degenerazione* (1994) and plays his own killers wherever anonymity will allow. DP

Dawn of the Dead (p)/1978 * *Demoni* (p)/1985 * *Demoni 2* (p)/1986 * *La chiesa* (p)/1989 * *La setta* (p)/1991 * *La maschera di cera* [*Wax Mask*] (p)/1996

Dario Argento, *Profondo thrilling* (1975); Maitland McDonagh, *Broken Mirrors/Broken Minds: The Dark Dreams of Dario Argento* (1991); Alan Jones, *Mondo Argento* (1996)

Arkoff, Samuel Z. (b. 1918)

American executive producer. In 1954 Arkoff founded American International Pictures with James H. **Nicholson**, backing movies aimed at teenage drive-in patrons. AIP distributed Herman **Cohen**'s *I Was a Teenage Werewolf* (1957), Roger **Corman**'s *The Fall of the House of Usher* (1960) and Mario **Bava**'s *La maschera del demonio* (1960), which began profitable cycles. Though reckoned less creative than Nicholson, Arkoff oversaw *Blacula* (1972), *The Amityville Horror* (1979) and *Dressed to Kill* (1980) after his partner's departure. Since leaving AIP (which became Filmways) in 1980, Arkoff has had credits on *Q* (1982) and *The Final Terror* (1983).

Samuel Z. Arkoff (with Richard Trubo), *Flying Through Hollywood by the Seat of My Pants* (1993)

Samuel Z. Arkoff (with cigar) and James H. Nicholson

Armstrong, Michael (b. 1947)

British writer, director. Having earned the dubious distinction of launching David **Bowie**'s film career with the ghost story short *The Image* (1967), Armstrong persuaded exploitationists Tigon to back *The Haunted House of Horror* (1969), which hit screens after producers interfered to up the youth appeal, and helmed the notorious *Hexen bis auf's Blut gequält* (*Mark of the Devil*, 1969) in Germany. Three later shorts, co-directed with Stanley Long, are lumped together in the drab *Screamtime* (1982). Armstrong wrote *House of Long Shadows* (1983) for Peter **Walker** and directed a 1990 prologue for a re-release of **The Phantom of the Opera** (1925). MA

Art

The chief horror tale about an uncanny portrait is Oscar **Wilde**'s **The Picture of Dorian Gray** (1891). More traditionally, pictures provide eyeholes for observing the innocent (*What a Carve Up!*, 1961) or visual reminders of dead characters about to manifest as ghosts (*The Uninvited*, 1944; *The Ghost and Mrs. Muir*, 1947). Paintings have the power of **voodoo** dolls in *Vault of Horror* (1973), depict hell in *L'aldilà* (*The Beyond*, 1981) and inspire tales in **Night Gallery** (1970–73).

An artist is blinded by acid in *Dead Man's Eyes* (1944) and another crippled by a critic in *Dr. Terror's House of Horrors* (1964), but most horror film artists are murderously aggressive. Painters kill in *Bluebeard* (1944) and *Blood Bath* (1966), while others use human **blood** for pigment in *Color Me Blood*

Red (1964) and *Blood Delirium* (1989). Sculptors are no better, using corpses for armatures in *A Bucket of Blood* (1959), *Diary of a Madman* (1963) and *El coleccionista de cadaveres* (*Cauldron of Blood*, 1967), while the maddest of the bunch (Martin **Kosleck**) makes a model of hideous and homicidal Rondo **Hatton** in *House of Horrors* (1946).

Dario **Argento** uses sculpture to kill a villain in *Tenebre* (*Tenebrae*, 1983), a trick stolen in *Dead Again* (1991), and hangs *La sindrome di Stendhal* (*The Stendhal Syndrome*, 1996) on an extreme psychological reaction to great art. Also taking a cue perhaps from Argento, who choreographs death as if he were a *grand guignol* Busby Berkeley, is the killer of *Se7en* (1995), for whom serial killing is explicitly a form of performance art. LD

Ashton, Roy (1909–95)

Australian-born British make-up artist. Ashton assisted Philip **Leakey** at **Hammer Films** on *Dracula* (1958) before becoming their in-house monster specialist. He successfully transformed Christopher **Lee** in *The Mummy* (1959) and Oliver **Reed** in *The Curse of the Werewolf* (1960) and made an interesting if odd snake-lady of Jacqueline **Pearce** in *The Reptile* (1966), but his classic monsters in **The Phantom of the Opera** (1963), *The Gorgon* (1964) and *The Evil of Frankenstein* (1964) are flakily makeshift. MS

The Man Who Changed His Mind/1936 * *Fire Maidens From Outer Space*/1957 * *The Abominable Snowman*/1958 * *The Hound of the Baskervilles*/*The Man Who Could Cheat Death*/*The Ugly Duckling*/1959 * *The Stranglers of Bombay*/*The Two Faces of Dr. Jekyll*/*The Brides of Dracula*/1960 * *The Shadow of the Cat*/*The Terror of the Tongs*/*Taste of Fear*/1961 * *Captain Clegg*/1962 * *The Damned*/*Paranoiac*/*Kiss of the Vampire*/*The Old Dark House*/1963 * *Nightmare*/*Curse of the Mummy's Tomb*/*Dr. Terror's House of Horrors*/1964 * *Fanatic*/*The Plague of Zombies*/*She*/*Hysteria*/*Dracula – Prince of Darkness*/*Rasputin the Mad Monk*/*The Skull* (u)/1965 * *The Devil Rides Out* (u)/1967 * *Tales From the Crypt*/*Jane Eyre*/*Hands of the Ripper* (u)/*The Devils* (u)/1971 * *Asylum*/*The Creeping Flesh*/1972 * *Vault of Horror*/*Persecution*/1973 * *The Ghoul*/*Legend of the Werewolf*/1974 * *The Monster Club*/1981

TV: *Frankenstein: The True Story*/1973

Astin, John (b. 1930)

American actor. Gomez in **The Addams Family** (1964–6) and animated reprises (1973, 1992–3).

Roy Ashton's handiwork: Christopher Lee, Peter Cushing, *The Mummy* (1959)

The Spirit is Willing/1966 * *Teen Wolf Too*/1987 * *Return of the Killer Tomatoes*/1988 * *Night Life*/1989 * *Gremlins 2: The New Batch*/1990 * *Killer Tomatoes Strike Back*/1991 * *Killer Tomatoes Eat France*/*Stepmonster*/1992 * *The Silence of the Hams*/1993 * *The Frighteners*/1996

TV: *The Twilight Zone*: 'A Hundred Yards Over the Rim'/1961 * *Wild Wild West*: 'The Night of the Tartar'/1967 * *Night Gallery*: 'The House' (d)/1970; 'A Fear of Spiders' (d)/'The Dark Boy' (d)/'Pamela's Voice'/'Hell's Bells'/1971; 'The Girl With the Hungry Eyes'/1972 * *The New Scooby-Doo Movies*: 'Scooby-Doo Meets the Addams Family' (v)/1972 * *Circle of Fear*: 'Graveyard Shift'/1973 * *Halloween With the Addams Family*/1977 * *Disney Movie*: 'Mr. Boogedy'/1986 * *The Charmings*: 'The Witch of Van Oaks'/1987 * *Eerie, Indiana*/1991–2 * *Tales From the Crypt*: 'Top Billing'/1991

Astral Projection * See: **Out of Body Experiences**

Asylums

An almost superstitious fear of madness makes it a key component in many horror films, with the asylum serving as the haunted house of the mind. 'The System of Dr. Tarr and Prof. Fether' (1845), **Poe**'s tale of inmates taking over the asylum, was first adapted comically by Edison (*Lunatics in Power*, 1909) and seriously by Maurice Tourneur (*Le système du Doctor Goudron et du Professeur Plume*, 1912). Variations on this theme include *The Monster* (1925), *Don't Look in the Basement* (1972) and *Silent Night, Bloody Night* (1973), and deciding which residents are sane is crucial to ***Das Cabinet des Dr. Caligari*** (1919), *Asylum* (1972) and *Tales That Witness Madness* (1972). The most famous inmate in horror is **Renfield**, resident madman and aspiring **vampire**, but Dr **Mabuse** often manipulates others from his solitary cell, perhaps inspiring Thomas **Harris**'s Hannibal Lecter.

Paranoid fears of being a sane person incarcerated by brutal keepers are exploited in *Bedlam* (1946), *Behind Locked Doors* (1948), *Shock* (1946), *Shock Corridor* (1963), *Shock Treatment* (1964), *Asylum of Satan* (1971), *The Dead Pit* (1989) and *Disturbed* (1990). Nevertheless, madhouses are most commonly used as places from which **psychopaths** escape or are prematurely released: ***The Cat and the Canary*** (1927), *Night of Terror* (1933), *Maniac* (1963), *Strait-Jacket* (1964), **Halloween** (1978), *Alone in the Dark* (1982), *Psycho II* (1983), *Silent Madness* (1984), *Psycho Girls* (1985). LD

Atkins, Peter (b. 1955)
British writer. His talents have been turned to *Hellraiser* sequels and the narration of *Dust Devil* (1992). His promising first novels are *Morningstar* (1992) and *Big Thunder* (1996). As an actor, he is flayed alive in Clive **Barker**'s *The Forbidden* (1975–8).

Hellbound: Hellraiser II/1988 * *Nightbreed* (2nd unit d)/1990 * *Hellraiser III: Hell on Earth* (+a)/1992 * *Fist of the North Star*/1995 * *Hellraiser: Bloodline*/1996

Asylums: Peter Breck, *Shock Corridor*

Atwill, Lionel (1885–1946)

British actor, cast as stocky **mad scientists**, police inspectors or burgomasters. Memorable as the mad **artist** of *Mystery of the Wax Museum* (1932), the red herring of *Doctor X* (1932), the one-armed Inspector Krogh in *Son of Frankenstein* (1939), and Moriarty in *Sherlock Holmes and the Secret Weapon* (1942). SJ

The Vampire Bat/Murders in the Zoo/Secret of the Blue Room/The Sphinx/1933 * *The Man Who Reclaimed His Head/Mark of the Vampire*/1935 * *The Hound of the Baskervilles/The Gorilla*/1939 * *Man Made Monster*/1941 * *The Ghost of Frankenstein/The Strange Case of Dr. Rx/Night Monster/The Mad Doctor of Market Street*/1942 * *Frankenstein Meets the Wolf Man*/1943 * *Fog Island/Captain America/House of Frankenstein*/1944 * *House of Dracula*/1945 * *Genius at Work*/1946

Aured, Carlos (b. 1937)

Spanish director, producer. Aured progressed from directing silly Paul **Naschy** films to producing ersatz Americana like Alice **Cooper**'s bid for horror stardom, *Monster Dog* (*Leviatan*, 1985).

El espanto surge de la tumba [*Horror Rises From the Tomb*]/1972 * *Los ojos azules de la muñeca rota* [*House of Psychotic Women*]/*La venganza de la momia/El retorno de Walpurgis* [*Curse of the Devil*]/1973

Australia

Horror films made in Australia have the same problem as everything else made in Australia: koalas and gum trees. Not even Peter **Weir**'s seminal *Picnic at Hanging Rock* (1975) is immune. But the landscape also provides the force behind some remarkable entries in the field. Early Australian cinema drew inspiration from bush life: *The Kelly Gang* (1906) is a contender for the world's first feature film. *The Guyra Ghost Mystery* (1921), *Fischer's Ghost* (1924) and *The Haunted Barn* (1931) are sporadic examples of genre, whereas *For the Term of His Natural Life* (1927) is an overblown gothic romance containing several episodes of effective horror, and *On the Beach* (1959) is one of the nastier cold war/end-of-the-world movies.

The field expanded, along with the rest of the industry, in the mid-70s, with Weir's *The Cars That Ate Paris* (1974), *Picnic*, and George Miller's influential *Mad Max* (1979). The contemporary Australian horror film is characterised by life in the bush gone wrong, struggling against a hostile environment. *Long Weekend* (1979), *Razorback* (1984) and *Dead Calm* (1988) have humans at the mercy of, respectively, a beach, a giant pig and the ocean (plus Billy Zane). In Rolf De Heer's *Incident at Raven's Gate* (1988), alienation is suggested literally. This fear can also come from the uneasy relationship of the settlers with the original inhabitants, though there is little pure Aboriginal mythology on screen. The likes of *Kadaicha* (1988) are simply **Nightmare on Elm Street** (1985) with body paint; in *The Dreaming* (1988) and the frenetic *beDevil* (1993), the white man, by various twists, does the haunting.

Weir's vision of **apocalypse**, *The Last Wave* (1977), makes perhaps the best use of the possibilities. The *Mad Max* series, sire of a hundred post-nuclear action movies, is a different vision of the apocalypse, within a different nightmarish landscape. The original has more in common with Ray Lawrence's *Bliss* (1985), a horrific satire on modern life and the retreat to the bush (and a direct influence on *Howling 3: The Marsupials*, 1987). *Bliss* is also an excellent example of what seems the defining characteristic of Australian film, a surreal but pragmatic sensibility – found in Weir's and Miller's work, and also 'straight' horror films like *Patrick* (1978), the **vampire** film *Thirst* (1979), the excellent thriller *Road Games* (1981) and the unclassifiable *Celia* (1988).

Combining these characteristics within the apocalyptic landscape of the modern city are such vehement stars as *Ghosts . . . of the Civil Dead* (1988), De Heer's *Bad Boy Bubby* (1994) and Geoffrey Wright's magnificent decadents, *Romper Stomper* (1992) and *Metal Skin* (1995). Australian directors who have essayed horror overseas include Jim Sharman (*The Rocky Horror Picture Show*, 1975), Richard **Franklin** (*Psycho 2*, 1983), Russell **Mulcahy** (*Highlander*, 1986), George Miller (*The Witches of Eastwick*, 1987) and Alex Proyas (*The Crow*, 1994). Attempts to emulate American **stalk-and-slash** have not been a great success: *Bloodmoon* (1990) is competent but boring, whereas *Zombie Brigade* (1988) has the opposite problem. Perhaps the best, certainly most interesting, treatment is Philip Brophy's *Body Melt* (1993), part of a fan-driven resurgence in the genre. If there is a single Australian horror icon, it would have to be a more succinct image: The Grim Reaper at the bowling alley, bowling down men, women and children to promote AIDS awareness in the mid-80s. KW/DC

Avati, Pupi (b. 1938)

Italian director, writer. Avati began a cinema career with the neo-gothic *Balsamus, l'uomo di Satana* (1968). The sprit-themed *Thomas* (1970) remains unreleased, but he achieved huge success with *La casa dalle finestre che ridono* (1976), the most accomplished Italian horror film of the 70s. *Tutti defunti tranne . . . i morti* pokes fun at **giallo** conventions, while *Zeder* (1982) is a superbly atmospheric exploration of **zombie** territory. He has directed mainstream fare to international acclaim: *Noi tre* (1984), *Bix* (1990), *Magnificat* (1993). Avati remade *La casa* in America as *Bitter Chamber* (1995), and backed an atmospheric TV serial *Voci notturne* (1995). MA

Il bacio (w)/1974 * *Il cavalier Costante Nicosia demoniaco ovvero Dracula in Brianza* (w)/1975 * *Macabro* [*Macabre*] (w)/1980 * *Dove comincia la notte* (w)/1991 * *La stanza accanto* (w)/1994 * *L'arcano incantatore* [*The Arcane Enchanter*]/1996

The Avengers (UK TV series, 1961–9)

Suavely bowler-hatted John Steed (Patrick **Macnee**) investigates bizarre mysteries with a succession of sidekicks, Dr David Keel (Ian**Hendry**), Cathy Gale (Honor Blackman), Emma Peel (Diana Rigg) and Tara King (Linda Thorson). *The New Avengers* (1976–7) partners Steed with Purdey (Joanna Lumley) and Gambit (Gareth Hunt).

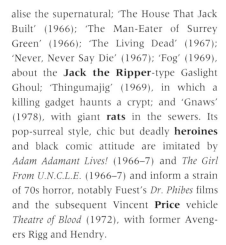

Patrick MacNee as John Steed, *The Avengers*

Notionally a crime show with a sophisticated comic streak, *The Avengers* frequently dallies with the weird and fantastical, employing genre stalwarts like writer Brian **Clemens**, actors Peter **Cushing**, Christopher **Lee** and Michael **Gough**, and directors Roy Ward **Baker**, Don **Sharp** and Robert **Fuest**. Horror episodes: 'Warlock' (1963), a **voodoo** story which unusually does not ration-

alise the supernatural; 'The House That Jack Built' (1966); 'The Man-Eater of Surrey Green' (1966); 'The Living Dead' (1967); 'Never, Never Say Die' (1967); 'Fog' (1969), about the **Jack the Ripper**-type Gaslight Ghoul; 'Thingumajig' (1969), in which a killing gadget haunts a crypt; and 'Gnaws' (1978), with giant **rats** in the sewers. Its pop-surreal style, chic but deadly **heroines** and black comic attitude are imitated by *Adam Adamant Lives!* (1966-7) and *The Girl From U.N.C.L.E.* (1966-7) and inform a strain of 70s horror, notably Fuest's *Dr. Phibes* films and the subsequent Vincent **Price** vehicle *Theatre of Blood* (1972), with former Avengers Rigg and Hendry.

Dave Rogers, *The Avengers* (1983), *The Avengers Anew* (1985), *The Complete Avengers* (1995)

B

Babcock, Dwight V. (1909–79)

American writer. A *Black Mask* contributor and mystery novelist (*The Gorgeous Ghoul*, 1941), Babcock joined Universal's B unit in 1943 and toiled on **Mummy**, **Inner Sanctum**, Ape Woman and Creeper films. He also worked on Columbia's *I Love a Mystery* series and added macabre touches to Bulldog Drummond (*13 Lead Soldiers*, 1948) and Jungle Jim (*Jungle Moon Men*, *Devil Goddess*, 1955) programmers. The **psycho noir** *So Dark the Night* (1946) is notable.

Dead Men's Eyes/1944 * *The Mummy's Curse*/*Jungle Captive*/*Pillow of Death*/1945 * *House of Horrors*/*She-Wolf of London*/*The Devil's Mask*/*The Unknown*/*The Brute Man*/1946

Babies * See: Children and Babies; It's Alive

Baker, Rick (b. 1950)

American make-up artist. The first of a generation of monster-makers inspired in childhood by *Famous Monsters of Filmland* and Dick **Smith**'s *Monster Make-Up Handbook* (1965), Baker became Smith's protégé and assisted on *The Exorcist* (1973). Having worked with John **Landis** on *Schlock* (1973), Baker won an Oscar for the **werewolf** transformations of *An American Werewolf in London* (1981) and reprised the act in 'Thriller' (1983). A lifelong obsession to create the perfect **ape** has seen him make *and*

LEFT Australia: *Razorback*

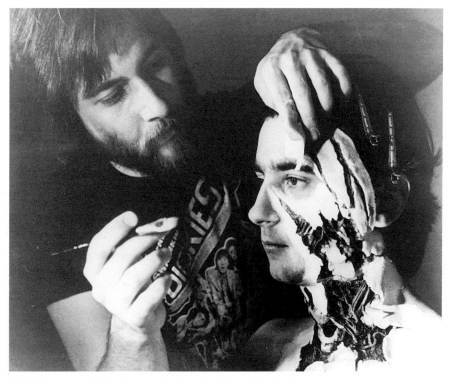

Rick Baker (and Griffin Dunne), *An American Werewolf in London*

play gorillas in **King Kong** (1976), *The Kentucky Fried Movie* (1977) and *The Incredible Shrinking Woman* (1981). Other highpoints: **mutant babies** (*It's Alive*, 1975), a cow creature (*The Funhouse*, 1981), the new flesh (*Videodrome*, 1982), realistic primates (*Greystoke: The Legend of Tarzan, Lord of the Apes*, 1984), Bigfoot (*Harry and the Hender-sons*, 1987), Martin **Landau** as **Lugosi** (*Ed Wood*, 1994). He cameos in Landis's *Into the Night* (1985). MS

Octaman/1971 * *The Thing With Two Heads*/ 1972 * *Track of the Moon Beast*/1976 * *The Fury*/1977 * *Gremlins II: The New Batch*/1990 * *Wolf*/1994 * *The Nutty Professor*/*The Frighteners*/*Escape From LA*/1996

TV: *Werewolf*/1987-8 * *Beauty and the Beast*/ 1987–90 * *Something Is Out There*/1990

Baker, Robert S. (b. 1916) and Berman, Monty (b. 1913)

British producers. Baker and Berman produced many low-budget features from 1948 to the early 60s, mostly thrillers directed by Baker himself, John **Gilling** or Henry Cass. They dabbled in horror following the success of **Hammer**, though never to any great effect. Cass's *Blood of the Vampire* (1958), a messily bombastic period piece featuring **mad scientist** Donald Wolfit, serves only to underline the surgical coldness of Hammer's more successful approach. However, Gilling's *The Flesh and the Fiends* (1959) is the best **Burke and Hare** movie. In the 60s, Baker and Berman switched to television series: *The Saint* (1962–9), *The Champions* (1968–9), **Randall and Hopkirk (Deceased)** (1969–71). PH

The Trollenberg Terror/1958 * *Jack the Ripper*/ 1959 * *What a Carve Up!*/1961

Baker, Roy Ward (b. 1916)

British director. By the time he started making horror films, Baker had proved himself prolific but rather uneven, alternating the accomplished with the workmanlike. Oddities include the US-produced Marilyn Monroe film *Don't Bother to Knock* (1952) and the gothic/**camp** *The Singer Not the Song* (1960). His horror for both **Hammer** and **Amicus** is of much the same order: always professional, sometimes above average, on other occasions routine. For Hammer, *Quatermass and the Pit* (1967) and *The Vampire Lovers* (1970) are polished if impersonal productions which treat their sources, Nigel **Kneale**'s 1959 TV series and **Le Fanu**'s **'Carmilla'** (1871), with more respect than

RIGHT Roy Ward Baker

usually expected from British horror. For the same studio, *Scars of Dracula* (1970) is a decidedly below-par entry in the **Dracula** cycle, while the more interesting *Dr. Jekyll and Sister Hyde* (1971) combines impressively perverse sequences with irritating, very unfunny **comedy**. Similarly, he made one of the best Amicus **anthologies** (*Asylum*, 1972) and one of the weakest (*Vault of Horror*, 1973). Baker had the distinction of directing the maddeningly uneven *The Legend of the 7 Golden Vampires* (1974), Hammer's last period horror. PH

The Anniversary/1968 * *–And Now The Screaming Starts!*/1973 * *The Monster Club*/ 1980

TV: *Journey to the Unknown*: 'The Indian Spirit Guide'/1968 * *Randall and Hopkirk (Deceased)*: 'But What a Sweet Little Room'/'Who Killed Cock Robin?'/1969 * *Q.E.D.*: 'Infernal Device'/'Limehouse Connection'/1982 * *The Masks of Death*/1984

Balaban, Bob (b. 1945)

American director, actor. Having played bearded scientists in *Close Encounters of the Third Kind* (1978) and *Altered States* (1980), Balaban made a remarkable directorial debut with the 50s-set **cannibal** satire *Parents* (1989). With perfectly pitched performances from Randy Quaid and Mary Beth Hurt and a sense of the surreal that encompasses ground meat and kidney-shaped coffee tables, *Parents* effectively renders suburban **family values** deeply sinister.

My Boyfriend's Back (d)/1993

TV: *Tales From the Darkside*: 'Trick or Treat'/

1983 * *Amazing Stories*: 'Fine Tuning'/1985 * *Eerie, Indiana*: 'The Lost Hour'/1991; 'Marshall's Theory of Believability'/'Zombies in PJs'/1992

Balch, Antony (1937–80)

British director, producer. An apostle of sensationalist cinema, Balch became a distributor in 1963 to handle Tod **Browning**'s *Freaks* (1932). His film-making career began in advertising and continued with a trio of assaultive William Burroughs/Brion Gysin collaborations (*Towers Open Fire*, 1963; *The Cut-Ups*, 1967; *Bill and Tony*, 1968). He failed to unrealise a musical version of *Naked Lunch* (1959), but managed two ambitious exploitation features. *Secrets of Sex* (1970) is a morbid, satiric **anthology**; *Horror Hospital* (1973) pays breathlessly idiosyncratic homage to childhood passion Bela **Lugosi**. DP

Balderston, John L. (1889–1954)

American writer. After Broadway success as co-author with J.C. Squire of the twice-filmed time travel romance *Berkeley Square* (1928) and (adapting Hamilton Deane's British version) *Dracula: The Vampire Play* (1927), he worked on a handful of Hollywood classics. His contributions to *Frankenstein* (1931) and *Dracula's Daughter* (1936) were unused outlines, but he did write **The Mummy** (1932) and *Bride of Frankenstein* (1935). His sad final credit is *Red Planet Mars* (1952).

Dracula/*Drácula*/1930 * *The Mystery of Edwin Drood*/*Mad Love*/1935 * *The Man Who Lived Again*/1936

Baledón, Rafael (1???–??)

Mexican director, actor. His most notable film (for its use of Mexican folklore) is *La maldición de la llorona* (*Curse of the Crying Woman*, 1961). He tends to absurd variants on the familiar, offering **Faust** and Mr **Hyde** (*El hombre y el monstruo*, 1957), a **Waxworks** derivative (*El museo del horror*, 1964) and a female **werewolf** (*La loba*, 1964). Don Willis notes *El pantano de las animas* (*Swamp of the Lost Monsters*, 1965) is 'just another western-horror-mystery-comedy-musical'.

La venganza del ahorcado/1958 * *Orlak, el infierno de Frankenstein*/1960 * *Los fantasmas burlones*/1964

Band, Albert (b. 1924)

American producer, director. After directing the ambitious *I Bury the Living* (1958) and *Face of Fire* (1959), Band left horror until the silly *Dracula's Dog* (1977). Latterly, mostly a producer for son Charles **Band**.

Troll/*TerrorVision*/1986 * *Ghoulies II* (d)/1988 * *The Pit and the Pendulum*/1990 * *Doctor Mordrid* (d)/1992

Band, Charles (b. 1951)

American producer, director, son of Albert **Band**. Having grown up on movie sets in Rome in the 60s, Band made Warhol-inspired shorts while in school, but returned to the US determined to make genre movies. As a producer, Band dabbled briefly in X-rated pictures (*The Other Cinderella*, 1976; *Adult Fairy Tales*, 1978), but *Les yeux sans visage* knock-off *Mansion of the Doomed* (1976), directed by Michael **Pataki**, was the shape of things to come. As a producer-director-distributor of horror and fantasy films, Band parlayed witty titles and clever gimmicks into a low-budget empire. He was one of the first entrepreneurs to exploit the video market, forming Meda (now Media) Home Entertainment in 1977.

In the 80s, Band founded Empire International, then its successor, Full Moon Entertainment. Both generated a steady stream of low-budget genre pictures and relied heavily on ancillary markets. An inveterate huckster, Band's impish motto was '1000 films by the year 2000'. He has directed or co-directed more than a dozen films and had a hand in many more. His best work as a director is *Trancers* (1985), though Empire's most notable horror is Stuart **Gordon**'s *Re-Animator* (1986). He has exploited horror commodities from H.P. **Lovecraft** to **vampires**, but has a particular soft spot for diminutive menaces: puppets, **dolls**, little **aliens**, miniature dinosaurs. MM

Crash (d)/1977 * *Tourist Trap*/1979 * *The Alchemist* (d)/1981 * *Parasite* (d)/1982 * *The Dungeonmaster* (co-d)/1983 * *Ghoulies*/1984 * *Troll*/*From Beyond*/*Crawlspace*/1986 * *Dolls*/*Ghoulies II*/1987 * *Prison*/*Ghost Town*/*Pulse Pounders* (unfinished)/1988 * *Puppet Master*/*Shadowzone*/1989 * *Crash and Burn* (d)/*Meridian* (d)/*Catacombs*/*Puppet Master II*/*Demonic Toys*/*Netherworld*/*The Pit and the Pendulum*/1990 * *Trancers 2* (d)/*Puppet Master III*/*Subspecies*/1991 * *Doctor Mordrid* (co-d)/1992 * *Dollman vs. Demonic Toys* (d)/*Trancers III*/*SeedPeople*/*Bloodstone: Subspecies II*/1993 * *Arcade*/*Bloodlust: Subspecies III*/*Trancers 4: Jack of Swords*/*Puppet Master IV*/*The Lurking Fear*/*Dark Angel*/1994 * *Shrunken Heads*/*Puppet Master 5*/*Trancers 5: Sudden Deth*/*Castle Freak*/1995 * *Zakorr! The Invader*/*Blonde Heaven*/1996

Adrienne Barbeau, *Creepshow*

Barbeau, Adrienne (b. 1945)

American actress. Rescuing many a clunker from the brink of unwatchability, the hard-faced, dark-haired Barbeau has cornered the horror market for blowsy drunks and ball-breaking bitches. The TV movie *Someone's Watching Me!* (1978) initiated an association with sometime husband John **Carpenter**, for whom she is as an all-night DJ trapped in a lighthouse by *The Fog* (1980). Her ripe portrayal of a foul-mouthed, whisky-slugging campus wife is easily the best thing about *Creepshow* (1982), and she manages to breathe moments of precious life into **Romero**'s formulaic rendering of 'The Facts in the Case of Mr Valdemar' in *Due occhi diabolici* (*Two Evil Eyes*, 1989). She voices Catwoman on the animated **Batman** (1992–4) MA

Swamp Thing/1982 * *The Next One*/1984 * *Open House*/1987 * *Piranha Women*/1989 * *The Burial of the Rats*/1995

TV: *The Darker Side of Terror*/1979 * *The Twilight Zone*: 'Teacher's Aide'/1985 * *Bridge Across Time*/1986 * *Monsters*: 'All in a Day's Work'/1989

Barker, Clive (b. 1952)

British writer, producer, director. Anointed 'the future name in horror fiction' by Stephen **King**, Barker is a best seller whose high-flown novels continue to contribute to a redefining of the genre. *Hellraiser* (1987) and *Candyman* (1992) excepted, the films he has generated are less inspirational, perhaps bespeaking the limited possibilities of Hollywood horror.

Liverpudlian Barker moved to London in 1977 with members of his theatre group, founding The Dog Company to write and stage *Nightlives, Colossus, Subtle Bodies, The Magician, The Ecstasy* and the politicised fantasies *The History of the Devil* and *Frankenstein in Love*. In 1982, he withdrew from theatre to produce the literary, extreme and fearlessly revisionist horror stories published in the compendious *Books of Blood, Volumes I–VI* (1984–5). The **Faust**ian novel *The Damnation Game* (1985) further demonstrates a willingness to meet descriptive challenges sidestepped by his visionary predecessors, **Lovecraft** and **Machen**.

Cinema, with its visual imperatives, was a not unnatural progression. George Pavlou's *Underworld* (1985), a fatally British piece of s-f **film noir**, takes liberties with Barker's commissioned script; Pavlou's *Rawhead Rex* (1986), from the 1984 story, is less impoverished but even more thoroughly devoid of Barker's trademark audacity. Vetoing similar adaptations – though 'The Yattering and Jack' (1984) became a 1987 **Tales From the Darkside** – Barker opted to direct a feature version of the novella 'The Hellbound Heart' (1986). A striking explication of horror's sensualist subtext, *Hellraiser* presents a potent new set of monsters, and defers significantly to American financiers only in the matter of accents.

Shifting from **splatterpunk** to fabulist with the publication of *Weaveworld* (1987), Barker restricted his involvement in *Hellbound: Hellraiser II* (1988) to scenario and executive production. Scripted by long-time associate Peter **Atkins**, with Stateside liason Tony **Randel** at the helm, the sequel is an uncertain extrapolation of franchisable elements. Barker's own *Nightbreed* (1990), from the monsters-as-good-guys novel *Cabal* (1988), was intended as a Boschian 'Star Wars of horror'. After a difficult shoot, Fox sank a re-edited version with a deceptive slasher trailer, and a projected trilogy, in print and on film, remains uncompleted.

In a bid for greater cinematic control, Barker emigrated to Los Angeles in 1991: California had already provided the setting for *The Great and Secret Show* (1989), first in dream-life tryptych *The Art*. Bernard **Rose**'s *Candyman* increases the viability of the source-story 'The Forbidden' (1985) by translocating it from Liverpool to Chicago. With consequent access to a raft of **black** issues, Barker's urban meta-myth only benefits from the shift. Barker's own *Lord of Illusions* (1995), a variation on 'The Last Illusion' (1985), casts Scott Bakula as recurrent character Harry D'Amour. Rejigged after test screenings, the gumshoe hybrid disappointingly substitutes outré trimmings for any sterner sense of the uncanny. Synchronous video release of *avant garde* juvenilia *Salome* (1973) and *The Forbidden* (1975–8) provided a starkly experimental contrast. The gruesome *Hellraiser III: Hell on Earth* (1992), the flat *Candyman: Farewell to the Flesh* (1995) and the troubled *Hellraiser:* *Bloodline* (1995) continue the franchising, as does intro duty on *Clive Barker's A–Z of Horror* (1997). Other novels: *Imajica* (1991), *The Thief of Always* (1992), mooted as a cartoon feature, *Everville* (1994) and *Sacrament* (1996). DP

Sleepwalkers (a)/1992

Stephen Jones, *Clive Barker's Shadows in Eden* (1991)

Barrymore, Drew (b. 1975)

American actress, grand-daughter of John **Barrymore**. Noticed in *E.T.: The Extra-Terrestrial* (1982), Barrymore starred in Dino De Laurentiis Stephen **King** films before she was ten, as a chubby pyrokinetic in *Firestarter* (1984) and a pet owner in *Cat's Eye* (1985). An interesting young adult **psycho** in *Poison Ivy* (1992).

Altered States/1980 * *Far From Home*/1989 * *Waxwork II: Lost in Time*/1991 * *Doppelganger*/ 1992 * *Batman Forever*/1995 * *Scream*/1996

TV: *Amazing Stories*: 'The Ghost Train'/1985 * *Ray Bradbury Theatre*: 'The Screaming Woman'/1986

Barrymore, John [John Blythe] (1882–1942)

American actor, brother of Ethel and Lionel **Barrymore**. A matinée idol renowned for his 'great profile', he delighted in bizarre characters. His career ultimately floundered in alcoholism and self-parody. SJ

Dr. Jekyll and Mr. Hyde/1920 * *Sherlock Holmes*/1922 * *Svengali*/*The Mad Genius*/1931 * *Rasputin and the Empress*/1932 * *The Invisible Woman*/1941

Barrymore, Lionel [Lionel Blythe] (1878–1954)

American actor, director, brother of Ethel and John **Barrymore**. Remembered as crochety old men in *On Borrowed Time* (1939) and *It's a Wonderful Life* (1946). SJ

The Romance of Elaine/1915 * *The Devil's Garden*/1920 * *The Bells*/1926 * *The Show*/*The 13th Hour*/1927 * *West of Zanzibar*/1928 * *The Unholy Night* (d)/*Mysterious Island*/1929 * *Rasputin and the Empress*/1932 * *Mark of the Vampire*/*The Return of Peter Grimm*/1935 * *The Devil-Doll*/1936

Bartel, Paul (b. 1938)

American director, writer, actor. Bartel made his feature directorial debut with the **psycho** charade *Private Parts* (1972) and had hits

Clive Barker, *Hellraiser*

Drew Barrymore, *Firestarter*

John Barrymore, *Dr. Jekyll and Mr. Hyde* (1920)

Lionel Barrymore

with *Death Race 2000* (1975), a gross skit with David **Carradine** as **Frankenstein**, and *Eating Raoul* (1982), a delicious **cannibal comedy** co-starring Bartel and frequent collaborator Mary **Woronov**. Other directorial credits are spotty (*Cannonball*, 1976; *Lust in the Dust*, 1984; *Scenes From the Class Struggle in Beverly Hills*, 1989; *Shelf Life*, 1993) but include two *Amazing Stories* episodes: 'The Secret Cinema' (1986), a remake of his 1966 short, and 'Gershwin's Trunk' (1987). As a bit player, he is prissily loony in friends' films.

Hollywood Boulevard (a)/1976 * *Piranha* (a)/ 1978 * *Trick or Treats* (a)/*White Dog* (a)/1982 * *Frankenweenie* (s/a)/1984 * *Chopping Mall* (a)/ *Killer Party* (a)/1986 * *Munchies* (a)/1987 * *Mortuary Academy* (a/w)/1988 * *Out of the Dark* (a/p)/1989 * *Gremlins 2: The New Batch* (a)/1991 * *Soulmates* (a)/1992 * *Escape From LA* (a)/1996

TV: *Alfred Hitchcock Presents*: 'The Jar' (a)/ 1986

Bass, Saul (1920–96)

American designer. Known for remarkable titles sequences, Bass has a single directorial credit, the cerebral **insects**-on-the-rampage item *Phase IV* (1974). His claim to have directed the shower murder of *Psycho* (1960), on which he was a visual consultant, has been disputed by Janet **Leigh**. It seems unlikely that **Hitchcock** would have missed an opportunity to work closely with a naked blonde.

RIGHT Paul Bartel (and Mary Woronov), *Eating Raoul*

Vertigo/1958 * *Bunny Lake is Missing*/1965 * *Seconds*/1966 * *Cape Fear*/1991

Bates, Norman * See: Bloch Robert; Gein, Ed; Hitchcock, Alfred; Perkins, Anthony; *Psycho*; Stefano, Joseph

Bates, Ralph (1940–91)

British actor. **Hammer** unsuccessfully tried to promote him as a new horror star. SJ

Taste the Blood of Dracula/1969 * *The Horror of Frankenstein*/*Lust for a Vampire*/1970 * *Dr. Jekyll and Sister Hyde*/1971 * *Fear in the Night*/ 1972 * *Persecution*/1974 * *I Don't Want to Be Born*/1975

TV: *Thriller*: 'Murder Motel'/1975 * *Tales of the Unexpected*: 'Blue Marigold'/1982

Báthory, Erzsébet (1560–1614)

Slovakian mass murderess. Reputedly believ-

ing that bathing in virgins' **blood** would restore her youth, Countess Báthory suborned the **torture** murder of hundreds of children. An aristocratic **psychopath** on the model of Gilles de **Rais**, her case history is told in Sabine Baring-Gould's *The Book of Were-Wolves* (1865), Valentine Penrose's *Erzsébet Báthory: La comtesse sanglante* (1962) and Raymond T. McNally's *Dracula Was a Woman* (1983). A distant relationship with Vlad Tepes prompts her appearance in lurid fictions: Ray **Russell**'s 'Sanguinarius' (1967), Raymond Rudorff's *The Dracula Archives* (1971), John **Blackburn**'s *Our Lady of Pain* (1974), Dean Andersson's *Raw Pain Max* (1988), Elaine Bergstrom's *Daughter of the Night* (1992), Andrei Codrescu's *The Blood Countess* (1995).

Peter **Sasdy**'s *Countess Dracula* (1970), a **Hammer** Film with Ingrid **Pitt** as Erzsébet, is oddly unexcessive, featuring fewer than half a dozen victims. More bloodily indulgent countesses are Lucia Bosé in Jorge **Grau**'s *Ceremonia sangriento* (*The Legend of Blood Castle*, 1972) and Paloma Picasso in Walerian **Borowczyk**'s *Contes immoraux* (*Immoral Tales*, 1974). Báthory's crimes feature in the art movie *Necropolis* (1970), *Vampyros lesbos* (1970), *Mamma Dracula* (1979), *The Mysterious Death of Nina Chereau* (1988) and a Czech cartoon *Krvava pani* (1981). She appears as a **vampire** in Spanish films using variations on the historical name: *La noche de walpurgis* (1970), *El returno de walpurgis* (1973), *La orgia nocturna de los vampiros* (1973), *El retorno del hombre lobo* (1980). A Báthory descendent is seduced into bloodsucking in *Thirst* (1979), but the definitive vampire incarnation is Delphine Seyrig's marcelled lesbian adventuress in Harry **Kümel**'s *Le rouge aux lèvres* (*Daughters of Darkness*, 1971).

Most fictions dignify Báthory by turning her into a standard female **Dracula** or having her genuinely rejuvenated by blood-bathing. As is hinted by Kumel in a scene when Seyrig writhes in pleasure as she talks about her historical atrocities, she was actually a sexual sadist given enormous opportunities by wealth and position.

Batman

Created by Bob Kane and developed by Bill Finger, the vigilante superhero first appeared in the May 1939 number of *Detective Comics*. Darker than his friendly rival Superman, Batman drew inspiration from horror films:

Erzsébet Báthory, The Bloody Countess

his cowled look is modelled on *The Bat* (1926), while arch-enemy the Joker is a homage to *The Man Who Laughs* (1927) and second-string baddie Two-Face a **Jekyll and Hyde** character. In his early days in Gotham City, Batman tackled **vampires** and other fiends. He became decreasingly sinister when represented in the **serials** (*Batman*, 1943, *Batman and Robin*, 1949) and the cheerfully camp 1966–9 TV series and 1966 film with Adam West. In the 70s, writer Dennis O'Neil and artists Neal Adams and Dick Giordano

packed Robin the Boy Wonder off to college and brought back the darkness, introducing villains like the **Fu Manchu**-ish R'as al-Ghul, the **werewolf**-like Man-Bat and the vampire Nocturna.

Following Frank Miller Jr's revisionary *The Dark Knight Returns* (1986), DC have featured Batman in many comics with horrific or supernatural elements: *The Killing Joke* (1988), *Arkham Asylum* (1989), *Gotham By Gaslight* (1988), *Batman & Dracula: Red Rain* (1992), *The Devil's Worshop* (1993). Tim **Burton** launched a film franchise in *Batman* (1989) and *Batman Returns* (1992), with Michael Keaton as Bruce Wayne, then turned the series over to the less-interesting Joel Schumacher for *Batman Forever* (1995), with Val Kilmer. The films emphasise disfigured **Expressionist** villains: Jack **Nicholson**'s Joker, Danny DeVito's **Caligari**-ish Penguin, Michelle Pfeiffer's dominatrix Catwoman, Tommy Lee Jones's Two-Face, Jim Carrey's squirming Riddler. Also often trading in the monstrous is the excellent animated TV *Batman* (1992–4) and its feature-length spin-off *Batman: Mask of the Phantasm* (1993). Batman features in much associational material, including Joe Lansdale's fine were-cadillac novel *Captured By the Engines* (1991).

Bats

The real vampire bat, from South and Central America, is a much-feared creature

RIGHT Bats: *Nightwing*

linked for many centuries to European **vampire** mythology: the image of **Dracula** swirling his cape before flapping away as a bat is one of the most cherished in horror. Flocks of bats are used periodically for flesh-creeping effect: Dwight **Frye** is the bat keeper in *The Vampire Bat* (1933); imaginary bats are created by Charles **Gray** in *The Devil Rides Out* (1968) and real ones sent on a murder mission by Vincent **Price** in *The Abominable Dr. Phibes* (1971). Bats feature in a **dream** sequence in *Una lucertola con la pelle di donna* (*A Lizard in a Woman's Skin*, 1971), while *Chosen Survivors* (1974) and *Nightwing* (1979) are entirely concerned with humans menaced by vampire bats. Fantastic bat creatures enliven some programmers: **Lugosi** creates a giant bat in *The Devil Bat* (1940), sequelised in *Devil Bat's Daughter* (1945); extra-terrestrial bats appear in *Not of This Earth* (1956) and *Zontar the Thing From Venus* (1966) and Stewart Moss, imitating one of **Batman's** monster foes, becomes a man-bat in *The Bat People* (1974). No bat appears in *The Bat* (1926) and its first remake *The Bat Whispers* (1931), but there is one in the second, which reverts to the title *The Bat* (1958). DM

Bava, Lamberto (b. 1944)

Italian director. Son of Mario **Bava**, Lamberto became his father's assistant on *Terrore nello spazio* (*Planet of the Vampires*, 1966) and bolstered Mario's faltering career by scripting *Shock Transfert-Suspence-Hypnos* (*Shock*, 1977). It is said that Mario repeatedly feigned illness during production, allowing his son to gain experience at the helm. Subsequently, the Bavas co-directed a luminous TV production of Merimée's *La venere d'Ille* (1978). Mario lived to compliment his son's directorial debut, *Macabro* (*Macabre*, 1979), an allegedly fact-based story of a nymphomaniac who preserves her lover's severed **head**.

After Mario's death in 1980, Lamberto allied himself with Dario **Argento**, whom he assisted on *Inferno* (1980) and *Tenebre* (*Tenebrae*, 1982). Argento bankrolled Bava's second feature, *La casa con la scala nel buio* (*A Blade in the Dark*, 1983), a superior **giallo**, then produced the box office hit *Demoni* (*Demons*, 1985), a stylish headbanger's ball about a pus-infective breed of incubi that hatch from a movie audience during a midnight horrorfest. After the ill-advised, in-name-only remake *La maschera del demonio* (1989), he worked on the proposed TV series *Brivido giallo/Alta tenzione* (1989–90), directing *Il gioko* (*School of Fear*), *Testimone occulare*

(*Eyewitness*), *Il principe del terrore* (*The Master of Terror*) and an unrealized project of his father's, *L'uomo che non voleva morire* (*The Man Who Didn't Want to Die*). Unfortunately, the series never made it to air and these films (Bava's finest, most mature work in horror) have never been publicly shown.

He finally found his niche with *Fantaghirò* (1989), a winning, three-hour television **fantasy** inspired by Italo Calvino. Its enormous European success prompted four epic-length sequels, making him a wealthy and busy man. It is unlikely that he will return to horror in the immediate future, though *Corpo mosaico* (*Body Puzzle*, 1991) shows his affinity for the genre continuing to evolve into singularly dark and angry talent. TL

Shark: rosso nell'oceano [*Devouring Waves*]/ 1984 * *Morirai a mezzanotte*/*Le foto di Gioia* [*Delirium*]/*Demoni 2* [*Demons 2*]/1986

TV: *Brivido Caldo*: 'Per sempre, fini alla morte' [*Changeling 2*]/'Una notte nel cimitero' [*Graveyard Disturbance*]/'La casa dell'orco' [*Demons 3: The Ogre*]/'A cena con il vampiro' [*Dinner With the Vampire*]/1987

Bava, Mario (1914–1980)

Italian director, cinematographer. He learned his craft by assisting his father Eugenio Bava, a former cameraman (*Quo vadis?*, 1913) who headed the Instituto Luce's optical effects department. Bava became a director of photography in 1939 and shot films by Roberto Rossellini, G.W. Pabst and Raoul Walsh; his stylised lensing was critical in developing the screen personae of international stars Gina Lollobrigida and Steve Reeves.

Bava collaborated with Riccardo **Freda** on *I vampiri* (*Lust of the Vampire*, 1957), the first Italian horror film of the sound era, initially as cameraman and optical effects designer, then directing half of the film in only two days when Freda abandoned the project after being denied an extension on his twelve-day schedule. Rescuing other men's films became a habit with Bava: he directed a little of Pietro Francisci's *Le fatiche di Ercole* (*Hercules*, 1957) and even more of the Flash Gordon-inspired *Ercole e la regina di Lidia* (*Hercules Unchained*, 1958) 'while the director took his siestas'. Outraged by the way his unambitious friend was abused, Freda tricked Bava by hiring him to photograph *Caltiki il mostro immortale* (*Caltiki the Immortal Monster*, 1959), once again abandoning the director's chair after only two days.

Producer Lionello Santi rewarded Bava

for completing *Caltiki* by inviting him to select a property for his directorial debut. A devotée of Russian literature, Bava chose Nikolai Gogol's story 'Vij' (1835) as the foundation for *La maschera del demonio* (1960), an instant international success. The large-eyed British starlet Barbara **Steele** staggered audiences with iconic dual roles as the evil **witch** Asa and her twin descendant, the virtuous Katia, and overnight was crowned as the screen's first Queen of Horror. *La maschera* is a perfect conglomeration of nightmare and fairytale, parlaying the haunted forest ambience of Universal and the graphic **violence** of **Hammer** into something uniquely Italian. The film was extensively cut and rescored for release in America by AIP as *Black Sunday*; in Britain, BBFC certification was withheld until 1968 when *Black Sunday* was cut down and opened as *Revenge of the Vampire*; *The Mask of Satan*, the English-language version prepared and shelved in 1960, did not emerge until the late 80s. Instantly stereotyped as a black-and-white director, Bava demonstrated unparalleled Technicolor prowess with *Ercole al centro della terra* (*Hercules in the Haunted World*, 1961), a phantasmagorical descent into **Hell** improvised with leftover props from earlier Cinécittà productions. He returned to black-and-white a last time for *La ragazza che sapeva troppo* (*The Evil Eye*, 1962), an Alphabet Murder mystery filmed straight for the European market and more humorously for English-speaking territories.

His next three films show him at the height of his creative powers. *I tre volti della paura* (*Black Sabbath*, 1963), a three-part **anthology** which gave **Karloff** his last great horror role (as Gorka in 'The Wurdalak'), was often cited by Bava as his own personal favourite. *La frusta e il corpo* (*Night is the Phantom*, 1963) casts Dahlia Lavi and Christopher **Lee** in a vertiginously romantic period film about a masochist haunted by the ghost of her whip-wielding lover. And *Sei donne per l'assassino* (*Blood and Black Lace*, 1964) is the first great **giallo**, a deliriously colourful, nakedly sadistic whodunit about fashion models being murdered by a maniac in search of an incriminating diary. Made for adult audiences but sold abroad as scary kiddie fare, all three suffered from censorship problems, especially *I tre volti della paura* (ironically, the tamest of the three), which was rearranged, rescored, rewritten (to delete a **lesbian** subtext) and otherwise toned down by AIP. Bava's original cut, significant as the first horror film in which Evil explicitly wins out over Good, survives only in an Italian-language version.

With *Terrore nello spazio* (*Planet of the Vampires*, 1966), another victory for Evil in which the members of an exploratory space mission are physically invaded by the disembodied spirits of an **alien** race, Bava achieved a successful fusion of s-f and horror. A major influence on *Alien* (1979), the film's convincing otherworldly alien landscape is an ingenious smoke-and-mirrors confection of studio **fog**, coloured lighting and 'two rocks left over from a mythological epic'. After breaking his AIP contract with the disastrous *Le spie vengono dal semifreddo* (*Dr. Goldfoot & the Girl Bombs*, 1966), Bava rebounded with *Operazione paura* (*Curse of the Dead*, 1966), a low-budget, gothic masterpiece about villagers haunted by the ball-bouncing ghost of a little girl, whose apparition compels them to suicide. Oedipal and unsettling, with unexpected sequences of Escher-like dislocations of time and space, the film received a standing ovation at its Italian premiere from Luchino Visconti. *Operazione paura* is an admitted influence on later films by **Fellini** (*Toby Dammit*, 1967), Martin Scorsese (*The Last Temptation of Christ*, 1988) and David **Lynch** (*Twin Peaks Fire Walk with Me*, 1991).

Overworked, distressed by personal problems and upset by the death of his father and mentor in October 1966, Bava avoided the genre for the next two years. While preparing *Cry Nightmare*, an original *giallo* script by Tudor **Gates** later filmed by Antonio **Margheriti** as *Nude . . . si muore* (*The Young, the Evil and the Savage*, 1968), Bava was approached by Dino De Laurentiis with the biggest assignment of his career, *Diabolik* (*Danger: Diabolik*, 1968), based on the Giussani Sisters' popular *fumetti*. Budgeted at $3,000,000, *Diabolik* was completed by Bava for only $400,000. Accustomed to the freedom that came with low budgets, Bava found he disliked the production office interference and other pressures that came with hardball budgets and politely declined De Laurentiis's invitation to helm a sequel.

After collaborating with Carlo Rambaldi on the special effects for the miniseries *Odissea* (1968), Bava happily withdrew to familiar territory, directing the darkly comic *Il rosso segno della follia* (*A Hatchet for the Honeymoon*, 1969) in Barcelona. In the wake of Dario **Argento**'s *L'uccello dalle piume di cristallo* (1970), Bava returned to the newly fashionable *giallo* with *Cinque bambole e la luna d'Agosto* (*Five Dolls for an August Moon*, 1970). He then impishly extended, even obliterated, the frontiers of the sub-genre with *L'ecologia del delitto* (*A Bay of Blood*, 1971), a diabolical black **comedy** which boasts thirteen characters and thirteen outrageously splashy murders. Reviled at the time of its release, it proved prophetic when the imitative **Friday the 13th** (1980) launched a new generation of 'body count' movies.

Perhaps cowed by such excesses, Bava cooled down with *Gli orrori del castello di Norimberga* (*Baron Blood*, 1972), a minor work which so successfully resuscitated the Technicolor look and matinee feel of his American International period that AIP acquired it for distribution. The film's producer, Alfredo Leone, rewarded Bava with *carte blanche* on their next collaboration, which became the extraordinary *Lisa e il diavolo* (*Lisa and the Devil*, 1973). Based on memories of growing up among his father's sculptures, dialogue borrowed from Dostoevsky and an unrealised project about necrophile Viktor Ardisson, *Lisa e il diavolo* unfolds like a waking **dream**, following disoriented **heroine** Elke Sommer through a time-suspended labyrinth of love, sex and violent death. When the film proved unsalable at the 1973 Cannes Festival, Bava suffered the humiliation of painting a moustache on his own masterpiece: the sad result was *La casa dell'esorcismo* (*The House of Exorcism*, 1975), a bewildering, johnny-come-lately **Exorcist** rip-off combining *Lisa* footage with pea soup, priestly guilt and blasphemy. This abomination (credited to 'Mickey Lion') served its purpose, easing the original version out of the red, and has been forgotten, while *Lisa e il diavolo* has resurfaced on video to an overdue audience of admirers.

He found it harder to find directorial assignments after turning sixty and green-lighted projects also turned unlucky: *Cani arrabbiati* (1974) ran out of money on the eve of post-production and its footage was impounded for twenty years. It was bought and completed by co-star Lea Lander fifteen years after Bava's death and had its world premiere in 1996 under the title *Semaforo rosso*. As violent and foul-mouthed as any Quentin Tarantino caper, this kidnapping saga is unlike any other Bava film. Set almost entirely inside a speeding car and told in real time, it is one of his most exciting technical achievements. Troubled by his father's inactivity, son Lamberto **Bava** (his assistant since 1966) scripted what proved to be his final feature, *Shock Transfert-Suspence-Hypnos* (*Shock*, 1977), the harrowing story of a woman's mental collapse after returning to the house where she once lived with her late, drug-addicted husband. Bava storyboarded the entire film but directed only parts, feigning illness to help Lamberto gain directorial experience.

Father and son also share directorial credit

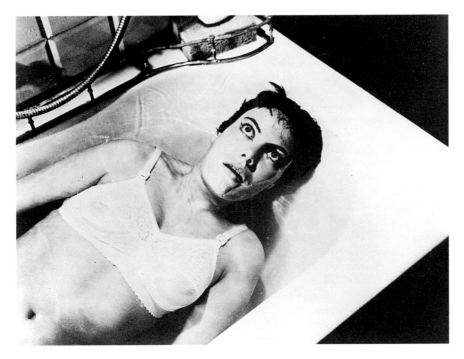

LEFT Mario Bava's *Sei donne per l'assassino*

for a lovely TV adaptation of Prosper Mérimée's *La venere d'Ille* (1978). Both projects star Daria **Nicolodi**, an acquaintance responsible for bringing the Bavas together with Italy's reigning horror *maestro*, Dario Argento. Lamberto was hired as assistant director on *Inferno* (1980), for which Mario was also recruited in an uncredited special effects capacity. Mario built maquettes, painted glass mattes and devised optical effects for the film (notably a momentous lunar eclipse). As Argento now admits, Mario also directed certain scenes in his absence when he was stricken with hepatitis. With an irony typical of his films, Bava died of a heart attack at sixty-six, within days of a medical check-up that found him to be in perfect health.

Bava's career placed him at the birth of virtually every style of film-making native to Italy: *neorealisme*, *telefono bianchi*, *operetta*, *pepla*, Italian horror, *gialli* and the Spaghetti Western. Perhaps more than any other figure, Bava 'was' the Italian cinema . . . yet it's unlikely that the full breadth of his achievement will ever be known. Since Bava's death, his filmography has continued to grow with disclosures from former colleagues of his uncredited involvement in numerous Italian productions as cinematographer, special effects artist and director. TL

Pascal Martinet, *Mario Bava* (1984)

Baxt, George (b. 1923)

American writer. Having worked mainly in British films, Baxt writes mystery novels with a gay (*A Queer Kind of Death*, 1966) or Hollywood (*The Alfred Hitchcock Murder Case*, 1986) background. His most notable credits (*Night of the Eagle*, 1962; *Vampire Circus*, 1971) are rewrite jobs, but his solo scripts are consistently perverse.

*Circus of Horrors/City of the Dead/1960 * The Shadow of the Cat/1961 * Strangler's Web/1965 * Tower of Evil/1972*

TV: *Tales of the Unexpected*: 'What Have You Been Up to Lately?'/1982

Baxter, Les (1922–96)

American composer, musician. A cool jazzman who worked with Nat King Cole, Mel Tormé, Yma Sumac and Martin Denny. AIP's in-house composer: besides scoring **Corman**'s **Poe**, he jazzed up American releases of Mario **Bava** movies.

*The Black Sleep/1956 * The Bride and the Beast/Pharaoh's Curse/Voodoo Island/1957 * Macabre/*

1958 * *The Fall of the House of Usher/La maschera del demonio* [*Black Sunday*]/1960 * *Pit and the Pendulum/1961 * Tales of Terror/The Raven/1962 * The Comedy of Terrors/I tre volti della paura* [*Black Sabbath*]/1963 * *Dr. Goldfoot and the Bikini Machine/1965 * Dr. Goldfoot and the Girl Bombs/The Ghost in the Invisible Bikini/1966 * The Dunwich Horror/1969 * Cry of the Banshee/1970 * Frogs/1971 * One Minute Before Death/1973 * The Beast Within/1981*

TV: *An Evening With Edgar Allan Poe/1973 * Cliffhangers/1979*

Beasts (UK TV series, 1975) * See: Kneale, Nigel

Beaudine, William (1892–1970)

American director. A silent era assistant to D.W. Griffith and director for Mary Pickford, 'One-Shot' Beaudine cranked out dozens of talkie Bs, from inferior vehicles for **Lugosi** (*The Ape Man*, 1943) and the East Side Kids (*Spook Busters*, 1946) to disappointingly dull freaks like *Bela Lugosi Meets a Brooklyn Gorilla* (1952) and *Jesse James Meets Frankenstein's Daughter* (1965). The crazed charm of *Voodoo Man* (1944), *The Face of Marble* (1946) and *Billy the Kid vs. Dracula* (1965) owes more to John **Carradine** than Beaudine's traffic cop direction. He worked on television's *The Green Hornet* (1966–7).

*Sparrows/1926 * Condemned Men/1940 * The Living Ghost/The Phantom Killer/Professor Creeps/1942 * Mystery of the 13th Guest/Ghosts on the Loose/1943 * /Mr. Hex/1946 * Ghost Chasers/1951*

Beaumont, Charles [Charles Nutt] (1929–67)

American writer. His short stories are often about damaged childhoods, as in the semi-autobiographical horror classic 'Miss Gentibelle' (1957), and secret identities, as with 'The Hunger' (1955), in which a willing victim seeks out her killer. Though scornful of television in his essay collection *Remember? Remember?* (1963), celebrating the golden era of **radio**, his sharp humour and skilful dialogues were ideal for the medium: he wrote many teleplays, notably for **The Twilight Zone** (1959–64).

Ironically, his first published story 'The Devil, You Say' (1951) was the basis for one of his last telescripts, 'Printer's Devil' (1963); illness forced him to employ friends to write for him. Probably Beaumont's finest feature script, based on his 1959 novel, is Roger

Corman's *The Intruder* (1962), in which he also acts. His screenplay *Paranoia*, written for Corman in 1963, was finally filmed by Adam Simon as *Brain Dead* (1990). Other solo scenarios, each with characteristic elements of parody, include *Queen of Outer Space* (1958), *The Haunted Palace* (1963), *7 Faces of Dr. Lao* (1964). PS

*The Premature Burial/Night of the Eagle/1962 * The Masque of the Red Death/1965*

TV: *The Twilight Zone*: 'Perchance to Dream'/1959; 'Elegy'/'Long Live Walter Jameson'/'A Nice Place to Visit'/'The Howling Man'/1960; 'Static'/'Prime Mover'/'Long Distance Call'/'Shadow Play'/'The Jungle'/1961; 'Dead Man's Shoes'/'The Fugitive'/'Person or Persons Unknown'/1962; 'In His Image'/'Valley of the Shadow'/'Miniature'/'Printer's Devil'/'The New Exhibit'/'Passage on the Lady Anne'/'Living Doll'/1963; 'Number Twelve Looks Just Like You'/'Queen of the Nile'/1964 * *Thriller*: 'Girl With a Secret'/1960; 'Guillotine'/1961; *Alfred Hitchcock Presents*: 'Backward, Turn Backward'/1960 * *Alfred Hitchcock Hour*: 'The Long Silence'/1963 * *The Outer Limits*: 'The Guests'/1964 * *Journey to the Unknown*: 'The New People' (st)/1968; 'Miss Belle'/1969 * *The Twilight Zone*: 'Dead Woman's Shoes' (st)/1985; 'Shadow Play' (st)/1986

Bergman, Ingmar (b. 1918)

Swedish director, writer. The macabre qualities evident in the **dream** sequence of *Musik i mörker* (*Night Is My Future*, 1947) are developed throughout his career. As portrayed in *Det sjunde inseglet* (*The Seventh Seal*, 1957), Death proved enduring enough to meet Bill and Ted and Arnold Schwarzenegger. *Smultronstället* (*Wild Strawberries*, 1957) begins with a dream no less terrifying for being introduced as one and set in daylight. *Ansiktet* (*The Face*, 1958) subjects skeptical Gunnar Björnstrand to a series of scary illusions: an eye in an inkwell, a comforting hand which proves to stop at the wrist.

A series of Bergman films has different protagonists retreat to an island only to be confronted by what they are fleeing. In *Såsom i en spegel* (*Through a Glass Darkly*, 1961), a young woman sees God in the form of a giant spider (in fact a helicopter descending to take her to the mainland). *Persona* (1966) concerns an actress who has attempted to take refuge in silence and who battens (in one scene literally) on the nurse attempting to care for her. *Vargtimmen* (*Hour of the Wolf*, 1968) is a **Hoffmann**esque goth-

Bengt Ekerot, Max Von Sydow, *Det sjunde inseglet*

ic tale in which a wife fails to save her artist husband from the demons which have followed him, and in *Skammen* (*Shame*, 1968) the same performers (Liv Ullmann, Max von **Sydow**) play musicians caught up in a civil war which destroys them morally. At several points in *Persona* the film ruptures to let in the horrors of the world, and *Skammen* is all about them.

After this purging bleakness Bergman was able, years later, to introduce a less threatening spectre than usual into *Fanny och Alexander* (*Fanny and Alexander*, 1982). Horror buffs no doubt know him best by reputation as the director of *Jungfrukällan* (*The Virgin Spring*, 1959), Wes **Craven**'s original source for *Last House on the Left* (1972). RC

Djävlens öga [*The Devil's Eye*]/1960 ∗ *En passion* [*L182: A Passion*]/1969 ∗ *Viskningar och rop* [*Cries and Whispers*]/1972 ∗ *The Magic Flute*/1974 ∗ *Das Schlangenei* [*The Serpent's Egg*]/1977 ∗ *Aus dem Leben der Marionetten* [*From the Life of the Marionettes*]/1980

Peter Cowie, *Ingmar Bergman* (1982, 1992)

Berman, Monty ∗
See: **Baker, Robert S.**

Bernard, James (b. 1925)
British film composer. A protégé and assistant of Benjamin Britten, Bernard's first scores were for BBC radio plays. He moved into film with **Hammer**'s *The Quatermass Experiment* (1954). During a long, successful association with the company, he composed scores of great melancholy beauty, jagged tension and gothic savagery. He co-wrote the original story of the nuclear thriller *Seven Days to Noon* (1950) and composed a 1995 symphony to accompany *Nosferatu* (1922). SL

Quatermass 2/*The Curse of Frankenstein*/*X-The Unknown*/1957 ∗ *Dracula*/1958 ∗ *The Hound of the Baskervilles*/1959 ∗ *The Stranglers of Bombay*/1960 ∗ *The Terror of the Tongs*/1961 ∗ *Kiss of the Vampire*/1963 ∗ *The Gorgon*/1964 ∗ *Dracula, Prince of Darkness*/*The Plague of the Zombies*/*She*/1965 ∗ *Frankenstein Created Woman*/*Torture Garden*/1967 ∗ *Dracula Has Risen From the Grave*/*The Devil Rides Out*/1968 ∗ *Frankenstein Must Be Destroyed*/*Taste the Blood of Dracula*/1969 ∗ *Scars of Dracula*/1970 ∗ *The Legend of the Seven Golden Vampires*/1973 ∗ *Frankenstein and the Monster From Hell*/1974

TV: *The Hammer House of Horror*: 'Witching Time'/'The House That Bled to Death'/1980

Berryman, Michael (b. 1948)
Bizarre-looking, bald American actor who made his debut in *One Flew Over the Cuckoo's Nest* (1975). The **cannibal** desert-dweller Pluto in Wes **Craven**'s *The Hills Have Eyes* (1977) and *The Hills Have Eyes Part II* (1984). SJ

Doc Savage The Man of Bronze/1975 ∗ *Deadly Blessing*/1980 ∗ *Weird Science*/*My Science Project*/*Inferno in diretta* [*Cut and Run*]/1985 ∗ *Saturday the 14th Strikes Back*/1988 ∗ *Evil Spirits*/*The Guyver*/1991 ∗ *Auntie Lee's Meat Pies*/1992 ∗ *The Crow* (scenes deleted)/*Double Dragon*/*Teenage Exorcist*/1994

TV: *Invitation to Hell*/1984 ∗ *Highway to Heaven*: 'The Devil and Jonathan'/1985 ∗ *Love and Curses*: 'Bride of the Wolfman/1991 ∗ *Tales from the Crypt*: 'The Reluctant Vampire'/1991 ∗ *The X Files*: 'Revelations'/1995

Best, Willie (1916–62)
Pop-eyed black actor. He began his career under the name 'Sleep 'n' Eat'. The archetypal frightened **comic relief** manservant ('My feets ain't gonna stand around to see my body abused!'). SJ

The Monster Walks/1932 ∗ *Mummy's Boys*/1936 ∗ *Super-Sleuth*/1937 ∗ *The Ghost Breakers*/1940 ∗ *The Body Disappears*/*The Smiling Ghost*/1941

Ingmar Bergman

Michael Berryman, *Deadly Blessing*

* *The Hidden Hand/A-Haunting We Will Go/
Whispering Ghosts/*1942 * *The Girl Who Dared/*
1944 * *The Monster and the Ape/*1945 * *The
Face of Marble/*1946

Beswick, Martine (b. 1941)
British actress, sometimes billed as 'Beswicke'. A Bond girl (*From Russia With Love*,
1964, *Thunderball*, 1965) and star of **Hammer**'s *Slave Girls* (1966), the dusky Beswick
steals *One Million Years B.C.* (1966) from
Raquel Welch. Her dark, sensuous looks and
high cheekbones serve well as Ralph **Bates**'s
provocative alter ego in *Dr. Jekyll and Sister
Hyde* (1971), and she is imperiously menacing as the Queen of Evil in *Seizure* (1974).
MA

*The Penthouse/*1967 * *Il bacio/*1974 * *From a
Whisper to a Scream/*1986 * *Trancers II/*1990 *
*Evil Spirits/*1991 * *Wide Sargasso Sea/*1993 *
*Night of the Scarecrow/*1995

TV: *Night Gallery*: 'The Last Laurel'/1971 *
*Devil Dog: The Hound of Hell/*1978 * *The Next
Step Beyond*: 'Woman in the Mirror'/1979

Bewitched (US TV series, 1964–72)
A **situation comedy** starring Elizabeth
Montgomery as Samantha, a nose-twitching
witch who marries a mortal, Darrin
Stephens (Dick York), and promises she will
give up using magic. Her vow is made more
difficult by her witch mother (Agnes
Moorehead), warlock father (Maurice Evans)
and scriptwriters intent on getting Darrin in

magical hot water. George Tobias and Alice
Pearce (later Sandra Gould) are the next-
door neighbours Abner and Gladys Kravitz;
and Dick Sargent took over from the ailing
York in 1969. Modelled on the film *I Married
A Witch* (1942), the show owes something to
Fritz **Leiber**'s oft-filmed novel *Conjure Wife*
(1943). Darrin and Samantha's daughter
grew up to have a spin-off *Tabitha* (1977-8),
starring Lisa Hartman. TM

Herbie J. Pilato, *The Bewitched Book* (1992)

Bey, Turhan (b. 1922)
Austrian-born Turkish actor. While many
established male stars were away during the
war, Bey served as an exotically handsome
Hollywood leading man. He later became a
photographer for soft-porn magazines but
returned to acting in the 90s, including an
appearance in *Babylon 5*, 'The Coming of
Shadows' (1995). SJ

*Shadows on the Stairs/*1941 * *The Mummy's
Tomb/*1942 * *The Mad Ghoul/Captive Wild
Woman* (v)/1943 * *The Climax/*1944 * *The
Spiritualist/*1948 * *Possessed By the Night/*1994
* *Grid Runners/*1995

Beyond Reality (US TV series, 1991–3)
Created by Richard Manning and Hans
Beimler, filmed in Canada by Paragon
Entertainment for the USA Network, and
supposedly 'based on reported incidents',
this **parapsychology**-themed show predates

Martine Beswick, *Slave Girls*

Turhan Bey, *Frisco Sal*

the more successful **The X Files** (1993–). Drs
Laura Wingate (Shari Belafonte) and J.J.
Stillman (Carl Marotte) investigate paranormal activities. 'The Passion' (1993), scripted
by Marc Scott Zicree, is a welcome variation
on the format: an 1888 flashback with the
heroes' lookalike ancestors defeating a **vampire Jack the Ripper**. SJ

Bierce, Ambrose (1842–1914?)
American writer. A cynic who turned to
humour (*The Devil's Dictionary*, 1906) and
horror, Bierce often uses the grotesque or
supernatural to provide cruel punch-lines.
His stories are collected in *Tales of Soldiers and
Civilians* (*In the Midst of Life*, 1891) and *Can
Such Things Be?* (1893). His disappearance in
Mexico inspired Carlos Fuentes's novel *El
viejo gringo* (*The Old Gringo*, 1985), filmed
with Gregory Peck (1989). Bierce has
inspired Robert Enrico's *La rivière du hibou*
(1961, from 'An Occurrence at Owl Creek
Bridge'), Sture Rydman's *The Man and the
Snake* (1972) and *The Return* (1973, from
'The Middle Toe of the Right Foot') and Noel
Black's 'The Eyes of the Panther' (1989,
Nightmare Classics). 'An Occurrence at Owl
Creek Bridge' was also a 1959 **Alfred
Hitchcock Presents**, and is much plagiarised
(*Black Angel*, 1980). Enrico's film was repack-
aged as an episode of **The Twilight Zone** and
included (with 'Chickamauga' and 'The
Mocking-Bird') in the omnibus *Au coeur de la
vie* (1962).

Carey McWilliams, *Ambrose Bierce: A*

Birds: *The Birds*

Biography (1929); Paul Fatout, *Ambrose Bierce: The Devil's Lexicographer* (1951)

Birds

Folklore is rich with tales of evil black birds and their particularly horrid penchant for pecking out human eyes. **Hitchcock**'s *The Birds* (1963) is, however, virtually a one-off, possibly because of the almost insurmountable problem of working with creatures given to flying off the set (trainer Ray Berwick was number one in a field of one). There was no further mass attack by birds until *Raptors* (*Killing Birds*, 1988), but a bland sequel, *The Birds II: Land's End* (1993), was made for television. **Poe**'s haunting 1845 poem **'The Raven'** has been considerably debased by the cinema: the 1935 film uses material from **'The Pit and the Pendulum'**

(1843), while the bird in the 1963 **comedy** is a transmuted Peter **Lorre** (and talks with his voice). However, ravens attack Elizabeth Shepherd in *Damien: Omen II* (1978) and Urbano Barberini in *Opera* (1987); Peter **Wyngarde** imagines he is attacked by an eagle in *Night of the Eagle* (1962); and the spirits of girls sacrificed to the Knights Templar return as gulls in *La noche de las gaviotas* (*Night of the Seagulls*, 1975). Among mythical birds, Quetzalcoatl is in *The Flying Serpent* (1946) and *Q* (1982). *The Giant Claw* (1957) is a bird from outer space and *The Vulture* (1966) is a bird man (Akim Tamiroff). The murders in *Deliria* (*Stagefright*, 1987) are committed by a man in a bird costume. DM

Bissell, Whit [Whitner] (1914–96)

Dependable, somewhat stuffy American character actor, often a scientist (sometimes **mad**) or other authority figure. On TV, he played General Heywood in *Time Tunnel* (1966–67). SJ

Lost Continent/1951 * *Creature from the Black Lagoon*/1954 * *Invasion of the Body Snatchers*/1956 * *I Was a Teenage Werewolf*/*I Was a Teenage Frankenstein*/1957 * *Monster on the Campus*/1958 * *The Manchurian Candidate*/1962 * *Soylent Green*/1973 * *Psychic Killer*/1976

TV: *One Step Beyond*: 'Brainwave'/1959 * *Alfred Hitchcock Presents*: 'Burglar Proof'/1962 * *The Outer Limits*: 'Nightmare'/1963 * *Alfred Hitchcock Hour*: 'Behind the Locked Door'/

RIGHT Boris Karloff, *The Black Cat* (1934)

1964 *The Invaders*: 'Dark Outpost'/1967 *
Darkroom: 'Lost in Translation'/1981

Blackburn, John (1923–93)
British writer. Combining the approaches of John Wyndham and Dennis **Wheatley**, Blackburn deals with English eco-catastrophe (*A Scent of New-Mown Hay*, 1958; *A Ring of Roses*, 1965) or the supernatural (*Bury Him Darkly*, 1970; *Our Lady of Pain*, 1974) within the police or espionage thriller. His strongest novel is the **Machen**-influenced *For Fear of Little Men* (1972). *Nothing But the Night* (1968) was filmed by Peter **Sasdy** in 1972.

'The Black Cat' (1843)
Edgar Allan **Poe**'s tale of madness and murder may be the single most-filmed short story. First adapted in *The Raven* (1912) and *The Avenging Conscience* (1914), then fully by Richard **Oswald** in 1919 in *Unheimliche Geschichten* (which he remade in 1932), 'The Black Cat' has inspired Edgar G. **Ulmer** (1934), Dwain Esper (*Maniac*, 1934), Albert Rogell (1941), Roger **Corman** (*Tales of Terror*, 1962), Harold Hoffmann (1966), Sergio **Martino** (*Il tuo vizio è una stanza chiusa e solo io ne ho la chiave*, 1972), Ralph Marsden (*Sabbat of the Black Cat*, 1974), Lucio **Fulci** (1982), Dario **Argento** (*Due occhi diabolici/ Two Evil Eyes*, 1990) and Luigi **Cozzi** (1991). Rob Green's 1994 short is a rare *faithful* version.

Black Horror
The segregated industry of the 30s and 40s produced 'race' horror films for black audiences, often using **voodoo** themes: *Drums O'Voodoo* (1934), *Ouanga* (1935), *Son of Ingagi* (1939), *Condemned Men* (1940). More common were films like the revealingly titled *White Zombie* (1932), which co-opts Haitian beliefs but has no significant black characters. *King of the Zombies* (1941) is built around comedian Mantan **Moreland** (top-billed in black theatres) but has white leads, ensuring release in regular cinemas.

With few exceptions, black actors in classic horror played native chiefs (Noble **Johnson**, *King Kong*, 1933), frightened servants (Willie **Best**, *The Ghost Breakers*, 1940) or bug-eyed **zombies** (Darby Jones, *I Walked With a Zombie*, 1943). Though the casting of Duane **Jones** in *Night of the Living Dead* (1968) was ground-breaking (and black actors play prominent, unstereotyped roles

in the sequels), black horror did not reappear until William **Crain**'s *Blacula* (1972), a funky post-*Shaft* (1971) soul movie with William **Marshall** as a reasonably dignified African **vampire**. The blaxploitation cycle yielded *Blackenstein* (1972), *Scream, Blacula, Scream* (1973), *The House on Skull Mountain* (1974), *Abby* (1974), *Sugar Hill* (1974), *Dr. Black Mr. Hyde* (1975) and *J.D.'s Revenge* (1976). Tangental are sincere efforts like Bill Gunn's *Ganja and Hess* (1973), a vampire movie that explores the clash of African religion and Afro-American gospel culture, and the occasional colour-blind casting of black actors in integrated horror films, like Calvin Lockhart in *The Beast Must Die* (1974).

In the 80s and 90s, with a revival of black cinema, there have been black horror films (James Bond III's *Def By Temptation*, 1990, *Tales From the Hood*, 1995) and more frequent black monsters (Grace Jones, *Vamp*, 1986; Tony **Todd**, *Candyman*, 1992;Eddie Murphy, *Vampire in Brooklyn*, 1995) and heroes (Brandon Adams, *The People Under the Stairs*, 1991; Cynda Williams, *The Killing Box*, 1993). Wes **Craven**'s *The Serpent and the Rainbow* (1988) and Richard Stanley's *Dust Devil* (1992) explore Haitian or African voodoo themes, with Zakes Mokae (in radically different roles) initiating bewildered whites. The nascent African film industry

RIGHT Black Horror: Darby Jones,
I Walked with a Zombie

has produced supernatural films, like Idrissa Ouedraogo's *Yaaba* (1989) from Burkina Faso, but these tend to a matter-of-fact approach antithetical to genuine horror. With *Tales From the Crypt: Demon Knight* (1994), Ernest Dickerson became the first black director to make a non-black-themed major release horror film.

Black, Karen [Karen Ziegeler] (b. 1942)
American leading lady. Once promising, with signature roles in *Five Easy Pieces* (1970) and *Nashville* (1975) and solid genre credits in the TV movie *Trilogy of Terror* (1975) and **Hitchcock**'s *Family Plot* (1976), now an exploitation fixture. SJ

*The Pyx/1973 * Burnt Offerings/1976 * Killer Fish/1979 * Inferno in diretta [Cut and Run]/ 1985 * It's Alive III: Island of the Alive/1986 * Eternal Evil/1987 * Out of the Dark/1989 * Mirror, Mirror/Night Angel/Overexposed/Twisted Justice/Children of the Night/1990 * Evil Spirits/ 1991 * Auntie Lee's Meat Pies/1992 * Death Before Sunrise/1995 * Crimetime/Plan 10 From Outer Space/Children of the Corn IV/1996*

TV: *The Invaders*: 'The Ransom'/1967 * *Ghost Story*: 'Bad Connection'/1972 * *The Strange Possession of Mrs. Oliver*/1977 * *The Hitchhiker*: 'Hired Help'/1985

Blackwood, Algernon (1869–1951)

British writer. A prolific author of supernatural fiction, collected in *The Empty House* (1906), *John Silence, Physician Extraordinary* (1908), *Incredible Adventures* (1914) and *The Dance of Death* (1928). A popular BBC **radio** voice, Blackwood read his own work on a primitive TV show, *Saturday Night Stories*

Karen Black, *Out of the Dark*

(1948–9). *Tales of Mystery* (1961–3), hosted by John Laurie, dramatised his stories. Other adaptations: 'The Wendigo' (**Great Ghost Tales**, 1961), 'The Listener' (**Mystery and Imagination**, 1968), 'The Doll' (**Night Gallery**, 1971), *Wendigo* (1978).

Blair, Linda (b. 1959)

American actress. A star at fourteen as the **possessed** Regan MacNeil in the blockbuster *The Exorcist* (1973), Blair swiftly downshifted into exploitation. The TV movie *Born Innocent* (1974) kicked off a string of

women-in-prison grinders (*Chained Heat*, 1983; *Red Heat*, 1987) which gained a sleazy cult following. Along with well-publicised drugs charges and ill-considered topless modelling, John Boorman's calamitous big-budget sequel *Exorcist II: The Heretic* (1977) destroyed her mainstream credibility. She attempts to lay the ghost of *The Exorcist* with the spoof *Repossessed* (1990); Brian Stoller's earlier (and reportedly superior) short parody, in which Blair plays all the original *Exorcist* characters, remains unreleased. MK

*Hell Night/1981 * Grotesque/1985 * The Chilling/Bad Blood/Witchery [Ghosthouse II]/ 1989 * Bedroom Eyes II/1990 * Dead Sleep/ 1991 * Phone (s)/1992*

TV: *Stranger in Our House*/1978 * *Fantasy Island*: 'Shadow Games'/1982 * *Monsters*: 'La Strega'/1989

Blanc, Erika [Enrica Bianchi] (b. 1945)

Italian actress. Blanc's horror baptism came with *La vendetta di Lady Morgan* (1966) and Mario **Bava**'s classic *Operazione paura* (*Curse of the Dead*, 1966). An early screen incarnation of Emmanuelle, her curvaceous figure and flame-haired Lady Penelope looks make her a natural for such shockers as *Così dolce . . . così perversa* (*So Sweet . . . So Perverse*, 1969), *La notte che Evelyn usci dalla tomba* (*The Night Evelyn Came Out of the Grave*, 1971), *Au service du diable* (*Devil's Nightmare*, 1971) and *La rossa dalla pelle che scotta* (*Sweet Spirits*, 1971). She blots her copy book with the appalling *Hexen – geschändet und zu Tode gequält* (*Mark of the Devil Part II*, 1972) and *Una libulela para cada muerto* (*A Dragonfly for Each Corpse*, 1973), but adds spice to an episode of **Argento**'s *La porta sul buio* TV series (1973). MA

*L'uomo più velenoso del cobra/1971 * Amore e morte nel giardino degli dei/1972 * Deadly Triangle/Giorni d'amore sul filo di una lama/ 1973 * Body Puzzle/1992*

Blatty, William Peter (b. 1928)

American writer, director. The leading contemporary exponent of 'theological thrillers' (and an underrated humorist), Blatty spins weighty philosophical tracts from populist paperback fictions. Schooled by Jesuits at Georgetown University, he became a writer of lightweight screen comedy (*A Shot in the Dark*, 1964) and satirical novels (*John Goldfarb Please Come Home*, 1962). Failing to gain church permission to write a factual

Linda Blair, *The Exorcist*

account of a 1949 exorcism, Blatty fictionalised the anecdote as *The Exorcist* (1971), a best-seller filmed in 1973 from his Oscar-winning screenplay.

Having toyed with a script for *One Flew Over the Cuckoo's Nest* (1976), Blatty expanded his novel *Twinkle, Twinkle, Killer Kane* (1966) into *The Ninth Configuration* (1979), his finest work, in which an army psychiatrist and mental patient discuss man's potential for selfless action as proof of God's existence. Blatty directed *The Ninth Configuration* (1981) from his own screenplay; the 118 minute version is his preferred cut. Blatty fought (and lost) a battle to prevent the reshooting, recutting and renaming of his film of his novel *Legion* (1983), which emerged as the sporadically impressive *The Exorcist III* (1990). MW

Blaxploitation * See: Black Horror

Bloch, Robert (1917–94)

American writer, famed for his novel *Psycho* (1959), basis for **Hitchcock**'s film (1960). Bloch published his first story at seventeen, encouraged by H.P. **Lovecraft**, and introduced to the **Cthulhu Mythos** the dreaded *De Vermis Mysteriis* (by Ludwig Prinn). Broadening his range from 1938, he imitated Thorne Smith and Damon Runyon, becoming an outrageous punster.

His horror yarn 'Yours Truly, Jack the Ripper' (1943) led to his adapting many of his own stories for **radio**'s *Stay Tuned for Terror* (1945). He also wrote Chandleresque mystery novels beginning with *The Scarf* (1947). He was in Hollywood preparing a screenplay for Warners (*The Couch*, 1962) and scripting for television when *Psycho* unexpectedly made his name: his response was a striking scenario in homage to silent cinema, *The Cabinet of Caligari* (1962). His career haunted by Norman Bates and The Ripper (who reappears in his 1967 *Star Trek* script 'Wolf in the Fold' and 1984 novel *Night of the Ripper*), Bloch's constant themes are the frenzied blade, the violently split personality and the Lovecraftian notion of evil as supernatural, possibly alien, entity.

His screenplays for William **Castle** (*Strait-Jacket*, 1963; *The Night Walker*, 1964) are less well served than amiably gruesome **anthology** scripts for **Amicus**: *Torture Garden* (1967), *The House That Dripped Blood* (1970), *Asylum* (1972). His novels include *Shooting Star* (1958), *Night-World* (1974), *American Gothic* (1975), *Strange Eons* (1979), *Psycho II* (1982), *Lori* (1989) and *The Jekyll Legacy* (with Andre Norton, 1990); among many story collections are *The Opener of the Way* (1945), *Yours Truly, Jack the Ripper: Tales of Horror* (1962), *The Skull of the Marquis de Sade and Other Stories* (1965) and *The Selected Stories of Robert Bloch* (1987). An 'unauthorised autobiography', *Once Around the Bloch*, appeared in 1993. PS

The Skull (st)/*The Psychopath*/1965

TV: *Alfred Hitchcock Presents*: 'The Cure' (st)/ 'Madame Mystery' (st)/'The Cuckoo Clock'/ 1960; 'A Change of Heart'/'The Greatest Monster of Them All'/'The Landlady'/'The Gloating Place'/1961; 'The Sorcerer's Apprentice'/'Bad Actor'/'The Big Kick'/1962 * *Bus Stop*: 'I Kiss Your Shadow'/1962 * *Thriller*: 'The Cheaters' (st)/1960; 'Yours Truly, Jack the Ripper'/'The Devil's Ticket'/ 'A Good Imagination'/'The Grim Reaper'/ 'The Weird Tailor'/1961; 'Waxworks'/'Til Death Do Us Part'/'Man of Mystery'/1962 * *Alfred Hitchcock Hour*: 'Annabel'/1962; 'A Home Away From Home'/1963; 'Sign of Satan' (st)/1964; 'Final Performance' (st)/ 'The Second Wife'/'Off Season'/1965 * *Star Trek*: 'What Are Little Girls Made Of?'/1966; 'Catspaw'/1967 * *Journey to the Unknown*: 'The Indian Spirit Guide'/'Girl of My Dreams'/1968 * *Night Gallery*: 'Logoda's Heads'/1971 * *Ghost Story*: 'House of Evil'/ 1972 * *The Cat Creature*/1973 * *The Dead Don't*

Blood: Christopher Lee, Melissa Stribling, *Dracula* (1958)

Die/1975 * *Tales of the Unexpected*: 'Fat Chance' (st)/1980 * *Darkroom*: 'The Bogeyman Will Get You'/'A Quiet Funeral'/ 'Catnip'/1981 * *Tales From the Darkside*: 'A Case of the Stubborns'/1984 * *Alfred Hitchcock Presents*: 'The Gloating Place' (st)/ 1986 * *Monsters*: 'The Legacy' (st)/1988

Blood

Anatomically, the oxygenating fluid that circulates in the bodies of higher animals; symbolically, the juice of life itself. The sustenance of **vampires**, the ink for **Faust** pacts and a substance spilled by **violence**, blood is central to the horror film, though the black-and-white era restricted it to a smudge on **Renfield**'s finger in *Dracula* (1931), a trickle under the door in *The Leopard Man* (1943) and coffee grounds swirling in the shower in

Psycho (1960). Even *Before I Hang* (1940), which hinges on transfusion, is reluctant to show any blood.

However, when Eastmancolor was introduced to the genre with **Hammer**'s *The Curse of Frankenstein* (1957) and *Dracula* (1958), Kensington gore fairly glowed from surgical incisions, nibbled necks and skewered vampires. H.G. **Lewis**'s *Blood Feast* (1964), precursor of the **splatter movie**, sloshes ketchup over severed mannequins and borrowed offal, and follow-up *Color Me Blood Red* (1966) concentrates on an **artist** who daubs in gore. Surprisingly few horror films spill as much blood as the squib-laden crime or **Western** apocalypses of *Bonnie and Clyde* (1967) and *The Wild Bunch* (1969), though the red stuff features in such startling moments as the elevator nightmare of *The*

Shining (1980), which may well feature the most blood ever seen in a single scene.

Dario **Argento**'s blood is almost scarlet neon in the stained-glass pictorialism of *Suspiria* (1977), while George **Romero**, having spilled monochrome gore in *Night of the Living Dead* (1968), opts for a muted, tomato soup-ish look for *Dawn of the Dead* (1979). Vampire films are oddly reluctant to use blood as anything more than a colour in the palette, but *Blood for Dracula* (1974) has the Count puke after gorging himself on nonvirgin blood, and both *¡Vampiros en la Habana!* (*Vampires in Havana*, 1985) and *Sundown: The Vampire in Retreat* (1989) feature vampires searching for a safe blood substitute. Erzsébet **Báthory**, who allegedly bathed in blood, has often been seen in films. Prefigured by the blood-powdering **disease** of *The Andromeda Strain* (1971), AIDS has made blood plagues fashionable bogeys.

Like 'Curse', 'Horror', 'Night' and 'Monster', 'Blood' is also a nifty if mostly meaningless word suitable for use in titles that signify 'yes indeed, this is a horror film': *Night of the Blood Beast* (1958), *Blood of the Vampire* (1958), *Blood of Dracula's Castle* (1967), *Taste the Blood of Dracula* (1968), *Blood on Satan's Claw* (1971), *Blood From the Mummy's Tomb* (1971), *Blood* (1973), *Blood Orgy of the She Devils* (1973), *Blood and Lace* (1974), *Nightmare in Blood* (1976), *Blood Beach* (1980), *Blood Freak* (1985), *Blood Diner* (1987).

Blue Demon [Alejandro Cruz] (b. 19??– 19??)

Mexican wrestler. Cruz appears in his civilian identity in *La maldición de la momia Azteca* (1959) and made his **monster-wrestling** debut in *El demonio azul* (1963). The blue-suited bruiser joined his chief rival in *Santo Contra Blue Demon en la Atlántida* (1968) and subsequently appeared only in tag teams.

Blue Demon contra el poder satánico/1964 * *Arañas infernales*/*La sombra del murciélago*/1966 * *Blue Demon contra cerebros infernales*/*Blue Demon contra las diabolicas*/1967 * *Blue Demon y las seductoras*/*El mundo de los muertos*/1968 * *Santo y Blue Demon contra los monstruos*/1969 * *Las momias de Guanajuato*/1970 * *Santo y Blue Demon contra el Dr. Frankenstein*/1971 * *Santo y Blue Demon contra Drácula y el Hombre Lobo*/*Santo y Blue Demon contra las bestias del terror*/*Blue Demon y Zóvek en la invasión de los muertos*/*Vuelven los campeones justicieros*/1972

Bodeen, DeWitt (1908–88)

American writer, associated with Val **Lewton**. His post-B career includes *The Enchanted Cottage* (1945) and *Twelve to the Moon* (1960).

Cat People/*The Seventh Victim*/1943 * *The Curse of the Cat People*/1944

Body-Snatching

An illegal trade in exhumed corpses to schools of anatomy flourished in Scotland, England and Ireland from the middle of the 18th century until 1832. Oddly, the most famous body-snatchers were not genuine resurrection men but mere murderers. Edinburgh-resident Irishmen William Burke and William Hare avoided the heavy work of entering a churchyard and digging up graves by smothering victims whom they then sold, mostly to Dr Robert Knox. When Burke and Hare were caught, Hare informed on his partner in return for exemption from prosecution and Burke was hanged (and dissected) in 1829. The furore was in part responsible for the Anatomy Acts of 1832, which ended the trade by making provision for unclaimed bodies to be donated to science and education.

Burke and Hare became lasting bogeymen, their story often retold and embroidered. R.L. **Stevenson**'s 'The Body Snatcher' (1884) features a Burke-like murderer and a Knox-style anatomist: it was filmed by Val **Lewton** and Robert **Wise** with **Karloff** and Henry **Daniell** in 1945 and remade on *Mystery and Imagination* (1966). James Bridie's play *The Anatomist* (1930) indicts the arrogance and culpability of Knox: it was filmed in 1961, with Alistair Sim, George Cole and Michael **Ripper**, and telecast with Andrew Cruickshank, W.G. Fay and Harry Hutchinson (1939), and Patrick Stewart (an especially fine Knox), Micky O'Donoghue and James Coyle (1980). Dylan Thomas's script *The Doctor and the Devils* (1941), published in 1953 but finally filmed (by Freddie **Francis**) in 1986, renames Burke and Hare as Fallon (Jonathan Pryce) and Broome (Stephen Rea) and, unlike Bridie, exonerates the Knox-like Dr Rock (Timothy Dalton).

British Censors in the 40s took a dim view of those who wanted to revive memories of Burke and Hare: they cut all mention of the names from *The Body Snatcher* and insisted a Tod **Slaughter** vehicle redub Burke and Hare as Moore and Hart, renaming the film *The Greed of William Hart* (1948). John Gilling, Slaughter's writer, mounted a more elaborate version which restored the historical names, *The Flesh and the Fiends* (1959), with Peter **Cushing** lending Knox a Frankenstein aspect and George Rose and Donald **Pleasence** as the murderers. Though

LEFT Body-snatching: Timothy Dalton, Stephen Rea, Jonathan Pryce, *The Doctor and the Devils*

The Body Snatcher is the best body-snatching film, *The Flesh and the Fiends*, with its Hogarthian Edinburgh atmospherics, is the definitive Burke-and-Hare movie, unchallenged by Vernon **Sewell**'s tits-and-gore knees-up *Burke & Hare* (1971), with Harry Andrews buying corpses from Derren Nesbitt and Glynn Edwards, and the tardy, dreary *Doctor and the Devils*. Liberated from historical context, Burke and Hare appear in *Dr. Jekyll and Sister Hyde* (1971), played by Ivor Dean and Tony Calvin, and *Nightmare in Blood* (1978).

Corridors of Blood (1958), with Karloff as a doctor who employs genuine body-snatcher Resurrection Joe (Christopher **Lee**), is a rare non-Burke-and-Hare film on the theme, (very) loosely based on the career of Dr Robert Liston, a pioneer of anaesthesia. Though reputable anatomists have had little use for body-snatchers since 1832, the cinema's **mad scientists** often employ unshaven, drunken, frequently hunchbacked **minions** for the purpose of supplying raw material for unhallowed experiments. *Frankenstein* (1931) opens with Colin **Clive** and Dwight **Frye** in a graveyard ready to dig up a just-buried corpse; Frye reprises the crime in *Bride of Frankenstein* (1935), in which he expresses the Burke-like opinion that body-snatching 'is no job for murderers'. Subsequent resurrectionists: Lionel Jeffries (*The Revenge of Frankenstein*, 1958), John Dierkes and Dick **Miller** (*The Premature Burial*, 1962), Dennis **Price** (*Horror of Frankenstein*, 1970), Walter Burke ('Deliveries in the Rear', **Night Gallery**, 1972), Patrick **Troughton** (*Frankenstein and the Monster From Hell*, 1973), Arthur Mullard (*Vault of Horror*, 1973).

George MacGregor, *The History of Burke and Hare, and of the Resurrectionist Times* (1884); Ruth Richardson, *Death, Dissection and the Destitute* (1987); Brian Bailey, *The Resurrection Men* (1991)

Borland, Carroll (1914–94)

American actress. Self-promoted protégé of Bela **Lugosi**, Borland is his striking mock **vampire** daughter in *Mark of the Vampire* (1935). A novel, *Countess Dracula*, written in 1928, was published in 1994.

Scalps/1982 * *Biohazard*/1984

Borowczyk, Walerian (b. 1932)

Polish director, writer. An animator who enjoyed collaborations with Jan Lenica (*Dom*, 1958) and Chris Marker (*Les astro-*

Carroll Borland, *Mark of the Vampire*

nautes, 1959) and whose feature debut is *Théâtre de Monsieur et Madame Kabal* (1967), Borowczyk relinquished his reputation to make untrammelled, iconoclastic, oddly ambivalent **sex** films that routinely flirt with horror: the **anthology** *Contes immoraux* (*Immoral Tales*, 1974) contains a **Báthory** segment; the expanded short *La bête* (*The Beast*, 1975) turns infamously on a dream of monster **rape**; while the Wedekind re-interpretation *Lulu* (1980) sees Udo **Kier** limn **Jack the Ripper**. The Warhol horror star is re-used in Borowczyk's most concertedly macabre entry, the polymorphously perverse *Dr. Jekyll et les femmes* (*The Blood of Dr. Jekyll*, 1981).

An interest in issues of pleasure and responsibility depraves the pre-softcore *Blanche* (1971), transforms the Ovidian *Ars amandi* (*The Art of Love*, 1983) into a murder movie, and produces untoward sex-death orchestrations even in Sylvie Kristel compromise *La marge* (*The Streetwalker*, 1975). Other para-horrors include *Interno di un convento* (*Behind Convent Walls*, 1977) and *Les heroines du mal* (*Three Immoral Women*, 1979). Fetishistically wrought, Borowczyk's erotica owes much to his harsh, enigmatic cartoons; his very persistence with **pornography** bespeaks a continued personal commitment. Disowning *Emmanuelle 5* (1986), the adoptive Parisian has not managed a film since the ironic *Cérémonie d'amour* (1988). DP

Boswell, Simon (b. 1956)

British composer. Boswell has scored for Lamberto **Bava**, **Argento**, Richard Stanley

and **Barker**. He also provided a score for the English-language version of *Baby Blood* (1990).

Phenomena [*Creepers*]/1984 * *Deliria* [*Stagefright*]/*Demoni 2* [*Demons 2*]/1986 * *Le foto di Gioia*/1987 * *La casa 3*/1988 * *L'uomo che non voleva morire*/*Maestro del terrore*/*Il gioco*/*Santa Sangre*/*La chiesa* [*The Church*]/ 1989 * *La maschara del demonio*/*Hardware*/*Eye Witness*/1990 * *Dust Devil*/*The Turn of the Screw*/*Children of the Corn II: The Final Sacrifice*/1992 * *Shallow Grave*/ 1994 * *Lord of Illusions*/1995

TV: *Brivido Caldo*: 'Per sempre, fini alla morte' [*Changeling 2*]/'Una notte nel cimitero' [*Graveyard Disturbance*]/'La casa dell'orco' [*Demons 3: The Ogre*]/'A cena con il vampiro' [*Dinner With the Vampire*]/1987

Bottin, Rob (b. 1959)

American make-up effects artist. Known for his surreal imagination and wildly outré creations, typified by the elaborate shapeshifting **alien** of John **Carpenter**'s *The Thing* (1982). A Rick **Baker** protégé, Bottin lived out of his mentor's house during his teenage years, assisting on *Star Wars* (1977) and *The Incredible Melting Man* (1978), and went solo with New World Pictures assignments: *Piranha* (1978), *Humanoids From the Deep* (1978), *Rock 'n' Roll High School* (1979). He even whipped up an effect for a trailer for *Screamers* (1981), an Americanised re-cut of *L'isola degli uomini pesce* (*Island of the Mutations*, 1978), that was spliced into some prints.

His first major credits are Joe **Dante**'s *The Howling* (1980), for which he produced **werewolf** transformations, and Carpenter's *The Fog* (1980), on which he was responsible

Walerian Borowczyk: Sirpa Lane, *La bête*

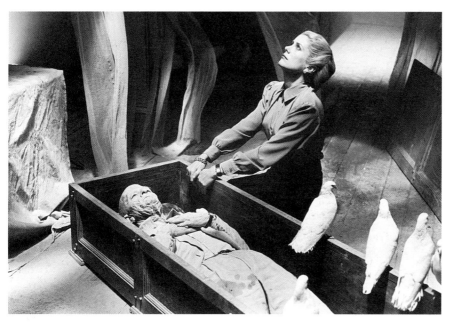

David Bowie (and Catherine Deneuve), *The Hunger*

for the leper effects and appears as the lead ghost pirate. He designed monstrous creations for Ridley Scott's *Legend* (1985), including the spectacular water witch Meg Mucklebones (played by regular Bottin man behind the mask, Robert Picardo) and the awe-inspiring horned Lord of Darkness (Tim Curry). After *Explorers* (1985), *RoboCop* (1987) and an Academy Award for *Total Recall* (1990), his work has become less outlandish and more mainstream (*Bugsy*, 1991; *Basic Instinct*, 1992). He provided the realistic corpses seen in *Se7en* (1995) and the disguises of *Mission: Impossible* (1996). MS

Twilight Zone: The Movie ('It's a Good Life')/ 1983 * *The Witches of Eastwick*/1987

Bowie, David [David Jones] (b. 1947)

British pop star, actor. As a musician Bowie is known for a chameleon quality, effortlessly moving from Ziggy Stardust via Aladdin Sane to the Thin White Duke. Lasting influences are Lindsay Kemp, whose mime troupe he joined at the end of 60s, and Michael **Armstrong**, for whom he starred in the short *The Image* (1967) and who tried to cast him as a **psycho** in *Haunted House of Horror* (1968). A fragmented film career has been secondary to music: from the mid-60s he tried on styles (British R&B, jazz, idiosyncratic pop *á la* Anthony Newley) as others tried on clothes. Whereas Bowie's ever-

changing musical identity is as much a matter of disguising his essentially androgynous image as keeping in tune with the music of the times, his screen persona focuses directly on intense otherness: an **alien** in *The Man Who Fell to Earth* (1976), a **vampire** in *The Hunger* (1983), a Billy Budd-like martyr in *Merry Christmas Mr. Lawrence* (1983). Less successful are films like *Labyrinth* (1986), in which he is merely asked to act: his goblin king is a cipher rather than an 'other'. PHa

Cat People (song)/1982 * *Ziggy Stardust and the Spiders From Mars*/1983 * *Twin Peaks Fire Walk With Me*/1992 * *Se7en* (song)/1995

Bradbury, Ray (b. 1920)

American writer who brought passion, poetry and nostalgia to Space-Age fiction, countering the hard science of his contemporaries with wholly non-technical visions of the near future. Determined from infancy to become a writer, driven by his enthusiasm for Buck Rogers, Edgar Rice Burroughs, **Poe** and Hemingway, he sold his first story (co-written with Henry Hasse) 'Pendulum' in 1941 and published his first collection *Dark Carnival* in 1947. Many appearing originally in **Weird Tales**, his stories use metaphor to explore childhood pleasures and fears: he constantly re-examines the distorted family unit, the child as **alien** species, the loss of innocence and individuality as the inevitable consequence of a malevolent future, the growing awareness and distrust of sexuality, the wisdom of old age and the treasure-trove provided by literature itself.

Bradbury's vividly visual writing has inspired many screenplays, few completed films and no unarguable screen triumphs. However, there is much to savour in Truffaut's 1966 version of *Fahrenheit 451* (1951) and Jack **Clayton**'s Disneyfield 1982 take on *Something Wicked This Way Comes* (1962). Perpetually recycled in the form of plays, comics (he was an **EC** mainstay),

RIGHT Doug Bradley, *Hellbound: Hellraiser II*

musicals, operas and fresh film concepts, Bradbury's output has formed intriguing television material: he wrote and introduced *The Ray Bradbury Theatre* (1985–9), which was part-reissued on video as *Ray Bradbury's Nightmares* and became the basis, in turn, for a whole new generation of comic-books. His important collections are *The Illustrated Man* (1951), *The October Country* (1955) and *The Stories of Ray Bradbury* (1980). PS

It Came From Outer Space/The Beast From 20,000 Fathoms (st)/1953

TV: *Alfred Hitchcock Presents*: 'Shopping for Death'/'And So Died Riabouchinska' (st)/ 1956; 'Design for Loving'/1958; 'Special Delivery'/1959; 'The Faith of Aaron Menefee'/1962 * *The Twilight Zone*: 'I Sing the Body Electric'/1962 * *Alfred Hitchcock Hour*: 'The Jar' (st)/'The Life Work of Juan Diaz'/1962 * *Out of the Unknown*: 'The Fox and the Forest'/1965 * *CBS Library*: 'Robbers, Rooftops and Witches' (st)/1982 * *The Twilight Zone*: 'The Burning Man' (st)/1985; 'The Elevator/1986 * *Alfred Hitchcock Presents*: 'The Jar' (st)/1986 * *The Halloween Tree*/1994 * *It Came From Outer Space 2* (st)/1996

Bradley, Doug (b. 1954)

British actor. A horror icon as Pinhead, lead Cenobite in schoolfriend Clive **Barker**'s *Hellraiser* series. The **vampire** Barlow in a BBC **radio** *Salem's Lot* (1994). SJ

The Forbidden/1975–8 * *Hellraiser*/1987 * *Hellbound Hellraiser II*/1988 * *Nightbreed*/1990 * *Hellraiser III Hell on Earth*/1992 * *Proteus*/ 1995 * *Hellraiser: Bloodline/The Killer Tongue*/ 1996

Brahm, John (1893–1982)

German director. After the **werewolf** B *The Undying Monster* (1942), Brahm made two lavish Victorian melodramas starring Laird **Cregar**, *The Lodger* (1944) and *Hangover Square* (1945). His career declined into self-imitation with the **3-D** Vincent **Price** vehicle *The Mad Magician* (1954), a cash-in on *House of Wax* (1953), itself influenced by Brahm's films. Later productive in television.

TV: *Alfred Hitchcock Presents*: 'A Night With the Boys'/'Dry Run'/1959; 'Madame Mystery'/'The Cuckoo Clock'/'The Hero'/ 'Insomnia'/'The Five Forty-Eight'/'Pen Pal'/ 1960; 'The Throwback'/1961 * *The Twilight Zone*: 'Time Enough at Last'/'Judgment Night'/1959; 'The Four of Us Are Dying'/ 'Mirror Image'/'A Nice Place to Visit'/1960; 'Mr Dingle, the Strong'/'Shadow Play'/1961;

Brains: Brain (and Dan Blom), *Mind Ripper*

'Person or Persons Unknown'/'Young Man's Fancy'/1962; 'The New Exhibit'/1963; 'You Drive'/'Queen of the Nile'/1964 * *Thriller*: 'The Watcher'/'The Prediction'/'The Cheaters'/1960; 'The Merriweather File'/ 'Well of Doom'/'A Good Imagination'/'Dark Legacy'/'The Remarkable Mrs Hawk'/1961; 'An Attractive Family'/'Waxworks'/'A Wig for Mrs DeVore'/'Cousin Tundifer'/'Flowers of Evil'/1962 * *Alfred Hitchcock Hour*: 'Don't Look Behind You'/1962; 'Death and the Joyful Woman'/1963; 'Murder Case'/1964; 'Final Performance'/'The Trap'/1965 * *The Outer Limits*: 'Zzzzz'/'The Bellero Shield'/ 1964

Brains

Centres of understanding not yet fully understood, brains are the archives for our deepest fears. Exposed, they excite a compulsive fascination. Early films, recalling both Darwin and **Frankenstein**, merrily exchange organs to produce *The Monkey Man* (1908) or, in *Go and Get It* (1920), an **ape** with a murderer's mind. Later variants include *The Monster and the Girl* (1941), *Return of the Ape Man* (1944) and the multiple transplants and regenerations of the **Captive Wild Woman** (1943) trilogy. Essence of brain, injected into a capuchin monkey in **Romero**'s *Monkey Shines* (1988), administered to student drop-outs in *Zombie High* (1987), distilled as a cure for sick Martians in

the TV-series *War of the Worlds* (1988), also prove to have remarkable qualities.

Brain preservation for the sake of longevity (*The Immortaliser*, 1990) has been a major attraction since *The Lady and the Monster* (1944), with Erich von **Stroheim** resuscitating a criminal millionaire in the first of three versions of Curt **Siodmak**'s *Donovan's Brain* (1943). Justifying the time and equipment devoted to them, brains that matter include those of **Nostradamus** (*The Man Without a Body*, 1957), Michel Simon (*The Head* (1959), a brilliant scientist (*The Colossus of New York*, 1958) and a waxen Führer (*They Saved Hitler's Brain*, 1963). On a more domestic level, a transplant specialist activates the beautiful head of his late fiancée in *The Brain That Wouldn't Die* (1959), a French surgeon finds himself in the body of his daughter's lover in *L'homme au cerveau greffé* (*The Man with the Transplanted Brain*, 1972) and Steve Martin sings duets with the jar containing his true love in *The Man with Two Brains* (1983). In the exuberant fantasy-land of *La cité des enfants perdus* (*The City of Lost Children*, 1995), Uncle Irvin's brain (voiced by Jean-Louis Trintignant) continues to endure birthdays and indigestion tablets while dominating the family from a battery of lenses and gramophone horns.

No longer the threat that it was in the era of Dan Dare's adversary The Mekon – probably because the giant craniums of *Invaders* from Mars (1953), This Island Earth (1995) and The Brain from Planet Arous (1958) look merely silly – the brain remains squirmingly at risk from evil consumers, as in The Brain Eaters (1958), El barón del terror (The Brainiac, 1962), Pánico en el Transiberiano (Horror Express, 1972) and Mind Ripper (1995). Rare benevolence (The Space Children, 1958) does little to protect against skull-crushing intrusion, trademark of the **Hammer Frankensteins**, with deranged consequences (The Creature With the Atom Brain, 1955; Nightmares in a Damaged Brain, 1981; Blood Diner, 1987). Guaranteed to disrupt any peace of mind, Angel Garcia del Val's Spanish horror-documentary Cada ver es (1981) shows real brains being sliced like fresh loaves for examination by medical students.

'Kill the brain and you kill the ghoul' cry the righteous rednecks of **Night of the Living Dead** (1968). Food for thought indeed, and thought can also become food, for the monster parasite Elmer who preys on brains in Frank **Henenlotter**'s Brain Damage (1987), which features the singular image of brains emerging string-like through an ear, as well as for the zombies in Return of the Living Dead (1985) and in From Beyond (1986). More ludicrously, in The Fiend Without a Face (1958), monstrous thoughts become real and the unconscious takes the shape of killer leaping brains preying on other brains. PS/LRW

Brandner, Gary (b. 1933)

American writer. Joe **Dante**'s **The Howling** (1981) uses so little of Brandner's paperback (1979) that John **Hough**'s Howling IV: The Original Nightmare (1988) was able to adapt it. He co-scripted Howling II: Stirba, Werewolf Bitch (1985) but gets only a spurious 'based on characters created by' tag for other series entries. The miniseries From the Dead of Night (1989) is based on Brandner's Walkers (1980). He scripted Cameron's Closet (1989) from his own novel (1987).

Briant, Shane (b. 1946)

British actor. Unmemorable youth in several **Hammer** films. Later moved to Australia. SJ

Demons of the Mind/Straight on Till Morning/ Captain Kronos Vampire Hunter/1972 * Frankenstein and the Monster from Hell/1973 * Cassandra/1987 * Out of the Body/1988 * Tunnel Vision/1995

TV: The Picture of Dorian Gray/1973

Tod Browning on the set of The Show

Briggs, Joe Bob [John Bloom] (b. 1953)

American reviewer, redneck iconoclast. Writer John Bloom's pseudonymous life as East Texan drive-in movie muncher Joe Bob Briggs began in 1972 in a weekly satirical film column for the Dallas Times Herald. He found fame, syndication and chagrin when his politically incorrect belief in the higher meaning of cinematic sleaze proved too much for the usual crowd of moralists and feminists. In addition to occasional film appearances (notably in Casino, 1995) and a stint as a television **horror host**, Joe Bob continues his philosophical discourse on D-cups and decapitation with a Swiftian wit that has been impaired only slightly by the ingestion of too much polio weed, if you know what I mean and I think you do. He published the magazines We Are the Weird (1985–93) and The Joe Bob Report (1993–5). DW

The Texas Chainsaw Massacre 2 (a)/1986 * Hollywood Boulevard 2 (a)/1989

TV: The Stand (a)/1994

Joe Bob Briggs, Joe Bob Goes to the Drive-In (1987), Joe Bob Goes Back to the Drive-In (1990)

Brown, Fredric (1906–72)

American writer, important in mystery (Night of the Jabberwock, 1951; Knock Three-One-Two, 1959) and s-f (What Mad Universe?, 1951; The Mind Thing, 1961). The Screaming Mimi (1949), officially filmed in 1958, is the uncredited source for Dario **Argento**'s pioneering **giallo** L'Uccello dalle piume di cristallo (The Bird With the Crystal Plumage, 1970). Brown's tart short stories are collected in Honeymoon in Hell (1958) and Nightmares and Geezenstacks (1961).

TV: Alfred Hitchcock Presents: 'The Cream of the Jest' (st)/'The Night the World Ended' (st)/'The Dangerous People' (st)/1957; 'The Human Interest Story'/1959 * Thriller: 'Knock Three-One-Two' (st)/1960 * Darkroom: 'Daisies' (st)/1981 * Alfred Hitchcock Presents: 'The Human Interest Story' (st)/1985 * Tales From the Darkside: 'The Geezenstacks' (st)/1986

Browning, Tod [Charles Albert Browning] (1880–1962)

American writer, producer, director. Effectively the major architect of Hollywood horror, Browning is both canonised and decried for his helmsmanship of **Dracula**

(1931) but his real value is revealed by a silent run of melodramas made with Lon **Chaney** at MGM. Notwithstanding the disastrous reception of their sound extension *Freaks* (1932), these form a vitally perverse preamble to the Golden Age of American Gothic.

Browning's biography connects cinema with its carnival beginnings: absconding with a travelling show in 1896, he clowned for the Ringling Brothers and performed a 'Hypnotic Living Corpse' act prior to stints in vaudeville and on a contortionist world tour. As a comedian, he plays an undertaker in D.W. Griffith's *Scenting a Terrible Crime* (1913) and moved to Hollywood with its maker. He made a directorial debut with the two-reel **comedy** *The Lucky Transfer* (1915), and followed up with shorts like *The Burned Hand* (1915) and *The Living Head* (1915). After assistance both in front and behind camera on *Intolerance* (1916), he made a feature debut with *Jim Bludso* (1917), a Mississippi marital drama, but the inheritance chiller *The Eyes of Mystery* (1918) is more typical of his later interests. *The Wicked Darling* (1919) and *Outside the Law* (1920), two of a series of Priscilla Dean movies made for Universal, are notable for initiating relations with Chaney.

Blackballed for alcoholism, Browning adapted a 1917 Tod Robbins best seller as his comeback feature, gaining MGM backing after representations from his briefly estranged wife Alice Wilson. *Ergo* a Lon Chaney vehicle, *The Unholy Three* (1925) makes an issue of its star's vaunted mimicry by way of Browning's **circus** background: the story of a sideshow trio who turn to jewel-theft, the film features Chaney as a **ventriloquist** who plays grandmother to midget Harry Earles's monstrously embittered 'baby'. *The Blackbird* (1926) takes even more ironic delight in charlatanry by casting the Man of a Thousand Faces as a crook whose back is snapped after posing as his paralysed, philanthropic twin. With Chaney as disfigured father rather than suitor, *The Road to Mandalay* (1926) varies the inconsummate love theme of previous efforts.

The Show (1927), a non-Chaney fairground film, has Lionel **Barrymore** attempt to decapitate romantic rival Cock Robin (John Gilbert): noting the castrative connotations of Browning's work, several have speculated on the injuries he suffered in a 1915 car-smash. Whatever the case, *The Unknown* (1927) presents the director at his most torridly Freudian: extrapolated from an autobiographical incident and scripted (with Browning's usual assistance) by regular writer Waldemar Young, it has Chaney, masquerading as an armless knife-thrower, elect for amputation in a bid to marry Joan **Crawford**'s sexual neurotic. In a use of frame that belies criticism of Browning's primitivist technique, Chaney's feet are doubled by bona fide freak Dismuki. Sentiment and sado-masochism again collide in the deeply mordant *West of Zanzibar* (1928), with Chaney as a cuckolded magician.

After the lost collaborations *London After Midnight* (1927) and *The Big City* (1928) and a final mutilation movie *Where East is East* (1929), Chaney and Browning succumbed seperately to talkies: the actor with a showpiece sonorisation of *The Unholy Three* (1930), the director with the transfixed theatricality of *The Thirteenth Chair* (1929), a fake **medium** mystery. *Dracula* suffers less from its eerily circumspect attitude to sound than from a disinterest seemingly derived from Chaney's death. The project appears ideal for Browning, but despite its bizarre psycho-sexual imperatives, the sequentially shot feature fades after a bracingly peculiar first half.

While *Dracula*'s success officially launched the horror movie, the balance of Browning's shockers stubbornly resist the trend for the supernatural. *Freaks* was meant as MGM's contribution to the vogue: an embellishment of Todd Robbins' 'Spurs' (1917) announced as early as 1929, the film is inarguably Browning's most assiduous. Its *vérité* castings and too-candid querying of notions of monstrosity however proved confounding. After reshoots, re-edits and a loss-making first run, a scandalised Louis Mayer consigned the property to roadshowman Dwain Esper. Sidelined, Browning nonetheless essayed a subsequent Metro contender *Mark of the Vampire* (1935), a remake of *London After Midnight*. Unpopularly, the director insisted on the original's **rationalised** conclusion, thus revealing **Lugosi** to be not a **vampire** but merely an actor. Begun as a colonialist **voodoo** adventure, *The Devil-Doll* (1936) ended up a bizarre *Bride of Frankenstein* (1935) admixture after British pre-production objections. In *Unholy Three* drag, Lionel Barrymore exacts revenge using a set of miniature people.

Henry Hull is the Chaney substitute in *Miracles for Sale* (1939), Browning's official, unprofitable finale; a murder mystery with debunking **magician** Robert Young as hero. Plans to film Horace McCoy's Depression text *They Shoot Horses, Don't They?* (1935) having failed, he retired in 1942 after a period of script-doctoring. *Variety* obituarised Browning two years later: his actual death followed a bout of the same throat cancer that did for his preferred star. Among many film tributes, *Blood From the Mummy's Tomb* (1971) names its hero (Mark Edwards) 'Tod Browning'. DP

An Interrupted Séance (a)/1914 * *The Mystery of the Leaping Fish* (w)/1916 * *The Mystic*/1925

David J. Skal and Elias Savada, *Dark Carnival: The Secret World of Tod Browning, Hollywood's Master of the Macabre* (1995)

Brownrigg, S.F. (b. 19??)

American director, producer. Until 1968 an employee of fellow Texan Larry **Buchanan**, Sherold Brownrigg helms distinctively despondent **rural horror** melodramas with psychologically imperilled women at their centres. Though talkbound and largely tensionless, they benefit from an unwholesome, forcefully performed sense of backwoods malaise. In 1990 Brownrigg announced a sequel to *Freaks* (1932). Wife Libby Hall stars in Buchanan's horror debut, *The Naked Witch* (1960). DP

Don't Look in the Basement/1973 * *Poor White Trash Part II*/1974 * *Don't Open the Door*/1979 * *Keep My Grave Open*/1980

Bruce, Nigel (1895–1953)

Mexican-born British actor. Bruce's dotty Watson partnered Basil **Rathbone**'s **Sherlock Holmes** in film and on **radio**.

She/1935 * *The Hound of the Baskervilles*/*The Adventures of Sherlock Holmes*/1939 * *Sherlock Holmes and the Voice of Terror*/*Sherlock Holmes and the Secret Weapon*/1942 * *Sherlock Holmes in Washington*/*Sherlock Holmes Faces Death*/*Crazy House*/1943 * *The Scarlet Claw*/*The Spider Woman*/*The Pearl of Death*/1944 * *The House of Fear*/*The Woman in Green*/*Pursuit to Algiers*/1945 * *Terror by Night*/*Dressed to Kill*/1946 * *The Two Mrs. Carrolls*/1947

Buchanan, Larry (b. 1923)

American director, writer, producer. After distributing Buchanan's profitable blaxploitationer *Free, White and 21* (1963), AIP contracted the Dallas-based film-maker to complete feature packages with colour product, ready for sale to TV. The murky 16mm quickies that resulted are mainly slavish remakes of older AIP monster movies; their combination of outmoded, po-faced dialogue

ABOVE Luis Buñuel
BELOW *Le charme discret de la bourgeoisie*

and soporifically exigent visuals has earnt acclaim from badfilm devotees. DP

The Naked Witch/1960 * *The Eye Creatures*/ 1965 * *Curse of the Swamp Creature*/*Year 2889*/ *Zontar – the Thing from Venus*/*Mars Needs Women*/1966 * *Creature of Destruction*/1967 * *It's Alive!*/1968 * *The Loch Ness Horror*/1982

Buechler, John Carl (b 19??)

American make-up artist, director. At the lower end of low-budget spectrum, Buechler (through his company Mechanical and Make-Up Imageries) has contributed to most of the franchise horrors. *Re-Animator* (1985) is the best of his many Charles **Band** credits, which are typified more by the clumping rubber monsters of *Ghoulies* (1984). His directorial efforts are hardly distinguished. MS

The Thing in the Basement (s)/197? * *The Island*/1980 * *Android*/*Mausoleum*/*Forbidden World*/1982 * *The Dungeonmaster* (+co-d)/ *Hard Rock Zombies*/1984 * *Trancers*/1985 * *From Beyond*/*Zone Troopers*/*Eliminators*/ *TerrorVision*/*Troll* (+d)/1986 * *Dolls*/*The Caller*/*Cellar Dweller* (+d)/*Crawlspace*/*Prison*/ 1987 * *Demonwarp* (+st)/*Friday 13th VII: The New Blood* (+d)/*Ghost Town*/*Ghoulies II*/*To Die For*/*The Caller*/*Halloween 4: The Return of Michael Myers*/*A Nightmare on Elm Street: The Dream Master*/1988 * *The Laughing Dead*/1989 * *Ghoulies Go To College* (+ d)/*The Sleeping Car*/1990 * *Bride of Re-Animator*/*Demonic Toys*/*Freddy's Dead: The Final Nightmare*/*Son of Darkness: To Die For II*/1991 * *Seed People*/ 1992 * *Dollman vs. Demonic Toys*/*Scanner Cop*/*Ghost in the Machine*/1993 * *Carnosaur*/ *Necronomicon*/1994 * *Carnosaur 2*/*Scanner Cop II: Volkin's Revenge*/*Halloween: The Curse of Michael Myers*/*Project: Metalbeast*/1995

TV: *The Darker Side of Terror*/1978

Bugs * See: **Insects and Arachnids**

Buñuel, Luis (1900–1983)

Spanish director. He announced his arrival in the cinema with the closeup slicing of an **eye**ball in *Un chien andalou* (1928). Two Mexican films are studies of outright psychosis: *El* (1952) is a landowner whose distorted romanticism drives him to consider the **Sade**an extreme of sewing up his wife's genitals; *Ensayo de un crimen* (*The Criminal Life of Archibaldo de la Cruz*, 1955) concerns Archibaldo de la Cruz and his blackly comic attempts to murder women for pure pleasure. *El angel exterminador* (*The Exterminating Angel*, 1962), in a device as surreal as it is satiric, robs its bourgeois characters of their ability to leave a room. A severed **hand** emerging from a cabinet appears to have crept in from *The Beast With Five Fingers* (1947), whose Spanish-language version Buñuel supervised.

Le charme discret de la bourgeoisie (*The Discreet Charm of the Bourgeoisie*, 1972) revels in the increasingly gothic (sometimes supernatural) devices with which its denies a group of friends the chance to meet for dinner. In Buñuel's world reality is liable at any moment to collapse into dream. In *Los olvidados* (*The Young and the Damned*, 1950), osten-

LEFT Victor Buono

Bank'/1971; 'Satisfaction Guaranteed/1972 * *Orson Welles' Great Mysteries*: 'Money to Burn'/1973 * *The Nancy Drew Mysteries*: 'A Haunting We Will Go'/1977 * *Fantasy Island*: 'With Affection, Jack the Ripper'/1980 * *Here's Boomer*: 'Camityville's Boomer'/1982

Burial Alive

Though the phenomenon of live burial is a folkloric source of the **vampire** myth, the theme enters horror fiction through **Poe**, who deploys it directly in **'The Fall of the House of Usher'** (1839), 'The Cask of Amontillado' (1846) and 'The Premature Burial' (1846) and tacitly in **'The Tell-Tale Heart'** (1843) and **'The Black Cat'** (1843). With the exception of the essay-like 'Premature Burial', these dwell not on the agonies of the victims but on the guilts of those who have half-deliberately buried others alive. 'The Premature Burial' is often filmed: *The Raven* (1912), *The Crime of Dr. Crespi* (1935), *The Premature Burial* (1962), a **Thriller** episode (1962), *Buried Alive* (1990).

Burial Alive: RIGHT *The Premature Burial*
BELOW Peter Lorre, Vincent Price, Joyce Jameson, *Tales of Terror*

Premature burial is so associated with Poe that Roger **Corman** even adds it to provide a punch-line for **Pit and the Pendulum** (1961). Though hardly the most visual of horrors (most movie victims are conveniently interred with matches to light the scene), other instances occur in *Black Orchids* (1916), Val **Lewton**'s *Isle of the Dead* (1945) and *Bedlam* (1946), *Macabre* (1958), *Dirty Harry*

sibly a piece of liberal realism, Buñuel was forbidden to introduce 'mad, completely incongruous' elements – but in the released version, nightmare and the everyday are indistinguishable. In Buñuel's best films social criticism and the wildest imagination are proved to be mutually supportive. RC

La chute de la Maison Usher (assistant)/1929 * *L'age d'or*/1930 * *Abismos de pasión*/1953 * *La mort en ce jardin*/1956 * *Viridiana*/1961 * *Simón del desierto* [*Simon of the Desert*]/1965 * *Belle de Jour*/1967 * *Tristana*/1970 * *Le Moine* [*The Monk*] (w)/1972 * *Le fantôme de la liberté* [*Phantom of Liberty*]/1974 * *Cet obscur objet du desir* [*That Obscure Object of Desire*]/1977
Luis Buñuel (Jean-Claude Carrière), *My Last Breath* (1984); Raymond Durgnat, *Luis Buñuel* (1990); John Baxter, *Buñuel* (1994)

Buono, Victor (1938–82)
Bulky American character actor, Oscar-nominated in his film debut as the piano player in *What Ever Happened to Baby Jane?* (1962). An outlandish TV villain: Count Manzeppi in *Wild Wild West* (1965–7), King Tut in *Batman* (1966–69), Mr Schubert in *The Man from Atlantis* (1977). He died unexpectedly after enjoying a particularly large Christmas dinner. SJ

The Strangler/1963 * *Hush . . . Hush, Sweet Charlotte*/1964 * *Beneath the Planet of the Apes*/1969 * *Moonchild*/*The Mad Butcher*/1972 * *Arnold*/1973 * *The Evil*/1978

TV: *Thriller*: 'Girl With a Secret'/1960; 'God Grante That She Lye Stille'/1961 * *Voyage to the Bottom of the Sea*: 'The Cyborg'/1965 * *Night Gallery*: 'A Midnight Visit to the Blood

(1971), *The Screaming Woman* (1972), *Vault ofHorror* (1973), another *Buried Alive* (1990) and both versions of *The Vanishing* (1988, 1992).

Burke and Hare * See: Body-Snatching

Burman, Tom (b. 1940)

American make-up artist. He began his career assisting John Chambers with the sapient simians of *Planet of the Apes* (1968), created **aliens** for *The Man Who Fell to Earth* (1976) and *Close Encounters of the Third Kind* (1977), and rivals the monster transformations of **Baker** and **Bottin** in *The Beast Within* (1981) and *Cat People* (1982). Many of his credits are in conjunction with his brother Ellis. His unusual directorial debut is the surreal *Life on the Edge* (1989). MS

The Thing With Two Heads/1972 * *The Boy Who Cried Werewolf*/1973 * *Phantom of the Paradise*/1974 * *The Devil's Rain*/*Food of the Gods*/1975

* *The Island of Dr. Moreau*/*Demon Seed*/*Empire of the Ants*/1977 * *Invasion of The Body Snatchers*/*The Manitou*/1978 * *My Bloody Valentine*/*The Hand*/*Altered States* (u)/*Happy Birthday to Me*/1981 * *Halloween III: Season of the Witch*/*One Dark Night*/1982 * *Teen Wolf*/1985 * *Teen Wolf Too*/1987 * *Scrooged*/1988 * *Dead Again*/1991 * *Body Snatchers*/1993

TV: *The Midnight Hour*/1985

Burr, Jeff (b. 1961)

American director. *From a Whisper to a Scream* (*The Offspring*, 1987), Burr's debut, is an ambitious, if nasty **anthology**. It is hard to note progress in Burr's run of 'sequels nobody wanted'.

Stepfather 2/1989 * *Leatherface: Texas Chainsaw Massacre III*/1990 * *Puppet Master 4*/*Things* (a)/1993 * *Puppet Master 5*/1994 * *Pumpkinhead II: Blood Wings*/1994 * *Night of the Scarecrow*/1995

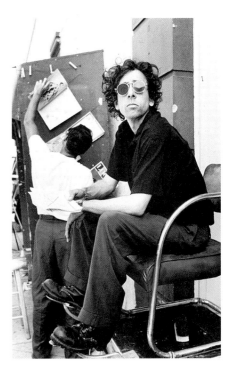

Tim Burton on the set of *Ed Wood*

Burton, Tim (b. 1960)

American director. California-born Burton grew up in suburban isolation, watching old horror movies on TV. He attended Cal Arts Institute on a **Disney** fellowship, training as an animator, then spent four years at Disney studios seeing his work rejected as too dark and depressing. Disney did, however, finance two shorts, *Vincent* (1982) and *Frankenweenie* (1984), that presage the curious mix of the cute and the macabre that informs Burton's features. He also conceived the stop-motion *The Nightmare Before Christmas* (1993), in which Halloweentown's Pumpkin King Jack Skellington kidnaps Santa Claus and hijacks Christmas. He pitched the project in the early 80s but it was only produced after *Batman* (1989) had commercially validated Burton's bizarre sensibilities.

Burton's vision is childlike in the darkest sense of the term: morbid, unselfconsciously alienated and deliciously ghoulish. His films are all fairytales, some (like *Edward Scissorhands*, 1990) more obviously than others. He made his feature debut with the playful *Pee-Wee's Big Adventure* (1985) and followed it with the macabre **comedy** *Beetle Juice* (1988). The melancholy, **Expressionist** *Batman* transformed him from weirdo artist into Hollywood money-making machine, apparently without corrupting his darkly whimsical imagination. MM

Johnny Depp, Tim Burton's *Edward Scissorhands*

Batman Returns/1992 * *Ed Wood*/1994 * *Batman Forever* (p)/1995 * *Mars Attacks*/1996

TV: *Alfred Hitchcock Presents*: 'The Jar'/1985
Mark Salisbury, *Burton on Burton* (1995)

The Bus

A technical term, derived from *Cat People* (1942), in which a suspenseful walk through a park climaxes with the sudden hiss of a bus's brakes. Strictly, a bus should be a false scare, like the broken window of *Halloween* (1978), which makes audiences and screen characters jump but turns out to be harmless. Often in **stalk-and-slash** (cf *Friday the 13th, Part 2*, 1981), a bus like the screech of a harmless cat will be followed swiftly by a genuine shock as the killer pounces.

Buttgereit, Jörg (b. 1963)

German writer, director. Fringe auteur Buttgereit gives let to his **sex**/death obsession in flagrant 16mm entries: *Nekromantik* (1987, some 8mm footage), *Der Todesking* (1990), *Nekromantik 2* (1991), *Schramm* (1993). Teutonically depressive, self-regarding art-sleaze leavened with queasily competent special effects, all are co-authored by Franz Rodenkirchen and produced by Manfred O. Jelinski. Their mirthless irony is foretold in Buttgereit's early, absurdist shorts, which often punkishly appropriate horror motifs (*Captain Berlin – Retter der Welt*, 1981, *J.B.'s Horror Heaven*, 1984). *Hot Love* (1985) is a transitional featurette. Buttgereit also directs the **vampire** Christ segment of Michael Brynntrup's *Jesus – der Film* (1986). In 1992, German authorities ordered the destruction of *Nekromantik 2*, accusing the perverse onanist epic of 'glorifying **violence**'. The praise heaped upon Buttgereit by some suggests gorehounds and censors view with the same salacious priorities. DP

David Kerekes, *Sex-Murder-Art: The Films of Jörg Buttgereit* (1994).

Byron, George Gordon (1788–1824)

British poet. Though he tackled fantastical themes in *The Giaour* (1813), *Manfred* (1817) and *Don Juan* (1819–24), Lord Byron's profile in horror has more to do with his presence at the Villa Diodati during the summer of 1816 when the Shelley-Byron circle held a ghost story contest which produced Mary **Shelley**'s *Frankenstein* (1818). Also present was John **Polidori**, Byron's physician, who wrote 'The Vampyre' (1819). Originally believed to be by Byron (and based on his 'Fragment of a Story', 1819), 'The Vampyre'

Lord Byron: Gabriel Byrne (with skull) as Byron, Natasha Richardson, Timothy Spall, Julian Sands, Miriam Cyr, *Gothic*

travesties the poet by representing him as a bloodsucker. It was influential enough to infuse the formerly repulsive **vampire** with a Byronic romanticism which has persisted: the **Dracula** of **Lugosi** or **Lee** owes more to the Byronic Ruthven than to **Stoker**'s hairy foreign brute.

Byron figures in fiction: Manly Wade **Wellman**'s 'The Black Drama' (1938), Guy Bolton's *The Olympians* (1961), Philip José Farmer's *Image of the Beast* (1968), Anne Edwards's *Haunted Summer* (1972), Brian Aldiss's *Frankenstein Unbound* (1973), Barbara Lynn Devlin's *I Am Mary Shelley* (1977), Kathryn Ptacek's *In Silence Sealed* (1988), Tim Powers's *The Stress of Her Regard* (1989), Paul West's *Lord Byron's Doctor* (1989), Tom Holland's *The Vampyre* (1995). Screen Byrons: Gavin Gordon (*Bride of Frankenstein*, 1935), Dennis **Price** (*The Bad Lord Byron*, 1951), Noel Willman (*Beau Brummell*, 1954), Richard Chamberlain (*Lady Caroline Lamb*, 1972), Tim McInnerny ('Frankenstein and Dracula', *The South Bank Show*, 1986), Gabriel Byrne (*Gothic*, 1986), Philip Anglim (*Haunted Summer*, 1988), Hugh Grant (*Rowing with the Wind*, 1989), Michael Hutchence (*Frankenstein Unbound*, 1990).

C

Das Cabinet des Dr. Caligari (1919)

Scripted by Carl **Mayer** and Hans Janowitz as an indictment of bourgeois hypocrisy, the film was transformed into the touchstone of German Expressionist horror when Fritz **Lang** suggested the story be framed as the raving of an **asylum** inmate, 'explaining' exaggerated sets and cartoon-like grotesque characters. Robert **Wiene** replaced Lang as director; Werner **Krauss** and Conrad **Veidt** play the scuttling **hypnotist-psychologist** Caligari and the svelte, white-faced somnambulist Cesare. Through the film's huge international impact, 'caligarism' became a synonym for **Expressionism**.

The bizarre look and **mad scientist/zombie** theme fed into classical horror via James **Whale**'s *Frankenstein* (1931) and Robert **Florey**'s *Murders in the Rue Morgue* (1932). Caligari is evoked by Roger Kay's *The Cabinet of Caligari* (1962), Stephen Sayadian's *Dr. Caligari* (1989) and Peter Sellars's *The Cabinet of Dr. Ramirez* (1991). Cesare (Curtis **Harrington**) features in Kenneth **Anger**'s *The Inauguration of the Pleasure Dome* (1954)

adjectives kitsch and tacky, embodying OTT taste rather than common taste. It's also an off-beat, quirky sensibility which can take possession of both effete Paul **Bartel** (*Eating Raoul*, 1982) and hyperactive Brian **De Palma** (*Phantom of the Paradise*, 1974). Other directors of horror camp: Paul **Morrissey** (*Flesh for Frankenstein*, 1973; *Blood for Dracula*, 1973), William **Castle** (especially *The Tingler*, 1959), Robert **Fuest** (*The Abominable Dr. Phibes*, 1971), Larry **Cohen** (*The Stuff*, 1985), Roger **Corman** (*The Little Shop of Horrors*, 1960).

Actors specialising in camp include John **Carradine** (*The Astro-Zombies*, 1968; *Nocturna*, 1979) and Vincent **Price** (every role apart from *Matthew Hopkins Witchfinder General*, 1968). Actress-wise, there's more scope through the sheer out-of-control Diva-dom of Joan **Crawford** (*Berserk*, 1967; *Trog*, 1970), Bette **Davis** (*Hush . . . Hush, Sweet Charlotte*, 1964; *The Anniversary*, 1968), Carroll Baker (*Paranoia*, 1968; *Baba Yaga*, 1973) and Susan Tyrrell (*Butcher Baker Nightmare Maker*, 1981). Davis and Crawford appear together in *What Ever Happened to Baby Jane?* (1962) while Baker and Tyrrell are matched in *Andy Warhol's Bad* (1977). Notable camp horrors: *The Killer Shrews* (1959), *The Horror of Party Beach* (1964), *Blood Freak* (1972), *The Giant Spider Invasion* (1975), *Dracula's Dog* (1978), *Zombie Island Massacre* (1985) and any Mexican **wrestling** horror. AJ

and Caligari reappears in Basil Copper's story 'Amber Print' (1968).

ABOVE Werner Krauss, *Das Cabinet des Dr. Caligari*

Siegfried Kracauer, *From Caligari to Hitler: A Psychological History of the German Film* (1947); S.S. Prawer, *Caligari's Children: The Film as Tale of Terror* (1980); Mike Budd, *The Cabinet of Dr. Caligari: Texts, Contexts, Histories* (1990)

BELOW Camp: Vincent Price, Robert Morley, *Theatre of Blood*

Cain, Paul * See: **Ruric, Peter**

Caligarism * See: *Das Cabinet des Dr. Caligari*; **Expressionism**

Campbell, Bruce (b. 1958)

American actor, producer. Comic-book handsome and an adept physical comedian,

Camp

The dictionary defines camp as 'affected, consciously artificial, vulgar or mannered'. Such a broad description could apply to everything from Tim **Burton**'s *Beetle Juice* (1988) to what's considered the all-time camp extravaganza, Ed **Wood**'s *Plan 9 From Outer Space* (1956). But for many critics camp is a catch-all represention of limited budgets, meandering plots, awful acting, hopeless direction and cheapjack special effects. So *Beetle Juice* is out of the loop? Wrong: Camp is a palpable atmosphere, as described by the

Bruce Campbell, *Evil Dead 2*

Campbell is battered, terrorised, possessed, mutilated and time-warped as the long-suffering Ash of Sam **Raimi**'s *The Evil Dead* (1982) and sequels. *The Adventures of Brisco County, Jr.* (1993–4), his TV Western, occasionally went weird.

CrimeWave/1984 * *Evil Dead 2*/1987 * *Moontrap*/*Maniac Cop*/*Intruder*/1989 * *Maniac Cop 2*/*Darkman*/*Sundown: The Vampire in Retreat*/1990 * *Lunatics: A Love Story*/*Waxwork II: Lost in Time*/1991 * *Mindwarp*/*Army of Darkness*/1992 * *The Hudsucker Proxy*/1994 * *Congo*/1995 * *Fargo*/*The Demolitionist* (u)/1996

TV: *American Gothic*: 'Meet the Beetles'/1995

Campbell, Ramsey [John] (b. 1946) British writer. Having absorbed and outgrown the influence of **Lovecraft**, Campbell is the finest, most important horror writer of his generation. His collections include *Demons By Daylight* (1973), *Dark Companions* (1982) and *Alone With the Horrors* (1992); among his novels are *The Doll Who Ate His Mother* (1976), *The Face That Must Die* (1979), *Incarnate* (1983), *Obsession* (1985), *Ancient Images* (1989) and *The One Safe Place* (1995). In 1977, as Carl Dreadstone, he novelised *Bride of Frankenstein* (1935), *Dracula's Daughter* (1936) and **The Wolf Man** (1941). He edited *New Terrors* (1980), *New Tales of the Cthulhu Mythos* (1980) and, with Stephen **Jones**, five volumes of *Best New Horror* (from 1990). A typical Campbell tale combines supernatural menace with human madness, observed with wit and sympathy.

RIGHT Cannibalism: *Emanuelle e gli ultimi cannibale*

Cannibalism

If one of horror's most upsetting revelations is that all we are is meat, then cannibalism is a central and subversive motif. Practised without exception by **vampires** and **werewolves**, it is a habit of **zombies** from *Night of the Living Dead* (1968) on, and makes milestones of *Doctor X* (1931) and *Sweeney Todd, the Demon Barber of Fleet Street* (1936). In **Hammer**'s audacious *The Revenge of Frankenstein* (1958), Michael **Gwynn** develops cannibal tendencies after receiving a hunchback's brain.

Integral to the gory inroads of H.G. **Lewis**'s *Blood Feast* (1963), anthropophagy is emblematic of a feral new brand of 70s horror. Following George **Romero**'s zombies, Tobe **Hooper**'s Ed **Gein**-inspired degenerates (*The Texas Chain Saw Massacre*, 1974) and Wes **Craven**'s Sawney Bean-following family (*The Hills Have Eyes*, 1977) demonstrate people-food equations to pole-axing effect. The quieter Gein derivative *Deranged* (1974) is hardly less impactful. Alan **Ormsby**, writer of *Deranged*, had already collaborated on the anthropophagoid Vietnamster *Dead of Night* (1972). Antonio **Margheriti**'s pacifist fancy *Apocalypse domani* (*Cannibal Apocalypse*, 1980) returns to the theme, while the Korean **War** explains Laurence Harvey's tastes in *Welcome to Arrow Beach* (1973).

The precocious comedies *Cannibal Girls* (1971), *The Folks at Red Wolf Inn* (1972) and *Motel Hell* (1980) are ham-fistedly adumbrated by *Shriek of the Mutilated* (1974) and *The Incredible Torture Show* (1976) and the mainstream correlative *Soylent Green* (1973). Non-American cannibal movies have varying flavours. In *Death Line* (1972), Gary **Sherman** brings a visceral American approach to bear on a British tradition of class-conscious horror. Peter **Walker** and David **McGillivray**'s *Frightmare* (1974) is more purely English, but impressively impolite nonetheless: its **family values** and **power tool** interests shadow those of *Texas Chain Saw*. By comparison *The Ghoul* (1974) is defeatistly retro, and *Tower of Evil* (1972) transitional kitsch. From Spain, Eloy De La Iglesia's engaged psycho-study *La semana del asesino* (*Cannibal Man*, 1972) grinds its victims with the abbatoir beef. René **Cardona** Jr's Mexican *Los supervivientes de los Andes* (*Survive!*, 1976) dramatises an event central to long-piggery: the devouring of corpses by a Uruguayan rugby team stranded in the Andes in 1972.

Flesh-eating is given frankest let in an Italian series that begins with Umberto **Lenzi**'s *Il paese del sesso selvaggio* (*Deep River Savages*, 1972). With the exception of Francesco Barilli's *La profumo della signora in nero* (*The Perfume of the Lady in Black*, 1974), the bulk of Italy's cannibal films mesh a long tradition of **jungle** thriller (**The Most Dangerous Game**, 1932) with the shorter

and more purely Roman one of sensational-ist travelogue (*Mondo cane*, 1962). Alternating inexorable special effects with unfaked animal cruelty amid Third World locations, the results are sullyingly confrontational. While *Il paese* is an Asian update of sado-Western *A Man Called Horse* (1971), Ruggero **Deodato**'s *L'ultimo mondo cannibale* (*Cannibal*, 1976) back-burners its adventurist narrative with a fiercesome new fixation on the (wo)man-eating process. The sexual implication of gormandised bodies that informs Sergio **Martino**'s Ursula Andress vehicle *La montagna del dio cannibale* (*Prisoner of the Cannibal God*, 1978) is yet more explicit in Aristide **Massaccesi**'s *Emanuelle e gli ultimi cannibale* (*Emanuelle and the Last Cannibals*, 1977). By the time of *Cannibal holocaust* (1979), rape features as a pre-prandial exercise.

Galvanising its *mondo* precursors, *holocaust* is Deodato's demythologising response to his own trend-setting entry and the acme of the sub-genre. The horrifically sustained cod-documentary shows a team of film-makers first catalysing Amazonian atrocities, then capturing their own deaths on camera. Lenzi's *Cannibal ferox* (1981) is a fag-end commodification of similar themes. Other jungle late-comers are Lucio **Fulci**'s *Dawn of the Dead* (1978) hybrid *Zombi 2* (*Zombie Flesh Eaters*, 1979), Marino Girolami's *Zombi 2* hybrid *Zombi holocaust* (*Zombie Holocaust*, 1980), and, courtesy of Eurociné, Jesús **Franco** and Julio Tabernero's desultory twins *Mondo cannibale* (*The Cannibals*, 1979) and *Terreur cannibale* (*Cannibal Terror*, 1981). Massaccesi's *Antropophagus* (*The Anthropo-phagous Beast*, 1980) deserves some sort of prize for its climactic auto-cannibalism.

An extensively prohibited image (the focus of much **video nasties** furore), cannibalism maintains a profile in edgy, high-toned parables like *Diyu wu men* (*We Are Going to Eat You*, 1980), *Eating Raoul* (1982), *Parents* (1988) and *The Cook the Thief His Wife & Her Lover* (1989), as well as such smirking prospects as *Cannibal Campout* (1988) and *Lucky Stiff* (1988). In *The Silence of the Lambs* (1991), Hannibal Lecter breaks the taboo to stress his superiority, while *Fried Green Tomatoes* (1991) may well be the most respectable cannibal movie ever made. Countering the sacrilege that haunts the act, the jocks of *Alive* (1993), Frank Marshall's wholesome remake of *Los supervivientes de los Andes*, gobble their fellows as if taking communion. DP

Cannom, Greg (b. 19??)

American make-up artist. Oscar winner for *Mrs. Doubtfire* (1993), adept at **vampires** and **werewolves**.

The Fury/1978 * *The Howling*/1981 * *Dreamscape*/1983 * *Vamp*/1986 * *The Lost Boys*/1987 * *Fright Night, Part 2*/1988 * *Meridian*/*Exorcist III*/*The Pit and the Pendulum*/ 1990 * *Bram Stoker's Dracula*/1992 * *The Puppet Masters*/*The Mask*/1994 * *Thinner*/1996

TV: *Werewolf*/1987-8 * *Monsters*: 'Fools' Gold' (d)/1989

Captive Wild Woman (1943)

A female version of *Dr. Renault's Secret* (1942), itself a remake of *The Wizard* (1927), Edward Dmytryk's film led off a brief Universal series. John **Carradine** surgically turns a gorilla into a woman, naming her Paula Dupree. **Acquanetta**'s Paula, sometimes in a Jack **Pierce** mask, returns in Reginald **LeBorg**'s *Jungle Woman* (1944), a silly *Cat People* (1942) clone with J. Carrol **Naish** in the lab coat. Vicky Lane is the **ape** woman in Harold **Young**'s even sillier *Jungle Captive* (1945), with Otto **Kruger** and Rondo **Hatton**. Denis Gifford notes that Paula 'left behind her, if not an interesting body of work, an interesting body'.

Cardona, René (1906–??)

Cuban-born Mexican producer-director fond of pitting wrestlers against **mad scientists** with **ape**, robot or **mummy minions**. Key films: *Las luchadoras contra el medico asesino* (*Doctor of Doom*, 1962), remade with added horror y sexo as *La horripilante bestia humana* (*Night of the Bloody Apes*, 1968), and *Las luchadoras contra la momia* (*Wrestling Women vs the Aztec Mummy*, 1964). The mix of Saturday matinee naiveté with ketchup and cheese-cake has **camp** appeal, but **wrestling** bouts invariably provide *longeurs* between monster madness.

El espectro de la novia/*La mujer sin cabeza*/1943 * *El as negre*/*El museo del crimen*/1944 * *The Living Idol* (assistant)/1956 * *La lorona*/1959 * *Santo contra el estrangulador*/*El espectro del estrangulador*/1963 * *El asesino invisible*/1964 * *Operación 67*/*Santo en el tesoro de Moctezuma*/ *Las mujeras panteras*/1966 * *La mujer murciéla-go*/*Santo en el tesoro de Drácula*/1967 * *Santo contra Capulina*/1968 * *Las luchadoras contra el robot asesino*/*Santo contra los cazadores de cabezas*/1969 * *Santo en la venganza de la momia*/1970 * *Blue Demon y Zóvek en la invasión de los muertos*/1972

Cardona Jr, René (b. 19??)

Mexican writer-director, son of Rene **Cardona**. Heir to a schlock dynasty, Cardona assisted his father on **Santo** pictures and wrote his lurid *La horripilante bestia humana* (*Night of the Bloody Apes*, 1968) before directing the crazed *La noche de los mil gatos* (*Night of a Thousand Cats*, 1972). He has exploited true-life horrors like the Andes plane crash (*Los supervivientes de los Andes*/*Survive!*, 1976) and the Jonestown massacre (*Guyana: Cult of the Damned*, 1980). *Tintorera* (1977) and *Beaks* (1987), imitations of *Jaws* (1977) and *The Birds* (1963), are in English with all-has-been casts.

Carewe, Arthur Edmund (1894–1937)

Armenian-born American actor: 'the Persian' in **The Phantom of the Opera** (1925), Svengali in **Trilby** (1923), a cocaine fiend in *Mystery of the Wax Museum* (1933). Often a sinister but ultimately innocent suspect.

The Ghost Breaker/1922 * *The Cat and the Canary*/1927 * *Doctor X*/1932 * *Charlie Chan's Secret*/1936

Carlson, Veronica (b. 1945)

British actress. Willowy, bland, blonde **Hammer** heroine, an English rose bitten by **Lee** in *Dracula Has Risen From the Grave* (1968), raped by **Cushing** in *Frankenstein Must Be Destroyed* (1969).

The Horror of Frankenstein/1970 * *The Ghoul*/ *Vampira*/1974 * *Fangs*/1993 * *Freakshow*/ 1995

TV: *Randall and Hopkirk (Deceased)*: 'The Ghost Who Broke the Bank at Monte Carlo'/ 1969

'Carmilla' (1871)

First published in *The Dark Blue* magazine and included in the collection *In a Glass Darkly* (1872), J. Sheridan **Le Fanu**'s 'Carmilla' concerns the seduction of a girl in Styria by a houseguest ultimately revealed as a **vampire**. The story influenced Bram **Stoker**'s *Dracula* (1897): Vordenberg, the stake-wielding occultist, is a **Van Helsing** prototype. Carmilla (Countess Mircalla Karnstein) is an ambiguous monster: her passionate involvement with female victims has been amplified into **lesbianism** by most readings.

Dreyer's *Vampyr* (1931), purportedly based on *In a Glass Darkly*, has only an oblique relationship with Le Fanu. Val

'Carmilla', Sybille Schmitz, *Vampyr*

Lewton planned in the 40s to make 'Carmilla' with a colonial setting, but the story only became much-filmed in the 60s and 70s. Official Carmillas: Annette Vadim (*. . . et mourir de plaisir/Blood and Roses*, 1960), Pier Ana Quaglia (*La cripta e l'incubo/Crypt of Horror*, 1964), Natasha Payne ('Carmilla', *Mystery and Imagination*, 1966), Ingrid **Pitt** (*The Vampire Lovers*, 1970), Yutte Stensgaard (*Lust for a Vampire*, 1970), Katya Wyeth (*Twins of Evil*, 1971), Alexandra Bastedo (*La novia ensangrentada/The Blood-Spattered Bride*, 1972), Meg Tilly ('Carmilla', *Nightmare Classics*, 1989).

Carmilla informs many lesbian-ish vampires: Dominique in *Le frisson des vampires* (*Sex and the Vampire*, 1970), Delphine Seyrig in *Le rouge aux lèvres* (*Daughters of Darkness*, 1971), Celeste **Yarnall** (as 'Diane Le Fanu') in *The Velvet Vampire* (1971), Britt Nichols (as 'Luisa Karlstein', *La fille de Dracula*, 1972), Wanda Ventham (as 'Countess Karstein') in *Captain Kronos Vampire Hunter* (1972), Lina Romay (as 'Countess Irina Karlstein') in *La comtesse noire* (*Female Vampire*, 1973), Marianne Morris and Anulka in *Vampyres* (1976) and Sophia Crawford (as 'Carmella') in *Night Hunter* (1995). *Poison Ivy* (1992), which omits vampire and lesbian themes, is close to Le Fanu's cuckoo-in-the-nest plot, with Drew **Barrymore** latching onto a family and edging out their real daughter.

Carnivals * See: **Circuses and Carnivals**

Carpenter, John (b. 1947)

American director, writer, composer, producer. Carpenter belongs to a generation of film-makers weaned on Hollywood movies. Unlike **Coppola** or Scorsese, who cut their teeth on genre but moved on to the artier edges of the mainstream, he has remained faithful to science fiction and horror. After the s-f skit *Dark Star* (1974) and the nightmare suspenser *Assault on Precinct 13* (1976), **Halloween** (1978), a model of pared-down horror, catapulted him into the bigtime. The plot revolves around a gaggle of small town **teenagers** picked off, one by one, by Michael Myers, aka 'The Shape', an escaped **psycho** in a **mask**. The sole survivor among her peer group is plucky Jamie Lee **Curtis**, marked out as virtuous (and therefore undeserving of death) by her decision to babysit rather than spend the evening having sex like her friends.

Many of Carpenter's ideas soon became **clichés** in the hands of lesser directors: the shock prologue (in which the murderer is revealed to be a small boy), the killer's point of view represented by **subjective camera**, the tendency for teenagers to die horribly after having sex, the dead bogeyman who keeps coming back to life. Later exponents of **stalk-and-slash** fail to emulate Carpenter's

ability to marshall widescreen effects so that the film seems far more violent and bloody than it actually is. In the end, *Halloween* is little more than a well-oiled machine designed to make its audience jump; but by stripping its story to the bone, Carpenter invests it with the quality of urban myth, an impression enhanced by the presence of Donald **Pleasence** as a sort of psychiatric Captain Ahab obsessed with tracking the psychopath.

As well as a slew of inferior imitations (**Friday the 13th**, 1980, et al), *Halloween* spawned sequels of decreasing merit. Carpenter produced and co-wrote *Halloween II* (1981), set in the hospital where Curtis is taken immediately after the events of the original, and produced *Halloween III: Season of the Witch* (1983), a bid (unsuccessful, as it turned out) to continue the series with a Myers-free storyline (by an uncredited Nigel **Kneale**). His only involvement with later sequels is that they use his distinctive synthesised Shape theme. *The Fog* (1981), about a Californian coastal town terrorised by the shades of long-dead mariners, is a creditable attempt to revive the **ghost story**. *Escape from New York* (1981) is an amusing s-f action picture with favoured star Kurt Russell, whom Carpenter had cast in the mini-series *Elvis* (1979) and who would return for *Escape From LA* (1996).

The Thing (1982) is not so much a remake of the Howard Hawks/Christian Nyby *The Thing From Another World* (1951) as a return to John W. Campbell Jr's original story, 'Who Goes There?' (1938): an isolated group is infiltrated by a shapeshifting **alien**, and no-one can be sure which of the others is human. A bleak all-male horror film (inevitably starring Russell) set in an Antarctic research station, it features imaginative special effects (by Rob **Bottin**) as the alien sporadically erupts out of its host bodies. Its box-office failure, at a time when the public warmed to the more cuddlesome *ET: The Extra-Terrestrial* (1982), marked the beginning of a downward spiral in Carpenter's fortunes.

Christine (1983) is an effective Stephen **King** adaptation about a demonic Plymouth Fury which turns its wimpy owner (Keith Gordon) into the baddest boy on the block, but *Big Trouble in Little China* (1986) is a botched attempt to Americanise the Hong Kong supernatural action movie. Between big studio blandnesses *Starman* (1984) and *Memoirs of an Invisible Man* (1992), Carpenter made a concerted effort to return to independent roots with *Prince of Darkness* (1987), a Kneale variation in which the **Devil** is discovered trapped in a sort of giant lava lamp in the basement of a Los Angeles church, and the satirical alien invasion of *They Live* (1988).

Carpenter appears as the cadaverous coroner host in the framing scenes of the made-for-cable **anthology** *Body Bags*, also directing two out of three segments: a standard woman-in-periller set at an isolated gas station, and a black comedy in which Stacy Keach's hair transplants turn out to have a life of their own. *In the Mouth of Madness* (1994) is an inventive **recursive** yarn about a private detective (Sam Neill) on the trail of a missing horror writer. Again, Carpenter is heavily influenced by other writers; notably Jonathan Carroll, whose *The Land of Laughs* (1980) and *A Child Across the Sky* (1989) deal with similar themes, and **Lovecraft**. *Village of the Damned* (1995) is a serviceable, if uninspired, remake of the 1960 adaptation of John Wyndham's *The Midwich Cuckoos* (1957). AB

The Eyes of Laura Mars (w)/1978 * *The Philadelphia Experiment* (w)/1984 * *Black Moon Rising* (w)/1985 * *The Silence of the Hams* (a)/1993

TV: *Someone's Watching Me!*/1978

Robert C. Cumbow, *Order in the Universe: The Films of John Carpenter* (1990)

Carradine, David (b. 1940)

American actor, son of John **Carradine**. Best known as Caine of *Kung Fu* (1972–5), which occasionally relieves the diet of bigoted Sheriffs with Chinese demons, Carradine is an exploitation regular. He is a futuristic **Frankenstein** in *Death Race 2000* (1975) and, in homage to his father, a gunslinging **Dracula** in *Sundown: The Vampire in Retreat* (1990). His horrors range from the lead in Ingmar **Bergman**'s *Das Schlangenei* (*The Serpent's Egg*, 1977) to an unconventional cop in Larry **Cohen**'s *Q* (1982). He directed the gently fantastical *Americana* (1981).

Trick or Treats/1982 * *Sonny Boy*/1989 * *Evil Toons*/1990 * *Waxwork II: Lost in Time*/1991

TV: *Alfred Hitchcock Presents*: 'Thou Still Unravished Bride'/1965 * *The Name of the Game*: 'Tarot'/1970 * *Night Gallery*: 'The Phantom Farmhouse'/1971 * *Darkroom*: 'The

Partnership'/1981 * *Hammer House of Mystery and Suspense*: 'A Distant Scream'/1984 * *The Bad Seed*/1985 * *Kung Fu: The Movie*/1986 * *Amazing Stories*: 'Thanksgiving'/1986 * *Ray Bradbury Theatre*: 'And the Moon Be Still as Bright'/1991

Carradine, John [Richmond Reed Carradine] (1906–88)

American actor. With a face like a gnawed bone and a voice of basso fleshiness, Carradine physically towered over his contemporaries. He was an erudite maverick whose Shakespearian intensity made him a natural for horror movies at a time when to be educated was to be alien and, thus, frightening. A New York-born painter and sculptor, he began as a set-designer for Cecil B. DeMille but took to acting 'to save my sanity'.

The Invisible Man (1933) and *Bride of Frankenstein* (1935) were a respectable entrée into horror by way of the good graces of James **Whale**. Thereafter, though, he became a second-string **Lugosi**: many programmers would send goose-pimples not squawking but sniggering if not for Carradine's distinguished, dignified presence. Titles like *Whispering Ghosts* (1942), ***Captive Wild Woman*** (1943), *Revenge of the Zombies* (1943) give the truth to the kind of genre-collapsed movies they are. That Carradine's impressive deportment is associated with them does more for their schlock than his

reputation. Incarnadine Carradine chose not wisely but what would pay the rent: having fathered five sons (including actors David, Keith and Robert) over three marriages, he took any kind of work to pay alimonies.

Though there is a sense in which he seems to be mocking that in which he appears, such as *Horror of the Blood Monsters* (1970), condescension came late in his career after a welter of such dubious roles. His attempts at **Dracula**, for instance, begin with the sober earnestness of *House of Frankenstein* (1944) and a 1956 television adaptation but proceed to the inane *Billy the Kid vs Dracula* (1967) and degenerate into the camp of *Nocturna* (1979). This can be counted as an analogue of the way his acting went downhill, so that by the end he was locked into rotten movies (*The Sentinel*, 1976; *Vampire Hookers*, 1978) with all the painful rigidity with which arthritis gripped his hands in his last years.

The expectations he aroused in the early 30s became dismal achievements in a Hollywood which treated him as a freak reputed to stalk the streets declaiming Shakespeare. There is a story that John Ford wanted him to play the down-and-out actor in *My Darling Clementine* (1940), forced to recite Hamlet to the accompaniment of cowboys' bullets, but thought it struck too near the bone of what had happened to Carradine and hired Alan Mowbray instead. For Ford,

RIGHT John Carradine (and Sheila Keith), *House of the Long Shadows*

RIGHT John Carradine, *The Sentinel*

Carradine's most paradoxically chilling performance is as John Steinbeck's a-hollering and a-leaping mad preacher in *The Grapes of Wrath* (1940). There is to this ultimate boondocks style an indication of over-the-top humanity which could have been brought to many of his horror roles with advantage, a sense of a loosed mania.

What, in fact, he brought to the screen was the dignity of **Karloff** and the obsessiveness of Lugosi; both those qualities were already taken care of by their prime movers, so he found himself out of the big leagues. For all his educated talents, Carradine played safe with what producers and audiences expected of lank and looming menace, a distinctly hollow man without the sinister substance that would have made him so much more than the joke he became. It is good to report, then, that among his last films are *The Howling* (1981), a thoroughly respectable exemplar of the genre which treated him so badly through a long and intensive career, and *The Scarecrow* (1982), a rare thoughtful feature built around his eerie presence. Hollywood producers had looked down on him for so long, it was a delight that he could look down on them. His height, at last, had not been cut down to size. TH

Murders in the Rue Morgue/1932 * *The Black Cat*/1934 * *The Hound of the Baskervilles*/1939 * *All That Money Can Buy*/ *Man Hunt*/1941 * *Voodoo Man*/*The Invisible Man's Revenge*/*Return of the Ape Man*/*The Mummy's Ghost*/*Bluebeard*/ *Jungle Woman* (reused footage from *Captive Wild Woman*)/1944 * *House of Dracula*/1945 * *Face of Marble*/1946 * *The Black Sleep*/*Female Jungle*/ 1956 * *The Unearthly*/*Half Human*/ 1957 * *Invisible Invaders*/1959 * *Invasion of the Animal People*/1962 * *Curse of the Stone Hand*/ *House of the Black Death*/*The Wizard of Mars*/ 1965 * *Munster, Go Home!*/1966 * *Hillbillys in a Haunted House*/*Dr. Terror's Gallery of Horrors*/ *La señora muerte*/*Autopsia de un fantasma*/1967 * *Pacto diabólico*/*The Astro Zombies*/*Enigma de muerte*/1968 * *Blood of Dracula's Castle*/*Las vampiras*/1969 * *Five Bloody Graves*/1970 * *The Mummy and the Curse of the Jackal*/*Blood of Ghastly Horror* [*Fiend With the Electronic Brain*]/*Threshold* (s)/1971 * *Moonchild*/*Shadow House* (s)/*Legend of Sleepy Hollow* (s/v)/*Every Thing You Always Wanted to Know About Sex * But Were Afraid to Ask*/*Silent Night, Bloody Night*/1972 * *Hex*/*Legacy of Blood*/*The House of the Seven Corpses*/*Blood of the Iron Maiden*/ *Terror in the Wax Museum*/1973 * *Mary, Mary,*

Bloody Mary/1975 * *Crash!*/*The Killer Inside Me*/1976 * *Shock Waves*/*Doctor Dracula*/*The White Buffalo*/*Satan's Cheerleaders*/*Journey to the Beyond* (v)/1977 * *The Bees*/1978 * *Monster*/1979 * *The Boogey Man*/*The Monster Club*/1980 * *The Nesting*/*The Best of Sex and Violence*/*Satan's Mistress*/*Frankenstein Island*/ 1981 * *House of the Long Shadows*/*Evils of the Night*/*Boogeyman II* (reused footage from *The Boogey Man*)/*Monster in the Closet*/1983 * *The Tomb*/1985 * *The Revenge*/*Hollywood Ghost Stories*/1986 * *Demented Death Farm Massacre . . . the Movie*/*Evil Spawn*/1987 * *Buried Alive*/ *Teenage Exorcist*/1990 * *Jack-O*/1995

TV: *Lights Out*: 'The Half-Pint Flask'/1950; 'The Meddlers'/1951; 'The Lonely Albatross'/ 1952 * *Suspense*: 'Come Into My Parlor'/1953 * *The Adventures of Fu Manchu*/1954 * *Matinee Theatre*: 'The House of the Seven Gables'/ 'Dracula'/1956; 'Daniel Webster and the Sea Serpent'/1957 * *The Twilight Zone*: 'The Howling Man'/1960 * *Thriller*: 'Masquerade'/ 'The Remarkable Mrs Hawk'/1961 * *Alfred Hitchcock Hour*: 'Death Scene'/1965 * *The Munsters*: 'Herman's Raise'/1965; 'Tone Deaf Eddie'/1966 * *Girl From U.N.C.L.E.*: 'The Montori Device Affair'/1966 * *The Green Hornet*: 'Alias the Scarf'/1967 * *The Man From U.N.C.L.E.*: 'The Prince of Darkness Affair'/ 1967 * *Land of the Giants*: 'Comeback'/1969 * *Daughter of the Mind*/1969 * *Crowhaven Farm*/1970 * *Night Gallery*: 'The Big Surprise'/1971 * *The Night Strangler*/1973 * *Kung Fu*: 'The Nature of Evil'/1974 * *The Cat Creature*/1975 * *Death at Love House*/1976 *

McCloud: 'McCloud Meets Dracula'/1977 * *The New Adventures of Wonder Woman*: 'Gault's Brain' (v)/1978 * *B.J. and the Bear*: 'A Coffin With a View'/1978 * *Goliath Awaits*/1981 * *The Twilight Zone*: 'Still Life'/1986 * *Blacke's Magic*: 'Breathing Room'/1986

Carreras, James (1909–90)

British studio head. Managing director of **Hammer Films**. Carreras's aggressive showmanship defined Hammer's public image until control of the company passed to his son Michael **Carreras** in the early 70s. Once quoted as saying 'I'm prepared to make Strauss waltzes tomorrow if they'll make money', he showed little interest in the production of the films themselves, concentrating on finance and distribution. He mastered the trick of pre-selling a film on the basis of title and poster (usually before a script had been commissioned) and was one of the first post-war industry figures to embrace opportunities offered by co-operation with American majors. Without his indefatigable efforts, Hammer would undoubtedly not have achieved the success it did. PH

Carreras, Michael (1927–94)

British studio executive, son of James **Carreras**. He worked as executive producer on the classic **Hammer** horrors of the 50s and early 60s with Anthony **Hinds** as producer and Terence **Fisher** as director. He was himself a producer, director and writer for Hammer (sometimes under the name Henry Younger, a riposte to Hinds' pseudonym, John Elder), with occasional diversions into independent production. Though efficient and spirited, his films never display the style and personality of those associated with Fisher and Hinds. In the early 70s, he took control of Hammer but was unable to reverse the studio's decline. PH

The Mummy (p)/1959 * *The Two Faces of Dr. Jekyll* (p)/1960 * *Maniac* (d)/1963 * *The Curse of the Mummy's Tomb* (p/d/w)/1964 * *The Lost Continent* (p/d)/1968 * *Crescendo* (p)/1969 * *Blood from the Mummy's Tomb* (co-d/u)/1971

Cars

While the horse and carriage are part of the trappings of gothic horror, their successor has achieved no such place of honour. Even as an instrument of death (for Candace Hilligoss in *Carnival of Souls*, 1962, or Julie Harris in *The Haunting*, 1963) or maiming (for Joan **Crawford** in *What Ever Happened to Baby Jane?*, 1962, or Michael **Gough** in *Dr.*

Terror's House of Horrors, 1964), the car has a subsidiary role. Steven **Spielberg**'s highly original *Duel* (1971) is the first film in which motor vehicles take precedence over actors. It inspired generally less effective films in which cars (or other motor vehicles) are **possessed** by demons, spirits of the dead and extra-terrestrial intelligence: 'One Deadly Owner' (*Thriller*, 1974), *Killdozer* (1974), *Crash!* (1976), *The Car* (1977), *The Hearse* (1980), *Nightmares* (1983) *Christine* (1983), *Mr Wrong* (1984), *Maximum Overdrive* (1985). In *The Cars That Ate Paris* (1974), a town is

TV: *The Avengers*: 'Second Sight'/1963; 'Dial a Deadly Number'/1966 * *Adam Adamant Lives!*: 'The League of Uncharitable Ladies'/1966 * *Thriller*: 'Possession'/1973 * *Schmoedipus*/1974 * *The New Avengers*: 'The Midas Touch'/1978 * *Hammer House of Horror*: 'Guardian of the Abyss'/1980 * *Doctor Who*: 'Snakedance'/1983

Castles

A fortified residence is central to Horace Walpole's *The Castle of Otranto* (1764), the first English **gothic novel**, and became the

The most peculiar castle, memorable for its mysterious spiral staircase, is that designed by William Cameron **Menzies** for *The Maze* (1953), and the most elusive, of course, that of Franz **Kafka**'s novel *Das Schloss* (1926). Ruined castles are hideouts for *The Gorgon* (1964) and *The Devil's Men* (1976). From the 50s, castles were favoured chiefly by the producers of low-budget second features in which visitors are slaughtered by a madman and women chained up in the torture chamber. In recent years, the traditional Gothic castle is mainly the subject of parody: *Young Frankenstein* (1974), *The Rocky Horror Picture Show* (1975), *Transylvania Twist* (1989). A rare serious modern horror film using a castle setting is *The Keep* (1983). Interestingly, real castles are rarely used as locations. The real thing, it seems, cannot measure up to the fantasy cultivated by Hollywood. DM

Cars: *The Cars That Ate Paris*

controlled by delinquents driving mutant cars. Car chases are uncommon in horror, but *Race With the Devil* (1975) is constructed around one. Hitchhikers feature in *Autostop rosso sangue* (*Hitch-Hike*) (1977), the short *Panic* (1978), *Road Games* (1981), *The Hitcher* (1986), *The Hitchhiker* (1983–91) and *Dust Devil* (1992). DM

Carson, John (b. 1927)

British actor, **Hammer** stalwart. The dastardly squire of *Plague of the Zombies* (1966).

The Night Caller/1965 * *Taste the Blood of Dracula*/*The Man Who Haunted Himself*/1970 * *Captain Kronos Vampire Hunter*/1972

sine qua non of the genre. Also obligatory are bad weather, a sinister manservant, an outwardly genial host, creaking doors, **bat**-infested turrets and a secret room. The cinema pounced on these picturesque details and one's impression is that every horror film made between 1930 and 1970 begins with a yokel warning the hero, 'no one goes up to the castle after dark', and ends with torch-wielding **peasants** storming the castle and killing its villainous occupant. **Dracula** is perhaps the character most readily identified with his habitat, but monster-making (and other crazy scientific experiments), haunting and physical cruelty also retain strong associations with the castle.

Castle, William [William Schloss Jr.] (1914–77)

American producer, director, 'P.T. Barnum of horror'. Castle's horror films make unique connections between commercialism and creativity. Famously gimmicky, they are driven by an anxiety to entertain that at best combines delirious left-field plotting with a carnivalesque assault on the fourth wall.

Castle's most useful collaborator is screenwriter Robb **White** and their most outrageous movie is *The Tingler* (1959), in which a fear-fed worm that can only be killed by screaming escapes from its mute host's spine into a silent movie theatre as actual *Tingler* patrons are buzzed by the 'Percepto' device beneath their seats. Other novelty features are: *Macabre* (1958, an insurance policy covers death by fright); *The House on Haunted Hill* (1959, 'Emergo' enables Vincent **Price** to crank a skeleton to across the auditorium); *13 Ghosts* (1960, 'Illusion-O' spectacles reveal the eponymous spooks); *Homicidal* (1961, a 'Fright Break' gives cowards the chance of a refund); *Mr. Sardonicus* (1961, a 'Punishment Poll' decides the ending); and *I Saw What You Did* (1965, theatre 'shock sections' fitted with safety belts).

Strait-Jacket (1963) contents itself with the surprise of Joan **Crawford**; Barbara Stanwyck features in *The Night Walker* (1964); while Marcel Marceau stars (twice) in the minimally dialogued *Shanks* (1974). Plans for roach-mimicking, floor-level windscreen wipers were nixed for *Bug* (1975), Castle's final production. Keen to include a

William Castle

affected even Dario **Argento**, Castle haunts Alan **Ormsby**'s *Popcorn* (1991) and is honoured in Joe **Dante**'s *Matinee* (1992). DP

*The Whistler/Mark of the Whistler/1944 * The Crime Doctor's Warning/Voice of the Whistler/ 1945 * Just Before Dawn/Mysterious Intruder/ The Crime Doctor's Manhunt/1946 * The Crime Doctor's Gamble/1947*

William Castle, *Step Right Up! I'm Gonna Scare the Pants off America* (1976)

The Cat and the Canary (1922)

With Earl Derr Biggers and George M. Cohan's *Seven Keys to Baldpate* (1913) and Mary Roberts Rinehart and Avery Hopwood's *The Bat* (1920), John Willard's stage hit, which he novelised in 1927, was one of

a run of **Old Dark House** thrillers popular on Broadway in the 20s. The decrepit mansions, wills read at midnight, murdered heirs, imperilled flappers, sombre suspects, secret passages, concealed corpses, wisecracking heroes and masked psychos of these plays fed a cinema tradition that culminated with James **Whale**'s *The Old Dark House* (1932), at once a last word on and an ultimate skit of the genre. *The Cat and the Canary* was filmed by Paul **Leni** with Creighton Hale and Laura La Plante (1927); by Rupert Julian with Helen Twelvetrees (*The Cat Creeps*, 1930); by George Melford with Lupita Tovar (*La voluntad del muerto*, 1930, a Spanish version of *The Cat Creeps*); by Elliott Nugent with Bob Hope and Paulette Goddard (1939); for the *Dow Hour of Great*

participatory element in theatre productions *Dracula* (1929) and *Meet a Body* (1944), he showed a penchant for the dynamics of fright in his several contributions to Columbia's Crime Doctor and Whistler series. As pertinently, *It's a Small World* (1950), *The Fat Man* (1951) and early success *When Strangers Marry* (1944) make use of fairground/circus backdrops. Footage from *The Phantom of the Opera* (1925) is redeployed by Castle in *Hollywood Story* (1951). 'I'm not a director, I'm a great pitcher,' he declared on completing *Fort Ti* (1953), the first of three stereoscopic costumers. Sensationalist, post-**3-D** retorts to television, Castle's horrors nonetheless accrue from a long-standing showmanliness. *Homicidal*, the first of Castle's **Psycho** (1960) exacerbations, is prefaced by one of several on-screen addresses that compare to the TV appearances of both **Hitchcock** and **Disney**. This showiness, furthered by cameos in *The Day of the Locust* (1975) and *Shampoo* (1976), culminates when, as producer of the **Ghost Story** (1972–3) series, he appears as a studio head in the episode 'The Graveyard Shift' (1973).

A school-age fan club explains the explicitly childish *Zotz!* (1962) and such outright comedies as *Let's Kill Uncle* (1966) and *The Spirit is Willing* (1967). The **Hammer** disaster *The Old Dark House* (1962) stresses the shortcomings of Castle's avuncular, chutzpah-heavy approach. On acquiring the rights to Ira **Levin**'s *Rosemary's Baby* (1967), he was firmly dissuaded from its direction by Paramount. An undervalued stylist who has

RIGHT Mystery Man, Paulette Goddard, *The Cat and the Canary* (1939)

Mysteries (1960) with Collin Wilcox and Andrew Duggan; and by Radley Metzger with Michael Callan and Carol Lynley (1978).

Cat People (1942)

The first of Val **Lewton**'s important RKO Bs, directed by Jacques **Tourneur**, with Simone **Simon** as Irena Dubrovna, a Serbian convinced she turns into a leopard when aroused. A radical break from the fairytale tone of Universal's **The Wolf Man** (1941), it has a contemporary New York setting, characters of some depth and sustained scenes of menace as the supposedly transformed Simon stalks Jane Randolph, her husband's girlfriend, through Central Park or in a swimming pool. It also marks the first use of Lewton's favourite shock device, the **bus**.

A tangential sequel *The Curse of the Cat People* (1944), directed by Gunther von Fritsch and Robert **Wise**, has Irena's ghost (Simon) befriend the lonely daughter (Ann Carter) of her former husband (Kent Smith). Mark **Robson**'s *The Seventh Victim* (1943) revives suavely lecherous psychologist Louis Judd (Tom **Conway**), killed in *Cat People* and more heroic in his second outing. *Cat People* was much imitated: **heroines** tormented by a belief in hereditary curses that turn them into wolves, **cats**, **apes** or mermaids appear in *Cry of the Werewolf* (1943), *Jungle Woman* (1944), *She-Wolf of London* (1946), *The Creeper* (1948), *Cat Girl* (1957), *Daughter of Dr. Jekyll* (1957), *Cult of the Cobra* (1955), *The Bride and the Beast* (1958) and *Night Tide* (1961). Paul Schrader remade *Cat People* (1982) with Nastassja **Kinski** and Malcolm **McDowell** as incestuous werecat siblings, straining for eroticism, gore and significance. Even less reputable is John Leslie's porno *The Cat Woman* (1988), with Kathleen Gentry; Leslie shows a touch of awareness by calling his sequel, with Selena Steele, *The Curse of the Cat Woman* (1990).

Cats

Currently the number one choice among pet-lovers, the lovable pussy-cat is still in horror fiction the devil creature it was in the Middle Ages. Ruthlessly killed during witch-hunts, the black cat became an object of great superstition and was immortalised by **Poe** in the much-filmed **'The Black Cat'** (1843). The cat inhabited by the spirit of a dead woman is the subject of *The Cat Creeps* (1946) and (loosely based on Poe) *The Tomb of Ligeia* (1964). Women transform into cats (domestic and jungle) in **Cat People** (1942), *The Undead* (1956), *Cat Girl* (1957) and *Sleepwalkers* (1992), and a cat turns into a woman in *Serpent's Lair* (1995).

Men are less likely to turn feline, but do so in *The Creeper* (1948) and the remake of

Cats: art deco cat on the set of *The Black Cat* (1934)

Cat People (1982). Several versions of **The Cat and the Canary** (1922) feature an alleged maniac known as 'The Cat', but a more successful adoption of the cat as a totemic model is made by Julie Newmar and Michelle Pfeiffer as **Batman**'s provocative foe Catwoman. A popular concept is the vengeful or malign cat: *The Shadow of the Cat* (1961), *Torture Garden* (1967), *Eye of the Cat* (1969), *La noche de los mil gatos* (*Night of the Thousand Cats*, 1972), *Persecution* (1974), *The Uncanny* (1977), *Tales from the Darkside: The Movie* (1991), *Strays* (1991). *Cat's Eye* (1984) has a rare good guy cat. Memorable cats chase Grant Williams in *The Incredible Shrinking Man* (1957), are accidently killed then embalmed in *A Bucket of Blood* (1959), turn killer after eating Lotus cat food in *The Corpse Grinders* (1971), survive at the end of **Alien** (1979) and (though obviously fake) revivify in *Re-Animator* (1985). DM

Censorship

Now overt political censorship of films has more or less disappeared in the West, the topics which most concern modern censors are bad language, **sex** and **violence**. Horror movies are particularly vulnerable: most contain the third ingredient, and a good number (especially European ones) are apt to spice it with the second.

Different countries have different standards – America tends to be tough on sex and liberal about violence, while in Scandinavia it is usually the other way round – but there can be little doubt that

Cat People (1982)

horror, after **pornography**, is film's second most censored genre. In its early days in Britain and America, cinema was hedged about by a series of 'thou shalt nots' which made the production and exhibition of horror films extremely difficult, though not impossible. The Hays Code stated that 'brutal killings are not to be presented in detail' and, in more general terms, 'the treatment of low, disgusting, unpleasant, though not necessarily evil, subjects should be guided always by the dictates of good taste and a proper regard for the sensibilities of the audience'.

The British Board of Film Censors operated a vast code of prohibitions which forbade, *inter alia*, 'the exhibition of profuse bleeding', 'gruesome murders and strangulation scenes' and 'cruelty to young infants and excessive cruelty and torture to adults, especially women'. Thanks to these rules the British pre-war public were unable to see *Nosferatu* (1922), *Freaks* (1932) and *Island of Lost Souls* (1933) at all, and only cut versions of *Dr. Jekyll and Mr. Hyde* (1931) and *M* (1931). By the late 50s, censorship standards became more liberal in the West, but less thoroughgoingly in Britain than in most other countries. Matters were not helped by the BBFC's patronising attitude to horror ('nobody took these films seriously; this included the people who made them as well as the audiences' said John Trevelyan, one of the Board's more *enlightened* Secretaries) and the hostility of a bitterly censorious press (including, unfortunately, critics). Victims of cuts included now-acknowledged masterpieces like *Les yeux sans visage* (1959), *Psycho* (1960), *Peeping Tom* (1960), *Rosemary's Baby* (1968) and *Matthew Hopkins Witchfinder General* (1968).

Numerous horror films were banned outright: *La maschera del demonio* (*The Mask of Satan*, 1960, released cut as *Revenge of the Vampire*, 1968), *Hexen bis auf's Blut gequält* (*Mark of the Devil*, 1969), **The Texas Chain Saw Massacre** (1974) and *Lo squartatore di New York* (*The New York Ripper*, 1982). Thanks to the stringent regulations of the BBFC, the British public were protected from the murkier depths of the American and Italian exploitation industries, with their bizarre cast of **cannibals**, maniacs, **Nazis** and women in prison, until the floodgates were opened by the advent of home video in the early 80s. There then followed the **video nasty** panic and an increased toughening of censorship standards, especially in the area of the much-maligned horror film. Britain now has the strictest censorship of the genre in the Western world. JP

Chaney, Lon [Leonidas]
(1883–1930)

American actor. He piled on the agony with the make-up. Known as 'the Man of a Thousand Faces' because he chameleoned from one guise to another, he learned the art of mime as the son of deaf mute parents. Body-language was a mode of expression he used with immaculate expertise through his comparatively short career. He became the family provider when his mother was stricken by rheumatism; then, after a period in a draper's store, joined his younger brother's travelling theatre.

Abraded by the pain of his childhood, his reputation as a dramatic masochist began and grew from *The Penalty* (1920), in which he bound his calves to his thighs to play a legless criminal. His kind of horror was for audiences appalled and fascinated by disfigurement: it has all the geek quality of low-class carnival, in which creatures with three heads and foetuses with five were alluring hex-objects, reminders to ordinary people how flesh could melt and mutate into weird carcasses. Chaney's success was in achieving this as a kind of psychic self-mutilation. But with grace.

As *The Hunchback of Notre Dame* (1923), he is as poignant as he is fearsome. In its way, the performance criticises the taste of those who made him a box-office icon as much as those who throng to see him flogged in the film's narrative. To create Quasimodo, Chaney wore a plaster hump, a leather harness which kept him from standing upright and a dental device which stopped him closing his mouth. That he still manages to suggest a pitiable human being through these surgical appliances is the mark of his enormous talent. With similar and obsessive inventiveness he created his own prosthetics for **The Phantom of the Opera** (1925). The revelation of a hideous skull-like face when he turns to the camera, and the **heroine**, is one of the great, most formidable, unmaskings in cinema. This, again, required a most painful technique in facial adjustment.

Such tuggings and pullings about of his body were necessary, he wrote, 'because I want picturegoers to be bewildered and stirred by what they see'. Not only cinematic observers, but his Hollywood colleagues. 'Don't step on it, it may be Lon Chaney' was the joke of the time, while his flesh-crawling personality went into music hall songs of the era. His most frequent and fruitful collaborator, along the road of his Calvary crippleage, was director Tod **Browning** who perhaps saw in Chaney a forerunner of his contro-

Lon Chaney, *The Hunchback of Notre Dame* (1923)

Lon Chaney Jr

versial *Freaks* (1932) and wanted him to play **Dracula** but settled for **Lugosi** after Chaney's death. Chaney's best work belongs to the silent age though the sound remake of *The Unholy Three* (1930), reveals an actor as flexible of voice as of body. Tragically, it was his last film – he had throat cancer and died at the age of forty-seven.

What he bestowed upon horror movies was a cruel elegance and an understanding of how the body could be morphed, before that technique had been invented. He shocked because he took body manipulation beyond the confines of what flesh had imposed upon it. James Cagney plays Chaney in *The Man of a Thousand Faces* (1957), a tribute which salutes its hero in ways that do not align with his artistry: it sees the sensation and not the sensibility. Like **Houdini**, Chaney was the kind of showman who believed in punishing the flesh to achieve purification through transfiguration. When he died it was, after a lifetime of elected bondage, to reach unfettered release. It was a liberty he never really wanted. TH

*A Night of Thrills/The Forbidden Room/*1914 * *Stronger Than Death/*1915 * *The Miracle Man/* 1919 * *Outside the Law/*1921 * *A Blind Bargain/*1922 * *While Paris Sleeps/*1923 * *The Monster/The Unholy Three/*1925 * *The Black Bird/The Road to Mandalay/*1926 * *Mr Wu/The Unknown/London After Midnight/*1927 * *West of Zanzibar/*1928 * *Where East is East/*1929

Robert G. Anderson, *Faces, Forms, Films: The Artistry of Lon Chaney* (1971); Forrest J.

Ackerman, *Lon of a Thousand Faces* (1983); Michael F. Blake, *Lon Chaney: The Man Behind the Thousand Faces* (1993), *A Thousand Faces: Lon Chaney's Unique Artistry in Motion Pictures* (1996)

Chaney Jr, Lon [Creighton Chaney] (1906–73)

American actor, son of Lon **Chaney**. It is a truth universally acknowledged in the world of the creative arts that the shadows of famous fathers lie heavy on their children. None was so smothered by parental celebrity than Creighton, who assumed his father's name for reasons of profession if not pride. Hulkingly brutish (six foot, two inches), he had little of his father's grace and became a low-grade feature player in Universal's cheapo horrors. He proved himself a useful character actor outside the genre, notably the retarded Lenny in John Steinbeck's *Of Mice and Men* (1939), but was considered a star for those programmers desirous of cashing in on a name which meant so much in terms of thrills and appalled audiences.

Though Chaney Senior forbade his son access to the acting profession, young Chaney took up work as an extra and stuntman after his father's death. Cut from **The Most Dangerous Game** (1932), he made his horror debut in an aquatic atrocity, the serial *Undersea Kingdom* (1936). He is a caveman of unpleasant hairiness in *One Million B.C.* (1940), a forecast of the way he was typecast by Universal Studios for **The Wolf Man** (1941). 'I think that I must have played that character more than any other actor,' he said with a tinge of melancholy. He also played the **Frankenstein** Monster, **Dracula**'s son and the **Mummy**, in descending order of merit.

Of all his deplorable B movies, the best suited to his talent for a haunted-eye pathos, imprisoned within a huge frame, is *Man Made Monster* (1941), in which **mad scientist** Lionel **Atwill** converts Chaney into a man invulnerable to electricity but able to shock people to death with his touch. In the way of **King Kong** and **Karloff**, he manages to give a pitiable dignity to a creature who has no choice about the way his life has been created and directed. This melancholic sense of a fated existence, over which the Chaney-creature has no control, became more and more evident in the roles accepted, from (**Abbott and Costello**) *Meet Frankenstein* (1947) via *La casa del terror* (*Face of the Screaming Werewolf*, 1959) to *The Haunted Palace* (1963).

Among later credits, only *Spider Baby* (1964) has much merit, with Chaney as the chauffeur to a monstrously sick family. He even croons the title-song; in terms of what he had filmed, he did not have much to sing about. His on-screen pathos was matched by a tragic private life in which alcoholism took hold and his body bloated to display the effects of the addiction. His last genre film was *Dracula vs. Frankenstein* (1970), in itself a shrewd comment on what had happened to Chaney Jr. The success of the father was not passed on to the following generation: trying to live up to his parent's reputation was something that, in the long term, brought him low. As a wolfman he always seemed to be the underdog. Instead of frightening audiences they came to regard him with the kind of affection you bestow upon a well-loved pet. In *Man of a Thousand Faces* (1957), he is played by Roger Smith. TH

*A Scream in the Night/*1935 * *Killer at Large/* 1936 * *Ghost of Frankenstein/The Mummy's Tomb/*1942 * *Frankenstein Meets the Wolf Man/ The Mummy's Ghost/Son of Dracula/Calling Dr. Death/*1943 * *Weird Woman/The Ghost Catchers/The Mummy's Curse/Dead Man's Eyes/ House of Frankenstein/*1944 * *House of Dracula/ Strange Confession/Pillow of Death/The Frozen Ghost/*1945 * *Bride of the Gorilla/*1951 * *The Black Castle/*1952 * *Manfish/Indestructible Man/ The Black Sleep/*1956 * *The Cyclops/*1957 * *The Alligator People/*1959 * *The Devil's Messenger/* 1962 * *Witchcraft/*1964 * *House of the Black Death/*1965 * *Dr. Terror's Gallery of Horrors/ Hillbillys in a Haunted House/*1967

TV: *Tales of Tomorrow*: 'Frankenstein'/1952 * *The Whistler*: 'Backfire'/1954 * *Zane Gray Theater*: 'Warm Day in Heaven'/1961 * *Route 66*: 'Lizard's Leg and Owlet's Wing'/1962 * *The Phantom/*1963

Don G. Smith, *Lon Chaney, Jr: Horror Film Star, 1906–1973* (1996)

Charnas, Suzy McKee (b. 1939)

American writer. *The Vampire Tapestry* (1980) is the single best **vampire** novel in two decades. *Dorothea Dreams* (1986), also excellent, is a **ghost story**.

Chetwynd-Hayes, Ronald (b. 1919)

British writer. His short stories, some with a slapstick streak, are collected in *The Elemental* (1974), *The Monster Club* (1975) and *The House of Dracula* (1987). *From Beyond the Grave* (1974) and *The Monster Club* (1980), produced by Milton **Subotsky**, are adaptations. His 'Housebound' (1968) became a **Night Gallery** ('Something in the Wood-work', 1973). In *The Monster Club*, he is cadaverously played by John **Carradine**.

Children and Babies

The young were once emblems of innocence: trusting little girls offer poignant contrast to menaces in *Der Golem* (1920), **Frankenstein** (1931), *Ghost of Frankenstein* (1942) and *Curse of the Cat People* (1944), while the dreams of small boys explain the somewhat incoherent scenarios of *Invaders from Mars* (1953) and *Robot Monster* (1953). Things changed in 1956, when *The Bad Seed*, derived via Broadway from a novel by William March, depicted an angelic blonde child (Patty McCormack) as a **serial killer**. A small army of towheads, sired by **aliens** and bent on destruction, appear in *Village of the Damned* (1960, 1995) but are whitewashed in *Children of the Damned* (1963), while *The Damned* (1963) are radioactive kids created as a government experiment.

A vindictive child's ghost, heralded by a bouncing ball, is chilling in Mario **Bava**'s

ABOVE Children: Pamela Franklin, *The Innocents*

BELOW Children: Charlotte Burke, Elliott Spears, *Paperhouse*

Operazione Paura (*Kill, Baby, Kill*, 1966), immediately echoed in **Fellini**'s acclaimed segment of *Histoires extraordinaires* (*Spirits of the Dead*, 1967) and still influential in *The Changeling* (1980). Evil kids became big business and booted horror up to a new level of respectability, beginning with the conception of Satan's son in *Rosemary's Baby* (1968). Then *The Exorcist* (1973) with its possessed girl became one of the biggest hits in history, while *The Omen* (1978) was another blockbuster about a demonic child. An onslaught of naughty youngsters was unleashed: *The Other* (1972), *Nothing But the Night* (1972), *It's Alive* (1974), *Quien puede matar un niño?* (1975), *I Don't Want to Be Born* (1975), *Full Circle* (1976), *The Brood* (1979), *The Children* (1980), *Bloody Birthday* (1980), *The Godsend* (1980), *The Good Son* (1993).

The homicidal child at the start of **Halloween** (1978) had a few imitators, but kids of the coming era were most influenced by author Stephen **King**, whose heroic children appear in *Salem's Lot* (1979), *The Shining* (1980), *Cujo* (1983), *Firestarter* (1985) and *Silver Bullet* (1985), though trouble-

makers emerge in *The Children of the Corn* (1984) and *Pet Sematary* (1989). Good kids were back in **Poltergeist** (1982), *Something Wicked This Way Comes* (1983), *Flowers in the Attic* (1987), *The Monster Squad* (1987), *Lady in White* (1988) and *Parents* (1989), while Demi Moore spawns the second coming in *The Seventh Sign* (1988). A more thoughtful depiction of youth is suggested by *Paperhouse* (1988) and *The Reflecting Skin* (1991), while spooky kids are spoofed in *The Addams Family* (1991) and *Casper* (1995). LD

Child's Play (1988)

An effective, slick variant of Tom **Holland**'s habitual boy who cried wolf theme: Alex Vincent can't convince adults that his **doll** Chucky is **possessed** by **voodoo serial killer** Brad **Dourif**, who wants to migrate to Vincent's body. Written by John Lafia and Don Mancini, the film combines mild satire of the toy industry with the killer doll theme and slyly conservative family values. Lafia directed *Child's Play 2* (1990) and Jack Bender contributed *Child's Play 3* (1991). The films typify middle-of-the-road horror but became controversial in Britain in the early 90s when the press made spurious links between them and several murder cases.

LEFT Chucky, Alex Vincent, *Child's Play*

Imitations: *Dolly Dearest* (1991), *Demonic Toys* (1991), *Revenge of the Red Baron* (1993).

Chiller (UK TV series, 1995)

A lacklustre series of well-produced, feebly plotted supernatural stories. 'Prophecy', a cut-down of Peter **James**'s 1992 novel, opened the series, followed by originals from Stephen **Gallagher** ('Here Comes the Mirror Man'), Anthony Horowitz ('The Man Who Doesn't Believe in Ghosts', 'Number Six') and Glenn Chandler ('Toby'). Produced by Lawrence **Gordon Clark**.

China

Most Chinese horror films are inspired by popular legends, Cantonese operas or literature (novelist Pu Songling, known for **ghost stories**, is a favourite). Many Chinese still believe in spirits and sorcerers, making it easier for film-makers to scare them. Allegedly, the first Chinese horror film is *Yanzhi* (1925), Li Behai's romantic ghost story, which inaugurated a genre lost to history because most examples were destroyed after World War II. **Hammer** and Hong Kong's Shaw Brothers collaborated on *The Legend of the 7 Golden Vampires* (1972), directed by Roy Ward **Baker** featuring Peter **Cushing** and David Chiang: though this gothic-*kung-fu* crossbreed was unique, a new era of Chinese horror soon followed.

Samo **Hung**'s *Gui Da Gui* (*Encounters of the Spooky Kind*, 1980), a mix of horror, comedy and martial arts was a success in Asia, inspiring box-office hits like *Ren Xia Ren* (*The Dead and the Deadly*, 1982) and the *Jiangshi Xiansheng*/*Mr. Vampire* series (1985–8). China's distinctive fiend is the hopping **vampire** (or **jiangshi**). In the mid-80s, **Tsui** Hark changed HK film by mixing modern film techniques with classic legends. Founding his own studios, Tsui directed *Dap Bin* (*Butterfly Murders*, 1979) and *San Susan Gimgap* (*Zu Warriors from the Magic Mountain*, 1983) and produced **Ching** Siu-Tung's *Chinese Ghost Story* movies (1987, 1990, 1991) and *Yaoshou Dushi* (*The Wicked City*, 1993). The popularity of these romantic fantasy dramas made way for a plethora of copies, including Wu Ma's *Huazhongxian* (*Portrait of a Nymph*, 1988) and Ronny Yu's *Bai Fa Mo Nu Zhuan* (*The Bride With White Hair*, 1993). Stanley Kwan followed with the much acclaimed *Yanzhi Kou* (*Rouge*, 1987) and Ringo Lam set a ghost story in contem-

Mel Martin, 'The Man Who Didn't Believe in Ghosts', *Chiller*

porary Hong Kong with *Yinyang Cuo* (*Esprit d'Amour*, 1983).

All aspects of horror have been shown in Far East cinema: softcore (Nam Nai Choy's *Liao Zhai Yantan*/*Erotic Ghost Story*, 1990), comedy (Billy Chan's *Crazy Safari*, 1991), period adventure (Po Chih Leong's *Ye Jing Hun*/*He Lives By Night*, 1982; Sun Chung's *Renpi danglong*/*Human Skin Lanterns*, 1982), black magic (**Gui** Zhihong's *Xie*/*Hex*, 1980) and sleazy gore (Keith Li's *Centipede Horror*, 1988). CV

Ching Siu-Tung (b. 1953)

Chinese director. After directing the disappointing *Qi Yuan* (*The Witch from Nepal*, 1985), Ching choreographed fights for **Tsui** Hark's *San Susan Gimgap* (*Zu Warriors from Magic Mountain* (1983), which prompted Tsui to give him another shot at directing with *Qian Nu Youhoun* (*A Chinese Ghost Story*, 1987). The movie which made many Westerners discover Hong Kong horror cinema was unsurprisingly followed by sequels. He also directed *Tseun Yung* (*A Terra-Cotta Warrior*, 1989), a lovely fantasy romance shot in China, starring Zhang Yimou and Gong Li. Co-director with Ann Hui, King Hu and Raymond Lee of the Hark-produced *Xiao Ao Jiang Hu* (*Swordsman*, 1989), he exerts more influence on the sequels. If Tsui is the Chinese **Spielberg**, Ching might well be the Asian **Zemeckis**: a talented filmmaker but nothing of a visionary. CV

Yangan Dou [*A Chinese Ghost Story II*]/1990 * *Qian Nu Youhun III Dao Dao Dao* [*A Chinese Ghost Story II*]/1991

Christensen, Benjamin (1879–1959)

Danish director. Christensen was summoned by Hollywood on the strength of the demented pseudo-documentary *Häxan* (*Witchcraft Through the Ages*, 1922). After directing Lon **Chaney** in the melodrama *Mockery* (1927),

he made three haunted house mysteries probably partially written by Cornell **Woolrich**. Only *Seven Footprints to Satan* (1929), based on A. Merritt's 1927 novel, survives. Dismissed from the troubled *The Mysterious Island* (1929), Christensen returned to Denmark and worked infrequently in the sound era. His films are characterised by perversity and humour. In *Häxan*, he literally plays the **Devil**.

The Mysterious X/1913 * *Night of Revenge*/1915 * *The Haunted House*/1928 * *The House of Horror*/1929

Christie, Agatha (1891–1976)

British writer. Remembered as the mistress

ABOVE Benjamin Christensen
LEFT Benjamin Christensen's *Häxan*

of the whodunit, Christie is also influential in horror. *Ten Little Niggers* (1939), republished (for obvious reasons) as *And Then There Were None* or *Ten Little Indians*, with an isolated group of **victims** dying gruesomely one by one in macabre enactment of a children's rhyme, is the template for many a 'body count' from *Cinque bambole per la luna d'agosto* (1970) to *The Abominable Dr. Phibes* (1971). The novel has been filmed successfully by René Clair (*And Then There Were None*, 1945) and unsuccessfully (thrice) by Harry Alan **Towers** (*Ten Little Indians*, 1966; *And Then There Were None*, 1975; *Ten Little Indians*, 1989). The presence of rational (and irritating) persons like Hercule Poirot and Miss Marple excludes the supernatural from the bulk of her work, but she experimented with the **ghost story** (in the collection *The Hound of Death*, 1933) and the psycho thriller (*Endless Night*, 1967; filmed 1971). *The Agatha Christie Hour* (1982), a TV anthology, featured weird stories: 'The Fourth Man', 'The Mystery of the Blue Jar', 'The Red Signal', 'In a Glass Darkly'.

Christmas

The Victorian tradition of ghosts for Christmas found ultimate expression in Charles Dickens's *A Christmas Carol* (1843). Filmed under its own title in 1908, 1910, 1914 and 1938 and as *Scrooge* in 1901, 1913, 1935, 1951 and 1970, it is also adapted as *The Dream of Old Scrooge* (1910), *The Right to be*

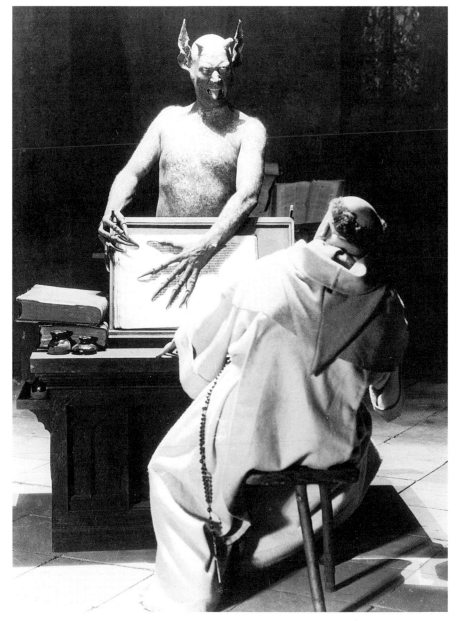

Christmas

other menaces. *Don't Open Till Christmas* (1984) makes victims of Santas, while *36:15 – Code Père Noël* (1989), a French template for *Home Alone* (1990), pits another crazed Father Christmas against a resourceful kid. In a different vein, Tim **Burton**'s animated fable *The Nightmare Before Christmas* (1994) shows Hallowe'en characters creating their own odd brand of Yuletide cheer. LD

Ciannelli, Eduardo (1887–1969)
Italian-born American actor. Sinister looks typed him as a villain or red herring. SJ

The Scoundrel/1935 * *Super-Sleuth*/1937 * *Mysterious Dr. Satan*/*The Mummy's Hand*/1940 * *The Lost Moment*/*Seven Keys to Baldpate*/1947 * *The Creeper*/1948

TV: *Matinee Theatre*: 'The Fall of the House of Usher'/1956; 'The Cask of Amontillado'/1957 * *Thriller*: 'Man in the Cage'/1961; 'The Bride Who Died Twice'/1962 * *Alfred Hitchcock Presents*: 'Strange Miracle'/'The Test'/1962 * *Time Tunnel*: 'The Ghost of Nero'/1967

Cinefantastique

American film magazine, published and edited by Frederick S. Clarke. This respected journal began in 1965 as a mimeographed fanzine, *Garden Ghouls Gazette*. In 1967, Clarke changed the title; in 1970, the magazine became professional. Serious, sometimes pretentious, always readable, it attempts to cover all aspects of fantasy cinema. Rapidly establishing itself as a market leader, *CFQ* has never been afraid of controversy in reports, interviews or critiques. If a film is greeted with a critical mauling, Clarke frequently allocates space for injured parties to defend themselves but seldom prints retractions. By the late 70s, more and more space was given over to detailed reports on the making of each new special effects spectacular, only for the films to be shredded in reviews. The magazine went into decline in the early 90s, due to an obsessive interest in **Star Trek**. *Imagi-Movies*, a companion publication, was launched in 1993 to cover films that would once have routinely been in the 'old' *Cinefantastique*; after two years, it was incorporated into the parent. MW

Circle of Fear * See: *Ghost Story*

Circuses

With a surface of tawdry glamour masking a milieu marked by danger, depravity and

Happy (1916), animated as *Mickey's Christmas Carol* (1983) and *The Muppet Christmas Carol* (1992) and updated as *Scrooged* (1988). The best version, Brian Desmond Hurst's *Scrooge* (1951), shows Alastair Sim a genuinely disturbing fate. Dickens aside, cinema offers Yuletide murder in *The Brighton Strangler* (1945), a vivid vignette like the cruel treatment of Christmas carolers in **The Addams Family** (1991), or a tale of Santa stuck up the chimney in *Gremlins* (1984), uncredited but apparently based on a Gahan Wilson cartoon.

The crucial moment came when Johnny Craig's **EC Comics** story 'And All Through the House' (*The Vault of Horror*, 1954) was adapted for *Tales from the Crypt* (1972): the image of a murderer in a Santa suit gradually permeated American culture. Just the idea of horror on holidays is enough for *Silent Night, Bloody Night* (1972) and *Black Christmas* (1972), but 1980 put the killer into the crimson costume for *To All a Goodnight* and the ungrammatical *You Better Watch Out*. The deluge came with *Silent Night, Deadly Night* (1984), which roused public protest and spawned four numbered sequels. Before the end, the series replaced the killer Claus with

deformity, circuses and carnivals provide a colourful background for horror. *Das Cabinet des Dr. Caligari* (1919) presents its menaces as fairground attractions, and the first major Hollywood horror director, Tod **Browning**, spent years with the circus and used it as background for the Lon **Chaney** vehicle *The Unknown* (1927) and the uniquely confrontational *Freaks* (1932). Trained animals become killers in *The Leopard Lady* (1928), **Murders in the Rue Morgue** (1932), *Murders in the Zoo* (1933), *The Ape* (1940) and *Black Zoo* (1963), while travelling shows touch base with classic **monsters** in *House of Frankenstein* (1944), *The Evil of Frankenstein* (1964) and the inventive *Vampire Circus* (1971).

Performers are transformed into monsters in *Man Made Monster* (1941), **Captive Wild Woman** (1943), *The She Creature* (1956) and *She Freak* (1966), while fairgrounds provide colourful backgrounds for climaxes in *The Beast from 20,000 Fathoms* (1953), *Horrors of the Black Museum* (1958), *Gorgo* (1959), *Carnival of Souls* (1962) and *The Incredibly Strange Creatures Who Stopped Living and Became Mixed-Up Zombies!!?* (1964). A key film, Sidney **Hayers**'s *Circus of Horrors* (1960), depicts a deranged **plastic surgeon** (Anton **Diffring**) who creates beauties with his knife, then kills them in staged accidents before paying crowds. Frankly exploitive, it surpasses imitators like *Berserk!* (1967), which even uses the same real circus.

The ambitious *Something Wicked This Way Comes* (1982) fails to translate Ray **Bradbury**'s atmosphere to the screen, *Howling VI: The Freaks* (1990) and *Freaked* (1993) are just silly, and *Killer Klowns from Outer Space* (1987) and *Clownhouse* (1989) at least do their job. Tobe **Hooper**'s *The Funhouse* (1981), a nicely paced thriller about kids trapped in the eponymous structure with a deformed maniac, may be the best recent use of the carnival setting. Still, little is as disturbing as Tyrone Power taking a job as a geek in *Nightmare Alley* (1947). LD

Clare, Diane (b. 1938)

British actress. Small-faced heroine: a spirited gel in *Plague of the Zombies* (1965).

The Haunting/1963 * *Witchcraft*/1964 * *The Vulture*/*The Hand of Night*/1966

TV: *The Avengers*: 'Death at Bargain Prices'/ 1966

Clarens, Carlos (1936–87)

Cuban-born American critic. *An Illustrated History of the Horror Film* (*Horror Movies*, 1967), the first full-length genre study, remains esssential. *Crime Movies* (1980) is also considerable.

Clark, Bob [Benjamin] (b. 1939)

American director, producer, writer. After *The She Man* (1967) and *The Emperor's New Clothes* (1967), Clark joined writer-actor Alan **Ormsby** to make two 'living dead' films, *Children Shouldn't Play With Dead Things* (1972) and *Dead of Night* (1973). The latter

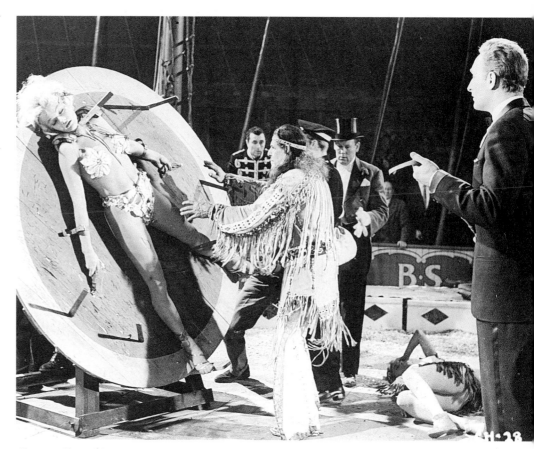

Circuses: *Circus of Horrors*

weds Vietnam fears with **'The Monkey's Paw'** (1902) in a surprisingly timely horror-tragedy. Clark removed his producer credit from *Deranged* (1974), Ormsby's superb directorial debut. The genuinely scary **psycho**-in-the-attic shocker *Black Christmas* (1974) was followed by *Murder By Decree* (1979), an effective **Sherlock Holmes** vs. **Jack the Ripper** piece embracing Stephen Knight's conspiracy theories and an all-star cast. He abandoned horrors to pursue mainstream success with *Porky's* (1982) and *A Christmas Story* (1983). Clark briefly reunited with Ormsby and the genre as uncredited

co-writer and 'supervisor' of the ill-fated *Popcorn* (1991). SB/DW

Clark, Greydon (b. 1943)

American director. After acting for Al Adamson (*Dracula vs. Frankenstein*, 1970) and writing Ray **Danton**'s interesting *Psychic Killer* (1975), Clark became a grindhouse director, employing down-on-their-luck vets John Ireland, John **Carradine** and Yvonne **DeCarlo** (*Satan's Cheerleaders*, 1976) and Jack **Palance**, Martin **Landau** and Cameron

Mitchell (*Without Warning*, 1980). His films tend to choppy tedium and are unkind to their stars. *Wacko* (1982), a **stalk-and-slash** parody about a lawnmower killer, is fitfully amusing.

Uninvited/1988 * *Out of Sight, Out of Mind*/ 1990 * *Dance Macabre*/1991

Clayton, Jack (1921–95)

British director. Clayton embodied the angriness of *Room at the Top* (1958) before turning to the eerie, if psychologically reputable, *The Innocents* (1961), from **'The Turn of the**

Screw' (1898). The uneasily macabre *Our Mother's House* (1967) is underrated, but *Something Wicked This Way Comes* (1983), from Ray **Bradbury**'s 1963 novel, is a severe let-down.

The Queen of Spades (associate p)/1948 * *The Bespoke Overcoat* (s)/1955

Clemens, Brian (b. 1931)

British writer, producer. Clemens did not create **The Avengers** (1961–9), but as writer and producer set the show's witty, bizarre, weird style. He wrote many feature-length suspense and horror teleplays, often re-broadcast as TV movies, for his series *Thriller* (1973–5): 'Someone at the Top of the Stairs' (1973) has an **immortal** murderer in a boarding house; 'One Deadly Owner' (1973) has a **car** possessed by a previous owner who was murdered in it; 'Nurse Will Make It Better' (1975), with witchy Diana Dors taking over the household of an American ambassador, is a dry run for **The Omen** (1976). His most notable films are **Hammer**'s *Dr. Jekyll and Sister Hyde* (1971) and *Captain Kronos Vampire Hunter* (1972). *Kronos* is his single directorial credit.

The Tell-Tale Heart/1960 * *The Watcher in the Woods*/1980 * *Highlander II: The Quickening*/1992

TV: *Adam Adamant Lives!*: 'The Terribly Happy Embalmers'/'A Slight Case of Reincarnation'/1966 * *Darkroom*: 'Who's There?'/'1982 * *Hammer House of Mystery and Suspense*: 'The Sweet Scent of Death'/1988 * *Worlds Beyond*: 'The Eye of Yemanja'/'Voice From the Gallows'/1987 * *Highlander*: 'See No Evil'/1993

Clichés

A genre is defined, at least in part, by recurring motifs and devices, which may be exalted as tropes or archetypes but often are rendered so devoid of meaning that they become clichés. One especially annoying early example was the very denial of a narrative's validity by its dismissal as a **dream** (*Life Without Soul*, 1915) or a delusion (*Das Cabinet des Dr. Caligari*, 1919). Even the revelation that such a dream was coming true grew tedious, as when the end title of *Incubo sulla città contaminata* (*Nightmare City*, 1980) proclaims 'The Nightmare Becomes Reality.' Equally irritating are films like *The Mark of the Vampire* (1935), in which an uncanny menace turns out to be an elaborate hoax. Gradually the fantastic themes of

Jack Clayton

horror films became more acceptable, with driven protagonists making genuine forays into unknown realms of science or the supernatural.

The **Faustian** theme was rapidly reduced to a commonplace by reiterated remarks such as 'there are things beyond us, things we're not meant to understand' (*The Manster*, 1960). When *Dracula* (1931) became a hit, it established almost subliminally the concept that a proper horror plot would revolve around the Oedipal struggle between a good young man and an evil older one for the love of a desirable woman. This provided basic structure for years, but after half a century was joined by a solipsistic variation in which a young woman survives when every other character in the story has been slaughtered (*Alien*, 1979). Visual clichés in early films range from the corpse falling out of the closet (**The Cat and the Canary**, 1927) to the climactic, purging fire (**Frankenstein**, 1931). The sound effect of a heartbeat was introduced in *Dr. Jekyll and Mr. Hyde* (1931) but only became omnipre-sent decades later.

Recurring plot points include the sinister mastermind whose dimwitted **minion**, having committed countless atrocities, suddenly develops a conscience and revolts at story's end (*Dark Eyes of London*, 1939); the **immortal** fiend who's attracted to the glamorous **heroine** because she looks like someone he loved centuries ago (**The Mummy**, 1932); and the heroine inexplicably recoiling in dismay when a villain offers eternal life, unless she's the sensible Louise Allbritton in *Son of*

Brian Clemens

Dracula (1943). And incidentally, what do those marks on her neck mean, doctor? In modern times, the success of **Halloween** (1978) made it a fount of clichés for uninspired imitators, institutionalising the idea of a prologue set years before the main action and also the concept of the resilient **psychopath** who pops up again each time he seems to have been finally dispatched. The most obvious of the many visual aids provided for unimaginative directors by *Halloween* is the shot of a victim's feet lifted off the floor to demonstrate the murderer's maniacal strength.

Other current clichés include electronically altered bass voices which emerge from the most unlikely characters to prove they've been **possessed** (*Evil Toons*, 1990) and the omnipresent animated blue lightning which twinkles around uncanny objects (*Lifeforce*, 1985). Contrary to what casual commentators like to say, **sex** is not really punished by death in modern horror movies: it only looks like cause and effect because producers want to show both, and sex before death is more practical. LD

Clive, Colin [Colin Clive-Greig] (1900–1937)

Sensitive French-born British stage actor, in Hollywood from 1930. His friend James **Whale** cast him as an hysterical Henry Frankenstein ('It's alive!'). SJ

Frankenstein/1931 * *Jane Eyre*/1934 * *Bride of Frankenstein*/*Mad Love*/1935

Coen, Joel (b. 1958)

American director, writer. An editor on *Fear No Evil* (1981) and *The Evil Dead* (1982), Coen (with producer brother Ethan) scripted Sam **Raimi**'s *Crimewave* (1985) and creates consistently surprising, challenging post-modern movies. The Coens' essays in screwball comedy and thriller remarkably incorporate the demonic, represented by private eye M. Emmet Walsh (*Blood Simple*, 1984), biker Randall Tex Cobb (*Raising Arizona*, 1984), Mephistophelean squealer John Turturro (*Miller's Crossing*, 1990), salesman-serial killer John Goodman (*Barton Fink*, 1991), handyman Harry Bugin (*The Hudsucker Proxy*, 1994) and axe-and-wood-chipper murderer Peter Stormare (*Fargo*, 1996). Unconfined by but interested in genre, Coen's most nightmarish work is *Barton Fink*, a Hollywood horror story which requires its **Devil** savagely to attack the complacency of Turturro's tourist-with-a-typewriter playwright.

Cohen, Herman (b. 1928)

American producer. An associate on *Bride of the Gorilla* (1951) and *Bela Lugosi Meets a Brooklyn Gorilla* (1952), Cohen turned producer with the British-shot *Ghost Ship* (1952) and the robot invasion quickie *Target Earth* (1954). He hit a streak for AIP with the archetypally American *I Was a Teenage Werewolf* (1957) and another with the British-made *Horrors of the Black Museum* (1959). His films obsessively reuse evil parent figures who turn young partners into monstrous murderers, emphasising semi-gay relationships between **mad scientists** and their hypnotised pupils, while his **heroines** are often callously killed off. Far more than **Hammer**, he was responsible for the introduction of graphic **violence** to horror cinema, whether in the blackly comic organ-switching of *I Was a Teenage Frankenstein* (1958) or the gruesome **torture** murders of nubile women in *Black Museum*. His most likable film is the **Holmes**/**Jack the Ripper** *A Study in Terror* (1965). He made a minor icon of Michael **Gough**, an unrestrained sadist in many Cohen films.

Blood of Dracula/1957 * *How to Make a Monster*/1958 * *The Headless Ghost*/1959 * *Circus of Horrors*/1960 * *Konga*/1961 * *Black Zoo*/1963 * *Berserk!*/1968 * *Trog*/1970 * *Craze*/1974

Cohen, Larry (b. 1936)

American writer, director, producer. The mind behind our favourite movies about Aztec gods nesting in the Chrysler building (*Q*, 1982), **mutant babies** (*It's Alive*, 1974), hermaphrodite **alien** messiahs (*God Told Me To*, 1976) and killer dessert (*The Stuff*, 1986) belongs to talented but erratic New York City native Larry Cohen. 'They're not your run-of-the-mill ideas, huh?' he asks, a bit defiantly. 'I don't like to imitate other people's ideas or do homages to other people's films. My pictures are mine: they're individual and special.'

Cohen began his career in 1958, fresh out of college: while a page at NBC, he sold scripts to the network's *Kraft Television Theatre*, a prestigious anthology show, and progressed to writing for dramatic series (*The Defenders, The Rat Patrol, Columbo*). He created the paranoid Western *Branded* (1965–6) and the popular s-f series *The Invaders* (1967–8), and entered cinema with the script for *Return of the Seven* (1966). Though known for horror, Cohen has also written and/or directed mysteries, comedies, thrillers, Westerns and gangster pictures. *The Private Files of J. Edgar Hoover* (1977) is a masterpiece of prurient paranoia. *Black Caesar* (1973) and its sequel *Hell Up in Harlem* (1973) are high-water marks in Blaxploitation, to which he returns with *Original Gangstas* (1996).

Stubborn, idiosyncratic and sharp-tongued, Cohen is consistently an inventive writer and a mediocre director. His greatest directing talent seems to be doggedness and manic invention in the face of apparent disaster: when an ailing Bette **Davis** bowed out of *Wicked Stepmother* (1989) halfway through production, Cohen managed to rework her part so it could be picked up by Barbara Carrera. A Catherine's wheel of ideas (an amazing number of them good), he is regularly tripped up by the follow-through. He thrives on the autonomy of low-budget filmmaking but lacks the skills to make a million dollars look like more and the patience to coax consistent performances from his always idiosyncratic casts (alumni include Michael **Moriarty**, Richard **Lynch**, Eric Bogosian, Zoe Tamerlis, Anne Carlisle, Andrew Duggan, Laurene Landon, James Earl Jones and Sam Fuller). He is most highly praised by critics willing to weight ideas and ideology higher than technical execu-

LEFT Ethan Cohen, Joel Cohen, on the set of *Barton Fink*

tion. 'I know I'm a lucky guy, I get to write my stories and make my pictures.' MM

Daddy's Gone A-Hunting (w)/1969 * *Bone* (+w/p)/1970 * *It Lives Again* (+w/p)/1978 * *Full Moon High* (+w/p)/1981 * *Perfect Strangers* (+w/p)/*Special Effects* (+w/p)/1986 * *It's Alive III: Island of the Alive* (+w/p)/*A Return to Salem's Lot* (+w/p)/1987 * *Maniac Cop* (w)/ 1988 * *Maniac Cop II* (w)/1990 * *The Ambulance* (+w)/1991 * *Maniac Cop III: Badge of Silence* (w)/1992 * *Guilty as Sin* (w)/1993 * *Body Snatchers* (w)/1994 * *Invasion of Privacy* (w)/*Uncle Sam* (w)/1996

TV: *Way Out*: 'False Face'/1961 * *In Broad Daylight* (w)/1971 * *See China and Die* (+w)/ 1981 * *As Good as Dead* (+w/p)/1995 * *The Invaders* (st)/1996

Cohen, Lawrence D. (b. 1947)

American screenwriter who adapts best selling novels, latterly into TV mini-series. He did *Carrie* as hit film (1976) and famously disastrous stage **musical** (1988).

Ghost Story/1981

TV: *It*/1990 * *The Tommyknockers*/1993

Collins, Barnabas * See: **Cross, Ben; Curtis, Dan;** *Dark Shadows;* **Frid, Jonathan; Vampirism**

Combs, Jeffrey (b. 19??)

American actor. Memorable as insensitive mad scientist Herbert West in *Re-Animator* (1985) and *Bride of Re-Animator* (1991). In *Necronomicon* (1994), he plays H.P. **Lovecraft**. SJ

From Beyond/1986 * *Cellar Dweller/The Phantom Empire*/1987 * *Pulse Pounders* (unfinished)/1988 * *Trancers II: The Return of Jack Deth/The Pit and the Pendulum*/1990 * *The Guyver*/1991 * *Doctor Mordrid*/1992 * *Lurking Fear*/1994 * *Castle Freak*/1995 * *The Frighteners*/1996

TV: *Beauty and the Beast*: 'No Way Down'/1987 * *Freddy's Nightmares*: 'Love Stinks'/1989 * *Perversions of Science*/1996

Comedy

Horror films that work as comedies are usually parodies. Even **Old Dark House** films, the first group of horror movies to contain large doses of humour, are burlesques of gothic conventions established in literature and drama. It was only after sound arrived and horror was gradually established as an identifiable genre that parody became a real possibility. There were quite a few comedies about hauntings (*The Ghost Goes West*, 1935; *Topper*, 1937; *Blithe Spirit*, 1945), but these are urbane fantasies quite outside the realm of terror. Comedian Harold Lloyd's penultimate feature, *Professor Beware* (1938), opens with a surprising recreation of the ancient Egyptian rituals presented in **The Mummy** (1932) but abandons its **reincarnation**

Jeffrey Combs, *Bride of Re-Animator*

theme for a series of pointless chases. More to the point is *The Ghost Breakers* (1940), Bob Hope's follow up to his successful **The Cat and the Canary** (1939). What sets *The Ghost Breakers* apart is its Caribbean setting and the use of a **zombie** as the principal menace. The film was a hit, and an inferior remake, *Scared Stiff* (1953), became a vehicle for the team of Dean Martin and Jerry Lewis, with Hope dropping in for a cameo as the final, unbearable horror.

As remarkable in its way is *Zombies on Broadway* (1945), with Wally Brown and Alan Carney burlesquing the poetic *I Walked with a Zombie* (1943) to the extent of reusing key performers and a song. **Lugosi** is also on board, and in the **jungle** horror *Bela Lugosi Meets a Brooklyn Gorilla* (1952) he faces shockingly bad Martin and Lewis imitators. Mercilessly, he was then cast in *Old Mother Riley Meets the Vampire* (1952). **Karloff** and **Lorre** fare marginally better as addled scientists building super soldiers for the war effort in *The Boogie Man Will Get You* (1944), while radio actor Harold Peary faces **apes**, mad doctors and an invisible woman in *Gildersleeve's Ghost* (1944). More original is *Murder, He Says* (1945), pitting Fred MacMurray against a clan of iridescent, homicidal hillbillies.

ÉPOUVANTE SUR NEW-YORK

LEFT Larry Cohen's *Q*

Key figures in establishing horror comedy were Bud **Abbott** and Lou **Costello**, at one point in the 40s the most popular movie stars in America. They visit the usual haunted house in *Hold That Ghost* (1941), but break new ground with (Abbott and Costello) *Meet Frankenstein* (1948). The team was in a slump, as were the **monsters** made famous by their home studio, Universal, so the **Frankenstein** Monster (Glenn **Strange**), **Dracula** (Lugosi) and the **Wolf Man** (Lon **Chaney Jr**) were revived for a spoof that made millions, prompting encounters between the stars and the **Invisible Man** (1951), **Jekyll and Hyde** (1953) and the **Mummy** (1955). Universal cast its other top comedian, Francis the Talking Mule, in *Francis in the Haunted House* (1956).

The next wave of parodies came from AIP, the studio that picked up the banner of low-budget horror in the USA. Their ace director Roger **Corman** created a cult favourite with his quickie about a talking, man-eating plant, *The Little Shop of Horrors* (1960), but its companion piece *A Bucket of Blood* (1959) is even better, a send-up of California beatniks with a dead-on script by Charles **Griffith** and delirious performances by Dick **Miller** and Julian Burton. AIP produced a couple of hackneyed **teenage** horror comedies, *The Headless Ghost* (1959) and

The Ghost of Dragstrip Hollow (1959), then went up-market with Corman's colour adaptations of Edgar Allan **Poe**. When writer Richard **Matheson** grew tired of the formula, he burlesqued it with *The Raven* (1963),

featuring **Price**, Lorre and Karloff as addled medieval wizards. The three returned, joined by Basil **Rathbone**, for Jacques **Tourneur**'s graverobbing caper *The Comedy of Terrors* (1964).

AIP's English counterpart, **Hammer Films**, awkwardly sent up its groundbreaking *The Curse of Frankenstein* (1957) with *The Horror of Frankenstein* (1970); more satisfying, at least on its own terms, is the frankly tawdry *Carry On Screaming* (1966). The most elegant offering of the era is Roman **Polanski**'s tribute to **Hammer**, *Dance of the Vampires* (1967). The horror parody reached out to general audiences with the 1964 debut of the TV series ***The Addams Family*** and its lookalike ***The Munsters***. Jerry Lewis earned raves and revenue with *The Nutty Professor* (1963) while Mel Brooks had his finest hour (and three quarters) with *Young Frankenstein* (1974), a lovingly photographed parody of the Universal **Frankenstein** cycle. *Vampira* (1974), later called *Old Dracula*, is a ham-handed hash starring David Niven, and *Love at First Bite* (1979), with George Hamilton, and Brooks's *Dracula – Dead and Loving It* (1995), with Leslie Nielsen, aren't much better.

Comedy: Gene Wilder, *Haunted Honeymoon*

The **stalk-and-slash** cycle inspired weak parodies (*Student Bodies*, 1981; *Pandemonium*, 1982) but *Saturday the 14th* (1981) is a misnamed throwback. **Cannibalism** is the theme of *The Microwave Massacre* (1979), *Motel Hell* (1980) and the perversely charming *Delicatessen* (1991), while ultra-**violence** is exaggerated for comic effect in *Re-Animator* (1985), *Return of the Living Dead* (1985), *The Toxic Avenger* (1985), *Dead Heat* (1988), *Frankenhooker* (1990) and Peter **Jackson**'s especially outrageous *Braindead* (1992). Repeating the Abbott and Costello formula of top comedians and state-of-the-art effects, Ivan **Reitman**'s *Ghostbusters* (1984) was a huge success, as was Joe **Dante**'s fable about the cutely creepy *Gremlins* (1984). These made horror comedy big business, though sequels came too late. Neil **Jordan**'s fey *High Spirits* (1988) flopped but Tim **Burton**'s *Beetle Juice* (1988) scored with its brilliantly twisted view of the afterlife, while *Death Becomes Her* (1992) cast Oscar-winners Meryl Streep and Goldie Hawn as ludicrous walking corpses. On the other hand, most recent horror spoofs are desperately-titled direct-to-video disasters: *Hollywood Chainsaw Hookers* (1987), *Sorority Babes in the Slimeball Bowl-A-Rama* (1988), *Chopper Chicks in Zombie Town* (1991). Devoid of chills or chuckles, they do not bode well. LD

Comic Relief

Light moments intended as contrast to dark-er drama go back at least as far as the drunken porter in *Macbeth* (1606), and are usually created by supporting characters in subordinate positions. The **asylum** attendant in *Dracula* (1931) has his silly scenes, but so does the befuddled old baron in *Frankenstein* (1931). Una **O'Connor**'s hysterical reactions are a highlight in **The Invisible Man** (1933) and *Bride of Frankenstein* (1935), but James **Whale** also enjoyed joking with monsters and madmen, a progressive approach that eventually undercut the need for separate **comedy** relief characters.

The best remembered comic relief came from **black** actors who played frightened servants. Shocking when seen today is Stepin Fetchit (Lincoln Perry), who seems barely capable of thought or motion in *Charlie Chan in Egypt* (1935) but earned substantial success with his routines. Somewhat sprightlier is Willie **Best**, who made a specialty of spooky thrillers like *The Smiling Ghost* (1941) and *Face of Marble* (1946). He often played the servants of Caucasian comedians who could look braver by contrast, yet he had key roles: Jerry Lewis took Best's part rather than Bob Hope's when remaking *The Ghost Breakers* (1940) as *Scared Stiff* (1953). Usually deplored as racist stereotype, Best offers a healthy realism in the face of genre conventions demanding heroes who place themselves in jeopardy. 'You say you're going to invite the killer here tonight?' he says in *Super-Sleuth* (1937).

'Would an evening off be asking too much?' Mantan **Moreland** is more aggressive, stealing centre stage from white leads in *King of the Zombies* (1941). Eddie Anderson played Jack Benny's valet Rochester on the top-rated radio comedy program of the era, but his only horror is the polished *Topper Returns* (1941). La Wanda Page revived the tradition, now a baffling anachronism, in *Mausoleum* (1982).

Other notable comedy reliefs include wisecracking reporters like Lee Tracy in *Doctor X* (1932), Glenda Farrell in *Mystery of the Wax Museum* (1933) and Ted Healy in *Mad Love* (1935). The amiable idiot (Ralph Littlefield) wandering through *The Ape Man* (1943) turns out to be the screenwriter. Relief also comes from befuddled duffers like Ian **Wolfe** in *The Raven* (1935) and balmy dowagers like Spring Byington in *The WereWolf of London* (1935), but the best bet is a baffled **police** officer, a breed ranging from Lionel **Atwill**'s one-armed inspector in *Son of Frankenstein* (1939) to Bill Goodwin's lecherous lieutenant in *House of Horrors* (1946). Outstanding in British films is Miles **Malleson**, with wonderful bits as an addled bystander in **Dracula** (1958) and *The Hound of the Baskervilles* (1959). Comedy relief *per se* went out of style decades ago, as jokes are now so often combined with jolts, but especially amusing recent performers include Griffin Dunne in *An American Werewolf in London* (1981), Michael **Moriarty** in *Q* (1982), James Karen and Don Kalfa in *Return of the Living Dead* (1985) and Stephen Geoffreys in *Fright Night* (1985). LD

Comics

Like horror films, comic strips and comic books are sometimes viewed with disdain if not actual alarm. The media share a fondness for the lurid and the grotesque and influence one another's visual approach but comparatively few horror films are based on comics. *Lady Frankenstein* (1972) is an exception, apparently plagiarised from a *Vampirella* story, 'For the Love of Frankenstein' (1969).

Comics were initially adapted as **serials** shown to children at Saturday matinees; costumed heroes battle villains who wear sinister diguises and hatch nefarious schemes, but the effect is hardly horrific. The serials *Batman* (1943) and *Batman and Robin* (1948) lack the atmosphere of artist Bob Kane's work, and the screen version of Lee Falk's *Mandrake the Magician* (1939) is only marginally better. A feature, *Dick Tracy Meets Gruesome* (1947), employs **Karloff** and a rather lighter tone than Chester Gould's comic strip. *Tales from the Crypt* (1972), based on **EC**'s best-known book, remains the key work in this subgenre. Produced by **Amicus** and directed by Freddie **Francis**, this **anthology** adapts with some faithfulness a group of stories written for the four-colour page by William Gaines, Al Feldstein and Johnny Craig. A sister publication inspired *Vault of Horror* (1973). *Tales from the Crypt* became an HBO television series (1989–95): updated and endowed with a different sense of humour, it attracted directors like Walter Hill and Arnold Schwarzenegger, and offers such spectacles as Joe Pesci split lengthwise or Demi Moore stabbed an even dozen times.

A burlesque *Batman* series (1966–89) encouraged American television to invest in comic book heroes and *The Incredible Hulk* inaugurated a series (1977–82), but this Marvel Comics version of the **Jekyll and Hyde** theme went no deeper than endowing the hero with extra bulk. The pilot film *Dr. Strange* (1978), about Marvel's white magician, did not result in further episodes. *Swamp Thing*, created by Len Wein and Bernie Wrightson for DC Comics, was filmed by Wes **Craven** in 1982; a spoof sequel followed in 1989, and the mossy **monster** ended up as a cable television series. While these very mild horrors are predominantly juvenile, Europeans produce comic book erotica in film form: *Diabolik* (1967), *Baba Yaga* (1973), *Gwendoline* (1984) and *Valentina* (1989) have fetishistic horror incidents.

Tim **Burton**'s *Batman* (1989) finally catches the dark spirit of the original, and *Batman Returns* (1992) surpasses it, forcing a deliberate lightening of touch in Joel Schumacher's *Batman Forever* (1995). The **Batman** films each include monstrous, monomaniacal villains running amok amid picturesque urban decay, and by their tremendous popularity have defined comic books for the general public, influencing such subsequent comic-to-screen efforts as *Dick Tracy* (1990), *The Mask* (1994), *The Crow* (1994) and *Judge Dredd* (1995). Meanwhile, comics creators experience horrors in Oliver **Stone**'s ambitious failure *The Hand* (1981) not to mention the inconsequential *Cellar Dweller* (1987), a **Friday the 13th: The Series** episode ('Tales of the Undead', 1987) and Larry **Cohen**'s mild *The Ambulance* (1990). LD

Mike Benton, *Horror Comics: The Illustrated History* (1991)

Computer Games * See: **Interactive**

Connor, Kevin (b. 1940)
British director, editor. He turned director for **Amicus**'s *From Beyond the Grave* (1973), whose nasty humour subsequently surfaces only in *Motel Hell* (1980). Known for rubbery **monster** movies (*The Land That Time Forgot*, 1975), he has done competent, weird-tinged TV work (*Goliath Awaits*, 1981; *The Return of Sherlock Holmes*, 1987) and been stuck with *Diana: Her True Story* (1993).

The House Where Evil Dwells/1982

Conway, Tom [Thomas Sanders] (1904–67)
Undervalued Russian-born British leading man, brother of George Sanders. He gives stylish support in a trio of **Lewton** classics and played the Falcon's brother from 1942–6. SJ

Cat People/1942 * *I Walked With a Zombie*/*The Seventh Victim*/*The Falcon and the Co-Eds*/1943 * *Bride of the Gorilla*/1951 * *The She-Creature*/*Voodoo Woman*/1956 * *Atomic Submarine*/1959

TV: *20th Century-Fox Hour*: 'Stranger in the Night'/1956 * *Alfred Hitchcock Presents*: 'The Glass Eye'/1957; 'Relative Value'/1959

Cook Jr, Elisha (1903–95)
Weasely American character actor, remembered as the neurotic gunsel Wilmer in *The Maltese Falcon* (1941). He lent welcome support to a number of horror films, invariably as a **victim**. SJ

Stranger on the Third Floor/1940 * *Hellzapoppin'*/1941 * *A-Haunting We Will Go*/1942 * *Voodoo Island*/1957 * *House on Haunted Hill*/1959 * *The Haunted Palace*/*Black Zoo*/1963 * *Rosemary's Baby*/1968 * *Blacula*/1972 * *Messiah of Evil*/1973

TV: *Thriller*: 'The Fatal Impulse'/1960 * *Wild Wild West*: 'The Night of the Double-Edged Knife'/1965; 'The Night of the Bars of Hell'/1966 * *The Night Stalker*/1971 * *Hollywood Television Theatre*: 'The Scarecrow'/1972 * *The Phantom of Hollywood*/1974 * *Dead of Night*/1976 * *Terror at Alcatraz*/1978 * *Salem's Lot*/1979 * *The Twilight Zone*: 'Welcome to Winfield'/1986

Cooper, Alice [Vincent Fournier] (b. 1945)
American **rock** musician. Creator of at least one classic, 'School's Out' (1972), Cooper is nonetheless best remembered for bellowed

Comics: Brandon Lee, *The Crow*

vocals and simulated stage violence, involving the deaths of chickens and dolls. His mix of beer-soaked, chat show geniality and ashen-faced horror is exemplified perfectly by an appearance as himself in *Wayne's World* (1992). Formed in 1965, Alice Cooper the group made psychedelia-inflected albums for Frank Zappa's Straight Records before signing with Warners for the breakthrough *Love It to Death* (1972).

Subsequently, the group was a vehicle for Cooper's show-biz theatrics and producer Bob Ezrin's buzz-saw dramatics. Though album titles were horror inflected (*Welcome to My Nightmare*, 1975; *AC Goes To Hell*, 1976), it was not until the 80s, as his recording career declined, that Cooper became a fully fledged horror icon, recording theme songs ('He's Back', *Friday the 13th, Part 6: Jason Lives*, 1986) and appearing in films (*Freddy's Dead: The Final Nightmare*, 1991), sometimes doing both (*Prince of Darkness*, 1987). The Spanish-shot *Monster Dog* (*Leviatan*, 1985) is a shoddy vehicle, casting him as a rock star **werewolf** (like some traditional lycanthropes, he was born on Christmas Day). In the 90s, Cooper returned to recording with some success ('Hey Stoopid', 1991). In the manner of **KISS**, *The Last Temptation* (1994) was promoted with a Nail Gaiman-authored **comic book** which perfectly catches the fairground melodramatics of the album. PHa

TV: *The Snoop Sisters*: 'The Devil Made Me Do It'/1974

Cooper, Merian C. (1893–1973) and **Schoedsack, Ernest G.** (1893–1979)
American producers-directors. Deservedly immortal for *King Kong* (1933), Cooper and Schoedsack appear as the pilots who strafe the giant **ape** on the Empire State Building. Committed to adventure and the exotic rather than horror, the team also produced the pulpy grue of *The Most Dangerous Game* (*The Hounds of Zaroff*, 1932) and the mythic grandeur of *She* (1935). Seperately, Cooper produced *The Phantom of Crestwood* (1932) and Schoedsack directed *Dr. Cyclops* (1940).

The Son of Kong/1933 * *Mighty Joe Young*/1949

Coppola, Francis Ford (b. 1939)
American director, producer, writer. Coppola cut his teeth with producer Roger **Corman** before maturing into one of America's premiere film-makers. After editing work on Corman's Soviet acquisitions, turning *Sadko* into *The Magic Voyage of Sinbad* (1962) and enhancing *Nebo Zovyot* with rubber penis versus vagina monsters in *Battle Beyond the Sun* (1963), he graduated to hands-on assistant directing chores for *The Premature Burial* (1962) and the legendarily patchwork *The Terror* (1963). In Europe as an assistant on *The Young Racers* (1963), Coppola scripted and directed an effective Irish-set psychological gothic, *Dementia 13* (1963).

Having established himself in Hollywood with *Finian's Rainbow* (1968) and *The Godfather* (1971), Coppola founded his own production facility, American Zoetrope, where he produced George Lucas's dystopian s-f debut *THX-1138* (1971). Though Coppola did not return to genre proper until his flamboyant *Bram Stoker's Dracula* (1992), his career has included two masterpieces which spilled into, and indeed shaped, the parameters of the contemporary horror film: the high-tech surveillance parable *The Conversation* (1974); and a hallucinogenic reconfiguration of Joseph Conrad's *Heart of Darkness* (1902) for the Vietnam generation as the definitive **war**/horror epic *Apocalypse Now* (1979). SB

Alice Cooper, *Wayne's World*

Mary Shelley's Frankenstein (p)/1994 * *Haunted* (p)/1995

Peter Cowie, *Coppola* (1990)

Corman, Roger (b. 1926)
American producer, director, distributor. Even mainstream moviegoers have some vague idea that Roger Corman is a cut above the mass of genre film-makers. His extensive body of work has been the subject of books, papers, retrospectives and festivals. Corman's strengths include a head for business, an eye for popular preoccupations, good timing and a rock-solid sense of how to put a movie together. Protégé Paul **Bartel** once remarked slyly that Corman believed in the theory of the producer as auteur. While Bartel was complaining (if Corman wanted more bare breasts in a movie he had produced, the

director had little say), the observation contains a larger truth: Charles **Griffith**'s *Eat My Dust!* (1976), with its mix of **comedy** and high adventure, and Jonathan Kaplan's *Night Call Nurses* (1974), a naughty, sexy movie full of pretty girls and low laughs, are as much 'Roger Corman movies' as anything Corman actually directed.

Corman pictures are always watchable, but most are guilty pleasures and their charms are largely incidental: an early performance by a now-famous actor, a suspended fragment of popular culture in a particular place and time, a sense of dogged determination to make a movie no matter what. Corman's autobiography, *How I Made a Hundred Movies in Hollywood and Never Lost a Dime* (1990), is a cheerfully crass portrait of a man who did not feel compromised by having to keep his eye on the bottom line. Corman the savvy producer hired Corman the director because he knew he was fast, cheap and reliable. Early in his career,

ling the movie business from the ground up, rising from messenger to story analyst at 20th Century-Fox before becoming disillusioned with studio politics. He took a break to attend Oxford University on the GI Bill, and returned to LA in the early 50s. He quickly sold his first script, *Highway Dragnet* (1954), and later that year produced his first low-budget feature, *The Monster From the Ocean Floor*. Wyott Ordung, director of *Ocean Floor*, put him in touch with would-be moguls James H. **Nicholson** and Samuel Z. **Arkoff**, whose American Releasing Corporation (later American International Pictures) released the second feature Corman produced, *The Fast and the Furious* (1954), and a long and fruitful relationship began.

During the 50s and 60s, Corman produced and directed his way through just about all the popular low-budget genres: juvenile delinquent, rock 'n' roll, gangster, s-f, biker, horror, Western, hippie. He turned

into commodities and selling them with catchy titles, memorable ad campaigns and tempting trailers. Corman claims he only ever lost money once – on the sober, socially conscious racial drama *The Intruder* (1961) – and he never made that mistake again.

He stopped directing in 1970 after clashing with United Artists during the production of *Von Richthofen and Brown* (he made a brief, inglorious comeback with *Frankenstein Unbound*, 1990) and formed his own production and distribution company, New World Pictures, that same year. For more than a decade, Corman released an eclectic mix of exploitation and foreign art films: **Fellini**'s *Amarcord* rubbing shoulders with *Caged Heat* (both 1973), and *The Tin Drum* with *Humanoids From the Deep* (1980). Chafing under the responsibilities of running the increasingly unwieldy studio, Corman sold New World in 1982, created a new company, Millennium Pictures, and then in 1985 formed Concorde/New Horizons. With Con-

Francis Coppola's *Dementia 13*

Roger Corman

Corman thought nothing of directing four or five films a year; his personal best was eight, in 1957. But if he could get another director for less money, he almost always did.

Born in Detroit, Michigan, Corman moved with his family to Los Angeles in 1940 and attended Beverly Hills High School. The practical Corman earned a degree in engineering – interrupted by World War II military service – before tack-

out many mediocre films, some significant genre pieces – notably his **Poe** series with Vincent **Price** – and the occasional cult classic, like *The Little Shop of Horrors* (1960). Corman anticipated the seminal New Hollywood picture *Easy Rider* (1969) with *The Wild Angels* (1966) and *The Trip* (1967) but was primarily a dedicated follower of fashion, capitalising on trends. He excelled at seizing on topical concerns, turning them

corde, Corman – responding to the changing market for low-budget films – shifted his focus from theatrical releases to direct-to-video films.

Corman's real genius lies in spotting and exploiting (in the best and worst senses) talent in others. The list of those given first or early breaks by Corman includes producers Jon Davison, Menahem Golan, Gale Anne Hurd and Gary Kurtz; screenwriters Amy

Holden Jones, John Sayles and Robert Towne; and directors Allan Arkush, Bartel, Peter Bogdanovich, James Cameron, Francis **Coppola**, Joe **Dante**, Jonathan **Demme**, Monte Hellman, Ron Howard, Kaplan, Martin Scorsese and Adam Simon. Corman surrounded himself with gifted film-makers, and his glorious reputation is largely reflected. MM

The Day the World Ended (d)/*It Conquered the World* (d)/1956 * *Attack of the Crab Monsters* (d)/*Not of This Earth* (d)/*The Undead* (d)/1957 * *Night of the Blood Beast*/1958 * *A Bucket of Blood* (d)/*The Creature From Haunted Sea* (d)/ *The Wasp Woman* (d)/*Attack of the Giant Leeches*/*The Beast From Haunted Cave*/1959 * *The Fall of the House of Usher* (d)/1960 * *Pit and the Pendulum* (d)/1961 * *The Premature Burial* (d)/*Tales of Terror* (d)/*The Tower of London* (d)/1962 * *The Haunted Palace* (d)/*The Raven* (d)/*The Terror* (d)/*Dementia 13*/1963 * *The Masque of the Red Death* (d)/1964 * *Tomb of Ligeia* (d)/1965 * *Queen of Blood*/1966 * *Targets*/1967 * *De Sade* (uncredited co-d)/ 1969 * *The Dunwich Horror*/1970 * *Hollywood Blvd*/*Piranha*/1976 * *Saturday the 14th*/*The Howling* (a)/1981 * *Galaxy of Terror*/*The Slumber Party Massacre*/1982 * *Forbidden World*/1983 * *Munchies*/*The Slumber Party Massacre II*/1987 * *Not of This Earth*/*The Nest*/1988 * *The Terror Within*/*Transylvania Twist*/*Brain Dead*/*Masque of the Red Death*/ 1989 * *The Terror Within II*/*The Haunting of Morella*/*The Slumber Party Massacre III*/1990 * *The Unborn*/*The Silence of the Lambs* (a)/1991 * *Munchie*/1992 * *Stepmonster*/*Dracula Rising*/ *Carnosaur*/*The Unborn 2*/*Quake*/*Revenge of the Red Baron*/1993 * *Carnosaur 2*/*Of Unknown Origin*/1994 * *Carnosaur 3*/*Munchy Strikes Back*/1996

TV: *Body Bags* (a)/1993 * *Hellfire*/*Burial of the Rats*/*Alien Within*/*The Wasp Woman*/*Not of This Earth*/*Horror Cafe*/*Piranha*/*Sawbones*/*Not Like Us*/*Dark Secrets*/1995 * *Star Quest*/*Humanoids From the Deep*/*Vampirella*/*Not of This Earth II*/ *Mortal Challenge*/*House of the Damned*/*The Haunted Sea*/*Marquis de Sade*/*Visitors to a Strange Planet*/*Inhumanoid* /1996

Paul Willemen, David Will, *Roger Corman: The Millennic Vision* (1970); J. Philip di Franco, *The Movie World of Roger Corman* (1979); Ed Naha, *Roger Corman: Brilliance on a Budget* (1982); Stephane Bourgoin, *Roger Corman* (1983); Mark Thomas McGee, *Roger Corman: The Best of the Cheap Acts* (1988)

Corri, Adrienne (b. 1930)

British actress. With her archly refined looks and red hair, Corri was a useful asset in home-grown thrillers from the 50s onwards. She is impressive as the pretty **heroine** of *The Tell-Tale Heart* (1960), but really excels at more unconventional roles: splendidly chilling as the 'Gypsy Woman' in *Vampire Circus* (1971), and saving *Madhouse* (1972) from total disaster. Famously raped in *A Clockwork Orange* (1971). MA

Devil Girl From Mars/1954 * *Corridors of Blood*/1958 * *The Hellfire Club*/*The Anatomist*/ 1961 * *Bunny Lake Is Missing*/*A Study in Terror*/1965

TV: *One Step Beyond*: 'The Confession'/1961 * *Danger Man*: 'The Ubiquitous Mr. Lovegrove'/ 1965 * *Adam Adamant Lives!*: 'The Sweet Smell of Disaster'/1966 * *Journey to the Unkown*: 'The New People'/1968 * *Randall and Hopkirk (Deceased)*: 'All Work, No Play'/ 1969 * *Doctor Who*: 'Leisure Hive'/1980 * *The Demon Lover*/1986

Coscarelli, Don (b. 1952)

Libyan-born American writer, director. Orphaned Mike and balding ice-cream vendor Reggie battle chrome spheres, shrunken revenants and the lowering Tall Man (Angus **Scrimm**) in Coscarelli's sepulchral, consistently eccentric *Phantasm* series. Amazingly, *Phantasm* (1979) was the youngster's third feature; he made *Phantasm II* (1988) for Universal following career disappointments *The Beastmaster* (1982) and *Survival Quest* (1987). *Phantasm III* (1994) is, like the improvisational first, independently produced. Coscarelli hints at his interests in *Kenny & Co.* (1976), a Halloween **comedy**. DP

Costello, Lou * See: **Abbott, Bud** and **Costello, Lou**

Coulouris, George (1903–89)

British actor. After his debut in *Citizen Kane* (1941), seen in sinister or bumbling roles. An extravagant **mad scientist** in *Man Without a Body* (1957) and *Womaneater* (1957).

The Master Race/1944 * *The Verdict*/1946 * *Bluebeard's Ten Honeymoons*/1960 * *The Skull*/ 1965 * *The Assassination Bureau, Limited*/1969 * *Blood From the Mummy's Tomb*/*Tower of Evil*/ 1971 * *The Suicide Club*/1973 * *The Final Program*/*L'antecristo* [*The Antichrist*]/1974

TV: *Virus X*/1962 * *Doctor Who*: 'The Keys of Marinus'/1964 * *The Prisoner*: 'Checkmate'/ 1968 * *The Mind Beyond*: 'The Daedalus Equations'/1976

Court, Hazel (b. 1926)

British actress. Panoramic cleavage and regal looks cemented Court's position as one of the leading ladies of costume horror. Best appreciated for her work at **Hammer** and

Adrienne Corri, *Madhouse*

Arthur Crabtree

AIP, she also lent her talents to contemporary offerings like *Doctor Blood's Coffin* (1961). Though a convincing traditional **heroine** in *The Curse of Frankenstein* (1957), Court's finest hour is as the Devil worshipping noblewoman in **Corman**'s *The Masque of the Red Death* (1964), a logical extension of her scheming beauties in *The Premature Burial* (1962) and *The Raven* (1963). MA

Ghost Ship/1952 * *Devil Girl From Mars*/1954 * *The Man Who Could Cheat Death*/1959 * *The Final Conflict*/1981

TV: *Alfred Hitchcock Presents*: 'The Crocodile Case'/1958; 'The Avon Emeralds'/'Arthur'/1959; 'The Pearl Necklace'/1961 * *Thriller*: 'The Terror in Teakwood'/1961 * *The Twilight Zone*: 'The Fear'/1964 * *Wild Wild West*: 'The Night of the Returning Dead'/1966

Cox, Brian (b. 1946)
Scots actor. A powerful stage presence and increasingly frequent supporting player (*Rob Roy*, 1995; *Braveheart*, 1995), Cox won a place in the horror pantheon by originating the role of 'Hannibal Lektor' in *Manhunter* (1986), from Thomas **Harris**'s novel *Red Dragon* (1981). Cox's reading is subtler, wittier and creepier ('Would you give me your home phone number?') than Anthony **Hopkins**' 'Hannibal Lecter' in *The Silence of the Lambs* (1991).

TV: *Hammer House of Horror*: 'The Silent Scream'/1980 * *The Cloning of Joanna May*/1991

Cozzi, Luigi (b. 1947)
Italian director, writer. A prime exponent of trashily enjoyable sci-fi (*Scontri stellari oltre la terza dimensione*/*Starcrash*, 1978), Cozzi has also been active in the **Argento** camp, working as writer, production assistant and effects man on *Il gatto a nove code* (*The Cat O'Nine Tails*, 1970), *Quattro mosche di velluto grigio* (*Four Flies on Grey Velvet*, 1971), *Le cinque giornate* (1973), *Phenomena* (1985), *Due occhi diabolici* (*Two Evil Eyes*, 1989) and *La sindrome di Stendhal* (*The Stendhal Syndrome*, 1995). After the underground *Il tunnel sotto il mondo* (1969) and the TV **giallo** *Il vicino di casa* (1973), he directed the excellent *L'assassino è costretto ad uccidere ancora* (*The Dark is Death's Friend*, 1975) and the entertaining *Contamination* (1979). He returned to horror with the frenetically awful *Il violino che uccide* (*Paganini Horror*, 1988) and outrageously attempted to round off Argento's 'Three Mothers' trilogy in *Il gatto nero* (*Edgar Allan Poe's The Black Cat*, 1990). MA

Shark: rosso nell'oceano [*Devouring Waves*] (w)/1984 * *Nosferatu a Venezia* [*Vampire in Venice*] (fx/2nd unit d)/1988 * *Dario Argento's World of Horror 2*/1991

TV: *La porta sul buio*: 'Il testimone oculare' (w)/1972 * *Turno di notte*/'L'impronta dell'assassino'/'Ciak si muore'/'Sposari e un Stradivari'/'Giallo natale'/''Via delle streghe'/'Il taxi fantasma'/1987

Crabtree, Arthur (1900–75)
British director. His career is book-ended by delirium: his first film, after work as a cinematographer, is *Madonna of the Seven Moons* (1944), a lunatic Gainsborough period psycho-drama with Phyllis Calvert; his last are *Fiend Without a Face* (1958), with flying killer **brains**, and *Horrors of the Black Museum* (1959), with Michael **Gough** and eye-gouging binoculars.

Crain, William (b. 1943)
Black American director. Blaxploitation pioneer; more fustian than funky.

Blacula/1972 * *Dr. Black Mr. Hyde*/1976

Crampton, Barbara (b. 1962)
American actress. Receives slobbery cunnilingus from a severed **head** in *Re-Animator* (1985).

Body Double/1984 * *From Beyond*/*Chopping Mall*/1986 * *Pulse Pounders* (unfinished)/1988 * *Puppet Master*/1989 * *Trancers II*/1990 * *Castle Freak*/1995

Craven, Wes (b. 1949)
American director, writer, producer. The man who created Freddy Kreuger has mixed feelings about his success in horror, but never been able to shake his reputation as a shockmeister. Craven has a master's from John's Hopkins and once taught humanities at college level: intelligent and deeply serious, his analytical thoughtfulness is unusual among American genre film-makers and has led to accusations of self-importance; it has also probably contributed to his evident dissatisfaction with his career.

Though championed as a director whose work is highly original and distinguished by complex thematic underpinnings, his reputation rests on a handful of films: *Last House on the Left* (1972), *The Hills Have Eyes* (1977) and **A Nightmare on Elm Street** (1984), and to a lesser degree *The Serpent and the Rainbow* (1988) and *The People Under the Stairs* (1991). *Deadly Blessing* (1981), **Swamp Thing** (1982), *The Hills Have Eyes II* (1985), in which everyone has a flashback, including the dog, *Deadly Friend* (1986) and *Shocker* (1989) do not really lend themselves to substantive analysis.

He began in movies as an editor on low-budget features: *You've Got to Walk It Like You Talk It or You'll Lose That Beat* (1971), *It Happened in Hollywood* (1972) and Sean S. **Cunningham**'s softcore *Together* (1972). Cunningham produced Craven's directing debut, the exploitation landmark *Last House on the Left*, a crudely brutal revenge film with a conspicuous subtext of class hostility, loosely inspired by **Bergman**'s *Jungfrukällan*

Wes Craven, *Wes Craven's New Nightmare*

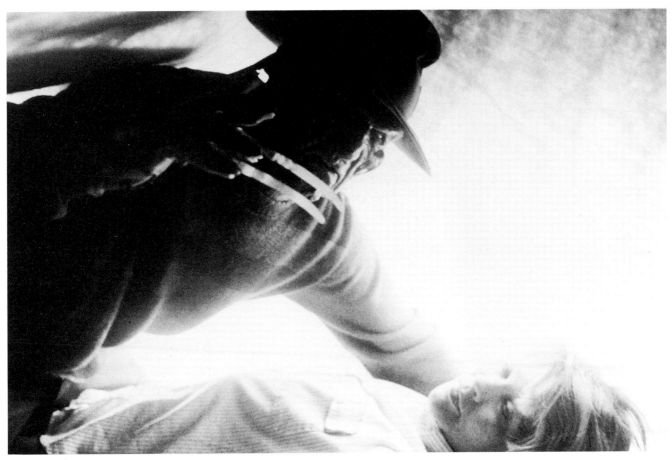

Robert Englund, Amanda Wyss, Wes Craven's *A Nightmare on Elm Street*

(*The Virgin Spring*, 1959). Twenty-five years later, *Last House* still packs a visceral wallop, and its advertising tag line ('Keep telling yourself it's only a movie . . .') has become a minor legend. Craven and Cunningham claim *Last House* had a profound effect on their lives and careers, making them social pariahs and stereotyping them as purveyors of viciously violent, second-rate films (Craven did some uncredited editing on *Friday the 13th*, 1980). After several frustrating years of trying to get other projects produced (the jungle thriller *Marimba* became Ruggero **Deodato**'s *Inferno in diretta*, 1985), Craven made the caustic *The Hills Have Eyes*, another shocker with a strong socio-political subtext. '[It] was hard making another violent film,' he says, 'because I was aware, even then, that I was going to be a horror/**violence** director and not some other kind. Not just a director. And that's proved to be true.'

Since the late 70s, Craven has switched back and forth between theatrical features and TV movies. *A Nightmare on Elm Street*, deservedly praised as an original and truly frightening film, launched one of the most profitable horror franchises: New Line Cinema benefited far more than Craven himself, and he feuded bitterly with the studio for years. With the exception of co-writing *A Nightmare on Elm Street 3: Dream Warriors* (1987), Craven had little to do with the *Elm Street* series for the better part of a decade. The films quickly degenerated into self-parody – Craven himself described the once fearsome Freddy as the 'Henny Youngman of horror' – until he returned with his name in the title for its seventh instalment, the **recursive** *Wes Craven's New Nightmare* (1994). Craven wrote, directed, co-produced and played himself, addressing the *Elm Street* phenomenon with rigour and wit.

Having directed episodes of the new **Twilight Zone**, Craven created his own anthology show, *Nightmare Cafe* (1992), featuring *Elm Street*'s Robert **Englund**, which only lasted six episodes. Craven's other TV credits include the light fantasy series *The People Next Door* (1989), which he executive produced, and the 'dark soap' pilot *Laurel Canyon* (1993), which he created. Though

Craven, like many other horror film-makers, often claims he would really like to do **comedy**, his best work has been bitterly dark and pessimistic. *Vampire in Brooklyn* (1995), an attempt at the style perfected by John **Landis** for *An American Werewolf in London* (1981), is an abject failure: gross, mean-spirited and not very funny. Craven's son Jonathan – whose balloon is burst by David **Hess** in *Last House* – co-wrote and co-produced *Mind Ripper* (1995), on which Wes has a 'presents' credit. MM

The Fear (a)/1995 * *Scream*/1996

TV: *Stranger in Our House*/1978 * *Invitation to Hell*/1984 * *Chiller*/1984 * *The Twilight Zone*: 'Shatterday'/'A Little Peace and Quiet'/ 'Wordplay'/'Chameleon'/'Children's Zoo' (a)/'Dealer's Choice'/'Her Pilgrim Soul'/ 1985; 'The Road Less Traveled'/1986 * *Night Visions*/1990

Crawford, Joan [Lucille LaSoeur, Lucile Le Sueur, Billie Cassin] (1904–77)
Archetypal Hollywood movie star. She began

her career as a showgirl before entering the movies as an extra in 1925. Two years later she was co-starring with Lon **Chaney Sr** in *The Unknown* (1927). After thirty years as a top box-office attraction, her declining career received a boost with the **ageing actress** psycho-thriller *What Ever Happened to Baby Jane?* (1962). sj

Strange Cargo/1940 * *Possessed*/1947 * *Strait-Jacket*/1964 * *I Saw What You Did*/1965 * *Berserk!*/1967 * *Trog*/1970

TV: *Night Gallery*/*Journey to the Unknown*/ 1969 * *The Sixth Sense*: 'Dear Joan, We're Going to Scare You to Death'/1972

Cregar, Laird [Samuel Laird Cregar] (1913–44)

Overweight American character actor. A suave **Devil** in *Heaven Can Wait* (1943), ideally cast as tortured **psychopaths** in *The Lodger* (1944), as **Jack the Ripper**, and *Hangover Square* (1945). Neurotically haunted by his **homosexuality**, his promising career was cut tragically short when he dieted himself to death. sj

Criticism

Horror has amassed a vast body of self-examination while being all but ignored by the critical world outside. The 'insider', often without adequate knowledge of wider fields of literature and film, is too easily pleased, while the 'outsider' sees only the generic label and moves quickly on to something else. As early as 1711, Joseph Addison's commentaries on supernatural horror in fiction and drama were appearing in *The Spectator*. Even then, a major argument was about the merits of subtlety and 'the higher reaches of terror' versus gratuitous **violence** and blood-letting. Addison was very much in favour of the former.

The title of Anna Letitia Barbault's essay 'On the Pleasure Derived From Objects of Terror' (1773) is self-explanatory. Nathan Drake, writing in 1798, found much to praise in the **gothic novel** but felt it would soon turn to parody and die out. Book-length studies began to appear during the first half of the 20th century, notably H.P. **Lovecraft**'s *Supernatural Horror in Literature* (1927) and Montague Summers's *The Gothic Quest* (1938). Dorothy Scarborough's *The Supernatural in Modern English Fiction* (1917) explores folklore in detail but fails to mention many important writers. Edmund Wilson, dean of literary critics, launched scathing attacks on the genre, 'A Treatise on

Joan Crawford, *What Ever Happened to Baby Jane?*

the Tales of Horror' and 'Tales of the Marvellous and the Ridiculous', collected in *Classics and Commercials* (1951).

The form survived to be investigated from a variety of viewpoints: Mario Praz's *La carne, la morte e il diavolo nella letteratura romantica* (*The Romantic Agony*, 1930) and Devendra P. Varma's *The Gothique Flame* (1957) rekindled interest in the gothic. Peter Penzoldt's *Supernatural in Fiction* (1952) uses the psychoanalytical approach, David Punter's *Literature of Terror* (1980) the Marxist. Julia Briggs's *Night Visitors* (1977) sets out to prove the **ghost story** dead, while Jack Sullivan argues in *Elegant Nightmares* (1978) that it is very much alive. The increased popularity of horror in the 70s brought forth a number of books, mostly coffee-table overviews like Les Daniels's *Living in Fear* (1975) and Sullivan's *Penguin Encyclopedia of Horror and the Supernatural* (1988). Stephen **King**'s *Danse Macabre* (1981) is a useful popular study, as is **Jones** and Newman's *Horror: 100 Best Books* (1988). By far the best critical writing on the genre is Douglas E. Winter's *Shadowings* (1983), expanded from a series of fanzine essays. It is in the magazines, fan and professional, that some of the best critical writing can be found. The British *Shadows*, edited by David Sutton, established a tradition in the 60s, followed by *Whispers*, *Fantasy Newsletter*, *Interzone* and especially the learned *Necrofile*, edited by Stefan Dziemianowicz, S.T. Joshi and Michael A. Morrison.

Just as early studies of horror fiction tend to concentrate on the safer, more respectable gothic era, so the earliest critical works on

horror films look to **expressionist** silent cinema, rendered more palatable by historic distance. Siegfried Kracauer's *From Caligari to Hitler* (1947) is 'A Psychological History of the German Film', and of necessity gives much space to horrific territory is covered in tighter focus by Lotte Eisner's *L'écran demoniaque* (*The Haunted Screen*, 1952). The first general overview of horror films was in French, *Le fantastique au cinéma* (1958) by Michael Laclos, a screen-shaped collection of (then) rare stills with introductory essay and extended picture captions.

The many magazines that proliferated in the wake of **Famous Monsters** were informative (some of the time) but almost wholly uncritical until, again in France, **Midi-Minuit Fantastique** began publishing in 1961, applying the *auteur* theory to the likes of **Corman**, **Fisher** and **Bava**. The American *Castle of Frankenstein*, initially a *Famous Monsters* clone, began running critical reviews and many fanzines soon followed. Even so, a book-length work on the subject did not appear in English until Carlos **Clarens**'s *Illustrated History of the Horror Film* (1967). Revised the following year as *Horror Movies*, this makes more than a few sweeping statements but offers little in the way of informed comment. However, an endless parade of 'Histories of the Horror Film' have appeared since, illustrated and otherwise, notably Ivan Butler's *The Horror Film* (1967; revised as *Horrror in the Cinema*, 1970) and Denis Gifford's *A Pictorial History of Horror Movies* (1973). Often essentially checklists, the tone of many of these books is of nostalgia: older films good, newer ones bad. There are a few exceptions: Phil Hardy's *The Aurum Encyclopedia of Horror* (1985; revised 1993) makes the best of an impossible job, taking the capsule comment format of John Stanley's *Creature Features Movie Guide* (1981; revised regularly) and Michael Weldon's *The Psychotronic Encyclopedia of Film* (1983) about as far as it can go. These are not just works of criticism, but also **reference books**.

Specialisation has also occurred: cultural (David J. **Skal**'s *The Monster Show*, 1993, David **Pirie**'s *A Heritage of Horror*, 1973); psychological (Charles Derry's *Dark Dreams*, 1977); and the reinvention of genre at specific points in time (Kim Newman's *Nightmare Movies*, 1984; revised 1988), as as well studies of individual studios, directors and films. Magazines, too, have diversified into different areas, typified by prozines like **Cinefantastique** and **Fangoria** and fanzines like *Sleazoid Express* and *Shock Xpress*.

Cronenberg, David

Following the *Famous Monsters* tradition, too much writing on horror film still relies on reportage rather than opinion; and, too often, a newer generation of film writers makes the same errors as the old, mistaking nostalgia for quality but moving the dates forward so that the 'classics' of the 30s and 40s are supplanted by those of the 50s and 60s. MW

Cronenberg, David (b. 1943)

Canadian director, writer, actor, producer. It is a misconception that Cronenberg's films display an attitude of disgust to the human body: anyone who can devise stories revolving around a parasite specially bred to take over the functions of diseased organs, a cable TV programmer with an organic VCR slot in his stomach, or a scientist who watches with ironic detachment as his ears and fingernails fall off, must surely be fascinated by the human body in every last one of its possible permutations. Cronenberg has said, 'I could conceive of a beauty contest where people could unzip themselves and show you the best spleen and the best-looking viscera.' He is one of the best advertisements the horror genre could have: working within it allows him to plunge without flinching into areas (death, decay, **disease**) where mainstream film-makers dare not tread. And he finds not just truth, but a terrible beauty in the inevitability of these things.

After studying biochemistry at Toronto University, Cronenberg switched to English literature, but ended up making two futuristic underground films, *Crimes of the Future* (1969) and *Stereo* (1969), which present in embryo many of the themes he develops in his later work: the father/scientist figure, telepathic mutation, faceless institutions, psychosexual disease. *Shivers* (1976) – also known as *They Came From Within* or *The Parasite Murders* – is about sexually transmitted sluglike parasites which turn the inhabitants of a luxury tower-block (not just young men and women, but, shockingly, old-age pensioners and children) into sex-crazed zombies. The title *They Came from Within* is a suitable description for the rest of his work, the 'threat' in his films coming not from the more usual horror movie maniacs or monsters, but from the mind itself, and from changes wrought on the human body by disease, decay and mutation.

In *Rabid* (1977), porno star Marilyn Chambers receives radical surgery after a motorbike accident and develops a phallic growth in her armpit which not only feeds on human **blood** but spreads a plague which turns half the inhabitants of Montreal into drooling psychopaths. In *The Brood* (1979), Cronenberg's version of *Kramer vs. Kramer* (1979), Oliver **Reed** runs a self-help therapy clinic which encourages its patients to vent their neuroses in physical form. Samantha Eggar, a patient involved in a bitter custody battle, takes it to extremes by giving birth to a pack of homicidal dwarves which dispatch anyone she considers a threat. It is tempting to read into this hints of the film-maker's own divorce and custody case, and *The Brood* remains one of his most discomforting movies. *Scanners* (1981), on

Stephen Lack, David Cronenberg's *Scanners*

the other hand, is his most upbeat offering, though it ends with the **hero** going up in flames after his eyeballs explode. Patrick McGoohan plays the father/scientist, whose responsibility for the distribution of an experimental pre-natal drug has resulted in his own sons developing telepathic powers. One (Michael **Ironside**) is now out of control; in the film's most famous set-piece, he uses his mental powers to blow up another telepath's **head**.

Cronenberg's work is prescient in its vision of the near future: *Videodrome* (1983) is remarkable in its anticipation of a world ruled by cable and satellite, and in its examination of the moral dilemmas which such a world would need to confront. Too much TV may lead to addiction and even brain tumours, but it also enables dead people to speak from beyond the grave. More than a decade after its release, *Videodrome*'s blend of reality and hallucination still looks daring. *The Dead Zone* (1983), adapted from Stephen **King**'s 1979 novel, is his most conventional movie: though it lacks the customary visceral effects, its bleak, snow-covered landscapes and haunting central performance from Christopher **Walken** as a schoolteacher cursed with second sight give it an overwhelming sense of melancholy which places it a long way from the mainstream.

With the big-budget remake of *The Fly* (1986), Cronenberg hit his stride, finally managing to reach a wide audience without compromising his personal vision. Scientist Seth Brundle (Jeff **Goldblum**) merges molecules with a fly during an experiment in the transportation of matter, and watches his own humanity fall away with parts of his body. Cronenberg seems much fonder of his

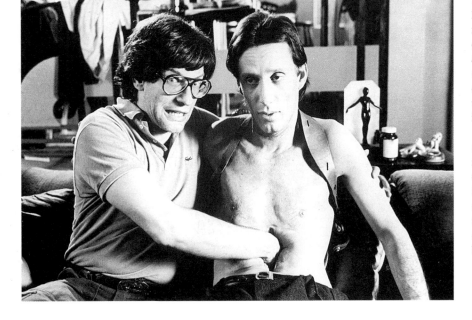

LEFT David Cronenberg, James Woods, on the set of *Videodrome*

characters than in the past and the touching relationship between Brundle and journalist Veronica Quaife (Geena Davis) makes this as much a tragic Hollywood love story with added gloopy effects, as a metaphor for disease or death. *Dead Ringers* (1988), with Jeremy Irons giving a *tour de force* double performance as twin gynaecologists, is in many ways a distillation of Cronenberg's work. Even sparer and more elegantly filmed than his previous work, set in the architectural spaces between cold concrete and studded with bold stylised touches such as the red surgical robes of the clinical staff, the story unfolds with the simplicity and inevitability of classical Greek tragedy. When one brother falls in love with an actress (Genevieve Bujold) who has a rare trifurcate womb, the twins' semi-telepathic relationship unravels, ending in disaster for them both.

Naked Lunch (1991) is a brave stab at William Burroughs' unfilmable novel, though it sorely misses the cracking narrative drive of Cronenberg's best work. After an ill-advised venture outside genre territory – an adaptation of the stage play *M. Butterfly* (1993) – Cronenberg returned to more congenial subject matter: *Crash*, adapted from the novel by J.G. Ballard, is an amalgam of deviant **sex** and fast cars – two of the film-maker's favourite subjects, though cars have so far cropped up only in his odd film out, the unabashed B-picture *Fast Company* (1979). As an actor, he has significant cameos in *Into the Night* (1985) and *To Die For* (1995) and plays the psycho analyst of *Nightbreed* (1989). He has minimal involvement with *The Fly II* (1989) and a *Scanners* cycle: *Scanners II: The New Order* (1991), *Scanners III: The Takeover* (1992), *Scanner Cop* (1993), *Scanner Cop II: Volkin's Revenge* (1995). AB

Transfer (s)/1966 * *From the Drain* (s)/1967

TV: *Programme X*: 'Secret Weapons'/1972 * *Peep Show*: 'The Victim'/'The Lie Chair'/1976 * *Teleplay*: 'The Italian Machine'/1976 * *Friday the 13th*: 'Faith Healer'/1988

Piers Handling, *The Shape of Rage: The Films of David Cronenberg* (1983); Wayne Drew, *BFI Dossier 21: David Cronenberg* (1984); Chris Rodley, *Cronenberg on Cronenberg* (1992)

Cross, Ben (b. 1948)
British actor. Known for *Chariots of Fire* (1981), Cross is a horror regular: **vampire** Barnabas in *Dark Shadows* (1991–2), a gloomy **Dracula** in *Nightlife* (1989).

The Unholy/1988 * *Paperhouse*/1989 * *Cold Sweat*/1993 * *Temptress*/1995 * *Hellfire/The House That Mary Bought*/1996

TV: *The Twilight Zone*: 'Devil's Alphabet'/1986 * *Ray Bradbury Theater*: 'The Concrete Mixer'/1992 * *Tales From the Crypt*: 'Seance'/1992

Crowley, Aleister [Edward] (1875–1947)
British magician, writer, mountaineer. Crowley's eccentric devotion to libertinism led him to leave the Hermetic Order of the Golden Dawn to found his own cult, the Argentum Astrum. He called his sexual form of Satanism 'magick' and imported the *I Ching* to Europe, but was perhaps most significantly a self-promoting charlatan, revelling in his reputation as 'the worst man in England'. Crowley's importance to horror is less as a writer than as the model for Satanist villains considerably less flamboyant and more powerful than he actually was. Crowley's bungled attempts to bring the **Devil**'s child into the world are allegorised in Somerset Maugham's *The Magician* (1908), Crowley's own *Moonchild* (1929), Dennis **Wheatley**'s *To the Devil a Daughter* (1953) and Ira **Levin**'s *Rosemary's Baby* (1967), in which he appears as 'Oliver Haddo', 'Simon Iff', 'Canon Copley-Syle' and 'Adrian Marcato'.

Other writers to base characters on Crowley include Dylan Thomas and John Davenport (*The Death of the King's Canary*, 1940), Anthony Powell (*A Dance to the Music of Time*, 1951–75) and Christopher Isherwood ('A Visit to Anselm Oakes', 1966), who use the names 'Hamish Corbie', 'Dr Trelawney' and 'Anselm Oakes'; even Ian Fleming, it is alleged, used elements of Crowley, emphasising espionage rather than magic, in creating the first James Bond villain, LeChiffre in *Casino Royale* (1953). Film Crowleys include Paul **Wegener** (*The Magician*, 1926), **Karloff** (*The Black Cat*, 1934), Niall MacGinnis (*Night of the Demon*, 1958), Charles **Gray** (*The Devil Rides Out*, 1967) and Curt Jurgens (*The Mephisto Waltz*, 1971). Disciple Kenneth **Anger** evokes Crowley in his 'Magick Lantern Cycle'.

John Symonds, *The Great Beast: The Magick and Life of Aleister Crowley* (1971); Colin Wilson, *Aleister Crowley: The Nature of the Beast* (1987)

Cthulhu Mythos
The major fictions of H.P. **Lovecraft** –

including 'The Call of Cthulhu' (1926), *The Case of Charles Dexter Ward* (1927), 'The Dunwich Horror' (1928), 'The Whisperer in Darkness' (1930), *At the Mountains of Madness* (1931), 'The Shadow Over Innsmouth' (1931) and 'The Shadow Out of Time' (1934–5) – share the premise that the Earth was once ruled by extra-terrestrial (or extra-dimensional) beings banished to make way for mankind. The Old Ones, remembered as gods by evil cults, constantly strive to re-establish their power.

Lovecraft, fond of borrowing suggestive bits from Ambrose **Bierce** or Robert Chambers, skilfully invents a pantheon of Old Ones (Nyarlathotep, Yog-Sothoth, and reinforces the (illusory) sense of an over-arching story connecting all his works with repeated references to locales like the Miskatonic University of Arkham and unholy books like 'the **Necronomicon** of the mad Arab Abdul al-Hazred'. With a larkishness overlooked by devotees, Lovecraft encouraged friends (Robert **Bloch**, Clark Ashton **Smith**, Robert E. Howard, Frank Belknap Long) to refer to his world in their works, paying them back by co-opting their universes. Typical is the tit-for-tat relationship of Bloch's 'The Shambler From the Stars' (1935) and Lovecraft's 'The Haunter of the Dark' (1935), in which the authors playfully murder each other.

Aleister Crowley

RIGHT Cthulhu Mythos, Artist: Dave Carson

Lovecraft intended philosophical, psychological and even social statements, but the train-spotting side of his personality was posthumously emphasised. August **Derleth**, his devoted promoter, made Lovecraft's loosely connected story cycle into a 'mythos' which was at once a marketing franchise and a secret history of horror fiction. Derleth elaborated Lovecraft fragments into novels and stories (*The Lurker at the Threshold*, 1945; *The Shuttered Room*, 1959), then produced new-minted stuff (*The Mask of Cthulhu*, 1958; *The Trail of Cthulhu*, 1962). With *Tales of the Cthulhu Mythos* (1969), Derleth opened the mythos to a new generation.

Among those to turn the mythos to their own ends were Ramsey **Campbell** (*Cold Print*, 1993), Colin Wilson (*The Mind Parasites*, 1967) and Brian **Lumley** (*The Burrowers Beneath*, 1974). Bloch's apocalyptic *Strange Aeons* (1978), in which the Old Ones triumph, was not enough to stem the flow. Even Stephen **King** wrote mythos tales ('Jerusalem's Lot', 1978). An enormous outpouring of fanzine-level material was encouraged by the success of a Cthulhu role-playing **game**. Many novels extrapolate (sometimes subtly) from Lovecraft: Graham **Masterton**'s *The Manitou* (1976), F. Paul **Wilson**'s *The Keep* (1981), Michael **McDowell**'s *Blackwater* (1982), T.E.D **Klein**'s *The Ceremonies* (1984), Umberto Eco's *Foucault's Pendulum* (1988), Whitley **Strieber**'s *The Forbidden Zone* (1993). The cream of the third- and fourth-generation mythos is in Campbell's *New Tales of the Cthulhu Mythos* (1980), Stephen **Jones**'s *Shadows Over Innsmouth* (1994) and Jim Turner's *Cthulhu 2000* (1995).

There are comparatively few Cthulhu movies, though Lovecraft adaptations (*The Haunted Palace*, 1963; *The Dunwich Horror*, 1969; *The Unnameable Returns*, 1992) usually mention the Great Old Ones or the *Necronomicon*. Original film contributions are limited to an odd *Night Gallery* episode ('Professor Peabody's Last Lecture', 1971) and the cable TV films *Cast a Deadly Spell* (1991) and *Witch Hunt* (1994), where private eye Philip Lovecraft (Fred Ward, Dennis Hopper) battles cultists in post-War Los Angeles. Nevertheless, the Mythos informs *The Last Wave* (1977), *Inferno* (1980), *L'aldilà* (*The Beyond*, 1980), *The Evil Dead* (1982), *Conan the Destroyer* (1984), *Ghostbusters* (1985), *Howard the Duck* (1986), *Urotsukudoji* (*Legend of the Overfiend*, 1989), *Twin Peaks Fire*

 # 88 of 200   *Dave Carson*

Walk With Me (1992), *Cthulhu Mansion* (1992), *Necronomicon* (1993) and *In the Mouth of Madness* (1994).

Lovecraft's premise that aliens once owned the Earth and are remembered as gods or devils, has been handled by many: Arthur C. Clarke (*Childhood's End*, 1950), Nigel **Kneale** (*Quatermass and the Pit*, 1959), Erich von Däniken (*Chariots of the Gods?*, 1969) and **Doctor Who** (*The Dæmons*, 1971; *Pyramids of Mars*, 1975; *The Curse of Fenric*, 1989). Currently, the Cthulhu Mythos, straddling horror and s-f, is not what Lovecraft intended, but has outgrown Derleth's craze for systemising chaos and remains an often fruitful if overworked area. Lin Carter, *Lovecraft: A Look Behind the Cthulhu Mythos* (1972)

Cunningham, Sean S. (b. 1941)

American producer, director. After working in the theatre, Cunningham broke into film by producing the quasi-documentary sex movies *The Art of Marriage* (1970) and *Together* (1971) and directing the **vampire porno** *The Case of the Full Moon Murders* (1973). He also produced the notorious *Last House on the Left* (1972), which launched the career of director Wes **Craven** and typed them both as vicious exploitation film-makers. After detouring into 'family' films (*Here Come the Tigers*, 1978), he sold **Friday the 13th** (1980), which he produced and directed, on the strength of the title and his *Last House* reputation: it spawned one of the most popular horror series of the 80s, though his involvement with the sequels was minimal.

He continues to direct occasionally, but more often produces. MM

Planeta ciega [*The People Who Own the Dark*]/ 1976 * *A Stranger is Watching* (d)/1981 * *The New Kids* (+d)/1985 * *House*/1986 * *House II: The Second Story*/*The Taste of Hemlock*/1987 * *DeepStar Six* (+d)/*The Horror Show* (*House III*)/ 1989 * *House IV*/1992 * *My Boyfriend's Back*/ *Jason Goes to Hell: The Final Friday*/1993

Curiel, Federico (1916–85)

Mexican director. The features *La maldición de Nostradamus*, *Nostradamus y el destructor de monstruos*, *Nostradamus, el genio de las tinieblas* and *La sangre de Nostradamus* (1959–60) and *El Enmascarado negro*, *Neutrón contra el Doctor Caronte*, *Los automatas de la muerte* (1959–60) repackage serials about the **vampire** Nostradamus (German **Robles**) and the **wrestler** Neutrón (Wolf **Ruvinskis**).

Santo contra el cerebro diabólico/*Santo contra el rey del crímen*/*Santo en hotel de la muerte*/1961 * *El fantasma de las nieves* (w)/1962 * *El sombra del murciélago*/*Arañas infernales*/*El empiro de Drácula*/1966 * *Las vampiras*/*Enigma de muerto*/1968 * *Santo en la venganza de las mujeres vampiro*/*Los canallas*/1969 * *Santo contra la mafia del vicio*/1970 * *Santo en misión suicida*/1971 * *Vuelven los campeones justicieros*/ *Santo contra los secuestradores*/1972 * *Santo en oro negro*/1974

Curtis, Dan (b. 1928)

American producer, director. Having seen the ratings of his gothic soap *Dark Shadows* (1966-71) soar thanks to a **vampire** character, Curtis produced mostly indifferent TV versions of horror classics. Written by Richard **Matheson** or William F. Nolan, the *Monsterpiece Theatre* films at least afford Jack **Palance** respectable shots at **Jekyll and Hyde** or **Dracula**. His contemporary TV movies are more distinctive, especially **The Night Stalker** (1971) and *The Night Strangler* (1972), which mix classic themes with 70s cynicism. The Matheson anthology *Trilogy of Terror* (1975) climaxes with a killer fetish sequence that represents Curtis's best work as a director. His theatrical showing is limited to *Dark Shadows* spin-offs and the patchy *Burnt Offerings* (1976). After *The Winds of War* (1983), Curtis revived *Dark Shadows* (1990) without matching its earlier success.

House of Dark Shadows/1970 * *Night of Dark Shadows*/1971

TV: *The Strange Case of Dr. Jekyll and Mr. Hyde*/ 1968 * *The Norliss Tapes*/*The Picture of Dorian*

Michael Curtiz

*Gray/Dracula/Frankenstein/1973 * The Turn of the Screw/Scream of the Wolf/1974 * Curse of the Black Widow/Dead of Night/1977 * Trilogy of Terror 2/1996*

Curtis, Jamie Lee (b. 1958)

American actress; daughter of Janet **Leigh** and Tony Curtis. Notably imperilled as Laurie Strode in **Halloween** (1978), Curtis was briefly a genre fixture as the screaming but resourceful **heroine**. She returned to the **psycho** field as a cop in *Blue Steel* (1990) and the mad mommy of *Mother's Boys* (1994).

*The Fog/Prom Night/Terror Train/1980 * Road Games/Halloween II/1982 * Coming Soon/1984*

Curtiz, Michael [Miháli Kertész] (1888–1962)

Hungarian director. Remembered for *The Adventures of Robin Hood* (1938), *Casablanca* (1943) and *Mildred Pierce* (1945), Curtiz contributed importantly to horror. *Doctor X* (1932) and *Mystery of the Wax Museum* (1933) set deformed fiends in wisecracking urban Warner Bros. locales, offering an American alternative to Universal's European approach. His psycho *guignols* offer demented roles to Edward G. Robinson (*The Sea Wolf*, 1941) or Claude **Rains** (*The Unsuspected*, 1947).

*Alraune/1919 * The Mad Genius/1931 * The Walking Dead/1935*

Cushing, Peter (1913–94)

British actor. Off-screen, he had the mild manners of an antiquarian bookseller, but the lean and skeletal style he imposed on the new kind of horror **Hammer** Films represented in the 50s was imperious and arrogant.

Cushing was a disciplined thespian, making Hollywood films in the late 30s (*The Man in the Iron Mask*, 1939, for James **Whale**) and appeared in Olivier's *Hamlet* (1948), then becoming a British TV Actor of the Year for his Winston Smith in Nigel **Kneale**'s BBC *1984* (1955). Cushing and Christopher **Lee** formed The Unholy Two, principal residents of the House of Horror created by Hammer at Bray studios, putting new blood into old vaults with *The Curse of Frankenstein* (1957). After playing life-tampering Baron Victor **Frankenstein**, he was typecast as an aloof and radical scientist meddling with unknown forces. Compared with Colin **Clive**'s Frankenstein (all camp hysteria and maniacal laughter), Cushing is cool and cultured. If the s-f films of the 50s are a paranoid reaction to the cold war, Cushing's wayward geniuses can be read as a metaphor for the real scientists who created the atomic bomb. After *Curse*, there was a brand-old monster to be put together by his baron for *The Revenge of Frankenstein* (1958) and six years later a semi-human encased in ice re-animated for *The Evil of Frankenstein* (1964). He came, topically, to gender-bending with *Frankenstein Created Woman* (1967), in which a drowning girl is revived with the heart of a guillotined murderer. In *Frankenstein Must Be Destroyed* (1969) and *Frankenstein and the Monster from Hell* (1973), he refines the role, exposing heartlessness beneath the dedication.

After *The Curse of Frankenstein*, Cushing was as prematurely coffined in that kind of casting as any Edgar Allan **Poe** neurosis. He no longer had the luxury of choice and knew he had sacrificed a career's fulfilment for the expediency of a contract. 'If I made *Hamlet* now, people would expect a horror story,' he said. Cushing had become the definitive Frankenstein and, in so doing, a universally acclaimed horror star. In yet another Hammer reworking of old glories, he switched tracks from bad to good with ***Dracula*** (1958) in which he is **Van Helsing**, the ghost-buster trying to save the Harkers from the inevitable corruption of the vampire Count (Lee). What became known as English gothic cinema was well under way with this Dracula, a vividly sensual count, as Freud and Krafft-Ebbing were trawled to scoop up psychological reasons to match supernatural causes. Social criticism about the explicit sex-and-death themes caused queues to form.

Though shackled to horrific roles, he shook his chains vigorously within the confines of this imprisonment. He ventures into more orthodox menace as a superb **Sherlock Holmes** in *Hound of the Baskervilles* (1959), is an eerily prophetic sage in *Dr. Terror's House of Horrors* (1964), makes a singularly dotty **Doctor Who** in *Dr. Who and the Daleks* (1965) and *Daleks' Invasion Earth 2150 AD* (1966) and pops up gauntly in *Star Wars* (1977) and *Biggles* (1986). Mostly, he appears in films in which the sensational expectations of the titles (*The Satanic Rites of Dracula*, 1973; *The Legend of the 7 Golden Vampires*, 1973) are never quite achieved by the content. Only Cushing was worth the watching as the Old Dark House of Hammer became the semi-detached villas of a more realistic British cinema.

RIGHT Peter Cushing, *Dracula* (1958)

Cushing said his career had been one of fame and futility. 'I suppose I'm really only a footnote to the kind of stage acting to which I once aspired. But I think that Baron Frankenstein – for which I know I'll be remembered – was a worthwhile creation. It shows how human beings can topple over the top of ambition when they try to play God. That's a lesson we should all learn.' A benign presence away from his horror films, he seemed to have to pull himself inside out to expose the chill cruelty of the many characters that he played. It is Cushing's achievement that he imbued that horror with a cold grace: in that world of colour, he was always frighteningly grey eminence. TH

The Abominable Snowman/1957 * *The Mummy*/ 1959 * *The Brides of Dracula*/1960 * *The Flesh and the Fiends*/1961 * *Captain Clegg*/1962 * *The Gorgon*/1964 * *She*/1965 * *Island of Terror*/ *The Skull*/1966 * *The Blood Beast Terror*/*Night of the Big Heat*/*Torture Garden*/1967 * *Corruption*/1968 * *Scream and Scream Again*/ 1969 * *The House That Dripped Blood*/*The Vampire Lovers*/*One More Time*/*I, Monster*/ *Incense for the Damned*/1970 * *Twins of Evil*/ 1971 * *Dracula A.D. 1972*/*Dr. Phibes Rises Again*/*Nothing But the Night*/*Tales From the Crypt*/*The Creeping Flesh*/*Asylum*/*Fear in the Night*/1972 * *From Beyond the Grave*/*The Beast Must Die*/*Pánico en el Transiberiano* [*Horror Express*]/—*And Now the Screaming Starts!*/ *Madhouse*/1974 * *The Ghoul*/*Legend of the Werewolf*/*Tendre Dracula*/1975 * *The Devil's Men*/1976 * *Shock Waves*/*The Uncanny*/1977 * *House of the Long Shadows*/1983

TV: *The Creature*/1955 * *Gaslight*/1957 * *The Cases of Sherlock Holmes*/1967–8 * *The Avengers*: 'Return of the Cybernauts'/1968 * *Orson Welles' Great Mysteries*: 'La Grande Bretèche'/1973 * *The New Avengers*: 'The Eagle's Nest'/1978 * *Hammer House of Horror*: 'The Silent Scream'/1980 * *Tales of the Unexpected*: 'The Vorpal Blade'/1983 * *The Masks of Death*/1984

Gary Parfitt, *The Films of Peter Cushing* (1975); Peter Cushing, *Peter Cushing: An Autobiography* (1986), *Past Forgetting: Memoirs of the Hammer Years* (1988); Deborah Del Vecchio, Tom Johnson, *Peter Cushing: The Gentle Man of Horror and His 91 Films* (1992); Mark A. Miller, *Christopher Lee and Peter Cushing and Horror Cinema* (1995)

LEFT Peter Cushing, *Frankenstein Must Be Destroyed*

Dahl, Roald (1916–90)

British writer. Though known for children's books (*Charlie and the Chocolate Factory*, 1964; *The BFG*, 1982), Dahl's cynical, sinister short stories, collected in *Someone Like You* (1953) and *Kiss Kiss* (1960), have been rich pickings for book, TV and **radio** horror anthologies. A mainstay of **Alfred Hitchcock Presents** (1955-63), Dahl presented **Way Out** (1961) and **Roald Dahl's Tales of the Unexpected** (1979–80). A ruthless touch shows in screenplays: *You Only Live Twice* (1967), *The Night Digger* (1971).

The Witches (st)/1990 * *James and the Giant Peach* (st)/*Matilda* (st)/1996

TV: *Alfred Hitchcock Presents*: 'Lamb to the Slaughter'/'A Dip in the Pool' (st)/'Poison' (st)/1958; 'Man From the South' (st)/'Mrs. Bixby and the Colonel's Coat' (st)/1960; 'The Landlady' (st)/1961 * *Suspicion*: 'The Way Up to Heaven' (st)/1958 * *Way Out*: 'William and Mary' (st)/1961 * *Late Night Horror*: 'William and Mary' (st)/1968 * *Tales of the Unexpected*: 'The Surgeon' (st)/1988 * *Roald Dahl's Little Red Riding Hood* (st)/1995 Jeremy Treglow, *Roald Dahl* (1994)

Daleks * See: *Doctor Who*

D'Amato, Joe * See: **Massaccesi, Aristide**

Daniell, Henry (1894–1963)

Fussy British actor, an urbane Hollywood villain during the 30s and 40s. Best as 'Toddy' MacFarlane, the doctor dominated by **Karloff** in *The Body Snatcher* (1945). SJ

The Thirteenth Chair/1937 * *Castle in the Desert*/1941 * *Sherlock Holmes and the Voice of Terror*/1942 * *Sherlock Holmes in Washington*/1943 * *The Woman in Green*/1945 * *The Four Skulls of Jonathan Drake*/1959

ABOVE Roald Dahl

BELOW Roald Dahl: Anjelica Huston, *The Witches*

D

D'Agostino, Albert S. (1893–1970)

American art director. Second fiddle to Charles D. **Hall** at Universal in the 30s, he did remarkable work with **Lewton** at RKO in the 40s, often redressing his sets from *The Magnificent Ambersons* (1942). More inclined to stylisation than gothic clutter, he carried the look of his horrors into *Murder, My Sweet* (1945), *The Stranger* (1946), *Notorious* (1946) and *They Live By Night* (1949).

The Man Who Reclaimed His Head/1934 * *The Mystery of Edwin Drood*/*The WereWolf of London*/*The Raven*/1935 * *The Invisible Ray*/*Dracula's Daughter*/1936 * *Stranger on the Third Floor*/1940 * *Cat People*/1942 * *I Walked With a Zombie*/*The Leopard Man*/*The Seventh Victim*/*The Ghost Ship*/*Gildersleeve's Ghost*/*Zombies on Broadway*/1943 * *Curse of the Cat People*/1944 * *A Game of Death*/*The Body Snatcher*/*Isle of the Dead*/1945 * *The Spiral Staircase*/*Bedlam*/*Genius at Work*/1946 * *Dick Tracy Meets Gruesome*/*Experiment Perilous*/1948 * *The Thing*/*The Whip Hand*/1951

Dagover, Lil [Marie Liletts] (1897–1980)

Dutch actress. The original white-night-gowned **heroine**, abducted in **Das Cabinet des Dr. Caligari** (1919).

Die Spinnen [*The Spiders*]/*Spiritismus*/1919 * *Das Medium*/*Der Müde Tod* [*Destiny*]/1920 * *Dr. Mabuse der Spieler*/*Phantom*/1922 * *Zur Chronik von Grieshuus*/1925

Henry Daniell, *The Woman in Green*

TV: *Lights Out*: 'Of Time and Third Avenue'/1951; 'The Perfect Servant'/1952 * *Thriller*: 'The Cheaters'/1960; 'Well of Doom'/ 'Prisoner in the Mirror'/'The Grim Reaper'/ 'God Grante That She Lye Stille'/1961

Daninsky, Waldemar * See: Naschy, Paul; Werewolves

Dante, Joe (b. 1947)

American director, writer, editor, critic. 'I always thought that if I could be as good a director as Jack Arnold, if I could have that kind of career, that I would be very happy.' Born too late for a career like Arnold's, Dante has done his best. A lifelong movie buff, TV addict and comics fan, he published articles in **Famous Monsters of Filmland** and *Castle of Frankenstein* while still in his early teens, and reviewed movies for *Film Bulletin* from 1968 to 1974. He studied to be a cartoonist and made his first foray into movie-making (of a sort) with the *All-Night-Once-in-a-Lifetime-Atomic-Movie-Orgy* (1975), a seven-hour compilation of movie and TV excerpts that played to an audience of fellow students.

His movie career began in earnest in the trailer department at Roger **Corman**'s New World Pictures, where he learned the tenets of exploitation trailer cutting: don't show too much of a bad movie, and 'almost anything makes a great cut to an exploding heli-copter'. He did uncredited editing on several Corman releases, including *I Never Promised You a Rose Garden* (1977), *Fast Charlie, the*

Moonbeam Rider (1978) and *Screamers* (1981) – an Americanised recut of *L'isola degli uomini pesce* (*Island of the Mutations*, 1978), for which he directed additional scenes as 'Dan T. Miller' – but not *The Arena* (1974), as is often reported. He and fellow wage slave Allan Arkush persuaded Corman to finace their *Hollywood Boulevard* (1976) by promising that it would be the cheapest movie ever made at New World. 'The great thing about working for Roger was that even the dumb-est person picked up a lot, because there were so many things that had to be done every day and nobody who knew how the hell to do them.'

In rapid succession, Dante directed *Piranha* (1978) – Steven **Spielberg** reported-ly considered it the best knock-off of *Jaws* (1975) – and the sardonic **werewolf** picture ***The Howling*** (1980). His first three pictures engendered sequels, none of which he directed. Spielberg produced Dante's ***Gremlins*** (1984), a monster hit that put him on the Hollywood map with a distinctive mix of satirical cruelty and Capra-esque whimsy. He had a run of commercial losers with the per-sonal and charming *Explorers* (1985), the anonymous *InnerSpace* (1987) and the biting *The 'Burbs* (1989), driving him to *MAD*-ish sequel, *Gremlins 2: The New Batch* (1990), itself a box-office disappointment. Since *Matinee* (1993), another skilful exercise in pointed genre nostalgia, he has worked in television, creating ***Eerie, Indiana*** (1991–2), and directing the TV movie *Runaway Daughters* (1994) and the pilot *The Osiris Chronicles* (1996). Dante is a vigorous sup-porter of film preservation and restoration. MM

The Slumber Party Massacre (a)/1982 * *Twilight Zone – The Movie* ('It's a Good Life')/1983 * *Amazon Women on the Moon* (co-d)/1987 * *Sleepwalkers* (a)/1992 * *The Silence of the Hams* (a)/1993

TV: *Twilight Zone*: 'The Shadow Man'/1985 * *Amazing Stories*: 'Boo'/'The Greibble'/1986 * *Eerie, Indiana*: 'Foreverware'/'The Retainer'/ 'The Losers'/'America's Scariest Home Video'/'Heart on a Chain'/'The Hole in the Head Gang'/1991

Danton, Ray (1931–92)

American actor, director. Hawk-faced star of Budd Boetticher's *The Rise and Fall of Legs Diamond* (1960), Danton slipped to Euro superspies (*New York appelle Super Dragon*, 1966) and off-Hollywood American psychos

(*The Centerfold Girls*, 1974). He directed hippie-flavoured horror pictures.

The Deathmaster/1972 * *Hannah, Queen of the Vampires*/1973 * *Psychic Killer*/1975

TV: *Night Gallery*: 'Miracle at Camafeo' (a)/ 1972 * *Tales of the Unexpected*: 'The Best Policy' (d)/1981; 'Turn of the Tide' (d)/1983; 'Bird of Prey' (d)/1984

Dark Shadows (US TV series, 1966–71)

Produced for ABC TV by Dan **Curtis**, *Dark Shadows* was the first daily, live gothic soap. Set in the present in the town of Collinsport, Maine, the series follows Victoria Winters (Alexandra Moltke), hired as a governess by the Collins family who live at 'Collinwood', a mansion presided over by matriarch Elizabeth Collins Stoddard (Joan Bennett). Earlier episodes stay with soap, but Curtis gradually introduced bizarre plots and char-acters, commencing with the arrival of **vam-pire** Barnabas Collins (Jonathan **Frid**). Recurring performers include David Selby (**werewolf** Quentin Collins), John Karlin (**minion** Willie Loomis), Lara Parker (sor-ceress Angelique), Grayson Hall (Dr Hoff-man, who tries to cure Barnabas) and Kathryn Leigh Scott (a waitress and her lookalike ancestress). 1,225 episodes were produced, hauling in **reincarnation** and **witchcraft**, plus elements of **'The Turn of the Screw'** (1898) and the Cthulhu **Mythos**.

Curtis produced and directed *House of Dark Shadows* (1970), a movie remake of the Barnabas storyline with most of the TV cast. *Night of Dark Shadows* (1971) is a new-mint-ed haunted house story which seems a dry run for Curtis's *Burnt Offerings* (1976). A popular fad, *Dark Shadows* spun off paper-backs by William Ross (under the pseudo-nym Marilyn Ross) and a comic book. Curtis

Joe Dante, *Twilight Zone – the Movie*

Jonathan Frid, David Selby, Joan Bennett, *Dark Shadows*

remade the series for prime-time (1990–1) with a new cast: Ben Cross (Barnabas), Lysette Anthony (Angelique), Barbara **Steele** (Dr Hoffman), Jean Simmons (Mrs Stoddard). The revival did not take and was cancelled on a cliffhanger. TM

Kathryn Leigh Scott, Jim Pierson, *The Dark Shadows Companion* (1990)

Darkroom (US TV series, 1982)

Introduced by James Coburn, this bland one-hour show, a 80s *Night Gallery*, presents two suspense-supernatural stories in each programme. Robert **Bloch** adapts three of his stories, while other tales come from Brian **Clemens**, Alan Brennert, Robert **McCammon**, Fredric **Brown** and Cornell **Woolrich**. Among the directors are Paul **Lynch** and Curtis **Harrington**. Cancelled after seven weeks. TM

Davis, Bette [Ruth Elizabeth Davis] (1908–89)

Hollywood star. Originally considered for the role of Elizabeth in *Frankenstein* (1931), she lost out to Mae Clarke. After three decades as a star, her flagging career (along with that of long-time rival Joan **Crawford**) was revitalised by an Oscar-nominated role in the **ageing actress** chiller *What Ever Happened to Baby Jane?* (1962). Her last role was a chain-smoking **witch** who transforms into Barbara Carrera (*Wicked Stepmother*, 1989). SJ

Hush . . . Hush, Sweet Charlotte/*Dead Ringer*/ 1964 * *The Nanny*/1965 * *The Anniversary*/

1968 * *Burnt Offerings*/1976 * *The Watcher in the Woods*/1980

TV: *Alfred Hitchcock Presents*: 'Out There – Darkness'/1959 * *Madame Sin*/1972 * *Scream Pretty Peggy*/1973 * *The Dark Secret of Harvest Home*/1978

Dawn, Vincent * See: Mattei, Bruno

Dawson, Anthony M. * See: Margheriti, Antonio

Day, Robert (b. 1922)

British director. A likeable journeyman, Day handled two lurid 1958 **Karloff**s (*The Haunted Strangler, Corridors of Blood*), **Hammer**'s *She* (1965) and several Tarzans (*Tarzan the Magnificent*, 1960).

First Man into Space/1959

TV: *The Avengers*: 'Never . . . Never Say Die'/ 1967; 'Mission: Highly Improbable'/'The Positive-Negative Man'/'Return of the Cybernauts'/The £50,000 Breakfast/1968 * *The Invaders*: 'The Peacemaker'/'The Miracle'/1968 * *Ritual of Evil*/1969 * *The Sixth Sense*: 'The Man Who Died at Three and Nine' (co-d)/'With This Ring, I Thee Kill'/

Bette Davis, *The Nanny*

'Shadow in the Well'/'With Affection, Jack the Ripper'/'The Eyes That Would Not Die'/ 1972

Deadman

Aerialist Boston Brand, allowed by goddess Rama Kushna to avenge his own murder, occasionally possesses people as he seeks justice. Created by artist Carmine Infantino (though Neal Adams soon took over) and writer Arnold Drake, Deadman made his debut in *Strange Adventures* (1967). A quirky addition to DC Comics' superhero stable, Deadman has had several series, and teamed up with **Batman** ('The Track of the Hook', *The Brave and the Bold*, 1968) and **Swamp Thing** ('Down Amongst the Dead Men', *Swamp Thing*, 1985). Writer Mike Baron and artist Kelley Jones develop an especially agonised, skeletal Deadman in *Love After Death* (1989) and *Exorcism* (1992).

Dead of Night (UK TV series, 1972)

Produced by the BBC. Seven stand-alone plays with supernatural themes. Its strongest entry is the first, writer-director Don Taylor's extremely frightening, socially relevant **ghost story** 'The Exorcism', later a stage play. Other episodes offer phantom aeroplanes ('Return Flight'), a famous murderer ('Smith') and traditional ghosts ('A Woman Sobbing').

Deadman (DC Comics), Artist: Kelley Jones

De Angelis, Fabrizio (b. 1941)

Italian producer, director. Founder of Fulvia Films, De Angelis turned director with *Thunder* (1983) and specialises in action pictures, sometimes under the name Larry Ludman. His personal favourite among his productions is Lucio **Fulci**'s *Lo squartatore di New York* (*The New York Ripper*, 1982), heralded in the trades with 'Fulvia Film Proudly Announces "Cutting Up Women Was His Pleasure"'.

Sette scialli di seta gialla [*The Crimes of the Black Cat*] (production manager)/1972 * *Una magnum special per Tony Saitta* [*Blazing Magnum*] (production manager)/*Emanuelle perché . . . violenza alla donne?* [*Emanuelle in America*]/ 1976 * *Emanuelle e gli ultimi cannibali* [*Emanuelle and the Last Cannibals*]/1977 * *Zombi 2* [*Zombie Flesh Eaters*]/1979 * *Zombi holocaust*/1980 * *L'aldilà* [*The Beyond*]/*Quella villa accanto al cimitero* [*The House by the Cemetary*]/1981 * *Manhattan Baby* [*Possessed*]/ 1982 * *Quella villa in fondo al parco* [*Ratman*]/ 1983 * *7 Hyden Park* [*Formula for a Murder*]/1985 * *Killer Crocodile* (d)/*Paganini Horror*/1988 * *Killer Crocodile 2*/1989 * *Breakfast With Dracula: A Vampire in Miami* (d)/1993

De Carlo, Yvonne [Peggy Middleton] (b. 1922)

Canadian-born Hollywood leading lady. Star of Bs during the 40s and 50s, known as Lily Munster in the **situation comedy** *The Munsters* (1964–6). SJ

Munster, Go Home!/1966 * *The Power*/1967 * *Satan's Cheerleaders*/1976 * *House of Shadows*/ 1977 * *Nocturna, Granddaughter of Dracula*/ 1979 * *Silent Scream*/1980 * *Play Dead*/1981 * *Cellar Dweller*/*American Gothic*/1987 * *Mirror, Mirror*/1990

TV: *Lights Out*: 'Another Country'/1952 * *The Munsters' Revenge*/1981 * *Tales From the Crypt*: 'Death of Some Salesmen'/1994 * *Here Come the Munsters*/1995

DeCoteau, David (b. 1962)

American producer, director, formerly in hardcore (as 'David McCabe'), prolific in direct-to-video schlock (sometimes as 'Ellen Cabot'). His titles are often more entertaining than his films, but *Puppet Master III: Toulon's Revenge* (1992), which he directed, is a modest achievement. 'What I really want to do is black-and-white, gay art movies,' he claims.

Galaxy of Terror (assistant)/1981 * *Dreamaniac*

(d)/1986 * *Creepozoids* (d)/*Sorority Babes in the Slime Ball Bowl-a-Rama* (d)/*Nightmare Sisters*/ *Assault of the Killer Bimbos*/1987 * *Deadly Embrace*/*Murder Weapon*/1988 * *Ghost Writer*/ 1989 * *Ghoul School*/*Linnea Quigley's Horror Workout*/*Puppet Master II*/*Skinned Alive*/*Steel and Lace*/*Crash and Burn*/*Kingdom of the Vampire*/1990 * *Zombie Cop*/*Reanimator Academy*/1991 * *Shock Cinema, Volumes One– Four*/*Trancers 2*/*Nightmare Asylum*/*Edgar Allen Poe's Madhouse*/1992 * *Virgin Hunters*/1994 * *Blonde Heaven*/1996

J.R. Bookwalter, *B-Movies in the 90s and Beyond* (1992)

DeFelitta, Frank (b. 1921)

American director, writer. Author of the **reincarnation** novel *Audrey Rose* (1976, filmed 1977), DeFelitta writes potboilers (*Golgotha Falls*, 1984; *Funeral March of the Marionettes*, 1990) and directs programmers. Lightly likable.

Scissors/1991

TV: *The Two Worlds of Jennie Logan*/1979 * *Dark Night of the Scarecrow*/1981

Deformity

Characters with birth defects have a long and not very honourable history in horror, where physical appearance is too often a clue to character. Still, the most famous story of deformity, Victor Hugo's *Notre Dame de Paris* (1831), often filmed as **The Hunchback of Notre Dame**, treats its initially repulsive hero with sympathy. Hateful hunchback **minions** appear in *Frankenstein* (1931) and *House of Frankenstein* (1944) but are replaced by a kindly nurse in *House of Dracula* (1945), then parodied in *Young Frankenstein* (1974).

Tod **Browning**'s *Freaks* (1932) uses real **circus** performers, wins audience sympathy for them, then turns them into a horde of crawling assassins. Not a likeable film, but in its ambivalence perhaps preferable to the Hollywood treatment accorded Rondo **Hatton**, an actor whose features were distorted by acromegaly. Totally talentless, he is cast as a moronic murderer in vehicles from *The Pearl of Death* (1944) to *The Brute Man* (1946). Make-up artists supply the acromegaly in *The Monster Maker* (1944), *Tarantula* (1955) and *Doomwatch* (1972), while real freaks play misunderstood outcasts in *House of the Damned* (1963) and refugees from **Hell** in *The Sentinel* (1977).

Deformity as the outward evidence of homicidal mania is dramatised in *A Face in

Robert De Niro, *Angel Heart*

the Fog (1936), **It's Alive** (1973), sequels to **Friday the 13th** (1980), *The Funhouse* (1981), *Phenomena* (1985) and *Batman Returns* (1992). Such conditions receive more sympathy in *The Maze* (1953), *Ratboy* (1987) and *Nightbreed* (1990), while ugly siblings are evil siblings in *The Face at the Window* (1939), *Dark Intruder* (1965), *Sisters* (1973) and *Basket Case* (1981). LD

Jack Hunter, *Inside Teradome: An Illustrated History of Freak Film* (1995)

Dein, Edward (1910–84)

American writer, director. A B scenarist who had a minor hand in *Cat People* (1942) and *The Leopard Man* (1943), Dein turned director with the McCarthyist *Shack out on 101* (1955), *Curse of the Undead* (1959), a **vampire** Western, and *The Leech Woman* (1960).

Calling Dr. Death/1943 * *Jungle Woman/The Soul of a Monster*/1944 * *The Cat Creeps*/1946

Dekker, Fred (b. 1959)

American director. He followed the lively **alien-zombie** quickie *Night of the Creeps* (1986) with the charming Universal homage *The Monster Squad* (1987) but has subsequently managed only the dull *Robocop 3* (1994).

TV: *Tales From the Crypt*: 'And All Through the House' (w)/'Only Sin Deep' (w)/1989; 'The Thing From the Grave' (+w)/'Lower

Berth' (w)/1990; 'Split Personality (w)/1992

de Leon, Gerardo * see: **Leon**
de Maupassant, Guy * See: **Maupassant**

Demme, Jonathan (b. 1944)

American director. Few A-list talents can boast of an early career that includes producing biker (*Angels Hard as They Come*, 1970) and sex (*The Hot Box*, 1972) films for **Corman** and being fired from directing a British skinflick starring Graham Stark, *Secrets of a Door-to-Door Salesman* (1973). Demme touches on psychosis in *Caged Heat* (1974), with Barbara **Steele** as a crippled lesbian prison warden, *Last Embrace* (1979) and *Something Wild* (1986), but was identified more with the quirky roadside comedy of *Crazy Mama* (1975), *Citizens Band* (1977) and *Melvin and Howard* (1980) until the box-office, critical and Academy Award smash of *The Silence of the Lambs* (1991). Adapted from Thomas **Harris**'s novel, this pitting of FBI trainee Jodie Foster against **serial killer** 'Buffalo Bill', with imprisoned mad genius Hannibal Lecter (Anthony **Hopkins**) sniping from the sidelines, was a breakout horror hit, re-energising a tired **stalk-and-slash** sub-genre for the 90s.

The Incredible Melting Man (a)/1978

De Niro, Robert (b. 1943)

American actor. After work for Brian **De Palma** (*Greetings*, 1968) and Roger **Corman** (*Bloody Mama*, 1970), De Niro hooked up with Martin Scorsese and became accepted as the finest screen actor of his generation. He essays major horror characters: the **Devil** (*Angel Heart*, 1987), an archetypal **psychopath** (*Cape Fear*, 1991), the Monster (*Mary Shelley's Frankenstein*, 1994). Nevertheless, his most horrifying roles are disturbed minds for Scorsese: *Mean Streets* (1973), *Taxi Driver* (1976), *Raging Bull* (1980), *The King of Comedy* (1983), *GoodFellas* (1990).

Deodato, Ruggero (b. 1939)

Italian director, known for his brilliant yet savage *Cannibal holocaust* (1980). His debut came when he briefly replaced Antonio **Margheriti** (who receives sole credit) on *Ursus il terrore dei Kirghisi* (1964), but it was not until *Ultimo mondo cannibale* (*Cannibal*, 1977) that Deodato found his mark with a genuinely horrific vision of first-world consumerism in conflict with third-world **cannibalism**. His crippled classic *Cannibal holo-*

caust portrays the search for a doomed camera crew (based on the infamous *mondo* documentary film-makers Jacopetti and Prosperi) whose film footage, recovered from the South American jungle, depicts their mad descent into death. Deodato returned to cannibal country in the grisly *Inferno in diretta* (*Cut and Run*, 1985).

Other efforts have embraced more mundane horrors, from the mean-spirited home invasion of *La casa sperduta nel parco* (*The House at the Edge of the Park*, 1980) and the **Friday the 13th** clone *Il camping del terrore* (*Body Count*, 1987) to the haunted telephone of *Minaccia d'amore* (*Dial: Help*, 1989) and his surreal anti-**giallo** *The Washing Machine* (1993). DW

Danza macabra [*Castle of Blood*] (assistant d)/ 1963 * *La vergine di Norimberga* [*Virgin of Nuremberg*] (assistant d)/1964 * *Fenomenal e il tesoro di Tutankamen*/1968 * *Un delitto poco comune* [*Phantom of Death*]/1988

de Ossorio, Amando * See: **Ossorio**

De Palma, Brian (b. 1940)

American director, writer. *Sisters* (1973) suggested Brian De Palma would be a genre film-maker to be reckoned with: if he has never lived up to this promise he has also never abandoned his roots, regularly returning to the psychological thriller on ever-increasing budgets. This side of his career is largely defined by his preoccupation with Alfred **Hitchcock**. *Obsession* (1976) is a close reworking of themes and images from *Vertigo* (1958); *Dressed to Kill* (1980) borrows from *Psycho* (1960). *Blow Out* (1981), *Body Double* (1984) and *Raising Cain* (1992) also strive mightily to be 'Hitchcockian', usually taken to mean technically polished, suspenseful, tricky and blackly humorous. De Palma 'quotes' liberally from Hitchcock; though his respect for the master is clear, he's a ham-handed acolyte, cruder and more obvious than his idol.

He regularly fields charges of sensationalism, misogyny and excessive reliance on **violence**, and seems to enjoy provocation for its own sake. The son of a surgeon, De Palma appeared headed for a career in science when he enrolled at Columbia University, but Hitchcock movies gave him the film-making bug. He transferred to Sarah Lawrence College, and began making short films. His first feature (co-directed with Wilford Leach and Cynthia Munroe) is the little-seen *The Wedding Party* (made between

1964 and 1966, released in 1969), featuring unknowns Robert **De Niro** and Jill Clayburgh. His second, *Murder a la Mod* (1967) is an erotic thriller, experimenting with multiple perspective. Typed as a hip young director, De Palma made trendy, youth-oriented pictures – counter-culture hits *Greetings* (1968) and *Hi, Mom!* (1970), theatrical documentary *Dionysus in '69* (1969) and the disastrous *Get to Know Your Rabbit* (1972) – before hitting his stride with the Hitchcockian *Sisters*.

Carrie (1976), the first Stephen **King** adaptation (and one of the best), helped launch a lasting vogue for double-twist endings, and is interestingly balanced between De Palma's callous technique and the humane efforts of an outstanding cast headed by Sissy Spacek and Piper Laurie. *The Fury* (1978), also dealing with **ESP**, is kinetic and entertaining but conspicuously less successful, prompting him to an increasingly chilly series of thrillers, often cross-breeding Hitchcock with Antonioni. As a gun for hire, De Palma has made gangster films (*Scarface*, 1983; *The Untouchables*, 1987; *Carlito's Way*, 1993), the bitter Vietnam war movie

LEFT Sissy Spacek, Brian De Palma's *Carrie*

Casualties of War (1988) and *Mission: Impossible* (1996).

He is least successful when trying to be funny: *The Phantom of the Paradise* (1974), a **rock** *Phantom of the Opera*, plays cleverly on genre conventions, but *Home Movies* (1980) and *Wise Guys* (1986) remain unknown, and *The Bonfire of the Vanities* (1990), from Tom Wolfe's wickedly satirical novel, is widely regarded as a monumental misfire. Once married to actress Nancy **Allen**, whom he frequently cast as a **prostitute**, he is now married to producer Gale Anne Hurd. MM

Laurent Bouzereau, *The De Palma Cut* (1988); Kenneth MacKinnon, *Misogyny in the Movies: The De Palma Question* (1990)

de Rais, Gilles * See: **Rais**

Derleth, August (1909–71)

American writer, editor. A member of the **Lovecraft** circle, Derleth founded Arkham House to perpetuate Lovecraft's reputation. An important anthologist (*Sleep No More*, 1944), Derleth was a prolific writer of varied fiction, including much slick but shallow horror. He embedded tiny fragments of HPL in stretches of whole cloth to produce posthumous 'collaborations' like the novel *The Lurker at the Threshold* (1945). *The Shuttered Room* (1966) is based on a Derleth-Lovecraft story.

TV: *The Unforeseen*: 'The Metronome' (st)/ 1960 * *Thriller*: 'The Incredible Doktor Markesan' (st)/1962 * *Night Gallery*: 'House – With Ghost' (st)/'The Dark Boy' (st)/ 'Logoda's Heads' (st)/1971

de Sade, Marquis * See: **Sade**

The Devil

Theologically speaking, the Devil bears the blame for most supernatural evil encountered in horror films, but he has proven camera-shy compared to his underlings, and when he does appear it is often in a comic guise. His traditional form, complete with horns and hooves, was most frequently displayed in silent films, from *Le manoir du diable* (1896) to *Häxan* (1922), but continued to reappear sporadically in movies like *The Devil Rides Out* (1968), *The Devil's Rain* (1975), *Fear No Evil* (1981) and *The Unholy* (1987). Inflated to titanic size, he makes a ripsnort-

ing monster in *Night of the Demon* (1957), despite Jacques **Tourneur**'s objections, but was never more impressive than when **Lugosi** posed for animators in the 'Night on Bald Mountain' segment of Walt **Disney**'s *Fantasia* (1941).

The Prince of Lies also gets something akin to classical treatment in many versions of **Faust**, while **Hell** is vividly delineated in a dream sequence from *Dante's Inferno* (1935). More often, the Devil is depicted as suave, worldly and all too human, played by George Arliss (*The Devil*, 1909, 1921), Osgood Perkins (*Puritan Passions*, 1923), Adolphe Menjou (*The Sorrows of Satan*, 1925), Walter Huston (superb as a sly rustic in *All That Money Can Buy*, 1941), Laird **Cregar** (*Heaven Can Wait*, 1943), Claude **Rains** (*Angel on My Shoulder*, 1946), Ray **Milland** (*Alias Nick Beal*, 1949), Richard Devon (*The Undead*, 1956), Vincent **Price** (*The Story of Mankind*, 1957), Lon **Chaney** Jr (*The Devil's Messenger*, 1962), Criswell (*Orgy of the Dead*, 1965), Peter Cook (*Bedazzled*, 1967), Burgess Meredith (*Torture Garden*, 1967), Telly Savalas (*Lisa e il diavolo*, 1972), Christopher **Lee** (*Poor Devil*, 1973), Victor **Buono** (*The Evil*, 1978), Jack **Nicholson** (*The Witches of Eastwick*, 1987), Robert **De Niro** (*Angel Heart*, 1987), Jeffrey Jones (*Stay Tuned*, 1992) and Viggo Mortensen (*The Prophecy*, 1995).

Cults of Satanists appear, without a look at their lord, in **The Black Cat** (1934), *The*

The Devil, *Fantasia*

The Devil, Emil Jannings, *Faust*

Seventh Victim (1943), *Blood on Satan's Claw* (1970) and *To the Devil a Daughter* (1976), but he can be glimpsed almost subliminally while impregnating Mia **Farrow** in Roman **Polanski**'s *Rosemary's Baby* (1968), which inaugurated a vogue for taking the Devil and his works seriously. Continuing the trend, William **Friedkin**'s *The Exorcist* (1973) became a blockbuster in cinema history, but the fiend **possessing** Linda **Blair** actually seems to be one of the minor demons and appears on screen only as a statue. *The Omen* (1976), another substantial success, concerns the Devil's son, while a very different view of the scion of Satan is presented in the African-American musical *Cabin in the Sky* (1943). Nigel **Kneale**'s *Quatermass and the Pit* (1959) suggests Satan may have come from outer space; John **Carpenter**'s tribute to Kneale, *Prince of Darkness* (1987), may have finally driven the Devil from the screen by attempting to explain him in terms of quantum physics. LD

Les diaboliques (1954)

A tale of murder, conspiracy and sadism set in a provincial school, Pierre Boileau and Thomas Narcejac's novel *Celle qui n'était plus* (*The Woman Who Was No More*, 1954) was superbly filmed by Henri-Georges **Clouzot** with Simone Signoret and Véra Clouzot. Known internationally as *The Fiends* or *Diabolique*, *Les diaboliques* prompted **Hitch-**cock to essay *Psycho* (1960) to regain his master of suspense title, one-upping Clouzot's bathtub drowning with the shower slashing. Clouzot added to horror's stock of **clichés**: if a character mentions a potentially fatal heart condition, it is a tip-off that any supernatural back-from-the-dead business is part of an it's-all-a-plot plot. It has been remade competently for TV (*Reflections of Murder*, 1974; *House of Secrets*, 1993) and direly for cinema (*Diabolique*, 1996, with Sharon Stone and Isabelle Adjani). Among many imitations: *The Tingler* (1958), *Taste of Fear* (1961), *Hush . . . Hush, Sweet Charlotte* (1964), *Games* (1967), *Fear in the Night* (1972), *Dominique* (1978), *Deathtrap* (1982), *Disturbed* (1990).

Diaz, Vic (b. 19??–????)

Filipino actor. Pudgy, moustached heavy, seemingly in every movie ever shot in the **Philippines**: the **Devil** in *Beast of the Yellow Night* (1970), a farting **vampire** wannabe in *Vampire Hookers* (1978).

Bloodthirst/1965 * *Daughters of Satan*/*Night of the Cobra Woman*/*Deathhead Virgin*/*Superbeast*/*Wonder Women*/1972 * *The Thirsty Dead*/1974 * *Raw Force*/1982

Dieterle, William [Wilhelm] (1893–1972)

German-born American director. Originally an actor, in *Das Wachsfigurenkabinett* (1924) and *Faust* (1926), Dieterle was associated with Warners biopics (*The Life of Emile Zola*, 1937; *Juarez*, 1939), but handled three classics of fantasy and horror: **The Hunchback of Notre Dame** (1939), *All That Money Can Buy* (1941) and David O. Selznick's folly *Portrait of Jennie* (1949). All are awash with eddies of **Expressionism** and memorably acted.

Diffring, Anton (1918–89)

German-born actor, often a **Nazi** in British films. **Frankenstein** in an unsold **Hammer** TV pilot (*Tales of Frankenstein*, 'The Face in the Tombstone Mirror', 1958), he is best remembered as the mad **plastic surgeon** in the sleazy *Circus of Horrors* (1960). He twice played Barré **Lyndon**'s long-lived villain, on television (*Hour of Mystery*, 'The Man in Half Moon Street', 1957) and for Hammer (*The Man Who Could Cheat Death*, 1959). SJ

La morte negli occhi del gatto [*Seven Dead in the Cat's Eyes*]/*Hexen-Geschändet und zu Tode gequält* [*Mark of the Devil Part II*]/1972 * *The Beast Must Die*/1974 * *Les prédateurs de la nuit* [*Faceless*]/1988

TV: *One Step Beyond*: 'The Prisoner'/1961 * *Thriller*: 'The Savage Curse'/1974 * *The Masks of Death*/1984 * *Doctor Who*: 'Silver Nemesis'/1988

Disease

Many horror narratives are concerned with infection: **possession** and transformation movies are full of the messy iconography of

Anton Diffring, *The Beast Must Die*

illness, while contagion is always of interest to the **vampire** and **werewolf** sub-genres, which subversively propose **immortality** as a disease. In *Nosferatu* (1921), **Dracula** is literally pestilential; Christopher **Lee** attempts suicide in *The Satanic Rites of Dracula* (1973) by unleashing plague upon his food source. Personified disease is found in versions of **Poe**'s **'The Masque of the Red Death'** (1842), as well as shockers that feature real-life acromegalic Rondo **Hatton**.

In the Richard **Matheson**-derived *The Last Man on Earth* (1964) and its remake (*The Omega Man*, 1971), the whole of humanity are viral monsters. Rabies infests *I Drink Your Blood* (1971), sickle-cell anaemia haunts *Ganja and Hess* (1973) and VD is behind the crimes in *Jack the Ripper* (1959). Carcinogenics and **sex** infection obsess David **Cronenberg**, especially in *Rabid* (1977) and *Dead Ringers* (1988). Disease paranoia is employed by numerous politically inflected items from *Isle of the Dead* (1945) on, and makes a comeback in AIDS-age entries like *Vampire's Kiss* (1989), *The Stand* (1993) and *Outbreak* (1995). The **brain**-sucking *übermensch* of *Mind Ripper* (1995) is a suicide reanimated by a retro-infection. DP

Disfigurement and Plastic Surgery

'Maybe if a man is ugly, he does ugly things,' suggests **Karloff** in *The Raven* (1935), just before **Lugosi** surgically transforms him into a **monster**. In the sinister cinema, a disfigured face provides the motive for villainy: most notoriously, **The Phantom of the Opera** is often portrayed as an acid-scarred

Disfigurement: Lionel Atwill, *The Mystery of the Wax Museum*

musician, though his origin is enigmatic in the 1925 movie and in Gaston **Leroux**'s 1911 novel. Later villains who go on a tear after losing face appear in *Mystery of the Wax Museum* (1933), its remake *House of Wax* (1953), *The Face Behind the Mask* (1941), *Mr. Sardonicus* (1961), *Pyro* (1963), *Something Weird* (1967), *I, Madman* (1989), ***Batman*** (1989) and *Batman Forever* (1995). Friendlier frazzled faces appear in *The Man Who Laughs* (1928), *Face of Fire* (1959) and *Darkman* (1990), while restorative surgery gives amnesiacs the wrong identity in *Shattered* (1991) and *Suture* (1993).

Another problem is losing limbs, but here disfigured fiends display considerable ingenuity: a missing arm is replaced by 'synthetic flesh' (*Doctor X*, 1932); legs are restored through meditation (*Night Monster*, 1942); arms are regrown through reptile gland injections (*The Alligator People*, 1959); a psychopath who has cut off his own hand carries a case of murderous attachments for the stump (*Chamber of Horrors*, 1966). Beautiful women with disfigured faces pose more problems: they endure in *Peeping Tom* (1960) and *The Brain That Wouldn't Die* (1960) but are cured and then killed by a sadistic plastic surgeon in *Circus of Horrors* (1959). In Georges **Franju**'s icily elegant *Les yeux sans visage* (1959), a doctor murders for flesh to restore a loved one's face; the theme is taken up in *Corruption* (1967), and by Jesús **Franco** in films from *Gritos en la noche* (*The Awful Dr. Orlof*, 1961) to *Les prédateurs de la nuit* (*Faceless*, 1988). LD

Disney, Walt (1900–66)

American animation (and live action) producer. A brand-name while its founder was alive, Disney lives on as an enormously powerful corporate empire. An innovator, Disney backed major ventures like the first sound cartoon *Steamboat Willie* (1928) and first full-length animated feature *Snow White and the Seven Dwarfs* (1937), then moved into television and built the pioneer theme park, Disneyland. His studio played safe for nearly two decades after his death, only revitalising its animation output after the disastrously overblown *The Black Cauldron* (1985). Though his name inevitably connotes family entertainment and bedrock Americana, horror runs through the Disney output.

The whimsical *Silly Symphonies* shorts *The Skeleton Dance* (1929), *Hell's Bells* (1929) and *Cannibal Capers* (1930) led to the darker *Midnight in a Toy Shop* (1930). Mickey Mouse went from the burlesque of *The Haunted*

Walt Disney

House (1929) to the domestic hell of *Mickey's Nightmare* (1932). *Snow White* has its wicked queen and a terrifying dark forest; the runaways of *Pinocchio* (1940) turn into donkeys on the theme park-like Pleasure Island; *Fantasia* (1940) features both 'Night On Bald Mountain' and 'The Sorcerer's Apprentice'; *Victory Through Air Power* (1943) shows Japan as monster octopus. Headless horsemen occur in *The Adventures of Ichabod and Mr Toad* (1949) and (the live action) *Darby O'Gill and the Little People* (1959). The icy Maleficent of *Sleeping Beauty* (1959) predates the gothic atmospherics of *Beauty and the Beast* (1991). Though Disney live-action is associated with harmless fantasy – *The Shaggy Dog* (1959) is the least threatening **werewolf** in the movies – the studio has occasionally dabbled in kid-friendly scariness: *The Watcher in the Woods* (1980), *Something Wicked This Way Comes* (1983). JC

Dumbo/1941 * *Bambi*/1942 * *Peter Pan*/1953 * *The Sword in the Stone*/1963 * *The Jungle Book*/ 1967 * *Aladdin*/1992 * *The Nightmare Before Christmas*/1993 * *The Hunchback of Notre Dame*/1996

Richard Schickel, *The Disney Version* (1985); Marc Eliot, *Walt Disney: Hollywood's Dark Prince* (1993)

Doctors

Doctors are indispensable to horror, even if they sometimes play minor roles. Of course many of horror's medical practitioners may be dismissed as mere **mad scientists**, embarked on outrageous experiments, yet a considerable number are actually practising their craft, or at least trying to. The dichotomy was embodied early on in ***Das Cabinet des Dr. Caligari*** (1919), whose title character is viewed by various characters as saint or sadist.

The genre's archetypal good physician is Dr **Van Helsing**, played stolidly in *Dracula* (1931) and *Dracula's Daughter* (1936) by Edward Van Sloan. His mantle was taken a generation later by Peter **Cushing**, a more dashing Van Helsing in four films beginning with ***Dracula*** (1958). Even **Lugosi** plays a kindly medical man in ***The Black Cat*** (1934), while **Karloff** is frequently well intentioned: his rampages in *The Ape* (1940) and *Black Friday* (1940) begin with sincere attempts to cure his patients, while in *The Man They Could Not Hang* (1939) and *The Man with Nine Lives* (1940) he is experimenting with artificial hearts and cryonics long before real doctors. He also serves as a pioneer in anesthesia in the period thriller *Corridors of Blood* (1958), one of a run of **body-snatching** dramas of doctors driven to distraction by hidebound contemporaries, including *The Body Snatcher* (1945) and *The Flesh and the Fiends* (1959).

As a masked man with a knife, a sawbones is already a frightening figure; serious

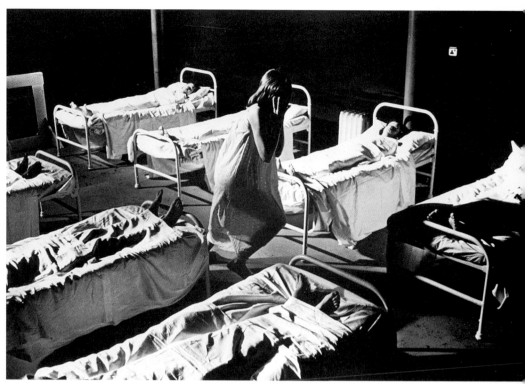

Doctors: *Horror Hospital*

surgeons deranged by sexual or romantic problems are portrayed by Peter **Lorre** (*Mad Love*, 1935), Erich von **Stroheim** (*The Crime of Dr. Crespi*, 1935), Bela Lugosi (***The Raven***, 1935), Robert **Flemyng** (*L'orribile segreto del dr. Hichcock*, 1962), Jeremy Irons (*Dead Ringers*, 1988), Julian Sands (*Boxing Helena*, 1993) and Sean Haberle (*Exquisite Tenderness*, 1995). On the other hand, surgeons are the victims of disgruntled patients in *Night Monster* (1942) and *The Abominable Dr. Phibes* (1971). Hospitals and clinics are settings for horror in *Doctor X* (1931), *Horror Hospital* (1973), *Visiting Hours* (1981), *X-Ray* (1982), *Flatliners* (1990), *Dr. Giggles* (1992) and *Riget* (*The Kingdom*, 1995). The Nobel Prize for medicine in horror films must go to Dr Franz Edelmann (Onslow **Stevens**), who in *House of Dracula* (1945) actually cures the **Wolf Man** of lycanthropy. LD

Dr Jekyll and Mr Hyde * See: **Jekyll and Hyde**

Dr Strange

Created by writer Stan Lee and artist Steve Ditko. Dr Stephen Strange, the amulet-wearing 'Master of the Mystic Arts', was introduced in 'Dr Strange, Master of Black Magic' (*Strange Tales*, 1963). Marvel Comics have several times given Strange his own title and

kept him busy as a guest star, defending Greenwich Village against such foes as Baron Mordo, the Dread Dormammu and Nightmare, at best inspiring artists to semi-surreal heights of mind-bending weirdness. Peter Hooten is a blandly blow-dried sorcerer in *Dr. Strange* (1978), a busted TV pilot, and Jeffrey Combs is a blatant steal in *Doctor Mordrid* (1992).

Doctor Who (UK TV series, 1963–)

The BBC's long-running flagship science fiction show. The Doctor, a Time Lord who travels time and space in a machine shaped like a police telephone box, is played in different regenerations by William Hartnell, Patrick **Troughton**, Jon Pertwee, Tom Baker, Peter Davison, Colin Baker, Sylvester McCoy and Paul McGann (not to mention Richard Hurndall, Michael Jayston and Peter **Cushing**). Originally intended as an educational show with the Doctor and companions touring historical events, it took off with the appearance of the Daleks, fascist mutants in robot casings. *Doctor Who* concentrated on monsters thereafter, driving a generation behind the sofa and upsetting Mary Whitehouse.

The series spun off feature films, radio shows, comics, books and much associational material. Informed by Nigel **Kneale**, *The*

Doctors: Boris Karloff, *Abbott and Costello Meet Dr. Jekyll and Mr. Hyde*

Outer Limits (1963–5) and **Lovecraft**, *Doctor Who* was often more horror than s-f (especially in the 70s), with thin rationales presented for **alien** elder gods or space **vampires** and odd attempts at genuine scariness. Horror-indebted serials are 'The Tomb of the Cybermen' (1967), 'The Claws of Axos' (1971), 'The Dæmons' (1971), 'The Ark in Space' (1975), 'Pyramids of Mars' (1975), 'The Brain of Morbius' (1976), 'The Talons of Weng-Chiang' (1977), 'Horror of Fang Rock' (1977), 'Image of the Fendahl' (1977), 'State of Decay' (1980), 'Black Orchid' (1982), 'Ghost Light' (1989) and 'The Curse of Fenric' (1989). Essential viewing for children of the 60s and 70s, *Doctor Who* may yet prove a major influence on British horror.
Jean-Marc Lofficier, *The Doctor Who Programme Guide* (1981, 1994); David Howe, Mark Stammers, Stephen James Walker, *Doctor Who: The Sixties* (1992), *Doctor Who: The Seventies* (1994), *Doctor Who: The Eighties* (1996); Adrian Rigelsford, *The Doctors: 30 Years of Time Travel* (1994).

Dogs

Man's best friend appears infrequently in horror, usually as a slavering hunting dog like Conan **Doyle**'s much-filmed *The Hound of the Baskervilles* (1901). Killer packs were briefly in vogue in the 70s: *Dogs* (1976), *The Pack* (1977), *The Boys from Brazil* (1978), *Rottweiler* (1981), *After Midnight* (1989). Unlike other creatures, the dog tends not to be the subject of transformation: exceptions are the dog turned wolf in *Monster on the Campus* (1958) and the dog turned monster in *The Thing* (1982). There are telepathic dogs (*A Boy and His Dog*, 1975), Devil sidekick dogs (*The Omen*, 1976), **vampire** dogs (*Dracula's Dog*, 1977), possessed dogs (*Devil Dog: The Hound of Hell*, 1978), robot dogs (*A Close Shave*, 1995), racist dogs (*White Dog*, 1983), rabid dogs (*Cujo*, 1983), genetically altered dogs (*Man's Best Friend*, 1993) and Cenobite dogs (*Hellraiser: Bloodline*, 1996). In *Theatre of Blood* (1973), Robert Morley unwittingly eats his pet poodles. Disturbing scenes occur in *Yojimbo* (1961) and *The Mad Room* (1969), in which dogs carry severed **hands** in their mouths, and *The Mephisto Waltz* (1971) and *Invasion of the Body Snatchers* (1978), in which dogs have or seem to have human **heads**. DM

Dolls

The doll is an innocent plaything, but also a mockery of the human form that children cheerfully imbue with life. For adults, a living doll is a figure of horror. In *The Devil-Doll* (1936) and its cheap imitator *Attack of the Puppet People* (1958), the little figures are actually miniaturised human beings. The killer dolls of *Asylum* (1972) are **ESP**-animated, but magic usually provides the motivating force, most memorably in the segment of Dan **Curtis**'s *Trilogy of Terror* (1975) where a ferocious Zuni fetish doll brutalises Karen **Black**. More dolls stalk the innocent in *Barbarella* (1967), *Serenata macabra* (*House of Evil*, 1968), **Poltergeist** (1982), *Screamtime* (1983), *Dolls* (1987), *Death Doll* (1988), *Dolly Dearest* (1991), *Demonic Toys* (1991) and *Pinocchio* (1996).

Tom **Holland**'s *Child's Play* (1988), about a mass-marketed toy called Chucky that is endowed with the spirit of a murderer, walks a familiar path but made considerable money and spawned sequels. An even longer series started with *Puppet Master* (1989), which introduces an entire team of gimmicky killer dolls who return in made-for-video sequels. Even more disturbing are department store mannequins: lifesized and sometimes hideously human-oid, they serve as macabre window dressing in *The Gruesome Twosome* (1968) and *Una hacha par la luna di miel* (*A Hatchet for the Honeymoon*, 1969), come to life in 'The After Hours' (*The Twilight Zone*, 1960) and *Mannequin* (1987) and kill at Chuck Connors' command in *Tourist Trap* (1978). Dolls also creep creepily in TV episodes: 'Living Doll' (*The Twilight Zone*, 1963), 'The Doll' (*Night Gallery*, 1971), 'Terror of the Autons' (*Doctor Who*, 1971). Non-living dolls are eerie set-dressing in *The Psychopath* (1966) and *Pin . . .* (1988). LD

Donner, Richard (b. 1939)

American director. A big budget hack (*Superman*, 1978; *Lethal Weapon*, 1987), Donner's

Doctor Who:
LEFT John Pertwee, Daleks
BELOW Carole Ann Ford, William Hartnell

Dogs: *Dracula's Dog*

first hit was the emptily theatrical ***The Omen*** (1976). More interesting is his work for ***The Twilight Zone***, which includes Richard **Matheson**'s classic 'gremlin' episode.

Ladyhawke/1985 * *The Lost Boys* (p)/1987 * *Scrooged*/1988 * *Tales From the Crypt: Demon Knight* (exec p)/1994 * *Tales From the Crypt: Bordello of Blood* (exec p)/1996

TV: *The Twilight Zone*: 'Nightmare at 20,000 Feet'/1963; 'From Agnes – With Love'/'The Jeopardy Room'/'The Brain Center at Whipple's'/'Come Wander With Me'/ 'Sounds and Silences'/1964 * *Wild Wild West*: 'Night of the Returning Dead'/1965 * *Ghost Story*: 'The Concrete Captain'/1972 * *Tales From the Crypt* (exec p)/1989–: 'Dig That Cat . . . He's Real Gone'/1989; 'The Ventriloquist's Dummy'/1990; 'Showdown'/1992

Donovan's Brain (1943)
Curt **Siodmak**'s novel is the archetypal **brain**-in-a-tank story, filmed as *The Lady and the Monster* (1944) with Erich von **Stroheim**, *Donovan's Brain* (1953) with Lew Ayres, 'Donovan's Brain' (*Studio One*, 1955) with Wendell Corey and *Vengeance* (1963) with Peter van Eyck. Billionaire Donovan dies in a plane crash, but is kept alive by a scientist who comes under his mental domination. Siodmak's *Hauser's Memory* (1968; filmed 1970) is a sequel. The premise appears in

embryo in *Charlie Chan in Honolulu* (1938), with red herring George **Zucco** keeping alive a criminal brain. Imitations tend to feature living severed **heads** (*Die Nackte und der Satan*, 1959; *They Saved Hitler's Brain*, 1964), but there are a few direct borrowings: *The Man With Two Brains* (1983), three TV versions of Roald **Dahl**'s 'William and Mary' (1959) and episodes of ***The Outer Limits*** ('The Brain of Colonel Barham', 1964), *Wild Wild West* ('The Night of the Druid's Blood', 1966) and *The New Adventures of Wonder Woman* ('Gault's Brain', 1978).

Doppelgängers
The true doppelgänger, a supernatural double whose presence indicates spiritual malaise, is comparatively rare in film. A classic literary version is **Poe**'s 'William Wilson' (1839), a source for German **Expressionist** cinema via H.H. **Ewers**'s oft-filmed *Der Student von Prag*. Closer to Poe is the vivid vignette of depravity in Louis Malle's portion of the **anthology** *Histoires extraordinaires* (*Spirits of the Dead*, 1967). Vincent **Price** discovers death has his own face in **Corman**'s ***The Masque of the Red Death*** (1964), while **Karloff**'s **monster** resembles his youthful self in *Frankenstein 1970* (1958). In *The Man Who Haunted Himself* (1970), the character

RIGHT Lew Ayres, *Donovan's Brain*

confronting his own soul is improbably enacted by Roger Moore. In *Single White Female* (1992), distantly following *3 Women* (1977), deranged roommate Jennifer Jason Leigh takes on the personality and appearance of Bridget Fonda, while *La double vie de Véronique* (1991) offers Irène Jacob as a French girl haunted by the death of an unmet Polish double.

More common is the 'evil twin', an identical relative who allows an actor to play dual roles: **Lugosi** (*Murder by Television*, 1935), George **Zucco** (*Dead Men Walk*, 1943), Olivia de Havilland (*The Dark Mirror*, 1946), Bette **Davis** (*Dead Ringer*, 1964). **Karloff** rises above the cliché in *The Black Room* (1935) and Jeremy Irons is astonishing as twin gynaecologists in David **Cronenberg**'s *Dead Ringers* (1988). Characters are also sometimes haunted by lookalike forebears: it happens to Vincent Price in *The Haunted Palace* (1964) and Chris **Sarandon** in *The Resurrected* (1991), while Barbara **Steele** goes through it twice in *La maschera de demonio* (*The Mask of Satan*, 1960) and *Amanti d'oltretomba* (*Nightmare Castle*, 1965). LD

Douglas, Melvyn [Melvyn Hesselberg] (1901–81)
Slightly stuffy Hollywood leading man of the 30s and 40s. In old age, a fine character actor. SJ

The Old Dark House/1932 * *The Vampire Bat*/ 1933 * *Le Locataire* [*The Tenant*]/1976 * *The Changeling*/1979 * *Ghost Story*/1981

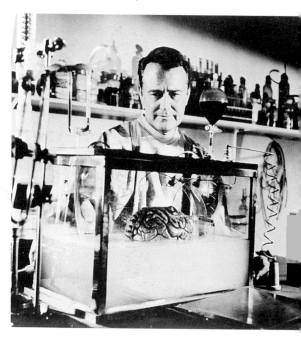

TV: *Lights Out*: 'Private, Keep Out'/1952 *
Drama Special: 'The Crucible'/1967 * *Death
Takes a Holiday*/1971 * *Ghost Story*: 'House of
Evil'/1972

Dourif, Brad (b. 1950)

American actor. The premier twitchy psycho
of his generation, Dourif was Oscar-nominated for *One Flew Over the Cuckoo's Nest*
(1976). The voice of Chucky in the **Child's
Play** films, he often adds entertainment
value to terrible pictures.

The Eyes of Laura Mars/1978 * *Wise Blood*/
1979 * *Blue Velvet*/*Impure Thoughts*/1986 *
Child's Play/1988 * *Exorcist III*/*Spontaneous
Combustion*/*Sonny Boy*/*Graveyard Shift*/*Grim
Prairie Tales*/*Child's Play 2*/1990 * *Child's Play
3*/*Body Parts*/1991 * *Critters 4*/1992 * *Trauma*/
1993 * *The Color of Night*/*Death Machine*/1994
* *Phoenix*/1995 * *Nightwatch*/1996

TV: *I, Desire*/1982 * *Tales of the Unexpected*:
'Number Eight'/1984 * *The Hitchhiker*: 'The
Legendary Billy B.'/1987 * *Tales From the
Crypt*: 'People Who Live in Brass Hearses'/
1992 * *The X Files*: 'Beyond the Sea'/1992

Doyle, Arthur Conan (1859–1930)

British writer. Known for the **Sherlock
Holmes** stories - of which *The Hound of the
Baskervilles* (1901) is the most horrific - and
the Professor Challenger series (*The Lost
World*, 1912), Doyle was passionately interested in spiritualism and the occult. Holmes
remains rational to the end, but Challenger
converts to table-rapping in *The Land of Mist*
(1924). Doyle produced a few capable ghost
and horror stories, including the **mummy**
story 'Lot 249' (1892; adapted for TV in
Conan Doyle, 1967, and film in *Tales From the
Darkside: The Movie*, 1990) and 'The Leather
Funnel' (1903; adapted for TV in **Orson
Welles' Great Mysteries**, 1974). Doyle figures
in novels: Robert Saffron's *The Demon Device*
(1979), Simon Hawke's *The Dracula Caper*
(1988), Mark Frost's *The List of Seven* (1993)
and *The 6 Messiahs* (1995), Steve Szilagyi's
Photographing Fairies (1993), William Hjortsberg's *Nevermore* (1994).

Dracula

Dracula is the most famous **vampire** novel
of all. One hundred years after first publication in June 1897 (in a fashionably decadent
yellow-covered edition of 3,000 copies), it is
more controversial than ever, with issues of

RIGHT Helen Chandler, Bela Lugosi,
Dracula (1931)

gender and sexuality high up on the cultural
agenda. The year 1897 was also Queen
Victoria's Diamond Jubilee, the high point of
the British Empire, and the year when
Sigmund Freud started his researches into
psychoanalysis.

It is likely that the Anglo-Irish author
Bram (or Abraham) **Stoker** saw the book as
an adventure story, intending a form of
turn-of-the-century techno-fiction with type-
writers, phonographs and blood-transfu-
sions. A gang of fine upstanding chaps protect their womenfolk from becoming harpies
and don't care much for the verminous
Eastern European Count who wants to suck
the Brits into his evil empire. The villain's
circle of friends includes gypsies, wolves,
rats and **Renfield**, a lunatic who lunches
on flies.

Freudians interpret the text as a parable
of repressed sexual desire and the dilution of
the sexual drive: one early 50s analyst called
it 'a kind of incestuous, necrophilious,
oral-anal-sadistic all-in wrestling match'.
Others relate Dracula to the Oedipus complex (the Count as Big Daddy), a defence of
traditional family values against the discon-
tents of modern civilisation and a yearning
to break just about every taboo you can
think of, especially taboos about **blood** and
menstruation. One of the reasons, it has
been argued, *Dracula* remains so astonishingly popular with adolescents (especially in the

darkened space of the cinema) is that it is
about sex from the neck *up*. It is also about a
pathological form of consumerism and one
of the great anti-vegetarians.

Feminist views range from the dismissive
(the novel as bible of 'the antifeminine
obsession') to the intrigued (the thesis that it
is at a deeper level about the empowerment
of the female character). The 'good strong
men' of the novel – Professor **Van Helsing**,
Lord Godalming, Dr John Seward, the cow-
boy-like Quincey Morris – who enthusiastically set about their task of putting creatures
of erotic desire back into their boxes, have
become, over time, the bad guys. Stoker
would not have been amused: the complete
absence of humour in his work was noted by
contemporary critics, and of the extant portrait photographs not one shows him even
attempting to smile. If the character of
Dracula is anything to go by, we may safely
assume Stoker believed too much indul-
gence leads to hairy palms, a pale complex-
ion and very bloodshot eyes.

The original idea for *Dracula* came to
Stoker in a nightmare (March 1890) about
three predatory females who kiss 'not on the
lips but on the throat', their young male **victim** who experiences 'some longing and . . .
some deadly fear', and an old Count who
stops the vampire brides in the nick of time
while hissing 'this man belongs to me!'. A
bizarre mixture of the witches from *Macbeth*

(a favourite of Stoker's employer, the actor-manager Henry Irving), Stoker's own anxieties about his masculinity (he liked to brag about his athletic prowess, but was puzzled by what he called 'the problem of **sex**') and a voyeur's fantasy. Exorcising this nightmare (if such it was) by turning it into a full-length novel was a seven-year project which Stoker approached with all the meticulousness of an ex-civil servant from Dublin Castle. He drew on the main traditions of vampire literature (the folkloric, the *femme fatale*, the demonic or Byronic aristocrat) and the watering places he visited for his annual summer holidays: Whitby, scene of the arrival of the phantom ship, and Cruden Bay on the Buchan coast of Scotland, possibly the inspiration for Castle Dracula.

The story was originally – like Sheridan **Le Fanu**'s **'Carmilla'** (1871) – to be set in Styria (part of the Austrian empire), but once he settled on **Transylvania** – to late-Victorian readers, synonymous with primitive superstitions driven from the rest of Europe by the march of science – Stoker did his background research. While preparing *Dracula*, he never personally ventured further east than the Yorkshire coast; whole paragraphs were transferred from travel guides to novel. Originally called (rather blandly) Count Wampyr, the villain picked up his immortal name when Stoker found scattered references in the British Museum library to Vlad Dracula, Voivode of Wallachia in the mid-15th century, who was also called 'the Impaler' because of the nasty things he did with Turkish prisoners.

Stoker's Dracula is a Count, he has a home in Transylvania and a **castle** near the Borgo Pass: Vlad was a prince, his home was in Wallachia and his castle in Poenari near Curtea des Arges, nowhere near the Transylvania-Bukovina border. The novel's gothic villain is a part tailor-made for Irving, veteran of **Faust**, The Flying Dutchman and Richard III. His physical description (probably based on a 1491 woodcut from the British Museum collection) is of an aged military commander with aquiline face, thin nose, arched nostrils, massive eyebrows and a heavy moustache. The only illustration Stoker is known to have seen (on the cover of the abridged 1901 paperback) shows the Count as a white-haired veteran (resembling C. Aubrey Smith) in a batlike cloak and oversized bare feet, shinning lizard-like down the stone walls of his castle, while a moustached solicitor's clerk observes in horror from a barred upper window.

The transformation from novel to film – the demobilisation of the Count into civilian evening dress, and the evolution of this rough castle lizard into the smooth lounge variety – was unusually fraught. Ten years after her husband's death, the sixty-four year old Florence Stoker tried to extract payment from the German company Prana films for the first film version, *Nosferatu: Eine Symphonie des Grauens* (1922): they had adapted the novel (like most future adaptations, with an emphasis on the early, Transylvanian section and the seduction of Mina Harker back in England) with a few changes of name (Harker became Hutter) but without asking anyone's permission. There was, in fact, a Hungarian *Drakula* (1921), but this film (now lost) appears to have been about Vlad rather than his fictional namesake.

Prana went bankrupt, so three years later Florence had to settle for the removal of *Nosferatu* from circulation: a German court ruled that all positive and negative copies be destroyed. But some prints escaped the purge. Count Orlok in F.W. **Murnau**'s film has a bald head, the ears of a **bat** and the teeth of a rat – and he belongs as much to the romantic world of writer E.T.A. **Hoffmann** and painter Caspar David Friedrich as to Stoker. He is a repulsive creature of folklore: the verdict of critics has ranged from 'a penis with teeth' to a walking peasant legend to an anti-semitic caricature.

But the Count Dracula of modern myth – a red-eyed smoothie with a Hungarian accent who dresses formally for dinner and is utterly irresistible to female characters – originated soon after, in the *Dracula* play which ran in London and New York. This play – written in 1924 by the barnstorming actor-manager Hamilton Deane and rewritten for Broadway three years later with journalist and playwright John L. **Balderston** – was sanctioned by Florence, introduced an opera cloak into the iconography, and provided the basis for the first Hollywood version. Bela **Lugosi** made the part his own, at the Fulton Theatre on 46th Street, after Raymond Huntley (who had played Dracula with Deane's company in London) turned it down.

When Tod **Browning**'s low-budget 1930 film of the play (with a low-budget actor in the lead) opened at the Roxy Theatre in New York, February 1931, it was accompanied by a ballet of high-kicking Roxyettes and billed as 'good to the last gasp!'. With Lugosi's first entrance as the Count – 'I (pause) am

Dracula. I bid you welcome' – standing on the steps of a gigantic cobwebby castle, with armadillos crawling at his feet, the story of Dracula at last flew away from the world of literature altogether. CF

Harry Ludlam, *A Biography of Dracula* (1962); Leonard Wolf, *A Dream of Dracula* (1972), *The Annotated Dracula* (1975); Gabriel Ronay, *The Dracula Myth* (1972); Raymond McNally, Radu Florescu, *In Search of Dracula* (1972); Daniel Farson, *Bram Stoker: The Man Who Wrote Dracula* (1975); Donald Glut, *The Dracula Book* (1975); Peter Haining, *The Dracula Scrapbook* (1976); Clive Leatherdale, *Dracula: The Novel and the Legend* (1985), *The Origins of Dracula* (1987); Gregory A. Waller, *The Living and the Undead* (1986); Margaret L. Carter, *Dracula: The Vampire and the Critics* (1988); Christopher Frayling, *Vampyres: Lord Byron to Count Dracula* (1990); David Skal, *Hollywood Gothic: The Tangled Web of 'Dracula' from Novel to Stage to Screen* (1990); Barbara Belford, *Bram Stoker: A Biography of the Author of Dracula* (1996)

Dracula (Universal)

Though *Dracula's Daughter* (1936) and *House of Dracula* (1945) are sequels respectively to *Dracula* (1931) and *House of Frankenstein* (1944), carrying over cast members and plot threads, Universal's **Dracula** series is less consistent than their **Frankenstein** cycle. Tod **Browning**'s *Dracula* is an adaptation of Hamilton Deane and John L. **Balderston**'s 1927 Broadway play rather than Bram **Stoker**'s 1897 novel. Its stars (Bela **Lugosi** as **Dracula** and Edward **Van Sloan** as **Van Helsing**) were recruited from the theatre. George Melford simultaneously directed a Spanish language version with Carlos Villarias as the Count. Lambert **Hillyer**'s *Dracula's Daughter* recalls Van Sloan as a slightly renamed 'von Helsing' and casts Gloria Holden as Countess Marya Zaleska. Robert **Siodmak**'s *Son of Dracula* (1943) stands alone, with Lon **Chaney Jr** as 'Count Alucard' and no reference to the earlier films. John **Carradine** is a dapper Dracula, disguised as Baron Latos, in Erle C. **Kenton**'s *House of Frankenstein* and *House of Dracula*, mixing with the **Wolf Man** and the Frankenstein Monster, but Lugosi returns to sign off the cycle with **Abbott and Costello** in *Meet Frankenstein* (1948).

By casting Lugosi and then Carradine, Universal decreed how Dracula and imitation vampires would look and act until the arrival of Christopher **Lee**, as demonstrated

Dracula (Hammer)

by Lugosi's turns in *Mark of the Vampire* (1935) and *Return of the Vampire* (1944) and even Carradine's straggling through *Billy the Kid vs. Dracula* (1966) and *Nocturna* (1979). There are footnotes: Philip Marshak's *Dracula Sucks* (1978), with Jamie Gillis, uses the bulk of the 1931 script; John Badham's *Dracula* (1979), with Frank **Langella**, is based on the Balderston-Deane play (and was a Universal release); Stan Dragoti's *Love at First Bite* (1979), with George Hamilton, establishes itself as a sequel to the Browning version; Fred **Dekker**'s *The Monster Squad* (1987), with Duncan Regehr, is a homage to the *House* films; and *Dracula – Dead and Loving It* (1995), with Leslie Nielsen, is *Dracula Sucks* without the porno. Because Universal retain the rights to the single-word title, **Hammer**'s *Dracula* (1958) is known in the US as *Horror of Dracula* and the 1974 and 1992 versions are officially called *Bram Stoker's Dracula*.

David J. Skal, *Hollywood Gothic: The Tangled Web of 'Dracula' from Novel to Stage to Screen* (1990)

Dracula (Hammer)

At first, **Hammer** Films took care with the continuity of their **Dracula** series, remembering how Christopher **Lee**'s Count had been killed off and using some imagination to have him resurrected for his next revenge. The initial cycle comprises of Terence **Fisher**'s *Dracula* (1958) and *Dracula, Prince of Darkness* (1965), Freddie **Francis**'s *Dracula Has Risen From the Grave* (1968), Peter **Sasdy**'s *Taste the Blood of Dracula* (1970) and Roy Ward **Baker**'s *Scars of Dracula* (1970). Lee is confined mainly to Berkshire Transylvania (he visits Victorian London in *Taste*) and, after losing to Peter **Cushing**'s **Van Helsing** in the first film, is opposed by a run of stuffy religious figures brandishing crucifixes and stakes. Notable fixtures are **inns** full of superstitious cockney Rumanian peasants and repressed maidens reincarnated as **vampire** hoydens.

Alan **Gibson**'s *Dracula A.D. 1972* (1972) and *The Satanic Rites of Dracula* (1973), with Lee revived in present-day London and tangling with Cushing as a Van Helsing descendent, start afresh: the prologue of *A.D. 1972* gives an alternative version of the battle seen in *Dracula*. Cushing's Van Helsing is bereft of Lee's Dracula in Fisher's *The Brides of Dracula* (1960), with David Peel as the swish Baron Meinster, and Baker's *Legend of the 7 Golden Vampires* (1973), with Cushing as the

Christopher Lee, *Dracula* (1958)

Lawrence Van Helsing seen in the prologue of *A.D. 1972* (though he dies in 1872 and *Legend* is set in 1904) and both John Forbes-Robertson and Chan Shen as incarnations of Dracula. Sasdy's *Countess Dracula* (1970), with Ingrid **Pitt** as Erzsbet **Báthory**, is linked to the cycle only by its opportunist title.

Elements of the Hammer series are parodied in *Tempi duri per i vampiri* (1959), *One More Time* (1970), *Dracula, père et fils* (1976), with Christopher Lee satirising himself. Roman **Polanski**'s *Dance of the Vampires* (1968) is a fond pastiche of Hammer with Jack MacGowran and Ferdy **Mayne** at once parodying and contradicting Cushing and Lee; the dud Reg Varney comedy *Go for a*

Take (1972) offers Dennis **Price** spoofing Lee as a weary actor coping with brainless victim Julie Ege; and *Dracula – Dead and Loving It* (1995) lampoons Fisher's style. Hammer's other vampire movies – Don **Sharp**'s *Kiss of the Vampire* (1964), Baker's *The Vampire Lovers* (1970), Robert Young's *Vampire Circus* (1971), Brian **Clemens**'s *Captain Kronos, Vampire Hunter* (1974) – follow *The Brides of Dracula* by trying to establish separate identities while reusing images, themes and characterisations from the series. The company was not above lifting glass shots of Castle Dracula or even close-ups of Lee's bloodshot eyes to beef up the non-Dracula likes of Jimmy **Sangster**'s *Lust for a Vampire* (1971).

Dracula (**Various**)

The most lasting renditions of the **Dracula** role have come from Max **Schreck** (*Nosferatu: Eine Symphonie des Grauens*, 1922), Bela **Lugosi** (*Dracula*, 1930) and Christopher Lee (*Dracula*, 1958). F.W. **Murnau**'s film casts a stylistic shadow over a few subsequent shockers, but only Universal's Lugosi and Hammer's Lee, abetted by directors Tod **Browning** and Terence **Fisher**, inspired sequel cycles. The cinema's one-off Draculas have found it hard to come up with an independent identity and tend overwhelmingly to echo the costume (cloak, dark suit) and manner (suave purrs, fanged hisses) of these major readings of the role.

A few players have essayed the role more than once, including John **Carradine** (*House of Frankenstein*, 1944; *House of Dracula*, 1945; *Billy the Kid vs. Dracula*, 1966; *Nocturna*, 1979), Howard **Vernon** (*Dracula, prisonnier de Frankenstein/Dracula, Prisoner of Frankenstein*, 1971; *La fille de Dracula*, 1971) and Jamie Gillis (*Dracula Sucks*, 1978; *Dracula Exotica*, 1981). Only Carradine, who also played Dracula on stage and television ('Dracula', *Matinee Theatre*, 1956), is really associated with the role, and he hardly matches the commitment of Lugosi and Lee though he resembles Stoker's description rather more than his rivals. Among the most serious interpretations, in 'straight' versions of the novel, are Carlos Villarias (*Drácula*,

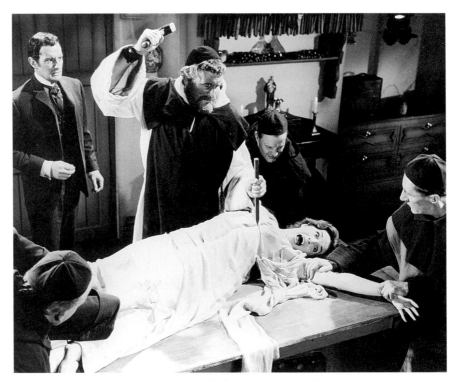

Francis Matthews, Andrew Keir, Barbara Shelley, *Dracula Prince of Darkness*

1930), Denholm **Elliott** ('Dracula', *Mystery and Imagination*, 1970), a non-Hammer Christopher Lee (*El conde Drácula*, 1970), Norman Welsh ('Dracula', *Purple Playhouse*, 1973), Jack **Palance** (*Dracula*, 1974), Louis **Jourdan** (*Count Dracula*, 1977), Klaus

Christopher Lee, Linda Hayden, *Taste the Blood of Dracula*

Kinski (*Nosferatu, Phantom der Nacht*, 1979), Frank **Langella** (*Dracula*, 1979) and Gary Oldman (*Bram Stoker's Dracula*, 1992).

Farther afield are takes on the part from Atif Kaptan (*Drakula Istanbulda*, 1953), Malcolm Rogers ('A Journey Into Terror', ***Doctor Who***, 1964), Eric del Castillo (*El imperio de Drácula*, 1966), Alex D'Arcy (*Blood of Dracula's Castle*, 1967), Carlos Agosti (*Santo y el tesoro de Drácula*, 1968), David Avizu (*Santo y Blue Demon vs. los monstruos*, 1969), Paul Albert Krumm (*Jonathan*, 1970), Des Roberts (*Guess What Happened to Count Dracula*, 1970), Charles Macaulay (*Blacula*, 1972), Aldo Monti (*Santo y Blue Demon contra Drácula y el hombre lobo*, 1972), Narciso Ibañez Menta (*La saga de los Dráculas*, 1972), Paul **Naschy** (*El gran amor del Conde Drácula*, 1972), John Forbes-Robertson (*The Legend of the 7 Golden Vampires*, 1974), Henry Polic II (*The Monster Squad*, 1976), Stephen Boyd (*Lady Dracula*, 1977), Michael **Pataki** (*Dracula's Dog*, 1977), Fabian Forte (*La dinastia Drácula*, 1978), Bent Borgesen (*Draculas ring*, 1978), Michael Nouri ('The Curse of Dracula', *Cliffhangers*, 1979), Duncan Regehr (*The Monster Squad*, 1987), David **Carradine** (*Sundown: The Vampire in Retreat*, 1988), Brendan Hughes (*To Die For*, 1988), Miles O'Keefe (*Waxwork*, 1988), Ben Cross (*Nightlife*, 1989), Geordi Johnson (*Dracula: The Series*, 1990-91), Michael Praed (*Son of Darkness: To Die For II*,

Dracula (Various)

1991) and Peter Fonda (*Nadja*, 1995). Of these second-string Counts, Francis Lederer (*The Return of Dracula*, 1958; 'The Devil is Not Mocked', **Night Gallery**, 1971) and Udo **Kier** (*Blood for Dracula*, 1974) acquit themselves well, escaping from the shadow of their rivals by offering genuinely fresh yet acceptable readings of the role; among stiff competition for the worst screen Dracula, the outstanding losers must be Mitch Evans (*Dr. Terror's Gallery of Horrors*, 1965), Vince Kelly (*Dracula the Dirty Old Man*, 1969) and Zandor Vorkov (*Dracula vs. Frankenstein*, 1970).

Granpa Munster (Al Lewis) of **The Munsters** (1964–6) may or may not be Dracula himself, but the Count has appeared in numberless skits, perversions and parodies played by an unlikely range of comedians: Jeffrey Smithers (*House on Bare Mountain*, 1962), a puppet (*Mad Monster Party?*, 1966), Cesar Romero ('A Matter of Semantics', *Night Gallery*, 1971), David Niven (*Vampira*, 1974), John Steiner (*Il Cav. Costante Nicosia demoniaco, ovvero: Dracula in Brianza*, 1975), Johnny Harden (*Star Virgin*, 1979), Gianni Garko (*Graf Dracula in Oberbayern*, 1979), Dick Shawn (*Mr. & Mrs. Dracula*, 1980), Jeffrey Tambor (*Saturday the 14th*, 1981), Charlie Callas (*Hysterical*, 1982), Edmond Purdom (*Fracchia contro Dracula*, 1985), Mike Horner (*Leena Meets Frankenstein*, 1993), Anthony Georghiou (*U.F.O.*, 1993), Leslie Nielsen (*Dracula: Dead and Loving It*, 1996). Best of this batch is George Hamilton (*Love at First Bite*, 1979), who makes his Lugosi-ish Count an unlikely romantic innocent; the worst – surprisingly given his heartfelt Dracula imitation in *Dance of the Vampires* (1967) – is Ferdy **Mayne** (*Gebissen wird nur nachts – Vampire Happening*, 1971), who arrives by helicopter and loses his trousers.

If Dracula himself is unavailable, sundry relatives have shown up: Gloria Holden (*Dracula's Daughter*, 1936), Lon **Chaney Jr** (*Son of Dracula*, 1943), Bill Rogers (*A Taste of Blood*, 1967), Soledad **Miranda** (*Vampyros lesbos*, 1970), Britt Nichols (*La Fille de Dracula*, 1971), Hope Stansbury (*Blood*, 1974), Harry Nilsson (*Son of Dracula*, 1974), Carlos Benpar (*El jovencito Drácula*, 1975), Bernard Menez (*Dracula, père et fils*, 1977), Geoffrey Land (*Doctor Dracula*, 1977), Nai Bonet (*Nocturna*, 1979), Louise **Fletcher** (*Mamma Dracula*, 1979), a cartoon (*Vampire Hunter D*, 1985), Sylvie Kristel (*Dracula's Widow*, 1988), Christopher Atkins (*Dracula Rising*, 1992), Elina Löwensohn (*Nadja*, 1995). Even the *name* of Dracula is enough for *Blood of Dracula* (1958), *Countess Dracula*

(1970), *The Mystery in Dracula's Castle* (1972), *Tendre Dracula* (1974), 'McCloud Meets Dracula' (*McCloud*, 1977) and 'A Dream of Dracula' (*Virtual Murder*, 1992), not to mention *Deafula* (1975), *Spermula* (1975), *Gayracula* (1983), *Rockula* (1990) and *Count Duckula* (1988).

Maybe it was the memory of Florence Stoker's vigorous pursuit of copyright-infringers, but no one got round to writing a Dracula spin-off until Manly Wade **Wellman**'s wartime anecdote 'The Devil is Not Mocked' (1942), and no full-length novel appeared until Otto Frederick's negli-

gible *Count Dracula's Canadian Affair* (1960). By contrast, the bone-pickers were at **Sherlock Holmes** almost before Arthur Conan **Doyle** left him alone. There have been whole *series* of Dracula sequels (or retellings) from Robert Lory (*Dracula Returns*, 1973), Fred Saberhagen (*The Dracula Tape*, 1975), Peter Tremayne (*Dracula Unborn*, 1977), R. **Chetwynd-Hayes** (*Dracula's Children*, 1987), Kim Newman (*Anno Dracula*, 1992), Jeanne Kalogridis (*Covenant With the Vampire*, 1994), and one-offs from Raymond Rudorff (*The Dracula Archives* (1971), Brian Hayles (the **radio** play *Prince Dracula*, 1972), Victor

Winona Ryder, Gary Oldman, *Bram Stoker's Dracula*

Samuels (*The Vampire Women*, 1973), Etienne Aubin (*Dracula and the Virgins of the Undead*, 1974), Gail Kimberley (*Dracula Began*, 1976), Loren D. Estleman (*Sherlock Holmes vs. Dracula*, 1978), John Shirley (*Dracula in Love*, 1979), Asa Drake (*Crimson Kisses*, 1981), Michael Corby and Michael Geare (*Dracula's Diary*, 1982), Brian Aldiss (*Dracula Unbound*, 1991), Dan Simmons (*Children of the Night*, 1993), Roderick Anscombe (*The Secret Life of Laszlo, Count Dracula*, 1994), Marie Kiraly (*Mina*, 1994) and Brian Stableford (*The Hunger and Ecstasy of Vampires*, 1996).

Also, there are rewrites for junior (Walter Gibson's 'Dracula the Vampire', *Monsters*, 1965) or adult (Amarantha Knight's *The Darker Passions: Dracula*, 1993) markets, and several runs of comic books (Marvel's *Tomb of Dracula*, 1972–80). Of all the genre's icons, Count Dracula is the most overworked and, perhaps, the most domesticated. While the **Frankenstein** monster has always had a doggily lovable streak that appeals especially to children, Dracula began as a double-dyed moustache-twirling villain and has over the years been reformed as a comical elderly relative or a haunted romantic. Dr **Polidori**'s Lord Ruthven and Anne **Rice**'s Lestat have perhaps overlapped with Stoker's monstrous brute, reshaping the popular image of the Count. It is, sadly, a long time since Dracula tried seriously to frighten anyone.

Dreams

The best horror films may be, in the fashionable terminology, 'oneiric', but most lack the true quality of nightmare. Failing that, their plots can be explained away as only a dream: examples range from D.W. Griffith's *The Avenging Conscience* (1914) to Phil Tucker's *Robot Monster* (1953). In a sophisticated variant, the dream begins to come true: this trick works for films from the classic *Dead of Night* (1945) to the forgettable *Incubo sulla città contaminata* (*Nightmare City*, 1980). Another device, in *Carrie* (1976), *Dressed to Kill* (1980) and **Friday the 13th** (1980), is to attach a shocking coda to the end of a thriller, then reveal the apparent return of the horror as a protagonist's nightmare. A dream can also be an atmospheric metaphor, used in **The Wolf Man** (1941), *Dr. Jekyll and Mr. Hyde* (1941) or *House of Dracula* (1945) to suggest metamorphosis into a monster. Similar dreams are also used to make the innocent seem guilty in *She-Wolf of London* (1946), *Devil Bat's Daughter* (1946) or *Daughter of Dr. Jekyll* (1957).

Nightmares are highlights of some horror

Dreams: *Spellbound*

films, like the burial in *Vampyr* (1931) or the resurrection in *The Plague of the Zombies* (1966); they also inject menace into mainstream movies: the hero's dream of death in **Bergman**'s *Smultronstället* (*Wild Strawberries*, 1957), or the delirium designed by Dali for **Hitchcock**'s *Spellbound* (1945). The intrusion of dreams into reality is a major theme in William **Castle**'s corny *The Night Walker* (1964), Oliver **Stone**'s heavy-handed *Seizure* (1973), Peter **Weir**'s ominous *The Last Wave* (1977), Joseph **Ruben**'s jolly *Dreamscape* (1984) and Bernard **Rose**'s poignant *Paperhouse* (1988); the idea spawned a pop culture franchise with the success of Wes **Craven**'s **A Nightmare on Elm Street** (1984), whose wisecracking dream killer Freddy Krueger reappears in sequels and inspires imitations like *Bad Dreams* (1988), *Dream Demon* (1988) and *SleepStalker: The Sandman's Last Rites* (1995). LD

Dreier, Hans (1885–1966)

German-born art director. Known for work with Josef von Sternberg (*The Scarlet Empress*, 1934) and Billy Wilder (*Sunset Blvd.*, 1950), Dreier was a specialist in the exotic, fantastical and weird.

The Hunchback of Notre Dame/1923 * *Dr. Jekyll and Mr. Hyde*/1932 * *Island of Lost Souls*/*Supernatural*/1933 * *Death Takes a Holiday*/1934 * *Maid of Salem*/1937 * *The Cat and the Canary*/1939 * *Dr. Cyclops*/*The Ghost Breakers*/1940 * *Among the Living*/*The Monster and the Girl*/1941 * *I Married a Witch*/1942 * *The Uninvited*/*The Man in Half Moon Street*/*Henry Aldrich Haunts a House*/1943 * *The Night Has a Thousand Eyes*/1948 * *Alias Nick Beal*/1949

Dreyer, Carl (1889–1968)

Danish director. *Vampyr* (1931), his only film capable of being subsumed in the horror genre, is one of the cinema's most mysterious evocations of the supernatural, nominally based on J. Sheridan **Le Fanu**'s novella 'Carmilla' (1871). Baron Nicholas de Gunzburg plays David Grey, who intervenes on behalf of two sisters under the spell of a female **vampire** and an evil doctor. In this haunted fogbound place shadows and reflections behave independently of their subjects, while the film's whiteness suggests it has been vampirised of shadow. Most copies of the film, which was shot in three languages, are incomplete and subtitled in language as dislocated as the narrative – all of which adds to the film's insidious power. *Vredens dag* (*Day of Wrath*, 1943) is a relentless study of religious superstition and **witch-hunting**, with an especially harrowing **torture** scene. RC

De Naede Fåergen (s)/1948

Tom Milne, *The Cinema of Carl Dreyer* (1971).

Drugs

Horror abounds in addicts. **Psychopaths** are compelled to kill as much as **zombies** are to devour flesh and **vampires** to drink **blood**. *Martin* (1976) supplies John Amplas with a syringe, while the curse of *The Vampire* (1958) comes in pill form and Christopher **Walken** in *The Addiction* (1995) has even got straight. In an image re-used by *Blood for Dracula* (1974) and *Cronos* (1992), *The Mummy's Hand* (1940) has its degraded, dependent monster suck tana juice from the temple floor. Marshall Thompson spends *Fiend Without a Face* (1958) speeding, *Corridors of Blood* (1958) stars **Karloff** as an anaesthetics fiend, and *The Tingler* (1959) sees Vincent **Price** mainline LSD. Hallucinogens drive *Matango* (1963), *The Trip* (1967), *I Drink Your Blood* (1971), *Blue Sunshine* (1977), *Killer's Moon* (1978), *Altered States* (1980) and *Brain Damage* (1987). Marijuana fuels the mystery of *La ragazza che sappeva troppo* (1962, but not that of Anglicisation *The Evil Eye*) and is also responsible for *Bloodeaters* (1979), but PCP in the water supply explains animals-and-children nasty *Wild*

Beasts (1983). Dr **Jekyll** is the genre's premiere user, but from *The Crimson Stain Mystery* (1916) on, a multiplicity of malfunctioning serums exist that suggest an awkward intimacy between mind and body. **Cronenberg**'s body-horrors are very much a product of the drug-wise 60s, as *Naked Lunch* (1991) emphasises. DP

du Maurier, Daphne (1907–89)

British writer. Two fine stories became important horror films by major directors, 'The Birds' (1952; filmed by **Hitchcock**, 1963) and 'Don't Look Now' (1971; filmed by Nicolas **Roeg**, 1973). *Rebecca* (1938), also filmed by Hitchcock (1940) and remade for television (1947, 1979, 1996), revives gothic romance for the 20th century. Her weird fiction is collected in *The Apple Tree* (1952) and *Echoes From the Macabre* (1976).

TV: *The Breakthrough*/1976 * *The Lifeforce Experiment*/1996

Dunn, Michael [Gary Neil Miller] (1935–74)

Talented American dwarf actor who always gave performances of stature. A semi-regular on **Wild Wild West** (1965–68) as diminutive **mad scientist** Dr Miguelito Loveless. SJ

No Way to Treat a Lady/1967 * *Murders in the Rue Morgue*/1971 * *The Mutations/The*

RIGHT Carl Dreyer

Werewolf of Washington/Il castello della paura [*Frankenstein's Castle of Freaks*]/1973

TV: *Voyage to the Bottom of the Sea*: 'The Wax Men'/1967 * *Night Gallery*: 'The Sins of the Fathers'/1972

Dyall, Valentine (1908–85)

Skeletal British character actor whose sepulchral voice made him famous as **radio**'s mysterious Man in Black on *Appointment with Fear* (1943–55), a role he reprised on TV and in film in 1949. A cruel lodger suspected of being **Jack the Ripper** in **Hammer**'s *Room to Let* (1950). SJ

Latin Quarter/1945 * *The Ghost of Rashmon Hall*/1947 * *Corridor of Mirrors/Queen of Spades*/1948 * *Dr Morelle: The Case of the Missing Heiress/The Man in Black/Helter Skelter*/1949 * *City of the Dead*/1960 * *The Haunting/The Horror of it All*/1963 * *Bizarre* (v)/1970 * *Britannia Hospital*/1982

TV: *Stranger From Space*/1951–2 * *The Avengers*: 'You'll Catch Your Death'/1968 * *Sapphire and Steel*: 'Doctor McDee Must Die'/1981 * *Doctor Who*: 'The Armageddon Factor'/1979; 'Mawdryn Undead'/ 'Terminus'/'Enlightenment'/1983

E

Eastern Europe

The austere relationship between art and **politics** in Eastern Europe has precluded the development of coherent genre horror in this large, culturally diverse cluster of nations. War and occupation have also played a part in the strife-torn population's disinterest in horror as entertainment.

Carl Dreyer's *Vampyr*

Czech Republic and Slovakia * Juraj Jakubisko's *Zbehovia a pútnici* (*The Deserter and the Nomads*, 1968) is an **apocalyptic** tale with numerous horror elements, including 'mondo' footage of a pig slaughter, the torture of hapless villagers by deranged soldiers and a personal appearance by Death in a fall-out shelter packed with ragged survivors. A borderline case is Oldrich Lipsky's *Stastny konec* (*Happy End,* 1966), a bizarre horror comedy which literally runs backwards, commencing with a murder victim's decapitated head rejoining her body. The killer unkills her, unplots against her, unmarries her and falls back in love with his dowdy girlfriend. Jan **Švankmajer**'s chilling, deeply weird animations include fragmented adaptations of **Poe**: *Zánik domu Usherů* (*The Fall of the House of Usher*, 1981), *Kyvadlo, jáma a naděje* (*The Pit, the Pendulum and Hope*, 1983). More fokloric are frequently nightmarish fairytales like Jaromil Jireš's *Valerie a týden divů* (*Valerie and Her Week of Wonders*, 1970), with its Nosferatu-faced **vampire**, and Juraj Herz's *Panna a netvor* (*Beauty and the Beast*, 1978), with its unusual bird monster. Czech emigrés of note include Hans Janovitz, co-scenarist of *Das Cabinet des Dr. Caligari* (1919), and Karl **Freund**, while Prague has been home to **Kafka**, **Faust**, the **Golem**.

Poland * Janusz Majewski worked in the horror genre several times. His short *Ja gore* (*I'm On Fire*, 1967) features a nobleman taunted by the hellbound ghost of his castle's previous owner. He adapted two Prosper Mérimée stories, *La vénère d'ille* (for Polish TV) and *Professor Wittembach's Manuscript* (as *Lokis/The Bear*, 1970). He also made *System* (1971), a short based on Poe's 'The System of Doctor Tarr and Prof. Fether' (1845). Jacek Koprowicz's *Medium* (1985) mixes *Patrick* (1978)-style psychic material with a plot that links occultism and fascism; Mariusz Grzegorzek's *Robak* (*The Worm*, 1988) is a nightmarish short about child abuse; and Janusz Zaorski's *Na dobranoc* (*A Good Night Story*, 1970) is a twenty five minute black and white parody of American horror films. Andrzej Zulawski's intense psychodramatic exorcisms frequently approach horror, though his 'art film' manners tended to alienate some fans who resented his 'intrusion' into the genre with the brilliant Franco-Polish *Possession* (1981). His *Diabel* (*The Devil*, 1972), set during the partition of Poland in the 18th century, focuses on cruelty and corruption, manipulated by a weirdly commonplace **Devil**. Acknowledging the warping lens of historical account, Zulaw-ski's wicked fairy tale adopts hallucinatory style: it was promptly banned by the authorities. At the edge of the genre is Krzysztof Kieslowski's *Krótki film o zabijaniu* (*A Short Film About Killing*, 1988), a gruelling exploration of nasty crime and even nastier punishment. Roman **Polanski** and Walerian **Borowczyk** eventually found refuge from the stifling communist old guard in Paris and the US and worked in horror.

Romania/Hungary * Ironically, the genre has been almost entirely disdained in these countries. Horror films were looked on as a 'low' culture import from the West, unsuitable for imitation. Vlad Tepes, the mediaeval prince considered the historic model for Bram **Stoker**'s **Dracula**, is a national hero to Romanians, who resent his portrayal as a monster. Dimitru Fernoaga's *Vlad Tepes* (*The True Life of Dracula*, 1980) is an official version, though the Hungarian-born Peter **Sasdy** fittingly dispenses with the Count's roots in *Taste the Blood of Dracula* (1969). Other Hungarian exports to Western horror are Michael **Curtiz**, Bela **Lugosi** and Peter **Lorre**. **Transylvania**, now part of Romania though historically Hungarian, is a setting for many Western horror films. With the collapse of communism, Romania has been the location as well as locale for a few vampire movies: *Subspecies* (1990) and sequels; *Daughter of Darkness* (1990).

(Former) Yugoslavia * There has been almost no engagement with horror film in this now blood-drenched territory, though Goran Markovic's *Vec videno* (*Déjà Vu*, 1987), a part satirical study of homicidal mania, and Serbian Slobodan Sijan's *Davitelj protiv davitelja* (*Strangler vs. Strangler*, 1984), a thriller with references to classical German and American horror, just about qualify.

All of these countries have produced politically themed films dealing with state **violence**, military conflict and the unrelenting misery of those living and dying under vicious regimes. While some examples undoubtedly have the power to horrify (the Pole Ryszard Bugajski's harrowing *Przesluchanie/Interrogation*, 1981), they fall outside the scope of genre. ST

Eastman, George * See: **Montefiori, Luigi**

EC Comics

Between 1950 and 1954, William M. Gaines published successful, innovative and influential **comics**. In the flagship titles (*Tales From the Crypt, The Vault of Horror, The Haunt of Fear*), horror stories are introduced by the Crypt Keeper, the Vault Keeper and the Old Witch, gruesome characters modelled on the hosts of **radio** shows like *Inner Sanctum* (1941–52) and *The Witch's Tale* (1931–8). EC also put out *Shock SuspenStories* and *Crime SuspenStories*, which concentrate on non-supernatural *contes cruels*, and *Weird Science* and *Weird Fantasy*, which often dress up horror plots in Flash Gordon spaceclothes. Mostly written by Gaines or Albert Feldstein, who were not above poaching a **Lovecraft** or **Bradbury** plot to meet a slew of monthly deadlines, EC stories afforded opportunities for the grotesque taken in different ways by artists Jack Davis, Graham 'Ghastly' Ingels, Johnny Craig, Jack Kamen, Reed Crandall, Wally Wood and Bernard Krigstein.

Early issues are basic in content but EC horrors swiftly developed a distinctive tone influenced by radio, **pulps** and ex-soldiers' acceptance of black comedy. EC stories feature rotting **zombies** or drooling homicidal maniacs and are rooted in a dark morality whereby wrong-doers are extravagantly, ironically and permanently punished. A backlash against explicit horrors served as children's reading coalesced around pop psychologist Fredric Wertham, whose *The Seduction of the Innocent* (1954) alleged a link between horror and crime comics and juvenile delinquency. In Fritz **Lang**'s *While the City Sleeps* (1956), strangler John Drew Barrymore is shown reading *Tales From the Crypt*. After congressional hearings, the industry imposed a self-regulating code which effectively outlawed horror from the medium until the 70s. The EC titles folded and Gaines and company directed their enthusiasms into *MAD*.

The repressed returned, inspiring film **anthologies** (*Tales From the Crypt*, 1972; *The Vault of Horror*, 1973), homages (*Creepshow*, 1982; *Creepshow 2*, 1987) and a cable TV show (*Tales From the Crypt*, 1989–) which in turn spun off movies (*Tales From the Crypt: Demon Knight*, 1995; *Tales From the Crypt: Bordello of Blood*, 1996) and an animated series (*Tales From the Cryptkeeper*, 1994–). The Crypt Keeper, voiced by John Kassir in the cable show, even has a guest spot in *Casper* (1995). Writers and film-makers Stephen **King**, George **Romero** and Sam **Raimi** admit an EC influence. Though *Death Trap* (1976) and *The Evil Dead* (1982) are hailed as tales of rotting backwoods horror in the EC tradition, it is less noticed that *Blood Simple* (1984) and *Shallow Grave* (1994) are descended from the SuspenStories.

Martin Barker, *A Haunt of Fears* (1984)

Eco-Horror

Nature is habitually bucked in horror, with disastrous results. Scientists forever try to circumvent the processes which, by definition, the supernatural must also flout. Anti-ecological positions are outlined in films ranging from the Darwinian *Balaoo* (1913) to nuclear nightmare *The Beast from 20,000 Fathoms* (1953); **zombies** (*No profanar el sueño de los muertos*, 1974), Godzilla (*Gojira tai Hedora*, 1971) and giant rabbits (*Night of the Lepus*, 1972) are all co-opted by the 70s shockers that sprang from 60s back-to-naturism. Though **Troma** has built an empire on *The Toxic Avenger* (1985) and Mario **Bava**'s *Ecologia del delitto* (*Bloodbath*, 1971) cannot be ignored, horror's most surprising environmentalist is Leatherface (**The Texas Chain Saw Massacre**, 1974), whose sole concern is to return man to the food-chain. The **cannibals** of *Motel Hell* (1980) even plant their victuals in the garden and are less ashamed of mass murder than of using artificial preservatives. Some movies ennoble nature by anthropomorphising monsters: *King Kong* (1933), *The Creature from the Black Lagoon* (1954), *Gorgo* (1961). Others apocalyptically stress nature's inscrutability: *The Birds* (1963), *Frogs* (1972), *Long Weekend* (1977), *Squirm* (1978). Gladly forsaking his rural idyll, the hero of *Arachnophobia* (1990) implies man will always be

at odds with the natural. The unlikely counter-argument is put in Dario **Argento**'s *Phenomena* (1985). DP

Eerie, Indiana (US TV series, 1991–92)

A **situation comedy** set in a Twin Peaks-cum-Mayberry small town stricken with supernatural phenomena: dental braces allow the wearer to read dogs' minds, a mummy actor escapes from a telecast movie, a sentient wind duels with a tornado hunter. In 'Reality Takes a Holiday', the town is seen to be the setting of a TV series and all the characters are actors. Joe **Dante** served as creative consultant and directed six episodes, co-opting kindred souls like Bob **Balaban** (*Parents*, 1989) and Tim Hunter (*River's Edge*, 1986) to fill out the run. Omri Katz stars as Marshall Teller, the teenager who seems to be the only resident who notices how odd things are. Likable and offbeat, but too clever to be a hit and not quite strange enough attract a cult.

Egyptology * See: **Mummies**; *The Mummy*

Eisner, Lotte (1896–1983)

German film historian. *L'ecran démoniaque* (*The Haunted Screen*, 1952) is the pioneering work on German **Expressionism**. Other important studies: *Murnau* (1973), *Fritz Lang* (1976).

Denholm Elliott, *To the Devil a Daughter*

Elder, John * See: **Anthony Hinds**

Elliott, Denholm (1922–92)

British actor. Often in literary horrors, he made a fine TV **Dracula**. SJ

The Night My Number Came Up/1955 * *The House That Dripped Blood*/1970 * *Vault of Horror*/1973 * *To the Devil a Daughter*/1976 * *The Hound of the Baskervilles*/1977 * *The Boys from Brazil*/1978 * *Raiders of the Lost Ark*/1981 * *Brimstone & Treacle*/1982 * *Underworld*/1985 * *Indiana Jones and the Last Crusade*/1989

TV: *Alfred Hitchcock Presents*: 'The Crocodile Case'/1958 * 'Relative Value'/1959 * *The Wednesday Thriller*: 'The House'/1965 * *Mystery and Imagination*: 'The Fall of the House of Usher'/1966; 'Dracula'/1969 * *The Strange Case of Dr. Jekyll and Mr. Hyde*/1968 * *Thriller*: 'The Crazy Kill'/1975 * *Brimstone & Treacle*/1976 * *A Ghost Story for Christmas*: 'The Signalman'/1976 * *Supernatural*: 'Lady Sybil'/1977 * *Tales of the Unexpected*: 'The Stinker'/1980 * *Hammer House of Horror*: 'Rude Awakening'/1980 * *The Hound of the Baskervilles*/1983 * *Ray Bradbury Theatre*: 'The Coffin'/1988

Ellison, Harlan (b. 1934)

American writer. Most associated with s-f, Ellison's baroque, intense short stories often have a horrific or demented edge. Among many collections, with bewilderingly overlapping contents: *Paingod* (1965), *Deathbird Stories* (1975), *The Essential Ellison* (1987). His post-apocalyptic 'A Boy and His Dog' (1969) was filmed in 1975. TV genre work includes

Eco-Horror: *Squirm*

superior time travel stories for **Star Trek** ('The City on the Edge of Forever', 1967) and **The Outer Limits** ('Demon With a Glass Hand', 1964; 'Soldier', 1964). His oddest credit is a **Jack the Ripper** episode of the Western *Cimarron Strip* ('Killer With a Knife', 1967), a spin-off from 'The Prowler in the City at the Edge of Forever' (1969). As 'creative consultant', he is attached to **The Twilight Zone** (1985–7) and the **Lovecraft**-tinged s-f series *Babylon 5* (1993–).

TV: *The Alfred Hitchcock Hour*: 'Memo From Purgatory'/1964 * *Voyage to the Bottom of the Sea*: 'The Price of Doom'/1964 * *The Man From U.N.C.L.E.*: 'The Sort of Do-It-Yourself Dreadful Affair'/1966; 'The Pieces of Fate Affair'/1967 * *Circle of Fear*: 'Earth, Air, Fire and Water'/1973 * *Curse of the Black Widow* (st-u)/1977 * *Tales From the Darkside*; 'D'jinn, No Chaser'/1984 * *The Twilight Zone*: 'Shatterday' (+st)/'Paladin of the Lost Hour' (+st)/ 'One Life, Furnished in Early Poverty' (st)/ 1985; 'Gramma'/1986; 'Crazy as a Soup Sandwich'/1989

Elmi, Nicoletta (b. 1965?)

Italian actress. A creepy, red-haired little girl, often a junior murderess. *Demoni* (1985) is a rare adult outing.

Ecologia del delitto [*Bay of Blood*]/1971 * *Gli orrori degli castello di Norimberga* [*Baron Blood*]/*Chi l'ha vista morire?* [*Who Saw Her Die?*]/1972 * *Flesh for Frankenstein*/*Profondo rosso* [*Deep Red*]/*Il medaglione insanguinato* [*Night Child*]/*Le orme*/1975

Elvira [Cassandra Peterson] (b. 1951)

American **horror host**. Black-beehived, deep-cleavaged, Elvira introduced and interrupted films on a TV show, *Movie Macabre*. Peterson starred in (and co-wrote) a weak vehicle, *Elvira, Mistress of the Dark* (1988). Her persona is a mix of **Vampira**, Morticia and Mae West.

Jekyll and Hyde . . . Together Again/1982 * *Stroker Ace*/1983

TV: *The Fall Guy*: 'October the 31st'/1984

Endore, Guy (1901–70)

American writer. Remembered for his novel *The Werewolf of Paris* (1933), filmed as *The Curse of the Werewolf* (1960), Endore contributed to interesting 30s horror films. He translated **Ewers**'s *Alraune* (1929) and wrote historical fiction (*Satan's Saint: A Novel About the Marquis de Sade*, 1965). *Methinks the Lady . . .* (1945), a thriller with psychic touches,

Robert Englund, *A Nightmare on Elm Street, Part 2: Freddy's Revenge*

was filmed by Otto Preminger as *Whirlpool* (1950). Blacklisted, he used the name 'Harry Relis' on *Captain Sindbad* (1963).

Mark of the Vampire/*Mad Love*/*The Raven*/1935 * *The Devil-Doll*/1936

Englund, Robert (b. 1949)

American actor. Freddy Krueger, a virtual cameo in **A Nightmare on Elm Street** (1984), turned bit-player Englund into a 80s horror star, though the short, nervy American is not well served by roles like **The Phantom of the Opera** (1989) or the Marquis de **Sade**

Elvira, Mistress of the Dark

(*Night Terrors*, 1993). Having dominated *Elm Street* sequels with wisecracks and extended the Freddy role to horror host status for *Freddy's Nightmares* (1989–90), he used his **Fangoria** coverboy clout to win a minor directing gig, *976-EVIL* (1989). In *Wes Craven's New Nightmare* (1994), he plays himself and Freddy.

Slashed Dreams/1974 * *Death Trap*/1976 * *Dead and Buried*/*Galaxy of Terror*/1981 * *A Nightmare on Elm Street, Part Two: Freddy's Revenge*/1985 * *Never Too Young to Die*/1986 * *A Nightmare on Elm Street 3: Dream Warriors*/ 1987 * *A Nightmare on Elm Street 4: The Dream Master*/1988 * *A Nightmare on Elm Street 5: The Dream Child*/1989 * *Freddy's Dead: The Final Nightmare*/*Danse Macabre*/1991 * *The Mangler*/ 1995 * *The Killer Tongue*/1996

TV: *Mind Over Murder*/1979 * *Manimal*: 'Night of the Beast' * *Freddy's Nightmares* (d): 'Cabin Fever'/'Monkey Dreams'/1989 * *Nightmare Cafe*/1991

ESP

For movie purposes, the most popular version of extra-sensory perception, an elusive talent, is mind control, the imposition of one will on another, much feared as an inevitable consequence of conformism and censorship. Often associated with the supernatural, mental displacement can result from proximity to a malevolent painting (*The Haunted Palace*, 1963), from acquiring second-hand limbs (*Orlacs Hände*, 1925), from encounters with vengeful ghosts (*The Possession*

ESP: Martin Stephens, *Village of the Damned*

of Joel Delaney, 1972; *Ruby*, 1977; *Audrey Rose*, 1977) or from invasion by parasites of all kinds (*Brain Damage*, 1988; *The Puppet Masters*, 1995).

Pleasantly lurid examples of mental manipulation, based on Stephen **King** stories, have been *It* (1990), featuring evil mesmerist clown Pennywise, and *The Tommyknockers* (1993), with a community spellbound by underground influences. King was also the source for *Carrie* (1976), an incendiary display of telekinesis – the ability to shift things by thought alone. The sight of inanimate objects on the move has fascinated audiences since the first trick films, but the transfixing of Piper Laurie by a broadside of kitchen cutlery prepared the way for new extremes of cinematic derangement. These were promptly staged by the same director, Brian **De Palma**, in the first 'exploding

head' film, *The Fury* (1978), emulated in the same year by *The Medusa Touch* (Richard Burton downs an airliner with one glare) and *Patrick* (comatose patient creates merry hell), and soon topped by **Cronenberg**'s *Scanners* (1980).

Precognition, the foreseeing of future events, has proved less photogenic: rare screen sightings have been *Sette Notte in Nero* (*The Psychic*, 1977), Stephen King's *The Dead Zone* (1983), *Out of the Body* (1988), *The Premonition* (1992), **Nostradamus** (1993), *Safe Passage* (1995) and **Spielberg**'s *Amazing Stories* episode 'You Gotta Believe Me (1985). Predictive elements occasionally feature in 'empathy' dramas, based on a supposed link – or 'calling' – between twins or close relatives. This has intrigued both De Palma (*Sisters*, 1972; *Raising Cain*, 1992) and Cronenberg (*Dead Ringers*, 1988), while the

psychic solving of crime has become staple teleplay material: *Visions* (1972), *Mind over Murder* (1979), *Fear* (1990), *Psychic* (1992).

Telepathy, the ultimate in communication, is an anticipated gift for man's distant future, whether taking the form of the Force in *Star Wars* (1977), an elitist matriarchy in *Dune* (1984), the Betazoids of *Star Trek: The Next Generation* (1987–94) or the troublemaking Psi-Corps of *Babylon 5* (1993–). Significantly, heightened mental skills are often seen as an uncontrolled youthful talent erupting in extreme crisis, as in *Carrie* and two other King stories, *The Shining* (1980) and *Firestarter* (1984). This linking of childhood with a violent conspirational power over adults extends from *The Space Children* (1958), *Village of the Damned* (1960, 1994) and *Children of the Damned* (1963) to *The Tomorrow People* (1973–79, 1992–95) and *The*

Secret World of Alex Mack (1994), which, unsurprisingly, are popular children's programs. PS

Etchison, Dennis (b. 1943)

American writer. A specialist in dark Californiana, Etchison's best is collected in *The Dark Country* (1982), *Red Dreams* (1985) and *The Blood Kiss* (1987). 'The Late Shift' (1980) was filmed as a short *Killing Time* (1986). Having novelised as 'Dennis Etchinson' (*The Fog*, 1980) and 'Jack Martin' (*Halloween II*, 1981; *Videodrome*, 1981; *Halloween III: Season of the Witch*, 1983), he ventured into long form with *Darkside* (1986), *Shadowman* (1993) and *California Gothic* (1995). As script doctor, consultant or first draft man, he contributed to **The Hitchhiker** (1983–91), *Halloween IV: The Return of Michael Myers* (1988), *Night Life* (1989), *Blood Ties* (1991), *La setta* (1991) and *Trauma* (1993). A character in *Prince of Darkness* (1987) is named 'Etchinson' in tribute to him.

Evans, Clifford (1912–85)

Welsh actor. As the fanatical **vampire** hunter Professor Zimmer, he proved himself a fair **Van Helsing** substitute in *The Kiss of the Vampire* (1962). SJ

House of Mystery/1939 * *The Curse of the Werewolf*/1960

TV: *Jack the Ripper*/1958 * *One Step Beyond*: 'Justice'/1961 * *The Avengers*: 'Death's Door'/1968 * *Randall and Hopkirk (Deceased)*: 'When Did You Stop Seeing Things?'/1969

Everson, William K. (1929–96)

British-born film historian, critic. *Classics of the Horror Film* (1974) is a cornerstone study of pre-50s horror film. *More Classics of the Horror Film* (1986) is less successful in covering recent material than in winkling out more from the period covered by the first volume. Also ground-breaking are *The Bad Guys* (1962) and *The Detective in Film* (1972).

The Evil Touch (Canadian TV series, 1973–4)

A cheap anthology on the **Twilight Zone** model, hosted by Anthony Quayle, with struggling American guest stars like Leslie Nielsen, Harry Guardino, Carol Lynley and Robert Lansing. The mix offers ghosts ('Death By Dreaming'), suspense ('Dear Carol, I'm Going to Kill You') and monsters

RIGHT Jason Miller, Max von Sydow, *The Exorcist*

('Heart to Heart'). It is likely Stephen **King** was among the tiny audience: *Misery* (1987) owes something to 'The Fans', with Vic Morrow (who also directs) as a horror star kidnapped by his greatest fans, while 'Children of the Corn' (1977) echoes 'They'.

Ewers, Hanns Heinz (1871–1943)

German writer, spy. His novel *Alraune* (1911), about a soulless woman fathered by artificial insemination, was filmed in 1918 (twice), 1928 and 1930 (with Brigitte Helm) and 1952 (with Hildegarde Knef). Ewers's alter ego Frank Braun also appears in *Der Zauberlehrling* (1907, *The Sorcerer's Apprentice*) and *Vampir* (1921, *Vampire*); his stories (which **Lovecraft** admired) are collected in *Das Grauen* (1907) and *Nachtmar* (1921). Ewers wrote 1913 and 1926 *doppelgänger* films *Der Student von Prag*, remade without him in 1935. Official biographer of Horst Wessel, Ewers was purged from the Nazi Party for pro-Semitism. He appears in Kim Newman's novel *The Bloody Red Baron* (1995).

Exorcism

A long-standing, multicultural rite in which an invading spirit or demon is cast from the body of a host by a wizard, holy man, priest, etc. Christian exorcists date back to Jesus Christ, who cast a 'legion' of demons from a Geresenes man, and ordered His disciples to do likewise. In the Middle Ages, Pope Gregory IX authorised the Dominican Order to pursue violent exorcisms against heretics and those beset by succubi, the popular demons **du jour**.

During the Inquisition, exorcisms were public spectacles, with 7,000 attending a 1566 ritual in Laon, while 30,000 people observed the mass exorcisms of Loudon. Urbain Grandier's torture and burning for the possession of Sister Jeanne of the Angels inspired Ken **Russell**'s *The Devils* (1971), from the writings of John Whiting and Aldous Huxley, and Jerzy Kawalerowicz's *Matka Joanna od aniołów* (*Mother Joan of the Angels*, 1960). Freud's 'The Neurosis of Demoniacal Possession in the Seventeenth Century' (1923) paved the way for psychological debunking of demonic **possession**. Modern Western exorcisms persist: a young boy exorcised in Maryland inspired the book (1971) and movie (1973) *The Exorcist*. In 1991, the televised exorcism of a young (and clearly disturbed) American girl led to widespread derision and public outcry, though furtive exorcisms continue both in Europe and America. MK

The Exorcist

As a novel and film, *The Exorcist* provoked widespread hysteria and sparked off a lucrative 70s horror boom. Having failed to gain clerical permission to pen a factual account of a Maryland boy's 1949 exorcism, writer William Peter **Blatty** devised his own

LEFT Expressionism, Conrad Veidt, Lil Dagover, *Das Cabinet des Dr. Caligari*

fictional tale of a girl's demonic **possession**. Fifty-five weeks on the US best-seller list, the 1971 novel was adapted for the screen in 1973 by writer-producer Blatty (who cameos in the movie as an irate producer) and Oscar-winning director William **Friedkin**. John Boorman's recklessly dismal *Exorcist II: The Heretic* (1977), with Linda **Blair** and Max von **Sydow** returning as possessee Regan and exorcist Father Merrin, was labelled 'the work of a demented mind' by Blatty and Friedkin. Blatty's *The Exorcist III* (1990), with Jason Miller reprising his Father Karras, is a heavily recut rendering of his sequel novel *Legion* (1983). Possession rip-offs ensued from Italy and elsewhere; parodies are *The Hound of the Baskervilles* (1977), *The Duxorcist* (1987) and *Repossessed* (1990). MK

William Peter Blatty on The Exorcist (1974); Peter Travis, Stephanie Reiff, *The Story Behind The Exorcist* (1974); Howard Newman, *The Exorcist: The Strange Story Behind The Film* (1974); Barbara Pallenberg, *The Making of Exorcist II: The Heretic* (1977); Thomas Allen, *Possessed* (1993)

Expressionism

An art movement responsible for the morbid stylisation of a number of German movies in the wake of World War I, expressionism exerts a delineating force on the horror film. Violently opposed to naturalism, expressionism addressed the latent significance of objects and actions through stark artifice. For cinema, this meant not only the importation of certain painterly, dramatic and novelistic devices, but also a harnessing of the angularity and *chiaroscuro* already at play in the work of Danes like Benjamin **Christensen** and Stellan Rye, together with a new recognition of the suspension of disbelief film uniquely affords.

All serrate distortion and painted shadow, with antagonists that derive alarmingly from their environment, **Das Cabinet des Dr. Caligari** (1919) is the first of the expressionist experiments. Despite the imposition of a normalising frame-story (and the fact that the crucial Hermann Warm/Walter Reimann/Walter Röhrig set designs were basically an afterthought) it is inarguably also the purest. Several subsequent movies attempted to ape the style, a pair (*Genuine*, 1920; *Raskolnikow*, 1923) directed by *Caligari*'s Robert **Wiene**. More used elements to enhance their sense of the uncanny: Conrad **Veidt**'s *Wahnsinn* (*Madness*, 1919), Paul **Wegener** and Carl Boese's *Der Golem, wie er in die Welt kam* (*The Golem*, 1920), Arthur Robison's *Schatten* (*Warning Shadows*, 1923), Paul **Leni**'s *Das Wachsfigurenkabinett* (*Waxworks*, 1924), Henrik **Galeen**'s *Der Student von Prag* (*The Student of Prague*, 1926) and a run of Fritz **Lang** entries.

A spiky shadowcaster tainting the landscapes he moves through, Max **Schreck** is an anomalously expressionist fiend in F.W. **Murnau**'s *Nosferatu, Eine Symphonie des Grauens* (*Nosferatu*, 1921). Released to America in 1921, *Caligari* moved Sam Goldwyn to produce the similarly World War I-informed freakshow *A Blind Bargain* (1922). The arrival of *Der Golem* catalysed both the spectacle and monstrosity of subsequent Lon **Chaney** vehicle **The Hunchback of Notre Dame** (1925). *Der Golem* also set obvious precedents for Universal's **Frankenstein** (1931): Robert **Florey** test reels dressed **Lugosi** up like Paul Wegener; eventual director James **Whale** rescreened the movie as a preparatory aid. **Karloff**'s performance owes much to the emotive robotics of the expressionist stage.

The haemorrhaging of European personnel into Hollywood also accounts for a spread of expressionist tropes: Paul **Leni**'s input animates a succession of Broadway-adapted comic-horrors, while Karl **Freund**'s contributions to the otherwise negligently theatrical **Dracula** (1931) make for a watch that almost palpably records the birth pangs of a new genre. It is therefore felicitous that when German horror was reinvented after the callousing experiences of World War II, Victor Trivas' formative *Die Nackte und der Satan* (*The Head*, 1959) featured design-work from expressionist linch-pin Hermann Warm. Recent homage is paid in the pre-centennial celebrations of Guy Maddin (*Tales from the Gimli Hospital*, 1987), Woody Allen (*Shadows and Fog*, 1991), Tim **Burton** (*Batman Returns*, 1992) and Francis Ford **Coppola** (*Bram Stoker's Dracula*, 1992). DP

Siegfried Kracauer, *From Caligari to Hitler: A Psychological History of German Film* (1947); Lotte **Eisner**, *L'ecran démoniaque* (*The Haunted Screen*, 1952); Francis Courtade and Henri Veyrier, *Cinéma expressioniste* (1984)

Eyes

Perhaps the first cinematic eye-penetration was perpetrated by **Méliès**'s famous rocket which lands sharply in the right eye of the Man in the Moon in *Le voyage dans la lune* (1903). This has been followed by a rich history of squeamishly disturbing moments of

RIGHT Eyes: *Un Chien Andalou*

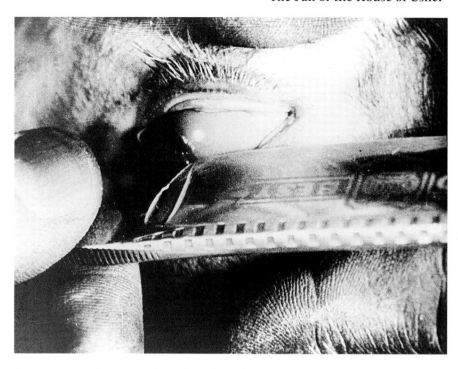

eye-**violence** that have tested audience tolerance and fear, as well as horror narratives fixing on the powers and disturbances of blindness.

Eyes are sliced by blades in Luis **Buñuel**'s *Un chien andalou* (1928) and Lucio **Fulci**'s *Lo squartatore di New York* (*The New York Ripper*, 1982); shot point-blank in Dario **Argento**'s *Opera* (1987); pecked out, gouged with needles, splinters or mirror shards in *The Birds* (1963), *Suspiria* (1976), *Zombi 2* (*Zombie Flesh Eaters*, 1979) and *Manhunter* (1986); forced open with metal clamps in *A Clockwork Orange* (1971). Schwarzenegger performs robotic self-surgery on his injured eye in *The Terminator* (1984), while in *The Funny Man* (1994) – echoing a serious stomping from *Matthew Hopkins Witchfinder General* (1968) – a character 'gets the point' with a stiletto heel in the eye.

A self-reflexive thread running through horror-thrillers aligns the viewer's point of view with the murderer's gaze, exemplified in a number of **stalk-and-slash** films since *Peeping Tom* (1960), which features the **subjective camera**-eye as weapon, as well as the blind woman as strange seer – a motif picked up in *Eyes of a Stranger* (1980). LRW

Eyes: Karl Bohm, *Peeping Tom*

F

'The Fall of the House of Usher'
(1839)

Edgar Allan **Poe**'s story is modelled on European gothic but reflects American psychology by rooting its curse in madness. Roderick Usher and his sister Madeline, whom he has **buried alive**, perish as the house which architecturally embodies the family's corruption crumbles into the tarn. There are adaptations by Jean Epstein (*La chute de la Maison Usher*, 1928), Melville Webber (1928), Ivan Barnett (1948), Curtis **Harrington** (1948), Arch **Oboler** (*Lights Out*, 1949), *Matinee Theatre* (1956), NBC-TV (1958), Roger **Corman** (1960), Kim Mills (*Tales of Mystery and Imagination*, 1966), James L. Conway (1978), Jan **Svankmajer** (*Zánik domu Usherů*, 1981), Jesús **Franco** (*El hundimiento de la Casa Usher*, 1983) and Alan Birkinshaw (*The House of Usher*, 1988). Rodericks include Vincent **Price**, Denholm **Elliott**, Martin **Landau**, Tom **Tryon**, Helmut Dantine and Oliver **Reed**. In *Due occhi diabolici* (*Two Evil Eyes*, 1990), Harvey Keitel's character is called 'Rod Usher'. *The Darker Passions: The Fall of the House of Usher* (1995) by Amarantha Knight [Nancy Kilpatrick] is an erotic rewrite, hampered by a porn morality that allows all manner of perversity save Poe's essential subtext, incest.

Family Values

The rise of the modern horror film can be charted in terms of the genre's changing family values. The genre's fantastic elements allow familial tensions to be expressed. Pervasive monster myths (**vampires**, **werewolves**, **Jekyll and Hyde**) conveniently allow individuals (usually patriarchal figures) to turn against their families while in a 'transformed' state.

Early films assert the moral supremacy of the nuclear family, monogamy and middle-class morality: monstrous seducers are defied by heterosexual couples protected by patriarchs in **Dracula** (1930), **The Mummy** (1932) and **The Black Cat** (1934), a pattern replicated a generation later by **Hammer**'s remakes **Dracula** (1958), **The Mummy** (1959) and *Kiss of the Vampire* (1964). **Lewton**'s 40s films stand out for an innovative relocating of horror within the family, from tragic sibling rivalry in *The Seventh Victim* (1943) to the competing attentions for Kent Smith in **Cat People** (1943). Familial rivalry and the tensions of motherhood are explored in *La llorona* (*The Crying Woman*, 1933) where a woman commits suicide following the familial murder of her four-year-old child, while *The Uninvited* (1945), a prototype of the **possession** movie, has Gail Russell haunted by alleged and actual mothers.

Within marriage, the mad husband is a popular melodramatic figure: *Murders in the Zoo* (1933), *Love From a Stranger* (1936), **Gaslight** (1940, 1944), *Secret Beyond the Door . . .* (1948), **Les diaboliques** (1955), *The Screaming Skull* (1958), *Sleeping with the Enemy* (1991). And a familial reworking of Jekyll and Hyde is explored in films featuring **twins**: *The Black Room* (1935), *Dead Men Walk* (1943), *Sisters* (1972), *Basket Case* (1981), *Dead Ringers* (1988), *Raising Cain* (1992). Families were under attack in the buttoned-down 50s: a child is orphaned by giant ants in the opening of *Them!* (1954); marriages are sundered by mutation in *The Quatermass Experiment* (1956), *The Fly* (1958) and *The Alligator People* (1959); and families are alien-infiltrated in *Invaders From Mars* (1954), **Invasion of the Body Snatchers** (1956) and *The Day Mars Invaded Earth* (1962).

The ground-breaking **Psycho** (1960) and *Peeping Tom* (1960) demonstrate families can create and nurture monsters, a theme developed by *What Ever Happened to Baby Jane?* (1962), *Fanatic* (1965), *The Psychopath* (1965), *The Beast in the Cellar* (1971) and *Taste the Blood of Dracula* (1971). The watershed films,

Family Values: Dana Wynter, King Donovan, Carlyn Jones. Kevin McCarthy, *Invasion of the Body Snatchers*

Rosemary's Baby (1968) and **Night of the Living Dead** (1968) challenge earlier assumptions by representing the 'normal' family as monstrous or useless. As horror became increasingly secular and familial, **cannibalism** became a popular theme (usually a familial/communal activity) and key films are dominated by demented families: **The Texas Chain Saw Massacre** (1974), *Frightmare* (1974), *The Hills Have Eyes* (1978).

The **stalk-and-slash** cycle popularised by **Halloween** (1978) and the **Friday the 13th** series (from 1980) has killers who emerge from normal or twisted families, though child molester Freddy Krueger, of the **A Nightmare on Elm Street** series (from 1985), 'bastard son of a hundred maniacs', is a predator *upon* weak families (note the procession of drunk or inadequate parents). In the 70s and 80s, the genre indicates how easily family becomes foe, and the disintegration of society due to **zombies** or **disease** is only a catalyst of the inherently unstable situation depicted in *The Shining* (1980). Psychotic parents, tormenting or possessing children, appear in *Hands of the Ripper* (1971), *Demons of the Mind* (1972), *The Fiend* (1972), *Night of Bloody Horror* (1973), *Carrie* (1976) and *Butcher, Baker, Nightmare*

Maker (1981). While monstrous **children**, often turning against parents, figure in *Night Hair Child* (1973), *It's Alive* (1975), **The Omen** (1976), *Bloody Birthday* (1980), *The Godsend* (1980), *Baby Blood* (1990) and *The Good Son* (1993).

Family members are forced to confront horror in their homes and take revenge in *Last House on the Left* (1972) and *La casa sperduta nel parco* (*The House at the Edge of the Park*, 1980). Family horror is literally internalised in films situated in the house (**The Amityville Horror**, 1979; **Poltergeist**, 1982), though here all strife within the family is put down to supernatural pressures and plot resolutions emphasise togetherness. Recently, horror has become more mainstream and melodramatic: *Fatal Attraction* (1987), *The Hand That Rocks the Cradle* (1991), *Cape Fear* (1991), *Poison Ivy* (1991) and *Unlawful Entry* (1992) have psychotic monsters threaten the family. **The Stepfather** (1986) bravely goes against the trend by representing the values of these films as monstrous. While psycho movies assume a pro-family stance, monster families are kitsch in *The Addams Family* (1991) or fairytale archetypes in the *The People Under the Stairs* (1991) and familial angst is supernaturally explained in *Pet*

Sematary (1989) and *Sleepwalkers* (1992). MP

Robin Wood, Richard Lippe, *The American Nightmare* (1979); Tony Williams, *Hearths of Darkness: The Family in the Aerican Horror Film* (1996)

Famous Monsters of Filmland
(1958–84)

American film magazine. Conceived by writer-editor Forrest **Ackerman** and publisher James Warren as a one-off to catch the *MAD* trade, *FM* arrived at exactly the right time to ride a wave of renewed interest in horror movies. Sales warranted quarterly, then bi-monthly publication, with Ackerman writing or rewriting every article and providing stills from his vast collection. Imitations appeared, but none matched the unique balance of fact and child-like, punning humour ('You axed for it!') that appealed to a predominantly eight to fourteen-year-old audience. Throughout the 60s, Ackerman tried to adopt a more adult approach, but sales dropped and Warren insisted on a return to pre-teen level. With the realisation that *FM* gained a new readership every few years came a canny programme of reprints that kept the magazine afloat until the eventual collapse of the Warren organisation. The title

was relaunched in 1993, but Ackerman – replicating with publisher Ray Ferry his relationship with Warren – resigned in 1996. MW

Fangoria (1979–)

American film magazine. Created as the horror offshoot of *Starlog* and originally announced as *Fantastica*, *Fangoria* has been edited by Ed Naha, Bob Martin and Tony Timpone. Though early issues were in the shade of the s-f-oriented parent (Mr Spock is on the cover of No. 4), it soon became the mouthpiece of the gorehound generation, devoting itself to the then new subgenre of **splatter movies**. Though never dealing exclusively with current films (Richard **Gordon** and Tom Weaver have written on older material), the 80s *Fangoria* too often resembled a glossy studio product handout, obsessively following the rubber-and-ketchup exploits of make-up men. Films get a critical raking (from 'Dr Cyclops') only after video release, though there have been tentative attempts to get more substantial work out of Douglas E. Winter, Mark Kermode, Maitland McDonagh and Caroline Vié. *GoreZone* (1988–9), a short-lived companion magazine, was apparently launched to flood the market and kill off competition.

Tim Lucas's *Video Watchdog* spun off from a column briefly carried by *GoreZone*, which also drew on the expertise of Steve Bissette and the bombast of Chas Balun. Imported into Britain, issues of both were reputed to have upset Margaret Thatcher. MW

Fantasy

Fantasy encompasses much if not all fiction, including horror. After the publication of J.R.R. Tolkien's *The Lord of the Rings* (1954–5), fantasy became recognised by fans, publishers and film-makers as a discrete genre. Obviously, stories about **werewolves, vampires** and **aliens** are essentially fantasy; questions of religious or spiritual belief aside, so are those featuring angels, **Hell** and ghosts. Much horror tries to avoid seeming like fantasy by putting the supernatural in a 'realistic' setting, whether contemporary, historic or futuristic.

Genre fantasy in literature and the cinema has two major strands: in one group (*Topper*, 1937; *It's a Wonderful Life*, 1946; *The Ghost and Mrs. Muir*, 1947; *Ghost*, 1990), supernatural beings impinge on the 'real' world as in horror but are not presented chiefly as frightening figures; in the other (*Babes in Toyland*, 1934; *The Thief of Bagdad*, 1940; *The Phantom Tollbooth*, 1970; *The Adventures of Baron Munchausen*, 1990), the world itself is fantastical, populated by magical beings benign and sinister. *Generic* fantasy (*Conan the Barbarian*, 1982; *The Black Cauldron*, 1985; *Legend*, 1985; *Willow*, 1988) descends from Arthurian legend and classical mythology via Tolkien and role-play **gaming**. The form is so ritualised that Terry Pratchett has made a career of parodying it.

Though it is a challenge to be frightening in the context of a world where magic is a commonplace, most fantasies feature demonically malevolent villains and monsters. Fantasy cinema has yielded powerful horror scenes like Ray Harryhausen's skeleton duels in *The 7th Voyage of Sinbad* (1958) and *Jason and the Argonauts* (1963) and truly frightening villains like the witches of *Snow White and the Seven Dwarfs* (1938) and *The Wizard of Oz* (1939).

Farmer, Mimsy (b. 1945)

American actress. Slim and blonde, Farmer essayed brittle, neurotic leads in continental horrors of the early 70s. Best known as

LEFT Family Values: Edwin Neal, Gunnar Hansen, Jim Siedow, *The Texas Chain Saw Massacre*

Mimsy Farmer

Michael Brandon's psychotic wife in **Argento**'s *Quattro mosche di velluto grigio* (*Four Flies on Grey Velvet*, 1971), she impresses as the frigid **heroine** of Armando Crispino's *Macchie solari* (*Autopsy*, 1974). In Francesco Barilli's extraordinary *Il profumo della signora in nero* (*The Perfume of the Lady in Black*, 1974), her gradually mounting hysteria is capped when she is **cannibalised** in a bizarre black magic ritual. MA

Il maestro e Margherita (*The Master and Margarita*)/1972 * *Il gatto nero* [*The Black Cat*]/1981 * *Sensi*/1986 * *Il camping del terrore* [*Body Count*]/1987

TV: *The Outer Limits*: 'Second Chance'/1964

Farris, John (b. 1936)
American writer. A skilful, prolific author of best seller-type books, several notches more ambitious than the sometimes similar Dean R. **Koontz**: *When Michael Calls* (1967), *Sharp Practice* (1974), *The Fury* (1976), *All Heads Turn When the Hunt Goes By* (1978), *The Uninvited* (1982), *Son of the Endless Night* (1985), *Wildwood* (1987), *Nightfall* (1987), *The Axman Cometh* (1989), *Fiends* (1990). Adaptations include the TV psycho thriller *When Michael Calls* (1969) and Brian **De Palma**'s *The Fury* (1977). He directed a low-budget horror *Dear Dead Delilah* (1972).

Farrow, Mia (b. 1945)
American actress. Less frequent a horror heroine than sister Tisa **Farrow**, she lends odd presence to weird or fantastical films.

RIGHT Mia Farrow: *Rosemary's Baby*

Her signature role is the mother of the Antichrist in *Rosemary's Baby* (1968).

Secret Ceremony/1968 * *Blind Terror*/1971 * *Full Circle*/1977 * *Zelig*/1983 * *Supergirl*/1984 * *The Purple Rose of Cairo*/1985 * *Alice*/1990 * *Shadows and Fog*/1992

Farrow, Tisa (b. 1951)
American actress. She had a brief shelf life as a Spaghetti Splatter heroine at the onset of the 80s, fulfilling obligations adequately in *Zombi 2* (*Zombie Flesh Eaters*, 1979) but floundering helplessly in the dreary depths of *Antrophagous* (*The Anthropophagous Beast*, 1980). MA

Some Call It Loving/1973 * *Un magnum special per Tony Saitta* [*Blazing Magnum*]/1976

TV: *The Initiation of Sarah*/1978

Father Christmas * See: Christmas

Faust
The German mountebank, conjurer and quack Georgius Faust (1480?–1540?) encouraged a rumour that he gained magic powers by selling his soul to the **Devil**. The story is told in an anonymous pamphlet

Historia von Iohañ Fausten (1587), translated into English by P.F. Gent as *The History of the Damnable Life, and Deserved Death of Doctor Iohn Faustus* (1592). In Christopher Marlowe's *The Tragical History of the Life and Death of Doctor Faustus* (date unknown, between 1588 and 1593), the scholar trades his soul to the demon Mephistophilis and is dragged into **Hell** when the debt is due. Johann Wolfgang Goethe's verse drama *Faust* (1808, 1832) breaks the contract and cheats Mephisto, allowing the necromancer to escape damnation. The Goethe became operas by Charles Gounod (*Faust*, 1860) and Arigo Boito (*Mefistofele*, 1868); the legend inspired music by Liszt, Berlioz, Wagner, Schumann, Louis Spohr and Randy Newman. The common link of the theme with music may reflect rumours that many a virtuoso, from Paganini to Robert Johnson, gained supernatural skill by a pact with the Devil.

Other German contributions are Nikolaus Lenau's epic *Faust* (1835) and Heinrich Heine's ballad *Faust* (1851). Thomas Mann's novel *Doktor Faustus* (1948; filmed 1982) conflates Faust with the composer Arnold Schönberg in the character of Adrian Leverkühn. István Szábo's *Mephisto* (1981),

Fausto (1969), the Romanian *Faust XX* (1966), Richard Burton's *Doctor Faustus* (1968), Clive Barker's underground *The Forbidden* (1975–8), the Argentine *El agujero en la pared* (1982), Jan **Švankmajer**'s Czech *Lekce Faust* (*Faust*, 1994).

A Faust puppet play features in *Bluebeard* (1944), opera stars **Karloff** and Willy the Whale play Mephisto in *Charlie Chan at the Opera* (1936) and *Make Mine Music* (1946) and Jack Buchanan goes broke turning a musical comedy into 'a modern Faust' in *The Band Wagon* (1953). Looser versions: *Bill Bumper's Bargain* (1911); *All That Money Can Buy* (1941), from Stephen Vincent Benét's *The Devil and Daniel Webster* (1937), with Walter Huston as Mr Scratch, an American down-home Devil; *Alias Nick Beal* (1949), with Ray **Milland** as a slouch-hatted Satan; 'Faust '57' (*Robert Montgomery Presents*, 1957); *Damn Yankees* (1958), with a baseball fan

selling his soul for a winning season; *Bedazzled* (1967), with Peter Cook tormenting Wimpy chef Dudley Moore; *Hammersmith is Out* (1972), with Richard Burton reincarnating Mephisto as an asylum inmate; and *Phantom of the Paradise* (1975), first of many rock 'n' roll Fausts, with Paul Williams as Faust-cum-Mephisto. In modern films, nerds sell souls for cool: *Oh God, You Devil* (1984), *Crossroads* (1986), *Trick or Treat* (1986), *Hunk* (1987), *976-EVIL* (1989), *Limit Up* (1989), *Shock 'Em Dead* (1990), *Outcast* (1991), *Brainscan* (1994).

Fellini, Federico (1920–93)

The whimsy running through Fellini's neo-realism (*I vitelloni*, 1953; *La strada*, 1954; *Le notti di Cabiria*, 1957) blossoms into magic in later work: *La dolce vita* (1960) ends with a sea monster dragged ashore; *8½* (1963) is haunted by **film-making** and Barbara **Steele**; *Giulietta degli spiriti* (*Juliet of the Spirits*, 1965) surrounds Giulietta Masina

based on a novel by Thomas Mann's son Klaus, models its protagonist Högen (Klaus Maria Brandauer), whose pact is with the Nazis, on stage star Gustaf Gründgens (Mephisto in a 1960 film *Faust*). The religious, philosophical or social interpretations are reinvented by each generation, permeating culture to such an extent that films like *The Little Shop of Horrors* (1960) and *Wall Street* (1987) are discussed in terms of 'Faustian bargains'.

Deal-with-the-Devil novels include Charles Maturin's *Melmoth the Wanderer* (1820), Marie Corelli's *The Sorrows of Satan* (1895), Clive **Barker**'s *The Damnation Game* (1985), Emma Tennant's *Faustine* (1992), Kim Newman's *The Quorum* (1994), Christopher Fowler's *Spanky* (1994) and Alan Judd's *The Devil's Own Work* (1995). Faust has been a film staple since the silents: there had been more than twenty five versions from Britain, France, Italy and America by the time F.W. **Murnau**'s Goethe-derived *Faust* (1926) offered Emil Jannings as Mephistopheles tempting Gösta Ekman. Other films: the British *Faust Fantasy* (1935), the Polish *Pan Tvardovski* (1937), the Italian *La leggenda di Faust* (1948) and *Mefisto Funk* (1986), the French *La beauté du diable* (1949) and *Marguerite de la nuit* (1955), the Spanish *Faustina* (1956) and *El extraño caso del Dr*

with pop-art bizarre; *Fellini Satyricon* (1970) is an ancient *Rocky Horror Show*; *Roma* (1972) has **Hammer** bit-player Marne Maitland discover fast-fading murals beneath the city; *Casanova* (1976) features automata; *La città delle donne* (*City of Women*, 1980) is pasta-stuffed Russ Meyer masculinism.

His purest genre excursions are episodes of **anthologies**: 'Le tentazioni del dottor Antonio' (*Boccaccio '70*, 1962) has Anita Ekberg as a living billboard inspired by *Attack of the 50 Foot Woman* (1958), and 'Toby Dammit' (*Histoires extraordinaires*, 1968) is a **Poe**-derived masterpiece with stoned Terence Stamp lured to death in his Ferrari by the **Devil** in the guise of a little girl. Like Steele, the demon child is borrowed from Mario **Bava** (*Operazione Paura*, 1966).

John Baxter, *Fellini* (1993)

Ferrara, Abel (b. 1951)

American director. 'I have this evil reputation,' says Ferrara, and he is right. Born in the Bronx, Ferrara was raised in then-rural Peekskill, New York, where he met screenwriter Nicholas St John (not as has been supposed a Ferrara pseudonym), his longtime collaborator.

Ferrara has worked in Hollywood, including a stint on *Miami Vice* and the pilot for *Crime Story* (1986), but he is too hard-edged for the American mainstream. His best work has been done in New York, the co-star of many of his films. From the **rape** revenge drama *Ms .45* (1980) through the Shakes-pearean crime tragedies of *China Girl* (1987) and *King of New York* (1990) to the philo-sophical **vampire** film *The Addiction* (1995), Ferrara straddles the worlds of exploitation and arthouse film-making. He has been called everything from the poet of the gutter to an opportunist hack with artistic pretensions. Inspired, he says, by Jean-Luc Godard, François Truffaut, Jean Vigo, Luis **Buñuel**, Robert Bresson and René Clair, Ferrara made his feature debut with *The Driller Killer* (1979), about a frustrated artist with a **power tool**. The wolfish Ferrara himself starred, hiding behind the pseudonym 'Jimmie Laine'.

Ferrara is a street romantic with darkly beguiling sensibilities. His films are distinguished by rich, evocative cinematography and a powerfully moral vision; even the viciosly degenerate *Bad Lieutenant* (1992) is searching for salvation, if in all the wrong places. MM

Fear City/1985 ∗ *Body Snatchers*/1994 ∗ *The Funeral*/1995

Ferrini, Franco (b. 1944)

Italian writer, director. Known for work on *Once Upon a Time in America* (1983) and contributions to Dario **Argento** projects, Ferrini turned director with a socially conscious **giallo**, *Caramelle da uno sconosciuto* (1987).

Enigma rosso [*Red Rings of Fear*]/1978 ∗ *Invito al viaggio*/1982 ∗ *Phenomena*/1984 ∗ *Sotto il vestito niente* [*Nothing Underneath*]/*Demoni* [*Demons*]/1985 ∗ *Demoni 2* [*Demons 2*]/1986 ∗

Opera/1987 ∗ *Due occhi diabolici* [*Two Evil Eyes*]/*Minaccia d'amore* [*Dial: Help*]/*La chiesa* [*The Church*]/1989 ∗ *Trauma*/1993 ∗ *La sindrome di Stendhal* [*The Stendhal Syndrome*]/1996

TV: *Turno di notte*/1980

Film-Making

Horror film-making is the backdrop for a handful of **recursive** films: *Frankenstein 1980* (1958), *House of the Seven Corpses* (1972), *Terror* (1979), *Screamplay* (1986), *Return to Horror High* (1987). TV shows: 'Sign of Satan' (**Alfred Hitchcock Presents**, 1964), 'Comeback' (*Land of the Giants* 1969), 'The Graveyard Shift (**Circle of Fear**, 1973), 'The Fans' (**The Evil Touch**, 1974), 'The Dummy' (*Beasts*, 1976), 'Master of Disguise' (**Friday the 13th**: The Series, 1988), 'Mummy Daddy' (**Amazing Stories**, 1985). A strain of Hollywood gothic touches on the horrific downside of the film capital, epitomised by Billy Wilder's *Sunset Blvd.* (1950) and Robert **Aldrich**'s *What Ever Happened to Baby Jane?* (1962), which hang **Old Dark Houses** with Hollywood tinsel, making monsters of **ageing actresses**.

Horror stars sometimes play horror stars conflated with their roles: Vincent **Price** (*Madhouse*, 1974), Peter **Cushing** (*Tendre Dracula*, 1974), Christopher **Lee** (*Dracula, père et fils*, 1976), Ferdy **Mayne** (*The Horror Star*, 1981) and Joe **Spinell** (*The Last Horror Film*, 1982). *Targets* (1968), with **Karloff**, is a more complex meditation on the role of screen bogey man. Ian Charleson and Liam Neeson play horror directors as callous swine in *Opera* (1987) and *The Dead Pool* (1988); movie star **vampires** appear in 'The Cloak' (*The House That Dripped Blood*, 1970) and *Nightmare in Blood* (1976); and Z film-making is mercilessly parodied in *Hollywood Boulevard* (1976) and *Get Shorty* (1995) but indulgently romanticised in *Matinee* (1993) and *Ed Wood* (1994). Self-reflexive serpent's tail-swallowing, distantly derived from *8½* (1963), features in Lucio **Fulci**'s *Un gatto nel cervello* (1990) and *Wes Craven's New Nightmare* (1994), which hop between levels of reality as film-makers (playing themselves) are touched by monsters they may have created.

Some novels intricately address the interface between film and real horror: Brock Brower's *The Late, Great Creature* (1971), Ramsey **Campbell**'s *Ancient Images* (1989), Theodore Roszak's *Flicker* (1991), Richard Christian **Matheson**'s *Created By* (1994), Stephen Laws's *Daemonic* (1995); Peter

Zoe Tamerlis, Abel Ferrara's *Ms .45*

Haining's *The Hollywood Nightmare* (1971) and David **Schow**'s *Silver Scream* (1988) collect film-related horror stories. Snuff movies, the probably legendary porno variants in which victims are killed on camera to provide a thrill for the jaded, often feature as plot devices or perverse frills: *Peeping Tom* (1960), *Emanuelle perché . . . violenza alla donne?* (*Emanuelle in America*, 1976), *Snuff* (1976), *Last House on Dead End Street* (1977), *Blue Nude* (1977), *Hardcore* (1978), *Whodunit* (1982), *Videodrome* (1982), *Final Cut* (1989), *Die Watching* (1993), *Mute Witness* (1995). Ruggero **Deodato**'s *Cannibal Holocaust* (1980) and Larry **Cohen**'s *Special Effects* (1984) explore the interface between death and documentary, explicated in David Kerekes and David Slater's book *Killing for Culture* (1993).

Film Noir

A type of thriller, identified by the French, which flourished in Hollywood in the 40s and 50s. Shaped by hard-boiled writers (Raymond Chandler, James M. Cain) and the **expressionist** style of émigré directors (Fritz **Lang**, Billy Wilder), plus topical fads like psychoanalysis and post-war cynicism, noir depicts a nightmare city of political corruption, doomed heroes, *femmes fatales*, pathetic losers and sadistic killers. The look recognisably fuses **Caligarism** with urban sleaze. Plots (especially if drawn from Cornell **Woolrich**) tend to the ironic and fatal.

The key figure at the intersection of horror and noir is Val **Lewton**: *Cat People* (1942), *The Leopard Man* (1943, from a Woolrich novel) and *The Seventh Victim* (1943) reshape both genres. A few noirs have explicitly horrific or supernatural themes: *Nightmare Alley* (1947), *Night Has a Thousand Eyes* (1948). Many feature grotesque psychotics and hallucinatory sequences: *Stranger on the Third Floor* (1940), *Phantom Lady* (1944), *Murder, My Sweet* (1944). The great noir horror is *Kiss Me Deadly* (1955), Robert **Aldrich**'s take on Mickey Spillane's Mike Hammer, which stirs in atom secrets and the face of Medusa. *Angel Heart* (1987), *Cast a Deadly Spell* (1991), *Witch Hunt* (1994), *Lord of Illusions* (1995) and *Se7en* (1995) are retro-noir horror hybrids. The ultimate neo-*noir* nightmare, voyaging into spiritual corruption, is Martin Scorsese's *Taxi Driver* (1976).

Findlay, Roberta (b. 19??)

American director, actress, cinematographer. A sexploitation diva, she co-directed with her husband Michael Findlay and performed under the name 'Anna Riva'. Their psychofetishist trilogy is *The Touch of Her Flesh* (1967), *The Curse of Her Flesh* (1968) and *The Kiss of Her Flesh* (1968). She shot her husband's *Shriek of the Mutilated* (1974) and *Slaughter* (*Snuff*, 1976) and, after his death, became a New York-based director-photographer of grainy occult movies.

*Blood Sisters/The Oracle/*1986 * *Lurkers/Prime Evil/*1988

Finley, William (b. 1944)

American actor. A twitchy regular for Brian **De Palma** and Tobe **Hooper**: the mad doctor of *Sisters* (1972), disfigured composer Winslow Leach in *Phantom of the Paradise* (1974), uncredited telephone voice of Michael Caine's *alter ego* in *Dressed to Kill* (1980).

Woton's Wake (s)/1962 * *Murder a la Mod/*1968 * *Dionysius in '69*/1969 * *Death Trap/*1976 * *The Fury/*1977 * *The Funhouse/*1981 * *Silent Rage/*1982 * *Night Terrors/*1993

Fisher, Terence (1904–80)

British director. After his debut *Colonel Bogey* (1947), Fisher spent ten years directing a wide range of low-budget fillers. A significant number were for **Hammer**, including the horror-like *Stolen Face* (1952) and *Four-Sided Triangle* (1953). However, he did not achieve any sort of status until *The Curse of Frankenstein* (1957), Hammer's first colour gothic. In the period following this success, a prolific Fisher was Hammer's principal director, responsible for **Dracula** (1958), probably his and Hammer's best work from this period, and *The Revenge of Frankenstein* (1958), *The Hound of the Baskervilles* (1959), *The Mummy* (1959), *The Curse of the Werewolf* (1960), *The Brides of Dracula* (1960) and *The Phantom of the Opera* (1962). Given the speed with which these were made, the quality is astonishing, more than making up for the less impressive but by no means disastrous *The Man Who Could Cheat Death* (1959) and *The Two Faces of Dr. Jekyll* (1960).

A survey of Fisher's entire body of work suggests claims made for him as some kind of supreme auteur are exaggerated. Rather he was a talented film-maker fortunate enough to be in the right place at the right time: in his case, Hammer in the 50s, working with producer-writer Anthony **Hinds**, writer Jimmy **Sangster**, cinematographer Jack **Asher** and others whose contributions are often eclipsed by an exclusive focus on the director. The films Fisher made away from Hammer are much less interesting: notably s-f/horrors *The Earth Dies Screaming* (1964), *Island of Terror* (1966) and *The Night of the Big Heat* (1967). Fisher's style is measured and undemonstrative, generally devoid of complicated camera movements, relying on precise and balanced compositions. In lesser hands, such an approach could become pedantic but Fisher carefully constructs the solid, thoroughly materialistic

David Prowse, Terence Fisher, on the set of *Frankenstein and the Monster From Hell*

Freddie Jones, Terence Fisher's *Frankenstein Must be Destroyed*

worlds which provide the characteristic settings for Hammer horror.

Not for Fisher the dreamlike atmospherics of Mario **Bava**'s Italian gothic or Roger **Corman**'s **Poe** adaptations. Instead, his drama has a physical energy that more than anything else is a defining quality of Hammer. Note the robustness of Dracula's first appearance, moving dynamically across the set towards an almost immobile camera to reveal himself as an articulate and attractive man, and the conclusion where Dracula and **Van Helsing** grapple with a **violence** until that time rarely seen in horror. Many of the themes found in Hammer horror can be assigned to various writers and producers rather than Fisher himself: for instance, the fascination with father figures coupled with a generally Manichaean view of the world. However, the manner in which these are presented, and in particular the characteristically brusque, no-nonsense tone, derives from Fisher's ability to stage action dynamically in relation to the camera: note the monsters crashing through framelike french windows in *Dracula*, *The Revenge of Frankenstein* and *The Mummy*.

Fisher worked less regularly for Hammer from the mid-60s but was responsible for their last uncomplicatedly outstanding films. *Frankenstein Created Woman* (1966), *The Devil*

Rides Out (1968) and *Frankenstein Must Be Destroyed* (1969) successfully combine the formal clarity of his earlier horrors with the troubled self-consciousness apparent elsewhere in the genre in this period. The younger directors who took over at Hammer often had more original ideas and were more ambitious; none ever succeeded in reproducing the dignity and gravitas of Fisher's best films. PH

Robert Flemyng

So Long at the Fair/1950 * *The Stranglers of Bombay*/1960 * *The Gorgon*/*The Horror of It All*/1964 * *Dracula, Prince of Darkness*/1965 * *Frankenstein and the Monster from Hell*/1973

David **Pirie**, *A Heritage of Horror* (1973); Stephane Bourgoin, *Terence Fisher* (1984); Wheeler Winston Dixon, *The Charm of Evil: The Life and Films of Terence Fisher* (1991)

Flemyng, Robert (1912–96)

British actor. Often an officer, usually a gentleman, Flemyng was familiar in services films when Riccardo **Freda** made him a horror immortal as the necrophile Dr Hichcock. 'The candle of his lust burnt brightest in the shadow of the grave.'

L'orribile segreto del dr. Hichcock [*The Terror of Dr. Hichcock*]/1962 * *The Blood Beast Terror*/1967 * *The Body Stealers*/1969 * *The Medusa Touch*/1978 * *Kafka*/1992

TV: *Elgin Hour*: 'A Sting of Death'/1955 * *Dow Hour of Great Mysteries*: 'The Woman in White'/1960 * *The Avengers*: 'You Have Just Been Murdered'/1968 * *The New Avengers*: 'To Catch a Rat'/1976 * *Rebecca*/1979

Fletcher, Louise (b. 1934)

American actress. Since a career-making turn as Nurse Ratched in *One Flew Over the Cuckoo's Nest* (1975), Fletcher has been cast as **Dracula**'s mother and a Martian frog-swallower.

Exorcist II: The Heretic/1977 * *Natural Enemies*/1979 * *Mamma Dracula*/1980 * *Strange Behavior*/1981 * *Strange Invaders*/1983 * *Firestarter*/1984 * *Invaders From Mars*/1985 * *Flowers in the Attic*/1987 * *Shadowzone*/1989 * *Blue Steel*/1990 * *Virtuosity*/*Frankenstein and Me*/1995

TV: *One Step Beyond*: 'The Open Window'/1959 * *The Twilight Zone*: 'The Hunters'/1988 * *Nightmare on the 13th Floor*/1990 * *The Hitchhiker*: 'Offspring'/1991 * *Tales From the Crypt*: 'Top Billing'/1991 * *The Haunting of Seacliff Inn*/1994

Florey, Robert (1900–1979)

French-born director. Originally slated for *Frankenstein* (1931) (and responsible for a fabled test reel with **Lugosi**), Florey was replaced by James **Whale**, but left his mark (the criminal **brain**, the windmill) on the script. As consolation, Florey and Lugosi were given *Murders in the Rue Morgue* (1932), a lesser but still weird Universal which borrows heavily from *Das Cabinet des*

Dr. Caligari (1919). In a shaky career, Florey made macabre Peter **Lorre** vehicles (*The Face Behind the Mask*, 1941; *The Beast With Five Fingers*, 1946) and horror-tinged mysteries (*The Florentine Dagger*, 1935; *The Preview Murder Mystery*, 1936). Ranging from the Marx Brothers' *The Cocoanuts* (1930) to *Tarzan and the Mermaids* (1947), his films have striking moments but are frequently awkward. His best horrors are episodes of **The Twilight Zone** ('Perchance to Dream', 1959) and **Thriller** ('The Incredible Doktor Markesan', 1962).

TV: *Alfred Hitchcock Presents*: 'Change of Heart'/'A Jury of Her Peers'/1961; 'Golden Opportunity'/'The Children of Alda Nuova'/ 'Where Beauty Lies'/1962 ✲ *The Twilight Zone*: 'The Long Morrow'/1964 ✲ *The Outer Limits*: 'Moonstone'/1964

Brian Taves, *Robert Florey: The French Expressionist* (1987)

Fog

The iconic horror weather, shrouding the London of **Sherlock Holmes** or the moors of *The Wolf Man* (1941). Alfred **Hitchcock**'s *The Lodger* (1926) is subtitled *A Story of the London Fog* but John **Brahm**'s 1944 remake makes more of its swirling dry ice. London fog features in most **Jack the Ripper** films

Louise Fletcher, *Strange Invaders*

though the Autumn of 1888 was fairly fog-free: influenced by black-and-white films, *Time After Time* (1979) and others show London pea-soup as white though it was actually yellow. Besides its eerie effect, fog serves to mask cheap studio sets in Edgar G. **Ulmer**'s *The Man From Planet X* (1951) and Mario **Bava**'s *Terrore nello spazio* (1965). James **Herbert**'s 1975 novel about a maddening bioweapon and John **Carpenter**'s

Robert Florey

1980 film about marine ghosts are both called *The Fog* and have rolling masses of the stuff. Major fog films: *The Scarlet Claw* (1944), *Fog Island* (1945), *Hangover Square* (1945), *She-Wolf of London* (1946), *The Slime People* (1963), *Tower of Evil* (1972), *Shadows and Fog* (1992), *Mary Reilly* (1996).

Forever Knight (Canadian TV series, 1992–5)

Nick Knight (aka *Midnight Cop*), a 1989 TV pilot directed by Farhad Khan from a script by James D. Parriott, features Rick Springfield as a 400-year-old **vampire** who works the nightshift as an LAPD detective and tangles with the less ethical bloodsucker Lacroix (Michael Nader) who turned him in the first place. Geraint Wyn Davies and Nigel Bennett take over as Nick and Lacroix in *Forever Knight*, a Canadian-shot cheapo cop-horror series.

Fort, Garrett (1898–1945)

American writer. Fort probably did more spadework on the screenplays of *Dracula* (1930) and *Frankenstein* (1931) than his credited collaborators.

On Time/1924 ✲ *Before Dawn*/1933 ✲ *Dracula's Daughter*/*The Devil-Doll*/1936 ✲ *Among the Living*/*Ladies in Retirement*/1941 ✲ *The Man in Half Moon Street*/1943

Foster, Meg (b. 1948)

American actress. An unusual beauty, intro

LEFT Robert Florey's *Murders in the Rue Morgue*

duced as a bell-bottomed hippie chick in *Welcome to Arrow Beach* (1973), Foster is often a villainess: Evil-Lyn in *Masters of the Universe* (1987), an earthling collaborator in *They Live* (1988), a lesbian gang boss in *Shrunken Heads* (1994).

The Wind/1987 * *Stepfather 2*/*Leviathan*/1989 * *Resort to Kill*/1994

TV: *The Sixth Sense*: 'Gallows in the Wind'/ 1972 * *Ghost Story*: 'At the Cradle Foot'/1972 * *Circle of Fear*: 'Spare Parts'/1973 * *The Legend of Sleepy Hollow*/1980 * *The Twilight Zone*: 'Dreams for Sale'/1985 * *The Hitchhiker*: 'The Martyr'/1989

1959 * *The Addams Family*: 'Lurch and His Harpsichord'/1965 * *The Monkees*: 'I Was a Teenage Monster'/1966 * *Wild Wild West*: 'The Night of the Juggernaut'/1968

Four In One: Night Gallery * See: *Night Gallery*

Francis, Freddie (b. 1917)

British director, cinematographer. To an extent, Francis has been overshadowed by Terence **Fisher**. Like Fisher, Francis had years of industry experience before turning to direction (as a camera operator then cinematographer) and began making horror

Ewan Hooper, Rupert Davies, Freddie Francis's *Dracula Has Risen From the Grave*

Foulger, Byron (1900–1970)

Timid American character actor, usually a bespectacled victim. SJ

Dick Tracy/1937 * *The Man They Could Not Hang*/1939 * *The Man With Nine Lives*/1940 * *Man Made Monster*/1941 * *The Black Raven*/ 1943 * *The Whistler*/1944 * *The Master Key*/ 1945 * *The Mysterious Mr. M*/*House of Horrors*/ *Dick Tracy vs. Cueball*/1946 * *The Magnetic Monster*/1953 * *The Devil's Partner*/1958 * *The Spirit is Willing*/1966

TV: *Rawhide*: 'Incident of the Druid Curse'/ 1959 * *The Twilight Zone*: 'Walking Distance'/

films for **Hammer**. Unlike Fisher, he did not stay long with Hammer and specialised in contemporary settings rather than period horror. He was the only director other than Fisher to contribute to both Hammer's **Frankenstein** and **Dracula** cycles. His *The Evil of Frankenstein* (1964) is a dull, by-the-numbers affair, but *Dracula Has Risen from the Grave* (1968) is much better: like most Hammer Draculas, it is not quite sure what to do with **Dracula** himself but boasts a grandiose conclusion in which he is staked with a huge crucifix and cries tears of blood. Francis also directed some of Hammer's psy-

chological thrillers (*Paranoiac*, 1962; *Nightmare*, 1963; *Hysteria*, 1964) but unlike Seth **Holt** (*Taste of Fear*, 1961) was unable to inject much life into mechanical plots.

Most of Francis's best work was done for Amicus. He directed the first of their horror **anthologies** *Dr. Terror's House of Horrors* (1964) and two of the follow-ups, *Torture Garden* (1967) and *Tales from the Crypt* (1972). These are all spirited fun, better than most of the other portmanteaux and proof that Francis's strength lies in the cinematic equivalent of the short story: though not very original, the episodes are never on screen long enough to bore and gain novelty from the use of contemporary British settings. However, Francis's other Amicus efforts are less successful, mingling impressive passages (a fine **dream** sequence in *The Skull*, 1965) with routine work. His most interesting single story film was actually made away from both Hammer and Amicus: *The Creeping Flesh* (1972) is an elegant and disturbing period piece which, rarely for British horror, utilises **Lovecraftian** ideas and deals with the themes of **incest** and female sexuality in a sustainedly intelligent way. *The Legend of the Werewolf* (1974) and *The Ghoul* (1975) are disappointing gothic throwbacks made for Tyburn, a company run by his son Kevin. PH

The Innocents (c)/1961 * *The Psychopath*/1965 * *The Deadly Bees*/1966 * *Mumsy, Nanny, Sonny and Girly*/1969 * *Trog*/1970 * *Gebissen wird nur nachts – Vampire-Happening* [*The Vampire Happening*]/1971 * *Tales That Witness Madness*/ *Craze*/1973 * *Son of Dracula*/1974 * *The Elephant Man* (c)/1981 * *The Doctor and the Devils*/1985 * *Dark Tower* (co-d with Ken Wiederhorn, credited to 'Ken Barnett')/1987 * *Cape Fear* (c)/1991

TV: *The Champions*: 'Shadow of the Panther'/ 1969 * *Tales from the Crypt*: 'Last Respects'/ 1996

Wheeler Winston Dixon, *The Films of Freddie Francis* (1991)

Franciosa, Anthony [Anthony Papaleo] (b. 1928)

Likeable Italian-American leading man. SJ

Nella stretta morsa del ragno [*Web of the Spider*]/ 1970 * *Daughter of Death*/1982 * *Tenebre* [*Tenebrae*]/1983 * *Death House*/1988 * *Ghost Writer*/*La morte è di moda*/1989

TV: *Curse of the Black Widow*/1977 * *Tales of the Unexpected*: 'A Woman's Help'/1981 * *Alfred Hitchcock Presents*: 'The 13th Floor'/

1988 * *The Twilight Zone*: 'Crazy as a Soup Sandwich'/1989 * *Night of the Hunter*/1991

Franco, Jesús (b. 1930)

Spanish film-maker. A hyperactive presence on the European film scene since *Tenemos 18 años* (1959), Franco has directed over 160 features (closer to 300, counting alternate soft- and hardcore versions of most post-1973 titles) making him by far the most prolific of all directors specializing in horror cinema. Franco's earliest (*Vampiresas 1930*, 1960) make playful reference to horror films, but he did not address the genre seriously until *Gritos en la noche* (*The Awful Dr. Orlof*, 1961), the story of a surgeon (Howard **Vernon**) determined to restore his daughter's ruined beauty with the skin of abducted women. Set in 1912, the handsomely crafted film borrows its villain's name from Bela **Lugosi** in *Dark Eyes of London* (1939), its music-hall ambience from John **Brahm**'s *Hangover Square* (1944) and its surgical scenario from Georges **Franju**'s *Les yeux sans visage* (1959); it also follows *Jack the Ripper* (1958) and *The Flesh and the Fiends* (1959) by adding sadoerotic flashes of female nudity filmed exclusively for the French market.

After Westerns, spy pictures and the odd Zorro film, Franco held true to his serial roots with *El segreto del Doctor Orloff* (*Dr. Orloff's Monster*, 1964), a modern-day story in which one of Orloff's disciples reactivates his dead brother's corpse to murder strippers and prostitutes. Franco continued to revive Orloff (and his humanoid assistant, Morpho) over the years in such non-sequitur sequels as *Los ojos siniestros del Doctor Orloff* (1973) and *El siniestro Dr. Orloff* (1982). Franco's most fascinating period commenced with *Miss Muerte* (*The Diabolical Dr. Z*, 1965), a bizarre and fetishistic reworking of Cornell **Woolrich**'s *The Bride Wore Black* (1940) scripted by Jean-Claude Carrière. Filmed in steely monochrome and scored with dolorous brass, the film strikes a unique chord of eros and melancholy, with Estella Blain unforgettable in her see-through, spider-crotched danceskin. After second unit on Orson **Welles**'s *Chimes at Midnight* (1965), Franco took his boldest step yet with *Necronomicon* (*Succubus*, 1967), a delirious slice of erotica which he described as an attempt to innovate a new genre of adult fantasy.

For the next few years, Franco busied himself with projects for producer Harry Alan **Towers**, including **Fu Manchu** sequels. The most widely seen of Franco's films, *Il conde Drácula* (*Count Dracula*,

1969), the making of which is covered in Pedro Portabella's avant-garde documentary *Cuadecuc (Vampir)* (1969), is the first attempt to adapt faithfully Bram **Stoker**'s novel. Unfortunately, this ambitious project was undertaken when Franco was averaging five or six features a year. While the components for a successful picture are mostly in place, they are recklessly filmed. Long considered a disaster, the film has excellent performances from Christopher **Lee** (**Dracula**), Klaus **Kinski** (**Renfield**) and Soledad **Miranda** (Lucy). Toward the end of his Towers tenure, Franco wrote and directed *Venus in Furs* (1968), the perfection of his proposed 'adult fantasy' genre, made even more strange in retrospect by its garish fashions, beatnik dialogue and lysergic Manfred Mann score. After breaking with Towers in 1970, Franco improvised five films around Miranda, each shot in two versions: mild for conservative Spain, sexually explicit for France and Germany. Traumatised by Miranda's death in a car accident, Franco threw himself into work, churning out product faster than ever before.

While making *La maldición de Frankenstein* (*The Erotic Rites of Frankenstein*, 1971) – in which **Frankenstein** meets Cagliostro, Dr Seward and Melissa the Bird Woman! – Franco met Rosa Maria Almirall, eighteen-year-old girlfriend of a production assistant cast in a minor role. Reminiscent of Miranda, Almirall was renamed 'Lina **Romay**' by Franco and cast in increasingly prominent roles in subsequent films. An exhibitionist willing to do almost anything in front of the camera, Romay was often called upon to provide material for the harder French and German versions. Her first starring role was the blood-sucking Countess Irina Karlstein in *La comtesse noire* (1973), though she enthusiastically partook of other bodily fluids in alternate versions, including the softcore *La comtesse aux seins nus* (*Female Vampire*) and the blatantly pornographic *Les avaleuses*. Between 1974 and 1979, Franco made dozens of bizarre **pornos**, but only two straight horror films: *Jack the Ripper* (1976) is a competent, if appallingly violent Kinski vehicle, while *Le sadique de Notre-Dame* (*Demoniac*, 1979) is a concoction of new and old footage (from *Exorcisme et messes noires*, 1974) about a religious zealot bent on purifying Paris by raping and killing its streetwalkers. Franco plays the maniac himself, giving an otherwise worthless effort the confessional allure of *Peeping Tom* (1960). He seemed to lose his edge after this orgasmic

height of self-exposure, mixing flaccid sex with endless genres, from **voodoo** (*Macumba sexual*, 1980) to **splatter** (*Die Säge des Todes*, 1980), from Emmanuelle (*Las orgias inconfessables de Emmanuelle*, 1982) to **Poe** (*El hundimiento de la Casa Usher*, 1983).

Les prédateurs de la nuit (*Faceless*, 1988), his first film with a full crew since 1969, was an unexpected comeback: not merely another retread of *Les yeux sans visage*, *Les prédateurs de la nuit* is also a sly and sentimental send-up of Franco's own career (with Vernon and Romay in cameos as Dr and Mrs Orloff). Its release coincided with a revival of interest in Franco's work, which had begun to surface around the world on home video. Franco fumbled his renaissance by turning to unsalable World War II/South American action cheapies, proving him terminally out-of-touch with his audience. He went into hiding until the 1992 Cannes Film Festival, where he premiered his disappointing assembly of Welles's legendary, unfinished *Don Quixote* (begun 1957).

Since 1989, he has written and directed at least two undistributed films – *Jungle of Fear* and *The Curse of the Evil Candle* (!), starring the late William Berger – and probably many more, returning to horror with the lesbian vampire film *Killer Barbys* (1996). Fortunately for his admirers, the bounty of Franco's available work is virtually inexhaustible and, for the tolerant of mind, endlessly fascinating. Pseudonyms include: Jess Frank, A.M. Franck, James P. Johnson, James Lee Johnson, Clifford Brown, Jack Griffin, Robert Griffin, James Gardner, Dan L. Simon, Roland Marceignac, Dave Tough, Joan Vincent, Lennie Hayden, Betty Carter, Cole Polly. TL

La mano de un hombre muerto/1962 * *Cartes sur table* [*Attack of the Robots*]/1966 * *El caso de las dos bellezas* [*Sadisterotica*]/*Besame, monstruo* [*Kiss Me Monster*]/1967 * *Die Sieben Männer der Sumuru* [*Rio 70*]/*El castillo de Fu Manchu* [*Castle of Fu Manchu*]/*Fu Manchu y el beso de la muerte* [*The Blood of Fu Manchu*]/*Justine*/1968 * *DeSade 70* [*Eugenie: The Story of Her Journey Into Perversion*]/*El proceso de las brujas* [*Night of the Blood Monsters*]/1969 * *Sie tötete in Ekstase* [*Mrs. Hyde*]/*Vampyros lesbos*/*Eugénie de Sade*/*Les cauchemars naissent la nuit*/*Una vergine tra i morti viventi* [*Virgin Among the Living Dead*]/*La venganza del Doctor Mabuse*/1970 * *Der Todesrächer von Soho*/*Dracula, prisonnier de Frankenstein* [*Dracula, Prisoner of Frankenstein*]/1971 * *La fille de Dracula*/*Os demonios* [*The Demons*]/*Un silencio de tumba*/ 1972 *

*Plaisir à trois [How to Seduce a Virgin]/ La comtesse perverse/Al otro lado del espejo/Les exploits érotiques de Maciste dans l'Atlantide/ Maciste contre la reine des Amazones/La noche de los asesinos/Mais qui donc a violé Linda?/1973 * Exorcisme/Lorna, l'exorciste/1974 * Shining Sex/De Sade's Juliette/1975 * Das Bildnis der Doriana Gray/1976 * Greta, Haus ohne Männer [Greta the Torturer]/1977 * Sinfonia eróti- ca/1979 * Mondo cannibale [The Cannibals]/Il cacciatore di uomini [Man Hunter]/Eugenia – historia di una perversion/1980 * La tumba de los muertos vivientes [Oasis of the Living Dead]/ 1981 * Gemidos de placer/Mil sexos tiene la noche/La casa de las mujeres perdidas/La man- sión de los muertos vivientes/1982 * Sola ante el terror/1983 * Voces de muerte/1984*

Lucas Balbo, Peter Blumenstock, Christian Kessler, Tim Lucas *Obsession: The Films of Jess Franco* (1993)

Franju, Georges (1912–87)

French director, writer whose second fea- ture, *Les yeux sans visage* (*Eyes Without a Face*, 1959), is seminal to post-war Euro-horror. A visually and emotionally lyric study in **dis- figurement and plastic surgery**, with defiant modern detail matched by unflinch- ing operating table gore, it owes much to the poetic documentary shorts Franju made in the aftermath of World War II. Early entries include brutal abattoir item *Le sang des bêtes* (1949) and the anti-militarist *Hôtel des Invalides* (1951). *Notre Dame, cathédrale de Paris* (1958) is a haunted architectural study. *Le grand Méliès* (1952) connects with the ear- liest moments of film imagination and speaks of its maker's archivist background. A troubled interest in fantasy maintains throughout Franju's fictive work, from psy- chiatric indictment *La tête contre les murs* (*The Keepers*, 1959) on. Like *Judex* (1964), theatri- cal finale *Nuits rouges* (*Shadowman*, 1973) and its TV extrapolation *L'homme sans visage* (1974) remember Feuillade's audacious pulp serials. DF

Raymond Durgnat, *Franju* (1967)

Frankenstein; or: The Modern Prometheus (1818)

Mary Wollstonecraft Godwin began to write her most famous novel on the 17th or 18th of June 1816, as part of a rainy day ghost story competition at the Villa Diodati on the shore of Lake Geneva. The circumstances of creation have become almost as famous as *Frankenstein* itself: see, among many others, the prologue to *Bride of Frankenstein* (1935) and *Gothic* (1986).

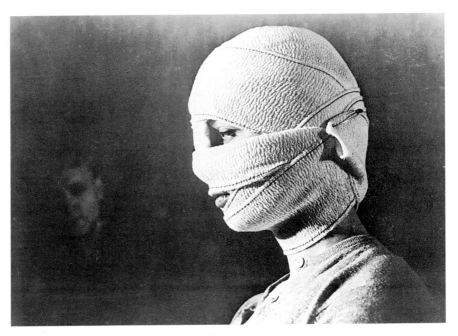

Edith Scob, Georges Franju's *Les yeux sans visage*

From 1931 onwards, the film versions entered the public realm as parallel texts to the novel, myths in their own right. The original has been interpreted as a feminist allegory of birthing (Mary was the daughter of the founding mother of women's libera- tion – who died shortly after the birth of puerperal fever), an attack on 'masculinist science' (or the Prometheanism of the poet Percy Shelley), a late example of female gothic, a transcription of Milton's *Paradise Lost* (with the creature as the new Adam, then the fallen angel), a reaction to the rise of the industrial proletariat, an enquiry into political justice (derived from the anarchism of William Godwin, Mary's estranged father), an example of Rousseau's ideas on education, and a dramatisation of then-cur- rent debates about the origins of the spark of life (or 'vitalism').

The stage – and most film – versions have turned all this into a simple **Faustian** moral- ity tale about the social responsibility of sci- ence (Frankenstein has a conscience from the word go) and about how people who look like Boris Karloff tend to get a negative reaction. In the book, the creature becomes ugly because he is treated as ugly: lacking a family of his own, he destroys his creator's brother, best friend and wife. Also because, though his limbs are individually beautiful, he does not 'work' as a complete human being and it shows in 'his watery eyes' (like the product of a drawing-by-numbers life class: Mary was herself learning to draw

when she wrote the bulk of her novel in Bath between September and February 1816–17). In most film versions, the creature behaves psychopathically from the moment he leaves the operating table. There is evi- dence that, in abridging her own 1818 novel, Mary herself cut out some of the scientific and political debates in favour of blood- and-thunder: and Frankenstein spoke for the first time of his 'presumption' in challenging the Almighty in the 1831 edition.

So Frankenstein was already on its jour- ney from novel to popular myth even before it left its author's control. The mythologies surrounding the novel's creation began at the same time, with Mary's introduction to the 1831 edition. Her memories of the Geneva summer of 1816 – storms, weird sci- ence, bizarre encounter groups involving Lord **Byron**, Percy Shelley, Dr John **Polidori** and Clare Clairmont with herself as a 'nearly silent' observer – present *Franken- stein* as a thoroughbred gothic novel (per- haps for marketing purposes), when in fact it is a great deal more than that. She turns her own role in the ghost-story session into a cliffhanger ('I busied myself to think of a story'); it now seems, though, that she was first to contribute and was an eager partici- pant in the proceedings. Mary Godwin – who became Mary **Shelley** at the end of December 1816 – had evidently been think- ing about the complex issues in her novel for some considerable time.

Her introduction (written fifteen years

after the events it purports to describe) reveals her struggle to establish maternity of her own story, as well as her dark memories of the men who had unwittingly contributed to its genesis: all of them were dead within eight years of summer 1816. By twenty-seven, the age when most scholars studying *Frankenstein* today (a growth industry, especially in the USA) are just finishing their postgraduate studies, Mary felt 'as an old woman might feel. I may not love any but the dead'. She had no way of knowing it, but one thing had survived that wet, dismal summer – to take on a life of its own which its creator would scarcely have recognised. The thing she called her 'hideous progeny', born in a dream. A creature with the full range of human emotions (that is his tragedy) who was eventually to become a cuddly addition to the playroom, a sitcom hero and an honorary member of the pantheon of high camp.

First published (anonymously) in spring 1818 (3 volumes; 500 copies), the book was and remains notoriously difficult to adapt to any other medium. It consists, in its original form, of Arctic explorer Robert Walton's letters, Victor Frankenstein's reminiscences and the creature's own autobiography: a novel within a novel within a novel, rather than a single linear narrative. To make things even more difficult, the creature – once he gets the hang of verbalising – is extremely talkative. There are also wild improbabilities and coincidences: for example, how does Victor create a being eight foot tall out of the body parts of ordinary people? How does the creature become so fluent in English and French, majoring in literature, in the space of less than a year? How exactly could the creature have found a cloak lying around that just happened to fit him?

There is a logic, but it is the logic of a dream: the 'creation' scene did in fact start life as a nightmare. As late as 1930, Hollywood scriptwriters were despairing of the property – though stage adaptations had by then been proliferating for just over a century. In the only illustration published during Mary's lifetime (at the beginning of the 1831 cut-down edition) the creature is beautiful as he is, at first, in the novel: his lustrous black hair, pearly white teeth and taut muscles suggest component parts have been selected with great care. His creator is a young research student who flees from his confused offspring in post-partum terror.

RIGHT *Frankenstein*, 1831 Frontispiece

But even in the earliest theatrical adaptation, *Presumption, or: The Fate of Frankenstein* (1823), the '**monster**' (as by then he was being called, even by politicians in the House of Commons) staggers around the stage and communicates only in grunts and whines. The scientist becomes a mature, fatherly figure and gains a comic **minion** in the form of a country bumpkin called Fritz. There are action scenes not in the book: a creation sequence with a lot of loud bangs and bright sparks (Mary was content with the perfunctory phrase 'I collected the instruments of life around me') and an avalanche at the final curtain which engulfs both the protagonists. In subsequent versions, the formula remains constant: while some details might change (instead of an avalanche, a polar

storm, a thunderstorm or Mount Etna), the basic linear structure, punctuated by action scenes, was established.

Inheriting this tradition, Thomas Edison's *Frankenstein* (1910) keeps the monster (Charles Ogle) crashing through some french windows (another staple ingredient), but adds an alchemical theme by having the **mad scientist** (Augustus Phillips) create him in a huge bubbling pot which transforms a skeleton into a somewhat overweight human being with frizzy hair. Another addition is the ending, in which the monster dissolves into a **mirror**. *Life Without Soul* (1915) is radical enough an adaptation to change its scientist's name to 'William Frawley' (William A. Cohill) and concentrates on a chase across Europe as the creator

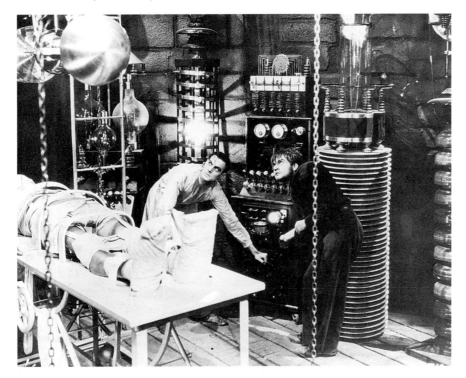

Daughter (1958). But the reworking that took was from Britain's **Hammer** Films, who started their series with *The Curse of Frankenstein* (1957), opting for colour, a period setting, surgical grue and cloak-swishing melodramatics. Peter **Cushing**'s ruthless Victor became the focus of a ***Frankenstein* (Hammer)** series that stretched until *Frankenstein and the Monster From Hell* (1973). CF

Don Glut, *The Frankenstein Legend* (1973), *The Frankenstein Catalog* (1984); Peter Haining, *The Frankenstein File* (1977); Leonard Wolf, *The Essential Frankenstein* (1977, revised 1993); Stephen Earl Forry, *Hideous Progenies: Dramatizations of Frankenstein from Mary Shelley to the Present* (1990); Stephen Bann, *Frankenstein, Creation and Monstrosity* (1994); Stephen Jones, *The Illustrated Frankenstein Movie Guide* (1994); David J. Skal, *Screams of Reason: Mad Science and Modern Culture* (1996)

Frankenstein (Universal)

James **Whale**'s *Frankenstein* (1931), with Colin **Clive** as Henry **Frankenstein** and Boris **Karloff** giving a definitive face to Mary **Shelley**'s creation, is the most important and influential of all horror films. All

pursues the 'Brute Man' (Percy Darrell Standing) who has slain his sister. *Il mostro di Frankenstein* (1920), with Luciano Albertini and Umberto Guarracino as Frankenstein and the *mostro*, is the first European film take on the story.

James **Whale**'s *Frankenstein* (1931) keeps Fritz (turning him into a hunchbacked, vertically challenged research assistant) and a grotesque, childlike, grunting monster (mimed, touchingly, by Boris **Karloff** – with a huge, dome-like forehead and big feet that make him look as though he is suffering from an acromegalic condition: an image of disability rather than of beauty). The original play's line 'It lives!' is changed into 'It's alive'; a jar containing 'Disfunctio Cerebri' or 'Abnormal Brain' is added; and the monster is destroyed at the fadeout in a burning mill. In this adaptation, Mary's seven-word description becomes a fully fledged laboratory sequence (inspired by *Metropolis*, 1926), complete with lightning-arc generators, bakelite dials, a giant voltaic battery and an adjustable metal hospital bed, a curious mixture of 1816 and 1931. Karloff gains stitches and a steel bolt through his neck to plug himself into while Henry Frankenstein is a manic Old Etonian (Colin **Clive**).

This set the tone for most future adaptations, up to Kenneth Branagh's *Mary Shelley's Frankenstein* (1994), which instead turns its creation sequence into a laboratory

birth from a metal womb full of amniotic fluid. Universal spun the franchise into a series that lasted until (**Abbott and Costello**) *Meet Frankenstein* (1948). A generation later, Frankenstein descendants revived the tradition in the drive-ins: *I Was a Teenage Frankenstein* (1957); *Frankenstein 1970* (1958), with Karloff as creator; *Frankenstein's*

Boris Karloff, Marilyn Harris, *Frankenstein* (1931)

Boris Karloff, Dwight Frye (extreme right), *Bride of Frankenstein*

subsequent versions must consider how plot, characterisations and make-up conform to or differ from Universal's template.

Whale, Karloff and Clive return for *Bride of Frankenstein* (1935), with Ernest **Thesiger** as Dr Pretorius and Elsa **Lanchester** as the **Monster**'s Mate. Karloff continues into Rowland V. **Lee**'s *Son of Frankenstein* (1939), with Basil **Rathbone** in the title role and Bela **Lugosi** as the broken-necked Ygor. Erle C. **Kenton**'s *Ghost of Frankenstein* (1942), with Lon **Chaney** Jr as the Monster and Cedric **Hardwicke** as Rathbone's brother, recalls Lugosi's Ygor, whose brain is transplanted by Lionel **Atwill** into the Monster's skull. Logically, Lugosi takes over the Monster role, with stunt man Eddie **Parker** doing most of the heavy lifting, in *Frankenstein Meets the Wolf Man* (1943), co-

starring Chaney as the werewolf and Ilona Massey as the last of the Frankensteins. Glenn **Strange** wears the flat head and electrodes for the studio's monster rallies: Kenton's *House of Frankenstein* (1944) and *House of Dracula* (1945) and Charles Barton's parody (**Abbott and Costello**) *Meet Frankenstein* (1948).

Universal's copyright on the Jack **Pierce** make-up forces most other films to take a different approach, but the Universal Monster is widely parodied, goofily caricatured as Herman Munster (Fred **Gwynne**) or given cameos in *Hellzapoppin'* (1941), *Abbott and Costello Meet Dr. Jekyll and Mr. Hyde* (1953) and *Casino Royale* (1967). Monsters conform roughly to the Karloff look in *Third Dimensional Murder* (1941), *Kiss Me Quick* (1963), **The Munsters** (1964–6), *Mad Monster*

Party? (1966), *Blackenstein* (1972) and *The Monster Squad* (1987). *Frankestein, el vampiro y cia* (1961) and *Leena Meets Frankenstein* (1993) are remakes of *Meet Frankenstein*, and *The Bride* (1985) is a partial reworking of *Bride of Frankenstein*.

Whale's films are homaged lovingly by Victor Erice's *El espíritu de la colmena* (*Spirit of the Beehive*, 1973), in which a little girl imagines a friendship with Karloff's Monster, Mel Brooks's *Young Frankenstein* (1975), which not only has Peter Boyle parodying Karloff but offers Gene Wilder and Kenneth Mars spoofing Rathbone and Atwill, and Tim **Burton**'s *Frankenweenie* (1984), in which ten-year-old Victor Frankenstein (Barret Oliver) revives his beloved dog. Christopher Bram's novel *Father of Frankenstein* (1995) is about Whale, while Thesiger's Pretorius haunts Paul J. McAuley's *Pasquale's Angel* (1995), 'The Temptation of Dr Stein' (1995) and 'The True History of Dr Pretorius' (1995).

Gregory William Mank, *It's Alive!* (1981)

Frankenstein (Hammer)

The continuing thread of Universal's Frankenstein series was the Monster, but **Hammer Films** chose to follow Victor **Frankenstein**, who returns to the drawing board with each film. Terence **Fisher**'s *The Curse of Frankenstein* (1957) and *The Revenge of Frankenstein* (1958), with Peter **Cushing**'s aristocratic scientist creating Christopher **Lee** (who beat Bernard Bresslaw for the part) and then Michael Gwynne, have a continuing storyline. Subsequent films tend to start afresh: Freddie **Francis**'s *The Evil of Frankenstein* (1964), with Kiwi Kingston as a **Karloff**ian Monster, has flashbacks which contradict *Curse*.

Fisher and Cushing stayed with the series: subtly varying the character of the Baron from heroic to villainous in *Frankenstein Created Woman* (1967), with Susan Denberg, *Frankenstein Must Be Destroyed* (1969), with Freddie **Jones**, and *Frankenstein and the Monster From Hell* (1973), with David **Prowse**. Jimmy **Sangster**'s *Horror of Frankenstein* (1970), with Ralph **Bates** as Victor and Prowse as the **Monster**, is a remake-cum-parody of the Sangster-scripted *Curse*. Cushing appears briefly as the Baron in *One More Time* (1969). Hammer's

Bela Lugosi, Boris Karloff, *Son of Frankenstein*

Frankensteins are is less often referenced than Universal's flathead version, but inform *Carry On Screaming* (1966), *La figlia di Frankenstein* (*Lady Frankenstein*, 1971) and *Flesh for Frankenstein* (1973).

Frankenstein (Various)

Mary Shelley's Frankenstein (1994), with Branagh creating Robert **DeNiro**, owes less to the Universal or **Hammer** takes on Mary **Shelley** than to a sincere run of mostly television versions that mendaciously claim to return to the original text: 'Frankenstein' (*Tales of Tomorrow*, 1952), with Lon **Chaney Jr** created by John **Newland**; 'Frankenstein' (*Matinee Theater*, 1957), with Primo Carnera as the monster; 'Frankenstein' (*Mystery and Imagination*, 1968), with Ian Holm as both monster and maker; 'Frankenstein' (*Once Upon a Time*, 1973), with Geoffrey Bayldon as maker and monster; *Frankenstein* (1973), with Robert Foxworth and Bo Svenson; *Frankenstein: The True Story* (1973), with Leonard Whiting and Michael Sarrazin, plus James Mason as an interpolated Dr **Polidori**; *Victor Frankenstein* (1976), with Leon Vitali and Per Oscarsson, a rare studious theatrical outing; 'Night of the Marionettes' (**Supernatural**, 1977); *Frankenstein* (1984), with Robert **Powell** and David **Warner**, adapted from the notorious one-night Broadway flop; *Frankenstein* (1992), with Patrick Bergin and Randy Quaid.

In on the act are updates, spin-offs, farces and pot-pourris: *Furankenshutain tai Baragon* (*Frankenstein Conquers the World*, 1964), *Jesse James Meets Frankenstein's Daughter* (1966), *Dr. Frankenstein on Campus* (1970), *Dracula vs. Frankenstein* (1970), *Frankenstein '80* (1972), *Il castello della paura* (*Frankenstein's Castle*

LEFT Elsa Lanchester, Boris Karloff, *Bride of Frankenstein*

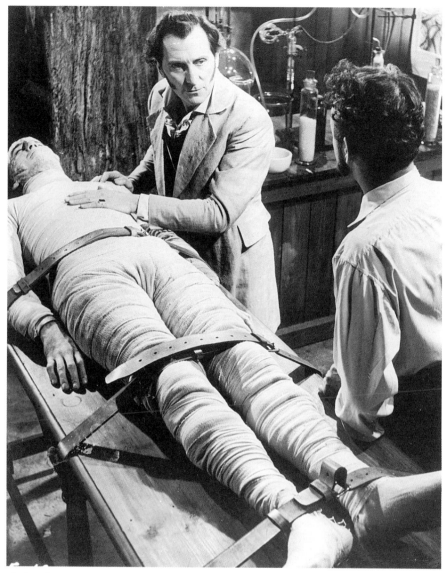

Christopher Lee, Peter Cushing, Robert Urquhart, *The Curse of Frankenstein*

of Freaks, 1973), *Frankenstein all'Italiana* (*Frankenstein – Italian Style*, 1975), *Death Race 2000* (1975), *Doctor Franken* (1980), *Frankenstein Island* (1981), *Frankenstein General Hospital* (1988), *Frankenstein: The College Years* (1991), *Frankenstein and Me* (1996). This activity hardly seems much less disreputable than the outright **pornography**: *House on Bare Mountain* (1962), *Kiss Me Quick* (1964), *Hollow-My-Weanie, Dr. Frankenstein* (1969), *The Sexual Life of Frankenstein* (1970), *La maldición de Frankenstein* (*The Erotic Rites of Frankenstein*, 1971), *Leena Meets Frankenstein* (1993), *Frankenstein* (1994).

Without even using the F word, the theme is knocked about by the likes of *Scream and Scream Again* (1969), *The Rocky Horror Picture Show* (1976), *Re-Animator*

(1985) and *Britannia Hospital* (1982). Though there have been pulpy novel sequels (Don Glut's *Frankenstein Lives Again*, 1971; Peter Tremayne's *Hound of Frankenstein*, 1977), several later novelists have revisited, reassessed and revised the original with some thought: Brian Aldiss's *Frankenstein Unbound* (1973; filmed 1990), Michael Bishop's *Brittle Innings* (1994), Hilary Bailey's *Frankenstein's Bride* (1995), Theodore Roszak's *The Memoirs of Elizabeth Frankenstein* (1995)

Franklin, Pamela (b. 1950)

British actress. A poised Flora in *The Innocents* (1961), Franklin grew into a pretty ingenue. Her best adult role is the psychic of *The Legend of Hell House* (1973).

The Nanny/1965 * *Our Mother's House*/1967 * *Night of the Following Day*/1968 * *And Soon the Darkness*/1970 * *Necromancy*/1971 * *Food of the Gods*/1975

TV: *The Strange Report*: 'Cult – Murder Shrieks Out'/1971 * *Ghost Story*: 'Half a Death'/1972 * *The Sixth Sense*: 'I Did Not Mean to Slay Thee'/1972 * *Satan's School for Girls*/1973 * *Thriller*: 'Won't Write Home, Mom – I'm Dead'/'Screamer'/1975

Franklin, Richard (b. 1948)

Australian director, **Hitchcock** devotee. At USC 1967–70, Franklin was an unfashionable champion then personal acquaintance of his idol; returning home, he followed failed Western *The True Story of Eskimo Nell* (1975) and sexploiter *Fantasm* (1976) with the telekinesis item *Patrick* (1980). *Road Games* (1981) earned *Psycho II* (1983), a witty, surprising sequel that yielded a further collaboration with writer Tom **Holland**, *Cloak and Dagger* (1984). Botching simian suspenser *Link* (1985), Franklin became a director-for-hire with the pilot of *Beauty and the Beast* (1987) and *FX2: The Deadly Art of Illusion* (1991). DP

Freaks * See: **Deformity; Disfigurement and Plastic Surgery**

Freda, Riccardo (b. 1909)

Egyptian-born Italian director. From his debut *Don Cesare di Bazan* (1942), Freda favoured historical dramas, swashbucklers and other costume pictures. After making the acquaintance of Mario **Bava**, uncredited cameraman on *Spartaco* (*The Sins of Rome*, 1952), he conceived the notion of making a horror film, a moribund genre in Italy since the silent days. *I vampiri* (*Lust of the Vampire*, 1957) has a beautiful *ducchesa* (memorably played by Freda's wife Gianna Maria Canale) kept young by the blood of abducted women. Freda directed only half the twelve-day production in ten days, abandoning it to Bava, whose technical ingenuity completed the film on schedule. *I vampiri* coined the look and obsessions of virtually every Italian horror film to follow, yet was not a box-office success in Italy. Freda blamed Italian audiences, who laughed at the idea of a spooky film made in sunny Italy.

The emergence of **Hammer** as an international phenomenon convinced Freda to try again with *Caltiki il mostro immortale* (*Caltiki the Immortal Monster*, 1959), inspired by the first **Quatermass** film, about a flesh-consuming blob discovered in an ancient

Riccardo Freda's *Lo spettro*

Mayan temple. This time, Freda convinced cast and crew to work pseudonymously to ensure the film's acceptance in Italy, himself adopting the *nom de l'ecran* 'Robert Hampton'. Once again, Freda argued with his producer and left Bava (aka 'Marie Foam') holding the bag; he later declared *Caltiki* should be considered Bava's directorial debut. Freda continued to make costume dramas under his own name, but revived 'Robert Hampton' for *L'orribile segreto del dr. Hichcock* (*Terror of Dr. Hichcock*, 1962) and *Lo spettro* (*The Ghost*, 1963), starring Bava's discovery Barbara **Steele**. The former is an outrageous period melodrama about a necrophile (Robert **Flemyng**) haunted by his dead wife, while the latter finds another Hichcock (Elio Jotta) faking his own death to entrap an adulterous wife (Steele): both are marvellous, highly fetishistic ruminations on sex and paralysis, ensuring Freda perpetual prominence in the history of Italian horror.

Equally delirious is *A doppia faccia* (*Double Face*, 1968), with Klaus **Kinski** as an industrialist searching the seedy underbelly of Swinging London for traces of his 'dead' wife after spotting her in a porno loop. A chief member of Italy's film censorship board for many years, Freda's subsequent work in the genre is disappointing as well as mysterious.

He denies involvement in *Estratto dagli archivi di polizia di una capitale europea* (1971), an intermittently effective ghost story that bears his name, while boasting paternity of *L'iguana dalla lingua di fuoco* (1970), an ugly *giallo* credited to 'Willy Pareto'. *Follia omicida* (*Murder Obsession*, 1980), evidently a swan song, adds chainsaw decapitations and explicit sex to his usual Victorian trappings with obvious discomfort. TL

Maciste all'inferno [*The Witch's Curse*] /1962
Riccardo Freda, *Divoratori de celluloide* (1981)

Freddy's Nightmares * See: *A Nightmare on Elm Street*

Freund, Karl (1890–1969)

German-born cinematographer, director. After photographing *Der **Golem*** (1920) and *Metropolis* (1926), Freund relocated to Hollywood and shot *Dracula* (1930) and **Murders in the Rue Morgue** (1932), bringing **expressionism** to Hollywood. His brief directorial career began and ended with major horror films, **The Mummy** (1932) and *Mad Love* (1935), but otherwise consists of forgotten items: *Moonlight and Pretzels* (1933), *The Countess of Monte Cristo* (1934), *The Gift of the Gab* (1934). *The Mummy*, a rethink of *Dracula* cut to suit **Karloff**, plays its mix of the eerie and the romantic better than Tod **Browning**'s film. *Mad Love*, a remake of **Les Mains d'Orlac**, is spirited **grand guignol** with Peter **Lorre** and Colin **Clive**, witty and gruesome in the manner of James **Whale**. As good-looking as expected, Freund's films are better-paced and more consistently acted

Karl Freund

than comparable efforts from established directors.

Satanas/1919 * *Der Januskopf*/*Der Bucklige und die Tänzerin*/*Die Spinnen*/1920 * *Der verlorene Schatten*/1921

Frid, Jonathan (b. 1924)

Canadian actor. Barnabas Collins in Dan **Curtis**'s gothic soap **Dark Shadows** (1966–71), Frid reprised the whining **vampire** in *House of Dark Shadows* (1970). His other notable credit is the haunted author of Oliver **Stone**'s *Seizure* (1974).

TV: *The Devil's Daughter*/1972

Friday the 13th

Despite running out of ideas twenty minutes into the first film, the *Friday* series was the most successful horror franchise of the 80s, though it took three films to get Jason Voorhees (originally the victim whose death motivated his mother to kill, a hulk with a bag on his head in *Part 2*) into his trademark hockey mask. Sean **Cunningham**'s *Friday the 13th* (1980), made with an uncredited editing assist from Wes **Craven** and gore from Tom **Savini**, borrows riffs from *Ecologia del delitto* (*A Bay of Blood*, 1971), *Carrie* (1976) and **Halloween** (1978) as a mystery killer plays **stalk and slash** with the teenagers of Camp Crystal Lake. Dozens more victims are claimed in Steve **Miner**'s *Friday the 13th, Part 2* (1981) and *Friday the 13th Part III in 3-D* (1982), Joseph **Zito**'s mendacious *Friday the 13th: The Final Chapter* (1984), Danny Steinmann's *Friday the 13th, Part V: A New Beginning* (1985), in which a copycat wields the knife, Tom **McLoughlin**'s *Friday the 13th, Part VI: Jason Lives* (1986), which brings Jason back as a **zombie**, John Carl **Buechler**'s *Friday the 13th, Part VII: The New Blood* (1988), Rob Hedden's *Friday the 13th, Part VIII: Jason Takes Manhattan* (1989) and Adam Marcus's *Jason Goes to Hell: The Final Friday* (1993), in which the killer turns out to be **possessed** by a body-hopping demon slug.

The series is parodied in *The Hand of Death, Part 25: Jackson's Back* (1989). Signature lines: 'You're all doomed' (*Friday the 13th*), 'so what were you going to be when you grew up?' (*Part VI*). Not part of the series are *Friday the 13th: The Orphan* (1979), an eerie adaptation of Saki's 'Sredni Vashtar' (1911), and a porno cycle beginning with *Friday the 13th* (1988). Paramount, who distributed all but the last of the run, also backed *Friday the 13th: The Series* (1987–90), a

Canadian-shot TV show about haunted antiques, which stars John D. Lemay, Robey and Chris Wiggins and takes a supernatural tack. David **Cronenberg** deigned to direct an episode ('Faith Healer', 1988) but the show more often made do with the likes of Armand **Mastroianni** and William **Fruet**; some episodes were recycled overseas as direct-to-video features: *Friday's Curse* (1988), *The Prophecies* (1989). Cultural fall-out includes Terrorvision's song 'Alice, What's the Matter?', which takes its title from a line of dialogue in *Part 2*. Eric Morse began a **young adult** series of tie-in novels with *Friday the 13th: Mother's Day* (1994).

Friday the 13th: The Series See: *Friday the 13th*

Friedkin, William (b. 1939)

American director. Following the success of *The French Connection* (1971), Friedkin directed **The Exorcist** (1973), from William Peter **Blatty**'s 1971 novel. A major hit, this triggered the **exorcism** cycle and led to such **Devil** Movies as *The Omen* (1976), though it is essentially a super-produced **Hammer** horror with added theology, best seller characterisations, broken taboos and grisly suspense effects. *The Guardian* (1990), a belated follow-up, is a silly, dire film about an evil tree and a Druid nanny. More interesting, if flawed, are the on-the-streets psycho movies *Cruising* (1980) and *Rampage* (1992). His best

pure horror credit is 'Nightcrawlers', a 1985 *Twilight Zone*.

Jade/1995

TV: *Alfred Hitchcock Hour*: 'Off Season'/1965 * *Tales From the Crypt*: 'On a Dead Man's Chest'/1992

Friedlander, Louis * See: Landers, Lew

Friedman, David F. (b. 1923)

American distributor, producer, writer. Friedman partnered H.G. **Lewis** on crude mould-breakers *Blood Feast* (1963) and *Two Thousand Maniacs!* (1964) and emerged the superior when he insisted the poorest parts of *Color Me Blood Red* (1965) be reshot. Resiting in California, he originated *She Freak* (1966) and sex fare including *The Defilers* (1965) and *The Adult Version of Jekyll and Hide* (1972). Friedman cameos in **Nazi** atrocity *Love Camp 7* (1967) and *Bikini Drive-In* (1994), but is only pseudonymously credited as producer of *Ilsa, She-Wolf of the SS* (1972). An exploitation barker of the old school, he recalls his early adventures in the impossibly vivid *A Youth in Babylon* (1990), co-written by Don De Nevi. DP

Fruet, William (b. 1933)

Canadian director. Better at hard suspense (*Death Weekend*, 1976; *Trapped*, 1982) than ridiculous monsters (*Spasms*, 1983; *Blue*

Friday the 13th – The Final Chapter

Monkey, 1987) but never more than competent.

Funeral Home/1981 * *Bedroom Eyes*/1984 * *Killer Party*/1986

TV: *Ray Bradbury Theatre*: 'The Playground'/ 1985 * *Alfred Hitchcock Presents*: 'If Looks Could Kill/1987 * *Friday the 13th*: 'The Inheritance'/1987; 'Scarecrow'/'Vanity's Mirror'/'The Doorway to Hell'/'Wax Magic'/ 1988; 'Face of Evil'/'The Shaman's Apprentice'/'Bad Penny'/1989; 'Repetition'/ 'The Tree of Life'/1990

Frye, Dwight (1899–1943)

American character actor. His portrayal of the fly-eating **Renfield** in *Dracula* (1930) quickly typecast him as madmen and hunchbacked **minions**, notably the sadistic Fritz in **Frankenstein** (1931) and the ghoulish Karl in *Bride of Frankenstein* (1935). Unable to find regular dramatic work, he was reduced to playing a voyeur in a stag film. SJ

LEFT *Friday the 13th*

*The Black Camel/1931 * The Vampire Bat/The Invisible Man/1933 * The Great Impersonation/The Crime of Dr. Crespi/1935 * The Shadow/1937 * Son of Frankenstein/1939 * Sky Bandits/Phantom Raiders/Drums of Fu Manchu/1940 * The Ghost of Frankenstein/1942 * Dead Men Walk/Frankenstein Meets the Wolf Man/1943*

Gregory William Mank, Jim Coughlin, Dwight D. Frye, *Dwight Frye's Last Laugh* (1996)

Fuest, Robert (b. 1927)

British director. Fuest worked on **The Avengers** and subsequently brought its flamboyant style to his cinema films. *The Abominable Dr. Phibes* (1971) features Vincent **Price** as a disfigured maniac who can only talk (and eat) through a hole in his neck. The minimal plot (Phibes avenges his wife's death) is merely a pretext for a series of killings based on biblical curses played out against Brian Eatwell's extravagant Art Deco sets. *Dr. Phibes Rises Again* (1972) is much the same, albeit slightly nastier. The films anticipate the **splatter movie** in their reliance on a series of spectacular deaths divorced from significant narrative context. PH

*And Soon the Darkness/1970 * The Final Program/1973 * The Devil's Rain/1976*

TV: *The Avengers*: 'Game'/'They Keep Killing Steed'/'The Rotters'/1968; 'My Wildest Dreams'/'Take Me to Your Leader'/'Pandora'/'Take-Over'/1969 * *Revenge of the Stepford Wives*/1980

Robert Fuest

Lucio Fulci's *L'aldilà*

Fulci, Lucio (1927–96)

Italian director, producer, writer. A journeyman whose pedigree included comedies, Westerns and musicals, Fulci directed *Zombi 2* (*Zombie Flesh Eaters*, 1979), an unauthorised sequel to George **Romero**'s *Dawn of the Dead* (*Zombi*, 1978). With its flamboyant imagery (including a stunningly choreographed **eye**-gouging) and stirring score, *Zombi 2* brought sudden acclaim and a new career to Fulci as major director of horror films. It was not his first in the field: he had made the cruel historical *Beatrice Cenci* (1969), the thriller *Una sull'altra* (*One on Top of the Other*, 1969), the animal-themed **gialli** *Una lucertola con la pelle di donna* (*A Lizard in a Woman's Skin*, 1971) and *Non si sevizia un paperino* (*Don't Torture a Duckling*, 1972), the parodic *Il Cav. Costante Nicosia demoniaco, ovvero: Dracula in Brianza* (1975) and the Edgar Allan **Poe**-inspired *Sette note in nero* (*The Psychic*, 1977).

Zombi 2 was followed by three other **zombie** films that comprise a loose tetralogy: the gaudily violent *Paura nella città dei morti viventi* (*City of the Living Dead*, 1980); *L'aldilà* (*The Beyond*, 1981), his finest achievement in horror cinema; and *Quella villa accanto al cimitero* (*The House by the Cemetery*, 1981), a revision of **Kubrick**'s *The Shining* (1980). He explored other themes in another Poe project, *Il gatto nero* (*The Black Cat*, 1981), and *Manhattan Baby* (*Possessed*

1982), and pushed his penchant for violence into the sordid **sex** of *Lo squartatore di New York* (*The New York Ripper*, 1982). After the primly budgeted but stylish sword-and-sorcery adventure *Conquest* (1983) and a generic futuristic actioner, *I guerrieri dell'anno 2072* (*Rome 2033: The Fighter Centurions*, 1983), Fulci turned away from the zombies and **violence** that had revitalised his career with the *Flashdance* (1983) inspired *giallo* *Murderock uccide a passo di danza* (1984), the psychological thriller *Il miele del Diavolo* (*The Devil's Honey*, 1986) and *Aenigma* (1987).

With his health failing, his planned return to his beloved zombies in *Zombi 3* (1988) was compromised, as Bruno **Mattei** replaced him during production. In the postmodern self-critique *Un gatto nel cervello* (*Nightmare Concert*, 1990), Fulci plays himself, wondering whether his obsession with horror is a mental illness that has led him to murder. His final films, sparsely budgeted and distributed, are a testament to his continued devotion to the cinema of fear. In 1995 Fulci began work on *La maschera di cera* (*Wax Mask*), a substantially budgeted **waxwork** movie produced by Dario **Argento**; he died just days before principal photography was to begin, and the project was assumed in 1996 by Sergio Stivaletti. DW

All'onorevole piacciono le donne [*The Eroticist*]/1972 * *Quando Alice ruppe lo specchio* [*Touch of*

*Death]/I fantasmi di Sodoma/1988 * Voci dal profondo [Voices from Beyond]/1990 * Le porte del silenzio/Demonia/1991*

TV: *La dolce casa degli orrori/La casa del tempo/*1989

Fu Manchu

There were insidious Chinese villains in popular literature before Fu-Manchu (the name was hyphenated at first) made his debut in *The Story-Teller* magazine in 1912. There were soon **pulp** imitations like Dr Yen Sin and Wu Fang, and even *Dr. No* (1958) – Ian Fleming admitted to being influenced by the devil doctor 'in my childhood' – but the popularity and impact of 'the yellow peril incarnate in one man' eclipsed all of them.

Birmingham-born Arthur Sarsfield Ward adopted the pseudonym 'Sax Rohmer' (which he reckoned meant 'freelance' in Anglo-Saxon) and wrote thirteen novels and several short stories about Fu Manchu between *The Mystery of Dr. Fu-Manchu* (1913) and *Emperor Fu Manchu* (1959). Each takes place roughly in the present, and chronicles an elaborate struggle between Sir Denis Nayland Smith – an ex-District Commissioner late of Mandalay, working with Scotland Yard – and Fu Manchu. The mastermind mobilises a small army of dacoits, thugs and **zombies** and an arsenal of rare poisons, exotic **insects** and such fiendish **torture** weapons as 'the Zayat Kiss' or 'the Coughing Horror'. At one level, the books are about a cosmic racial conflict between Wayland the Smith, the Anglo-Saxon folk-warrior, and a supervillain 'with all the cruel cunning of an entire Eastern race, accumulated in one giant intellect'. By implication, Fu Manchu is a representative of the recently (1911) overthrown Manchu dynasty, widely thought in the popular English press to have been the most inventively sadistic regime in recent Chinese history.

Rohmer claimed the idea came to him when he was sent on a magazine assignment for *Tit-Bits* to cover the dope-smuggling and white-slaving activities of a Mr King in Limehouse, East London's Chinatown. He never managed to find Mr King, but he did see a tall, lean and feline Chinaman entering a 'cheap-looking dwelling', and his fertile imagination did the rest: '[the dwelling] unknown to all but a chosen few [must have been] luxurious apartments, orientally furnished, cushioned and perfumed'. The books feed on exotic imaginings about what must be going on behind innocent-looking Limehouse shopfronts (for readers who were unlikely to visit the place for themselves) as well as Edwardian anxieties about 'Oriental' immigration and the awakening empires of the East. The pop-culture supervillain was Chinese rather than Japanese at that time and may also have had something to do with the West's troubled conscience.

The devil doctor's political ambitions seem to expand with Rohmer's readership: he promotes himself from small-time Limehouse crook who uses opium dens as a front to head of 'the Council of Seven' of the Si-Fan Secret Society (*The Daughter of Fu Manchu*, 1931), to self-styled controller of the balance of power in Europe against totalitarianism (*The Drums of Fu Manchu*, 1934, in which he sees off dictator 'Rudolph Adlon') to potential world dominator, armed with various ultimate deterrents (*The Island of Fu Manchu*, 1941). By 1959, months before Rohmer's death, Fu Manchu (like his creator) was intent on 'saving the world from the leprosy of Communism'. He also turns out to be a near-immortal dependent on an elixir of life and, in a bit of a cop-out, may not even be Chinese but ancient Egyptian.

At another level, the books owe less to the overthrow of the Manchu dynasty by Dr Sun Yat-sen and Yu'an Shih-kai (or the real-life kidnapping of a Chinese diplomat in London) than Rohmer's apprenticeship as a music-hall composer and lyricist for George Robey and Little Tich. The indestructible pantomime villain, complete with impossible Chinese name, impeccable manners, performing marmoset on his shoulder and surreal sense of the dramatic, is a master of illusion, disguise and the quick-change routine, and an ace escapologist to boot; Nayland Smith, meanwhile, tends to talk in the convoluted prose ('It is me, or rather it is I', he says in one tense scene) of George Robey's famous 'in other words' routine and Little Tich's 'so to speak' line in patter. Rohmer's formula was a combination of music hall, pop surrealism in docklands, detective fiction and paranoia about 'the yellow peril'. It has inspired sequels (Cay Van Ash's *Ten Years Beyond Baker Street*, 1984; *The Fires of Fu Manchu*, 1987) and pastiches (Richard Jaccoma's *Yellow Peril*, 1978). Fu has unbilled cameos in Rohmer's *The Golden Scorpion* (1919) and Kim Newman's *Anno Dracula* (1992). Unsurprisingly, he is a comics regular, sharing the early issues of *Detective Comics* with **Batman** in the 30s and dueling with his kung fu expert son in *The Hands of Shang-Chi* in the 70s.

Fu Manchu made his film debut in *The Mystery of Dr Fu-Manchu* (1923), a fifteen-part series starring Harry Agar Lyons, who returned insidiously in *The Further Mysteries of Dr Fu-Manchu* (1924). The role was taken up by Warner Oland for *The Mysterious Dr. Fu Manchu* (1929), *The Return of Dr. Fu Manchu* (1931), *Daughter of the Dragon* (1931), with Anna May Wong as the villain's daughter, and a comedy cameo in *Paramount on Parade*

RIGHT Henry Brandon, *The Drums of Fu Manchu*

Fu Manchu

(1930), mingling with **Sherlock Holmes** (Clive Brook) and Philo Vance (William Powell). More elaborate is *The Mask of Fu Manchu* (1932), which succeeds in mispronouncing 'Nayland', continues the cinematic tradition of having Fu in a long moustache (never once mentioned in the books), employs Myrna Loy as Fu's nymphomaniac daughter complete with pet python, and climaxes with Boris **Karloff** plus death ray exhorting the crazed mob to 'kill all the white men and take their women!' Needless to add, the Chinese embassy in Washington lodged a formal complaint. Rohmer said, in a finely balanced judgement – to say the least – that he found the film rather too crude.

The Henry Brandon serial version (*The Drums of Fu Manchu*, 1940) goes even further by introducing Burmese dacoits as vampire-fanged zombies, complete with lobotomy scars on their foreheads. *El otro Fu Manchu* (1945) features not the villain himself but a vaudeville **magician** namesake who fights crime in a run of Mexican low-budgeters. Though John **Carradine** starred in a 1954 TV pilot that led to a cheap series (*The Adventures of Fu Manchu*, 1956) with Glenn Gordon, the 'Lord of Strange Deaths' stayed off the big screen until Don **Sharp**'s *The Face of Fu Manchu* (1965). In the era of Chairman Mao, Fu (Christopher **Lee**) caught up with the imitator Dr No by entering the world of James Bond. Lee returns, accompanied by Tsai Chin and increasing desperation, in the Harry Alan Towers-produced *Brides of Fu*

ABOVE Boris Karloff, *The Mask of Fu Manchu*

LEFT Tsai Chin, Christopher Lee, *The Face of Fu Manchu*

Manchu (1966), *The Vengeance of Fu Manchu* (1967), *El castillo de Fu Manchu* (*Castle of Fu Manchu*, 1968) and *Fu Manchu y el beso de la muerte* (*The Blood of Fu Manchu*, 1968). Peter Sellers essays the roles of Fu and Smith in *The Fiendish Plot of Dr. Fu Manchu* (1980) and Paul **Naschy** takes his turn in *La hija de Fu Manchu* (1990).

Rohmer always thought Basil **Rathbone** would make the perfect Fu Manchu, because he was 'appropriately tall, cold and suave, and masterful even in pyjamas'. It never occurred to him, of course, that Fu could possibly be played by a Chinese actor. CF

Elizabeth Sax Rohmer, Cay Van Ash, *Master of Villainy* (1972)

G

Gale, David (19??–91)

British-born actor. The megalomaniac severed head of *Re-Animator* (1985).

The Brain/*Pulse Pounders* (unfinished)/1988 * *The First Power*/*Syngenor*/1990 * *Bride of Re-Animator*/*The Guyver*/1991

TV: *Tales From the Darkside*: 'Seymourlama' 1987

Galeen, Henrik (1881–1949)

German writer, director. The most important **expressionist** screenwriter, Galeen twice scripted *Der Golem* for Paul **Wegener**, acting and co-directing in 1913, merely writing in 1920. After 1933, in unproductive exile.

Der Student von Prag/1913 * *Peter Schlemihl*/1914 * *Nosferatu, eine Symphonie des Grauens*/1922 * *Das Wachsfigurenkabinett* [*Waxworks*]/1924 * *Der Student von Prag* (d)/1926 * *Alraune* (d)/1928

Gallagher, Stephen (b. 1954)

British author of horror novels with Nigel **Kneale**-like s-f premises or drizzly noir suspense: *Chimera* (1982), *Valley of Lights* (1987), *Down River* (1989), *Rain* (1990), *Nightmare, With Angel* (1992), *Red Red Robin* (1995).

TV: *Doctor Who*: 'Warrior's Gate'/1981; 'Terminus'/1983 * *Chimera*/1991 * *Chiller*: 'Prophecy'/'Here Comes the Mirror Man'/1995

Gaming

Role-Playing Games started with *Dungeons and Dragons* (1974), a **fantasy** system. This American college phenomenon prompted clones (*Tunnels and Trolls*, 1975) and excursions into s-f (*Metamorphosis Alpha*), Western (*Boot Hill*), swashbuckling (*Skulls & Crossbones*), crime (*Gangster!*), superheroes (*Superhero 2044*) and espionage (*Top Secret*). Strangely, the first horror role-playing game did not emerge until *Call of Cthulhu* (1981). This may be because most games systems already include horrific elements: the *Deities & DemiGods* (1980) manual for *Advanced Dungeons & Dragons* gave statistics for **Cthulhu Mythos** monsters before the **Lovecraft** estate gave the rights to Chaosium Games. *Call of Cthulhu* proved popular: with paranoia, insanity and tentacles, it was the perfect game for those raised on Reagan and Thatcher. *Chill*, another 80s system, also works on the premise that char-acters are trying to solve mysteries: as with *Call of Cthulhu*, the assumption is that players have to be 'good' or else become a dreaded 'NPC' (Non Player Character).

The mid-80s saw a general trend towards 'darker', more pessimistic games. *Cyberpunk* is the game of the 'dark future': landscapes are replicas of *Blade Runner* (1982) and everyone totes a big gun and a bad attitude. Again, the game is not overtly horrific but many of its trappings are. *Shadowrun* is a strange hybrid, a cross between *Cyberpunk* and *Dungeons & Dragons*: elves with guns. The horror content is potentially high, with long lists of monsters the characters can meet or turn into. The early 90s saw a major shift towards specifically horror games systems: *Nightlife* (1990), *Vampire: the Masquerade* (1991), *Kult* (1991). White Wolf's Goth-Punk *Vampire* was one of the first systems to allow gamers to play inherently evil creatures. White Wolf built a universe called 'The World of Darkness' and designed other games to slot into this cosmos (*Werewolf*, *Wraith*). Other companies followed the pattern: *Dark Conspiracy* mixes cyberpunk and horror, TSR's *Ravenloft* is a revamped horror world for its fantasy players. Horror role-playing has finally come into its own twilight world. MMcH

Garris, Mick (b. 1951)

American director, writer. Having paid dues with sequels and TV, Garris became Stephen **King**'s favoured director, coping well enough with the silly *Sleepwalkers* (1992) to land the epic job of *The Stand* (1994) and the hubris-stricken remake of *The Shining* (1996).

Coming Soon (s)/1984 * *Critters 2: The Main Course*/1988 * *The Fly II* (s)/1989 * *Hocus Pocus* (s)/1993

TV: *Amazing Stories* (s): 'The Main Attraction'/'The Amazing Falsworth'/1985 'The Sitter'/'No Day at the Beach'/'The Greibble'/'Life on Death Row' (+d)/'Go to the Head of the Class'/'Such Interesting Neighbours'/'Without Diana'/1986 * *Freddy's Nightmares*: 'Killer Instinct'/1988 * *Psycho IV: The Beginning* (d)/1991 * *She-Wolf of London* (*Love and Curses*, co-creator)/1992

Gas Light

Patrick Hamilton's *Gas Light: A Victorian Thriller* was first staged in Richmond in 1938, with Gwen Ffrancon-Davies and Dennis Arundell, transferred to the West End in 1939 and opened on Broadway, retitled *Angel Street*, in 1941, with Judith Evelyn and Vincent **Price**. The heroine is subtly tormented into madness by a cruel husband who has married her as part of a scheme to recover stolen jewels. The trappings are period chintz, but the psychological intensity is characteristic of Hamilton's modern despair. It was filmed twice as *Gaslight*: in 1940, by Thorold Dickinson with Diana Wynyard and Anton Walbrook; in 1944, by George Cukor with Ingrid Bergman and Charles Boyer. It was telecast by the BBC in 1939, with Ffrancon-Davies and Arundell, and 1947 (as *Gas Light*), with Catherine Lacey and Anthony Ireland; it was produced on *Matinee Theatre* (1958), as 'Angel Street', with Price

Mick Garris's Critters 2: The Main Course

Diana Wynyard, Anton Walbrook, *Gaslight*

and Evelyn. Other sadistic Victorian husbands (*Experiment Perilous*, 1944; *Sleep My Love*, 1948) are modelled on *Gas Light*, which also influenced the it's-all-a-plot school of **Les diaboliques** (1954).

Gates, Tudor (b. 1930)

British writer. In Italy, Gates worked with Mario **Bava** on *Diabolik* (1967) and a script (*Cry Nightmare*) which became Antonio **Margheriti**'s *Nude . . . si muore* (*The Young, the Evil and the Savage*, 1968). He contributed to *Barbarella* (1967) and wrote **Hammer**'s **'Carmilla'** films, which add softcore to the **vampire** formula.

The Vampire Lovers/1970 * *Lust for a Vampire*/ *Fright*/1971 * *Twins of Evil*/1972

Gein, Edward (1906–84)

American murderer. After the deaths of his overprotective mother and mad father, Wisconsin farmer Gein embarked on a body-snatching and homicide spree, allegedly practising necrophilia and **cannibalism**. When he was arrested for the murders of two middle-aged women, it was discovered that his isolated farmhouse was a repository of trophies made of female body parts. Obsessed with demented folk art, Gein procured materials for human skin masks and waistcoats, resorting to murder only after exhausting the possibilities of grave-robbery. Similarly, interest in him is down to unorthodox upholstery and home tailoring

rather than his comparatively minor status as a murderer.

Details percolate into significant works: Robert **Bloch**'s 1959 novel and **Hitchcock**'s 1960 film *Psycho*; Tobe **Hooper**'s *The Texas Chain Saw Massacre* (1974); Thomas **Harris**'s 1988 novel and Jonathan **Demme**'s 1991 film *The Silence of the Lambs*. Closer to the facts is Bob **Clark** and Alan **Ormsby**'s *Deranged* (1974), with Roberts Blossom as Ezra Cobb. Many mother-dominated, corpse-skinning, dungaree-wearing, baccy-chewing downhome maniacs derive from Gein: *3 on a Meathook* (1973), *Death Trap* (1976), *Motel Hell* (1980), *Tourist Trap* (1979), *Don't Go in the House* (1980), *Maniac* (1980), *The People Across the Lake* (1988). An Ed Gein Fan Club exists, encouraging idiotic merchandise from trading cards to busts.

Harold Schecter, *Deviant* (1989); Paul Anthony Woods, *Ed Gein – Psycho!* (1992)

Gemora, Charles (1903–61)

American mime. Aside from a turn as the Martian in *War of the Worlds* (1953), Gemora's horrors find him in a trusty **ape** suit, shambling for **mad scientists** or pursuing jungle lovelies.

Seven Footprints to Satan/1929 * *Ingagi*/1930 * *Savage Girl*/*Murders in the Rue Morgue*/1932 * *Island of Lost Souls*/1933 * *The Monster and the Girl*/1941 * *Gildersleeve's Ghost*/1943 * *Phantom of the Rue Morgue*/1953

Ghosts (UK TV series, 1994–)

Saturday night supernatural plays from the BBC, produced by Ruth Baumgarten and Andrée Molyneaux. More baffling than frightening, the series features originals from Stephen **Volk** ('I'll Be Watching You', 'Massage') and Terry Johnson ('The Chemistry Lesson') and adaptations of stories by Ellen Glasgow ('Shadowy Third') and Ronald Duncan ('Blood and Water'). The best episode is 'Three Miles Up', an **Aickman**-like canal story from Elizabeth Jane Howard, directed by Lesley Manning.

Ghost Story (US TV series, 1972–3)

Storyteller Winston Essex (Sebastian Cabot) introduces contemporary tales of horror. Horror pedigree was lent by creator Richard **Matheson**, executive producer William **Castle** and story editor Jimmy **Sangster**; writers include Henry Slesar, DC Fontana, Robert **Bloch** and Harlan **Ellison**. After thirteen weeks, Cabot was dropped and the title became *Circle of Fear*: the format change did not help the series survive. TM

The Ghost Story

One of the oldest forms of storytelling, verbal tales of supernatural activity are a folkloric commonplace. The telling of ghost tales, elaborated by atmospheric props and enhanced by darkness, remains a popular pastime among children and young adults. Supposedly 'true' ghost stories have been collected for years, but are mostly of a pathetic, gentle and benign nature. In fiction, ghosts are allowed to be malign. They abound in the plays of Seneca, inspiring the

Sebastian Cabot, *Ghost Story*

did most to define the ghost story as a separate entity within the wider field of horror fiction. He began composing ghost stories for his own amusement, reading aloud to friends at King's College every Christmas, and first collected them in *Ghost Stories of an Antiquary* (1904). He believed ghosts should be malevolent and appear in everyday surroundings: these rules, combined with the authority of his antiquarian knowledge, are demonstrated by much-reprinted classics like 'Oh, Whistle and I'll Come to You, My Lad' (1904), 'Lost Hearts' (1904) and 'Casting the Runes' (1911). Frederick Cowles, M.P. Dare, R.H. Maldon, E.G. Swain and, particularly, A.N.L. Munby all wrote in the Jamesian manner. Other masters, who break away from James, include H. Russell Wakefield, E.F. Benson and Algernon **Blackwood**.

Fritz **Leiber** did most to bring the ghost story into a modern urban setting: 'Smoke Ghost' (1941) and 'The Girl With the Hungry Eyes' (1949) influentially find the inexplicable at work in modern cities, while *Conjure Wife* (1953) and *Our Lady of Darkness* (1977) advance James's rules into the mid- and late-20th century. Notable followers of the Leiber tradition are Ramsey **Campbell**, Lisa Tuttle, Charles L. **Grant**, Karl Edward Wagner and Terry Lamsley. But Robert **Aickman** best deserves praise as master of the modern ghost story: he believed ghosts themselves less important than psychological effects they have upon the living. Aickman stories are the literary equivalent of the

admiring Elizabethans to fill their tragedies with supernatural characters. The spectre of a giant knight appears in Horace Walpole's *The Castle of Otranto* (1765), ensuring ghosts would feature in most subsequent **gothic novels**.

The ghost story came into its own in the 19th century. J. Sheridan **Le Fanu** entered the field with *The House by the Churchyard* (1863) and *Uncle Silas* (1864), gothics with occasional supernatural episodes, but his *In a Glass Darkly* (1886) employs the short form popular among Victorians, defining the **vampire** (**'Carmilla'**) and psychological ghost story ('Green Tea', 'The Familiar'), creating the psychic detective in the character of Dr Hesselius. Charles Dickens's *A Christmas Carol* (1843) popularised the 'ghost story for Christmas'. As well as writing stories of spectral vengeance ('The Trial for Murder', 1865) and warning ('The Signalman', 1866), Dickens encouraged Le Fanu, Wilkie Collins, Elizabeth Gaskell, Edward Bulwer-Lytton and others to produce ghost stories for Christmas issues of his magazine, *All the Year Round*. Bulwer-Lytton's 'The Haunted and the Hunters' or 'The House and the Brain' (1859) had already appeared in the rival *Blackwood's Magazine*; this story of the scientific investigation of a haunted house influences many later works: Richard **Matheson**'s *Hell House* (1971; filmed as *The Legend of Hell House*, 1973) and Nigel **Kneale**'s TV play *The Stone Tape* (1972).

Henry James's psychological ghost story **'The Turn of the Screw'** (1898; filmed as *The Innocents*, 1961) has children appear **possessed** by the spirits of dead servants. Cambridge scholar Montague Rhodes **James**

Ghost Stories: *The Fog*

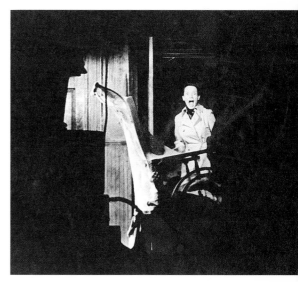

Ghost Stories: *The Changeling*

thing seen from the corner of the eye, not readily explicable. The ghost story is notoriously difficult to bring off at novel length: Shirley **Jackson**'s *The Haunting of Hill House* (filmed as *The Haunting*, 1963), where the psychological make-up of the characters and the inexplicable nature of the phenomenon are the whole of the plot, is a notable exception. Others have produced worthy ghost novels: Kingsley Amis (*The Green Man*, 1969), Bernard **Taylor** (*Sweetheart, Sweetheart*, 1977), Peter **Straub** (*Ghost Story*, 1979), Susan Hill (*The Woman in Black*, 1983), T.M. Wright (*A Manhattan Ghost Story*, 1984), Peter **James** (*Possession*, 1988), Jonathan Aycliffe (*Naomi's Room*, 1991).

Though classic ghost stories are often adapted for TV and **radio**, the cinema prefers sentimental (*The Ghost and Mrs. Muir*, 1947; *Field of Dreams*, 1989; *Ghost*, 1990) or funny (*Topper*, 1937; *Ghostbusters*, 1984; *Beetle Juice*, 1988) ghosts. Respectably scary ghosts include *The Uninvited* (1944), *Dead of Night* (1945), *Tormented* (1960), *Kwaidan* (1964), *Danza macabra* (1963), *The Other* (1972), *Ghost Story* (1974), *The Changeling* (1979), *The Fog* (1980), **Poltergeist** (1982) and *Lady in White* (1988). There are many nice-young-couple-buy-a-haunted-house efforts on the lines of **The Amityville Horror** (1979). Modern horror's most active ghost is Freddy Krueger (Robert **Englund**) of *A Nightmare on Elm Street* (1984). MW

Julia Briggs, *Night Visitors* (1977); Jack Sullivan, *Elegant Nightmares* (1978)

Giallo

A masked, black-gloved killer is stalking beautiful female **victims**. Suspicion is ubiquitous, because everyone is hiding something. Motivations are tenuous, murder methods grotesquely elaborate. Cinematic spectacle is foregrounded for its own sake, and there is a frankly perverse dwelling upon **violence**. An obstinate deferral of reliable plot information creates maximum confusion among a decadent, double-dealing cast of sleazy eccentrics. These are the characteristics of the Italian *giallo*, a film form which crossbreeds the murder mystery with horror.

The term *giallo* (literally, 'yellow') was first applied to crime fiction in the 30s, when a line of thrillers were issued with distinctive yellow covers. Bracketed as *gialli* on publication in Italy were works by such diverse fig-

ures as Agatha **Christie** and Cornell **Woolrich**. In the Italian cinema, Mario **Bava** made key contributions to the *giallo*'s development: *La ragazza che sapeva troppo* (*The Evil Eye*, 1962) is considered the first example of the genre, but Bava swifly eclipsed it with *Sei donne per l'assassino* (*Blood and Black Lace*, 1964). This Italian/West German co-production glancingly resembles the German-made *krimis*, crime thrillers derived from Edgar **Wallace**. However, Bava's chillingly irrational, violent and colour-drenched delirium make the black-and-white *krimis* seem relatively staid.

Dario **Argento** fuel-injected the format with his brilliant debut *L'uccello dalle piume di cristallo* (*The Bird With the Crystal Plumage*, 1969), an international commercial success which spawned a trend for similarly decorative titles. Argento's corkscrew plotting and bravura use of **subjective camera** to menace victims further refined the *giallo* style. Both he and Bava established hallmarks that would shape the better efforts of others in the field and escape the prosaic ambitions of the rest. Romolo Guerrieri's *Il dolce corpo di Deborah* (*The Sweet Body of Deborah*, 1968), which predates Argento's debut, also proved influential. Further highlights came from Lucio **Fulci**, who turned imaginatively to the genre with *Una lucertola con la pelle di donna* (*A Lizard in a Woman's Skin*, 1971) and excelled with the **rural horror** of *Non si*

sevizia un paperino (*Don't Torture a Duckling*, 1972), and Sergio **Martino**, whose numerous efforts include sexy frolics (*Il tuo vizio è una stanza chiusa e solo io ne ho la chiave/Gently Before She Dies*, 1972) and taut, salacious thrillers (*I corpi presentano tracce di violenza carnale/Torso*, 1973).

The *giallo poliziesco*, dominated by the cynical roughhouse of Umberto **Lenzi**, extend into sub-*Dirty Harry* (1971) terrain, but the principle 70s development was a clumsy mating with **pornography** in films like Silvio Amadio's *Alla ricerca del piacere* (*Hot Bed of Sex*, 1971) and Andrea Bianchi's *Nude per l'assassino* (*Strip Nude for Your Killer*, 1975). Other significant *gialli*: Sergio Bergonzelli's *Nelle pieghe della carne* (*Folds of the Flesh*, 1970), Massimo Dallamano's *Cosa avete fatto a Solange?* (*What Have You Done to Solange?*, 1971), Sergio Pastore's *Sette scialli di seta gialla* (*Crimes of the Black Cat*, 1972), Lenzi's *Sette orchidee macchiate di rosso* (1972), Giuliano Carnimeo's *Perché quelle strane gocce di sangue sul corpo di Jennifer?* (1972), Armando Crispino's *Macchie solari* (*Autopsy*, 1974), Lamberto **Bava**'s *La casa con la scala nel buio* (*A Blade in the Dark*, 1982), Carlo Vanzina's *Sotto il vestito niente* (*Nothing Underneath*, 1985), Michele **Soavi**'s *Deliria* (*Stagefright*, 1987), Piccio Raffanini's *Pathos, segreta inquietudine* (*Obsession: A Taste for Fear*, 1988). The tedium of flatly orchestrated murders and plodding investigations rotate endlessly in *giallo* purgatories: Riccardo **Freda**'s *L'iguana dalla lingua di fuoco* (1971), Alfonso Brescia's *Ragazza tutta nuda assassinata nel parco* (1972), Lenzi's *Gatti rossi in un laberinto di vetro* (*Eyeball*, 1974).

At the extremes, the most brutal entry is Mario Landi's outrageous *Giallo a Venezia* (1979), and creeping along as the strangest effort is Fernando Di Leo's too-weird-to-be-dull, too-stupid-to-be-good porno-asylum 'thriller' *La bestia uccide a sangue freddo* (*Cold Blooded Beast*, 1971). The genre's apotheosis is Argento's *Tenebre* (*Tenebrae*, 1982), a **recursive** *giallo* about a writer of murder thrillers that transcends the genre's limitations, rewrites its sexual politics and comments on its roots. The 'erotic thriller', exemplified by Brian **De Palma**'s *Body Double* (1984) and Paul Verhoeven's *Basic Instinct* (1992), is a Hollywood offshoot of the *giallo*, while the closest an American film has come to imitating the form is *Knight Moves* (1992). ST

Antonio Bruschini, Antonio Tentori, *Profonde tenebre – il cinema thrilling italiano 1962–1982* (1992)

Gibson, Alan (1938–87)
Canadian-born director. He worked for **Hammer** in the early 70s, when its formula was showing signs of wear, handling the last of Hammer's **Dracula** cycle, *Dracula A.D. 1972* (1972) and *The Satanic Rites of Dracula* (1973). In retrospect, both have a certain **camp** appeal (notably the outrageously unconvincing teenage stereotypes in *A.D. 1972*) but represent a sad retreat from the stately dignity of Terence **Fisher**'s *Dracula* (1958). PH

Crescendo/1969

TV: *Journey to the Unknown*: 'Jane Brown's Body'/'Somewhere in a Crowd'/'Poor Butterfly'/'The Killing Bottle'/1968 * *Orson Welles' Great Mysteries*: 'Captain Rogers'/'The Monkey's Paw'/'Money to Burn'/'Death of an Old-Fashioned Girl'/1973 * 'The Furnished Room'/'The Leather Funnel'/1974 * *Hammer House of Horror*: 'Silent Scream'/ 'The Two Faces of Evil'/1980

Giger, H.R. [Hansreudi] (b. 1940)
Swiss artist influenced by Bosch, Bocklin and the Surrealists. His paintings show life mutating into the mechanical. His third book, *H.R. Giger's Necronomicon* (1977), owing only its title to **Lovecraft**, led to a commission as designer for the aborted

Jodorowsky film of *Dune*. He was later hired to create the alien craft and title creature (typically phallic) of **Alien** (1979). He designed a composite spectre for *Poltergeist II: The Other Side* (1986) but was unhappy with its screen appearance. *Darkseed* (1992), a computer game, sends players into a dimension overrun by his monsters. *Species* (1995) saw his return to the cinema. RC

Swiss Made (s)/1969 * *Passagen* (s)/1971 * *Teito Monogatari* [*Tokyo: The Last Megalopolis*]/ 1987

Gilling, John (1912–84)
British writer, director. Known for **Hammer**'s 1966 Cornish duo *The Plague of the Zombies* and *The Reptile*, Gilling is a horrorist of surprising tenacity. His first script (*Black Memory*, 1946) earned writing credits on Tod **Slaughter**'s **Burke and Hare** perm *The Greed of William Hart* (1948), inaugural Hammer horrors *The Man in Black* (1949) and *Room to Let* (1949) and nascent psycho-thriller *Dark Interval* (1950). Early directorial efforts include *Mother Riley Meets the Vampire* (1952), arguably Britain's first **vampire** film, and the cold war **zombie** movie *The Gamma People* (1956).

A dispute over authorship of *Whispering Smith Hits London* (1951) damped his relationship with Hammer, but the canny *William Hart* upgrading *The Flesh and the Fiends* (1959) won him the devolved company project *The Shadow of the Cat* (1961), which reveals both reserves of style and an ability to deal with the risibilities of fantasy plotting. The Cornish films are notably forward-looking: each makes plain the political nature of their monster; *Plague*'s dream sequence presages a whole genre of paranoid **zombie** horror. In 1970, Gilling moved to Spain to paint and had a surprise career coda with one-time **Naschy** project *La cruz del diablo* (1974). DP

The Gorgon (w)/1964 * *The Night Caller*/1965 * *The Mummy's Shroud*/1967 * *Trog* (w)/1970

Girdler, William (1947–78)
American director, producer. After graduating from grindhouse to middle-budget productions, he died in a helicopter accident.

Abby/1972 * *3 on a Meathook*/1973 * *Grizzly*/ 1976 * *Day of the Animals*/1977 * *The Manitou*/1978

Goblin
Italian composers and performers. Goblin rose out of the progressive **rock** movement

of the early 70s when keyboardist Claudio Simonetti and drummer Walter Martino of Ritratto di Dorian Gray were joined by guitarist Massimo Morante of Era di Acquario and bass player Fabio Pignatelli of Rivelazioni to form film music's most influential rock-and-roll band. Goblin catapulted to fame with its thudding bass lines and keyboard flourishes for Dario **Argento**'s *Profondo rosso* (*Deep Red*, 1975). Though best known for its work with Argento, including *Suspiria* (1977), *Dawn of the Dead* (*Zombi*, 1979) and *Tenebre* (*Tenebrae*, 1982) (composed and performed by three of its members), the band recorded eight singles and thirteen albums in and out of film. Martino left to form I Libra and later scored Mario Bava's *Schock Transfert-Suspence-Hypnos* (*Shock*, 1977); he was replaced by Agostino Marangolo, while Maurizio Guarino provided additional keyboards.

The 1976 studio album *Roller* included themes for *Wampir*, the European release of **Romero**'s *Martin* (1978). After the concept album *Il fantastico viaggio del Bagarozzo Mark* (1977) and rescoring Richard **Franklin**'s *Patrick* (1978) for Europe, Goblin performed the soundtracks for Antonio Bido's *Solamente nero* (*Bloodstained Shadow*, 1978), Joe **D'Amato**'s *Buio omega* (*Buried Alive*, 1978) and Luigi **Cozzi**'s *Contamination* (*Alien Contamination*, 1979). After the studio album *Volo* (1982), the band scored *Notturno* (1983) and *Mount St. Helen's* (1987) before making its last appearance on the soundtrack of Michele **Soavi**'s *La chiesa* (*The Church*, 1988). *Phenomena* (1985) marked Simonetti's departure from Goblin for a solo career that has included music for *Conquest* (1983), *Demoni* (*Demons*, 1985), **Deodato**'s *Minaccia d'Amore* (*Dial: Help*, 1988), *The Washing Machine* (1993) and Argento's *Opera* (1987). His band, the Simonetti Project, has re-recorded several of the soundtrack themes for which Goblin is renowned. DW

Godwin, Mary * See: **Shelley, Mary Wollstonecraft**

Goldblum, Jeff (b. 1952)
American actor. Well cast as Ichabod Crane in **The Legend of Sleepy Hollow** (1980); outstanding as the mutating scientist of *The Fly* (1986).

The Sentinel/1977 * *Invasion of the Body Snatchers*/1978 * *Transylvania 6-5000*/1985 * *Vibes*/1988 * *Mister Frost*/*El mono loco* [*The Mad Monkey*]/1990 * *Fathers and Sons*/1992 *

Jurassic Park/1993 * *Hideaway*/*Powder*/1995 * *Independence Day*/1996

TV: *Ray Bradbury Theatre*: 'The Town Where No One Got Off'/1986

Goldsmith, Jerry (b. 1929)

American composer. Goldsmith earned a position at CBS radio in 1950, working on *Suspense* and *The Hallmark Hall of Fame*, graduated to television (*Playhouse 90*, *Dr Kildare*) and earned an Emmy nomination for **Thriller** (1960–62). Since *Black Patch* (1957), he has worked on many films. Versatile and gifted, he has composed for most major movie genres; his horror scores enhance superior work and save lesser efforts. He won an Academy Award for **The Omen** (1976) and plays a cameo role in *Gremlins II: The New Batch* (1990). Goldsmith library music from **The Twilight Zone** is used in *Kingdom of the Spiders* (1973) and *Alligator* (1980). SL

Seconds/1966 * *The Mephisto Waltz*/1971 * *The Other*/1972 * *The Reincarnation of Peter Proud*/1975 * *Coma*/*Magic*/*The Swarm*/*Damien: Omen II*/1978 * *Alien*/1979 * *The Final Conflict*/1981 * *Poltergeist*/1982 * *Psycho II*/*Twilight Zone: The Movie*/1983 * *Gremlins*/1984 * *Link*/*Poltergeist II: The Other Side*/1986 * *Warlock*/*The 'Burbs*/*Leviathan*/1989 * *Gremlins II: The New Batch*/1990 * *Congo*/*Powder*/1995

TV: *The Twilight Zone*: 'The Four of Us Are Dying'/'The Big Tall Wish'/'Nightmare as a Child'/'Nervous Man in a Four Dollar Room'/1960; 'Back There'/'Dust'/'The Invaders'/1961 * *Thriller*: 'Hay Fork and Bill Hook'/'Yours Truly, Jack the Ripper'/'Mr George'/'Terror in Teakwood'/1961.

The Golem

In the most familiar version of the Jewish legend, the golem is a man of clay animated by Rabbi Judah Loew ben Bezalel in the Prague ghetto. In some variants, the golem is a protector of its people while others make it a Frankensteinian menace. Among many works on the theme: Gustav Meyrink's *Der Golem* (1914), Bari Woods's *The Tribe* (1981), Marge Piercy's *He, She and It* (1991), Ernest Joselovitz's *Vilna's Got a Golem* (1996).

The Golem was the first recurring screen monster. Paul **Wegener** was the clay man thrice: revived in modern times in *Der Golem* (1913), playing himself impersonating the

OPPOSITE AND RIGHT Paul Wegener, *Der Golem, wie er in die Welt kam*

creature in *Der Golem und der Tänzerin* (1917), dramatising the original legend in *Der Golem, wie er in die Welt kam* (1920). Others: a Danish *The Golem* (1916), an Austrian skit *Der Dorfsgolem* (*The Golem's Last Adventure*, 1921), French movies called *Le Golem* (1936, 1966, 1971), the Czech *Císařův pekař – Pekařův císař* (*The Emperor's Baker*, 1951), *Pražské noci* (1968) and *Ze zivota deti* (1977), the British *It* (1967), the Polish *Golem* (1980), an animated *The Golem* (1987), the Italian *Miami Golem* (*Miami Horror*, 1987), 'Golem' (*Superboy*, 1991), Andy **Milligan**'s

Monstrosity (1991), Israeli Amos Gitai's *Golem, Spirit of Exile* (1992).

Gordon, Bert I. (b. 1922)

American producer, director, writer, cinematographer, effects artist. Born in Kenosha, Wisconsin, Orson **Welles**'s home town, Gordon is known for campy but dull big bug or person s-f. His horrors are more rewarding: *Tormented* (1960) is a creepy lighthouse-set ghost story; *Necromancy* (1972), reissued in an alternate version as *The Witching* (1981), has a false-nosed Welles raising the

Devil; *The Coming* (1983) mixes time travel and Salem **witchcraft**. His best is *The Mad Bomber* (1973), scripted by Marc Behm, with Chuck Connors as the **psychopath**.

Serpent Island (c)/1954 * *King Dinosaur*/1955 * *The Amazing Colossal Man*/*The Beginning of the End*/*The Cyclops*/1957 * *Attack of the Puppet People*/*War of the Colossal Beast*/*The Spider*/ 1958 * *The Magic Sword*/1962 * *Village of the Giants*/1965 * *Picture Mommy Dead*/1966 * *Food of the Gods*/1976 * *Empire of the Ants*/ 1977 * *Malediction*/1990

Gordon, Richard (b. 1925)

British producer. Twin brother of American-based producer Alex Gordon (*The She Creature*, 1957; *Voodoo Woman*, 1957), he works in the margins of the British film industry, combining lurid commercialism with the defiantly old-fashioned. It is hard not to enjoy such sly **camp** shudder pulps as *Fiend Without a Face* (1958), *Tower of Evil* (1971) and *Horror Hospital* (1973). The Gordons' enthusiasm for films they saw as children led them to work with their idols: Alex scripted **Lugosi**'s last star role (*Bride of the Monster*, 1955) while Richard brought **Karloff** to Britain in 1958 for *Grip of the Strangler* and *Corridors of Blood*. Otherwise, Gordon's regular leading man was Bryant Halliday, best as the evil **ventriloquist** of *Devil Doll* (1964).

Womaneater/1957 * *First Man into Space*/1959 * *Curse of Simba*/1964 * *The Projected Man*/ *Island of Terror*/*Naked Evil*/1966 * *The Cat and the Canary*/1978 * *Inseminoid*/1981

Gordon, Stuart (b. 1947)

American director, writer, producer Gordon burst on to the horror scene with *Re-Animator* (1985), a farcically gory adaptation of **Lovecraft**'s 'Herbert West – Re-Animator' (1922). He has an extensive and controversial background in theatre, dating back to obscenity charges levelled against a university *Peter Pan* in which Tinker Belle was gay, Peter Pan a flower child and the voyage to Never-Never Land an LSD trip. Gordon was co-founder and longtime artistic director of Chicago's famous Organic Theater, where his directing credits included the world premiere of David Mamet's *Sexual Perversity in Chicago* (1974). Gordon's makes low-budget horror and s-f movies, mostly in association with producers Charles **Band** and/or Brian **Yuzna**: none quite match his debut, though all have demented performances or the odd idea to recommend them. At Disney, he developed *Honey, I Shrunk the Kids* (1989) but was sidelined from directing the family hit by health trouble. Gordon and Paoli did a draft of the ***Invasion of the Body Snatchers*** remake eventually directed by Abel **Ferrara** as *Body Snatchers* (1992). MM

From Beyond/1986 * *Dolls*/1987 * *Robot Jox*/ 1989 * *The Pit and the Pendulum*/1990 * *Fortress*/1993 * *Castle Freak*/1995 * *Space Truckers*/1996

TV: *Daughter of Darkness*/1990

Gordon Clark, Lawrence (b. 19??)

British producer, director, writer. A TV specialist in the supernatural, Gordon Clark was behind the BBC's annual *Ghost Stories for Christmas* and has made earnest if sometimes elementary stabs at M.R. **James** and Stephen **Gallagher**.

TV: *A Ghost Story for Christmas*: 'The Stalls of Barchester'/1971; 'A Warning to the Curious'/1972; 'Lost Hearts'/1973; 'The Treasure of Abbot Thomas'/1974; 'The Ash Tree'/1975; The Signalman/1976; 'Stigma'/ 1977; 'The Ice House'/1978 * *Casting the Runes*/1979 * *Pattern of Roses*/1982 * *Chimera*/ 1991 * *Chiller*/1995

Gore * See: Blood; Decapitation;

Lewis, H.G.; Savini, Tom; Splatter Movies; Splatterpunk; Violence

Gorey, Edward (b. 1925)

American artist. A master of fey black humour, Gorey combines the approaches of Edward Lear, Saki, Hillaire Belloc and Charles **Addams**. His monochrome set designs for a 1975 Broadway **Dracula** brought mainstream attention. An influence on Tim **Burton**, his playroom decadence and violet callousness are distinctive. Collections: *Amphigorey* (1972), *Amphigorey Too* (1975), *Amphigorey Also* (1983).

Gorillas * See: Apes; *King Kong*; Minions

The Gothic Novel

The gothic novel arose out of a late-eighteenth-century fascination with the medieval and the barbaric: its characteristic settings are forbidding **castles**, dark forests and sinister monasteries peopled by brooding, mysterious aristocrats, repressive inquisitors and innocent young lovers. Coupling scenes of intense psychological terror with what to modern readers is cloying sentiment, the archetypal gothic novel is an unwieldy, uneven sprawl. Though literary critics found (and still find) the gothics something of an embarrassment, they proved hugely popular with the largely middle-class readership of the day and have influenced subsequent developments in horror, providing key themes and ideas.

The first major gothic is Horace Walpole's *The Castle of Otranto* (1764), a wildly Oedipal tale of familial jealousy replete with ghosts, curses, **torture** and dungeons. Notable followers include Anne **Radcliffe** (*The Mysteries of Udolpho*, 1794; *The Italian*, 1797), Matthew **Lewis** (*The Monk*, 1796), Mary **Shelley** (*Frankenstein*, 1818) and Charles Maturin (*Melmoth the Wanderer*, 1820). There are significant differences of approach (the sternly moralistic Radcliffe tends to **rationalised supernatural**, the brasher Lewis enthusiastically embraces dramatic possibilities offered by ghosts and **hell**) but together these writers and others enhanced the ability of literature generally to sustain long and complex narratives based on the psychologies of their characters. The intractably complicated plotting of most gothic novels means there has never been an entirely faithful cinematic adaptation of any of them, though *The Monk* has been tried twice and Jan **Švankmajer** did a fifteen-minute *Otranský zámek* (1973–7).

Gothic as a popular literary phenomenon faded in the early 19th century just as Jane Austen parodied it in *Northanger Abbey* (1817), though isolated works persisted (J. Sheridan **LeFanu**'s *Uncle Silas*, 1864) and many authors were marked by its influence (the Brontës, Bram **Stoker**). In the 20th century, the term 'gothic' has a variety of meanings: applied to horror films with a period setting; novels which refer in deliberately anachronistic way to earlier gothics (Peter Ackroyd's *Hawksmoor*, 1985); a type of romantic mystery fiction (Daphne **du Maurier**'s *Rebecca*, 1938); and, as 'goth' or 'gothic punk', a youth lifestyle distinguished by **vampire** fashion sense. PH

Mario Praz, *La carne, la morte e il diavolo nella letteratura Romantica* (*The Romantic Agony*, 1930); Montague Summers, *The Gothic Quest* (1938); Devendra P. Varma, *The Gothique Flame* (1957); Kate F. Ellis, *The Contested Castle: Gothic Novels and the Subversion of Domestic Ideology* (1989)

Gough, Michael (b. 1917)

British actor, equally at home in Ibsen on stage or as sadistic madmen in Z-features. Though a hysterical deadweight in *Dracula* (1958), he relishes the **mad scientist** of the **camp** *Horror Hospital* (1973) and is icily effective as the unsympathetic murder victim of *The Corpse* (1969). Unbilled as a mummified corpse in *The Legend of Hell House* (1973). SJ

Last Reunion/1955 * *The House in the Woods*/1957 * *Horrors of the Black Museum*/1959 * *Konga*/1960 * *What a Carve Up!*/1961 * *The Phantom of the Opera*/1962 * *Black Zoo*/1963 * *Dr. Terror's House of Horrors*/*The Skull*/1965 *

Berserk!/1967 * *Curse of the Crimson Altar*/1968 * *Trog*/1970 * *Satan's Slave*/1976 * *The Boys from Brazil*/1978 * *The Serpent and the Rainbow*/1987 * *Batman*/1989 * *Batman Returns*/1992 * *Batman Forever*/*Nostradamus*/1995

TV: *The New Adventures of Sherlock Holmes*: 'The Case of the Perfect Husband'/1955 * *Undermind*: 'Flowers of Havoc'/1965 * *The Avengers*: 'The Cybernauts'/1966; 'The Correct Way to Kill'/1967 * *Doctor Who*: 'The Celestial Toymaker'/1968; 'Arc of Infinity'/1983 * *Journey to the Unknown*: 'Eve'/1968 * *Omnibus*: 'The Need for Nightmare'/1974 * *A Christmas Carol*/1984

Grand-Guignol

A Paris theatre. Guignol, French equivalent of Mr Punch, was a marionette who figured in violent morality plays. Originally, the expression '*grand guignol*' described a tiny, box-like changing room: Oscar Méténier possibly chose the name for his Montmartre theatre as ironic comment on the smallness of the building. On opening in 1888, the theatre alternated melodrama with knockabout farce, but soon hit on horror. André de Lorde's *Le système du Docteur Goudron et du Professeur Plume*, freely adapted from the **Poe** story about lunatics taking over the asylum, was the theatre's first great hit and remained in the repertoire for years. De Lorde was the theatre's most prolific author, writing over one hundred of its plays: *Le système du Docteur Goudron et du Professeur Plume* became a 1912 film, first of a run of French spin-off adaptions. Reputedly a mild-mannered man, de Lorde always included the set pieces for which the Grand-Guignol was famous: an act of violence or dismemberment performed centre-stage in full view of the audience. A typical evening included cynical morality sketches, musical turns and low comedies in addition to the horrors.

The tiny stage saw adaptations from **Wilde**, **Maupassant**, **Kafka**, Gaston **Leroux**, Zola, Strindberg and Pirandello. True crime stories were also much used, allegedly taken from police records and mental institution files. Attempts to bring these forerunners of **splatter movies** to New York and London met with mixed results, partly because they were still performed in French. The theatre became a successful tourist attraction but closed in 1962, supposedly because horror in the real world had caught up with it.

RIGHT Michael Gough

Though the term is used somewhat loosely in the cinema, Grand-Guignol-inspired theatres appear in *Mad Love* (1935), *Theatre of Death* (1967), *The Wizard of Gore* (1970), *Murders in the Rue Morgue* (1971), *The Incredible Torture Show* (1977), *Dark Romances* (1986) and *Interview With the Vampire: The Vampire Chronicles* (1994). The establishment's wartime reputation as simultaneously an attraction for German officers and a hotbed of Resistance informs François Truffaut's *Le dernier métro* (*The Last Metro*, 1981). MW

Camillo Antona-Traversi, *L'histoire du Grand-Guignol* (1933); François Rivière, Gabrielle Wittkof, *Grand Guignol* (1979)

Grant, Arthur (1915–72)

British cinematographer. One of **Hammer**'s key men, borrowed by **Corman** for *Tomb of Ligeia* (1964). Typical are surreal eruptions of monstrosity in matter-of-fact settings: the reviving dead in the **dream** sequence of *The Plague of the Zombies* (1966), a corpse unearthed by a burst water pipe in *Frankenstein Must Be Destroyed* (1969). Fine in a different style is the black-and-white widescreen of Joseph Losey's *The Damned* (1961).

The Abominable Snowman/1957 * *The Spaniard's Curse*/1958 * *The Curse of the Werewolf*/*The Shadow of the Cat*/1961 * *Phantom of the Opera*/*Captain Clegg*/1962 * *The Old Dark House*/*Paranoiac*/1963 * *The Reptile*/1965 * *Frankenstein Created Woman*/*The Mummy's Shroud*/*The Witches*/1966 * *Quatermass and the Pit*/1967 * *The Devil Rides*

*Out/Dracula Has Risen From the Grave/1968 ∗
Taste the Blood of Dracula/1970 ∗ Blood From
the Mummy's Tomb/Demons of the Mind/1971*

Grant, Charles L. (b. 1942)

American writer, editor. Prolific under several names in s-f and romance, Grant is a master of understated horror, rooting supernatural terrors in a dismayed, faded modern America. Much of his fiction centres on the troubled Connecticut community of Oxrun Station, which features in *The Hour of the Oxrun Dead* (1977), *The Sound of Midnight* (1978), *Nightmare Seasons* (1982) and a trilogy written in homage to Universal monster movies: *The Soft Whisper of the Dead* (1982), *The Dark Cry of the Moon* (1986) and *The Long Night of the Grave* (1986). His novels include *The Nestling* (1982), *Night Songs* (1984), *The Tea Party* (1985), *For Fear of the Night* (1988), *Something Stirs* (1991) and *Jackals* (1994). His best single book is the collection *Tales From the Nightside* (1981). He has also written **young adult** horror (as Steven Charles) and *X Files* spin-offs (*Goblins*, 1994).

Grau, Jorge (b. 1930)

Spanish writer, director. Well-versed in the prohibitive nature of cinema under Franco, Grau made provoking contributions to the horror boom of the dictator's declining years. *Ceremonia sangrienta* (*The Legend of Blood Castle*, 1972) is an ambitious, politically minded appropriation of the **Báthory** story. The zestful *No profanar el sueño de los muertos* (*The Living Dead at the Manchester Morgue*, 1974) makes equally engaged demands of its borrowed **zombie** theme. DP

Graveyards and Mausolea

From the unsettling opening of *Night of the Living Dead* (1968) to the eerily green-tinted resurrection sequence of *The Plague of the Zombies* (1966), graveyards provide a classic backdrop for film-makers to summon instant menace and gloomy unease. Barbara **Steele** stalking around a mist-shrouded cemetery in *La maschera del demonio* (1960) and Rupert Everett shooting the rotting dead rising from their resting places in *Dellamorte Dellamore* (1994) are prime examples of art direction as narrative shorthand. So too are movies featuring **body snatchers** and **burial alive**. The **vampire** movie would miss out on easy atmospherics if coffins were placed in less starkly sinister surroundings. Mausolea, seen in *Phantasm* (1979) and *Mausoleum* (1982), add further claustrophobic darkness and have been used to good effect in more conventional chillers like Dario **Argento**'s *Il*

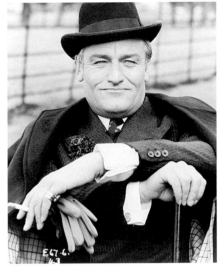

Charles Gray

gatto a nove code (1971). The ultimate mausoleum is the pyramid, starting point for practically every **Mummy** movie. AJ

Gray, Charles [Donald Gray] (b. 1928)

British actor. The smooth Satanist of *The Devil Rides Out* (1967) and the barely-suppressed Narrator ('it's just a jump to left . . .) of *The Rocky Horror Picture Show* (1975). Blofeld in *Diamonds Are Forever* (1971), Mycroft in *The Seven-Per-Cent Solution* (1976) and TV's *The Adventures of Sherlock Holmes* (1985) and *The Return of Sherlock Holmes* (1988). SJ

*The Beast Must Die/1974 ∗ The Legacy/1978 ∗
Shock Treatment/1981*

TV: *One Step Beyond*: 'The Return'/1960 ∗
Armchair Mystery Theatre: 'The Lodger'/1965 ∗
Orson Welles' Great Mysteries: 'A Time to
Remember'/1973 ∗ *Thriller*: 'Night is the
Time for Killing'/1975 ∗ *Schalcken the Painter*
(v)/1979

Great Ghost Tales (US TV series, 1961)

A colour series of mystery and suspense tales presented live by NBC-TV. Frank Gallup introduced stories from the work of famous authors: **Poe**'s 'William Wilson', with Robert Duvall; W.W. Jacobs's **'The Monkey's Paw'**, with Mildred Dunnock; Saki's 'Sredni Vashtar', with Richard Thomas; M.R. **James**'s 'Room 13'; Algernon **Blackwood**'s 'The Wendigo'. TM

LEFT Graveyards: Bette Davis, *Hush . . . Hush,
Sweet Charlotte*

Great Mysteries: See * *Orson Welles'*
Great Mysteries

Green, Nigel (1924–72)
British actor. Stiff-upper-lip type with a
roguish streak: Hercules in *Jason and the
Argonauts* (1963), Nayland Smith in *The Face
of Fu Manchu* (1965), the charmingly evil relative in *Let's Kill Uncle* (1966), a master villain in *Deadlier Than the Male* (1966), an
'electric messiah' in *The Ruling Class* (1971).
Stranger From Venus/1954 * *Corridors of Blood*/
1958 * *The Masque of the Red Death*/1964 * *The
Skull*/1966 * *Countess Dracula*/1970

TV: *Suspense*: 'Monsieur Vidocq'/1952 * *The
Cases of Sherlock Holmes*: 'Shoscombe Old
Place'/1968 * *The Avengers*: 'The Winged
Avenger'/1967; 'Fog'/1969

Greenaway, Peter (b. 1942)
British director, writer, painter. Though
Greenaway's early work owes more to post-
structuralist critical theory than cinema, he
has since *The Draughtsman's Contract* (1982)
formed an uneasy rapprochement with the
mainstream. Defiantly misanthropic, he is
able to attract curious filmgoers on a scale
unusual for such a formally and philosophi-
cally inclined artist. A high degree of shock
value perhaps provides the significant commercial factor, while playful intellectual
gamesmanship belies often aggressive pessimism. *The Cook The Thief His Wife & Her
Lover* (1989) rattles the teeth of the chattering classes: Michael Gambon's truly nightmarish 'Thief' is a bullying gangland monster
whose **violence** is both boorishly physical
and scatologically verbal on a relentless
scale. The 'Lover', Greenaway's surrogate, is
murdered, mouth stuffed with paged from
his beloved books, and the film climaxes
vengefully with enforced **cannibalism**. ST

The Falls/1980 * *A Zed & Two Noughts*/1986 *
The Belly of an Architect/1987 * *Drowning By
Numbers*/1988 * *Prospero's Books*/1991 * *The
Baby of Macôn*/1993 * *The Pillow Book*/1996

TV: *A TV Dante*/1990

Grefé, William (b. 19??)
American director. Based in Florida, Grefé is
responsible for the mind-numbing *Death
Curse of Tartu* (1966). Besides second-unit on
Live and Let Die (1973), his most notable
achievement is preserving William Shatner's
worst performance (and wardrobe) in *Impulse* (1975).

Sting of Death/1966 * *Stanley*/1972 * *Mako,
Jaws of Death*/1976

Griffith, Charles B. (b. 1930)
American writer, director. A **Corman** mainstay since the 50s, Griffith is the reliable if
cynical scenarist who reworked one story as
a South Sea epic (*Naked Paradise*, 1956), a
skiing gangster-monster movie (*The Beast
From Haunted Cave*, 1959), a mythic muscle
picture (*Atlas*, 1960) and a seafaring gangster-monster movie (*Creature From the
Haunted Sea*, 1961). His major works (which
have essentially the same plot) are Corman's
A Bucket of Blood (1959) and *The Little Shop of
Horrors* (1960), notable for beatnik/Catskills
humour and occasional poignance. His
scripts have been remade: *Zontar, the Thing
From Venus* (1968), *Little Shop of Horrors*
(1986), *Not of This Earth* (1988, 1995), *Horror
Cafe* (1995).

Not of This Earth/*The Undead*/*It Conquered the
World* (+a)/1956 * *Attack of the Crab Monsters*/
1957 * *Death Race 2000*/1975 * *Hollywood
Boulevard* (a)/1976 * *Up From the Depths*
(d)/1979 * *Dr. Heckyl and Mr. Hype* (d)/1980

Griffith, Hugh (1912–80)
Welsh actor. Flamboyantly eyebrowed sup-
porting player. SJ
The Three Weird Sisters/1947 * *Kind Hearts and
Coronets*/1949 * *Cry of the Banshee*/*Wuthering
Heights*/1970 * *Whoever Slew Auntie Roo?*/1971
* *The Abominable Dr. Phibes*/1971 * *Dr. Phibes
Rises Again*/1972 * *The Final Program*/1973 *
Legend of the Werewolf/*Craze*/1974 * *The Hound
of the Baskervilles*/1977

TV: *Lights Out*: 'The Borgia Lamp'/1952 *
Quatermass II/1955 * *Dow Hour of Great
Mysteries*: 'The Inn of the Flying Dragon'/
1960 * *Orson Welles' Great Mysteries*: 'The
Inspiration of Mr Budd'/1973

Grindé, Nick (1893–1979)
American director. Despite B credits from
Beyond the Sierras (1928) to *Road to Alcatraz*
(1945), Grindé is remembered (if not well)
for **mad scientist** movies with a sincere
Karloff extending the frontiers of medicine.

The Man They Could Not Hang/1939 * *The Man
With Nine Lives*/*Before I Hang*/1940

Gui Zhihong [Zuei Chich-hung]
(b. 1937)
Chinese director. Gui worked as an assistant
director in Taiwan before being hired by
Shaw Brothers in the early 70s. Hong Kong's
gothic specialist, his movies are often gifted
with oppressive atmosphere and a great
sense of suspense. CV

She Shashou [*The Killer Snakes*]/*The Eye Devil*/
1974 * *Spirit of the Raped*/1976 * *The
Teenager's Nightmare* (co-d)/1977 * *Wan Ren
Zhan* [*Killer Constable*]/*Xie* [*Hex*]/*Xie douxie*
[*Hex vs Witchcraft*]/1980 * *She Yao* [*Corpse
Mania*]/*Gu* [*Bewitched*]/1981 * *Hex after Hex*/
Curse of Evil/1982 * *Mo* [*The Boxer's Omen*]/
1983

Gwynn, Michael (1916–76)
British actor. Good as the twisted **cannibal**
in *The Revenge of Frankenstein* (1958). SJ

Village of the Damned/1960 * *What a Carve Up!*/
1961 * *The Deadly Bees*/1966 * *The Scars of
Dracula*/1970

TV: *Mystery and Imagination*: 'The Body
Snatcher'/1966 * *Adam Adamant Lives!*: 'Wish
You Were Here'/1967 * *Randall and Hopkirk
(Deceased)*: 'The Man from Nowhere'/1969 *
The Avengers: 'Take-Over'/1969

Gwynne, Fred (1924–93)
American comedian. The **Frankensteinian**
Herman in *The Munsters* (1964–6). SJ

Munster, Go Home!/1966 * *Fatal Attraction*/
1987 * *Pet Sematary*/1989 * *Shadows and Fog*/
1992

TV: *Drama Special*: 'Arsenic and Old Lace'/
1969 * *The Munsters' Revenge*/1981

Fred Gwynne, *The Munsters*

H

Haggard, Piers (b. 1939)

British director, great grand-nephew of H. Rider Haggard. Aside from *Blood on Satan's Claw* (1970), his major credits are TV mini-series: Dennis **Potter**'s *Pennies From Heaven* (1978), Nigel **Kneale**'s *Quatermass* (1980).

The Fiendish Plot of Dr. Fu Manchu/1980 * *Venom*/1982

TV: *Zodiac*: 'Sting, Sting, Scorpio!'/1974 * *Trilby*/1976 * *Heartstones*/1996 * *The Lifeforce Experiment*/1996

Haig, Sid (b. 1939)

American actor. A memorable bald geek in *Spider Baby* (1965).

Blood Bath/1966 * *The Womanhunt*/1972 * *Wonder Women*/1973 * *Galaxy of Terror*/1981 TV: *Get Smart*: 'Shock It to Me'/1969 * *Death Car on the Freeway*/1978 * *Werewolf*: 'King of the Road'/1988 * *The People Next Door*: 'Dream Date'/1989

Hall, Charles D. (1899–1968)

British-born art director. Designer of often-reused Universal sets: the opera house of ***Phantom of the Opera*** (1925), the European village of *All Quiet on the Western Front* (1930). He created crypts, laboratories, haunted hallways and moors for key horror films.

The Cat and the Canary/*The Man Who Laughs*/1927 * *The Last Warning*/1928 * *Dracula*/*Drácula*/1930 * *Frankenstein*/1931 * *The Old Dark House*/*Murders in the Rue Morgue*/1932 *

The Invisible Man/1933 * *The Black Cat*/1934 * *Bride of Frankenstein*/1935 * *Topper Takes a Trip*/1938

Haller, Daniel (b. 1928)

American art director, director. Having designed crypts for **Corman**'s **Poe** films, Haller directed a **Lovecraft** duo: *Die, Monster, Die!* (1965), from 'The Colour Out of Space' (1927), and *The Dunwich Horror* (1970).

War of the Satellites/1957 * *The Devil's Partner*/*Night of the Blood Beast*/1958 * *A Bucket of Blood*/*The Wasp Woman*/*Ghost of Dragstrip Hollow*/*Attack of the Giant Leeches*/*The Atomic Submarine*/1959 * *The Fall of the House of Usher*/*The Little Shop of Horrors*/1960 * *Pit and the Pendulum*/1961 * *Tower of London*/ *Tales of Terror*/*The Raven*/*The Premature Burial*/ *Diary of a Madman*/1962 * *The Haunted Palace*/ *The Comedy of Terrors*/*The Terror*/*The Man with X-Ray Eyes*/1963 * *Dr. Goldfoot and the Bikini Machine*/1965 * *The Ghost in the Invisible Bikini*/1966

TV: *Night Gallery*: 'I'll Never Leave You – Ever' (d)/1972 * *The Sixth Sense*: 'Face of Ice' (d)/1972 * *Manimal*: 'Illusions' (d)/'Night of the Scorpion' (d)/1983

Halloween (1978)

One of the most successful independent features of all time, John **Carpenter**'s terror trail-blazer is the seminal **stalk-and-slash** shocker. It inspired scores of inferior calendar date clones which substitute copious violence for the building of suspense via **subjective camera**, widescreen image placement, quick editing and driving music. Jamie Lee **Curtis** was elevated to Scream Queen status as the Haddonfield babysitter stalked by escaped **psychopath** Michael Myers, while Donald **Pleasence** is amusingly mannered as the obsessive psychiatrist Sam Loomis. Carpenter supervised Rick Rosenthal's *Halloween II* (1981) and Tommy Lee **Wallace**'s *Halloween III: Season of the Witch* (1983). *II* boasts a higher body count as Myers turns semi-supernatural, but little suspense; *III* bears no relation to the earlier movies, offering instead a nifty plot (by Nigel **Kneale**) about deranged toy-maker Dan O'Herlihy conspiring to massacre America's children. Pleasence, but not Curtis, returns for plodding follow-ups: Dwight H. Little's *Halloween 4: The Return of Michael Myers* (1988), Dominique Othenin-Girard's *Hallow-*

een 5 (1989), Joe Chappelle's *Halloween: The Curse of Michael Myers* (1995). AJ

Halperin, Victor (1894–19??)

American producer, director. In partnership with producer brother Edward, Halperin made the **Lugosi** vehicle *White Zombie* (1932). Aside from the **reincarnation** drama *Supernatural* (1933), with Carole Lombard, other credits have the ricketiness of *White Zombie* but not its occasional poetry.

Revolt of the Zombies/1936 * *Torture Ship*/1939

Hammer Films

One of the best-known brand names in the history of cinema, this small British production company led the world market in horror, inspired many imitations and today retains a significant hold on the affections of genre aficionados. Hammer was originally a production offshoot of Exclusive Films, a distribution company formed in the 30s by Enrique Carreras and William Hinds. There were a few Hammer productions in the 30s – including *The Mystery of the Marie Celeste* (1936), starring Bela **Lugosi** – but the company did not come into being in any meaningful sense until 1947. Throughout the late 40s and early 50s, Hammer turned out a range of low-budget thrillers and comedies, mostly routine adaptations of **radio** plays

LEFT Hammer Films: John Van Eyssen, *Dracula* (1958)

and serials (including films of *Dick Barton* and *PC 49*). Only a handful are fantasy oriented, notably the Terence **Fisher**-directed *Stolen Face* (1952) and *Four-Sided Triangle* (1953) and the macabre thrillers *The Man in Black* (1950) and *Room to Let* (1950).

The studio's first big success was its film of Nigel **Kneale**'s phenomenally popular 1953 BBC TV series *The Quatermass Experiment* (1955), initially sold as *The Quatermass Xperiment* to take advantage of the newly acceptable X certificate. Hammer made a move into both period horror and colour with *The Curse of Frankenstein* (1957), an epochal project which brought together for the first time actors Peter **Cushing** and Christopher **Lee** and director Terence Fisher. The film was a worldwide success and a series of gothic horrors quickly followed, including *Dracula* (1958), *The Mummy* (1959), *The Hound of the Baskervilles* (1959), *The Curse of the Werewolf* (1960), **The Phantom of the Opera** (1962) and further **Dracula**, **Frankenstein** and **Mummy** films. The company also branched out into a run of thrillers based on the success of **Les Diaboliques** (1955) and **Psycho** (1960), notably *Taste of Fear* (1961), *Paranoiac* (1962) and *The Nanny* (1965).

Throughout this period Hammer re-

mained a family-run firm with James **Carreras** (son of Enrique) presiding over what was in effect a repertory group of actors and technicians (directors, writers, cinematographers, composers, editors, production designers) based until 1967 at Bray Studio, a converted country house. Control of the company passed from Enrique Carreras to his son James and eventually, in the early 70s, to James's son Michael **Carreras**, with Anthony **Hinds**, son of William Hinds, also an important figure. It is appropriate given the importance of father-son relationships in the history of Hammer that father figures and their authority are privileged to such a great extent in films made by Hammer. Keenly aware of market trends, Hammer exploited both a relaxation in censorship and a growing public appetite for horror and fantasy projects. Hammer film-makers, seasoned professionals with years of industry experience, catered to this appetite with films whose apparently high production values bely meagre budgets.

Icons like Dracula, Frankenstein (and his monsters), the Mummy and the **werewolf**, last glimpsed in tawdry **Abbott and Costello** horror-**comedies**, were brought back to life in colour and with a measure of robustness and dandyism never seen before in the genre, soon joined by new creations such as *The Gorgon* (1964) and *The Reptile* (1966). Hammer's Dracula and Frankenstein

RIGHT Hammer Films: Bette Davis,
Wendy Craig, *The Nanny*

set the tone: ruthless, predatory creatures not much inclined to self-justification or self-pity. In 1968, Hammer received the Queen's Award for Industry, a recognition not only of the company's unprecedented international success but also that it had shifted from being the pariah of British cinema to being part of the establishment (albeit a somewhat embarrassing part). This period saw Hammer's departure from Bray and the production of three of the company's finest films, *Frankenstein Created Woman* (1966), *The Devil Rides Out* (1968) and *Frankenstein Must Be Destroyed* (1969). All were directed by Terence Fisher, Hammer's main director, and together they represent both a summation and a self-reflexive questioning of the themes and attitudes that had characterised earlier Hammer horrors. In particular, they display an ambivalence towards the paternalistic quality that underpins so many classic Hammers.

From the late 60s onwards, as Hammer sought to retain its hold on the youth market, many of its films, now often directed by younger film-makers such as Peter **Sasdy** and Peter **Sykes**, began to criticise patriarchal **family values**. Examples of revisionary Hammer horror include Sasdy's *Taste the Blood of Dracula* (1969) and *Hands of the Ripper* (1971) and Sykes's *Demons of the Mind* (1971), all of which show powerful fathers, the likely heroes of earlier Hammer films,

cruelly destroying their own families. The 70s also saw a growth in the overtly sexual element in Hammer horror with extensive female nudity featured in a trilogy based on J. Sheridan **Le Fanu's 'Carmilla'** (1871): *The Vampire Lovers* (1970), *Lust for a Vampire* (1970), *Twins of Evil* (1971). While much interesting work was done in this late period, these films did not share the commercial success of their predecessors. This was particularly so in America where locally produced horror films with contemporary settings were increasingly the order of the day.

Hammer ceased horror film production after of *To the Devil a Daughter* (1976). In the 80s, under new ownership, it produced TV series, *Hammer House of Horror* (1980) and *Hammer House of Mystery and Suspense* (1984). In 1993, Hammer Films announced plans to remake a number of its classics; to date, none have appeared, and it could be argued that *Bram Stoker's Dracula* (1992), *Mary Shelley's Frankenstein* (1994), *Mary Reilly* (1996) and even *Dracula: Dead and Loving It* (1995) are already effectively remakes of Hammer properties. PH

Allan Eyles, Robert Adkinson, Nicholas Fry, *The House of Horror* (1973); David Pirie, *A Heritage of Horror* (1973); Martini, Emanuela, *Hammer e Dintorni* (1990); Peter Hutchings, *Hammer and Beyond: The British Horror Film* (1993); Howard Maxford, *Hammer, House of*

Horror (1996); Tom Johnson, Deborah Del Vecchio, *Hammer Films: An Exhaustive Filmography* (1996); Denis Meikle, *A History of Horrors: The Rise and Fall of the House of Hammer* (1996)

Hammer House of Horror (UK TV series, 1980), *Hammer House of Mystery and Suspense* (UK TV series, 1984–5)

Like *Journey to the Unknown* (1968–9), these anthology series eschew the period gothic associated with **Hammer** horror. *Horror* consists of thirteen hour-long episodes, involving **witchcraft** ('Witching Time'), **werewolves** ('Children of the Full Moon'), ghosts ('The House That Bled to Death'), **dolls** ('Charlie Boy') and **cannibalism** ('The Thirteenth Reunion'). Directors Peter **Sasdy**, Alan **Gibson** and Don **Sharp** worked on the show, while stalwart British casting found roles for Jon Finch, Denholm **Elliott**, Diana Dors and, in his last work for Hammer, Peter **Cushing**. Like the quota quickies Hammer made in the early 50s, the *Mystery and Suspense* TV movies use American guest stars (David **Carradine**, Peter Graves, Dirk Benedict). Mostly bland thrillers, a few ('In Possession' 'Mark of the Devil', 'And the Wall Came Tumbling Down', 'Tennis Court') have supernatural themes. Old hands on the show were directors Sasdy, John **Hough**, Val **Guest** and Cyril Frankel and writers Don Houghton and Brian **Clemens**.

Hands

The hand bursting from an unsettled grave has become a staple shock motif, promising sequels or the return of the repressed – exemplary images featured in *Deliverance* (1972) and *Carrie* (1976). A great horror trope of the 20s, restaged often, is the hairy hand emerging from the wall above the heroine's bed in *The Cat and the Canary* (1926). But it is the hand, severed or transplanted, with a life and a mind of its own which has been established as the most reliable monstrous horror body part through multiple versions of Maurice Renard's **Les mains d'Orlac** (1920). Since hands are the means through which we engage most directly with the world, and since, when they go it alone, they can be animated in a range of scuttling, spidery ways to render their unnatural independence all the more sinister, they have been cast as villains in hand-horror gems as diverse Clive **Barker**'s short story 'The Body Politic' (1985), in which hands instigate the insurrection of

Peter Cushing, 'Silent Scream', *Hammer House of Horror*

Hands: Johnny Depp, *Edward Scissorhands*

body parts against the imperial govering self, and Sam **Raimi**'s *Evil Dead 2* (1987), where a possessed hand is chainsawed-off by its owner. Hands inch on fingers and clutch guilty throats in Guy de **Maupassant**'s 'La Main' (1883), W.F. Harvey's 'The Beast With Five Fingers' (1928) and Marc Brendel's *The Lizard's Tail* (1979), filmed respectively as *Le Sang des autres* (1972), *The Beast With Five Fingers* (1946) and Oliver **Stone**'s (yes – it is he!) offering *The Hand* (1981). The motif is recycled in *Espiritismo* (1961), *El angel exterminádor* (1962), *The Crawling Hand* (1963), *Dr. Terror's House of Horrors* (1965), *–And Now the Screaming Starts!* (1973), *Demonoid* (1979) and *Necropolis* (1987). Thing in **The Addams Family** offers a more benign image of the lively dismembered hand; *Edward Scissorhands* (1990) presents a gentler image of the wrong hands in the right place. LRW

The Hands of Orlac * See: *Les mains d'Orlac*

Hansen, Gunnar (b. 1947)
American actor. The hulk behind the **mask** as Leatherface in **The Texas Chain Saw Massacre** (1974).

The Demon Lover/1977 * *Hollywood Chainsaw Hookers*/1987 * *Mosquito*/1995

Hardwicke, Sir Cedric (1893–1964)
British actor, knighted in 1934 for outstanding performances on the London stage.

Often wasted in Hollywood as sophisticated villains. SJ

The Ghoul/1933 * *The Hunchback of Notre Dame*/*On Borrowed Time*/1939 * *The Invisible Man Returns*/1940 * *The Ghost of Frankenstein*/*Invisible Agent*/1942 * *The Lodger*/1944 * *The Picture of Dorian Gray* (v)/1945 * *Lured*/1947 * *The War of the Worlds* (v)/1953

TV: *Suspense*: 'Death in the Passing'/'The Interruption'/1953 * *Climax*: 'Dr. Jekyll and Mr. Hyde'/1955; 'Strange Deaths at Burnleigh'/1957 * *Alfred Hitchcock Presents*: 'Wet Saturday'/1956; 'A Man Greatly Beloved'/1957 * *Studio One*: 'The Other Place'/1958 * *The Twilight Zone*: 'Uncle Simon'/1963 * *The Outer Limits*: 'The Forms of Things Unknown'/1964

Hardy, Robin (b. 1929)
British director. *The Wicker Man* (1973) is a striking attempt to demythologise the supernatural. Written by advertising partner Anthony Shaffer and intended as a retort to **Hammer**, it probes Christian and Pagan verities in a rural *policier* format and concludes with genuine horror. Cult status was secured by a convoluted post-production history that also resulted in failure as a film-maker. His only other feature is the Dublin-set art-slasher *The Fantasist* (1986). DP

Harlin, Renny (b. 1958)
Finnish director. At odds with Helsinki cinema, the aspirant Harlin cobbled US backing

Sir Cedric Hardwicke

for his debut feature, *Born American* (1986), which led first to a haunted **prison** pic *Prison* (1987), then *A Nightmare on Elm Street IV: The Dream Master* (1988). Trading up horror credits, Harlin took Robert **Englund** out of make-up in the Andrew Dice Clay disaster *The Adventures of Ford Fairlane* (1990), and moved into *über*-actioners (*Die Hard 2*, 1990; *Cliffhanger*, 1993; *Cutthroat Island*, 1995). DP

Harrington, Curtis (b. 1928)
American director. Originally an avant gardiste, Harrington is known for a series of handsome, well-cast, relationship-inflected

Robin Hardy's *The Wicker Man*

Piper Laurie, Curtis Harrington's *Ruby*

horrors, typically graced by an interest in fey glamour. His precocious experimental work is consistently morbid and not uninfluential. *Fragment of Seeking* (1946), his first significant short, is an anxious piece of homoerotica featuring the director himself. His feature debut is the **Lewton**esque lorelei fantasy *Night Tide* (1961); distributed by Roger **Corman**, it led to *Queen of Blood* (1966), a haunting splice of Russian s-f footage and space **vampirism** that marked the beginning of a partnership with producer George Edwards. After the **Clouzot**-influenced *Games* (1967), he directed Debbie Reynolds, Shelley Winters and Ann Southern in the distressing **ageing actress** triumvurate *What's the Matter with Helen?* (1971), *Whoever Slew Auntie Roo?* (1971) and *The Killing Kind* (1973). The compromised **possession** item *Ruby* (1977) was completed by Stephanie **Rothman**. DP

The Fall of the House of Usher (s)/*Crescendo* (s)/1942 * *Renascence* (s)/1944 * *Picnic* (s)/ 1948 * *On the Edge* (s)/1949 * *Dangerous Houses* (s)/1952 * *The Assignation* (s)/1953 * *The Inauguration of the Pleasure Dome* (s/a)/ 1954 * *The Wormwood Star* (s)/1956 * *Voyage to the Prehistoric Planet* (co-d)/1966

TV: *How Awful About Allan*/1970 * *The Cat Creature*/1973 * *Killer Bees*/1974 * *The Dead Don't Die*/1975 * *Tales of the Unexpected*/'A Hand for Sonny Blue'/1977 * *Devil Dog: The Hound of Hell*/1978 * *Darkroom*/'A Quiet

Funeral'/'Make-Up'/1981 * *The Twilight Zone*/'Voices in the Earth'/1987

Harris, Thomas (b. 1940)

American novelist. Though his debut *Black Sunday* (1975) is merely good, Harris pitches fair to be the most influential horror *and* thriller writer of the 80s and 90s. *Red Dragon* (1981), filmed by Michael **Mann** as *Manhunter* (1986) and *The Silence of the Lambs* (1988), filmed by Jonathan **Demme** (1991), combine police procedural with flamboyant abnormal psychology as FBI agents Will Graham and Clarice Starling consult imprisoned genius Hannibal Lecter as they track **serial killers** Francis 'The Tooth Fairy' Dolarhyde and Jame 'Buffalo Bill' Gumb. Lecter is a monster for the era: Brian **Cox** and Anthony **Hopkins** are remarkable as the **psychologist**-cum-murderer but neither has the devil marks (maroon eyes, a seven-fingered hand) of the novels' character. Parodies: Jerry Butler (*Hannibal Lickter*, 1992), Ben Kingsley (*National Lampoon's Loaded Weapon 1*, 1993), Dom DeLuise (*The Silence of the Hams*, 1993).

Hartford-Davis, Robert (1923–77)

British director, a sexploitation pioneer who virtually invented the 'tabloid teaser' genre with *The Yellow Teddybears* (1963). His horror output is lavished with the same brand of lurid melodrama, reaching amorally sordid heights in *Corruption* (1967), a copy of *Les yeux sans visage* (1959). He signed the mod **vampire** redefinition *Incense for the Damned* (1970) with the pseudonym 'Michael Burrowes', arguably disowning his best film. Other odd credits: a short *A Christmas Carol*

John Turner, Heather Sears, Robert Hartford-Davis's *The Black Torment*

Herk Harvey, *Carnival of the Souls*

(1958), *Gonks Go Beat* (1965), the TV movie *Murder in Peyton Place* (1977). AJ

The Black Torment/1964 * *The Fiend*/1971

Harvey, Herk (1925–96)

American director. His sole film, *Carnival of Souls* (1962) was inspired by and shot in Saltair, an abandoned ballroom and amusement park. Like many prose classics but few genre films, it thus derives power from an actual landscape. After emerging from a car accident a young organist (Candace Hilligoss) experiences episodes outside reality and is haunted by drowned corpses (led by Harvey himself). The pasty-faced corpses prefigure the **zombies** of *Night of the Living Dead* (1968). While the acting ranges from enthusiastic amateurism to the Method, the film is atmospheric and frightening. RC

Hatton, Rondo (1894–1946)

American actor (to use the term loosely). Exposed to poison gas in World War I, Hatton suffered from the **disfiguring** disease acromegaly. Universal tastelessly cast him as a killer in low-budget horrors. He is a character called The Creeper in three otherwise unconnected productions: *The Pearl of Death* (1944), *House of Horrors* (1946), *The Brute Man* (1946). Latterly a cult figure to the 'Mondo Rondo' set, a hulking **minion** in *Rocketeer* (1991) is modelled on him. SJ

The Hunchback of Notre Dame/1939 * *The Jungle Captive*/1944 * *The Spider Woman Strikes Back*/1945

RIGHT Nathaniel Hawthorne

Hauer, Rutger (b. 1944)

Dutch actor. After appearing in the Dutch movies of director Paul Verhoeven, notably *Turkish Delight* (1973), Hauer made an incredible impact with his American debut as the albino replicant in *Blade Runner* (1982). He has been trying to live up to this benchmark ever since, coming close by sneering through *The Hitcher* (1986) as the archetypal 80s superpsycho. More a straight-to-video name now. AJ

Eureka/1983 * *Ladyhawke*/*Flesh + Blood*/1985 * *Split Second*/1992 * *Buffy the Vampire Slayer*/ 1992 * *Nostradamus*/*Surviving the Game*/1994 * *Angel of Death*/1995

TV: *The Edge*: 'Indian Poker'/1989 * *Mr Stitch*/ 1995

Haworth, Jill (b. 1945)

British actress. A nymphet for Otto Preminger (*Exodus*, 1960), Haworth became a frail, blonde heroine of kitsch horrors.

It/1966 * *The Haunted House of Horror*/1969 * *Tower of Evil*/1971 * *The Mutations*/1972

TV: *The Outer Limits*: 'The Sixth Finger'/1963 * *The Most Deadly Game*: 'Witches' Sabbath'/ 1970 * *Home for the Holidays*/1972

Hawthorne, Nathaniel (1804–64)

American writer. He recast the European **gothic novel** in colonial terms, building on the achievements of Charles Brockden Brown and clearing the way for his disciple, **Poe**. His major novels, shot through with the weird and the cruel, are *The Scarlet Letter* (1850), *The House of the Seven Gables* (1851),

Rutger Hauer, *The Hitcher*

The Blithedale Romance (1852) and *The Marble Faun* (1860); his stories are collected in

Twice-Told Tales (1837) and *Mosses from an Old Manse* (1846).

The House of the Seven Gables/1910 * *The House of the Seven Gables*/1940 * *Twice-Told Tales*/ 1963 * *Young Goodman Brown*/1993

TV: *Lights Out*: 'Dr. Heidegger's Experiment'/ 1950; 'Rappaccini's Daughter'/1951 * *Robert Montgomery Presents*: 'The House of the Seven Gables'/1951 * *Matinee Theatre*: 'The House of the Seven Gables'/1956 * *Shirley Temple Theatre*: 'The House of the Seven Gables'/ 1960 * *American Short Story*: 'Rappaccini's Daughter'/1980

Hayden, Linda (b. 1951)

British actress, adept at seeming innocence and hoyden cruelty: heroine of *Taste the Blood of Dracula* (1970), devil nymphet in *Blood on Satan's Claw* (1970).

Night Watch/1973 * *Madhouse*/1974 * *Exposed*/ 1975 * *Vampira*/1976 * *The Boys From Brazil*/ 1978

TV: *Hammer House of Mystery and Suspense*: 'Black Carrion'/1984

Hayers, Sidney (b. 1921)

British director. After the amazingly lurid *Circus of Horrors* (1960) and the excellent

149

Heads: *Scanners*

Fritz **Leiber** adaptation *Night of the Eagle* (1962), Hayers moved to TV, handling the outstanding **alien plant** episode of *The Avengers* ('Man-Eater of Surrey Green', 1966) before less rewarding US work on the likes of *Knight Rider* and *Super Force*.

The Malpas Mystery/1960 * *Assault*/*Revenge*/ 1971

TV: *The Avengers*: 'The Cybernauts'/'A Surfeit of H2O'/1966; 'The Hidden Tiger'/'The Superlative Seven'/'The Joker'/1967; 'Death's Door'/Dead Man's Treasure'/1968 * *The New Avengers*: 'Dead Men Are Dangerous'/'Hostage'/'Dirtier By the Dozen'/ 1978; 'The Last of the Cybernauts . . .?'/1979 * *Manimal*: 'High Stakes'/1984 * *Werewolf*: 'Eye of the Storm'/1987 * *Space Precinct*: 'Predator and Prey'/1994

Hayes, Allison [Mary Jane Haynes] (1930–77)
American actress. A cult Amazon for her starring role in *Attack of the 50 Foot Woman* (1958), striking for **Corman** as a Western villain of *Gunslinger* (1956) and a **witch** in *The Undead* (1956).

The Disembodied/*Zombies of Mora Tau*/*The Unearthly*/1957 * *The Hypnotic Eye*/1959 * *The Crawling Hand*/1963

Hayes, John (b. 19??)
American director, negligible aside from the

grim and unusual *Grave of the Vampire* (1972).

Garden of the Dead/1972 * *End of the World*/ 1977 * *Dream No Evil*/1980

TV: *Tales From the Darkside*: 'The Madness Room'/1985

Haze, Jonathan (b. 1935)
American actor. A 50s **Corman** regular in Jerrylewisian comic roles, notably the **Faust** florist of *The Little Shop of Horrors* (1960).

The Day the World Ended/*It Conquered the World*/1956 * *Not of This Earth*/1957 * *The Terror*/1963

Heads
The head is the body part which has been subject to the most lurid forms of violation in horror cinema. Heads explode (*Scanners*, 1980), rotate (*The Exorcist*, 1973) or are severed (*The Omen*, 1976). Decapitation is the surest way of 'saving' the victim of gothic malaise: Anthony **Hopkins** gathers a batch of vampire heads in *Bram Stoker's Dracula*, while the **werewolf** becomes a man again when his head plops into a pan of milk in *The Company of Wolves* (1984). Or severed heads are found in the wrong place: a fish tank (*The Silent Partner*, 1978, *He Knows You're Alone*, 1980) a toilet bowl (*The House on Sorority Row*, 1982), leaping into frame in a classic underwater shock (*Jaws*, 1975).

Even head-hunting rituals have offered the bare plot co-ordinates of *Night School* (1981). The wrong head appears on the right body (a fly's head on David Hedison's body, and vice versa, in the 1958 *The Fly*). The transplant theme usually focused on **hands** is doubled in *The Incredible Two-Headed Transplant* (1971), in which Orlac-like, a murderer's head is grafted onto the body of a simpleton, and *The Thing With Two Heads* (1972), which stitches a white racist's head onto a hulking black body. A head becomes a bowling ball in *Day of the Dead* (1985), while another sprouts spidery legs in *The Thing* (1982).

As a focus for our anxieties about the limits of the self and the body, the orifices of the head (**eyes**, mouth, ears) have been penetrated or as part of the unsettling effect of body horror, all the more disturbing when used to test or deconstruct the idea that the head is seat of the rational self, or home of the immortal soul. The **brain** embodies the paradox of the head as the ideal and the material combined: in horror, brains are both the most palpably gross of substances and the site of sublime ideas, and while schlock cinema might seem to relish the first more than the second (brains are the ultimate substance of 'splatter'), the genre has often intelligently investigated the double implications of head violation. Descartes's suggestion that the pineal gland is the seat of the soul hovers behind many of the anxieties evoked by gothic images of the headless but still animate body (what is the nature of a body if it is a body without a soul?) or the body attached to the 'wrong' head: think of John Cleese's brain in Robert **De Niro**'s body in *Mary Shelley's* **Frankenstein** (1994) – indeed, the multiple cinematic incarnations

Heads: David Gale, *Re-Animator*

Hell: *Dante's Inferno* (1924)

of Mary Shelley's novel trace these questions very clearly. LRW

Hell

Though neither as gruesome not as sadistic as the paintings by De Limburg or Bosch, Gustave Doré's illustrations (1861) to Dante's *Divine Comedy* have powerfully influenced how cinema pictures the fate of the damned. *L'inferno*, a five-reel Italian epic which sensationally brings Doré's images of torture and despair to life, was circulated in the USA in 1911 by the Warner Brothers, contributing appropriately to the rise of Hollywood and establishing a classical precedent for all scenes of the hereafter.

The Devil's Assistant (1917) features the River Styx and the hellhound Cerberus, *The Magician* (1926) molests its heroine with a nude Pan from the *Folies Bergère*, while two further versions of *Dante's Inferno* (1924, 1935) copy Doré's vistas of lost souls sprouting anguished branches, straining against boulders and toppling into furnaces (footage shamelessly recycled by Ken **Russell** for *Altered States*, 1981). Years later, the infernal ferryman is still toiling in *Soultaker* (1990), while Doré is studied in *Jacob's Ladder* (1990) prior to the wanderer's descent into a 'real' Hell with gut-splashed floors, deformed

observers and imminent vivisection by power-drill. He reappears, inescapably, in *Se7en* (1995).

More glimpsed than dwelled upon, Hell varies according to budget from pantomime in *Hellzapoppin'* (1942) – moustachioed demons cramming their prey into 'canned guy' and 'canned gal' containers – and, in much the same spirit, *Bill and Ted's Bogus Journey* (1991), to a bleak arena for the walking dead, their groans habitually

Clare Higgins, *Hellbound: Hellraiser II*

dubbed into American, as with *Ercole al centro della terra* (*Hercules at the Centre of the Earth*, 1961), *Maciste all'inferno* (*The Witch's Curse*, 1962), *Paura nella città dei morti viventi* (*City of the Living Dead*, 1980). The brink of the underworld forms a familiar battleground, easily reached through the local fair (*Carnival of Souls*, 1962), at the end of the garden (*The Gate*, 1986) or even in the kitchen (*The Refrigerator*, 1991). According to ***Hellraiser*** (1987) and sequels, contact with the beyond is achieved by a Magic Box enabling flayed tormentors to scramble into the streets hurling razor-edged CDs. Other points of access (as stated in a trio of 1987 productions: *Prince of Darkness*, *The Unholy*, *Angel Heart*) can be churches or an elevator in a seedy New Orleans hotel, descending into the gloom from a nasty case of blocked plumbing.

A subtler tone is suggested by Ernst Lubitsch's *Heaven Can Wait* (1943), where Satan (Laird **Cregar**) politely declines to drop Don Ameche through the trapdoor in his office floor. As Damien observes in *The Final Conflict* (1981): 'There is only one Hell – the leaden monotony of human existence', an interpretation with some affinity to the sepulchral bistro of *Totò all'inferno* (*Totò in Hell*, 1954), the interminable house-party of *Lurkers* (1988) and the roadhouse of *Highway to Hell* (1991), where Hitler has nothing better to do than wait to be joined by Jerry Lewis. Setting aside the burnings, gouges and skinners of Oriental shockers like *Jigoku* (*Hell*, 1960) and *Jigokuhen* (*Portrait of Hell*, 1969), the most plausible worst punishment might be as envisioned by Sartre and filmed as *Huis clos* (*Vicous Circle*, 1954) and *No Exit* (1962): spending eternity with three people in a single room. PS

Hellraiser (1986)

Author Clive **Barker** turned director with a chillingly perverse adaptation of his novella 'The Hellbound Heart' (1986). Exploring the pleasures and pain of death, *Hellraiser* takes bone-cracking, flesh-stretching, blood-and-guts transformations to gruesome new heights. The film made a horror icon of Barker's schoolfriend Doug **Bradley** as Pinhead, one of the demonic Cenobites, keeper of the Lament Configuration puzzle box which opens the gate to **Hell**. Acting weight is shouldered by Clare Higgins as a hammer-wielding murderess out to resurrect her lover. Sequels, written by Peter **Atkins**, are Tony **Randel**'s sicker and gorier *Hellbound: Hellraiser II* (1988), Anthony

Hickox's fun S&M spectacle *Hellraiser III: Hell on Earth* (1992) and Kevin **Yagher**'s *Hellraiser: Bloodline* (completed by Joe Chappelle, credited to 'Alan **Smithee**', 1996). There was a comic book spin-off, and a Pinhead joke features in *Transylvania Twist* (1989). AJ

Stephen Jones, *The Hellraiser Chronicles* (1992)

Hemmings, David (b. 1941)

British actor, director. Originally a swinging London icon in *Blowup* (1966), Hemmings is associated with horror through a run of weird parts, including an **Argento** hero in *Profondo rosso* (*Deep Red*, 1976) and the title roles in a decent TV *Dr. Jekyll and Mr. Hyde* (1980). As a director, he gravitates to genre, turning out the undistinguished *The Survivor* (1981) and pilots for **Werewolf** (1987) and *Quantum Leap* (1989).

Eye of the Devil/1967 * *Unman, Wittering and Zigo*/*Fragment of Fear*/1971 * *Voices*/1973 * *Murder by Decree*/*Thirst*/1979 * *Harlequin*/1980

TV: *Out of the Unknown*: 'The Counterfeit Man'/1965 * *Werewolf* (d): 'Nightwatch'/'The Wolf Who Thought He Was a Man'/'Nothing Evil in These Woods'/'Friendly Haven'/'Nightmare at Braine Hotel'/'Blood Ties'/'Nightmare in Blue'/1987 * *Nightmare Classics*: 'The Turn of the Screw'/1989 * *Tales From the Crypt*: 'Loved to Death'/1991

Hendry, Ian (1931–84)

British actor, often in seedy roles. Balding, with 'eyes like pissholes in the snow' (*Get*

David Hemmings

Carter, 1972). Unusually a hero in *Theatre of Blood* (1972).

Children of the Damned/1963 * *Repulsion*/1965 * *Tales From the Crypt*/1971 * *Captain Kronos Vampire Hunter*/1972 * *Damien: Omen II*/1978

TV: *The Avengers*/1961–2: *Thriller*: 'Killer With Two Faces'/1974 * *Supernatural*: 'Countess Ilona'/'The Werewolf Reunion'/1977 * *The New Avengers*: 'To Catch a Rat'/1979

Henenlotter, Frank (b. 1950)

American director, writer. A would-be cultist whose comedy horrors mitigate offbeam sleaze with an endearing line in monsters, Henenlotter has never properly capitalised on the success of Siamese-twin shocker *Basket Case* (1981). Its scabrous invention is shared by **drug**-themed follow-up *Brain Damage* (1987), but financial disappointments resulted in *Basket Case 2* (1990), which eschews the Bowery for a more fancifully freakish backdrop. *Basket Case 3* (1991) is at least more perversely goofy; the intervening *Frankenhooker* (1990) is mere t&a guffaw. Henenlotter's early, home-made horrors include *Gorilla Queen*, *Lurid Women* and *Son of Psycho*. The 16mm short *Slash of the Knife* was once mooted to support *Pink Flamingos* (1973). DP

Henriksen, Lance (b. 1939)

American actor. His best horror roles are as a **vampire** in *Near Dark* (1987) and Torquemada in **The Pit and the Pendulum** (1990). SJ

Mansion of the Doomed/1976 * *The Visitor*/*Damien: Omen II*/1978 * *Piranha II: The Spawning*/1981 * *Nightmares*/1983 * *The Terminator*/1984 * *Jagged Edge*/1985 * *Aliens*/1986 * *Pumpkinhead*/1988 * *The Horror Show*/1989 * *Alien3*/*Jennifer 8*/1992 * *Man's Best Friend*/*Hard Target*/1993 * *The Color of Night*/*Nature of the Beast*/1994 * *Mind Ripper*/*Powder*/*Dead Man*/1995

TV: *Tales from the Crypt*: 'Cutting Cards'/1990; 'Yellow'/1991

Herbert, Holmes [Edward Sanger] (1882–1956)

British actor in Hollywood. Often a stuffy aristocrat, doctor, judge or butler.

The Terror/1928 * *The Thirteenth Chair*/1929 * *Dr. Jekyll and Mr. Hyde*/*Daughter of the Dragon*/1931 * *Mystery of the Wax Museum*/*The Invisible Man*/1933 * *Mark of the Vampire*/1935 * *House of Secrets*/1936 * *The Thirteenth Chair*/1937 *

The Adventures of Sherlock Holmes/1939 * *Ghost of Frankenstein*/*The Undying Monster*/*Invisible Agent*/1942 * *Sherlock Holmes Faces Death*/*Calling Dr. Death*/1943 * *The Uninvited*/*The Mummy's Curse*/*Pearl of Death*/1944 * *House of Fear*/1945 * *Son of Dr. Jekyll*/1951

Herbert, James (b. 1943)

British writer. The term 'nasty' in application to horror was coined for Herbert's paperbacks *The Rats* (1974) and *The Fog* (1975), which intersperse disaster plots with unpleasant set-pieces, opening the creepy-crawly way for imitators Guy N. Smith (*Night of the Crabs*, 1976) and Shaun Hutson (*Slugs*, 1982). He has written rat sequels (*Lair*, 1979; *Domain*, 1984), but also moved to the less gruesome: *The Survivor* (1976), *Fluke* (1977), *Moon* (1985), *The Magic Cottage* (1986), *Haunted* (1988), *Creed* (1990), *The Ghosts of Sleath* (1994), *'48* (1996). He has succeeded Dennis **Wheatley** as the Default British Horror Writer, but some express a preference for his early, funny books. Herbert films are largely undistinguished: *The Rats* (1980), *The Survivor* (1982), *Haunted* (1995), *Fluke* (1995).

Stephen Jones, *James Herbert: By Horror Haunted* (1992)

Heroes

Because classic horror is structured around the conflict between **monster** and savant, archetypally represented by **Dracula** and **Van Helsing**, male romantic leads often seem feeble and superfluous, rarely embodying virile, righteous **violence** as do the heroes of crime films or **Westerns**. Overshadowed by monsters and older authority figures ('You *fool*, Rex,' Christopher **Lee** repeatedly snaps at Leon Greene in *The Devil Rides Out*, 1967), horror heroes do little except ask stupid questions, refuse to believe in the supernatural and hug the rescued girl at the fade-out. Among these unmemorable fellows are Norman Kerry (*The Phantom of the Opera*, 1926), David **Manners** (*Dracula*, 1931; **The Black Cat**, 1934), John Boles (**Frankenstein**, 1931) and Kent Smith (**Cat People**, 1942).

In **Old Dark House** films, there is a tendency to cast comedians, from Creighton Hale and Bob Hope in the 1927 and 1939 versions of *The Cat and the Canary* to Red Skelton in *Whistling in Dixie* (1942) and Kenneth Connor in *What a Carve Up!* (1961), which enables the leads to show convincing cowardice, wisecrack and blunder towards a off. In a few recent instances, monsters are able to fulfil the function of genuine heroes, using their powers against more monstrous villains: Rick Springfield as vampire cop *Nick Knight* (1989), Brendan Hughes as a heroic vampire in *To Die For* (1989) and **werewolf** in *Howling VI: The Freaks* (1990).

Heroines

The plot function of woman as trophy, sqaubbled over by **hero** and **monster**, was established as early as the abduction and rescue of the sometimes literally catatonic Jane (Lil **Dagover**) of *Das Cabinet des Dr. Caligari* (1919). Nina (Greta Schroeder) of *Nosferatu* (1922) has self-sacrificing spiritual strength enough to destroy the **vampire**, but the pallid Mina (Helen Chandler) of *Dracula* (1931) is differentiated from **victim** Lucy only by slight resistance to the monster's will and a Jonathan who comes to her rescue. Jane and Mina typify the fainting, abducted, desired, passive heroine; even *Mystery of the Wax Museum* (1932), which has Glenda Farrell as a hard-drinking, wisecracking, investigative heroine and sissifies its male hero, retains archetypal Fay **Wray** to be kidnapped by the monster and scream at his hideousness.

The ritual of classic horror requires almost characterless heroines (Evelyn **Ankers** specialised in this role). Suggestions of independence are often squashed by matrimonial finales: 'I don't want to be an art critic any more, darling,' chirrups Virginia Grey in *House of Horrors* (1946), retiring from the profession that has got her mixed up with murder. Rare non-stereotype heroines are offered in **Lewton** films by Betsy Dee (*I Walked With a Zombie*, 1943), Kim Hunter (*The Seventh Victim*, 1943) and Anna Lee (*Bedlam*, 1946); Lewton's impatience with cliché is also shown by Jane Randolph's *unsympathetic* heroine in *Cat People* (1942). The monster movies of the 50s allow heroines to be professional, but give them cute male nicknames to signify slightly unwomanly status: Nikki (Margaret Sheridan) of *The Thing* (1951) is a Hawksian team member, but supposed big brains Lesley (Faith Domergue, *It Came From Beneath the Sea*, 1953), Pat (Joan Weldon, *Them!*, 1954) and Steve (Mara Corday, *Tarantula*, 1955) make coffee, totter around labs on high heels and scream.

The housewife ingenues of **Hammer** fall back into classic mode, treated as prizes: again, Mina (Melissa Stribling, *Dracula*, 1958) is the touchstone, wooed into vam

Hero and Heroine: Fay Wray, Bruce Cabot, *King Kong (1932)*

solution and even the occasional romantic pairing, though the traditional unmanliness of the **comedy** hero often finds them maternally dominated by sensible **heroines** or even relegated to jokey semi-**homosexual** relationships (Connor shares a bedroom with Sid James). The Bs of the 40s offer a succession of two-fisted cops and newspapermen to tangle with **mad scientists** or **Nazi** monsters, but one would be hard-pressed to rank Dave O'Brien (*The Devil Bat*, 1940), Johnny Downs (*The Mad Monster*, 1942) or Robert Lowery (*The Mummy's Ghost*, 1944) alongside Bogart, Gable or Wayne as an epitome of masculine values.

In the 50s, heroes became more heroic, as military men (Kenneth Tobey, *The Thing From Another World*, 1951) or doctors (John Agar, *Tarantula*, 1955) mix action and intellect, and even an occasional young, good-looking scientist (Rhodes Reason, *This Island Earth*, 1955; Hugh Marlowe, *Earth vs. the Flying Saucers*, 1956) combining the function of Van Helsing and romantic lead. However, the gothic revival brought about a return of the feeble, fainting hero: Michael **Gough** (*Dracula*, 1958), Mark Damon (*The Fall of the House of Usher*, 1960), John Richardson (*La maschera del demonio*, 1960), Edward de Souza (*The Phantom of the Opera*, 1963), Trevor Eve (*Dracula*, 1979), Keanu Reeves (*Bram Stoker's Dracula*, 1992).

Duane **Jones** of *Night of the Living Dead* (1968) is notable as the first **black** horror hero, but the film deconstructs the type of competent survivor played by Rod Taylor (*The Birds*, 1963), showing all Jones's valiant efforts to be ultimately futile. This depressing tradition dates back to paranoid Kevin McCarthy of *Invasion of the Body Snatchers* (1956), is parodied by Roman **Polanski** in *Dance of the Vampires* (1967) and was common in the 70s: among leads who succumb in shock finales are Roger Perry (*Count Yorga, Vampire*, 1970), Jason Miller (*The Exorcist*, 1973), Paul Hampton (*Shivers*, 1974) and Gregory Peck (*The Omen*, 1976). More subtly disturbing *Matthew Hopkins Witchfinder General* (1968), *Straw Dogs* (1972), *The Hills Have Eyes* (1976) and *Se7en* (1995) where heroes are ultimately corrupted by violence into which they have been seduced by mirror image villains.

With the **stalk-and-slash** craze, heroes vanish almost entirely: the surviving girls of the *Halloween*, *Friday the 13th* and *Nightmare on Elm Street* series often have no love interest or are partnered by disposable male **victims** whose passing is not much noted. *The Burning* (1980), *A Nightmare on Elm Street, Part 2: Freddy's Revenge* (1985) and *Fright Night* (1985) are rare instances of modern horror films with male protagonists: girlfriends are sidelined and feminised heroes enter into semi-gay flirtations with monsters. A minor strain of horror, which begins with *The Wolf Man* (1941), poses the monster as tragic hero, usually keeping a spare man around to be partnered with the girl after the protagonist has been finished

Heroine: Nancy Allen, *Strange Invaders*

pirism but redeemed by others' heroism. The greater emphasis on **sex** allows **Hammer** heroines to dominate in relationships with weaker men: Mina's rescuer is **Van Helsing** while her husband is sidelined; Yvonne Furneaux in *The Mummy* (1959), married to cripple Peter **Cushing**, finally saves *him* by impersonating the mummy's imperious ex-lover; Jennifer Daniel in *Kiss of the Vampire* (1962) and *The Reptile* (1964) is a kittenish newly-wed, bantering with jovial dullard

husbands. The radical changes of the late 60s did not liberate heroines but let them suffer more: Veronica **Carlson** of *Frankenstein Must Be Destroyed* (1967) is exploited as home help and sex slave by the Baron and meaninglessly murdered; Hilary Dwyer of *Matthew Hopkins Witchfinder General* (1968) sleeps with Vincent **Price** in an effort to save her father, prompting the hero to a vengeance craze that ultimately drives her insane; Judith O'Dea of *Night of the Living Dead* (1968) convincingly lapses into catatonia after the death of her brother.

When the lady-in-peril genre of the 40s (*Phantom Lady*, 1944; *The Spiral Staircase*, 1946) became the **stalk-and-slash** of the 70s, the harrowed but surviving heroine predominated, typified by Jamie Lee **Curtis** (**Halloween**, 1978) and Sigourney Weaver (**Alien**, 1979). Ostensible heroes (Tom Skerritt in *Alien*) are enfeebled and often killed off, leaving love interests to fend for themselves. These heroines sometimes critique the machismo of heroes – Fran (Gaylen Ross) of *Dawn of the Dead* (1979) declares 'I won't play den mother for you guys' – and often embody slightly square virtues: in *Halloween*, the virginal Laurie (Curtis) survives while promiscuous friends fall victim; high schooler Nancy (Heather Langenkamp) of **A Nightmare on Elm Street** (1984) is surrounded by feeble-minded adults and doomed peers. *Aliens* (1986)

brings out a maternal dimension in Weaver's Ripley, considerably deepening the character, though an attempt to pull a similar trick with Langenkamp in *Wes Craven's New Nightmare* (1994) is hindered by the actress's limitations. Though the 'final girl' or 'surviving heroine' of the 70s remains a common cliché, there has been a drift back towards tradition.

A hooker (Nancy **Allen**, *Dressed to Kill*, 1980), a vampire (Anne Parillaud, *Innocent Blood*, 1992) or an FBI agent (Jodie Foster, *The Silence of the Lambs*, 1992) can be an active heroine, with male partners treated as subsidiary and vulnerable adjuncts. More common are Mina clones like Amanda Bearse (*Fright Night*, 1985), Jamie Gertz (*The Lost Boys*, 1987), Jenny Wright (*Near Dark*, 1987) or Helena Bonham Carter (*Mary Shelley's Frankenstein*, 1994), seduced into monstrousness but won back as minor goals in an ongoing conflict which is, with a homoerotic subtext foregrounded, between men. Only *Bram Stoker's Dracula* (1992) plays this story while emphasising the motivations and feelings of Mina (Winona Ryder) rather than Jonathan.

Carol Clover, *Men, Women and Chain Saws: Gender in the Modern Horror Film* (1992)

Herrmann, Bernard (1911–75)

American composer, of enormous significance in horror/suspense, responsible for the seminal strings-only score of **Psycho** (1960). Herrmann has a reputation as a serious composer (best known for the opera *Wuthering*

Heroine: Jodie Foster, *The Silence of the Lambs*

Heights, 1950) but never regarded his cinema work as an aesthetically poor relation and was passionate about motion-picture scoring. He served a long apprenticeship at CBS radio, forming an association with Orson **Welles** that led to his first film score, *Citizen Kane* (1941). A relationship with Alfred **Hitchcock** resulted in classic scores for *The Trouble with Harry* (1955), *Vertigo* (1958), *The Birds* (1963) – on which Herrmann orchestrated bird-sounds – and *Marnie* (1964) but ended when the director rejected his score for *Torn Curtain* (1966). He resigned in disgust from the MPAAA in 1968 as the symphonic film score fell out of vogue, but in his last years worked with a new breed of young, independent film-makers like Brian **De Palma**. His final score was for Martin Scorsese's *Taxi Driver* (1976), but he has posthumous credits thanks to the reprise of themes in **It's Alive** and *Psycho* sequels, the *Cape Fear* remake (1992) and, jokily, *Re-Animator* (1986). SL

All That Money Can Buy/1940 * *Hangover Square*/1944 * *The Ghost and Mrs. Muir*/1947 * *Portrait of Jennie*/1948 * *Cape Fear*/1962 * *Twisted Nerve*/1969 * *The Night Digger*/*Endless Night*/1971 * *Sisters*/1973 * *It's Alive*/1974 * *Obsession*/1976

TV: *A Christmas Carol*/1954 * *Companions in Nightmare*/1968 * *The Twilight Zone*: 'Where is Everybody'/'The Lonely'/'Walking Distance'/1959; 'The Eye of the Beholder'/1960; 'Little Girl Lost'/1962; 'Living Doll'/'Ninety Years Without Slumbering'/1963 * *Alfred Hitchcock Hour*: 'The Life Work of Juan Diaz'/'The Jar'/'The McGregor Affair'/1964 'Where the Woodbine Twineth'/1965

Herzog, Werner (b. 1942)
German director. Of the New Wave film-makers of the 70s, Herzog is most indebted to the fantastic tradition, as signified by his poised, faintly embalmed **Murnau** remake, *Nosferatu, Phantom der Nacht* (*Nosferatu the Vampyre*, 1979). Elsewhere, he trades in gimmicks like an all-midget cast (*Auch Zwerge haben klein angefangen*/*Even Dwarfs Started Small*, 1970) and hypnotising his actors (*Herz aus Glas*/*Heart of Glass*, 1976). Klaus **Kinski**, his rat-faced **Dracula**, began an antagonistic collaboration with the director as the visionary madman of *Aguirre, der Zorn Gottes* (*Aguirre, Wrath of God*, 1972), Herzog's best film, and returned to decreasing effect in *Woyzeck* (1978), *Fitzcarraldo* (1982) and *Cobra Verde* (1988). Though films like *Jeder für sich und Gott gegen alle* (*The Enigma of Kaspar*

Hauser, 1974) are remarkable, strange achievements, Herzog has run out of steam in recent years, turning to documentary doodles.

Man of Flowers (a)/1983

Hess, David (b. 1942)
American actor. The repulsive Krug Stillo of *Last House on the Left* (1972), and a regular villain for Wes **Craven** and Ruggiero **Deodato**.

Autostop rosso sangue [*Hitch-Hike*]/1977 * *La casa sperduta nel parco* [*The House at the Edge of the Park*]/*To All a Goodnight* (d)/1980 * *Swamp Thing*/1982 * *Il camping del terrore* [*Body Count*]/1987 * *Omicidio a luci blu*/1991

TV: *Manimal*: 'Illusions'/1983

Hessler, Gordon (b. 1930)
German-born director, writer. A story editor then producer on **Hitchcock**'s TV shows, Hessler based *Catacombs* (1964), his debut feature, on a novella rejected by *Alfred Hitchcock Hour* (1962–5). As a producer for AIP-London, he was thrown off *De Sade* (1969), then allowed to direct *The Oblong Box* (1969) when Michael **Reeves** withdrew. Three more revisionist horrors followed, all with writer Christopher **Wicking**. Hessler's raucous, slightly unkempt style made a modish paranoid classic of *Scream and Scream Again* (1969). After the adequate *Cry of the Banshee* (1970), AIP recut the radical, oneiric **Murders in the Rue Morgue** (1971). A comparable fate befell the restrained Richard Adams adaptation *The Girl in a Swing* (1988). DP

TV: *Alfred Hitchcock Presents*: 'Final Ambition'/1961 * *Scream Pretty Peggy*/1973 * *The Night Stalker*: 'The Spanish Moss Murders'/1974 * *The Strange Possession of Mrs Oliver*/1977 * *KISS Meets the Phantom of the Park*/*The New Adventures of Wonder Woman*: 'Gault's Brain'/1978 * *Tales of the Haunted*: 'Evil Stalks this House'/1981 * *Tales of the Unexpected*: 'People Don't Do Such Things'/1985

Hewitt, David L. (b. 19??)
American director, writer, producer, effects artist. Noticed by Forrest **Ackerman**, travelling **magician** Hewitt worked with Ib Melchior before making the carny-style short *Monsters Crash the Pyjama Party* (1964). *Dr. Terror's Gallery of Horrors* (1966) is an unconvincing attempt to exploit **Amicus**'s success with **anthology** format. Its mix of stasis and stock footage is characteristic of Hewitt's cheeseparing. DP

The Wizard of Mars/1964 * *Journey to the Centre of Time*/1968 * *The Mighty Gorga*/1969 * *The Lucifer Complex*/1978

Hickox, Anthony (b. 1959)
British director, writer. A horror fan with an eye for pretty heroines, Hickox made three over-ingratiating homages (*Waxwork*, 1988; *Sundown: The Vampire in Retreat*, 1989; *Waxwork II: Lost in Time*, 1992) before lending **Hellraiser** *III: Hell on Earth* (1992) slick professionalism. He cameos in his own films and takes a major role in *Lobster Man From Mars* (1989). DP

The Turn of the Screw (p)/1992 * *Return of the Living Dead III* (a)/*Warlock: The Armageddon*/1993 * *Full Eclipse*/1994 * *The Granny* (a)/*Children of the Corn III: Urban Harvest* (exec p)/1995 * *Invasion of Privacy*/1996

Hill, Jack (b. 1933)
American director, writer. A **Corman** associate, notable for fringe-work like writing and doing pick-ups on *The Terror* (1963), passing the baton on *Blood Bath* (1966) and American-shot scenes of **Karloff**'s last four films. A rare solo credit is *Spider Baby* (1965), a uniquely twisted horror farce.

Dementia 13 (2nd unit)/1963 * *La camara del terror* [*The Fear Chamber*]/*La muerte viviente* [*The Snake People*]/*La invasión siniestra* [*The Incredible Invasion*]/*Serenata macabra* [*House of Evil*]/1968 * *The Bees* (w/u)/1978 * *Death Ship* (st)/1980

Anthony Hickox, *Waxwork*

Hillyer, Lambert (1893–1969)

American director of many Westerns from 1917 to 1949. *Batman* (1943) is a serial with J. Carrol **Naish**'s electric **zombies**, but Hillyer did far better by a 1936 Universal pair, the s-f **Karloff**-**Lugosi** outing *The Invisible Ray* and the underrated *Dracula's Daughter*.

Before Midnight/1933

Hinds, Anthony (b. 1922)

British producer, writer. Hinds was the son of **Hammer**'s co-founder Will Hinds (whose stage name of Will Hammer gave the company its name). He and Michael **Carreras** (grandson of Hammer's other founder, Enrique Carreras) were Hammer's main producers throughout the 50s and early 60s. From 1960 on, Hinds was also a prolific screenwriter under the name John Elder. When dealing with collaborative enterprises, it is difficult to ascertain who contributed what to the final product: however, it seems the moral Manichaeanism that underpins so much Hammer horror (often attributed by auteurists to house director Terence **Fisher**) was as much to do with Hinds as anyone else. Certainly, the Hammer view of sexuality as an evil and bestial but also dangerously attractive force finds its fullest expression in Elder screenplays ranging from *The Curse of the Werewolf* (1960; he also produced) to *The Reptile* (1966), which probably stands as Hinds' best work as writer. PH

The Quatermass Experiment (p)/1955 * *X – The Unknown* (p)/1956 * *The Curse of Frankenstein* (p)/*Quatermass II* (p)/1957 * *Dracula* (p)/*The Revenge of Frankenstein* (p)/1958 * *The Hound of the Baskervilles* (p)/*The Man Who Could Cheat Death* (p)/1959 * *The Brides of Dracula* (p)/*The Stranglers of Bombay* (p)/1960 * *The Phantom of the Opera* (p/w)/*The Old Dark House* (p)/ *Paranoiac* (p)/1962 * *Kiss of the Vampire* (p/w)/*The Evil of Frankenstein* (p/w)/1964 * *Fanatic* (p)/1965 * *Rasputin, The Mad Monk* (w)/*Frankenstein Created Woman* (w)/1966 * *Dracula Has Risen from the Grave* (w)/1968 * *Taste the Blood of Dracula* (w)/1969 * *Scars of Dracula* (w)/1970 * *Frankenstein and the Monster from Hell* (w)/1973 * *The Legend of the Werewolf* (w)/1974 * *The Ghoul* (w)/1975

TV: *Hammer House of Horror*: 'Visitor from the Grave' (w)/1980

Hitchcock, Alfred (1899–1980)

British-born American director. From early in his career Hitchcock was advertised as 'the master of suspense', but his work becomes increasingly concerned with abnormal psychological states. Films which prefigure his official entries in the horror genre include *Murder!* (1930), with its grotesque revelation of the killer as a transvestite; *Suspicion* (1941), whose final visualisation of Cary Grant's innocence is exactly as reliable as Joan Fontaine's earlier paranoia about him; *Spellbound* (1945), with its seductively gleaming razor and its dream-landscapes designed by Salvador Dali; the claustrophobic *Rope* (1948), which imprisons the audience in an apartment with a concealed corpse; *Rear Window* (1954), with Raymond Burr trudging out at night with parcels of his wife's body; the **Kafka**esque nightmare of *The Wrong Man* (1957). *Rich and Strange* (1932) shows his black humour at its cruel-est in a scene where a young couple are confronted with the skin of the ship's cat they have just enjoyed as a meal, but Hitchcock regarded *Psycho* (1960) as his blackest joke. In fact most of the jokes come from Robert **Bloch**'s 1959 novel, and it is the organisation of the material which is Hitchcock's. The film crucially expands the role of Marion Crane to implicate the audience in her pathetic crime. The shower murder (which Hitchcock told Truffaut was the only reason he chose to film the book) is the single most unimaginatively imitated scene in all horror cinema. *Psycho* is Hitchcock's most densely constructed film in terms of images: the recurring journey into darkness (the opening track in from a cityscape into a dark room leads to Janet **Leigh**'s drive into night) becomes a

Alfred Hitchcock, Janet Leigh, on the set of *Psycho*

plunge into darkness: the car into the swamp, Martin Balsam's down the stairs, Vera Miles's descent into the cellars; indeed, this recurrence seems to be the justification for the otherwise inexplicable unnerving track through the darkened hardware store toward Miles. The film shares with *Peeping Tom* (1960) a preoccupation with looking and with **eyes**, and the journeys into darkness lead into the black gaze (even blacker than the motorcycle cop's) of Mrs Bates, who stares at us out of Norman's eyes in the final seconds of the film: here, as Robin Wood points out, the audience has become 'the cruel eyes studying you' which Norman (Anthony **Perkins**) earlier described as one of the horrors of being institutionalised. It is the most poetically organised of Hitchcock's films, and a triumphant vindication of genre.

The Birds (1963) marks a shift of interest from basing films on plot to building them around a situation, a method which also revives the monster-on-the-loose structure of 50s. *Torn Curtain* (1966), an espionage thriller which ultimately loses its nerve and justifies its protagonist, contains an especially protracted and disturbing murder by amateurs. The scene in *Frenzy* (1972) in which Barry Foster rapes and murders Barbara Leigh-Hunt is the most extreme expression of the misogyny underlying much of Hitchcock's work, and indeed is trimmed on British video. Some of the disturbing quality of the scene relates to the charm with which Foster plays the character throughout the film, as another of the attractive villains with whom Hitchcock appears to have felt some identification.

The sexual implications of Hitchcock's direction of his actresses are most fruitfully explored in *Vertigo* (1958), his masterpiece, which develops from a study of obsession into a nightmare of subjugation, with a final reel that is as harrowing intellectually as emotionally. Though Hitchcock's overt horror films are few, his influence on the genre is considerable. *Psycho* in particular is crucial to the development of the genre because of its ruthless determination to be as frightening as possible, a task to which Hitchcock applied all the techniques he regarded as pure cinema. Some of Dario **Argento**'s stylistic flourishes derive from Hitchcock, while several of Brian **De Palma**'s movies are variations on specific Hitchcock films, much as Robert Simpson wrote a set of string quartets commenting on Beethoven's. RC

The Lodger/1926 * *Young and Innocent*/1937 *

Rebecca/1940 * *Shadow of a Doubt*/1943 * *Strangers on a Train*/1951 * *The Trouble With Harry*/1955 * *Family Plot*/1976

TV: *Alfred Hitchcock Presents*/1955–62 * *Suspicion*/1957–8 * *The Alfred Hitchcock Hour*/ 1962–5 * *Alfred Hitchcock Presents*/1985–8

François Truffaut, *Hitchcock* (1967); Raymond Durgnat, *The Strange Case of Alfred Hitchcock* (1974); Donald Spoto, *The Art of Alfred Hitchcock* (1976), *The Dark Side of Genius: The Life of Alfred Hitchcock* (1983); John Russell Taylor, *Hitch: The Life and Times of Alfred Hitchcock* (1978); Robin Wood, *Hitchcock's Films Revisited* (1989)

The Hitchhiker (Canadian TV series, 1983–91)

A cable anthology of horror stories, linked by a sinister hitch-hiker. **Cronenberg** regular Nicholas Campbell was the first thumb-tripper in 1983, replaced by Page Fletcher for the rest of the run. Despite attracting interesting directors (Mai Zetterling, Phillip Noyce, Roger **Vadim**, Paul Verhoeven) and actors (Klaus **Kinski**, Franco Nero, Sandra Bernhard, Willem Dafoe), the show was never more than adequate, thanks to dreary scripts structured around nudity and violence. Later seasons rely on Canadian B directors (George **Mihalka**, Christian Duguay, Jorge Montesi, Gerard Ciccoritti) and downwardly mobile stars (Robby Benson, C. Thomas Howell, David Soul, Scott Valentine).

Hobbes, Halliwell [Herbert Hobbes] (1877–1962)

British actor in Hollywood, adept at baronets and butlers, good as the scheming servant of *Sherlock Holmes Faces Death* (1943).

Dr. Jekyll and Mr. Hyde/1931 * *The Double Door*/1934 * *Dracula's Daughter*/1936 * *Maid of Salem*/1937 * *The Undying Monster*/1943 * *The Invisible Man's Revenge*/1944

TV: *Lights Out*: 'Dr. Heidegger's Experiment'/ 1950

Hodder, Kane (b. 1955)

American stunt co-ordinator, the only actor to have played Jason of *Friday the 13th* more than once. His machete-wielding is hardly more distinctive than the hackwork of his anonymous predecessors.

House/1986 * *House 2: The Second Story*/*Prison*/ *Friday the 13th, Part VII: The New Blood*/ *Waxwork*/*Ghost Town*/1988 * *DeepStar 6*/*Friday*

the 13th, Part VIII: Jason Takes Manhattan*/*The Horror Show*/1989 * *Alligator II: The Mutation*/ *Waxwork 2: Lost in Time*/*Leatherface: Texas Chainsaw Massacre III*/1990 * *The Rapture*/ *House IV*/1991 * *Jason Goes to Hell: The Final Friday*/1993 * *Project: Metalbeast*/*Pumpkinhead II: Blood Wings*/1994 * *Scanner Cop II: Volkin's Revenge*/1995

Hodgson, William Hope (1877–1918)

British writer. Hodgson's novels are *The Boats of the 'Glen Carrig'* (1907), *The House on the Borderland* (1908), *The Ghost Pirates* (1909) and *The Night Land* (1912). From his seafaring days, Hodgson developed a sense of the awesome malevolence of the universe. His protagonists wander into regions where vast and monstrous forces impinge on reality. A key influence on **Lovecraft**, he also provided material for other writers: Dennis **Wheatley**'s *Uncharted Seas* (1938) draws on *'Glen Carrig'* and Iain Sinclair's *Radon Daughters* (1994) searches for a lost sequel to *Borderland*. Hodgson's most conventional book, *Carnacki the Ghost Finder* (1913), concerns a Holmesian psychic detective: Carnacki is played by Donald **Pleasence** in 'The Horse of the Invisible', an episode of *The Rivals of Sherlock Holmes* (1971); Rick Kennett and A.F. Kidd have extended the canon with pastiches in *No. 472 Cheyne Walk* (1992). Inoshiro Honda's *Matango* (1963) is loosely inspired by Hodgson's masterly 'The Voice in the Night' (1907).

Hoffmann, Ernst Theodor Amadeus (1776–1822)

German writer. If he did not create the short horror story, Hoffmann refined and mastered the form, opening the way for **Poe**, Gogol, **Maupassant** and **Bierce**. His collections are *Fantaisiestücke* (Fantasy Pieces, 1814–5), *Nachtstücke* (Night Pieces, 1816–7) and *Die Serapionsbruder* (The Serapion Brothers, 1818–21); his only completed novel is *Die Elixiere des Teufels* (The Devil's Elixir, 1815–16). His persistent themes are automata, **doppelgängers**, pacts with the **Devil**, alchemy and obsession. The most lasting Hoffmann adaptations are Delibes's ballet *Coppélia* (1870), Offenbach's opera *Les Contes d'Hoffmann* (1880) and Tchaikovsky's ballet *The Nutcracker* (1891–2). Michael **Powell** and Emeric Pressburger's *Tales of Hoffmann* (1951) is the major Hoffmann movie, with Robert Rounseville as the writer and a remarkable Moira Shearer as the automaton Olympia.

Tales of Hoffmann: ABOVE Moira Shearer
LEFT Frederick Ashton, Robert Helpmann,
Leonid Massine

La Poupée/1899 * *Coppelia, the Animated Doll*/
1900 * *Hoffmanns Erzählungen* [*Tales of
Hoffmann*]/1914 * *Das Hexenlied*/1919 *
Elixiere des Teufels/1921 * *Coppélia*/1964 * *Dr
Coppelius*/1966

Holland, Tom (b. 1943)

American director, writer. Though styling
himself a maker of polished 'adult' entertainments, Holland is important for the teen
sensibility of fx-laden hits *Fright Night* (1985)
and *Child's Play* (1988). He obsessively
returns to the theme of 'The Boy Who Cried
Wolf'. An actor who turned to writing as a
means to direct, he first scripted the messy
transformationer *The Beast Within* (1982).
Class of 1984 (1982) was better treated, and
his *Scream for Help* (1984) script snagged the
opportunity of *Psycho II* (1983), which
engages admirably with its prequel, and
Cloak and Dagger (1984). Directorial debut
Fright Night also toys with precursors by
sending **horror host** 'Peter Vincent' into the
vampire fray. Associated with Stephen
King on TV (*The Langoliers*, 1995) and film
(*Thinner*, 1996), he has a bit in *The Stand*
(1994). DP

The Temp/1993

TV: *Amazing Stories*: 'Miscalculation'/1986 *

Tales from the Crypt: 'Lover Come Hack to
Me'/1989; 'King of the Road'/1992; 'Four-
Sided Triangle' (+w)/1990 * *The Stranger
Within*/1990

Holmes, Sherlock * See **Sherlock Holmes**

Holt, Seth (1923–71)

British director. Holt only completed six
films before his premature death during the
production of *Blood from the Mummy's Tomb*
(1971; completed by Michael **Carreras**) but
established himself as one of British cinema's
most accomplished stylists. Holt first made
his name as an editor and associate producer
at Ealing Studios (where he worked on *The
Ladykillers* in 1955) and was one of the few
film-makers to move from the gentle waters
of Ealing into the somewhat more robust
world of **Hammer** horror.

He was the only director to do anything
interesting with Hammer's series of psychological thrillers. *Taste of Fear* (1961), first of
the run, is already hampered by what were
to become the usual plot twists, but in the
face of such absurdity Holt manages to convey in a surprisingly delicate way a sense of
his characters' fears and emotional frailties,
mainly through a subtle use of camera

movement. *The Nanny* (1965) is less burdened with plot twists and consequently a
more consistent success, covering much the
same ground as Joseph Losey's *The Servant*
(1963) but in a defter, less ponderous manner. *Blood from the Mummy's Tomb* is uneven,
not surprisingly given the circumstances, but
again demonstrates ability to conjure menace from ostensibly mundane situations and
settings. PH

Homicidal Mania * See: **Asylums**; **Psychopaths**

Homosexuality (also **Lesbianism, Transvestism** & **Transsexuality**)

The *raison d'être* for gay characters in horror
films is mostly to depict homosexuality as a
predatory weakness (cf: the murderous lesbian ghost of *The Uninvited*, 1944), but
homosexual parallels also arise in horror
movies when a monster is seen in allegorical
terms as antisocial misfit. In *Frankenstein*
(1931) and *Bride of Frankenstein* (1935),
James **Whale** arguably incorporated sexually
suspect subtext (Ernest **Thesiger**'s sissy Dr
Pretorious in *Bride*) on purpose. Though the
vampire film lends itself to a hidden gay
agenda (homoerotic neck-biting, the sado-
masochistic relationship between **Dracula**
and **Renfield**), the first gay male bloodsucker was featured in Roman **Polanski**'s *Dance
of the Vampires* (1967) and has since become
a stereotype: cf: the weak decadent faggot
bitten by *Blacula* (1972), effete Udo **Kier** in
Blood for Dracula (1974), the male-couplings
of *Interview with the Vampire* (1995). A fum-

bled satirical twist is Mark **Pirro**'s **werewolf** parody *Curse of the Queerwolf* (1987), whose hero turns gay by the light of the full moon.

As in society, female homosexuality is far more acceptable in film (especially with the lipstick lesbian vogue) because heterosexuals find it a turn-on. Lesbianism is the subtle reason why Gloria Holden stalks Soho for young girls in *Dracula's Daughter* (1936). 'She knew strange fierce pleasures that no other woman could ever feel!' screamed the poster for **Cat People** (1945), leaving Simone **Simon**'s obsession open to sexual interpretation. And so do *Screaming Mimi* (1958), *. . . et mourir de plaisir* (1960) and *The Haunting* (1963), in which Claire Bloom hugs Julie Harris rather a lot. European horror leant toward the Sapphic area – as in the work of French stylist Jean **Rollin**, especially *Le frisson des vampires* (1970), and Harry **Kümel**'s *Le rouge aux lèvres* (1971) – paving the way for **Hammer**'s explicit **'Carmilla'** trilogy (*The Vampire Lovers*, 1970; *Lust for a Vampire*, 1970; *Twins of Evil*, 1971), *Vampyres* (1974) and *The Hunger* (1983). Now it's unusual *not* to feature lesbians in vampire movies.

Homosexuality-transvestism-transsexuality as a plot device can be found in *The Devil-Doll* (1936) with Lionel **Barrymore** masquerading as an old lady, Ralph **Bates** becoming Martine **Beswicke** in *Dr. Jekyll and Sister Hyde* (1972), Robert Morley as a gay critic murdered in *Theatre of Blood* (1973) and Tim Daly transforming into Sean Young in *Dr. Jekyll and Ms. Hyde* (1995). It is the subtext of *A Nightmare on Elm Street Part 2: Freddy's Revenge* (1985) and *Fright Night*

Homosexuality: Little Nell, Patricia Quinn, Tim Curry, Richard O'Brien, *The Rocky Horror Picture Show*

(1985) and as a shock twist fuels the horror whodunnits **Psycho** (1960), *Homicidal* (1961), *The Haunted House of Horror* (1969), *Private Parts* (1972), *Dressed to Kill* (1980), *Terror Train* (1980), *Deadly Blessing* (1981) and *Whispers* (1990). The ultimate gay horror movie, where every pansexual/drag theme is cross-dressed with movie cliche, is Jim

Sharman's *The Rocky Horror Picture Show* (1975), based on Richard **O'Brien**'s crossover stage success and a unique cult film in its own right. Openly gay horror auteurs include writers M.G. **Lewis**, Oscar **Wilde** and Michael **McDowell** and directors F.W. **Murnau**, James **Whale**, Paul **Bartel**, Andy **Milligan**, Clive **Barker** and David **De-Coteau**. AJ

Hooper, Tobe (b. 1943)

American director. *The Texas Chain Saw Massacre* (1974), coming from a director who had made only the underground *Eggshells* (1970) and a Peter, Paul and Mary TV special, was a startling genre debut, establishing Hooper as a talent on a par with **Romero**, **Craven**, **Carpenter** or **Cronenberg**. While his peers have progressed unevenly from remarkable early work through artistic and commercial ups and downs, Hooper has been on the slide ever since *Chain Saw*. A ferocious, relentless and shattering film, touching on Ed **Gein** and **power tools**, *Chain Saw* is a genuine regional nightmare, steeped in an atmosphere of rotting meat, **rural** decline and twisted **fam-**

LEFT Homosexuality: Susan Sarandon, Catherine Deneuve, *The Hunger*

Anthony Hopkins, *The Elephant Man*

ily values. The credit immediately won him lesser but by-no-means contemptible projects: the **EC Comics**-style swamp fable *Death Trap* (1977), the Stephen **King** miniseries *Salem's Lot* (1979), the impressive but affectless **stalk and slash** *The Funhouse* (1981). In this period, he had a few false starts, replaced by John Bud Cardos and Piers **Haggard** on *The Dark* (1979) and *Venom* (1982).

Poltergeist (1982), his watershed credit, is a combination **ghost story**, light show and rollercoaster, but its successes were attributed to producer Steven **Spielberg**. Hooper's career crisis came in a three-picture deal with Cannon which yielded a laughably endearing Quatermass knock-off (*Lifeforce*, 1985), a disastrous remake (*Invaders From Mars* 1986) and a botched sequel (*The Texas Chainsaw Massacre 2*, 1986). The two franchises he launched retain enough lustre to win him gigs like TV pilots for *Freddy's Nightmares* ('No More Mr Nice Guy', 1988), *Nowhere Man* (1995) and *Dark Skies* (1996). *I'm Dangerous Tonight* (1990), a TV movie from a Cornell Woolrich novella, is modestly effective, but 90s theatrical efforts (*Spontaneous Combustion*, 1990; *Night Terrors*, 1994; *The Mangler*, 1995) not only seem the work of someone who did not make *Chain Saw* but might have been directed by someone who never saw it. Doomed to collaborations with

other career-spirallers like Robert **Englund** or John Carpenter (*Body Bags*, 1993), Hooper remains missing in action.

Sleepwalkers (a)/1992

TV: *Amazing Stories*: 'Miss Stardust'/1987 * *Tales From the Crypt*: 'Dead Wait'/1991 * *Haunted Lives . . . True Ghost Stories*/1991

Hopkins, Anthony (b. 1937)

British actor. A specialist in middle-aged

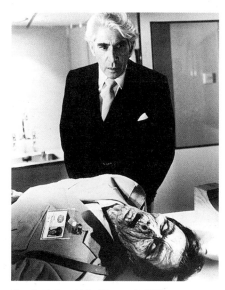

Frank Finlay, Tobe Hooper's *Lifeforce*

repression (*84 Charing Cross Road*, 1987; *Shadowlands*, 1993; *The Remains of the Day*, 1993), Hopkins pulls out stops on horrors, essaying classic roles (Quasimodo in *The Hunchback of Notre Dame*, 1982; **Van Helsing** in *Bram Stoker's Dracula*, 1992), winning an Oscar as a liver-eating genius bogeyman for the 90s, Hannibal Lecter in *The Silence of the Lambs* (1991). Masterly enough to get away with a little ham, he is at his best when restrained.

Audrey Rose/1977 * *Magic*/1978 * *The Elephant Man*/1980 * *The Trial*/1993

Hopley, George * See: **Woolrich, Cornell**

Horror Hosts

Radio and TV anthology shows like *Lights Out* and *Inner Sanctum* and **comics** like *Tales From the Crypt* and *The Haunt of Fear* all have a creepy narrator. When horror films were first televised in America, it seemed natural to use similar if more comical characters to introduce (and interrupt) the presentation. The first horror hostess was **Vampira**, a Morticia-like glamour ghoul who began on Los Angeles's KABC-TV in 1954, presenting the minor films then available for broadcast, injecting velvet camp into works which seemed creaky by the tail-finned standards of the decade.

When the Shock Theatre package, including the Universal films that had become legendary in an era when rare theatrical reissues were the only way audiences could catch up with old movies, was released to dozens of local TV stations in 1957, many horror hosts sprang up: Roland/**Zacherley** in Philadelphia and New York, Gorgon (Bill Camfield) in Texas, Tarantula Ghoul (Suzanne Waldron) in Oregon, Selwin (Roy Sparenberg) in Indiana, the Outsider (John Burke) in Florida (a rare 'serious' host) and Ghoulardi (Ernie Anderson) in Ohio. Zacherley changed the host role by splicing himself *into* the films, first appearing in a cutaway shot as a cultist in *The Black Cat* (1934). Eventually, films became secondary to the antics of hosts, who would sneer at their short-comings and dub over snatches of rock music or cut in snippets of stock footage, concentrating on macabre skits. Purists objected, and the **comedy** of most hosts was every bit as pathetic and drivelsome as the horror of the average William **Beaudine** or Al **Adamson** movie.

There were stragglers into the 70s: Chilly Billy Cardille of Pittsburgh, who appears in *Night of the Living Dead* (1968), Dr

Cadaverino (Jack Du Blon) of Milwaukee, Seymour (Larry Vincent) of Los Angeles, Son of Svengoolie (Rich Koz) of Chicago. The local horror host died out with the usurping of their favoured slot by *Saturday Night Live* (1975–) and a general decline of regional programming. A survivor is **Elvira**, who began in Los Angeles in 1981 and has a continuing career in many outlets, including the feature *Elvira, Mistress of the Dark* (1988). The final evolution of the horror host show is *Mystery Science Theatre 2000* (1992–), which screens movies with continuous comic chatter from on-screen silhouettes, ideal viewing for people whose friends aren't witty enough to think of a funny remark during *Teenage Caveman* (1958). Dr Terror (Guy Henry) became Britain's first nationwide horror host on the BBC in 1992.

Vampira and Zacherley had minor film careers and Dr Morgus (Sid Rideau) of New Orleans starred in his own film, *The Wacky World of Dr. Morgus* (1961). Lisa Marie impersonates Vampira in *Ed Wood* (1994) and fictional horror hosts are played by Roddy McDowell (*Fright Night*, 1985), Julie Carmen (*Fright Night II*, 1989), Robert Prosky (*Gremlins 2: The New Batch*, 1990) and Danny DeVito (*Jack the Bear*, 1993).

Elena M. Watson, *Television Horror Movie Hosts* (1991)

Hospitals * See: **Asylums; Doctors; Disfigurement and Plastic Surgery**

Houdini, Harry [Erich Weiss] (1874–1926)

Hungarian escapologist, **magician**. An early action star, Houdini recreated his famous stunts in bizarre silent melodramas. A debunker of fraudulent **mediums** and investigator of psychic phenomena, he features in horror fictions: H.P. **Lovecraft** ghostwrote a weird tale 'Under the Pyramids' (1924) for Houdini, and Richard Lupoff worked the escapologist into his novel about HPL, *Lovecraft's Book* (1985). William Hjortsberg's *Nevermore* (1995) is about his historical association with Arthur Conan **Doyle** and Daniel Stashower's *The Adventure of the Ectoplasmic Man* (1985) teams him with **Sherlock Holmes**; the comic *The Devil's Workshop* (1993), by Howard Chaykin, John Moore and Mark Chiarullo, teams him with **Batman**; Tim Powers's *Expiration Date* (1995) features his mummified thumb.

Harry Houdini

Biopics with Tony Curtis (*Houdini*, 1953) and Paul Michael Glaser (*The Great Houdinis*, 1976) touch on his paranormal interests, but his celebrity, as enshrined in E.L. Doctorow's *Ragtime* (1975), rests on his stage act.

The Master Mystery/1918 * *The Grim Game*/1919 * *Terror Island*/1920 * *The Man From Beyond*/1921

Hough, John (b. 1941)

British director. Hough has maintained a profile through a transitional period in horror; in consequence, his later contributions are problematic. A TV habitué, he sold *Wolfshead: The Legend of Robin Hood* (1969) to Hammer and returned to the studio for

Twins of Evil (1971), the ambitious conclusion to the **'Carmilla'** trilogy. As with trend-straddling American co-production *The Legend of Hell House* (1973), it is improved by his brisk, broad-stroked captaincy. Successfully relocating Stateside, Hough made s-f thrillers for **Disney**: the horror-styled *Watcher in the Woods* (1980) was recut and newly appended. After the uncertain monster-**rape** item *Incubus* (1981), taken from Ray Russell's 1976 novel, he proceeded to unintentionally childish shockers *American Gothic* (1987) and *Howling IV: The Original Nightmare* (1988). He includes a ghost in *Triumphs of a Man Called Horse* (1984) and oversaw Peter **Cushing**'s swansong, *Biggles* (1985). DP

TV: *The Avengers*: 'The Super-Secret Cypher Snatch'/1968; 'The Morning After'/'Fog'/'Homicide and Old Lace'/1969 * *The New Avengers*: 'Cat Amongst the Pigeons'/1978 * *Hammer House of Mystery and Suspense*: 'Czech Mate'/'A Distant Scream'/'Black Carrion'/1984

The Hound of the Baskervilles * See **Sherlock Holmes**

House (1986)

Producer Sean S. **Cunningham** and director Steve **Miner** attempted to repeat the franchise success of the ***Friday the 13th*** series by updating the haunted house scenario with fright farce, **EC Comic** wind-ups, animatronic creatures and spooky suspense. Novelist William Katt is plagued by Vietnam nightmares and cute dream demons after

RIGHT *House*

moving into an old mansion. The non-threatening excess formula proved popular and Arye Gross took up residence to fight off the otherworldly evil in *House II: The Second Story* (1987), directed by the screewriter of the original, Ethan Wiley. Though planned as *House III: The Horror Show*, James Isaac's supernatural thriller lost the *House* tag in some territories because of its gruesomeness. Katt returns as a ghost in Lewis Abernathy's routine *House 4: The Repossession* (1991). AJ

Hoven, Adrian (Peter Hofkirchner) (1922–81)

Austrian actor, producer, writer, director. A German matinee idol whose fading credits include the Edgar **Wallace** *krimi Das Rätsel der roten Orchidee* (*The Secret of the Red Orchid*, 1962) and *Der Fluch Der grünen Augen* (*Cave of the Living Dead*, 1964), Hoven turned to production and enabled a trio of Jesús **Franco** films. *Succubus* (*Necronomicon*, 1967), the most important, influenced his own gory, pretentious *Im Schloss der blütigen Begierde* (*Castle of Lust*, 1967). Hoven rowed sufficiently with Michael **Armstrong** to co-direct reviled **witch hunt** opus *Hexen bis auf's Blut gequält* (*Mark of the Devil*, 1969), and found third wind as a featured player for Fassbinder (*Martha*, 1973). DP

Der Mörder mit dem Seidenschal (d)/1965 * *Küß mich, Monster/Rote Lippen* (p)/1967 * *Hexen – geschändet und zu Tode gequält* (d)/1973

The Howling (1981)

In conjunction with John **Landis**'s *An American Werewolf in London* (1981), Joe **Dante**'s hip horror parody revitalised the moribund **werewolf** genre. Both movies feature state-of-the-art transformation scenes, with Rob **Bottin** conceiving the *Howling* creature prosthetics. Based on a 1979 airport novel by Gary **Brandner**, maestro scripter John **Sayles** packed his tongue-in-cheek adaptation with stylish scares, off-beat characters, horror references and inside jokes. Dante added cameos from Roger **Corman** and Forrest J. **Ackerman** alongside star turns from Kevin McCarthy, John **Carradine**, Dick **Miller**, Patrick **MacNee**, Dee Wallace and Christopher Stone.

Though an amazingly successful video franchise, subsequent sequels (shot on four continents) do not match the original in terms of sly humour balanced with creepy shocks, though they often plumb depths of eccentric silliness: Philippe **Mora**'s Hammer-influenced *Howling II: Stirba – Werewolf Bitch*

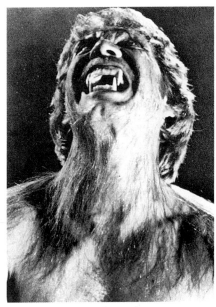

Christopher Stone, *The Howling*

(1986), with Christopher **Lee** and Sybil Danning; Mora's perverse farce *The Marsupials: Howling III* (1987); John **Hough**'s shoddy *Howling IV: The Original Nightmare* (1988); Neal Sundstrom's **Old Dark House** variant *Howling V: The Rebirth* (1989); Hope Perello's marginally intriguing werewolf-vs-**vampire** *Howling VI: The Freaks* (1990); Clive Turner's sub-amateur country and western bore *Howling VII: Mystery Woman* (1995). AJ

The Hunchback of Notre Dame

Victor Hugo's *Notre-Dame de Paris* (1831) is not merely, or perhaps even, a horror novel, but a vast historical tapestry set around the cathedral in 1482. A shift in public percep

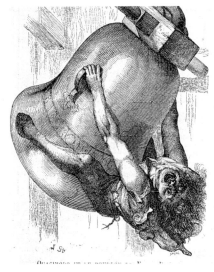

The Hunchback of Notre Dame (1872)

tion began with the retitling of the book in English translation, giving equal billing with the cathedral to Quasimodo, the **disfigured** bellringer. Quasimodo loves the gypsy Esmeralda, as do Claude Frollo, a scheming priest, and Phoebus, a handsome soldier. When Frollo murders Phoebus, Esmeralda is convicted of the crime. Quasimodo rescues her from the scaffold and claims sanctuary in Notre Dame. The ending is not happy: when Esmeralda is hanged, Quasimodo kills Frollo and steals his beloved's body. Quasimodo dies of a broken heart, leaving his skeleton entwined with Esmeralda's. Most films can't bear to be as depressing: in some silents, Quasimodo is even handsome enough to be a suitable partner for Esmeralda; in most talkies, the gypsy survives to be paired off with a deserving male.

Adaptations are *Esmeralda* (1906), with Henry Vorins; *Notre-Dame de Paris* (1911) with Henri Krauss; *Notre Dame* (1913); *The Darling of Paris* (1916), with Glen White and Theda Bara; *Esmeralda* (1922), with Booth Conway; *The Hunchback of Notre Dame* (1923), with Lon **Chaney**; *The Dancer of Paris* (1926), which omits Quasimodo; Indian versions called *Dhanwan* (1937), *Nav Jawan* (1937) and *Badshah Dampati* (1953); *The Hunchback of Notre Dame* (1939), with Charles **Laughton** and Maureen O'Hara; on *Robert Montgomery Presents* (1954), with Robert Ellenshaw; *Notre-Dame de Paris* (*The Hunchback of Notre Dame*, 1956), with Anthony Quinn and Gina Lollobrigida; *The Hunchback of Notre Dame* (1965) with Peter Woodthorpe; *The Hunchback of Notre Dame* (1978), with Warren Clarke; *The Hunchback of Notre Dame* (1981), with Anthony **Hopkins**; an Australian TV cartoon *The Hunchback of Notre Dame* (1985), with the voice of Tom Burlinson; and **Disney**'s more elaborately animated *The Hunchback of Notre Dame* (1996), with the voice of Tom Hulce. Quasimodo cameos include *Santo en el museo de cera* (1963) and *Mad Monster Party?* (1967).

There are also imitations and parodies: *The Hunchback* (1909), *Hugo the Hunchback* (1910), *The Loves of a Hunchback* (1910), *The Halfback of Notre Dame* (1923), *Big Man on Campus* (*The Hunchback of UCLA*, 1989), *Paul Norman's Hunchback of Notre Dame* (1991), *The Halfback of Notre Dame* (1996). Chaney's look is recreated in the 'Lon Chaney's Gonna Get You If You Don't Watch Out' number of *Hollywood Review of 1929* (1929), the cartoon *Mickey's Gala Premiere* (1933), the James Cagney Chaney biopic *Man of a Thousand Faces* (1957) and by Lon **Chaney Jr** in a

Cedric Hardwicke, Charles Laughton, *The Hunchback of Notre Dame* (1939)

Route 66 episode ('Lizard's Leg and Owlet's Wing', 1966). A *Way Out* episode ('Face in the Mirror', 1961) has actor Alfred Ryder transforming into Quasimodo for a play and finding his face stuck in a Dick **Smith** make-up.

Quasimodo entered the *Famous Monsters* pantheon because Chaney created one of his most elaborately disfigured make-up jobs for the 1923 movie. Laughton's successful re-reading of the role in William **Dieterle**'s fine film is less monstrous, but even more pathetic. If nothing else, Hugo changed the image of

hunchbacks: previously *Richard III*-style villains, they now tend to be ugly but devoted **minions** doing the bidding of mad authority figures like Frollo as they pine for lovely **heroines**. Exemplars in horror in-clude J. Carrol **Naish** in *House of Franken-stein* (1945) and Paul **Naschy** in *El jorobado de la morgue* (1972).

Hung, Samo [Hung Kim-Bo] (b. 1950) Hong Kong Chinese actor, director, producer, nicknamed Samo (literally 'four hair') for a comic book character. He studied Peking

Opera with classmate Jackie Chan before working as a stuntman, fight choreographer and popular star, then showed talented as an action actor/director. His facial scars and rotund body make him the most unusual fig-ure of Hong Kong martial arts cinema. He created the kung-fu-ghost comedy genre with *Gui Da Gui* (*Encounters of the Spooky Kind*, 1980), sequelised in *Gui Yao Gui* (*Encounters of the Spooky Kind II*, 1990). Wu Ma's *Ren Xia Ren* (*The Dead and the Deadly*, 1982) is one of his best vehicles, though *Gui Meng Jiao* (*Spooky! Spooky!*, 1986), *Gambling*

163

Hypnotism: Andrée Lafayette, Arthur Edmund Carewe, *Trilby* (1923)

Ghost (1991) and *Wufuxing Zhong Gui* (*Ghost Punting*, 1993) are easily forgotten. He acts in **Tsui** Hark's *San Susan Gimgap* (*Zu Warriors from the Magic Mountain*, 1983) and King Hu's *Hua Pi Zhi Yinyang Fawang* (*Painted Skin*, 1992), and produced but did not star in the *Jiangshi Xiansheng*/*Mr. Vampire* series (1985–92). CV

Ren Xia Gui [*Hocus Pocus*] (p)/1986

Hurst, Brandon (1866–1947)

British actor. A silent dastard, dashing as John **Barrymore**'s decadent mentor in *Dr. Jekyll and Mr. Hyde* (1920), Hurst became a character player in the talkies. A thin villain in **The Hunchback of Notre Dame** (1923) and *The Thief of Bagdad* (1924).

Legally Dead/1923 * *The Man Who Laughs*/ 1927 * *Murders in the Rue Morgue*/*White Zombie*/1932 * *The House of Mystery*/1934 * *The Great Impersonation*/1935 * *The Man in Half Moon Street*/1944 * *House of Frankenstein*/ 1945

Mr Hyde * See: Jekyll and Hyde

Hypnotism

From the unhelpful tinkerer who preserves a man beyond death in **Poe**'s 'The Facts in the Case of M. Valdemar' (1845) through vil-

lains like **Dracula**, **Svengali**, **Rasputin**, **Caligari** and **Mabuse**, mesmerists have a bad reputation. Evil hypnotists feature in *Dr. Mesner's Fatal Prescription* (1910), *Max Hypnotize* (1910), *In the Grip of a Charlatan* (1913), *The Magician* (1926), *The Climax* (1944), *The Woman in Green* (1945), *The Mask of Dijon* (1946), *Whirlpool* (1950), *Tales of Hoffmann* (1951), *The She-Creature* (1956), *I Was a Teenage Werewolf* (1957), *Blood of Dracula* (1957), *Horrors of the Black Museum* (1959), *The Hypnotic Eye* (1960), *Evil of Frankenstein* (1964), *The Devil Rides Out* (1968) and *Vampire at Midnight* (1988). Aside from the neutral **reincarnation** regression specialists of *The Search for Bridey Murphy* (1956), *The Undead* (1956) and *On a Clear Day You Can See Forever* (1970), rare good guy hypnotists force murderers to confess in *The Bells* (1913, 1914, 1914, 1918, 1926), *London After Midnight* (1927), *Calling Dr. Death* (1943) and *The Frozen Ghost* (1945).

I

I Love a Mystery (1939–52)

Created by Carlton E. Morse, this American **radio** show (sometimes *I Love Adventure*) follows Jack Packard, Doc Long and Reggie York of the A-1 Detective Agency in **pulp**-style macabre, exotic adventures. The origi-

nal cast was Michael Raffetto, Barton Yarbrough and Walter Patterson; subsequent voices included John McIntire, Jim Boles and Tony Randall. Typical serials: 'The Fear That Creeps Like a Cat', 'Bury Your Dead, Arizona', 'Temple of Vampires', 'Bride of the Werewolf'. Jim Bannon is Packard, with Yarbrough's Doc, in three decently weird 1945 Columbia Bs: *I Love a Mystery* (from 'The Decapitation of Jefferson Monk'), *The Unknown* (from 'The Thing That Cries in the Night') and *The Devil's Mask*. Les Crane, David Hartman and Hegan Beggs are the A-1 detectives in the **camp** unsold pilot *I Love a Mystery* (1966), a loose remake of *The Unknown*.

Image Animation

British special make-up effects partnership founded by Bob Keen and Geoff Portass to work on Clive **Barker**'s *Hellraiser* (1987). Veterans of *The Keep* (1984), *Lifeforce* (1985) and *Highlander* (1986), Keen has turned to direction (*To Catch a Yeti*, 1993, *Proteus*, 1995) and Portass is the creator of the BBC's **horror host** Dr Terror. Under the banner of 'Image Animation International', Gary Tunnicliffe handled *SleepStalker: The Sandman's Last Rites* (1995).

The Unholy/1987 * *The Lair of the White Worm*/ *Hellbound: Hellraiser II*/*Waxwork*/1988 * *The Hand of Death*/1989 * *Nightbreed*/*Hardware*/ *Hellgate*/*I Bought a Vampire Motorcycle*/1990 * *Hellraiser III: Hell on Earth*/*Waxwork II: Lost in Time*/*Candyman*/*Children of the Corn II: The Final Sacrifice*/1992 * *Cyborg Cop*/1993 * *Interview With the Vampire: The Vampire Chronicles*/1994 * *Lord of Illusions*/1995

TV: *Jekyll & Hyde*/1990 * *Chimera*/1991 * *Frankenstein*/1992

Immortality

The desire for immortality is universal but myth and literature tend, perhaps through frustration, to depict eternal life as a burden. Melmoth, Ayesha and **Dracula** could potentially live forever, but stories end with their deaths. True immortality is reserved for those doomed to suffer eternally, the **Wandering Jew** and the Flying Dutchman. Mike Resnick concludes in 'How I Wrote the New Testament, Ushered in the Renaissance, and Birdied the 17th Hole at Pebble Beach' (1991), 'as curses go, this is one of the better ones'. The issue is debated in Swift's *Gulliver's Travels* (1726), Shaw's *Back to Methuselah* (1921), Karel Capek's *The Makropoulos Secret* (1925), Huxley's *After*

Many a Summer (1939), Suzy McKee **Charnas**'s *The Vampire Tapestry* (1980) and Brian Stableford's *The Empire of Fear* (1988).

Highlander (1986), and sequels and spin-offs, mangles the old theme of a secret society of immortals; again, frequent decapitation deaths among these folk reveal them to be merely long-lived. A world-weary immortal seeking only death appears in *The Curse of the Mummy's Tomb* (1964); such death wishes afflict Dracula and the Wandering Jew in *The Satanic Rites of Dracula* (1973) and *The Seventh Sign* (1988). Mere longevity is achieved through science or magic in *The Man in Half Moon Street* (1944), *The Man Who Turned to Stone* (1957), *The Unearthly* (1957), *The Man Who Could Cheat Death* (1958), *Dr. Phibes Rises Again* (1972), *The Night Strangler* (1973), *Dr. Death: Seeker of Souls* (1973), *The Asphyx* (1972), 'Someone at the Top of the Stairs' (*Thriller*, 1973), *Lifespan* (1975) and *The Hunger* (1983).

Less ambitious are characters, always women, interested not in long life but renewed youth: *The Young Diana* (1922), *Black Oxen* (1923), *Vanity's Price* (1924), *One Way Street* (1925), *I vampiri* (*Lust of the Vampire*, 1957), *The Wasp Woman* (1960, 1995), *The Leech Woman* (1960), *La señora muerte* (1968), *Evil Spawn* (1987), *Rejuvenatrix* (1988), *The Immortaliser* (1989), *Death Becomes Her* (1992). Invariably, finales have the years catch up as supposed immortals do a gunk-dissolve to putrescence.

Incest

In *Dreadful Pleasures: An Anatomy of Modern Horror* (1985), academic James Twitchell suggests 'the fear of incest underlies all horror myths in our culture'. He believes **Dracula**, **Frankenstein** and the **werewolf** 'enjoy a long life because, within the horror that surrounds these monsters, there is a sexual truth preserved by our culture: a truth about incest so important that we feel uneasy explaining it, let alone even dreaming it'. He amasses supporting arguments but his thesis is too reductive. Possibly, Stephen **King**'s depiction of incestuous monsters in *Sleepwalkers* (1991) was influenced not by deep-rooted taboos but by a reading of Twitchell.

Nevertheless, incest is a distinct gothic theme: explicit in *The Monk* (1796), as Ambrosio is duped into raping his sister, implicit in **'The Fall of the House of Usher'** (1839), which turns on the 'unnatural' relationship of Roderick and Madeline. *Psycho* (1960) implies an incest actually depicted in *Psycho IV: The Beginning* (1990). More upsetting perhaps is *Twin Peaks Fire Walk With Me* (1993), which examines the wrecked life of Laura Palmer (Sheryl Lee), who has been often raped by her perhaps-possessed father. Child abuse, frequently involving incest, obsessively recurs in 90s horror, examined by Peter **Straub** (the 'Blue Rose' cycle), King ('The Library Police', 1990; *Dolores Claiborne*, 1992) and many lesser talents.

India

Though ancient epics *Ramayana* and *Mahabarata* feature hosts of **vampires**, ghouls and shapeshifters, censorship and social codes made Indian film a horror-free zone until the 70s, when violence and sex began to appear on screen. Pioneers Tulsi and Shyam **Ramsay** directed *Do Gaz Zameen Ke Neeche* (1972), India's first Western-style horror film. Others tentatively followed the lead. *Jaani Dushman* (1977) and *Jadu Tona* (1979), both briefly banned, conveniently typify the two Indian approaches to the genre: the first is a monster film, with a man murdered on his wedding night returning to prey on virgin brides; the second an *Exorcist* (1973) inspired possession drama.

Following a loosening of censorship in the mid-80s, a handful of horror specialists emerged. Vinod Talwar's *Raat Ke Andhere Mein* (1987), *Wohi Bhayaanak Raat* (1988) and *Hatyarin* (1991) are fast-paced and feature sex scenes that push the boundaries of censorship to their limits. Writer-producer-director Mohan Bhakri's *Kabrastan* (1988),

Roohani Taaqat (1991) and *Insaan Bana Shaitaan* (1992) are more hit and miss, but his *Khooni Mahal* (1987) is one of the liveliest Indian horrors. *Woh Phir Aayegi* (1987), *Bhayaanak Mahal* (1988) and *Kafan* (1990) are horror-filled versions of the **rape**-revenge stories that were an Indian staple throughout the 80s. Modern Indian horror cinema runs the gamut from the silly (*Andheri Raat*, 1990) to the sophisticated (*100 Days*, 1991). Ramgopal Varma's *Raat* (1992), with its prowling camera and low-key atmospherics, reveals the increasing European influence among a new generation of horror film-makers. PT

Indians * See: **American Indians**

Inner Sanctum

Inner Sanctum Mysteries (1941–52) was a popular **radio** horror anthology, hosted by hollow-voiced Raymond Johnson. The name was also used for pulp novels, a 1947 B, a 1954 TV series presented by Paul McGrath (Johnson's radio successor) and a 1991 erotic thriller. Universal produced *Inner Sanctum* mysteries with horror overtones, hosted by a head in a crystal ball (David Huffman), with Lon **Chaney Jr** often miscast as an intellectual: *Calling Dr. Death* (1943), *Weird Woman* (1944), *Dead Man's Eyes* (1944), *The Frozen Ghost* (1945), *Strange Confession* (1945), *Pillow of Death* (1945). *MAD*'s Wally Wood did a notable parody, 'Outer Sanctum'.

Inns

From Universal's 30s horrors to the **Hammer** Films of the 1950s, the Tran-

Inns: *Dracula's Daughter*

Insect and Arachnids

sylvanian or Olde Englande inn is an important set for the traditional monster movie. James **Whale**, Terence **Fisher** and a slew of character actors populate these inns with whiskery peasants, tipsy policemen, mumbling **body-snatchers**, superstitious *babushkas* and gibbering loons, all ready to cease chatter when an unwary traveller asks directions to Castle **Dracula**, eager to dispense ominous warnings, crucifixes and garlic. Last of these traditional hostelries is 'The Slaughtered Lamb' of *An American Werewolf in London* (1981). Pubs are primary settings for *The Invisible Man* (1933), *The Black Raven* (1943), *Devil Girl From Mars* (1954), *The Strange World of Planet X* (1958) and *Revenge* (1971). Michael **Ripper**, a soak in *The Mummy* (1959) and *The Curse of the Werewolf* (1961), a publican in *The Reptile* (1966) and *Scars of Dracula* (1970), spent a career in inns. American equivalents are less popular, but there is a memorable road house massacre in *Near Dark* (1987) and *From Dusk Till Dawn* (1996) is set in a topless bar.

Insanity * See: **Psychopaths**.

Insects and Arachnids

The giant ants of *Them!* (1954) were part of an inspired and, at the time, all too feasible science-fiction concept. With the equally

Insects: Joan Weldon, Edmund Gwenn, *Them!*

alarming *Tarantula!* (1955), *Them!* tends now to be lumped together with the many monster B-movies that followed as the most risible evidence of Atomic Age paranoia: *The Beginning of the End* (1957), *The Deadly Mantis* (1957), *Monster From Green Hell* (1957), *The*

Insects: Al Hedison, Patricia Owens, *The Fly* (1958)

Spider (1958). Occasionally revived (*The Giant Spider Invasion*, 1975; *Empire of the Ants*, 1977), giant bugs are absurdly old-fashioned, even in a 90s mini-boom: *Ticks* (1993), *Skeeter* (1994), *Mosquito* (1995).

The catastrophic experiment of *The Fly* (1958) was another horrible idea that fired public imagination; two sequels ensued. In 1986, the original was remade with typical ferocity by David **Cronenberg**; this too produced a sequel. *The Fly* is parodied in 'Mant!', the film-within-a-film of *Matinee* (1993). Other human-to-bug transformations, less challenging than that of **Kafka**'s 'Die Verwandlung' ('Metamorphosis', 1915), appear in *The Wasp Woman* (1959), *The Blood Beast Terror* (1968), *Invasion of the Bee Girls* (1973), *The Nest* (1987), *A Nightmare on Elm Street, Part IV: The Dream Master* (1988) and *The Wasp Woman* (1995). Uniquely, *Meet the Applegates* (1990) has insect-to-human transformations.

Swarms of malevolent, often super-intelligent (normal-sized) bugs have appeared since the 60s: *Phase IV* (1973), *Bug* (1975), *Kingdom of the Spiders* (1977), *Dap Bin* (*Butterfly Murders*, 1979), *Arachnophobia* (1990). The most durable entomological threat comes from the bee: *The Deadly Bees* (1967), *Killer Bees* (1974), *The Savage Bees* (1976), *The Swarm* (1978), *The Bees* (1978), *Terror Out of the Sky* (1978), *Deadly Invasion: The Killer Bee Nightmare* (1994). Bug/human communication features in *Kiss of the*

Tarantula (1972) and *Phenomena* (1984). Probably the most hated insect, the cockroach, features surprisingly rarely in horror, and usually as a shock effect: in the climax of *Creepshow* (1982), cockroaches crawl out of E.G. Marshall's body. DM

Interactive

Though video games have been around since the late 70s, horror has been slow to reach the format. The rise of second-generation console machines like the Sega Saturn and Sony Playstation, together with developments in CD-ROM-led technology have opened the field, offering heightened graphics and sound. In addition, the more adult content of video games has, in the mid-90s, led to the introduction of censorship guidelines similar to those imposed on film. A game showing excessive violence or horrific content can be rated as being for certain age groups only, or alternatively given a BBFC film certificate. Though violence in what is still considered a medium for children may be frowned upon, a ratings system allows more freedom for graphic content.

Perhaps the best use of horror in the video game is *Doom* (1992), whose simple but effective formula offers the player a chance to escape a fearsome creature by blasting away everything. Despite a violence quotient that proved too much for some, *Doom* quickly became a smash hit: one American company eventually had to ban it from their office computers after lunchtime playing sessions among the staff spiralled into the afternoon and beyond. *Doom II* (1993) made its mark on the public psyche thanks to an advertisement featuring the game against a backdrop of bloodstained offal. Many imitations have failed to match *Doom*'s impact, though the Sony Playstation's *Kileak the Blood* (1995) is superior.

Other notable video game horrors: the interactive movie *Hell* (1994), starring Dennis Hopper; a remarkable, graphically perfect PC retelling of **Frankenstein**, in which the player has to take on the role of the creature brought to life by a cackling Tim Curry; and *Phantasmagoria* (1995), a role-playing game so extreme that it comes complete with a gore button embedded in code form deep within the game, allowing users to shield younger players from the bloody mayhem on offer. CW

Invasion of the Body Snatchers
Jack Finney's novel *The Body Snatchers* (1955), ostensibly s-f as **alien** seedpods sprout doubles which replace humans, is actually a horror fantasy on the ***doppelgänger*** theme. One of the most durable myths of the late 20th century, it is open to political, social, psychological and philosophical interpretations. It was filmed as *Invasion of the Body Snatchers* (1956, 1978), by Don Siegel with Kevin McCarthy and Phil Kaufman with Donald Sutherland, and as *Body Snatchers* (1993) by Abel **Ferrara** with Gabrielle Anwar. The Siegel, which uses Finney's small-town setting, is a paranoid classic, climaxing as McCarthy shrieks 'you're next' at the audience. The remakes function also as sequels and revisions: Kaufman extends the pod invasion to the big city of San Francisco and Ferrara uses an army base, catching the moods of their decades as Siegel, with screenwriter Daniel Mainwaring, catches the unease of the 50s.

There are aliens-among-us precursors, homages and rip-offs, some using mind control rather than replacement: *Invaders From Mars* (1954), *It Conquered the World* (1956), *I Married a Monster From Outer Space* (1958), *Quatermass 2* (1958), *The Day Mars Invaded the Earth* (1963), *The Invaders* (1967–8), *The Body Stealers* (1969), 'Amazing Stories' (*Red Letter Day*, 1976), *Strange Invaders* (1983), *They Live* (1988), *Seedpeople* (1992), *The Puppet Masters* (1994). Ira **Levin**'s *The Stepford Wives* (1972; filmed 1974) is a rare reuse of the theme to a specific end, addressing sexual paranoia as suburban husbands willingly replace wives with home-making bunnies.

The Invisible Man (1897)
H.G. **Wells**'s novel offers a scientific rationale for an old magic theme. James **Whale**'s 1932 film, with Claude **Rains** as transparent scientist Jack Griffin, coined the visual **clichés** of the genre: unwinding bandages revealing empty space, faces briefly outlined by smoke or rain, slow fades to or from nothing. Universal spun a minor franchise: *The Invisible Man Returns* (1940), with Vincent **Price**, *Invisible Agent* (1942) and *The Invisible Man's Revenge* (1944), with Jon Hall, and parodies *The Invisible Woman* (1940) and (**Abbott and Costello**) *. . . Meet the Invisible Man* (1951). Strictly, the series belongs to s-f, though there is a strain of *guignol* in the side-effects of the drug monocaine, which drives Griffin and his successors to madness and murder, and settings, players and plots crossover with other Universal monster cycles. Spin-offs include (Abbott and Costello) *Meet Frankenstein* (1948), with an uncredited, unseen Price cameo; *El hombre que lobro ser invisible* (*H.G. Wells' New Invisible Man*, 1957), a remake of *The Invisible Man Returns*; and *Amazon Women on the Moon* (1987), with Ed

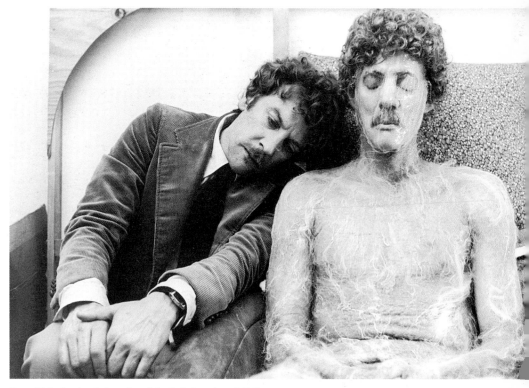

Donald Sutherland, *Invasion of the Body Snatchers* (1978)

Begley Jr doing Rains's voice as 'Son of the Invisible Man'

The novel was remade on *Hour of Mystery* (1957) with Chet Stratton (1957) and for the BBC as a 1984 serial with Philip Donaghy, and lent its name to unrelated adventure series in 1958, with Tim Turner, and 1975, with David McCallum. Related invisibles: *The Body Disappears* (1941), *The Invisible Monster* (1950), *The Amazing Transparant Man* (1960), *Die Ünsichtbaren Krallen des Dr. Mabuse* (*The Invisible Dr. Mabuse*, 1962), *Der unsichtbare* (*The Invisible Terror*, 1963), *El enmascadaro de ora contra el asesino invisible* (*The Invisible Murderer*, 1964), *El hombre invisible ataca* (1967), *Orloff y el hombre invisible* (*The Invisible Dead*, 1970), *Memoirs of an Invisible Man* (1993), *Invisible: The Chronicles of Benjamin Knight* (1993). Invisibility features in outright horrors like *The Invisible Maniac* (1990), advertised with 'out of sight and out of his mind', and as a budget-cutting measure in the likes of *Phantom From Space* (1953) and *El sonido prehistorico* (*The Sound of Horror*, 1965), which feature invisible aliens and dinosaurs.

Irish, William * See: **Woolrich, Cornell**

Ironside, Michael (b. 1950)

Balding, forceful Canadian actor. Since his skull-popping first impression as the evil psychic of *Scanners* (1981), a regular villain and

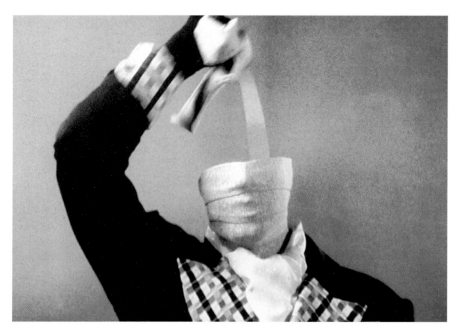

Invisibility: Chevy Chase, *Memoirs of an Invisible Man*

occasional cop. Despite high-profile gigs in *Total Recall* (1990) and *Highlander 2: The Quickening* (1991), happiest as a low-budget maniac.

American Nightmare/1981 * *Visiting Hours*/1982 * *The Surrogate*/1984 * *Hello Mary Lou: Prom Night 2*/1987 * *Watchers*/1988 * *Destiny to Order*/1989 * *Mindfield*/1990 * *Drop Dead Gorgeous*/1991 * *The Vagrant*/*Sweet Killing*/1992 * *Night Trap*/1993 * *Starship Troopers*/1996

TV: *The Sins of Dorian Gray*/1983 * *The Hitchhiker*: 'Dead Man's Curve'/1986 * *Alfred Hitchcock Presents*: 'Man on the Edge'/1987 * *Ray Bradbury Theatre*: 'The Fruit at the Bottom of the Bowl'/1988 * *Tales From the Crypt*: 'The Sacrifice'/1990

The Island of Dr. Moreau (1896)

H.G. **Wells**'s novel combines Darwinian evolutionary parabola, Swiftian human-beast satire, the **Frankenstein/mad scientist** character, vivisection horror and South Seas adventure as the shipwrecked Edward Prendick discovers scientific tinkerer Moreau surgically raising beasts to semi-humanity in his House of Pain but despairing as they regress to a brutishness that may be as typical of humankind as their love of ritual and law. It's a brilliant work, and a gift to cinema: Erle C. **Kenton**'s *Island of Lost Souls*

LEFT Invisibility: Claude Rains, *The Invisible Man* (1932)

(1932) has Charles **Laughton** as a flabby, whip-wielding scientist lecherously prizing Panther Woman Kathleen Burke and whipping fuzz-faced Sayer of the Law **Lugosi**.

Remakes using Wells's title came in 1977, with Don Taylor directing and Burt Lancaster transforming Michael York, and 1995, with John Frankenheimer taking over direction from writer Richard Stanley and Marlon Brando's Moreau collaborating with Val Kilmer in the creation of Fairuza Balk. Unofficial passes: *Ilê d'epouvante* (1913), *Terror is a Man* (1959), *The Mad Doctor of Blood Island* (1969), *The Twilight People* (1972). Literary footnotes come from Gene Wolfe ('The Island of Dr. Death and Other Stories', 1970), Brian Aldiss (*Moreau's Other Island*, (1980) and Kim Newman (*Anno Dracula*, 1992).

Islands

The uncharted island, either deserted or inhabited by strange creatures, human or animal, is the stuff of legend. Some outstanding horror films are associated with islands: *Island of Lost Souls* (1932), **The Most Dangerous Game** (1932), **King Kong** (1933), *I Walked with a Zombie* (1943), *Isle of the Dead* (1945), *Lord of the Flies* (1963, 1990), *Jurassic Park* (1993). Cult trash set on islands: *Attack of the Crab Monsters* (1957), *The Flesh Eaters* (1961), *They Saved Hitler's Brain* (1963), *The Mad Doctor of Blood Island* (1969), *Tower of Evil* (1971), *Zombi 2* (*Zombie Flesh Eaters*, 1979).

Agatha **Christie** may have been first (in

Ten Little Niggers, 1939) to isolate a murderer and his victims on an island, but the first of countless films on this theme is *Horror Island* (1941). Other oddities deserving of mention include the monster-invaded islands of *Island of Terror* (1967) and *Night of the Big Heat* (1967); *The Island* (1980), with Michael Caine held prisoner by a primitive pirate society; and *It's Alive III: Island of the Alive* (1986), on which the famous monster kids are quarantined. Actual islands are seldom used as locations (apart from establishing shots); exceptions are Staten Island, where director Andy **Milligan** shot many of his early films, and the Greek locales favoured by Nico **Mastorakis**. DM

It's Alive

Larry **Cohen** has directed, produced and written three pictures combining sensationalist monster horror with social issues: *It's Alive* (1975), *It Lives Again* (1978) and *It's Alive III: Island of the Alive* (1986). In the trilogy, **mutant babies** are born and run murderously amok, but parents and authorites are forced to assess their responsibility for the monsters. The films benefit from interesting leading men (John Ryan, Frederic Forrest, Michael **Moriarty**), a reused Bernard **Herrmann** score and a Rick **Baker** make-up monstrosity at its most effective when kept in the shadows.

J

Jackson, Peter (b. 1961)

New Zealand director, writer. The hand-to-mouth, in-your-face *Bad Taste* (1987) and *Brain Dead* (1992) take Sam **Raimi**'s already extreme splatsick **comedy** style to the outer limits of **splatter**. Unlike *Meet the Feebles* (1989), Jackson's mean-spirited Muppet parody, these hit-or-miss movies are doggily endearing, their kiwi sensibility represented by jokes about sheep and *The Archers*. *Heavenly Creatures* (1994), based on a New Zealand murder case of the 50s, follows a strange schoolgirl relationship: it is a major advance, sensitive where the earlier films are bludgeoning, entering a private fantasy at once magical and sinister. *The Frighteners* (1996), a more genial horror comedy, also locates a perverse killer couple at the heart of its CGI-lit darkness. In 1996, he announced a remake of *King Kong* (1933).

RIGHT Islands: Fay Wray, Minion, Leslie Banks, *The Most Dangerous Game*

Michael Ironside, *Highlander II: The Quickening*

Jackson, Shirley (1919–65)

American writer. Though her slim *oeuvre* is remarkable for consistent, quiet brilliance, Jackson retains a genre profile on the strength of 'The Lottery' (1945), a perfect *conte cruel* (adapted on *Robert Herridge Theatre*, 1961), and *The Haunting of Hill House* (1959), a **ghost story** (filmed as *The Haunting*, 1963). The typical Jackson protagonist is a middle-aged woman persecuted by insecurities which spiral into the horrific or the supernatural. *The Bird's Nest* (1954), a psychological study filmed as *Lizzie* (1957), and *We Have Always Lived in the Castle* (1962) are ambitious and strange.

Lenemaja Friedman, *Shirley Jackson* (1975)

Jack the Ripper

British (at least, British-based) murderer (or murderers). Though the deaths of between up to nine **prostitutes** have been attributed to him (or her) from 1887 to 1893, his six most likely **victims** were claimed in Whitechapel, in the East End of London, in the late summer and autumn of 1888. Known at first as 'Leather Apron' or 'The Whitechapel Murderer', the **serial murderer** gained his 'trade name' from (probably spurious) letters purporting to be from the killer sent to a news agency. Never caught or identified, he was freed from history to become a recurrent bogeyman, transforming in the popular imagination from the savage foreigner described by those who wished to deny such a fiend could be English into a bourgeois **psychopath** (perhaps a surgeon, maybe a Royal) whose sexual **violence** epitomises Victorian hypocrisy.

The first non-fiction books on the case had appeared by the end of 1888, almost before Mary Kelly (last and most extensively dissected victim) was buried: the anonymous

Jack the Ripper

The Whitechapel Murders, or: The Mysteries of the East End, Richard Kyle Fox's *The History of the Whitechapel Murders: A Full and Authentic Narrative of the Above Murders with Sketches*. For over a century, the facts have been studied (and distorted) by serious historians, sensationalist journalists and sheer cranks. William Stewart's *Jack the Ripper: A New Theory* (1939) is the foundation of many volumes of true crime writing, which mostly serve to elevate an author's pet suspect and frequently transgress the strict limits of the non-fiction category.

The most famous, and most arrantly fraudulent, examples are Stephen Knight's *Jack the Ripper: The Final Solution* (1976), which puts forth a Masonic conspiracy theory indicting Queen Victoria's court physician Sir William Gull, and the anonymous *The Diary of Jack the Ripper* (1993), which presents itself as the confession of a famous murder *victim*, James Maybrick. Both have been a spur to honest fiction: the diary affair is cleverly fictionalised by Peter Ackroyd's *Dan Leno and the Limehouse Golem* (1994). Among the useful books of 'Ripperology' (Colin Wilson's coinage): Paul Begg, Martin Fido and Keith Skinner's *The Jack the Ripper A to Z* (1991), Philip Sugden's *The Complete History of Jack the Ripper* (1994). Film and TV documentaries include *Primitive London* (1965), *The London Nobody Knows* (1967), *The Secret Identity of Jack the Ripper* (1988), 'Shadow of the Ripper' (*Timewatch*, 1988), 'Who Was Jack the Ripper?' (*Crime Monthly Special*, 1990), *The Diary of Jack the Ripper* (1993), 'The Whitechapel Murders' (*Secret History*, 1996).

The first fictionalising of the case, discounting fanciful articles in the *Police Gazette*, is J.F. Brewer's *The Curse Upon Mitre Square* (1889), a precursor to *The Hidden* (1988) in which the ghost of a mad monk possesses a series of weak-willed individuals and drives them to murder. The first literary heavyweight to tackle Jack is Frank Wedekind, who uses the Ripper to dispose of Lulu, minx heroine of his plays *Erdgeist* (1895) and *Die Büchse der Pandora* (1902). Alban Berg made these into an opera, *Lulu* (1937), and the story is oft-filmed, most importantly by G.W. Pabst as *Die Büchse der Pandora* (*Pandora's Box*, 1928) with Louise Brooks as Lulu and Gustav Diessl as Jack. Other versions: *Erdgeist* (1923), *Lulu* (*No Orchids for Lulu*, 1962), the minimalist *Lulu* (1978), a

French TV *Lulu* (1978), a televised opera *Lulu* (1979) and **Borowczyk**'s *Lulu* (1980) with Udo **Kier**.

Marie Belloc Lowndes's 'The Lodger' (1911), which she expanded into a 1913 novel, has an ordinary family suspect that Mr Sleuth, their mysterious lodger, is the murderer stalking London. *The Lodger: A Story of the London Fog* (1927), Alfred **Hitchcock**'s first notable film, has Ivor Novello as a lodger who turns out not to be the murderer known as the Avenger but a victim's relative out to track down the killer. Novello stars again in Maurice Elvey's 1932 remake (aka *The Phantom Fiend*) but John **Brahm**'s definitive *The Lodger* (1944) is the first explicitly to make its villain Jack the Ripper, with Laird **Cregar** as the sinister Mr Slade and claustrophobic use of Victorian clutter. Hugo Fregonese's *Man in the Attic* (1953), with Jack **Palance**, is an exact remake. A TV version of Phyllis Tait's opera of *The Lodger* appeared in 1964, and Charles **Gray** took the title role for an episode of *Armchair Mystery Theatre* (1965). *Room to Let* (1949), from a **radio** play by Margery Allingham, is a variation, with Valentine **Dyall** as Dr Fell, a sinister lodger revealed as Jack the Ripper.

Among the historical novels dealing with

the case are Patrice Chaplin's *By Flower and Dean Street* (1976), Richard Gordon's *The Private Life of Jack the Ripper* (1980), Robert **Bloch**'s *Night of the Ripper* (1984), Pamela West's *Yours Truly, Jack the Ripper* (1987), Alan Moore and Eddy Campbell's comic *From Hell* (1990-), Paul West's *The Women of Whitechapel* (1991), *The Cry From Street to Street* (1992) and Richard **Laymon**'s *Savage* (1993). Ripper stories are collected in Michel **Parry**'s *Jack the Knife: Tales of Jack the Ripper* (1975), Martin H. Greenberg, Charles Waugh and Frank McSherry's *Red Jack* (1988) and Susan Casper and Gardner Dozois's *Jack the Ripper* (1988). Ron Pember and Denis Marne staged a musical *Jack the Ripper* (1974), while Screaming Lord Sutch and Link Wray both cut 1963 hits called 'Jack the Ripper' (1963) and DJ Cool weighed in with an inevitable 'Jack the Rapper' (1988).

The murders resonate down the years in Colin Wilson's *Ritual in the Dark* (1960), Frederick Lindsay's *Jill Rips* (1987), Terence Lore Smith's *Yours Truly, From Hell* (1987), Iain Sinclair's *White Chappell, Scarlet Tracings* (1988); the films *Jack el destripador de Londres* (1971), *The Ruling Class* (1972), *Jack's Back* (1988), *Fatal Exposure* (1989) and *Deadly Advice* (1994); and the TV episodes 'Alias the

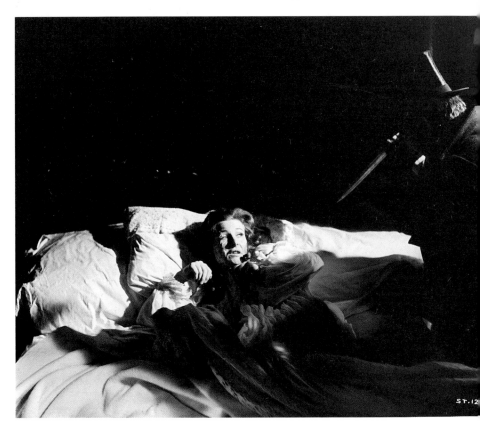

RIGHT Jack the Ripper: Adrienne Corri, John Fraser, *A Study in Terror*

Scarf' (*The Green Hornet*, 1967), 'Fog' (***The Avengers***, 1969), 'Ghost of the Ripper' (*Vega$*, 1979) and 'Dr. Ziegler's Casebook' (*Jemima Shore Investigates*, 1983). These mostly have the Ripper influencing copycat killings – sometimes on anniversaries of the original murders – but Bloch's short story 'Yours Truly, Jack the Ripper' (1943), adapted as a 1961 ***Thriller***, renders the murderer himself immortal by a magical blood rite.

Bloch later carried Jack into the future through time travel in the story 'A Toy for Juliette' (1967), which Harlan **Ellison** sequelised in 'The Prowler in the City at the Edge of Forever' (1969), and **alien possession** in 'Wolf in the Fold' (*Star Trek*, 1967). This approach is reused by writers R. **Chetwynd-Hayes** ('The Gatecrasher', 1971; filmed in *From Beyond the Grave*, 1973), Philip José Farmer (*The Gods of Riverworld*, 1984); films *Time After Time* (1979), with David **Warner** as a definitive Jack, *Bridge Across Time* (1986) and *The Ripper* (1985); and TV episodes 'The Ripper' (*Kolchak: The Night Stalker*, 1974) and 'Comes an Inquisitor' (*Babylon 5*, 1994).

Jack has been mixed up with Tarzan (Philip José Farmer's *A Feast Unknown*, 1969), **Batman** (*Gotham By Gaslight*, 1988) and **Dracula** (Kim Newman's *Anno Dracula*, 1992), but his most lasting fictional association is with **Sherlock Holmes**. The Great Detective was first set to catch the killer by W.S. Baring-Gould in *Sherlock Holmes: A Biography of the World's First Consulting Detective* (1962). Subsequent stabs are Michael Dibdin's *The Last Sherlock Holmes Story* (1978), Arthur Byron Cover's *An East Wind Coming* (1979), Ray Walsh's *The Mycroft Memoranda* (1984), M.J. Trow's *Lestrade and the Ripper* (1988), Edward B. Hanna's *The Whitechapel Horrors* (1992) and Geoffrey A. Landis's 'The Singular Habits of Wasps' (1994). Films on the theme are *A Study in Terror* (1965), with John Neville apprehending John Fraser, and *Murder By Decree* (1979), with Christopher Plummer and James Mason exposing the Masonic conspiracy.

Murder By Decree is based on a TV docudrama *Jack the Ripper* (1974), in which the sleuths who solve the case are the BBC's own 60s coppers Barlow (Stratford Johns) and Watt (Frank Windsor). Producer David Wickes returned with the centenary miniseries *Jack the Ripper* (1988), which ditches the discredited Mason business but still

accuses Gull (Ray McAnally). One of the trumped-up suspects is the actor Richard Mansfield (Armand Assante), who was appearing in London in the roles of **Jekyll and Hyde** in 1888. An identification between the real murderer and R.L. **Stevenson**'s split personality was made at the time, especially by those who felt Jack was more likely to be a distinguished surgeon than an immigrant dockyard layabout. Hyde is actually shown to be the guilty party in the persons of Martine **Beswick** (*Dr. Jekyll and Sister Hyde*, 1971) and Anthony **Perkins** (*Edge of Sanity*, 1988).

The mad surgeon theory is spotlighted by *Room to Let*, the first film actually to use the victims' real names, and 'Jack the Ripper' (1958), an episode of a TV series *The Veil* recycled as an anthology feature *Jack the Ripper*, which dramatises an anecdote about the psychic Robert James Lees, who features in *Murder By Decree* and *Jack the Ripper*

(1988), and is the first treatment even to attempt historical accuracy. Far less scrupulous are *Jack the Ripper* (1959), with Ewen Solon, *Das Ungeheuer von London* (*The Monster of London City*, 1964) and *Jack the Ripper* (1976), with Klaus **Kinski**, which reshuffle in increasingly gory manner archetypal images of swirling **fog**, East End knees-ups, cockney trollops, black bags of scalpels, glowering doctors and whistle-tooting bobbies.

Since *Farmer Spudd and His Missus Take a Trip to Town* (1915), a statue of Jack has been mandatory for **waxwork** films; Paul **Wegener** plays one which comes to life in *Das Wachsfigurenkabinett* (*Waxworks*, 1924). Witness: 'The New Exhibit' (***The Twilight Zone***, 1963), *Terror in the Wax Museum* (1973), *Waxwork* (1988) and *Waxwork II: Lost in Time* (1992). The Ripper has stalked series TV, turning up unexpectedly in the Western 'Killer With a Knife' (*Cimarron Strip*, 1967) but more familiarly in **Alfred Hitchcock Presents** ('The Hands of Mr. Ottermole', 1957), **The Sixth Sense** ('With Affection, Jack the Ripper', 1972), *Cribb* ('Swing, Swing Together', 1980), *Fantasy Island* ('With Affection, Jack the Ripper', 1980) and **Beyond Reality** ('The Passion', 1993).

Hammer's *Hands of the Ripper* (1971), from Edward Spencer Shew's novel, with Angharad Rees as Jack's possessed daughter, is a rare thoughtful take on the story, albeit punctuated by hatpin eye-gougings. More typical of the way a once-feared murderer has become something of a clown are *Here Come the Girls* (1953), with Robert Strauss as Jack the Slasher, and *The Wrong Box* (1966), with Tutte Lemkow as the Brighton Strangler, the sex films *What the Swedish Butler Saw* (1974) and *Jack the Stripper* (1991), Sterling Hayden as General Jack D. Ripper in *Dr. Strangelove; or: How I Learned to Stop Worrying and Love the Bomb* (1964) and the perhaps apocryphal *Black the Ripper* (1975). All this, and a great deal of allegedly more serious scholarship, is best encapsulated by the 'Bullshit or Not' segment of *Amazon Women on the Moon* (1986), in which Henry **Silva** asks, 'Was the Loch Ness Monster Jack the Ripper?'

Judith R. Wilkowitz, *City of Dreadful Delight: Narratives of Sexual Danger in Late Victorian London* (1992); Christopher Frayling, *The House That Jack Built* (1997)

James, Montague Rhodes
(1862–1936)

Famous for **ghost stories** (he wrote no other fiction), James treated them as a hobby, devoting himself to biblical scholarship and duties as provost of Eton. His collections are *Ghost Stories of an Antiquary* (1904), *More Ghost Stories of an Antiquary* (1911), *A Thin Ghost, and Others* (1919) and *A Warning to the Curious* (1925). His stature within a limited field is such that purists claim any ghost story not modelled on his template does not count.

His cosy chilliness prompts some to seek deeper neurosis in his finely constructed scary stories while others suggest he is exactly the mild-mannered Crypt Keeper he seems. Jonathan Miller, who directed 'Whistle and I'll Come to You' (a 1968 episode of the arts documentary series *Omnibus*, from 'Oh Whistle and I'll Come to You, My Lad', 1905), is a prober, drawing from Michael Hordern a performance suggesting quivering depths underlying English

eccentricity. S.T. Joshi's revisionary essay in *The Weird Tale* (1990) tries to limit James's reputation in order to elevate more ambitious writers.

Steeped in arcane scholarship, queer detail and convincing historical furniture, James's stories are distinctive and eerie, though his supposed mastery of subtle horror (like Val **Lewton**'s) is trumpeted by those who ignore an emphasis on the physically repellent scattered throughout the works. Like **Lovecraft**, James emphasises the intangible to such a degree that he is not often filmed, though Jacques **Tourneur**'s *Night of the Demon* (*Curse of the Demon*, 1958) is a masterly elaboration on 'Casting the Runes' (1911). Unsurprisingly, James is a mainstay of **radio** horror: a 40s 'Oh Whistle and I'll Come to You, My Lad' hosted by Valentine **Dyall** on *Appointment With Fear* has stayed with listeners for a lifetime.

TV: *Great Ghost Tales*: 'Room 13'/1961 * *Mystery and Imagination*: 'The Tractate Middoth'/'Lost Hearts'/'Number 13'/1966; 'Casting the Runes'/1968 * *A Ghost Story for Christmas*: 'The Stalls of Barchester'/1971; 'A Warning to the Curious'/1972; 'Lost Hearts'/1973; 'The Treasure of Abbot Thomas'/1974; 'The Ash Tree'/1975 * *Casting the Runes*/1979 * *Classic Ghost Stories*/1986

R.W. Pfaff, *Montague Rhodes James* (1980); Michael Cox, *M.R. James: An Informal Portrait* (1983)

James, Peter (b. 1948)

British writer. Originally a Canadian-based producer with a hand in *Dead of Night* (1972), *Blue Blood* (1973), *Sunday in the Country* (1975) and *Biggles* (1986), James turned novelist with the thriller *Dead Letter Drop* (1981). He specialises in meticulously researched, pleasingly melodramatic horror: *Possession* (1988), *Dreamer* (1989), *Sweet Heart* (190), *Twilight* (1991), *Prophecy* (1992), *Host* (1993), *Alchemist* (1996).

TV: *Chiller*: 'Prophecy' (st)/1995 * *The Shining* (a)/1996

Jane Eyre (1847)

Charlotte Brontë's romance has gothic trappings, like the mad wife in the attic who embodies the suffocating sins of the past, which tip adaptations into semi-horror. Jane and Rochester are played by Ethel Grandin and Irving Cummings (1914), Virginia Bruce and Colin **Clive** (1934), Joan Fontaine and Orson **Welles** (1943), Susannah York and

George C. Scott (1971), Zelah Clarke and Timothy Dalton (1983) and Charlotte Gainsbourg and William Hurt (1995). Jean Rhys's **voodoo**-haunted *Wide Sargasso Sea* (1966), filmed in 1992 with Karina Lombard and Nathaniel Parker, is about the first Mrs Rochester.

Japan

Japanese cinema is a cinema of genres. The **ghost story** (*kaidan eiga*) has been one of the most popular, with dozens of films produced during the 40s and 50s. Often based on kabuki stage pieces, they were released in the clammy summer months to coincide with O-Bon (the festival of the dead). *Tokaido Yotsuya Kaidan* (*Story of the Yotsuya Ghost*) has been filmed numerous times, most famously in 1959 by Nobuo Nakagawa, the foremost Japanese horror specialist. Nakagawa also directed *Onna Kyuketsuki* (1959), a rare **vampire** film, and the startling *Jigoku* (*Hell*, 1960). Japanese ghosts can also take the form of animals: **snakes**, foxes and above all **cats**. Female cat vampires feature in *Kaibyo Ranbu* (1956), *Kaibyo Noroi No Kabe* (1958) and *Kuroneko* (1968), the latter directed by Kaneto Shindo, who made the atmospheric *Onibaba* (1964). Another popular ghost story from an ancient Chinese source is the *Botan Doro* (*Peony Lantern*): this tale of a man in love with a dead woman has inspired many films, including Kenji Mizoguchi's classic *Ugetsu Monogatari* (*Tales of the Pale Moon After Rain*, 1953) and an episode of Masaki Kobayashi's highly stylised *Kwaidan* (1964).

The cruel tales of horror pioneer Edogawa Rampo form the basis for *Kyofu Kikei Ningen* (1969), *Moju* (1969) and Noboru Tanaka's *Yaneura no Sanposha* (*Stroller in the Attic*, 1976), one of the 'roman(tic) porno' series produced by the Nikkatsu company. The sado-horror hybrid also gave rise to *Hiroku Onnaro* (1967), *Tokugawa Onna Keibatsushi* (1968) and many films by the controversial Koji Wakamatsu (*Okasareta Byakui*/*Violated Angels*, 1967; *Sekusu Jakku*/*Sex Jack*, 1970). More Western influenced is the vampire trilogy of Michio Yamamoto: *Chi o Suu Ningyo* (*The Vampire Doll*, 1970), *Chi o Suu Me* (*Lake of Dracula*, 1971) and *Chi o Suu Bara* (*Evil of Dracula*, 1975). Outer space vampires feature in the gruesome *Kyuketsuki Gokemidoro* (*Goké, Bodysnatcher From Hell*, 1968) directed by B-movie maestro Hajime Sato.

From the late 60s there was a mixing of genres: *Kairyu Daikessen* (*The Magic Serpent*,

1966) includes giant monsters, swordplay and evil wizards; *Kurotokage* (*Black Lizard*, 1968), based on another Rampo story, is a camp, art/horror extravaganza; *Makai Tensho* (*Samurai Reincarnation*, 1981) unites historical, martial arts and horror genres; Nobuhiko Obayashi's *Ijintachi Tono Natsu* (*The Discarnates*, 1989) is a gore-drenched but subtle ghost story, with dead parents and a suicide teaching an insensitive writer lessons. Theatre director Takeshi Kawamura revised two classic Western horror myths in *Rasuto Furankenshutain* (*The Last Frankenstein*, 1991) and *Kamitsukitai* (*My Soul is Slashed*, 1990), the latter featuring a transfusion of **Dracula**'s blood.

Comics (*manga*) have inspired many films, including the **animated** (*anime*) *Vampire Hunter D* (1985) and *Urotsukidoji* (*Legend of the Overfiend*, 1989) and the live action *Teito Monogatari* (*Tokyo: The Last Megalopolis*, 1987) and *Rapeman* (1990). With the collapse of the big studio system, much Japanese horror is now made by low budget independents. These range from the bizarre (*Shojo no Harawata*/*Entrails of a Virgin*, 1985) to the even more bizarre (*Tetsuo*, 1988). Shinya Tsukamoto's combination of live action, animation and experimental technique led to a bigger budget sequel *Tetsuo 2: Body Hammer* (1992) and a more conventional teen horror *Hiruko* (*Hiruko the Goblin*, 1992). Shimako Sato followed her UK co-production, *Tale of a Vampire* (1993) with a high-school horror story, *Eko Eko Azaraku* (*Wizard of Darkness*, 1995). PT

Jaws * See: **Sharks**

Jay, Griffin (1905–54)

American writer. B man Jay invented most **Mummy clichés**, including tana leaves and the evil high priest.

The Mummy's Hand/1940 * *The Mummy's Tomb*/1942 * *Captive Wild Woman*/1943 * *Return of the Vampire*/*The Mummy's Ghost*/*Cry of the Werewolf*/1944

Jayne, Jennifer [Jay Firbank] (b. 1932)

British actress, writer. Minor starlet Jayne – Donald Sutherland's **vampire** wife in *Dr. Terror's House of Horrors* (1964) – wrote the makeshift *Tales That Witness Madness* (1973).

The Trollenberg Terror/1958 * *Hysteria*/1964 * *They Came From Beyond Space*/1967 * *The Medusa Touch*/1978 * *The Doctor and the Devils*/1985

Jennifer Jayne

TV: *Adam Adamant Lives!*: 'Allah is Not Always With You'/1966

Jekyll and Hyde

At the beginning of 1886, a story was published which redrew the map of horror. Instead of demons outside, *Strange Case of Dr. Jekyll and Mr. Hyde* (later editions add '*The*') dealt explicitly with demons inside, and in the process added a new phrase to the English language. There were earlier stories about 'man's double being' – usually expressed through personified consciences such as 'twins', '**mirrors**' or 'automata' – and the best **doppelgänger** tales (by **Hoffmann**, James Hogg and **Poe**) were influential, but *Dr. Jekyll and Mr. Hyde* was about 'the identity with difficulty preserved' and a journey within one person from Victorian complacency towards chaos and disintegration. As Andrew Lang observed 'we would welcome a spectre, a ghoul, or even a **vampire** gladly' rather than meet the villain of this piece.

The twenty-five year old Edinburgh-born author Robert Louis **Stevenson**, then living in a suburban villa in Bournemouth, won commercial success with his 'fine bogey tale'. The book confused the critics: it looked downmarket in fawn-coloured paper covers, but the contents – two personal memoirs, a newspaper-style report and a third-party narrative based on hearsay, all describing Dr Henry Jekyll's steady descent into the heart of darkness – were far from the usual fare. In

Jekyll and Hyde

summarising the plot, critics concentrated (like most adaptations) on the first-person chapter which gives Jekyll's full statement of the case (the last fifth of the text), ignoring the perspectives of his fellow bachelors Gabriel Utterson (his lawyer), Richard Enfield ('a man about town') and Dr Hastie Lanyon (his friend). Stevenson intended all these viewpoints as subtle variations on the theme of 'the Hypocrite' and 'that damned old business of the war in the members'. They also add to the strangeness, providing a series of out-of-focus glimpses of Edward Hyde and delaying until just before the denouement the revelation that Jekyll and Hyde are in fact the same person. It is difficult to imagine now, but readers in 1886 did not know that yet.

The literati tended to see the story as 'Poe with the addition of a moral sense', a parable of the struggle between good and evil which was, in the end, optimistic. A famous sermon on the subject was preached in St Paul's Cathedral, no less. Stevenson rejected this: the strange case happened, he reiterated, because 'the Hypocrite let out the beast of Hyde'; Hyde was in Jekyll just as Jekyll was in Hyde. Shilling-shocker readers enjoyed Jekyll and Hyde as a Christmas thriller and an internalised horror story. These two publics have been going in separate directions ever since.

In common with other classic nineteenth-

Louis Wolheim, John Barrymore, *Dr. Jekyll and Mr. Hyde* (1920)

century horrors (**Frankenstein**, **Dracula**), the origins of Jekyll and Hyde have themselves become part of the folklore. Jekyll and Hyde began with a fevered nightmare about Jekyll involuntarily transforming into Hyde, dreamed as Stevenson was confined to his bed suffering from haemorrhaging of the lungs. Legend, for which there is no contemporary evidence, has it that he wrote a first draft 'at a red heat', that it was much nastier, and that he burned the manuscript at the insistence of his wife Fanny then rewrote the story in three days flat. In fact, Stevenson wrote *Jekyll and Hyde* between the end of September and the end of October 1885, and surviving manuscripts show he carefully made the story more respectable as he went along. In a subsequently excised passage from his notebook draft, he had Jekyll admit 'from an early age, I become in secret the slave of disgraceful pleasures . . . at once criminal in the sight of the law and abhorrent in themselves.'

In Stevenson's strange case, the *Treasure Island* (1883) side of his posterity has battled it out with the Jekyll side for over a century. Thomas Russell Sullivan's dramatised play *Dr Jekyll and Mr Hyde*, written for American actor Richard Mansfield, opened in New York in 1887 and at the Lyceum in London a year later. Stevenson warned Sullivan that

adaptation 'appears to me a difficult undertaking', given the multilayering of the book. Though the play has disappeared, it can be reconstructed from two biographies of Mansfield: Jekyll is given a girlfriend (daughter of Sir Danvers Carew, an elderly MP) and Hyde a motive (he is so jealous of Agnes that he murders her father); there is a supernatural dimension (Carew's ghost opens a locked door) and the 'scene at the window' (Stevenson's nightmare) becomes a lovers' last farewell.

The play crucially expands the story beyond Stevenson's all-male world, but a more important change arises from Mansfield's desire to play both Jekyll and Hyde, founding a virtuoso tradition. In the book, Hyde is smaller than Jekyll, a different being who comes from within the doctor and who looks grotesque partly because his clothes are several sizes too large. In the play, and most film versions, he is the same person in elaborate make-up. To heighten the contrast between the two, to make them as he put it more 'distinctively individual', Mansfield made Jekyll more saintly and Hyde much more of a pantomime villain, distracting from the key theme of hypocrisy. The trans

RIGHT Frederic March, Miriam Hopkins, *Dr. Jekyll and Mr. Hyde* (1932)

formations in Acts Three and Four – on stage, without the use of doubles or hiding places, though Armand Assante in the mini-series *Jack the Ripper* (1988) falls back on bladder effects rather than authentic recreation of Mansfield's method – turned Dr Jekyll and Mr Hyde into an international hit.

Stevenson was upset: 'Hyde was the younger of the two', he wrote, not 'a mere voluptuary' who disapproves of Agnes Carew or embodies Jekyll's buried desires; the story was not about **sex** at all. But it was too late. Most film adaptations follow the outlines of Sullivan's version. And Mansfield's pronunciation – Jekyll rather Jeekyll – has stuck as well. Stevenson complained that 1880s critics read sexuality into everything, but he hadn't seen anything yet: the story has been deconstructed as really about homosexual panic, the father/son relationship, the adolescent boy inside the grown man, the eroticisation of the working man, impotence, misogyny, the dark side of patriarchy and (in general) everything late-Victorian single gentlemen could conceivably squeeze into the closets. A convincing recent interpretation sees the story as representing two sides of Stevenson's own personality: the man of action inside his head; the disabled artist he saw in the mirror.

Apart from the Sullivan play, the key influence – in the public realm – was the Whitechapel murders of autumn 1888. If readers felt short-changed by Hyde's behav-

Tony Calvin, *Dr. Jekyll and Sister Hyde*

iour in the story – as not 'bestial' enough – the confusion of Jekyll and Hyde with **Jack the Ripper** has more than made up for it. The first of the murders happened as Sullivan's play was running in the West End, and the sixteenth edition of Stevenson's paper-covered story was on sale in the bookshops: in public consciousness, Hyde became a 'lust-murderer' (the lust being Jekyll's), a killer of prostitutes (or 'dance hall girls' in Hollywood parlance) and a fiend who haunts the **fog**-shrouded East End of London (rather than Soho). The equation of Jack and Jekyll seemed somehow to 'fit' as a way of explaining the inexplicable. So, in addition to the sweet Agnes Carew, stage and screen Hydes began to consort with a tart-with-a-heart. Jekyll and Hyde became the story the public wanted to see, rather than the one Stevenson actually wrote.

Since the American *Dr. Jekyll and Mr. Hyde* (1908) and the British *The Duality of Man* (1910), the role has afforded opportunity for facial distortion to many actors: Alwin Neuss (*Den skaebnesvangre opfindelse*, 1910), James Cruze (1912), King Baggot (1913), Albert Bassermann (*Der Andere*, 1913), John **Barrymore** (1920), Sheldon **Lewis** (1920), Conrad **Veidt** (*Der Januskopf*, 1920), Fredric March (1931), Spencer Tracy (1941), Mario Scoffi (*Il dottor Jekyll*, 1951), Basil **Rathbone** ('Dr. Jekyll and Mr. Hyde', *Suspense*, 1951), **Karloff** (*Abbott and Costello Meet Dr. Jekyll and*

Mr. Hyde, 1953), Michael Rennie ('Dr. Jekyll and Mr. Hyde', *Climax*, 1955), Douglass Montgomery ('Dr. Jekyll and Mr. Hyde', *Matinee Theatre*, 1957), Jean-Louis Barrault (*Le testament du Dr. Cordelier/Experiment in Evil*, 1959), Paul Massie (*The Two Faces of Dr. Jekyll*, 1960), a puppet (*Mad Monster Party?*, 1965), Jack **Palance** (*The Strange Case of Dr. Jekyll and Mr. Hyde*, 1967), Denis DeMarne (*The Man With Two Heads*, 1971), Ralph **Bates** and Martine **Beswick** (*Dr. Jekyll and Sister Hyde*, 1971), Christopher **Lee** (*I, Monster*, 1971), Adam West ('With Apologies to Mr. Hyde, **Night Gallery**', 1971), Jack **Taylor** and Paul **Naschy** (*El doctor Jekyll y el hombre lobo/Dr. Jekyll and the Werewolf*, 1971), Kirk Douglas (1973), David **Hemmings** (1980), Udo **Kier** (*Dr. Jekyll et les femmes/ Blood of Dr. Jekyll*, 1981), Chris Harris ('Dr. Jekyll and Mrs. Hyde', *Into the Labyrinth*, 1982), Innokenti Smoktunovsky and Alexander Felikstov (*Strannyar Istoryar Doktora Dzehila i Mistera Khaida*, 1987), Anthony Andrews ('The Strange Case of Dr. Jekyll and Mr. Hyde,' *Nightmare Classics*, 1989), Anthony **Perkins** (*Edge of Sanity*, 1989), Michael Caine (*Jekyll & Hyde*, 1990), Leonard Nimoy (*The Pagemaster*, 1994), John Malkovich (*Mary Reilly*, 1996).

Relatives, dependents, imitations, pornography and parodies: *Dr. Pickle and Mr. Pride* (Stan Laurel, 1925), *Son of Dr. Jekyll* (Louis Hayward, 1951), *Daughter of Dr. Jekyll* (Gloria **Talbott,** 1957), *Horrors of the Black Museum* (1959), *The Ugly Duckling* (Bernard Bresslaw, 1959), *The Nutty Professor* (Jerry Lewis, 1963), *Dr. Sexual and Mr. Hyde* (1971), *The Adult Version of Jekyll and Hide* (1971), *Horror High* (1974), *Oversexed* (1974), *Dr. Black Mr. White* (Bernie Casey, 1975), *The Erotic Dr. Jekyll* (1976), *Dottor Jekyll e il gentile signora* (1979), *Dr. Heckyl & Mr. Hype* (Oliver **Reed**, 1980), 'Dr. Jekyll and Miss Hyde' (*Fantasy Island*, 1980), *Dr. Jekyll's Dungeon of Death* (James Mathers, 1982), *Jekyll & Hyde . . . Together Again* (Mark Blankfield, 1982), *The Lust Potion of Dr. F* (1986), *Dr. Jeckel and Ms. Hide* (1990), *Julia Jekyll and Harriet Hyde* (1995), *Dr. Jekyll and Ms. Hyde* (Tim Daly, Sean Young, 1995) and *The Nutty Professor* (Eddie Murphy, 1996). Valerie Martin's *Mary Reilly* (1990) is the most distinguished literary reprise, but Jekyll and/or Hyde figure in Loren D. Estleman's *Dr. Jekyll and Mr. Holmes* (1979), Samantha Lee's *Dr. Jekyll and Mr. Hyde* (1986), John A. Sanford's *The Strange Trial of Mr Hyde* (1987), Robert **Bloch** and André Norton's *The Jekyll Legacy* (1990) and Kim Newman's *Anno Dracula* (1992). CF

Ingrid Bergman, Spencer Tracy, *Dr. Jekyll and Mr. Hyde* (1941)

Jiangshi

Jiangshi (Chinese **vampires**) have little to do with Western bloodsuckers. Easily identified because they move with an amazing hopping motion, they usually wear mandarin clothing complete with feathered hat and track down victims by smelling their breath. Taoist monks can destroy them with incantations, wooden swords or dogs' blood. *Jiangshi* can be tamed by sticking a sheet of Chinese scripture to their foreheads and be commanded by ringing a bell. Hopping vampire movies: *Pao Dan Fei Che* (*The Trail*, 1983), *Jiangshi Xiansheng* (*Mr. Vampire*, 1985) and four sequels (1986, 1987, 1988, 1992), *Jiangshi Fansheng* (*New Mr. Vampire*, 1986), *The First Vampire in China* (1986), *Jiangshi Papa* (*Close Encounter of the Vampire*, 1986), *Vampire vs. Vampire* (1989), *Crazy Safari* (1991), *Yimeo daogu* (*Vampires Settle on the Police Camp*, 1991). A lone American entry is *The Jitters* (1988). CV

Johnson, Noble (1897–1978)

Black American character actor. Often cast as a mute or savage, notably as the Native Chief of Skull Island in **King Kong** (1933) and *The Son of Kong* (1933). He menaces Bob

Hope as a **zombie** in *The Ghost Breakers* (1940). SJ

Something Always Happens/1928 * *The Mysterious Dr. Fu Manchu*/*Black Waters*/1929 * *Murders in the Rue Morgue*/*The Most Dangerous Game*/*The Mummy*/*Mystery Ranch*/1932 * *She*/1935 * *Lost Horizon*/1937 * *The Mad Doctor of Market Street*/1942 * *A Game of Death*/1945

Johnson, Steve (b. 1960)

American special make-up effects artist. An assistant on *Humanoids From the Deep* (1980),

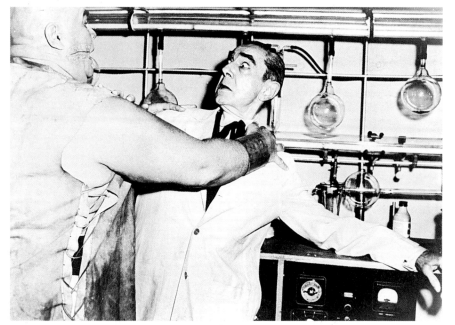

Tor Johnson, Bela Lugosi, *Bride of the Monster*

The Fog (1980), *An American Werewolf in London* (1981), *Videodrome* (1983) and *Ghostbusters* (1984), he has become a utility monster man.

Fright Night/1985 * *Howling II: Stirba, Werewolf Bitch*/1986 * *A Nightmare on Elm Street IV: The Dream Master*/*Dead Heat*/*Night of the Demons*/*Howling IV: The Original Nightmare*/*Night Angel*/1988 * *Howling VI: The Freaks*/1990 * *Highway to Hell*/*Playroom*/1991 * *Innocent Blood* (+a)/*Pet Sematary II*/1992 * *Freaked*/*Return of the Living Dead III*/1993 * *Brainscan*/*Evolver*/*Night of the Demons 2*/*Necronomicon*/1994 * *Exquisite Tenderness*/*Species*/*Lord of Illusions*/1995 * *Fotogrammi mortali (Fatal Frames)*/*Thor*/*Nightwatch*/*Anaconda*/1996

TV: *The Stand*/1993 * *The Langoliers*/*Here Come the Munsters*/1995 * *The Shining*/1996

Johnson, Tor (1903–71)

Swedish-born professional **wrestler** who toured America as the Super Swedish Angel and made his film debut in W.C. Fields's *The Man on the Flying Trapeze* (1935). After retiring from the ring, the bald, hulking actor became typecast as a quickie monster. In *Bride of the Monster* (1954), *The Unearthly* (1957) and *Night of the Ghouls* (1959), he plays 'Lobo'. Tor Johnson masks are still a popular Halloween item; one is worn by a hypnotised killer in *Strange Behavior* (1981). George Steele plays Tor in *Ed Wood* (1994). SJ

Ghost Catchers/1944 * *Behind Locked Doors*/1948 * *Carousel*/1956 * *The Black Sleep*/1956 * *Plan 9 from Outer Space*/1958 * *The Beast of Yucca Flats*/1961 * *Head*/1968

Jones, Carolyn (1929–83)

American actress, the vampish Morticia of **The Addams Family** (1964–66). SJ

House of Wax/1953 * *Invasion of the Body Snatchers*/1956 * *Eaten Alive*/1976

TV: *Alfred Hitchcock Presents*: 'The Cheney Vase'/1955 * *Ghost Story*: 'The Summer House'/1972 * *The New Scooby-Doo Movies*: 'Scooby-Doo Meets the Addams Family' (v)/1972 * *Ironside*: 'Raise the Devil'/1974 * *Kolchak: The Night Stalker*: 'Demon in Lace'/1975 * *Halloween With the Addams Family*/1977 * *Midnight Lace*/1981

Jones, Duane (1937–88)

American actor. In **Night of the Living Dead** (1968), Jones is Ben, the competent **black** hero who gets everyone killed. His other major role is the American professor overtaken by an African curse in *Ganja and Hess* (1973).

Vampires/1988 * *To Die For*/1989

Jones, Freddie (b. 1927)

British actor. In **Hammer**'s *Frankenstein Must Be Destroyed* (1969) he is remarkably sympathetic as a victim of a **brain** transplant. Later, the Baron himself in *Son of Dracula* (1974). SJ

The Persecution and Assassination of Jean-Paul Marat as Performed by the Inmates of the Asylum at Charenton Under the Direction of the Marquis de Sade/1966 * *The Man Who Haunted Himself*/*Goodbye Gemini*/1970 * *The Satanic Rites of Dracula*/1973 * *Vampira*/1974 * *The Elephant Man*/1980 * *Krull*/1983 * *Firestarter*/1984 * *The Black Cauldron*/*Young Sherlock Holmes*/1985 * *Consuming Passions*/1988 * *Wild at Heart*/1990 * *The Mystery of Edwin Drood*/1993

TV: *Mystery and Imagination*: 'Lost Hearts'/1966; 'The Tell-Tale Heart'/1968; 'Sweeney Todd'/1970 * *The Avengers*: 'Who's Who???'/1967 * *Randall and Hopkirk (Deceased)*: 'For the Girl Who Has Everything'/1969 * *Thriller*: 'A Midsummer Nightmare'/1976 *

Carolyn Jones

ary'. A lacklustre 1987 reprise had Scott Menville, Dan Messick and Granville Van Dusen voice the leads. TM

Jordan, Neil (b. 1950)
Irish writer, director. A novelist whose movies have literary aspirations, Jordan has exploited horror freedoms. *The Company of Wolves* (1984) combines Angela Carter's fairy-tale critique with marquee-value **werewolves** to *sui generis* effect. The supernatural comedy *High Spirits* (1988) was Jordan's first attempt at Hollywood parlay: its blend of American bluffness and Irish whimsy is predictably doctored. A happier compromise is struck in *Interview With the Vampire: The Vampire Chronicles* (1994). A big-budget adaptation of Anne **Rice**'s kinky 1976 novel, the film mixes adequate **homosexual**/paedophile inferences with verbal/ visual flourishes and an enjoyably fulsome turn from Tom Cruise. DP

Children of the Stones/1977 * *King of the Castle*/ 1978 * *The Return of Sherlock Holmes*: 'Wisteria Lodge'/1988 * *Hotel Room*/*The Last Vampyre*/ 1992 * *The Young Indiana Jones Chronicles*: 'Young Indiana Jones and the Phantom Train of Doom'/1993 * *Neverwhere*/1996

Jones, Stephen (b. 1953)
British book editor, publicist. Jones edits the annual *Best New Horror* (with Ramsey **Campbell**, from 1990), and many anthologies (*The Mammoth Book of Vampires*, 1992; *Shadows Over Innsmouth*, 1994). His non-fiction includes *Horror: 100 Best Books* (with Kim Newman, 1988), *Clive Barker's Shadows in Eden* (1991), *James Herbert: By Horror Haunted* (1992) and the *Illustrated Movie Guide* series.

Jonny Quest (US TV series, 1964–5)
This thirty minute prime-time animated show was produced for ABC TV by cartoon kings William Hanna and Joseph Barbera. Young Jonny Quest and his scientist father are protected by Roger Race Bannon, a government agent whose task is made difficult by the Quests' penchant for encountering foreign agents, lizard men, lost South American temples, ray guns and voodoo cults. Tim Matheson is the voice of Jonny, with John Stephenson as Dr Quest and Mike

Road as Roger Bannon. Though lacking the superior animation of earlier Hanna-Barbera work, it is often surprisingly strong **pulp** adventure. Typical episodes: 'The Curse of Anubis', 'Werewolf of the Timberland', 'Attack of the Tree People'. 'The House of Seven Gargoyles', 'Monster in the Monast-

Jourdan, Louis [Louis Gendre] (b. 1919)
French actor. The regulation smoothie of *Gigi* (1958) is interesting as a lizardy romantic **vampire** in the BBC's *Count Dracula* (1977). His is David Sorel, the psychic investigator of *Fear No Evil* (1969) and *Ritual of*

RIGHT Teddy Bear, Georgia Slowe, Neil Jordan's *The Company of Wolves*

Evil (1970), and Arcane, villain of *Swamp Thing* (1982) and *Return of Swamp Thing* (1989).

Journey to the Unknown (UK-US TV series, 1968–9)

This ITV show was produced by Anthony **Hinds** for **Hammer** and 20th Century-Fox, with **Hitchcock**'s right-hand woman, Joan Harrison, as executive producer. With modish settings and American guest stars, the show distanced itself from the traditional Hammer gothic style and was more a forerunner of *Night Gallery* (1970–73) or Brian Clemens's *Thriller* (1973–5). Authors adapted include L.P. Hartley ('The Killing Bottle'), Richard **Matheson** ('Girl of My Dreams'), Cornell **Woolrich** ('Jane Brown's Body'), Charles **Beaumont** ('The New People', 'Miss Belle') and Robert **Bloch** ('Matakitas is Coming'). In 'Eve', from John Collier's story, Dennis Waterman becomes obsessed with a shop window mannequin (Carol Lynley) which appears to come to life. In 'The Beckoning Fair One', from Oliver Onions's story, a painting of a dead woman fascinates artist Robert Lansing, who falls under her evil influence. Directors include Peter **Sasdy**, Alan **Gibson**, Gerry O'Hara and Roy Ward **Baker**. Episodes were fixed up into TV movies introduced by Joan **Crawford** (*Journey to the Unknown*), Patrick McGoohan (*Journey Into Darkness*) and Sebastian Cabot (*Journey to Midnight*). TM

Julian, Rupert (1886–1943)

American director. The hack who replaced Erich von **Stroheim** on *Merry-Go-Round* (1923), his major credit is ***The Phantom of the Opera*** (1925): Lon **Chaney**'s performance and the delirious imagery are sometimes hampered by his stolidity.

The Leopard Lady/1928 * *The Cat Creeps*/1930

Jungle

The jungle has provided a setting for most categories of horror film despite the fact that, until relatively recently, suspension of belief was rendered nigh on impossible by patently fabricated studio sets. Victims are pursued through undergrowth by killers from ***The Most Dangerous Game*** (1932) to *Predator* (1987), while the odd **cannibal** tribe, evil fetish or prehistoric monster adds a horror touch to many a Tarzan or white hunter adventure. From the 40s, the craze for **voodoo** and **zombie** pictures kept the studio greensmen busy, and there is even a **vampire** jungle movie *The Vampire's Ghost* (1945). As late as 1965, the British second feature *Naked Evil* attempted to recreate a South African jungle on Hampstead Heath.

By the 60s, the jungles of the **Philippines** had been invaded by partnerships of local and Hollywood producers for various low-grade action pictures, often horrors starring John **Ashley**. Ruggero **Deodato** went to the Philippines to shoot *L'ultimo mondo cannibale* (*Cannibal*, 1977), the first in a notorious cycle of cannibal movies. In stark contrast to the early jungle pictures, everything now looked so authentic that many newspapers believed the ridiculous planted rumours that the killings staged in *Cannibal Holocaust* (1979) were real. An island and a jungle, but no zombies, appear in *Zombie Island Massacre* (1984), while a mythic jungle invades New Hampshire in *Jumanji* (1995). DM

K

Kafka, Franz (1883–1924)

Jewish Czech writer. Though none of his novels – *Der Prozess* (*The Trial*, 1925), *Das Schloss* (*The Castle*, 1926), *Amerika* (1927) – was completed or published in his lifetime, Kafka is a major twentieth-century writer. The adjective 'Kafkaesque' (applied, for instance, to *Brazil*, 1985, or *Barton Fink*, 1991) connotes nightmare bureaucracy. His world is constructed for the oppression of the individual, a metaphor as psychological as it is political.

Never considered merely a horror writer, Kafka's imaginings are nevertheless consistently horrific: note 'Die Verwandlung' ('Metamorphosis', 1915), in which Gregor Samsa copes with transformation into a giant **insect**, and 'In der Strafkolonie' ('In

LEFT Joseph Cotten, Judy Parfitt, 'Do Me a Favour and Kill Me', *Journey to the Unknown*

Franz Kafka

between Colin **Clive**'s Henry Frankenstein and Boris Karloff's **Monster** in *Frankenstein* (1931). Just as Jeeves ministered to Bertie Wooster's sartorial needs and Captain Hastings to Hercule Poirot's ego, so the Monster was of a lower level of creation than his maker, Frankenstein, and meant to be a biological colonial for a higher, and more masterful, species. Karloff's neck-bolted *lusus naturai*, though, because of misappropriated body-parts, rebels in epic fashion. The implication in Frankenstein's 'In the name of God. Now I know what it feels like to be God!' is that the Monster is meant to be a worshipping, subservient creature. But the role achieved higher things for Karloff: it

made him one of the century's most remarkable icons, the Monster's menace leavened to arouse pity as well as terror. The scene in which he floats flowers with a little girl before killing her, became a much imitated legend in his own lifetime and beyond, a symbol of brute strength striving for compassion but succumbing to its own nature.

Born in Camberwell, South London, William Henry Pratt's first and foremost preoccupation was always with cricket, an obsession which lasted through Canadian repertory, work as labourer and reaching Hollywood as an indomitable redskin in *The Last of the Mohicans* (1920). The coming of sound suited the whispered threat of his lisp

the Penal Colony', 1919), about a surreal **torture** device (filmed as *Kafka: la colonia penale*, 1988). *The Trial* was filmed in 1963 by Orson **Welles** (with Anthony **Perkins** as Joseph K) and from a Harold Pinter script in 1993 (with Kyle MacLachlan), *The Castle* was made in 1968 (with Maximilian Schell as K), and 'Metamorphosis' in 1951, 1953, 1964 (the Yugoslav *Metamorfoza*) and 1975 (the Swedish *Förvandlingen*).

In fantastical embroideries on the author's life and work, Kafka is played by John Wood ('Kafka's Castle', *Omnibus*, 1974), Daniel Day-Lewis (*The Insurance Man*, 1985), Tim Roth ('Franz Kafka's The Trial', *The Modern World: Ten Great Writers*, 1988), Jeremy Irons (*Kafka*, 1991), a puppet (*Franz Kafka*, 1991) and Richard E. Grant (*Franz Kafka's It's a Wonderful Life* (1994).

Ernst Pawel, *The Nightmare of Reason: A Life of Franz Kafka* (1984); Pietro Citati, *Franz Kafka* (1990)

Karloff, Boris [William Henry Pratt] (1887–1969)

British actor. Of all the literary master-servant relationships that proliferated in the 30s, the least detected (because hidden by the gaudy apparatuses of horror) was that

Una O'Connor, Boris Karloff, *Bride of Frankenstein*

Myrna Loy, Charles Starrett, Boris Karloff, *The Mask of Fu Manchu*

in the prison melodrama *The Criminal Code* (1931) but it was British director James **Whale** who cast him as the Monster, billing him as ? but making him a household name. Whale chose Karloff over Bela **Lugosi**, and besides creating a chilling ambience, allowed Karloff a lumbering dignity for which Karloff was always grateful: 'I was allowed honesty. I wasn't just a golem with no real human characteristics. I saw the character as innocent as a baby, even if the results of what he did were evil.'

Though Karloff made mainstream films (*Scarface*, 1932), audiences and studios now saw him as a horror star: he was reunited with James Whale for the adaptation J.B. Priestley's *Benighted* (1927) as **The Old Dark House** (1932), a mansion full of grotesques of which Karloff's murderous butler is still the most haunting. In the same year, he was a Chinese archfiend for *The Mask of* **Fu Manchu** and a papyrus-faced sorcerer in **The Mummy**. This was followed, in Britain, by *The Ghoul* (1933), as an Egyptologist returned from the tomb to uncover lost jewels and a murderer. At the insistence of Whale, Karloff's monster re-emerged in *Bride of Frankenstein* (1935) in which Frankenstein (Clive again) is blackmailed by Ernest **Thesiger**'s Dr Pretorius into assembling a mate for his vast creation. There is all

the sizzling and crackling of electrical equipment but this is horror as black comedy (a fright-wigged Elsa **Lanchester** is the Bride rejecting her would be-lover) though Karloff himself wondered 'just how many liberties you can take with an idea like that.' 'We belong dead' is the Monster's seemingly final speech as he blows them all up. By that time Karloff lived in audiences' minds, if not his own, with horrors such as *The Black Cat* (1934) and *The Raven* (1935).

What Karloff imparts via his menace is the kind of *tendresse* which Jeeves might have bestowed upon Wooster if the relationship had been conceived in terms of philosophical sadism. In *The Tower of London* (1939) he plays Mord the Executioner to Basil **Rathbone**'s Richard III: his **torture** scenes are all the more horrific because he gently places crushing weights on the bodies of racked victims with an air of tender authority which makes Karloff an ogre beyond all others. This is further confirmed in *Son of Frankenstein* (1939), last of the 30s trilogy, in which he is reunited with Rathbone as the Baron's son, dabbling in resurrection techniques with the aid of a vindictive shepherd (Lugosi). Through these years Karloff represents a kind of thinking-man's monster, keeping to a kind of honour in whatever species of colossus he is embod-

ied – 'I got so sick and tired of all the make-up which took hours to plaster on me before I started work.'

The sensational nature of the titles tell of the subjects in which he was cast: *The Man They Could Not Hang* (1939), *Before I Hang* (1940), *The Ape* (1940), *The Devil Commands* (1941) and a brilliantly eerie threesome of low-budgeters for Val **Lewton**: *The Body Snatcher* (1945), *Isle of the Dead* (1945) and *Bedlam* (1946). In a sense his great days were over and he was winding down, but there were uplifts such as another reflight of *The Raven* (1962) for schlockmeister Roger **Corman** in which he was as mad magician pitted against another wizard, Vincent **Price**. So no more mighty tombs to unearth, no more splendid short-circuits to the birthing device of lightning? Not so.

Peter Bogdanovich's *Targets* (1968) is a magnificent tribute to Karloff's career, casting him as antique Byron Orlok, a venerable horror star appalled at a sniper's senseless slaughter during a screening of his own *The Terror* (1962). That difference between escapist horror and the real thing fascinated Karloff who, in his last years, was occasionally confined to a wheelchair because of crippling arthritis, and who had returned to London, mainly for the cricket. 'The contrast between what is possible and what might be probable intrigues me. Jim Whale had to use a wheelchair all the time. And he fell into

Boris Karloff, *The Black Cat* (1934)

the shallow end of his swimming pool and drowned. Now there' – giving one of his short-tongued chuckles – 'was real horror. And it's what we try to get away from throughout our lives,' he said, pouring tea for his guest with all the deferential expertise of a manservant who knows his place – which is still as one of the greatest of all superstars. He edited, at least in name, two fine anthologies *Tales of Terror* (1943) and *And the Darkness Falls* (1946). TH

The Hope Diamond Mystery/1921 * *The Bells*/ 1926 * *The Fatal Warning*/*King of the Congo*/ *The Unholy Night*/1929 * *The Sea Bat*/1930 * *The Mad Genius*/1931 * *Behind the Mask*/*Alias the Doctor* (role deleted)/1932 * *The Black Room*/1935 * *The Invisible Ray*/*The Walking Dead*/*The Man Who Changed His Mind*/ *Juggernaut*/1936 * *Charlie Chan at the Opera*/ *Night Key*/*West of Shanghai*/1937 * *The Invisible Menace*/1938 * *Black Friday*/*You'll Find Out*/1941 * *The Boogie Man Will Get You*/1942 * *House of Frankenstein*/1944 * *Lured*/ *Dick Tracy Meets Gruesome*/1947 * *Meet the Killer*/1949 * *The Strange Door*/1951 * *The Black Castle*/1952 * *Abbott and Costello Meet Dr. Jekyll and Mr. Hyde*/*Sabaka*/1953 * *Voodoo Island*/1957 * *Grip of the Strangler*/*Corridors of Blood*/*Frankenstein 1970*/1958 * *The Comedy of Terrors*/*I tre volti della paura* [*Black Sabbath*]/ 1964 * *Die, Monster, Die!*/1965 * *The Ghost in the Invisible Bikini*/1966 * *The Sorcerers*/*Mad*

Monster Party (v)/*El coleccionista de cadavares* [*Cauldron of Blood*]/1967 * *La camara del terror* [*The Fear Chamber*]/*La muerte viviente* [*The Snake People*]/*La invasión siniestra* [*The Incredible Invasion*]/*Serenata macabra* [*House of Evil*]/1968 * *Madhouse*/1973 * *Transylvania Twist*/1991

TV: *Starring Boris Karloff* (1949) * *Lights Out*: 'The Leopard Lady'/1950 * *Suspense*: 'The Lonely Place'/1951; 'The Black Prophet'/'The Signal Man'/1953 * *Lux Video Theatre*: 'The Jest of Hahalaba'/1951 * *Tales of Tomorrow*: 'Memento'/1952 * *Curtain Call*: 'Soul of the Great Bell'/1952 * *Schlitz Playhouse of the Stars*: 'Death House'/1952 * *Plymouth Playhouse*: 'The Chase'/1953 * *The Rheingold Theatre*: 'House of Death'/1953 * *Climax!*: 'The White Carnation'/1954; 'Bury Me Later'/1956 * *Colonel March of Scotland Yard*/ 1954–5 * *The Best of Broadway*: 'Arsenic and Old Lace'/1955 * *The Elgin TV Hour*: 'Sting of Death'/1955 * *Playhouse 90*: 'Rendezvous in Black'/1956; 'Heart of Darkness'/1958 * *Suspicion*: 'The Deadly Game'/1957 * *Shirley Temple's Storybook*: 'The Legend of Sleepy Hollow'/1958 * *The Veil*/1958 * *Thriller*/ 1960–2 * *Out of This World*/1962 * *The Hallmark Hall of Fame*: 'Arsenic and Old Lace'/1962 * *Route 66*: 'Lizard's Leg and Owlet's Wing'/1962 * *Wild Wild West*: 'Night of the Golden Cobra'/1966 * *The Girl From U.N.C.L.E.*: 'The Mother Muffin Affair'/1966

Sam Katzman

Forrest Ackerman, *The Frankenscience Monster* (1969); Peter Underwood, *Karloff* (1972); Denis Gifford, *Karloff: The Man, the Monster, the Movies* (1973); Paul Jensen, *Boris Karloff and His Films* (1974), Richard Bojarski, Kenneth Beale, *The Films of Boris Karloff* (1974); Cynthia Lindsay, *Dear Boris: The Life of William Henry Pratt a.k.a. Boris Karloff* (1975); Gregory William Mank, *Karloff and Lugosi: The Story of a Haunting Collaboration* (1990); Scott Allen Nolan, *Boris Karloff* (1991)

Karnstein, Countess Mircalla * See: **'Carmilla'; Homosexuality; Le Fanu, J.S.; Pitt, Ingrid; Vampirism**

Katzman, Sam (1901–73)
American producer. Longtime grindhouse fixture, known as 'Jungle Sam' for his Johnny Weissmuller *Jungle Jim* series, alleged coiner of the term 'beatnik'. His 50s quickies, notably *The Werewolf* (1958), are better than his 40s **Lugosi**/East Side Kids efforts, but *The Giant Claw* (1957) is especially shoddy. His big hit was *Rock Around the Clock* (1956); few remember *Calypso Heat Wave* (1957) or *Twist Around the Clock* (1961).

Shadow of Chinatown/1934 * *A Face in the Fog*/1936 * *Blake of Scotland Yard*/1937 * *The Ghost Creeps*/1940 * *Spooks Run Wild*/*The Invisible Ghost*/1941 * *The Corpse Vanishes*/ 1942 * *The Ape Man*/*Ghosts on the Loose*/1943 * *The Return of the Ape Man*/*Voodoo Man*/1944 * *The Creature With the Atom Brain*/*It Came From Beneath the Sea*/1955 * *The Man Who Turned to Stone*/1956 * *Earth vs. the Flying*

Boris Karloff, *The Body Snatcher*

*Saucers/Zombies of Mora Tau/1957 * Cult of the Damned/1969*

Kaufman, Lloyd (b. 1945)

American producer, director (as 'Samuel Weil'), writer. Mastermind of the dumbing of American horror via **Troma**, maker of the Toxic Avenger and Nuke 'Em High series and less successful franchise wannabes *Troma's War* (1988), *Sgt. Kabukiman NYPD* (1992) and *Tromeo and Juliet* (1996). *Rabid Grannies* (1988), *Stuff Stephanie in the Incinerator* (1987) and *A Nymphoid Barbarian in*

Lloyd Kaufman

Dinosaur Hell (1990) are unmistakably Kaufman titles, but the films are pick-ups merely distributed by Troma. His brother Charles directed *Mother's Day* (1980).

*The Toxic Avenger/1984 * Class of Nuke 'Em High/1986 * The Toxic Avenger, Part II/The Toxic Avenger, Part III: The Last Temptation of Toxie/1989 * Class of Nuke 'Em High, Part II: Subhumanoid Meltdown/1991 * Class of Nuke 'Em High, Part III: The Good, the Bad and the Subhumanoid/1993*

Keir, Andrew (b. 1926)

British character actor. Keir made his **Hammer** debut in an early thriller, *The Lady Craved Excitement* (1950), returning in substantial roles like the **vampire**-hunting Father Sandor in *Dracula, Prince of Darkness*

(1965). Earthier and more avuncular than other patriarchs, he brought a warmth to his performances that Hammer, never inclined to sentiment, often lacked. He recreated his *Quatermass and the Pit* (1967) role for Radio 3's *The Quatermass Memoirs* (1996). PH

*Daleks Invasion Earth 2150 AD/1966 * Blood from the Mummy's Tomb/The Night Visitor/1971 * Absolution/1978*

TV: *The Avengers*: 'The Fear Merchants'/1967; 'Get-a-Way'/1968 * *The Adventures of Sherlock Holmes*: 'The Speckled Band'/1984

Keith, Sheila (b. 1920)

British actress. Often a harridan for Pete **Walker**, especially grim as the Black-and-Decker **cannibal** of *Frightmare* (1974).

*House of Whipcord/1974 * House of Mortal Sin/1975 * The Comeback/1977 * House of the Long Shadows/1983*

Kelljan, Robert (1930–82)

American director. One-trick pony Kelljan gave the **vampire** movie a jolt with the Yorga films, which mix **Hammer clichés** with California hip and post-**Romero** intensity. He reprises the effect in *Scream, Blacula, Scream* (1973) and 'Vampire' (1976), a *Starsky and Hutch* with John **Saxon** as an apparently genuine bloodsucker.

*Count Yorga, Vampire/1970 * The Return of Count Yorga/1971 * Act of Vengeance/1974*

Kendall, Suzy [Freda Harrison] (b. 1944)

British actress. The extremely photogenic Kendall started out as a model but graduated to film and TV roles. After **Argento**'s trendsetting *L'uccello dalle piume di cristallo* (*The Bird with the Crystal Plumage*, 1969), she was briefly in vogue as a blonde heroine in Italian shockers where her performances were often considerably helped by the dubbing process. MA

*Circus of Fear/1966 * The Penthouse/1967 * Assault/1971 * I corpi presentano tracce di violenza carnale [Torso]/Craze/Tales That Witness Madness/1973 * Spasmo/1974*

Kenton, Erle C. (1896–1980)

American director. A prolific journeyman, Kenton turned to horror with the hallucinatory and committed *Island of Lost Souls* (1933), with Charles **Laughton** and disturbing beast people, and then as a 40s Universal reliable, marshalling much-loved performers and characters in efficient, cosy programmers. A former actor, he appears in his own *End of the Trail* (1936) as Teddy Roosevelt.

*Ghost of Frankenstein/1942 * House of Frankenstein/1944 * House of Dracula/1945 * The Cat Creeps/1946*

Kier, Udo (b. 1944)

German actor. Continental sleaze specialist, distinctively **camp** and highly eccentric, a rare actor to play both Count **Dracula** (*Blood for Dracula*, 1973) and Baron **Frankenstein**

Suzy Kendall

Dominique Darel, Udo Kier, *Blood for Dracula*

(*Flesh for Frankenstein*, 1973). Discovered by pop singer/director Mike Sarne for *The Road to St. Tropez* (1966), Kier's variable career ranges wildly between the art-house quickies of Rainer Werner Fassbinder (*Lili Marleen*, 1980), the up-scale sexual fantasies of Gus Van Sant (*My Own Private Idaho*, 1991) and the politico-gore of Christoph **Schlingensief**: *100 Jahre Adolf Hitler* (*100 Years of Adolf Hitler*, 1989), *Das deutsche Kettensägenmassaker* (*The German Chainsaw Massacre*, 1991), *Terror 2000* (1993), *Die Spalte* (*The Slit*, 1995). For Walerian **Borowczyk**, Kier has played **Jack the Ripper** (*Lulu*, 1980) and Dr **Jekyll** (*Dr. Jekyll et les femmes/Blood of Dr. Jekyll*, 1981). Famous quote (as Frankenstein): 'To know death, Otto, you have to fuck life in the gall bladder.' AJ

Hexen bis auf's Blut gequält [*Mark of the Devil*]/ 1969 * *Pan*/1971 * *Exposé/Spermula*/1975 * *Suspiria*/1976 * *Die Insel der blutigen Plantage* [*Escape From Blood Plantation*]/1983 * *Epidemic*/1987 * *Europa*/1992 * *Rotwang muss weg!*/1994 * *Johnny Mnemonic*/1995

TV: *Olipant*/1972 * *Riget* [*The Kingdom*]/1995 * *Riget: Blok 2* [*The Kingdom 2*]/1996

King, George (1899–1966)

British director, producer. The job of director on Tod **Slaughter** films was presumably to stand back and turn the star loose. After pro-

ducing Milton Rosmer's *Maria Marten* (1935), King saw no reason not to direct the rest of Slaughter's major films himself. In a typical moment from *The Crimes of Stephen Hawke* (1937), a child finds Slaughter lurking in the shrubbery and declares 'my father doesn't keep a garden for nasty common people like you to look at' just before the cackling fiend snaps his spine. In *The Case of the Frightened Lady* (1940), Marius Goring takes over scenery-chewing as a gay aristo strangler.

Sweeney Todd, the Demon Barber of Fleet Street/ 1936 * *The Ticket of Leave Man/Sexton Blake and the Hooded Terror*/1938 * *The Face at the Window*/1939 * *Crimes at the Dark House*/1940

King, Stephen (b. 1947)

American writer. For twenty years, King has permeated horror to such an extent that he serves to define the modern genre. He has written science fiction (*The Long Walk*, 1979; *The Running Man*, 1982), suspense (*Rage*, 1977; *Roadwork*, 1981), fantasy (*The Dark Tower: The Gunslinger*, 1982; *The Eyes of the Dragon*, 1984) and literary fiction (*Different Seasons*, 1982; *Dolores Claiborne*, 1992), but all these are darkened by King's horror inclinations. *Carrie* (1974), his breakthrough debut, could have been packaged as s-f with its near-future setting and **ESP** theme. It is King's emotional investment in the hell-is-a-schoolyard setting and the nightmare home life of its telekinetic protagonist, as much as any supernatural content, that marks the novel as horror.

King's horror oscillates between supernatural (*'Salem's Lot*, 1975; *The Shining*, 1977; *Christine*, 1983; *Cycle of the Werewolf*, 1983; *Pet Sematary*, 1983; *Thinner*, 1984; *It*, 1986; *The Dark Half*, 1989; *Needful Things*, 1991), *guignol* suspense (*Cujo*, 1981; *Misery*, 1987; *Gerald's Game*, 1992) and s-f (*The Dead Zone*, 1979; *Firestarter*, 1980; *The Tommyknockers*, 1987). *The Stand* (1978) and *The Talisman* (with Peter **Straub**, 1984) encompass s-f, horror, crime, fantasy and social satire, as do the collections *Night Shift* (1978), *Skeleton Crew* (1985), *Four Past Midnight* (1990) and *Nightmares and Dreamscapes* (1993). Setting stories often in his home state of Maine, returning frequently to his disaster-prone town of Castle Rock, King can claim to be a major regional writer, while his recurrent interests in religious fanaticism and child abuse (much imitated in post-King

RIGHT George King

horror) afford avenues into consistent probing of America's unhealthy underside. Though of a left-liberal disposition, King often demonises the deprived while making compromised heroes of struggling middle-class characters.

He is not averse to tackling literally generic material like the **vampires** of *'Salem's Lot* or the haunted house of *The Shining*, and has even constructed an entire novel (*The Tommyknockers*) on the skeleton of another work (Nigel **Kneale**'s *Quatermass and the Pit*, 1959) while treading in a tradition of American best selling fiction that includes Grace Metalious, John Steinbeck, John D. MacDonald and James Jones. Nevertheless, it is a mistake to deem him merely a dresser-up of elderly concepts in mini-series dump-bin form. King's recent work tends to bloat with verbiage, but at his best (*Carrie, Different Seasons, Misery*) he achieves considerable effects, in an evocation of fantastical dread and the pecking monstrousness of everyday America. Neither as literary as Peter **Straub** nor as schlocky as Dean **Koontz**, King is surprisingly demanding for a writer of his enormous popular standing and is capable of unsettling rigour.

Brian **De Palma**'s *Carrie* (1976) was certainly a powerful impetus to King's career. Few subsequent film adaptations are as mindful of their source or in tune with the special qualities of King's work, but an assortment of remarkable directors have tackled the *oeuvre*. The hits include Stanley Kubrick's controversial *The Shining* (1980), Rob Reiner's *Stand By Me* (1986) and *Misery* (1990), 'Gramma' (***The Twilight Zone***,

1986), Larry **Cohen**'s revisionary *A Return to Salem's Lot* (1987), Frank Darabont's *The Shawshank Redemption* (1994), Taylor Hackford's *Dolores Claiborne* (1995) and Bryan Singer's *Apt Pupil* (1997). Directors closely associated with the horror field have tended to turn out tame items: Tobe **Hooper**'s *Salem's Lot* (1979) and *The Mangler* (1995), George **Romero**'s *Creepshow* (192) and *The Dark Half* (1993), John **Carpenter**'s *Christine* (1983), David **Cronenberg**'s *The Dead Zone* (1983). Wes **Craven**, the only major horror auteur never to have tackled King, comes closer in *A Nightmare on Elm Street* (1985) to catching the author's small town horror than any of the above-cited adaptations.

King's own film credits – scripts for *Cat's Eye* (1984), *Silver Bullet* (1985), 'Sorry, Right Number' (**Tales From the Darkside**, 1987), *Pet Sematary* (1989), *Golden Years* (1991), *Sleepwalkers* (1992), *The Stand* (1994) and *The Shining* (1996), writing and directing *Maximum Overdrive* (1986) – are not much above the level of the TV and film hackwork derived from his stories, many of which have the possessory credit *Stephen King's* appended to the title. *Carrie* was also a notorious flop as a 1988 Broadway musical, while *Misery* was hardly better served by a 1992 stage adaption. As his books get fat and his films get skimpy, it becomes harder to remember the strengths of the best of King. King acts in *Knightriders* (1980), *Creepshow, Creepshow 2, Maximum Overdrive, Pet Sematary, Sleepwalkers, The Stand, The Langoliers* and *Thinner*. *Danse*

Macabre (1981) is a notable, free-wheeling study of horror in many media, and offers more insight than the clutter of associational material that has sprung up around him.

Disciples of the Corn (s)/*Cujo*/1983 * *The Devil's Gift* (uncredited, from 'The Monkey')/*Children of the Corn*/1984 * *The Boogeyman* (s)/*The Woman in the Room* (s)/1985 * *Creepshow 2*/*The Running Man*/1987 * *Graveyard Shift*/*Tales From the Darkside: The Movie*/1990 * *The Lawnmower Man*/*Children of the Corn II*/*Pet Sematary II*/1992 * *Needful Things*/1993 * *Children of the Corn III*/1994 * *Lawnmower Man 2: Beyond Cyberspace*/1995 * *Children of the Corn IV*/1996

TV: *Tales From the Darkside*: 'The Word Processor of the Gods'/1985 * *It*/1990 * *Sometimes They Come Back*/1991 * *The Tommyknockers*/1993 * *Sometimes They Come Back Again*/*The Langoliers*/1995

Douglas Winter, *Stephen King: The Art of Darkness* (1984); Don Herron, *Reign of Fear* (1988); George Beahm, *The Stephen King Companion* (1989); Tim Underwood, Chuck Miller, *Fear Itself* (1982), *Kingdom of Fear* (1986), *Bare Bones* (1988)

King Kong (1933)

Produced and directed by Ernest B. **Schoedsack** and Merian C. **Cooper** with effects by Willis O'Brien, *King Kong* straddles adventure, fantasy, s-f and horror. Kong, giant gorilla god of Skull Island, falls for Fay

Wray and fights dinosaurs. Brought to civilisation by movie producer Robert Armstrong, Kong rampages through New York in search of his blonde and is finally martyred atop the Empire State building by buzzing biplanes. At once the culmination of a 'lost world' tradition that stretches back to Swift, Rider Haggard and Conan **Doyle** and the progenitor of the city-smashing radioactive monsters of the 50s, *King Kong* is a Depression era fable that has entered and re-entered popular culture with each reissue and re-evaluation. Though O'Brien instils Kong with a sympathetic personality, he is also a savage monster, squashing native babies and discarding rejected brunettes from a great height in oft-trimmed scenes. Skull Island (the sets also feature in Cooper-Schoedsack's **The Most Dangerous Game**, 1932) is one of the cinema's great **jungle** hells.

Sequels, spin-offs, rip-offs, parodies and remakes: *King Klunk* (1933), *The Son of Kong* (1933), *Mighty Joe Young* (1948), *Konga* (1960), *King Kong* (a TV cartoon series, 1966), *Mad Monster Party?* (1966), *Kingu Kongu No Gyakushu* (*King Kong Escapes*, 1967), *Eva, la venere selvaggia* (*King of Kong Island*, 1968), *King Kong* (1976), *A*P*E* (1976), *The Mighty Gorga* (1969), *Queen Kong* (1976), *Goliathon* (1977), *Bye Bye Monkey* (1978), *King Dong* (1984) and *King Kong Lives* (1986). A further remake, from Peter **Jackson**, was announced in 1996. Footnotes range from Bob Newhart's 'Night Watchman' monologue to Philip José Farmer's short story 'After King Kong Fell' (1973). Kong cannot be claimed exclusively for horror, but remains the movies' greatest **monster**.

Orville Goldner, George E. Turner, *The Making of King Kong* (1975); Richard Gottesman and Harry Geduld, *The Girl in the Hairy Paw* (1976)

Kinski, Klaus [Klaus-Günther Nakszynski] (1926–91)

Polish-born actor. Best known to mainstream audiences as Werner **Herzog**'s collaborator and nemesis – auteur and actor worked together on *Aguirre, der Zorn Gottes* (*Aguirre, Wrath of God*, 1973) and repeatedly thereafter, fighting endlessly – Kinski made art films, exploitation movies and at least one pornographic picture, playing leads, supporting roles and cameos with equal gusto. Over three decades, he appeared in more than 120 pictures. An actor of unnerving intensity, Kinski delivered many vivid performances, but his utter contempt for acting

Stephen King: *Creepshow*

King Kong (1932)

– addressed at length in his outrageous auto-biography *All I Need is Love* (1989) – led him to make terrible films in which he was no better than he ought to have been. He was an especially effective lunatic, and his eccentricities inspired rumours that he was, in fact, quite mad. He said he only did it for the money. Kinski's early credits include a number of German *krimis* and Spaghetti Westerns, notably as a depraved hunchback in Sergio Leone's *Per qualche dollaro in più* (*For a Few Dollars More*, 1966).

He made several films with exploitation phenomenon Jesús **Franco**, playing de **Sade** in *Justine* (1968) and *Jack the Ripper* (1976). **Renfield** in Franco's *El conde Drácula* (*Count Dracula*, 1970), he graduated to **Dracula** himself in **Herzog**'s dreamy *Nosferatu, Phantom der Nacht* (*Nosferatu the Vampyre*, 1978). Other roles include Edgar **Poe** (*Nella stretta morsa del ragno*, 1971), the half-title in *Faery*

Klaus Kinski

Tale Theatre's 'Beauty and the Beast' (1984), a **Nazi** psycho in *Crawlspace* (1986) and the self-directed *Paganini* (1989). Kinski made many bad films, but seldom failed to steal a scene. MM

*Die Toten Augen von London/1961 * Der schwarze Abt/Scotland Yard jagt Doktor Mabuse/ 1963 * Circus of Fear/1966 * Die blaue Hand/ 1967 * A doppia faccia [Double Face]/1968 * La bestia uccide a sangue freddo [Slaughter Hotel]/ 1971 * La morte sorride all'assassino/1973 * Lifespan/1974 * Schizoid/1980 * Venom/1981 * Android/1982 * Titan Find/1984 * Nosferatu a Venezia [Vampire in Venice]/1988*

TV: *The Hitchhiker*: 'Lovesounds'/1984

Kinski, Nastassia [Nastassja Nakszynski] (b. 1961)
German actress; daughter of Klaus **Kinski**. Before her official discovery by Roman

Christopher Lee, Nastassia Kinski, *To the Devil a Daughter*

Polanski for *Tess* (1980), Kinski appeared as a nude novice in *To the Devil a Daughter* (1976). She took the Simone **Simon** role, also nude, in the remake of *Cat People* (1982). Her genetic weirdness is exploited variously by *One From the Heart* (1982), *La lune dans le caniveau* (*The Moon in the Gutter*, 1983) and *In weiter ferne, so nah!* (*Faraway, So Close!*, 1993).

KISS

Rock group. In March 1996, white blues guitarists John and Edgar Winter filed suit against DC Comics claiming that in the comic *Jonah Hex: Riders of the Worm and Such* (1995), they were falsely portrayed under the names Johnny and Edgar Autumn as 'vile, depraved, stupid, cowardly, subhuman individuals who engage in wanton acts of **violence**, murder and bestiality for pleasure'. In the era of glam rock, KISS adopted superhero **comic book** identities (notably Gene Simmons, plus lolling tongue, as 'Demon' and Paul Stanley as 'Lover') and were never photographed or filmed without make-up. Far gentler, but equally theatrical, versions of Alice **Cooper**, they followed up the superior *Destroyer* (1976) and lesser *Love Gun* (1977) albums by appearing in a Marvel comic and Gordon **Hessler**'s telefilm *KISS Meets the Phantom of the Park* (1978). They abandoned make-up in 1980 for the lacklustre *Unmasked*. Simmons detoured into a minor film career: *Runaway* (1984), *Never Too Young To Die* (1986), *Trick or Treat* (1986). KISS predictably reformed (minus the late Eric Carr) and recorded 'God Gave Rock'n'Roll to You' for *Bill and Ted's Bogus Journey* (1992). PHa

Klein, T.E.D. (b. 1947)

American writer. Author of a notable novel *The Ceremonies* (1984) and novellas collected in *Dark Gods* (1985), Klein served time editing *Rod Serling's Twilight Zone Magazine* and has a credit as co-writer of Dario **Argento**'s *Trauma* (1993).

Klein Rogge, Rudolf (1888–1955)

German actor, fire-eyed evil mastermind for Fritz **Lang**, the definitive **Mabuse**. Also the metal-armed Rotwang, **mad scientist** of *Metropolis* (1926), and Attila the Hun in *Die Nibelungen: Kriemhilds Rache* (1922).

Das Cabinet des Dr. Caligari/1919 * *Der müde Tod*/1921 * *Dr. Mabuse, der Spieler*/1922 * *Spione*/1928 * *Das Testament des Dr. Mabuse*/1933

Klimovsky, León (b. 1906)

Argentine-born Spanish director. A hack who guided Paul **Naschy** through medallion-man **werewolf** movies. His Naschy-less **vampire** films deal more interestingly with murderous undead families: *La saga de los Dráculas* (*The Dracula Saga*, 1972), *La orgia nocturna de los vampiros* (*The Vampires' Night Orgy*, 1975).

El pendiente/1951 * *Maleficio*/1954 * *La noche de Walpurgis* [*Shadow of the Werewolf*]/1970 * *El doctor Jekyll y el hombre lobo* [*Dr. Jekyll and the Werewolf*]/1971 * *La rebelión de las muertas* [*Vengeance of the Zombies*]/1972 * *Odio mi cuerpo*/1973 * *Planeta Ciego*/1975

Knaggs, Skelton (1911–55)

Emaciated British-born character actor and former Shakespearian mime, usually a scheming provocateur or angry villager in Hollywood movies. SJ

Torture Ship/1939 * *The Ghost Ship*/1943 * *The Invisible Man's Revenge*/*The Lodger*/1944 * *The Picture of Dorian Gray*/*Isle of the Dead*/*House of Dracula*/1945 * *Dick Tracy vs. Cueball*/*Terror By Night*/*Bedlam*/1946 * *Dick Tracy Meets Gruesome*/1947 * *Master Minds*/1949

KNB FX Group

American special make-up effects partnership founded in 1989 by Robert Kurtzman, Greg Nicotero and Howard Berger, who had worked together on *Evil Dead II* (1987). Though they have a reputation for 'realistic' effects (the buffalo in *Dances With Wolves*, 1990; the cattle birth from *City Slickers*, 1991), KNB have a sound horror pedigree, ranging from cheapies like *Intruder* (1989) and *Halloween 5* (1989) to the bigger-budgeted *Army of Darkness* (1993) and *Vampire in Brooklyn* (1995). KNB was also responsible for the infamous ear slicing in Quentin Tarantino's *Reservoir Dogs* (1991); Kurtzman provided the original story for the Tarantino-scripted *From Dusk Till Dawn* (1995) and made a directorial debut with *The Demolitionist* (1996). MS

A Nightmare on Elm Street: The Dream Child/*The Horror Show*/*Dr. Hackenstein*/*Nightwish*/1989 * *Leatherface: Texas Chainsaw Massacre III*/*Tales From the Darkside: The Movie*/*The Borrower*/1990 * *Bride of Re-Animator*/*The People Under the Stairs*/*Misery*/1991 * *Dr. Giggles*/*Doppelganger*/*Mindwarp*/*Children of the Night*/*Severed Ties*/*Amityville 1992: It's About Time*/1992 * *Cyborg 2: Glass Shadow*/*Jason Goes to Hell: The Final Friday*/*Ticks*/1993 * *Ed and His Dead Mother*/*In the Mouth of Madness*/*Wes Craven's New Nightmare*/*Pumpkinhead II: Blood Wings*/*My Boyfriend's Back*/1994 * *Skinner*/*Village of the Damned*/*Tales From the Hood*/*Lord of Illusions*/1995 * *Witchboard III: The Possession*/*The Relic*/*DNA*/*The Eighteenth Angel*/*The Crow: City of Angels*/1996

TV: *Body Bags*/1993

theme (infected astronauts, **alien** body-snatchers, ancient astronauts, the yeti, a haunted house) and treats it with more depth than anyone else, frequently influencing subsequent approaches to related material. Homages, ranging from the slavish to the canny, can be found in a run of Quatermass wannabes – Hammer's *X–The Unknown* (1958) was scripted as a Quatermass sequel until Kneale objected to the use of his character, and other imitations include *The First Man Into Space* (1958), *The Trollenberg Terror* (1958) and 'The Dæmons' (**Doctor Who**, 1971) – and a surprising number of novels: Robert Holdstock's *Mythago Wood* (1984), Stephen **King**'s *The Tommyknockers* (1987), Stephen Laws's *The Frighteners* (1990), Kim Newman's *Jago* (1991). *Poltergeist* (1982) is indebted to *The Stone Tape* and the short story 'Minuke' (1949); John **Carpenter**'s *Prince of Darkness* (1987), which claims to be scripted by 'Martin Quatermass', combines *Quatermass and the Pit* with *The Stone Tape*.

Kneale's other significant genre contributions include 'The Chopper' (**Out of the Unknown**, 1971), about a haunted motorcycle; 'Murrain' (*Against the Grain*, 1975), a rural English take on **Dreyer**'s *Vredens dag* (*Day of Wrath*, 1943); six plays packaged under the title *Beasts* (1975), which suffer from overstated performances but manage chilling and intriguing moments; uncredited work on *Halloween III: Season of the Witch* (1983), though the most 'Nigel Kneale' aspects (involving Stonehenge) are not in his draft; and a straightforward TV adaptation of Susan Hill's ghost story *The Woman in Black* (1989).

The Witches/1966

TV: *Wuthering Heights*/1953 * *Wuthering Heights*/1962 * *Bedtime Stories*: 'Jack and the Beanstalk'/1974

ABOVE Richard Wordsworth, Nigel Kneale's *The Quatermas Experiment*

BELOW Nigel Kneale, *on the set of Qutermas II* (1955)

Kneale, Nigel [Thomas] (b. 1922)

Manx writer. Though he came to attention with *Tomato Cain* (1949), a collection of short stories, Kneale's reputation rests upon work for television and, to a lesser extent, film. His signature creation is Professor Bernard Quatermass, the rocket boffin of his BBC serials *The Quatermass Experiment* (1953), *Quatermass II* (1955) and *Quatermass and the Pit* (1959), filmed by **Hammer** in 1955, 1957 and 1967; the late-coming *Quatermass* (1978), edited into a feature as *The Quatermass Conclusion*; and radio's *The Quatermass Memoirs* (1996).

Associated with s-f for TV (*1984*, 1954; *The Year of the Sex Olympics*, 1968) and film (*The First Men in the Moon*, 1964) and even social realism (*Look Back in Anger*, 1959; *The Entertainer*, 1960), Kneale has always been drawn to the **ghost story**. Much of his s-f involves the collision of rational discourse with the apparent supernatural, a theme intelligently and provocatively examined in *The Creature* (1955; filmed as *The Abominable Snowman*, 1957), *Quatermass and the Pit*, *The Road* (1963) and his masterpiece *The Stone Tape* (1972). In all these, scientific methods are brought to bear on primal horrors for which they are ultimately held responsible.

Kneale's achievements in and out of genre are on a par with or superior to those of Rod **Serling**. He often takes a hokey

Knight, Harry Adam

British pseudonym, used by John Brosnan (b. 1947) and Leroy Kettle (b. 1949) on *Slimer* (1983), *Carnosaur* (Brosnan solo, 1984), *The Fungus* (1985) and *Bedlam* (1992). As Simon Ian Childer, Brosnan and Kettle wrote *Tendrils* (1986) and (Brosnan solo) *Worm* (1987); as James Blackstone, Brosnan and John Baxter (b. 1939) wrote *Torched* (1986). Constructed on the James **Herbert** disaster-as-horror model, the HAKs and SICs mix contemporary British settings, imaginative science (*Carnosaur*'s genengineering predates *Jurassic Park*, 1990), sly humour, appalling grue, and downbeat, often alcohol-

Otto Kruger

driven, characters. In the 90s, the movies discovered HAK: *Carnosaur* (1993), *Beyond Bedlam* (1994, from *Bedlam*), *Carnosaur 2* (1994), *Proteus* (1995; from *Slimer*), *Carnosaur 3* (1995). Connoisseurs rate *The Fungus* as the best B-novel of the 80s. Under his own name, Brosnan has written genre-related non-fiction: *The Horror People* (1976), *Future Tense: The Cinema of Science Fiction* (1978) and *The Primal Screen: A History of Science Fiction Film* (1991).

Kolchak, Carl * See: **Curtis, Dan; McGavin, Darren; Matheson, Richard**; *The Night Stalker*

Kolchak: The Night Stalker * See: ***The Night Stalker***

Koontz, Dean (b. 1945)
American writer. In the 80s, after two decades of productivity under various names and in many genres, Koontz challenged Stephen **King**'s pre-eminence as horror's big-selling craftsman. Proficient in spinning old concepts into slick, thick novels, Koontz often takes s-f material (**alien** abduction in *Strangers*, 1986; time travel in *Lightning*, 1988), but is most adept at psychosis (*The Face of Fear*, 1977; *The Voice of the Night*, 1980) and extravagant **monster** epics (*Phantoms*, 1983; *Midnight*, 1989). His novels often read like TV movies: success has inevitably led to a plethora of mainly makeshift films. As 'Owen West', he novelised *The Funhouse* (1980).

Demon Seed/1977 * *Watchers*/1988 * *Watchers II*/1990 * *Whispers/The Servants of Twilight*/1991 * *Watchers 3/Hideaway*/1994

TV: *The Face of Fear*/1990

Kosleck, Martin [Nicolai Yoshkin] (1907–94)
Russian character actor and former artist, on stage in Germany under Max Reinhardt before arriving in Hollywood in 1932. Usually **Nazis**, weaselish killers or homicidal maniacs, he is Joseph Goebbels in three different movies: memorable as Basil **Rathbone**'s **minion**-lover in *The Mad Doctor* (1940) and the swish fascist sculptor of *House of Horrors* (1946). SJ

Alraune/1930 * *Strange Holiday*/1942 * *The Mummy's Curse/The Great Alaskan Mystery*/1944 * *The Frozen Ghost/Pursuit to Algiers*/1945 * *She-Wolf of London*/1946 * *The Flesh Eaters*/1964

TV: *Dow Hour of Great Mysteries*: 'The Great Impersonation'/1960 * *Thriller*: 'Waxworks'/1962 * *Voyage to the Bottom of the Sea*: 'The Fear Makers'/1964 * *The Outer Limits*: 'The Brain of Colonel Barham'/1964 * *Get Smart*: 'Weekend Vampire'/1965 * *The Wild, Wild West*: 'The Night of the Diva'/1969 * *Night Gallery*: 'The Devil is Not Mocked'/1971

Krauss, Werner (1884–1959)
German actor, unforgettable as the scuttling, tubby mountebank of ***Das Cabinet des Dr. Caligari*** (1919). He had other significant

LEFT Stanley Kubrick, on the set of *A Clockwork Orange*.
ABOVE Malcolm McDowell, *A Clockwork Orange*

expressionist roles: **Jack the Ripper** in *Das Wachsfigurenkabinett* (*Waxworks*, 1924), the mephistophelean tempter of *Der Student von Prag* (*The Student of Prague*, 1926). Star of the anti-Semitic *Jud Süss* (1940), he was appointed an Actor of the State by the Nazis.

*Hoffmanns Erzählungen/Nächte des Grauens/ 1916 * Tötentanz/1919 * Das Medium/1921 * Geheiminisse einer Seele [Secrets of a Soul]/1926 * Paracelsus/1943*

Krueger, Freddy * See: **Craven, Wes**; **Englund, Robert**; *A Nightmare on Elm Street*

Kruger, Otto (1885–1974)
American actor, a suave leading man during the 30s and 40s. A bogus psychic in *Murder, My Sweet* (1944). SJ

*Dracula's Daughter/1936 * Hidden Menace/ 1938 * Tarzan's Desert Mystery/1943 * The Jungle Captive/1944 * Escape in the Fog/Woman Who Came Back/1945 * The Colossus of New York/1958*

TV: *Suspense*: 'After Dinner Story'/'Help Wanted'/1949 * *Lights Out*: 'Curtain Call'/ 1955 * *Thriller*: 'An Attractive Family'/1962

Kubrick, Stanley (b. 1928)
American writer, producer, director. A mordant visionary whose bleakly absurd work is all the more notable for being studio-derived, Kubrick veered increasingly to horror following relocation to Britain in 1961. *Lolita* (1962) mocks its hero's jailbait fixation with a phallic insert from *The Curse of Frankenstein* (1957) and *Dr. Strangelove, or How I Learned to Stop Worrying and Love the Bomb* (1964) tracks a holocaust brought on by one General Jack D. Ripper. *2001: A Space Odyssey* (1968), an investigation of man in imperious fantasy terms, preludes explicit horrors *A Clockwork Orange* (1971) and *The Shining* (1980). Misanthropic yet brilliantly ingratiating, *A Clockwork Orange* (Kubrick's most vitally British film) touched enough nerves to merit a viewing by the Home Secretary. A perversely anti-climactic record of insanity-from-failure within the lofty Overlook Hotel, *The Shining* is at times hardly less devastating: of annoyance to aficionados both of Stephen **King** and the supernatural, it however suggests the limits of Kubrick's interest in the genre. *Full Metal Jacket* (1987) is instead a war film that flips idiosyncratically to psycho mode. DP

Kümel, Harry (b. 1940)
Belgian director. *Le rouge aux lèvres* (*Daughters of Darkness*, 1971), Kümel's second feature, reinterpreted the Countess **Báthory** myth as a glorious cocktail of Belgian surrealism, Hollywood camp and lesbian chic. Delphine Seyrig, dominating the movie like a psychopathic Dietrich, targets a pair of not-so-innocent honeymooners overnighting at an off-season hotel on the Ostend seafront. Traditional **vampire** banes such as stakes and running water are in evidence, but the film dispenses with fangs – they would have mussed up ¬the lady's perfect *maquillage*. Kümel's other films include *Malpertuis* (1972), in which Orson **Welles** presides over an **Old Dark House** of superannuated Greek gods. AB

Laemmle Jr, Carl (1908–79)
American production executive, son of the German-born mogul who founded Universal Pictures. Head of production at 21, 'Junior' overcame the studio's catchpenny reputation with *All Quiet on the Western Front* (1930). He presided over *Dracula* (1930) and *Frankenstein* (1931) but was unseated in 1936 during a slump in Universal's fortunes.

LaLoggia, Frank (b. 1955)
American director, writer, composer, producer. LaLoggia made a precocious debut with *Fear No Evil* (1981), an Antichrist entry that (distributor-imposed re-edit by Joel **Coen** notwithstanding) contrives something serious-minded from conventional elements. Frustrated by the industry, LaLoggia turned gamekeeper as film doctor on hard-sells like *The Power* (1984). *Lady in White* (1987) is an impressively personal **ghost story**, muddying small-town nostalgia with infanticide and racism while locating childhood as a place of genuine wonder. DP

Mother/1995

Lam Ching-Ying [Lin Zhengying] (b. 1952)
Hong Kong Chinese actor, martial artist. After stuntwork with Bruce Lee, Lam became a star as a Taoist vampire hunter in producer Samo **Hung**'s *Jianghsi Xiansheng/ Mr. Vampire* series (1985, 1986, 1987, 1988, 1992). He co-stars with Hung in *Gui Da Gui* (*Encounters of the Spooky Kind*, 1981), *Ren Xia Ren* (*The Dead and the Deadly*, 1982) and *Encounters of the Spooky Kind II* (1990), and N'Xau (of *The Gods Must Be Crazy*, 1981) in the **comedy** horror *Crazy Safari* (1991). CV

*Vampire vs Vampire (+d)/1989 * Qumo Jingcha [Magic Cop]/Gambling Ghost/Skin-Stripper/ 1991 * Exorcist Master/1993*

Lanchester, Elsa [Elizabeth Sullivan] (1902–86)
British actress, wife of Charles **Laughton**. Mary **Shelley** and the Monster's unforgettable shock-haired mate in *Bride of Frankenstein* (1935). SJ

*The Ghost Goes West/1936 * Ladies in Retirement/1942 * The Spiral Staircase/1945 * Bell Book and Candle/1958 * Mary Poppins/ 1964 * Blackbeard's Ghost/1968 * Willard/ 1971 * Terror in the Wax Museum/Arnold/1973 * Murder By Death/1976*

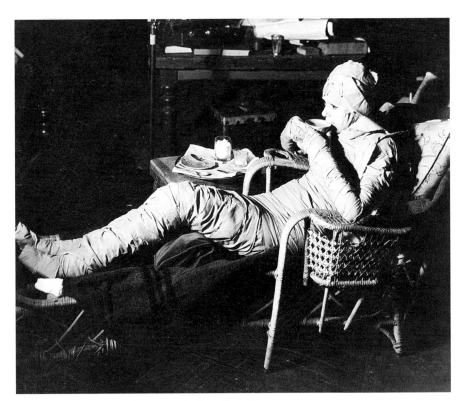

LEFT AND ABOVE Elsa Lanchester, *Bride of Frankenstein*

TV: *Lux Video Theatre*: 'Ladies in Retirement'/ 1954 * *20th Century-Fox Hour*: 'Stranger in the Night'/1956 * *Alfred Hitchcock Hour*: 'The McGregor Affair'/1964 * *Night Gallery*: 'Green Fingers'/1972

Elsa Lanchester, *Elsa Lanchester Herself* (1983)

Landau, Martin (b. 1928)

American actor. Powerful and versatile, Landau impresses as the gay spy in *North By Northwest* (1958) and the disguise expert of *Mission: Impossible* (1966–9). His best horror

work is for TV, notably outstanding *Outer Limits* episodes ('The Man Who Was Never Born' 1963; 'The Bellero Shield' 1964) and a **camp** vampire on *The Man From U.N.C.L.E.* ('The Bat Cave Affair', 1966). He followed Supporting Actor nominations (*Tucker*, 1988; *Crimes and Misdemeanors*, 1989) by taking home an Oscar for a remarkable interpretation of the aged Bela **Lugosi** ('nobody gives two focks for Bela') in *Ed Wood* (1994). Landau's understanding of Lugosi may come, in part, from his own period in unworthy schlock.

Without Warning/1980 * *Alone in the Dark*/ 1982 * *The Being*/1983

TV: *The Twilight Zone*: 'Mr Denton on Doomsday'/1959; 'The Jeopardy Room'/

1964 * *Shirley Temple Theatre*: 'The House of the Seven Gables'/1960 * *Alfred Hitchcock Hour*: 'Second Verdict'/1964 * *Mission: Impossible*: 'Zubrovnik's Ghost'/1966; 'The Psychic'/1967 * *The Fall of the House of Usher*/ 1979 * *The Twilight Zone*: 'The Beacon'/1985 * *Alfred Hitchcock Presents*: 'The Final Twist'/ 1987

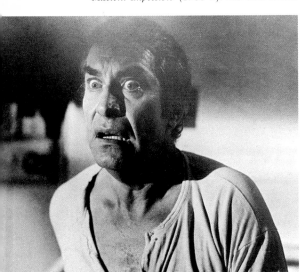

LEFT Martin Landau, *Alone in the Dark*

Landers, Lew [Louis Friedlander] (1901–62)

American director. Though *The Raven* (1935), signed Friedlander, is a shaky 'A' with **Lugosi** and **Karloff** going for *guignol*, Landers worked mainly in the B-hive: typical of his output are *Sing, Dance, Plenty Hot* (1940), *After Midnight With Boston Blackie* (1943) and *Cowboy Canteen* (1944). *Return of the Vampire* (1943), with Lugosi, is Columbia's effective Universal imitation, and *The Mask of Dijon* (1946) gives Erich von **Stroheim** the PRC treatment.

The Vanishing Shadow/1934 * *The Boogie Man Will Get You*/1942 * *The Power of the Whistler*/ 1945 * *Seven Keys to Baldpate*/1947 * *Inner Sanctum*/1948 * *Man in the Dark*/1953 * *Terrified!*/1962

Landis, John (b. 1950)

American director, writer. A fanboy from the time he saw *The 7th Voyage of Sinbad* (1958), Landis dropped out of school to be a director. He landed a job in the 20th Century-Fox mailroom, then paid his own way to Yugoslavia to work as a gofer on *Kelly's Heroes* (1970). After a year in Italy as a stuntman, the twenty-year-old Landis was broke, depressed and living with his mother. A true product of junk culture, his conspicuous influences include horror, s-f and martial arts movies, as well as trashy television. *Schlock* (1972), his first feature, is a low-budget lampoon in which he also plays an **ape** man in a Rick **Baker** gorilla suit. Having made a name as a comedy director with *National Lampoon's Animal House* (1978) and *The Blues Brothers* (1980), he peaked early with *An American Werewolf in London* (1981), which walks the thin line between black comedy and potent horror with remarkable aplomb.

When in doubt, he will always go for the laugh, and most of his films are outright – and unsubtle – comedies: *Trading Places* (1983), *Spies Like Us* (1985), *¡Three Amigos!* (1986), *The Stupids* (1995). He directed the video for Michael Jackson's 'Thriller' (1983), a teen horror movie spoof, complete with dancing **zombies**, narrated by Vincent **Price**, and did not return to horror until *Innocent Blood* (1993), an unsuccessful hybrid **vampire**-mafia movie. Landis's reputation was seriously tarnished when Vic Morrow and two child actors were killed during the filming of his segment of *Twilight Zone: The Movie* (1983); indicted on charges of manslaughter in 1983, he was acquitted in 1987. Fond of casting other directors in cameo roles, he has himself played bit parts. MM

Eating Raoul (a)/1982 * *Coming Soon* (p)/1984 * *Amazon Women on the Moon* (co-d)/1987 * *Spontaneous Combustion* (a)/1989 * *Darkman* (a)/1990 * *Sleepwalkers* (a)/*Body Chemistry 2* (a)/1991 * *The Silence of the Hams* (a)/1993

John Landis

Fritz Lang

TV: *The Stand* (a)/1994 * *Here Come the Munsters* (executive p)/1995

Landres, Paul (b. 1912)

American director. A specialist in musicals (*Rhythm Inn*, 1951) and Westerns (*Frontier Gun*, 1958), Landres made two minor but interesting **vampire** pictures with contemporary small-town settings

The Vampire/1957 * *The Return of Dracula*/*The Flame Barrier*/1958

Lang, Fritz (1890–1976)

Austrian director, writer. Lang was replaced by Robert **Weine** as director of ***Das Cabinet des Dr. Caligari*** (1919). He contributed the notion of the **asylum** frame which 'explains' the visual excesses of the art direction: as this suggests, he was less concerned with **expressionism** than a combination of visual imagination and commercial accessibility.

In the 20s, he specialised in the bizarre, mounting the fable-like *Der müde Tod* (*Destiny*, 1921), the legendry of the two-part *Die Nibelungen* (1924), the macabre serial-style thrills of *Die Spinnen* (1919), *Dr. Mabuse der Spieler* (1922) and *Spione* (*Spies*, 1928), and a vision of the future as gothic inferno in *Metropolis* (1927). With its steel-handed mad scientist and *Alraune*-like robotrix seductress, *Metropolis* was at least as influential on Universal's ***Frankenstein*** cycle as on other dystopias. *M* (1931), with Peter **Lorre** as a whistling child-murderer, and *Das*

Testament des Dr Mabuse (*The Last Will of Dr. Mabuse*, 1933), which confines **Mabuse** to an **asylum**, are **urban horrors**, haunted by a madness as much social as individual, reflecting the half-Jewish Lang's feelings upon learning that Goebbels and Hitler were admirers of *Metropolis*.

Abandoning Nazi wife and scenarist Thea von Harbou, Lang decamped to France, where he made the fantasy *Liliom* (1934), then to Hollywood, where he began a career in **film noir** with *Fury* (1936). His American films lack the supernatural spin of European efforts, but are shot through with nocturnal pursuits, psychological excess and incidences of unforgettable **violence**: *You Only Live Once* (1937), *Man Hunt* (1941), *The Ministry of Fear* (1944), *Scarlet Street* (1945), *Secret Beyond the Door . . .* (1947), *House By the River* (1950), *The Big Heat* (1953), *While the City Sleeps* (1956), *Beyond a Reasonable Doubt* (1956). At the end of his career, he returned to Germany and extravagant pulp poetry with *Der Tiger von Eschnapur* and *Das Indische Grabmal* (1959), a remake of his 1921 script, and *Die tausend Augen des Dr. Mabuse* (*The Thousand Eyes of Dr Mabuse*, 1960), which revived the character for a new series.

Hilde Warren und der Tod (w/a)/1917 * *Tötentanz* (w)/*Lilith und Ly* (w)/*Die Pest in Florenz* (w)/1919 * *Das indische Grabmal* (w)/ 1919

Lotte Eisner, *Fritz Lang* (1976)

Langella, Frank (b. 1940)

American actor. A romantic Latin **Dracula** in the 1975 Broadway revival, Langella repeated his Count, somewhat indebted to Valentino and Travolta, in John Badham's elegant but superfluous *Dracula* (1979). Subsequent career highlight: Skeletor in *Masters of the Universe* (1987).

Sphinx/1981 * *Body of Evidence*/1994 * *Brainscan*/1994

TV: *Sherlock Holmes*/1981

Larraz, Joseph [José Ramón Larraz] (b. 1929)

Spanish director. A self-exile, Larraz thrived in Paris as a comics artist and fashion photographer before moving to Britain to start his film career with the voyeuristic *Whirlpool* (1969). *Symptoms* (1974) is the least lurid of his sleazy, spottily striking **sex**-horrors. *Vampyres* (1974), his best-known entry, crosses the exploitation sensibility of **Hammer**'s *Carmilla* series with Jean **Rollin** oneirics. Subsequent Spanish-financed items are mostly dreadful. DP

Deviation/1971 * *Scream and Die*/*Emma, puertos oscuras*/1973 * *La muerta incierta*/1977 * *La visita del vicio* [*Violation of the Bitch*]/1978 * *Polvos magicos*/1979 * *Estigma*/*La momia nacional*/*Los ritos sexuales del diablo* [*Black Candles*]/1981 * *Descanse en piezas*/1987 * *Filo del hacha*/1988 * *Deadly Manor*/1990

Late Night Horror (UK TV series, 1968)
A six-part taped colour BBC series, mixing fine performances with classic stories. Brenda Bruce and Donald Sinden juggle **brains** in Roald **Dahl**'s 'William and Mary'; Michele Dotrice and Ronald Hines hear Robert **Aickman**'s 'The Bells of Hell'; Diane Cilento and Roy Dotrice exchange Arthur Conan **Doyle**'s 'The Kiss of Blood'; Claire Bloom and Nora Nicholson are haunted by H. Russell Wakefield's 'The Triumph of Death'; Richard **Matheson** demonstrates there is 'No Such Thing as a Vampire' and John Burke proves 'The Corpse Can't Play'. TM

ABOVE Robert Mitchum, *Night of the Hunter*
LEFT Charles Laughton on the set of *Night of the Hunter*

Laughton, Charles (1899–1962)
British actor. Outstanding as the sadistic, whip-cracking Moreau in *Island of Lost Souls* (1933) and the sympathetic bellringer in **The Hunchback of Notre Dame** (1939). *The Night of the Hunter* (1955), his only film as a director, is a remarkably eerie evocation of childhood menace, stalked by Robert Mitchum's evil preacher. SJ

The Old Dark House/1932 * *The Canterville Ghost*/1943 * *The Strange Door*/1951

Elsa Lanchester, *Charles Laughton and I* (1938); Charles Higham, *Charles Laughton: An Intimate Biography* (1976); Simon Callow, *Charles Laughton: A Difficult Actor* (1987)

Laymon, Richard (b. 1947)
American writer. Prolific author of spare, nasty horror novels more influenced by films like *The Hills Have Eyes* (1977) than earlier literature. His output includes *The Captive* (1980), *The Beast House* (1981), *Out Are the Lights* (1982), *One Rainy Night* (1991) and the **Jack the Ripper** Western *Savage* (1993).

Leakey, Philip (1908–92)
British make-up artist, employed by **Hammer Films** from 1947 to 1958. He designed the

creature makeup worn by Christopher **Lee** in *The Curse of Frankenstein* (1957). The sub-tler look used on Lee in *Dracula* (1958) pop-ularised **vampire** fangs. MS

Room to Let/1949 * *The Quatermass Experiment*/1955 * *Quatermass 2*/*The Abominable Snowman*/1957 * *X-The Unknown*/*The Revenge of Frankenstein*/*The Hound of the Baskervilles*/1958 * *The Eyes of Annie Jones*/1963 * *Vampira*/1974

Leap in the Dark (UK TV series, 1973–80)

A low-key supernatural series from BBC Bristol. Originally trading, like **One Step Beyond** (1959–61), in reconstructions of alleged actual events, with introductions from Colin Wilson and serious debate about **parapsychology**, it offered in its 1980 sea-son original plays from Fay Weldon ('Watch-ing Me, Watching You'), Alan Garner ('To Kill a King'), David Pownall ('Room for an Inwad Light'), Russell Hoban ('Come and Find Me') and David Rudkin ('The Living Grave'). The bulk of the series was directed by Colin Godman.

LeBorg, Reginald (1902–88)

Austrian-born American director. Identified with horror through Universal's 40s **Inner Sanctum** Bs, LeBorg was periodically given charge of poverty-row vehicles unworthy of their casts. *The Black Sleep* (1954) – with **Rathbone**, **Chaney Jr**, **Lugosi** and **Carradine** – is creditable if stuffy, but *Voodoo Island* (1957), with **Karloff**, and *Diary of a Madman* (1963), with **Price**, are dreary, and

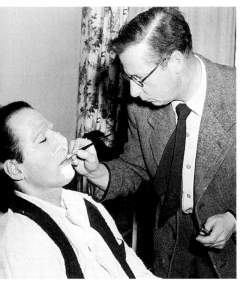

Christopher Lee, Philip Leakey, *The Curse of Frankenstein*

Christopher Lee, *Dracula Has Risen From the Grave*

House of the Black Death (co-directed with Harold Daniels, 1965), with Chaney Jr and Carradine, is a disaster.

Calling Dr. Death/1943 * *Dead Man's Eyes*/*Weird Woman*/*Jungle Woman*/*Destiny*/*The Mummy's Ghost*/1944 * *The Eyes of Annie Jones*/1964 * *So Evil, My Sister*/1973

Wheeler W. Dixon, *The Films of Reginald LeBorg* (1992)

Lecter, Hannibal * See: Cox, Brian; Demme, Jonathan; Harris, Thomas; Hopkins, Anthony; Mann, Michael

Lee, Christopher (b. 1922)

British actor. Of *Dracula* (1958), Terence **Fisher** said: 'of course, **Dracula** had to be an aristocrat . . . but Christopher Lee imposed himself on you just as though he were a high priest or bishop, demanding worship or allegiance. That was Christopher Lee's great strength as Dracula: he was always in command.'

In the 50s, Lee was a little-known but phenomenally busy actor pursuing a very varied career in a flurry of British movies,

usually as upper-class villains cursed with low motives and an even lower voice. Then **Hammer** picked him over Bernard Bresslaw for the man-made creature in *The Curse of Frankenstein* (1957) with Peter **Cushing** as Victor **Frankenstein**. It was the role which **Karloff** had made so very much his own, implying a degree of melancholy within the massive frame. Little compassion was allowed into the new-style Hammer crea-ture: he is all malice with no sense of self-reproach. Denied Universal's copyrighted make-up, the new face presented to an appalled and entertained world allows little room for expression to externalise the thoughts within. Lee did not think much would follow: 'My face was hidden by scar-ring tissue, my body by bandage-wrapping; I was nothing but a mobile parcel. But then Dracula came along and I knew this was going to be a long-term career if I wanted to follow in its path.'

The Curse of Frankenstein had the advan-tage of being the right escapist movie in the right escapist time, a British horror film made in colour. It was the biggest dollar earner made in Britain in that year. *Dracula* goes straight for the jugular of explicit bodily take-over, with Dracula's victims seeming to relish his throat-biting nuzzles. Meeting the vampire on his own terms, if not his own ground, **Van Helsing** forces Dracula into a lethal ray of sunlight: only dust, a wisp of hair and signet ring is left. So the Count is gone, but, of course, not forgotten. Lee returned as a **vampire** in an Italian movie, *Tempi duri per i vampiri* (*Uncle Was a Vampire*, 1959): the blood-letter became part of the family. Lee had taken on the universal (as opposed to Universal!) role of Dracula. Studio portraits depict him with a chic drool of blood leaking from his mouth in the manner of a displaced kiss-curl: *Dracula, Prince of Darkness* (1965), *Dracula Has Risen From the Grave* (1968), *Taste the Blood of Dracula* (1969), *Scars of Dracula* (1970).

Lee ventures back under shrouding bandages in the remake of **The Mummy** (1959) and takes sneery stooge roles for *The Hound of The Baskervilles* (1959), *The Man Who Could Cheat Death* (1959) and *The Two Faces of Dr. Jekyll* (1960). The aristo-vampire pursued him throughout his career, taking in a non-Hammer stab from Jesús **Franco** (*El conde Drácula*, 1971), though there was also the moustache-drooping Oriental evil mastermind **Fu Manchu** (*The Face of Fu Manchu*, 1965), *Rasputin, the Mad Monk* (1966), **Jekyll and Hyde** (*I, Monster*, 1971) and several essays at **Sherlock Holmes** (*Sherlock Holmes und das Halsband des Todes/Sherlock Holmes and the Deadly Necklace*, 1962; *Sherlock Holmes: The Golden Years*, 1991). Among his best genre efforts are Mario **Bava**'s *La frusta e il corpo* (*The Whip and the Flesh*, 1963), **Fisher**'s *The Devil Rides Out* (1967) and Robin **Hardy**'s *The Wicker Man* (1973). Lee was always trying to divert his career from the specific bloodstream into the more generalised mainstream. While Cushing seemed mainly content to stick to Hammer horrors, Lee ventured in other directions: Mycroft (*The Private Life of Sherlock Holmes*, 1970), Rochefort (*The Three Musketeers*, 1974), a Bond villain (*The Man With the Golden Gun*, 1974). However, unlike Cushing or Vincent **Price**, Lee accepted marquee value non-entity parts in pay-the-rent horrors, providing as uncommitted a turn in films excellent (*Scream and Scream Again*, 1969; *Death Line*, 1972), ordinary (*The Oblong Box*, 1970; *Dark Places*, 1972) and dire (*DeSade 70/Eugenie: The Story of Her Journey Into Perversion*, 1969; *Hollywood Meatcleaver Massacre*, 1977). As repetition thinned the original terrors, a touch of self-mockery crept in with *Dracula A.D.*

1972 (1972) and *The Satanic Rites of Dracula* (1973), turning to outright parody in *Dracula, père et fils* (1976).

What Lee brings to horror is a sense of authority and, as Fisher declared, command. He is no maimed casualty of fate, but a man totally in control. In a way it is a pity he himself became as much a dramatic martyr to the Count as any of his victims. Who knows what Lee would have become if it hadn't been for such typecasting. After all, in an astonishing vice-versa of circumstance, Lee's career was regenerated by Dracula – the fresh blood of a wholly irresistible character pumped back into its host. Making him one of horror's authentic superstars. TH

Christopher Lee

Corridor of Mirrors/1948 * *The Mirror and Markheim*/1954 * *Alias John Preston*/1955 * *Corridors of Blood*/1958 * *City of the Dead*/1959 * *The Hands of Orlac*/1960 * *Terror of the Tongs/Taste of Fear/Ercole al centro della terra* [*Hercules in the Haunted World*]/1961 * *La cripta e l'incubo* [*Crypt of Terror*]/*La vergine di Norimberga* [*The Virgin of Nuremberg*]/1963 * *Il castello dei morti vivi* [*Castle of the Living Dead*]/*The Gorgon/Dr. Terror's House of Horrors*/1964 * *She/The Skull*/1965 * *Theatre of Death/Brides of Fu Manchu*/1966 * *Das Schlangengrube und das Pendel* [*Blood Demon*]/*Circus of Fear/Victims of Terror* (s)/*The Vengeance of Fu Manchu/Night of the Big Heat*/1967 * *El castillo de Fu Manchu* [*Castle of Fu Manchu*]/*Fu Manchu y el beso de la muerte* [*The Blood of Fu Manchu*]/*Curse of the Crimson Altar*/1968 * *The Magic Christian*/1969 * *The House That Dripped Blood/One More Time/Vampyr/El proceso de las brujas* [*Night of the*

Blood Monsters]/1970 * *Nothing But the Night/The Creeping Flesh*/1972 * *Pánico en el Transiberiano* [*Horror Express*]/*In Search of Dracula* (s)/1974 * *To the Devil a Daughter/The Keeper*/1976 * *End of the World*/1977 * *House of the Long Shadows*/1983 * *New Magic* (s)/1984 * *Howling II: Stirba, Werewolf Bitch*/1985 * *Mask of Murder*/1989 * *Gremlins 2: The New Batch/The Rainbow Thief*/1990 * *Curse III: Blood Sacrifice*/1991 * *The Funny Man*/1994 * *Sorrellina*/1995

TV: *Colonel March Investigates*: 'At Night All Cats Are Gray'/1954 * *One Step Beyond*: 'The Sorcerer'/1961 * *Alfred Hitchcock Hour*: 'Sign of Satan'/1964 * *The Avengers*: 'Never Never Say Die'/1967; 'The Interrogators'/1969 * *Orson Welles' Great Mysteries*: 'The Leather Funnel'/1974 * *Poor Devil*/1973 * *Goliath Awaits*/1981 * *Tales of the Haunted*: 'Evil Stalks This House'/1981 * *Faerie Tale Theatre*: 'The Boy Who Left Home to Find Out About the Shivers'/1984 * *The Tomorrow People*: 'The Rameses Connection'/1995 * *Masque of the Red Death*/1996

Christopher Lee, *Tall, Dark and Gruesome* (1977); Robert W. Pohle Jr, Douglas C. Hart, *The Films of Christopher Lee* (1983); Mark A. Miller, *Christopher Lee and Peter Cushing and Horror Cinema* (1995).

Lee, Rowland V. (1891–1975)

American director, producer. Having directed Warner Oland's **Fu Manchu** (*The Mysterious Dr. Fu Manchu*, 1929; *The Return of Dr. Fu Manchu*, 1930) and produced an early **Sherlock Holmes** (*The Sign of Four*, 1932), Lee blossomed with the surrealist romance of *Zoo in Budapest* (1933) and the stagy suspense of *Love From a Stranger* (1936). Universal's *Son of Frankenstein* (1939) is a super-production, even more bizarre visually than the James **Whale** films it imitates, with witty work from **Rathbone**, **Atwill** and **Lugosi**. *Tower of London* (1939), a **Karloff**-Rathbone follow-up, adds grotesque touches to the swashbuckling Lee practises in *The Count of Monte Cristo* (1934) and *The Three Musketeers* (1935).

Le Fanu, J. Sheridan (1814–73)

Irish writer. Le Fanu inherited the gothic tradition but altered it, valuing abnormal psychology and genuine supernatural over melodrama and trickery, laying the foundations for the classic age of the **ghost story** and the modern horror tale. His novels are picaresque (*The House By the Churchyard*, 1863) or claustrophobic (*Uncle Silas*, 1864)

Rowland V. Lee

gothics, but his shorter fictions (*Ghost Stories and Tales of Mystery*, 1851, *In a Glass Darkly*, 1872) are striking exercises in supernatural horror. Among his best, most anthologised stories are 'Schalken the Painter' (1839), 'Ultor de Lacy' (1861), 'Squire Toby's Will' (1868), 'Green Tea' (1869), 'The Haunted Baronet' (1870), 'The Room in the Dragon Volant' (1872) and the oft-filmed vampire piece **'Carmilla'** (1871).

*Uncle Silas/El mysterioso tio Silas/*1947 * *Sleep of Death/*1978

TV: *Dow Hour of Great Mysteries*: 'The Inn of the Flying Dragon'/1960 * *Mystery and Imagination*: 'The Flying Dragon'/1966; 'Uncle Silas'/1968 * *Omnibus*: 'Schalcken the Painter'/1979 * *The Dark Angel*/1989

Michael Holroyd, *Sheridan Le Fanu and Victorian Ireland* (1980).

'The Legend of Sleepy Hollow'

First published in *The Sketch-Book of Geoffrey Crayon* (1819–20), Washington Irving's story centres on the encounter between Ichabod Crane, a superstitious schoolmaster, and the Headless Horseman, a supposed ghost. The most memorable screen adaptation is the retelling by Julia Dean in *Curse of the Cat People* (1944), but there are versions from 1908, 1912, 1922 (*The Headless Horseman*), 1949 (**Disney**'s *The Adventures of Ichabod and Mr Toad*, narrated by Bing Crosby), 1958 (on

Shirley Temple Theatre, narrated by **Karloff**), 1972 (a cartoon narrated by John **Carradine**), 1979 (a segment of *CBS Library* with Rene Auberjonois) and 1980 (a TV movie with Jeff **Goldblum**). While the spectre of *The Headless Ghost* (1959) is of the 'head tucked underneath her arm' variety, a few other spurious screen spooks follow Irving's **rationalised supernatural** pattern, notably the ghost of *Ask a Policeman* (1938). The *Ghost of Dragstrip Hollow* (1959) is make-up man Paul Blaisdell in his *She-Creature* (1956) suit.

Leiber, Fritz (1910–92)

American writer. Known for fantasy (the 'Fafhrd and Grey Mouser' series) and science fiction (*The Big Time*, 1958), Leiber was also a major supernatural writer. The s-f novel *Gather, Darkness!* (1943) and the horror novel *Conjure Wife* (1943) deal with cabals of **witches**, undermining a future theocracy or the marriage of a professor. The stories collected in *Night's Black Agents* (1947) and the late novel *Our Lady of Darkness* (1977) are remarkable post-**Lovecraft** weird fictions, unusually sensitive and subtly creepy though not without dark humour. *Conjure Wife* has been filmed as *Weird Woman* (1944),

an episode of *Moment of Fear* (1960), *Night of the Eagle* (*Burn, Witch, Burn!*, 1962), *Witches' Brew*, 1980) and (very loosely) *Bewitched* (1964–72). 'The Girl With the Hungry Eyes' (1949), a psychic **vampire** story, became a 1972 *Night Gallery* and a 1994 feature. The son of actor Fritz Leiber Sr (*The Hunchback of Notre Dame*, 1939; *Cry of the Werewolf*, 1944), he appears in *Equinox* (1971).

Leigh, Janet [Jeanette Morrison] (b. 1927)

American actress. Having survived menace in a motel room in *Touch of Evil* (1958), Leigh became a horror icon by dying in a motel bathroom. The shower-stall fate of Marion Crane, the ostensible heroine of **Psycho** (1960), demonstrated that in the uncertain universe **Hitchcock** opened for modern horror anyone could be a **victim**. Her daughters by Tony Curtis are actresses Jamie Lee **Curtis** and Kelly Curtis (*La setta*, 1992).

*Houdini/*1953 * *The Vikings/*1958 * *The Manchurian Candidate/*1962 * *Night of the Lepus/*1972 * *The Fog/*1980

TV: *Honeymoon with a Stranger/*1969 * *The Deadly Dream/*1971 * *Circle of Fear*: 'Death's

Janet Leigh, *Psycho*

Head'/1973 * *Roald Dahl's Tales of the Unexpected*: 'Light Fingers'/1982 * *The Twilight Zone*: 'Rendezvous in a Dark Place'/1989

Janet Leigh, Christopher Nickens, *Psycho: Behind the Scenes of the Classic Thriller* (1995)

Leni, Paul (1885–1929)

German director. Originally an art director, first in the theatre (for Max Reinhardt) and then the cinema, Leni made a directorial debut with *Der Feldarzt* (1917) and co-directed (with Leopold Jessner) *Hintertreppe* (*Backstairs*, 1921), a key film in the social realist strand of **expressionist** cinema. After the flamboyant **anthology** *Das Wachsfigur-enk-abinett* (*Waxworks*, 1924) – with Haroun al-Raschid, Ivan the Terrible and **Jack the Ripper** played by icons Emil Jannings, Conrad **Veidt** and Paul **Wegener** – Leni left for Hollywood, where he brought his love of shadowed sets and penchant for stories of psychotic cruelty to the archetypal **Old Dark House** of *The Cat and the Canary* (1927). *The Man Who Laughs* (1928), which tries to make Veidt a rival for Lon **Chaney**, is a more imaginative setting for the title grotesque (an ever-grinning mediaeval freak) than the stuffy pictures mounted for Chaney. Leni's career was cut short by fatal blood poisoning before he could make a talkie.

The Chinese Parrot/1927 * *The Last Warning*/1929

Lenzi, Umberto (b. 1931)

Italian director. After a debut with *Le avventure di Mary Read* (1961), Lenzi was known in the 60s for action films and thrillers, including the Carroll Baker vehicles *Orgasmo* (*Paranoia*, 1968) and *Paranoia* (*A Quiet Place to Kill*, 1970). His films took on a darker tone with a reworking of *The Spiral Staircase* (1946), *Il coltello di ghiaccio* (1972), the **gialli** *Sette orchidee macchiate di rosso* (1972) and *Spasmo* (1974) and several violent entries in the brief-lived *polizia* cycle. Lenzi claims to have invented the **cannibal** genre with *Il paese del sesso selvaggio* (*Man from Deep River*, 1972), a brutal revision of *A Man Called Horse* (1970). The graphic intensity of his cannibal trilogy, completed by the dissolute *Mangiati vivi!* (*Eaten Alive*, 1980) and the vengeful *Cannibal ferox* (1981), has waned with time while Ruggero **Deodato**'s subversive *Cannibal holocaust* (1980) proves the genuine classic of the subgenre. Lenzi also helmed an antic entry in the **zombie** arena, *Incubo sulla città contaminata* (*Nightmare City*, 1980). His later work is relatively tepid. Pseudonym: Humphrey Humbert. DW

Kriminal/1967 * *La Casa 3* [*Ghosthouse*]/1987 * *Le porte dell'inferno* [*Hell's Gate*]/*Paura nel buio* [*Hitcher in the Dark*]/*Nightmare Beach: La spiaggia del terrore* [*Welcome to Spring Break*] (supervisor)/1989 * *Demoni 3* [*Black Demons*]/1990

RIGHT Paul Leni

Leon, Gerardo de (1913–81)

Filipino director. DeLeon adds a Catholic twist to **vampirism** in *The Blood Drinkers* (1966) and *Curse of the Vampires* (1970) and kicks off the **Philippines**' 'Blood Island' saga with *Terror is a Man* (1959) and its loonier remake *The Mad Doctor of Blood Island* (1969). He passed the torch to co-director Eddie **Romero**, who continued the cycle.

Leroux, Gaston (1868–1927)

French writer. Though remembered for *Le fantôme de l'opéra* (**The Phantom of the Opera**, 1911), Leroux wrote other significant novels: *Balaoo* (1912) – filmed as *Balaoo* (1913), *The Wizard* (1927) and *Dr. Renault's Secret1* (1942) – has a Moreau-ish scientist humanising an **ape**; *Le mystére de la chambre jaune* (*The Mystery of the Yellow Room*, 1908), filmed by Marcel L'Herbier in 1930, is an influential locked-room mystery. L'Herbier also filmed Leroux's 1909 mystery *La parfum de la dame en noir* (1930), whose title was borrowed for a 1974 Italian horror film. *The Phantom of Paris* (1931) has John Gilbert as Leroux's illusionist adventurer Cheri-Bibi.

Lesbianism * See: Homosexuality

Levin, Ira (b. 1929)

American writer. *Rosemary's Baby* (1967, filmed 1968) founded the best selling horror genre, though its Satanism and Antichrist themes merely spotlight a concern with marital betrayal and pregnancy paranoia. *The Stepford Wives* (1972; filmed 1974) uses robotics to tackle similar feminist issues. Other works: *A Kiss Before Dying* (1953; filmed 1956, 1991), a 'trick' mystery; *This Perfect Day* (1970), a dystopian vision; *The Boys From Brazil* (1976; filmed 1978), about cloning Hitler; *Deathtrap* (1978; filmed 1982), a play crossbreeding **Les diaboliques** (1954) and *Sleuth* (1970); and *Sliver* (1991; filmed 1993), a high-tech psycho thriller. TV spin-offs: *Dr. Cook's Garden* (1970; from a 1967 play), with Bing Crosby as a folksy mass murderer; *Look What Happened to Rosemary's Baby* (1976); *Revenge of the Stepford Wives* (1980) and *The Stepford Children* (1988).

TV: *Alfred Hitchcock Presents*: 'Sylvia' (st)/1958

Lewin, Albert (1894–1968)

American director, producer, writer. An MGM employee who worked as a writer (*The Actress*, 1928) and producer (*Mutiny on the Bounty*, 1935) under the influence of Irving Thalberg, Lewin turned director and graced Paramount with three literary adap-

Albert Lewin

tations which combine taste with delirium and spotlight George **Sanders** at his most suavely snide. Lewin's take on **Wilde**'s *The Picture of Dorian Gray* (1945) is, oddly but aptly, no more nor less fantastical than his versions of Maugham (*The Moon and Sixpence*, 1942) and **Maupassant** (*The Private Affairs of Bel Ami*, 1947). His most amazing film, fulfilling the promise of the Technicolor portrait in the monochrome *Dorian Gray*, is *Pandora and the Flying Dutchman* (1951), with Ava Gardner and James Mason conducting supernatural *amour fou* in a surreal Spain. *Saadia* (1957) and *The Living Idol* (1957), magic romances set in Morocco and Mexico, are as preposterous, if stuffier and less fun.

Lewis, Fiona (b. 1946)

Brunette British actress. Her best horror role is a deliciously sensuous Lucy in Dan **Curtis**'s stolid *Dracula* (1973), but she plays second fiddle to Susan George in *Tintorera*, wasted as scantily-clad shark fodder. Striking as a **mad scientist** in Michael Laughlin's *Strange Behaviour* (1981) and an **alien** Avon Lady in his follow-up *Strange Invaders* (1983). MA

Dance of the Vampires/1967 * *Blue Blood*/*Dr. Phibes Rises Again*/1972 * *Lisztomania*/1975 * *The Fury*/1977

TV: *Hart to Hart*: 'Murder Wrap'/1983 * *Alfred Hitchcock Presents*: 'The Jar'/1986

RIGHT Fiona Lewis

Lewis, Herschell Gordon (b. 1926)

American director, writer, producer, 'godfather of gore'. With sometime partner David **Friedman**, H.G. Lewis is credited with inventing the gore film, forerunner of the **splatter movie**. A humanities lecturer who switched to advertising, Lewis made commercials and utility shorts in Chicago before turning to features. His first success was the episodic no-budget nudie *The Adventures of Lucky Pierre* (1961), produced and co-written by distributor Friedman. Further sexploiters include *Boin-n-g!* (1963), a movie-movie that mocks the genre, and early 'roughie' *Scum of the Earth* (1963).

Blood Feast (1963) was the result of an urge to delve new subject areas, its McGuffin plot (about a **cannibal** Egyptian caterer) excusing in pornographic manner a series of explicit, offal-heavy female mutilations. A grindhouse/drive-in smash, the film provided a template for *Two Thousand Maniacs!* (1964), *Color Me Blood Red* (1965), *The Gruesome Twosome* (1967), *Boin-n-g!* equivalent *The Wizard of Gore* (1970) and swansong *The Gore-Gore Girls* (1972). It also informed his less brutal *Something Weird* (1967), more mainstream *A Taste of Blood* (1967) and non-horror items like *She-Devils on Wheels* (1968). Concerned only with gruesome

money-shots, Lewis's shockers are outrageous but cynical burlesques, negligently fabricated and performed. He shot *The Psychic* (1968) and re-edited Bill **Rebane**'s *Terror at Halfday* into *Monster a-Go-Go* (1965).

Fans include John Waters, Frank **Henenlotter**, Jonathan Ross and Jackie Kong (*Blood Diner*, 1988); *Dr. Gore* (1975) is by assistant Pat Patterson. Lewis re-emerged in the 80s as a direct marketing millionaire, gleefully admitting his obsession with profit.
DP

Daniel Krogh, John **McCarty**, *The Amazing Herschell Gordon Lewis and His World of Exploitation Films* (1983)

Lewis, Matthew (1775–1818)

British writer. Setting out to shock, the young Lewis wrote *The Monk: A Romance* (1796) as an explicit answer to the tasteful **gothic novels** of Anne **Radcliffe**. He wallows in the tale of Ambrosio, a virtuous monk corrupted by a Satanic seductress, lacing the narrative with rape, torture, **incest**, necrophilia, hellfire, the **Wandering Jew** and a spectre called 'the Bleeding Nun'. Though not without ridiculous aspects, the novel was admired by de **Sade** and **Byron**. *The Monk* has been filmed twice, in 1972 (as *Le Moine*) by Ado Kyrou from a script by Luis **Buñuel** and Jean-Claude Carrière with

Franco Nero ensnared by Nathalie Delon, and in 1991 by Paco Lara, with Paul McGann succumbing to Sophie Ward. Lewis also wrote the novels *The Bravo of Venice* (1805) and *Feudal Tyrants* (1806), the collections *Tales of Terror* (1799) and *Tales of Wonder* (1801) and the play *The Castle Spectre* (1797), much admired for spectacular spook effects.

Lewis, Sheldon (1868–1958)

American actor. One of the screen's first horror stars, Lewis was famous as 'the Clutching Hand', villain of the serial *The Exploits of Elaine* (1914). Cast in a *Dr. Jekyll and Mr. Hyde* (1920) intended as a 'spoiler' for the **Barrymore** version, Lewis recreated his Clutching Hand look for the Hyde half of the title role.

*The Pursuing Vengeance/The Iron Claw/*1916 * *The Hidden Hand/*1917 * *The Chinatown Mystery/*1928 * *Seven Footprints to Satan/*1929 * *The Monster Walks/*1932

Lewton, Val [Vladimir Ivan Leventon] (1904–51)

Russian-born American producer, writer, considered the acme of good taste by those who regret the explicitness of modern horror. The nine chillers Lewton produced for RKO are a sophisticatedly funereal group,

often at subversive odds with the escapist demands of the period. Visually understated, informed by an interest in **psychology**, with a brooding **film noir** aesthetic and evocative sound, they eschew the cartoonish monsters of propagandist wartime rivals. The shock high-points (or **buses**) of early features are crucially derived from everyday moments, while later shudders are social. The high tone and moral radicalism of Lewton's horrors result from disdain for the genre's standards. 'Remember – no messages,' the consistently lowbrow RKO advised of *Isle of the Dead* (1945). 'I'm sorry but we do have a message,' the cultured, somewhat rarefied producer replied, 'and our message is that death is good.'

Raised in New York, where his mother lived with actress sister Alla Nazimova, Lewton was a prodigal talent who later grew anxious to stay in work. His first sustained job was with MGM publicity (1926–32), churning out movie adaptations for radio and magazine use. Having published a clutch of novels (along with non-fiction, poetry, porn and a sale to **Weird Tales**), Lewton crossed the US in 1933 to become David O. Selznick's story editor. Nine years later, with considerable reluctance, he left the bullying perfectionist for RKO, where production chief Charles Koerner was mounting a challenge to Universal's horror lead, intending to recoup losses incurred on Orson **Welles** with $150,000 programmers extrapolated from pre-tested titles. Lewton, in contrast, saw a chance to surprise his way into A features and, *à la* Selznick, set about building a creative team that would respond to close supervision.

Credited as 'Carlos Keith' on the unit's final two scripts, Lewton in fact co-wrote all. *Cat People* (1942) quickly dumped a period source (Algernon **Blackwood**'s 'Ancient Sorceries', 1908), along with a draft where a Panzer division is ravaged by Balkan were-cats. RKO despised the final version, in which Simone **Simon**'s belief that she will transform on consummating her New York marriage is presented with trademark ambiguity. Doubtless due to an astonishing sexual subtext, the film nevertheless saved the studio from bankruptcy. Lewton's avowedly libidinous approach to terror ('Our formula is simple: a love story, three scenes of suggested horror and one of actual **violence**') found match in director Jacques **Tourneur**, whose coolly sensual style is even more pronounced in *I Walked with a Zombie* (1943). Ostensibly based on an *American Weekly*

Val Lewton's *Cat People* (1942)

series but actually a **voodoo** *Jane Eyre* (1847), the film mocks its catchpenny title in a voiced prologue and uses the slave inheritance of an eerie West Indies to gloss the unhealthy emotional entanglements of a plantation-owning family.

The Leopard Man (1943), a **cat**-conscious renaming of Cornell **Woolrich**'s *Black Alibi* (1942), mutes its central romance and instead brims with casual cruelties. Memorably orchestrating the death of a teenager beyond her mother's locked door, the movie reveals feline-attributed killings as the work of a mild-mannered necrophile. As a reward for first year profits, RKO promoted Tourneur and vouchsafed *The Seventh Victim* (1943) extra funds until Lewton insisted that regular editor Mark **Robson** direct. Consequently missing scenes, the film remains a work of extraordinary, sustained morbidity. Telling of a suicidal Manhattan beauty hounded to death by devil-worshippers, it pointedly reverses the lust-for-life of DeWitt **Bodeen**'s scrapped original story, which has the threatened heroine racing to identify her potential killer. *The Ghost Ship* (1943) is a rather more expedient achievement: made to exploit an expensive standing set, the movie's shipboard locale forces Lewton to refocus on a claustrophobic male environment, yielding a brutal, idiosyncratic study in power and paranoia.

Often seeding his films with autobiography, Lewton (an ailurophobe) confounded expectations for *The Curse of the Cat People* (1944), importing details from childhood and his own strained relationship with daughter Nina. Lewton's obvious desire to vacate the genre was met with the opportunity to make the awkward early juvenile delinquent item *Youth Runs Wild* (1944). After the downbeat war costumier *Mademoiselle Fifi* (1944), B boss Jack Gross pushed for a return to horror by signing **Karloff** to three films. In the event, Karloff took to Lewton, relishing parts further complicated by his new producer's sense of entrapment. Already expressed in failed *Seventh Victim* poet Jason Hoag, Lewton's anxiety now informed the Greek freedom fighter of *Isle of the Dead*, who cannot escape an atavistic belief in **vampires**, and the eminent surgeon of *The Body Snatcher* (1945) who is unable to flee his **body-snatching** partner. The prestigious Hogarth homage *Bedlam* (1946) gives fullest flesh to Lewton's frustrations. As master of the eighteenth-century asylum, Karloff plays a literal gaoler and sadistic author manqué: among his loonies is

a man who glimpses cinema in the pages of a flick book.

The increased pedantry of these final films earned Lewton enough mainstream plaudits to plan a variety of As, but nothing (including psycho-thriller *Die Gently Stranger*) was realised. Periods at Paramount and MGM were followed by an equally frustrating attempt at independence with RKO collaborators Robson and Robert **Wise**, and a return to low-budget with *Apache Drums* (1951). Suffering a third and fatal heart attack shortly after joining the Kramer Company, Lewton died in the early stages of psychiatric melodrama *My Six Convicts* (1952). *Woman on the Beach* (1947), *Bride of Vengeance* (1949) and *Blackbeard, the Pirate* (1952) are all bastardised one-time projects, the latter to have starred Karloff. RKO's telling *Zombies on Broadway* (1945) re-uses sets and support from *I Walked with a Zombie*. DP

Joel E. Siegel, *Val Lewton: The Reality of Terror* (1972); Ed Bansak, *Fearing the Dark: The Val Lewton Career* (1995).

Lieberman, Jeff (b. 1947)

American director, writer. Lieberman's three horrors are driven by a nonsensical sensibility that improves paranoiac 70s subgenres. *Squirm* (1976) is an **eco-horror** that, in one witty scene, has worms rather than water drop from the shower-head; for-hire job *Just Before Dawn* (1980) is rural **stalk-and-slash** rescripted so its climactic psychopath chokes to death on the heroine's fist. The most wilful of the trio is *Blue Sunshine* (1977): in this ultimate hippy nightmare, professional-class Americans lose their hair and kill because of acid dropped a decade before. Lieberman co-wrote karate *policier Stone* (1972), shared author/director chores on Marvin Chomsky's TV pilot *Doctor Franken* (1980) and scripted the infantile *The Neverending Story 3* (1994). The failed *Remote Control* (1987) is a typically topical item about the dangers of home video. DP

Lights Out (US radio series, 1934–47)

Created by Willis Cooper (screenwriter of *Son of Frankenstein*, 1939) but most famously written by Arch **Oboler**, this was a **radio** horror highlight. 'The Chicken Heart That Ate the World', the best-known episode, predates both the devouring blob s-f films of the 50s and *MAD*'s satires of the genre. The show came to television briefly in 1946, and became a TV series (1949–52) hosted by Jack

LaRue and then Frank Gallup. Episodes were built around guest stars **Karloff** ('The Leopard Lady', 1950), Vincent **Price** ('The Third Door', 1952) and John **Carradine** ('The Lonely Albatross', 1952), but there were also adaptations of famous stories: **Poe**'s 'The Fall of the House of Usher' (1949), 'The Masque of the Red Death' (1951), **Hawthorne**'s 'Dr. Heidegger's Experiment' (1950) and 'Rappaccini's Daughter' (1951). A 1972 pilot episode ('When Widows Weep') did not lead to a revival.

Line, Helga [Helga Lina Stern] (b. 1932)

German actress. Best remembered for her engaging cameo as a glamorous spy in *Pánico en el Transiberiano* (*Horror Express*, 1972), Line began her illustrious exploitation career as a dancer and acrobat in a Portugese circus, graduating to films after modelling assignments. One of Spanish horror's most consistent leading ladies, her aristocratic beauty enhances lumpen offerings. MA

Horror [*The Blancheville Monster*]/1962 * *Gli amanti d'oltretomba* [*Nightmare Castle*]/1965 * *Così dolce . . . Così perversa* [*So Sweet . . . So Perverse*]/1968 * *Mio caro assassino* [*My Dear Killer*]/*Santo contra el Dr. Muerto*/*La saga de los Draculas* [*The Dracula Saga*]/*El espanto surge de la tumba* [*Horror Rises From the Tomb*]]/*Las garras de Lorelei* [*The Lorelei's Grasp*]/*La orgia nocturna de los vampiros* [*The Vampire's Night Orgy*/1972 * *La venganza de la momia*/1973 * *El aesesino de muñecas*/1974 * *Estigma* [*Stigma*]/*Los ritos sexuales del diablo* [*Black Candles*]/1981 * *Pulsacions* [*Shape Up*]/1984.

Lloyd, Doris (1900–1968)

English-born American actress. A bit player as stuffy ladies or nurses, Lloyd was a regular in Universal horrors.

A Study in Scarlet/1933 * *The Man Who Reclaimed His Head*/1934 * *The Black Doll*/1938 * *The Wolf Man*/1941 * *Night Monster*/*The Ghost of Frankenstein*/1942 * *Frankenstein Meets the Wolf Man*/*Flesh and Fantasy*/1943 * *Phantom Lady*/*The Lodger*/*The Invisible Man's Revenge*/1944 * *Tarzan and the Leopard Woman*/1945 * *Son of Dr. Jekyll*/1951

TV: *Matinee Theatre*: 'The Others'/1957 * *Alfred Hitchcock Presents*: 'A Dip in the Pool'/ 'Impromptu Murder'/'Safety for the Witness'/1958; 'The Schartz-Metterklume Method'/1960 * *One Step Beyond*: 'The Haunting'/1960 * *Thriller*: 'Dark Legacy'/ 1961 * *Alfred Hitchcock Hour*: 'The Dark Pool'/ 'Hay-Fork and Bill-Hook'/1963; 'Isabel'/ 1964

Doris Lloyd

The Lodger * See: Jack the Ripper

Lom, Herbert [Herbert Charles Angelo Kuchaevich ze Schluderpacheru] (b. 1917)

Czech-born actor, in Britain from 1939. Often a villainous foreigner or an authority figure, such as a doctor or psychiatrist. Best known as Inspector Dreyfus in the *Pink Panther* series, of which only *The Pink Panther Strikes Back* (1976) has any horror content. He has played Captain Nemo (*Mysterious Island*, 1961), **The Phantom of the Opera** (1963) and **Van Helsing** (*El conde Drácula* [*Count Dracula*], 1970). SJ

The Dark Tower/1943 * *The Seventh Veil*/1945 * *Hexen bis auf's Blut gequält* [*Mark of the Devil*]/1969 * *Cuadecuc (Vampir)/Dorian Gray/* 1970 * *Murders in the Rue Morgue*/1971 * *Asylum*/1972 * *Dark Places/– And Now the Screaming Starts!*/1973 * *And Then There Were None*/1974 * *The Dead Zone*/1983 * *Ten Little Indians/The Masque of the Red Death*/1989 * *La setta* [*The Sect*]/1990

TV: *Play of the Month*: 'I Have Been Here Before'/1982

Lommel, Ulli (b. 1944)

German director, writer, producer. An actor-auteur under Rainer Werner Fass-binder, Lommel made his directorial debut with *M* (1930) tribute *Zärtlichkeit der Wölfe* (*The Tenderness of Wolves*, 1973). In the US, punk-informed experiments (including Warhol's *Cocaine Cowboys*, 1979) preceded exploitation explorations. With star/wife/

co-writer Suzanna Love, Lommel is responsible for five useful 80s horrors that make idiosyncratic hay of **possession** and **stalk-and-slash** themes. *The Boogeyman* (1980) is a post-*Halloween* (1978) item distinguished by parochial atmosphere and haunted **mirror** plot. A massively wayward meta-sequel *Boogeyman 2* (1982) follows the invigoratingly peculiar *Olivia* (1981) and near-conformist *Brainwaves* (1982), while forthright feminist **witch hunt** flick *The Devonsville Terror* (1983) closes the run. Minus Love's imput, he has capitulated to impersonal action fare: cryonics fantasy *Strangers in Paradise* (1985) is Lommel's last interesting film. DP

Death Before Sunrise/1995

Lorre, Peter [Ladislav Loewenstein] (1904–64)

Hungarian actor. When Peter Lorre screams, before a 'court' of criminals in the finale of Fritz **Lang**'s *M* (1931), that he couldn't help his killing compulsion, it is a cry from a heart already broken by knowledge of inadequacy. With only twelve lines of dialogue, the film made him a star. Its memory lingered on: there is something heart-wounded about his roles, even at his most menacing.

Leaving Hungary, he worked in Swiss, Austrian and German theatres, where he was spotted by Lang for the role of the Düsseldorf child-murderer. Though admired by Hitler and Goebbels, he fled the Nazis in 1933. Chillingly bizarre for **Hitchcock** in *The Man Who Knew Too Much* (1934) and *The Secret Agent* (1936), he is at his most formidable in Hollywood's take on **Les Mains d'Orlac** (1920), *Mad Love* (1935). His melodramatic love-crazed surgeon slides into credibility on a streak of vulnerability. A squat and pop-eyed presence, combined with his most distinctive whine of voice, became most apparent in eight Mr Moto movies in which he played a gentle, judo-expert Japanese private detective, then led him to partner a vast Sydney Greenstreet at Warner Bros. He escaped Greenstreet's bulk to suggest a sad sensibility for *The Face Behind The Mask* (1941), as an immigrant disfigured by fire who turns to crime.

He shudders memorably and campily in *The Maltese Falcon* (1941) and is a character-diversion from the lovers in *Casablanca* (1943). But horror beckons digitally once more with *The Beast With Five Fingers* (1947), in which the disembodied hand creeps and crawls through the mansion in which Lorre sits and waits, as though transfixed by a fate

to come from that strangling hold. Becoming more and more obese, Lorre came late to authentic horror for Roger **Corman**: his horror reputation really resides in a whimpering **comedy** emerging in grotesque circumstances. In *Tales of Terror* (1962), four Edgar Allan **Poe** stories are merged, with Lorre's drunken Montresor walling up a prissy Vincent **Price**. *The Raven* (1963) has three sorcerers (Price, **Karloff**, Lorre) duel with big-scale magic. Half spoof, half truth, inspired by a Poe poem, it is elaborately conceived, with a running joke that has Lorre forever being turned into the monstrous bird of ill omen. Jacques **Tourneur**'s *The Comedy of Terrors* (1963) is not so successful: Price as an undertaker and Lorre as his assistant do their best to fill more coffins by killing off a few victims.

His genre output seems never to have been a matter of deliberate policy, but was tangential to his career as an actor. A return to Germany to direct *Der Verlorene* (*The Lost One*, 1951) might well have extended his creative range if it had been more successful. As a screen personality he was inimitable and yet most imitated (by Paul Frees, for instance, in the Spike Jones recording of 'My Old Flame', 1947) as a figure of fun, shading into absurd futility along with his hissing range of voice. He was the only monster with an inferiority complex; you felt a sadness for him as though he were a pet who would have to be put down. His threat is

Herbert Lom

Peter Lorre, Colin Clive, *Mad Love*

Peter Lorre

always edged with being only too human, whimsically part of our species and yet aware of an alien nature. We always feel the pathos within him can only be externalised in attempted menace; we are also aware of his **Kafka**esque search for meaning. Few horror stars are so likeable. Perhaps because he is ourselves through a distorting glass darkly. He can't help it, you see. TH

*Stranger on the Third Floor/You'll Find Out/ Strange Cargo/Island of Doomed Men/1940 * The Boogie Man Will Get You/Invisible Agent/1942 * Arsenic and Old Lace/1944 * Three Strangers/ Black Angel/The Verdict/1946 * 20,000 Leagues Under the Sea/1954*

TV: *Suspense*: 'The Tortured Hand'/1952 * *The Best of Broadway*: 'Arsenic and Old Lace'/1955 * *Alfred Hitchcock Presents*: 'The Diplomatic Corpse'/1957; 'The Man From the South'/ 1960 * *Route 66*: 'Lizard's Leg and Owlet's Wing'/1962

Love and Curses * See: *She Wolf of London*

Lovecraft, H.P. [Howard Phillips] (1890–1937)
American writer. His work unites the British and American traditions of weird fiction and, in its later developments, often approaches science fiction in its sense of the cosmos.

His early work is influenced by Edgar Allan **Poe**, in such stories as 'The Tomb' (1917) and 'Dagon' (1917), and Lord Dunsany, in such tales as 'The White Ship' (1919) and 'The Cats of Ulthar' (1920). 'Dagon', however, also suggests a first draft of his later invention, the **Cthulhu Mythos** (not Lovecraft's name for it). This myth-cycle is often identified by detractors as Lovecraft's only achievement, and not much of one at that, but like his resort throughout to his career to extended metaphors and to certain favourite words, it is only one of his attempts to communicate 'dread suspense' (his phrase) and to perfect a form for the weird tale. In fact, he tried many different styles: documentary reportage ('Facts Concerning the Late Arthur Jermyn and His Family', 1920), incantatory repetition and orchestration of language ('The Hound', 1922), conversational ('Pickman's Model', 1926).

As a body his stories represent a survey of all the underlying themes of the genre. Important tales from his pre-Mythos period include 'The Picture in the House' (1920), with its hints of **cannibalism**; 'The Nameless City' (1921), which introduces his famous creation, the *Necronomicon*, suggested by Robert W. Chambers' equally fictitious and forbidden *King in Yellow*; 'The Outsider' (1921), both his most Poe-esque story and a metaphor for his fear of his own supposed ugliness; 'The Rats in the Walls' (1923), a sustained crescendo of terror; 'The Shunned House' (1924), a vampire story with a thoroughly inhuman monster; 'Cool Air' (1926), reversing his own aversion to low temperatures in order to create something worse. 'The Call of Cthulhu' (1926) is the central story of his invented mythos, deriving its form from **Machen**'s 'Great God Pan' (1894). The following year, however, he was to achieve at least as much cosmic terror in 'The Colour Out of Space' without any reference to the mythos, in a continuing search for ways to convey a sense of a universe inhabited by alien forces indifferent to man.

He often inserted references to the mythos into stories he revised for clients, most of the plots and prose ending up wholly Lovecraft's, unlike the so-called posthumous collaborations with August **Derleth**, which (apart from the 1957 story 'The Lamp of Alhazred') contain little or no Lovecraft. Of the revisions, 'The Curse of Yig' (1928) and 'The Mound' (1929–30), both with Zealia Bishop, and 'Out of the Aeons' (1933), with Hazel Heald, are worth reading. He was increasingly using real landscapes as a source of atmosphere, as shown by Poe and the gothics: New England, with 'Arkham' standing in for Salem, or his beloved birthplace Providence, most autobiographically used in *The Case of Charles Dexter Ward* (1927). The growing sobriety of his style in 'The Dunwich Horror' (1928) and 'The Whisperer in Darkness' (1930) culminates in the scientific reportage of *At the Mountains of Madness* (1931). This derives much of its power from his having had to imagine a landscape (the Antarctic) just as he had to envision Australia for 'The Shadow Out of Time' (1935). Two of his most visionary stories, these were rejected by **Weird Tales**, his favoured market, but appeared severely edited in *Astounding Stories*, where they met considerable hostility from s-f readers.

Meanwhile his major writing included 'The Shadow Over Innsmouth' (1931), which progresses from supernatural thriller to Dunsanian fantasy; 'The Dreams in the Witch House' (1932), uniting black magic and interplanetary s-f; and 'The Thing on the Doorstep' (1933), a choice example of 'loathsome fright' (another Lovecraft phrase from his essential study of the genre, 'Supernatural Horror in Literature'). However, his opinion of his work – never high – was sinking, and it took his destruction in a

ABOVE Edward Sloan, Bela Lugosi, *Dracula*

LEFT Bela Lugosi

story by his youthful correspondent Robert **Bloch** to provoke him into writing 'The Haunter of the Dark' (1935) as an amiable revenge, killing off 'Robert Blake'. His last tale, the 1936 'The Night Ocean' (with R.H. Barlow) finally shakes off the over-explicitness which he had always seen as his besetting flaw.

He remains one of the most important and influential twentieth-century authors in the genre; writers who have subsumed his influence include Bloch, Fritz **Leiber**, Stephen **King**, T.E.D. **Klein**, Thomas Ligotti, Brian **Lumley** and Ramsey **Campbell**. RC

The Haunted Palace/1963 ∗ *Die, Monster, Die!*/

1965 * *Curse of the Crimson Altar*/1968 * *The Dunwich Horror*/1970 * *Re-Animator*/1985 * *From Beyond*/1986 * *The Curse*/1987 * *Pulse Pounders* (unfinished)/*The Unnameable*/1988 * *The Resurrected*/1991 * *The Unnameable Returns*/1992 * *Beyond the Wall of Sleep*/*Necronomicon*/1993 * *Lurking Fear*/1994

L. Sprague de Camp, *Lovecraft: A Biography* (1975)

Lubin, Arthur (1901–95)

American director. A plodder who struck it rich with **Abbott and Costello**'s *Buck Privates* (1941) and *Hold That Ghost* (1941), Lubin was entrusted with Universal's lavishly dull Technicolor ***Phantom of the Opera*** (1943). As boring, if cheaper, are quickies like the **Karloff**-**Lugosi** *Black Friday* (1940) and the Gale **Sondergaard**-Rondo **Hatton** *The Spider Woman Strikes Back* (1946). His winning streak came with talking animals, first in the Francis the Mule series, which did as well for Universal in the 50s as Bud and Lou had a decade earlier, and then the *Mr. Ed* (1961–5) TV show.

Lugosi, Bela [Belá Blaskó] (1882–1956)

Hungarian actor. For an actor whose **Dracula** yearned for the big sleep of forgetfulness ('To die, to be really dead, that might be glorious'), Tim **Burton** may have seemed an unwelcome resurrection man. Paying tribute to the world's worst film-maker with *Ed Wood* (1995), Burton also revives Lugosi, played by Martin **Landau**, showing him as a soured, drug-addicted left-over from Universal's great days. This Lugosi is a macabre memory brought to life from the entombment of cinema history. Yet this vision hardly needs Burton: once seen, how can Lugosi's thick-tongued accent and richly overplayed presence ever really be forgotten? Though Christopher **Lee** took up the mantle of Head Vampire with handsome *élan*, Lugosi's weirdly exotic nature still galvanises the mind with the horrific threat of overplayed innuendoes: 'I never drink . . . wine.'

Like Peter **Lorre**, he was born in Hungary, made films in Germany and came to America to work on the stage and in small roles in movies such as *The Silent Command* (1923), *The Rejected Woman* (1924) and *The Midnight Girl* (1925). He played Dracula in a 1927 Broadway adaptation of Bram **Stoker** (a play brought to Britain in his declining years) and replaced the just-dead Lon **Chaney** in Tod **Browning**'s *Dracula* (1931).

His first words in the character are pronounced with slow-motion diction: 'I . . . am . . . Dracula.' He was, indeed, once and future King of Vampires. An interesting variation on the evil dominance theme is Victor **Halperin**'s *White Zombie* (1932), with Lugosi as Murder Legendre, master of the living dead, a species of Haitian slave labour. Lugosi remembered this as 'different from the usual horror as it was a kind of fairy-tale of the sort remembered from my old country.' Low-slung mists and a continual chorus of frogs help that atmosphere, though the movie does not wear well.

It became harder to distinguish the real man from the fictitious **monster** as, with few exceptions such as *Ninotchka* (1939), he was forever caught within the catacombs of horror. The blood-money poured in through *The Death Kiss* (1932), *Island of Lost Souls* (1933) and *Night of Terror* (1933); a fruitful teaming with rival **Karloff** yielded ***The Black Cat*** (1934), *Gift of the Gab* (1934), *The Raven* (1935) and *The Invisible Ray* (1936); and it was back to never giving a suck an even break with *Mark of the Vampire* (1935) and *Return of the Vampire* (1943). **Frankenstein** claimed him for three movies: the broken-necked Ygor of *Son of Frankenstein* (1939) and *Ghost of Frankenstein* (1942) and a weak Monster in *Frankenstein Meets the Wolf Man* (1943). A supporting stooge at majors as sinister butlers and red herrings (*The Gorilla*, 1939; *Black Friday*, 1940; *Night Monster*, 1942), he could at least win top billing and plentiful dialogue on poverty row, reigning in Hell from *The Devil Bat* (1940) through *The Corpse Vanishes* (1942) to *Return of the Ape Man* (1944).

Spoof humiliations soon predominated: *Zombies on Broadway* (1945), (**Abbott and Costello**) *Meet Frankenstein* (1948), the British *Old Mother Riley meets the Vampire* (1952), *Bela Lugosi Meets a Brooklyn Gorilla* (1952). At least Milton's Satan was spared that kind of ignominy. In *The Black Sleep* (1956), Lugosi's final full feature, he and his co-featured horror-actors (Basil **Rathbone**, Lon **Chaney Jr**, John **Carradine**) might well be counting their curses. It is a whimper of an exit contrasted with the fanfare which had greeted him as Dracula. But, then, Lugosi rarely knew trumpets in his later years, having to make do with a death-interrupted cameo in **Wood**'s *Plan 9 From Outer Space* (1956).

He had, along with Karloff, become one of the great icons of the early 20th century. He survived ridicule and laughter by a belief in himself and what he had done. Perhaps, as Burton's film suggests, he took himself too seriously: but how else are you to take yourself if you are such a supernatural being in such a secular age? TH

Lulu/1918 * *Der Januskopf*/*Die Teufelsanbeter*/1920 * *The Thirteenth Chair*/1929 * *Murders in the Rue Morgue*/*Chandu the Magician*/1932 * *The Whispering Shadow*/1933 * *The Return of Chandu*/1934 * *The Mysterious Mr Wong*/*Murder By Television*/*The Mystery of the Marie Celeste*/1935 * *Shadow of Chinatown*/*Postal Inspector*/1936 * *S.O.S. Coastguard*/1937 * *The Phantom Creeps*/*Dark Eyes of London*/1939 * *You'll Find Out*/1940 * *The Invisible Ghost*/*The Black Cat*/*Spooks Run Wild*/*The Wolf Man*/1941 * *Black Dragons*/*Bowery at Midnight*/1942 * *The Ape Man*/*Ghosts on the Loose*/1943 * *Voodoo Man*/*One Body Too Many*/1944 * *The Body Snatcher*/1945 * *Genius at Work*/1946 * *Scared to Death*/1947 * *Glen or Glenda?*/1953 * *Bride of the Monster*/1954 * *Lock Up Your Daughters*/1958

Arthur Lennig, *The Count: The Life and Times of Bela 'Dracula' Lugosi* (1974); Robert Cremer, *Lugosi: The Man Behind the Cape* (1976), Richard Bojarski, *The Films of Bela Lugosi* (1980).

Lumley, Brian (b. 1937)

British writer. A vigorous pulpster who began his career with **Cthulhu Mythos** spin-offs (*The Burrowers Beneath*, 1974; *The Transition of Titus Crow*, 1975), Lumley had great success with *Necroscope* (1986), an unusual **vampire**-espionage-psychic saga, and has extensively devoted himself to sequelising it.

Luna, Bigas [José Juan Bigas Luna] (b. 1946)

Spanish writer, director. A post-Franco auteur whose early, sexually explicit features imaginatively explore the freedoms of the new regime, Luna made two determinedly odd international productions in the 80s. *Renacida* (*Reborn*, 1981) has Dennis Hopper as an astronaut-obsessed evangelist whose plans founder when Christ's rebirth follows far from immaculate conception; the **recursive** *Angustia* (*Anguish*, 1987) features an **eye**-gouging psycho (Michael Lerner) who is actually a character in a movie watched by an audience plagued by a copycat killer. Chasing Pedro Almodóvar's success, Luna has returned to earthy Iberian satire: *Jamón jamón* (1992), *Huevos de oro* (1993), *La teta y la luna* (*The Tit and the Moon*, 1994). DP

Caniche/1979

Lustig, William (b. 1955)

American director, producer. After pseudo-nymous hardcore, Lustig debuted with the vilified **stalk-and-slash** *Maniac* (1980), a singular, upsetting mix of downbeat sadism and psychotic fantasy shot with a porno-graphic eye, top-lining writer Joe **Spinell** and scream queen Caroline **Munro**. Leaving New York in 1985, Lustig reversed the poli-tics of formula action pic *Vigilante* (1983) with the high-concept horrors of *Maniac Cop* (1988). Writer Larry **Cohen** collaborated on two applied sequels: *Maniac Cop II* (1990), *Maniac Cop III: Badge of Silence* (1992). He dis-owns the producer-distorted latter and is not connected with any of the follow-ups (1991, 1992, 1994) to his killer-thriller *Relentless* (1989), but was peripherally involved with Dario **Argento**'s *Tenebre* (*Tenebrae*, 1982). DP

Army of Darkness (a)/1992 * *Uncle Sam*/1996

Lycanthropy * See: **Werewolves**

Lynch, David (b. 1946)

American director, writer. Like Curtis **Harrington**, Paul **Morrissey**, David **Cronen-berg** and John Waters, Lynch emerged from the underground/avant garde to distinguish himself in mainstream cinema as a unique stylist. Consistent with his background as a painter and experimental film-maker, linear narrative logic is secondary to ambience, atmosphere and the surreal in his work.

In 1965, Lynch filmed an untitled loop projected over a screen/sculpture featuring six figures whose stomachs swell and heads erupt into flame before they all vomit. He then employed live-action, **animation** and pixillation in *The Alphabet* (1968) and *The Grandmother* (1970), establishing the themes and images that define his later work: mon-strous domesticity and self-consuming **fami-lies**; a tactile fascination with fecundity, **dis-ease**, decay and organic life; the transcen-dent solace of netherworlds yearned for in **dream** but achieved only in death. Working with sound designer Alan Splet, Lynch established a fresh approach to aural as well as visual horror in these short films and his first feature, *Eraserhead* (1977), a genre mas-terpiece which found its audience in 'mid-night movie' venues. Protagonist Henry (Jack Nance) lives in a squalid apartment with his offspring, a horribly fragile (and convincingly alive) creature wrapped in gauze which wails incessantly as Henry dreams of a better life with a diseased waif

David Lynch, on the set of *Blue Velvet*

who lives behind his radiator, squashing fetuses beneath her heels as she meekly sings 'In Heaven, Everything is Fine'. Ultimately succumbing to madness or death, Henry embraces the Radiator Lady in a radi-ant afterlife. Lynch never again submerged himself so completely in dream-logic unen-cumbered by narrative conventions or restraints.

Producer Mel Brooks gambled on Lynch to direct a remarkable feature based on the life of John Merrick, *The Elephant Man* (1980), earning critical and box-office suc-cess. The subsequent failure of Lynch's big-budget adaption of Frank Herbert's s-f classic *Dune* (1985) forced Lynch back to more modest and fertile imaginings, yielding another masterwork, *Blue Velvet* (1986). This exploration of the seamy, steamy underbelly of illusory suburban American bliss struck a cultural nerve, launching an evocative, quirky vein of contemporary **film noir** which Lynch continued to tap with *Wild at Heart* (1990) and the television series **Twin Peaks** (1990–91; co-created with Mark Frost). The audacious wedding of TV soap opera and detective traditions with **incest**, **serial murder** and the supernatural was celebrated, then vehemently rejected, by viewers, culminating in the commercial sui-cide of a theatrical prequel, *Twin Peaks Fire Walk With Me* (1992).

During this period, Lynch collaborated with regular composer Angelo Badalamenti and singer Julee Cruise on the nightmarish *Industrial Symphony No. 1 – The Dream of the*

Brokenhearted (1990) for theatre and video, and further dabbled in TV with the bizarro sit-com *On the Air* (1992) and the documen-tary series *American Chronicles* (1991). Jennifer Lynch, his daughter, wrote a *Twin Peaks* spin-off (*The Secret Diary of Laura Palmer*, 1990) and made a controversial debut as a director with *Boxing Helena* (1993). SB

Nadja (p/a)/1995 * *Lost Highway*/1996

TV: *Hotel Room* (co-d)/1992

John Alexander, *The Films of David Lynch* (1993)

Lynch, Paul (b. 1946)

Canadian director. After 'little' Canadian pic-tures (*The Hard Part Begins*, 1973; *Blood and Guts*, 1978), Lynch made typical 80s **stalk-and-slash** movies, including the derivative but popular *Prom Night* (1980), and proceed-ed directly to TV, where he became a main-stay of *Star Trek: The Next Generation* (1987-94) and cable suspensers (*Murder By Night*, 1989; *Drop Dead Gorgeous*, 1991).

Humongous/1982 * *Bullies*/1987

TV: *Darkroom*: 'Stay Tuned, We'll Be Right Back'/'Needlepoint'/'Daisies'/1981 * *Ray Bradbury Theatre*: 'Marionettes, Inc.'/1985; 'The Long Years'/1990 * *The Twilight Zone*: 'Examination Day'/'A Message From Charity'/'Wong's Lost and Found Emporium'/1985 'Need to Know'/'Shadow Play'/The Storyteller'/'The World Next Door'/1986 'The Crossing'/'The Hunters'/ 1988; 'Crazy as a Soup Sandwich'/1989 * *Really Weird Tales*: 'All's Well That Ends Strange'/1986 * *The Twilight Zone*: 'Crazy as a Soup Sandwich'/1989 * *Dark Shadows*: 'Episode Four'/'Episode Five'/1991 * *The Outer Limits*: 'The Second Soul'/'Dark Matters'/1995

Lynch, Richard (b. 1936)

American actor. The sardonic, scarfaced Lynch has been guest villain on seemingly every TV series made since 1970. He leers evilly in low-budgeters, typically as Jim Jones's right-hand man (*Inferno in diretta*/*Cut and Run*, 1985) or a Russian infiltrator taking a flamethrower to Christmas (*Invasion U.S.A.*, 1985). *Bad Dreams* (1988) tastelessly exploits real-life facial burns by casting him as the ghost of a self-immolated cult leader. His most unusual role is the hermaphrodite alien messiah in *God Told Me To* (*Demon*, 1978), but he is traditionally effective in the TV movie *Vampire* (1979).

Open Season/1974 * *The Premonition*/1976 * *The Ninth Configuration*/1980 * *The Sword and the Sorcerer*/1982 * *Trancers II*/*Puppet Master III: Toulon's Revenge*/1990 * *Alligator 2: The Mutation*/1991 * *October 32nd*/1992 * *Necronomicon*/1993 * *Scanner Cop*/1994 * *Arizona Werewolf*/1996

TV: *Good Against Evil*/1977 * *Manimal*: 'Illusions'/1983 * *Werewolf*: 'Nightmare at Braine Hotel'/1987

Lyndon, Barré (1896–1972)

British writer. A successful playwright (*The Amazing Dr. Clitterhouse*, 1936), Lyndon's film career was heavy on Victorian melodrama. His *The Man in Half Moon Street* was filmed in 1944, done on *Kraft Theatre* (1949, 1953), *Matinee Theatre* (1957) and *Hour of Mystery* (1957), and remade as *The Man Who Could Cheat Death* (1958). He scripted John **Brahm**'s *The Lodger* (1941) – thus, by default, its close remake *Man in the Attic* (1953) – and *Hangover Square* (1945). Also eerie are his Cornell **Woolrich** adaptation *Night Has a Thousand Eyes* (1948) and the shudder pulp TV pilot *Dark Intruder* (1965).

They Came By Night/1940 * *War of the Worlds*/1953

TV: *Thriller*: 'Trio for Terror'/1961 * *The Alfred Hitchcock Hour*: 'Don't Look Behind You'/1962; 'Sign of Satan'/1964

Das Testament des Dr. Mabuse (1932)

M

Dr Mabuse

Created by novelist Norbert Jacques, the **hypnotist**-criminal mastermind Mabuse is incarnated by master-of-disguise Rudolf **Klein-Rogge** in Fritz **Lang**'s two-part *Dr. Mabuse, der Spieler* (*Dr. Mabuse*, 1922), which consists of *Der grosse Spieler* and *Inferno, ein Spiel von Menschen*. Maddened by apparitions, Klein-Rogge's Mabuse is confined to the **asylum** where he is found in Lang's *Das Testament des Dr. Mabuse* (*The Last Will of Dr Mabuse*, 1933), imposing his mind on a **Caligari**-ish psychiatrist and tangling with Lohmann (Otto Wernicke), the policeman from *M* (1931).

Producer Artur Brauner persuaded Lang to make *Die tausend Augen des Dr. Mabuse* (*The Thousand Eyes of Dr. Mabuse*, 1960), in which another madman (Wolfgang **Preiss**) takes over Mabuse's methods. Brauner had Preiss return, as Mabuse himself, with Wernicke-lookalike Gert Fröbe as Lohmann: *Im Stahlnetz des Dr. Mabuse* (*The Return of Dr. Mabuse*, 1961), *Die unsichtbaren Krallen des Dr. Mabuse* (*The Invisible Dr. Mabuse*, 1961), *Das Testament des Dr. Mabuse* (*The Testament of Dr. Mabuse*, 1962), *Scotland Yard jagt Dr. Mabuse* (1963), *Die Todesstrahlen des Dr. Mabuse* (1964). Jesús **Franco** cast Jack **Taylor** in the disreputable *La venganza del Dr. Mabuse* (1970), in fact a remake of his own *Gritos en la noche* (*The Awful Dr. Orlof*, 1961).

Mabuse is pastiched by no less than Ingmar **Bergman** in *Das Schlangenei* (*The Serpent's Egg*, 1977), with Heinz Bennent

LEFT Richard Lynch,
Invasion U.S.A.

as Dr Vergerus, and by Claude Chabrol in *Dr. M* (1989), with Alan Bates as Dr Marsfeldt. Willy Loman, tragic hero of Arthur Miller's *Death of a Salesman* (1949), is named for Mabuse's archenemy.

McCammon, Robert R. (b. 1952)

American writer. Since the pulpy *Baal* (1978) and *The Night Boat* (1980), McCammon's novels have grown more ambitious, offering apocalyptic scope in *They Thirst* (1981) and *Swan Song* (1987), playing cleverly with familiar themes in *Mystery Walk* (1983), *Usher's Passing* (1984), *The Wolf's Hour* (1989) and *Stinger* (1988). More recent novels move from the supernatural into suspense: *Mine* (1990), *Boy's Life* (1991), *Gone South* (1992). His stories 'Makeup' (1981) and 'Nightcrawlers' (1984) were adapted on **Darkroom** (1981) and **The Twilight Zone** (1985).

McCarty, John (b. 1944)

American critic. *Splatter Movies* (1981, revised 1984) is a study of graphic horror. McCarty has specialised in the field: writing *The Amazing Herschell Gordon Lewis and His World of Exploitation Films* (with Daniel Krogh, 1983) and *The Modern Horror Film* (1990), and editing *The Fearmakers* (1994) and *The Sleaze Merchants* (1995).

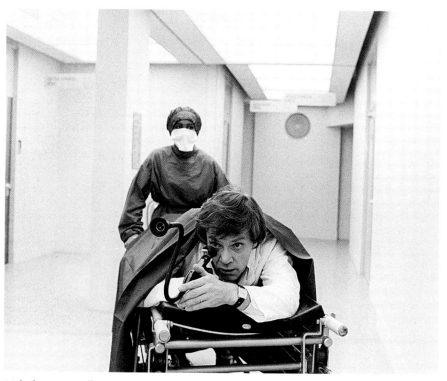

Malcolm McDowell, *Britannia Hopital*

Roddy McDowell, *Fright Night, Part 2*

McDowall, Roddy (b. 1928)

British actor, in Hollywood from 1940. A former child actor, his roles tend to the bizarre or psychotic. Star of the *Planet of the Apes* film and TV series (playing intelligent simians), he is ham **horror host** Peter Vincent in *Fright Night* (1985) and *Fright Night Part 2* (1988). SJ

Macbeth/1948 * *Midnight Lace*/1960 * *Shock*

Treatment/1964 * *The Loved One*/1965 * *It!*/1966 * *Tam Lin* (d)/1970 * *The Legend of Hell House*/Arnold/1973 * *Embryo*/1975 * *The Silent Flute*/1978 * *Charlie Chan and the Curse of the Dragon Queen*/1980 * *Class of 1984*/1982 * *Dead of Winter*/1987 * *Cutting Class*/1989

TV: *Playhouse 90*: 'Heart of Darkness'/1958 * *Hallmark Hall of Fame*: 'The Tempest'/1960 * *The Twilight Zone*: 'People Are Alike All Over'/1960 * *Alfred Hitchcock Hour*: 'The Gentleman Caller'/'See the Monkey Dance'/1964 * *The Invaders*: 'The Experiment'/1967 * *Journey to the Unknown*: 'The Killing Bottle'/1969 * *Night Gallery*/1969 * *A Taste of Evil*/1971 * *The Snoop Sisters*: 'A Black Day for Bluebeard'/1973 * *Fantasy Island*: 'The Devil and Mandy Breem'/1980; 'The Devil and Mr. Roarke'/1981 * *Nightmare Classics*: 'Carmilla'/1989 * *Deadly Game*/1991 * *Dead Man's Island*/1995

McDowell, Malcolm (b. 1944)

British actor, prominent as a young rebel in *If. . .* (1969), *A Clockwork Orange* (1971) and *O Lucky Man!* (1973). Since moving to Hollywood he has developed a career in weirdos and psychotics. SJ

Time After Time/1979 * *Cat People*/*Britannia Hospital*/1982 * *The Caller*/1987 * *Class of 1999*/*Mortacci*/1989 * *Disturbed*/1990 * *Fist of the North Star*/*Exquisite Tenderness*/*Hysteria*/1995 * *Where the Truth Lies*/*Asylum*/1996

TV: *Faerie Tale Theatre*: 'Little Red Riding Hood'/1983 * *Tales from the Crypt*: 'The Reluctant Vampire'/1991 * *Batman: The Animated Series*: 'Showdown' (v)/1994 * *Spider-Man:* 'Blade, the Vampire Hunter' (v)/1994

McDowell, Michael (b. 1950)

American writer. An important horror novelist (*The Amulet*, 1979; *Cold Moon Over Babylon*, 1980; *The Elementals*, 1981; *Blackwater*, 1982), McDowell's major film credits are *Beetle Juice* (1988) and *The Nightmare Before Christmas* (1993).

High Spirits/1988 * *Tales From the Darkside: The Movie*/1990 * *Thinner*/1986

TV: *Tales From the Darkside*: 'Inside the Closet'/'Word Processor of the Gods'/'Slippage'/1984; 'Answer Me'/'Bigalow's Last Smoke'/'Halloween Candy'/1985; 'A New Lease on Life'/'The Last Car'/'Black Widows'/'Seasons of Belief' (+d)/1986; 'The Moth' (d)/1987; 'The Cutty Black Sow'/1988 * *Amazing Stories*: 'Miscalculation'/1986; 'Such Interesting Neighbours'/1987

McGavin, Darren (b. 1922)

American actor. Utility leading man, often

on TV. Cast as pushy, rumpled reporter Carl Kolchak in *The Night Stalker* (1971), he reprised the role in *The Night Strangler* (1972) and the *Kolchak: The Night Stalker* series (1974–5). His single directorial credit is a psycho thriller, *Happy Mother's Day, Love George* (1973).

The Natural/1984 * *Dead Heat*/1988 * *Hell Night*/1991

TV: *Tales of Tomorrow*: 'The Duplicates'/1952 * *Alfred Hitchcock Presents*: 'Triggers in Leash'/ 'The Cheney Vase'/1955 * *Alfred Hitchcock Hour*: 'A Matter of Murder'/1964 * *Something Evil*/1972 * *The Evil Touch*: 'A Game of Hearts'/'George'/'Gornak's Prison'/1973 * *The Martian Chronicles*/1979 * *The Hitchhiker*: 'Nightshift'/1985 * *Tales From the Darkside*: 'Distant Signals'/1985 * *Monsters*: 'Portrait of the Artist'/1989

McGillivray, David (b. 1948)

British writer, critic. After interviewing sexploitation director Pete **Walker** for *Films and Filming*, McGillivray was asked to script his first 'Terror' film, *House of Whipcord* (1974). He brings deadpan humour to the nasty Home Counties horrors he wrote for Walker and Norman J. **Warren**. Dabbling in the British **sex** film industry with such classics as *I'm Not Feeling Myself Tonight* (1975), he wrote *Doing Rude Things* (1992), definitive book on the subject, basis of a 1995 BBC documentary. AJ

Frightmare/1974 * *House of Mortal Sin*/*Schizo*/ 1975 * *Satan's Slave*/1976 * *Terror*/1978 * *Turnaround*/1986

Machen, Arthur (1863–1947)

Welsh writer. Though he wrote mystic-tinged mainstream fiction (*The Hill of Dreams*, 1907) and much other matter including journalism and translation, Machen is remembered for supernatural stories: *The Great God Pan and The Inmost Light* (1894), *The Three Imposters* (1895), *The House of Souls* (1906), *The Terror* (1917). His outstanding stories – 'The Great God Pan' (1890), 'The Novel of the Black Seal' (1895), 'The White People' (1904) – deal with the rediscovery of ancient evils, whether pagan gods or a race of sinister 'little people', in modern times. 'The Bowmen' (1914), though a lesser story, has a permanent place in popular culture for inspiring the archetypal modern legend, that ghostly bowmen aided the allies during the battle of Mons. His influence, chanelled through H.P. **Lovecraft** or T.E.D. **Klein**,

remains strong in weird fiction. 'The Shining Pyramid' (1925) was filmed for the TV series *Border Country* in 1979. The Mexican black comedy *El esquelito de la Señora Morales* (1959) is based on Machen's true crime article 'The Islington Mystery' (1927).

McLoughlin, Tom (b. 1950)

American director, writer. As a mime artist, he plays a robot in *Sleeper* (1973) and *The Black Hole* (1979), the 'Pizza Bear' in *Prophecy* (1979) and the Jabberwocky in Irwin Allen's *Alice in Wonderland* (1985). He directed the funhouse zombie fest *One Dark Night* (1982), the James Bond-style gore parody **Friday the 13th**, *Part VI: Jason Lives* (1986), the endearing fantasy *Date With an Angel* (1987) and the cable Stephen **King** picture *Sometimes They Come Back* (1991). AJ

TV: *Amazing Stories*: 'Go to the Head of the Class' (w)/'Such Interesting Neighbors' (w)/ 1987 * *Freddy's Nightmares*: 'It's a Miserable Life'/1988 * *She-Wolf of London* (*Love and Curses*, co-creator)/1992

McNaughton, John (b. 1949)

American director. *Henry: Portrait of a Serial Killer* (1990) is an exceptional debut, spotlighting extremely unnerving performances from Michael Rooker and Tom Towles. Relentlessly horrific, its documentary style and lack of easy answers makes it impossible to subsume comfortably into the horror or thriller genres. McNaughton's subsequent films include the trashily fun s-f shocker *The Borrower* (1991) and the more mainstream *Mad Dog and Glory* (1992).

MacNee, Patrick (b. 1922)

Sophisticated British actor, the dapper John Steed in **The Avengers** (1960–68). For the UK video releases of volumes of **Tales From the Darkside**, Macnee taped Rod **Serling**-style introductions. SJ

The Fatal Night/1948 * *A Christmas Carol*/1951 * *Three Cases of Murder*/1953 * *Incense for the Damned*/1970 * *The Howling*/1980 * *The Creature Wasn't Nice*/1981 * *Transformations*/ *Waxwork*/1988 * *Lobster Man from Mars*/ *Masque of the Red Death*/1989 * *Waxwork II Lost in Time*/1991

TV: *Matinee Theatre*: 'Dr. Jekyll and Mr. Hyde'/1957 * *Suspicion*: 'The Voice in the Night'/*The Veil*/1958 * *One Step Beyond*: 'The Night of April 14th'/1959 * *Alfred Hitchcock*

RIGHT Patrick MacNee, *The Howling*

Presents: 'Arthur'/'The Crystal Trench'/1959 * *The Twilight Zone*: 'Judgment Night'/1959 * *Night Gallery*: 'Logoda's Heads'/1971 * *Orson Welles' Great Mysteries*: 'A Time to Remember'/1973 * *Sherlock Holmes in New York*/1976 * *The New Avengers*/1976–7 * *Dead of Night*/1976 * *Comedy of Horrors*/1981 * *Ray Bradbury Theatre*: 'Usher II'/1990 * *Sherlock Holmes and the Leading Lady*/1990 * *Incident at Victoria Falls*/1991

Macready, George (1909–73)

Scar-faced American actor, ran an art gallery in partnership with Vincent **Price**. Equally adept at hissible villains or weak-willed victims, his career highlight is *Gilda* (1946). His final role was as a batty vampire hunter in *The Return of Count Yorga* (1971), produced by his son Michael. SJ

The Missing Juror/*The Soul of a Monster*/1944 * *I Love a Mystery*/*The Monster and the Ape*/1945 * *Alias Nick Beal*/*Johnny Allegro*/1949 * *The Alligator People*/1959 * *Dead Ringer*/1964 * *The Human Duplicators*/1965

TV: *Alfred Hitchcock Presents*: 'Premonition'/ 'The Cheney Vase'/1955 * *Dow Hour of Great Mysteries*: 'The Cat and the Canary'/1960 * *Thriller*: 'The Weird Tailor'/1961 * *The Twilight Zone*: 'The Long Morrow'/1964 * *The Outer Limits*: 'The Invisibles'/'Production and Decay of Strange Particles'/1964 * *Alfred Hitchcock Hour*: 'The Ordeal of Mrs Snow'/ 1964 * *Night Gallery*/*Daughter of the Mind*/ 1969

Madness * See: **Asylums**; **Mad Scientists**; **Psychiatry**; **Psychopaths**

Mad Scientist: Gene Wilder, Peter Boyle, *Young Frankenstein*

Mad Scientists

Deranged scientists and their improbable experiments are among the key figures in horror films, simultaneously embodying the **Faust** theme and manufacturing a variety of photogenic abominations. The big names in the field, like Doctors **Jekyll**, **Fu Manchu** and **Frankenstein**, represent only the tip of the iceberg. Both a rebel against society and ruler of his hideous progeny, the mad scientist is a rich role, and many genre actors have repeatedly made a meal of it.

Stars who specialised include the brutally businesslike **Chaney** (*The Monster*, 1925), the benevolent but implacable **Karloff** (*The Devil Commands*, 1940), the beleaguered and bombastic **Lugosi** (*The Devil Bat*, 1941), the hypocritically avuncular **Atwill** (*The Mad Doctor of Market Street*, 1942), the bald and beady-eyed **Zucco** (*The Mad Monster*, 1942), the theatrically threatening **Carradine** (*The Unearthly*, 1957) and the gentlemanly but jittery **Cushing** (*The Creeping Flesh*, 1972). Other performers who have memorably helped themselves to the ham include Charles **Laughton** (*Island of Lost Souls*,

Patrick Magee

1932), Ernest **Thesiger** (*Bride of Frankenstein*, 1935), Humphrey Bogart (*The Return of Dr. X*, 1939), Albert Dekker (*Dr. Cyclops*, 1940), Erich von **Stroheim** (*The Lady and the Monster*, 1943), Basil **Rathbone** (*The Black Sleep*, 1956), Whit **Bissell** (*I Was a Teenage Werewolf*, 1957), Anton **Diffring** (*The Man Who Could Cheat Death*, 1958), Michael **Gough** (*Konga*, 1961), Martin **Kosleck** (*The Flesh Eaters*, 1964), Donald **Pleasence** (*The Mutations*, 1973), Barbara **Steele** (*Piranha*, 1978) and Jeffrey **Combs** (*From Beyond*, 1986). These are among the most enjoyably theatrical turns in the history of the genre.

S.J. Perelman once asked about a cinematic mad scientist, 'What does this guy do for a living?' One popular job is raising the dead, attempted in *Maniac* (1934), *The Mad Ghoul* (1943), *Face of Marble* (1946), *The Brain That Wouldn't Die* (1960), *Doctor Blood's Coffin* (1961) and *Re-Animator* (1985). Reclaiming youth is all the rage in *Before I Hang* (1940), *The Corpse Vanishes* (1942), *The Man in Half Moon Street* (1944), *I vampiri* (1956) and *The Sorcerers* (1967). Attempts to create a super species are conducted with no government grants in *Man Made Monster* (1941), *Mesa of Lost Women* (1952), *Bride of the Monster* (1955), *The Astro-Zombies* (1968), *Scream and Scream Again* (1970) and *Carnosaur* (1993). And Darwin-obsessed screenwriters invent bizarre **ape** experiments for *The Wizard* (1927), **Murders in the Rue Morgue** (1932), *The Monster and the Girl* (1941), *Dr. Renault's Secret* (1942), *The Ape Man* (1943), **Captive Wild Woman** (1943) and *Bela Lugosi Meets a Brooklyn Gorilla* (1952). The most creative of mad scientists are the inventions of writer-director David **Cronenberg**, whose ideas range from a venereal disease that is also an aphrodisiac in *Shivers* (1975), to a television signal that gives perverts brain tumors in *Videodrome* (1982). LD

Magee, Patrick (1924–82)

Irish actor with piercing eyes and sibilant voice. Associated on stage with Beckett and Pinter, his film roles include de **Sade** in *The Persecution and Assassination of Jean-Paul Marat as Performed by the Inmates of the Asylum at Charenton Under the Direction of the Marquis de Sade* (1966) and the writer in *A Clockwork Orange* (1971). Crucified in *The Fiend* (1971), he perpetrates memorable revenges on Nigel Patrick and Herbert **Lom** in *Tales from the Crypt* (1972) and *Asylum* (1972). Often cast as a sinister doctor. SJ

*The Very Edge/1962 * Dementia 13/1963 * The*

Magician: Cesar Romero, Connie Stevens, *Two on a Guillotine*

Masque of the Red Death/*Seance on a Wet Afternoon*/1964 * *The Skull*/*Die, Monster, Die!*/ 1965 * *Demons of the Mind*/1972 * *The Final Program*/ – *And Now the Screaming Starts!*/1973 * *Sleep of Death*/1978 * *Dr. Jekyll et les femmes* [*Blood of Dr. Jekyll*]/1979 * *Il gatto nero* [*The Black Cat*]/*The Monster Club*/*Sir Henry at Rawlinson End*/1980

TV: *The Murder Club*/1961 * *The Avengers*: 'Killer Whale'/'The Gilded Cage'/1963 * *Orson Welles' Great Mysteries*: 'The Monkey's Paw'/1973 * *Thriller*: 'A Killer in Every Corner'/1974 * *Beasts*: 'What Big Eyes You Have'/1975

LEFT Magician: *Ansiktet*

Magicians

The very existence of fantastic cinema owes much to a magician, Georges **Méliès**, who discovered the camera's capabilities for creating illusion. Harry **Houdini**, best-known conjuror of his era, starred in silent films (*Terror Island*, 1920) and his work exposing fraudulent spiritualists encouraged the cinema to mix magicians with mediums. Stage magicians who followed Houdini into film include Dante in *A-Haunting We Will Go* (1942) and David Copperfield in *Terror Train* (1980).

The idea of prestidigitators killing their assistants while performing dangerous tricks is exploited in *The Last Performance* (1929) and *The Wizard of Gore* (1970), while *Miracles for Sale* (1939) and *Ace of Wands* (1970–2) offer a magicain detectives. A magician joins the expedition that revived Kharis in *The Mummy's Hand* (1940), a Satanist performs parlour tricks in *Night of the Demon* (1958), a conjuror pursues the Indian Rope Trick in *Vault of Horror* (1973), an inebriated illusionist performs at a sideshow in *The Funhouse* (1981) and a stage performer acquires paranormal powers in *Lord of Illusions* (1995). Veteran villains who play masters of legerdemain include Cesar Romero (*Charlie Chan at Treasure Island*, 1939; *Two on a Guillotine*, 1965), Erich von **Stroheim** (*The Mask of Dijon*, 1946), Bela **Lugosi** (*Spooks Run Wild*, 1941; *Scared to Death*, 1946), Vincent **Price** (*The Mad Magician*, 1954) and Christopher **Lee** (*The Hands of Orlac*, 1960).

The theme also produced more serious films: in Edmund Goulding's offbeat *Night-mare Alley* (1947), Tyrone Power inflates a mindreading act into fraudulent spiritualism but collapses into total degeneracy. Ingmar **Bergman**'s *Ansiktet* (*The Face*, 1958) depicts a travelling troupe of entertainers as alternately frightening, funny and tragic. Beautifully photographed and acted, *Ansiktet* is an authentic masterpiece of the horror cinema.
LD

Les mains d'Orlac (1920)

Maurice Renard's novel, translated as *The Hands of Orlac* (1929), is one of the warhorses of horror: pianist Stephen Orlac apparently loses his **hands** in a railway accident and a **mad scientist** seemingly grafts on a new pair taken from an executed knife-murderer, wherupon Orlac's hands display murderous urges. There are adaptations from Robert **Wiene** (*Orlacs Hände*, 1925) with Conrad **Veidt**, Karl **Freund** (*Mad Love*, 1935) with

Mel Ferrer, *The Hands of Orlac* (1960)

Colin **Clive** and Peter **Lorre**, Edmond T. Gréville (*The Hands of Orlac*, 1960) with Mel Ferrer and Christopher **Lee**, and Newton Arnold (*Hands of a Stranger*, 1962) with Paul Lukather. *Mad Love* is the most impressive, though, like the rest, it is flawed by a fudged ending that tries unsuccessfully to impose a rational interpretation. Riffs on the story are 'The Terror in Teakwood' (*Thriller*, 1961) and *Body Parts* (1991).

Malleson, Miles (1888–1969)

British actor. Malleson's first brush with horror was as the spectral undertaker in *Dead of Night* (1945). He appeared in four of Terence **Fisher**'s **Hammer** films, usually playing an amiable old duffer: one has a sense of the director indulging this charming man, allowing him to make scene-stealing turns out of thankless bit parts. By contrast, Michael **Powell**, for whom Malleson wrote and acted in *The Thief of Bagdad* (1940), cast him as the smut-buying pervert of *Peeping Tom* (1960). PH

The Sign of Four/1932 * *Queen of Spades*/1948 * *Dracula*/1958 * *The Hound of the Baskervilles*/1959 * *The Brides of Dracula*/1960 * *The Phantom of the Opera*/*Vengeance*/1962

Mander, Miles [Lionel Mander] (1888–1946)

British actor. An excellent **Sherlock Holmes** villain in *The Pearl of Death* (1944). SJ

Tower of London/*Wuthering Heights*/1939 * *The House of the Seven Gables*/1940 * *Fingers at the Window*/*Shadows on the Stairs*/1941 * *Phantom of the Opera*/*The Return of the Vampire*/1943 * *The Scarlet Claw*/1944 * *The Picture of Dorian Gray*/*The Brighton Strangler*/1945

Mann, Michael (b. 1943)

American director, writer, producer. The box-office failure of Mann's sophomore features *The Keep* (1983) and *Manhunter* (1986) illustrates 80s hostility toward serious-minded horror. Though not free from glossy pos

turing, both films deploy source novels with ambitious, authentic insight. Pitting Nazis against a Nietzschian beast, *The Keep* is a politicised rendering of F. Paul **Wilson**'s 1983 book complete with surprise gestures to **expressionism**. *Manhunter* is a coolly disturbing adaptation of Thomas **Harris**' *Red Dragon* (1981). Its televisual style (copped from the Mann-produced *Miami Vice*, 1984–9) avoids the bandstanding of *The Silence of the Lambs* (1991). Mann eventually achieved big-screen success with *The Last of the Mohicans* (1992) and *Heat* (1995), which share the intelligent, downbeat drive of his earlier work. DP

Manners, David [Rauff de Ryther Duan Acklom] (b. 1901)

Canadian-born actor. A rather bland, if stalwart romantic leading man in 30s horror classics. SJ

Dracula/1930 * *The Mummy*/*The Death Kiss*/1932 * *The Black Cat*/*The Moonstone*/1934 * *Mystery of Edwin Drood*/1935

Manson, Charles (b. 1934)

American cult leader. Head of the drop-out group known as the Family and mastermind of the Tate-LaBianca murders of 1969, Manson remains an American boogeyman.

David Manners

His thousand-yard stare, **Rasputin**-like enslavement of hippie girls and philosophical justifications for random slaughter made him the counterculture flipside of the baby-faced Lieutenant Calley.

A born ham who clearly enjoyed his show trial and has raved from jail in televised interviews ever since his death sentence was commuted, Manson features directly in a few pictures: played powerfully by Steve Railsback in the docudrama *Helter Skelter* (1976), from prosecutor Vincent Bugliosi's 1974 book (with Curt Gentry), and as the subject of underground efforts like *Manson Family Movies* (1984). Before the Tate-LaBianca murders were solved, John **Waters** used the case in *Multiple Maniacs* (1970). The shadow of Charlie extends to the murderous cults and monster messiahs of *I Drink Your Blood* (1971), *Sweet Savior* (1971; with Troy Donahue), *The Deathmaster* (1972; with Robert **Quarry** as a **vampire** guru), *The Night God Screamed* (1973), *Snuff* (1974), *Thou Shalt Not Kill . . . Except* (1987; with Sam **Raimi**), *Bad Dreams* (1988; with Richard **Lynch**), *La setta* (1991) and *Lord of Illusions* (1995). Even Oliver **Stone**'s *Natural Born Killers* (1994) recognises Manson as the Elvis of Mass Murder.

Margheriti, Antonio (b. 1930)

Italian director. Commencing his directorial career in pulp s-f (*Space Men*, 1960), the genial Margheriti moved into horror with the lurid brutalities of *La vergine di Norimberga* (*The Virgin of Nuremberg*, 1964) and the stately atmospherics of the Barbara

Stephen Lang, Tom Noonan, Michael Mann's *Manhunter*

Steele vehicles *Danza macabra* (*Castle of Blood*, 1963) and *I lunghi capelli della morte* (*The Long Hair of Death*, 1964). After the **giallo** *Nude . . . si muore* (*The Young, the Evil and the Savage*, 1968), Margheriti returned to classical territory with *Contronatura* (*The Unnaturals*, 1969), *Nella stretta morsa del ragno* (*Web of the Spider*, 1971), an inferior remake of *Danza macabra*, and *La morte negli occhi del gatto* (*Seven Deaths in the Cat's Eye*, 1973). Concentrating on routinely professional imitations of recent hits, he turned out *Killer Fish* (1978) and the ultra-gory *Apocalypse domani* (*Cannibal Apocalypse* (1980). For union reasons, he is credited with *Il mostro è in tavola, barone . . . Frankenstein* and *Dracula cerca sangue di vergine . . . e morì di sete*, the Italian versions of Paul **Morrissey**'s *Flesh for Frankenstein* (1973) and *Blood for Dracula* (1973). Active on the international scene, Margheriti often signs his work 'Anthony Dawson'. MA

Marins, José Mojica (b. 1929)

Brazilian director, actor, writer. Prolific, wild, mad as a hatter, Marins is a real one-off. His shoestring budgets, theatrical persona and cracked surrealism merge Catholic fears with cosmic dissertations on the Void, Eternity and Will. The odd giblet of Nietzsche and de **Sade** sits uneasily with grotesque depictions of **Hell** and **torture** (some authentically nasty). His principle efforts are marshalled around alter-ego Zé do Caixao (or 'Joseph of the Grave'), a devilish dandy and libertine whose contempt for the world leads him to inflict varied sufferings on lesser mortals. Zé first appeared in *A meia noite levarei sua alma* (*At Midnight I Will Steal Your Soul*, 1963), as a scornful atheist undertaker who commits rape and taunts the spirit world into punishing him. The follow-up *Esta noite encarnerei no teu cadaver* (*Tonight I Will Make Your Corpse Turn Red*, 1966) offers a horribly cramped, childishly sadistic vision of Hell, composed of crucified figures, human staircases and tortured souls beset by (real) poisonous spiders.

Later films show Pirandellian ambitions as Marins begins to play both himself, the film-maker, and his creation, Zé. Self-referentiality is amplified by a habit of chucking clips from earlier movies into the story. In the very weird *Delírios de um anormal* (*Hallucinations of a Deranged Mind*, 1977), Marins is approached by psychiatrists who want him to help a patient who is convinced Zé is real and out to get him. The director toys with the viewer's apprehension that he may actually be as mad as the characters he

plays. However, *Estupro* (*Perversion*, 1978) is entirely set in the 'real' world, with Marins as a wealthy mutilator of women who gets off in court only to be castrated by the one he loves.

Chaotic deep-echo soundtracks, penchant for cheap but jolting effects and berserk visual inspiration combine amateur Jodorowsky, ragged Cocteau camera magic and Ed **Wood** senselessness. Some effects look chillingly real – a throat piercing in *O estranho mundo de Zé do Caixao* (1968) – but a tendency to repetition and longeur, as well as appallingly cheap production values, can undo his grotty delirium. ST

Trilogia de terror (co-d/w)/1968 * *Ritual dos sádicos* [*The Awakening of the Beast*] (d/w/a)/ 1969 * *Finis Hominis* (d/st/a)/1971 * *Quando os deuses adormecem* (d/w/a)/1972 * *Exorcismo negro* (d/w/a)/1974 * *A estrana hospedaria dos prazeres* (co-d/s/a)/1975 * *Como consolar viúvas* (d)/*Inferno carnal* (d/s/a)/1976 * *O universo de Mojica Marins* (a/s)/*O segredo da múmia* (a)/ 1978 * *A praga* (d/w, unfinished)/1980 * *Homem vs. máquina* (d/w/s)/*Brincadeira fatal* (d/w/s)/1981 * *A quinta dimensao do sexo* (d)/1983 * *A hora do medo* (co-d)/*A duas faces de um psicopata* (d)/*Demônios e maravilhas* (d/w/a, uncompleted)/*A Ultimo sessao de cinema* (s/a)/1986 * *A seita dos espíritos malditos* (d/w/a)/1992 * *Allucinaçao macabra* (d/w/a)/ *Zé do Caixao na cidade do terror* (a)/1993

Marshall, William (b. 1924)

American actor, briefly a horror star as the **black vampire** Prince Mamuwalde.

Blacula/1972 * *Scream, Blacula Scream*/1973 * *Abby*/1974

TV: *Alfred Hitchcock Hour*: 'The Jar'/1964 * *Wild Wild West*: 'The Night of the Egyptian Queen'/1968

Martin, Eugenio (b. 1925)

Spanish director. A former assistant to Nicholas Ray and Roy Ward **Baker**, Martin demonstrates significantly more technical polish than colleagues in the Spanish shocker. *Hipnosis* (*Hypnosis*, 1962) lead some to consider him an embryo **Hitchcock**, but his best venture remains the exciting 'monster on the loose' romp *Pánico en el Transiberiano* (*Horror Express*, 1972). *Una vela para el diablo* (*A Candle for the Devil*, 1973) uses sexual repression and religious bigotry as the basis for a gruesome murder tale, but the atmospheric *Aquella casa de las afueras* (1980) is tainted by nauseating anti-abortion undertones. MA

L'última señora Anderson/1970 * *Sobrenatural* [*Supernatural*]/1980

Martino, Sergio (b. 1938)

Italian director. During the 60s, Martino worked in various capacities for his producer brother Luciano, before a directorial debut with the **mondo** shockumentary *Mille peccati . . . nessuna virtù* (1969). Subsequently he ventured onto **giallo** terrain with *Lo strano vizio della signora Wardh* (*Blade of the Ripper*, 1970), *Tutti i colori del buio* (*All the Colours of Darkness*, 1972), *Il tuo vizio è una stanza chiusa e solo io ne ho la chiave* (*Gently Before She Dies*, 1972) and *I corpi presentano tracce di violenza carnale* (*Torso*, 1973). This slew of salacious shockers established Martino's commercial style, mixing lip-smacking eroticism with endearing vitality and an assuredly professional gloss. Active in many genres, he returned to horror with *La montagna del dio cannibale* (*Prisoners of the Cannibal God*, 1978) and *Il fiume del grande caimano* (*The Great Alligator*, 1979). One of his best is the Moreau-inspired *L'isola degli uomini pesce* (*Island of the Mutations*, 1978), which has a recent sequel, *The Fish Men and Their Queen* (1995). MA

La coda dello scorpione [*The Case of the Scorpion's Tail*]/1971 * *Assassinio al cimitero etrusco*/1982 * *Vendetta dal futuro* [*Fists of Steel*]/1986 * *American risciò*/1989 * *Delitti privati*/*Graffiante desiderio* [*Craving Desire*]/1993

Masks

The central props of Greek theatre and much pagan ritual, masks are recurrent in horror, worn by **disfigured** fiends (***The Phantom of the Opera***, 1926; *Mystery of the Wax Museum*, 1932; *The Face Behind the Mask*, 1941; *The Abominable Dr. Phibes*, 1971; *The Funhouse*, 1981) or used to conceal the identity of villains (***The Cat and the Canary***, 1927; *Quattro mosche di velluto grigio*, 1972; *Madhouse*, 1974; *The Toolbox Murders*, 1977; *Terror Train*, 1980). Leatherface of the **Texas Chain Saw Massacre** films, Michael of the **Halloween** series and Jason of the **Friday the 13th** sequels are characterised almost solely by featureless masks, but more subtle use of false faces and the mutilations they conceal is demonstrated by *Les yeux sans visage* (1959), in which Edith Scob emotes remarkably through a blank mask, and *Onibaba* (1965), with its magical samurai demon mask.

Douglass Dumbrille in *Castle in the Desert* (1942) and Christopher **Lee** in *Circus of Fear*

Unmasked: Vincent Price, Virginia North, *The Abominable Dr. Phibes*

(1966) wear masks to conceal that they are *not* disfigured. Masks are hammered on to Barbara **Steele**'s face (*La maschera del demonio*, 1960), trigger **3-D** hallucinations (*The Mask*, 1961), help Liam Neeson pass for normal (*Darkman*, 1990) or turn Jim Carrey into an anarchic toon (*The Mask*, 1994). Many great horror characters and actors, of course, are literally masked by their make-ups: the unmasking of **Chaney**'s Phantom merely reveals a more horrific mask beneath.

'The Masque of the Red Death' (1842)

Edgar Allan **Poe**'s mediaeval fable has Prince Prospero host a party in his enclosed castle while the plague ravages the country outside, only to be confronted by a red spectre who spreads the **disease** to the worthless revellers. It is one of Poe's most-adapted stories, with versions in 1911 (an Italian *Mask of the Red Death*), 1919 (the German *Die Pest in Florenz*), 1923 (the Soviet *Prizak Borodit po Yevrope*), 1951 (on **Lights Out**, with Hurd Hatfield), 1964 (by Roger **Corman** with Vincent **Price**, stirring Poe's 1849 'Hop-Frog' into the story), 1969 (the Yugoslav animated *Maska crvene smrti*), 1989 (a Corman-produced remake), 1990 (a feeble Harry Allan **Towers** whodunit), and 1996 (a South African-shot TV movie with Christopher **Lee**). In the Technicolor sequence of *The Phantom of the Opera* (1926), Lon **Chaney** attends the Opera Ball as Poe's Red Death.

LEFT Masked: Edith Scob, Georges Franju's *Les yeux sans visage*

Massaccesi, Aristide (b. 1936)

Italian producer, director, cinematographer, writer whose many pseudonyms include Joe D'Amato, David Hills and Kevin Mancuso. The unbelievably prolific Massaccesi is perhaps best known for the 70s *Black Emanuelle* films with Laura Gemser. *La morte ha sorriso all'assassino* (*Death Smiles on a Murderer*, 1973), his first horror film as a director, marks a particular obsession with necrophilia which also powers his best feature, *Buio omega* (*Buried Alive*, 1978). Massaccesi freely associates **sex** and death in his more infamous productions: *Emanuelle perché . . . violenza alla donne?* (*Emanuelle in America*, 1976), *Emanuelle e gli ultimi cannibali* (*Emanuelle and the Last Cannibals*, 1977), *Notti erotiche dei morti viventi* (1980), *Antropophagus* (*The Anthropophagous Beast*, 1980), *Rosso sangue* (*Absurd*, 1981) and the aptly titled *Porno holocaust* (1980). His morbid output slowed in the mid-80s as he turned to sword-and-sorcery (*Ator l'invincibile/Ator the Fighting Eagle*, 1982) and futuristic (*Anno 2020 i gladiatori del futuro/2020 Texas Gladiators*, 1983) fare, as well as hard (*Super hardcore*, 1982) and soft (*Il piacere/The Pleasure*, 1985) **pornography**. DW

Il plenilunio delle vergini [*The Devil's Wedding Night*] (c)/1973 * *L'anticristo* [*The Antichrist*] (c)/1974 * *Emanuelle e Françoise, le sorelline* [*Blood Vengeance*] (d)/1975 * *Deliria* [*Stagefright*] (p)/*La casa 3* [*Ghosthouse*] (p)/*Raptors* [*Killing Birds*] (p)/1987 * *La casa 4* [*Witchery*]/1988 * *DNA formula letale* [*Metamorphosis*] (p)/*Paura nel buio* [*Hitcher in the Dark*] (p)/1989 * *Troll 2* (p)/*La casa 5* [*Beyond Darkness*] (p)/1990 * *Il diavello nella carne* (d)/*Ossessione fatale* (d)/1991 * *Ritorno dalla morte* [*Frankenstein 2000*] (d)/1992

Masterton, Graham (b. 1946)

British writer. Masterton made his debut with *The Manitou* (1976), an **American Indian** curse story with **Cthulhu Mythos** overtones, filmed in 1978. A prolific author of slick, gruesome supernatural novels: *The Djinn* (1977), *The Pariah* (1983), *Death Dream* (1988), *Mirror* (1988), *The Hymn* (1991). He edited *Scare Care* (1989), a charity anthology.

Mastorakis, Nico (b. 1941)

Greek director, writer, producer. After the auspiciously sleazy tourist nasty *Island of Death* (1975), Mastorakis progressed to muddled **stalk-and-slash** derivatives. His films are international affairs often kinked with Grecian colour. DP

Jane Asher, Roger Corman, Vincent Price, on the set of *Masque of the Red Death*

Death Has Blue Eyes/1974 * *Blood Tide* (p)/ 1980 * *Blind Date*/1984 * *The Zero Boys*/1986 * *Nightmare at Noon*/*The Wind*/1987 * *Grand-mother's House* (p)/1988 * *In the Cold of the Night*/1990

Mastroianni, Armand (b. 1950)

American director; cousin of Marcello Mastroianni. Mastroianni jumped on the **stalk-and-slash** bandwagon with the heavy-handed *He Knows You're Alone* (1980). Confined to blandly derivative material, he has failed to give a modicum of style, or put a personal trademark, on any subsequent work. AJ

The Killing Hour/1982 * *The Supernaturals*/ 1986 * *Distortions*/1987 * *Cameron's Closet*/ 1989

TV: *Tales From the Darkside*: 'Pain Killer'/ 1984; 'If the Shoe Fits . . .'/'The Impression-ist'/1985; 'Social Climber'/1987 * *Friday the 13th: The Series*: 'Better Off Dead'/ 'Mesmer's Bauble'/'The Prisoner'/ 'Demonhunter'/ 'Night Prey'/1989; 'Mightier Than the Sword'/'My Wife as a Dog'/'The Charnel Pit'/1990 * *Nightmare Cafe*: 'Dying Well is the Best Revenge'/'Sanctuary for a Child'/1992

Matheson, Richard (b. 1926)

American writer. 'Born of Man and Woman' (1950), Matheson's first published story, established him as articulate champion of the isolated loner in a hostile universe. Similar paranoia underscores his detective thrillers (*Someone is Bleeding*, 1953; *Fury on Sunday*, 1953; *Ride the Nightmare*, 1959), the based-on-personal-experience war story *The Beardless Warriors* (1960), magnificent horror novels *I Am Legend* (1954) and *The Shrinking Man* (1956), screenplays on **Poe** themes for Roger **Corman** and the road-rage *Duel* (1971), famously filmed by the young Steven **Spielberg**. Since *Hell House* (1971), he has written novels on spiritual and romantic themes (*Bid Time Return*, 1975; *What Dreams May Come*, 1978) and unexpect-edly turned to the Western (*Journal of the Gun Years*, 1992).

Matheson greatly influenced **The Twi-light Zone** (1959–64), with stories typically centring on challenged identities and twists in time. Adapting his own novels, Matheson has scripted *The Incredible Shrinking Man* (1957), *The Last Man on Earth* (as 'Logan Swanson', 1964), *The Young Warriors* (1966), *The Legend of Hell House* (1973) and *Somewhere in Time* (1980), from *The Shrinking Man*, *I Am Legend*, *The Beardless Warriors* and *Hell House*. He adapted Kerouac's *The Beat Generation* (1959), Jules Verne's *Master of the World* (1961), Fritz **Leiber**'s *Conjure Wife* (1953) as *Night of the Eagle* (1962), Anne Blaisdell's *Nightmare* (1961) as *Fanatic* (1965) and Dennis **Wheatley**'s *The Devil Rides Out* (1968). His original scripts include 'The Comedy of Terrors* (1963), *De Sade* (1969) and, with his son Richard Christian **Matheson**, *Loose Cannons* (1990). PS

The Fall of the House of Usher/1960 * *Pit and the Pendulum*/1961 * *Tales of Terror*/1962 * *The Raven*/1963 * *The Omega Man* (st)/1971 * *Twilight Zone: The Movie*/*Jaws 3-D*/1983

TV: *The Twilight Zone*: 'And When the Sky Was Opened' (st)/1959; 'Third From the Sun' (st)/'The Last Flight'/'A World of Difference'/'A World of His Own'/'Nick of Time'/1960; 'The Invaders'/'Once Upon a Time'/1961; 'Little Girl Lost'/'Young Man's Fancy'/1962; 'Mute'/'Death Ship'/'Steel'/ 'Nightmare at 20,000 Feet'/1963; 'Night Call'/'Spur of the Moment'/1964 * *Thriller*:

'The Return of Andrew Bentley'/1961 *
Alfred Hitchcock Hour: 'Ride the Nightmare'/
1962 * *Journey to the Unknown*: 'Girl of My
Dreams' (st)/1968 * *Late Night Horror*: 'No
Such Thing as a Vampire' (st)/1968 * *Night
Gallery*: 'The Big Surprise'/1971; 'The
Funeral'/1972 * *Ghost Story*: 'The New
House'/1972 * *The Night Stalker*/1972 * *The
Night Strangler/Dying Room Only/Dracula*/1973
* *Scream of the Wolf/The Stranger Within*/1974
* *Trilogy of Terror*/1975 * *Dead of Night*/1977 *
The Strange Possession of Mrs Oliver/1977 * *The
Martian Chronicles*/1979 * *The Twilight Zone*:
'Button, Button'/1986 * *Amazing Stories*: 'The
Doll' (st)/'One for the Books'/1986 * *Twilight
Zone: Rod Serling's Lost Classics*/1994 * *The
Outer Limits*: 'The First Anniversary' (st)/
1996 * *Trilogy of Terror 2* (st)/1996

Matheson, Richard Christian
(b. 1953)

American writer; son of Richard **Matheson**.
Active in film and TV, Matheson's most serious work is the distinctive short fiction collected in *Scars and Other Distinguishing Marks*
(1987). *Created By* (1993), his first novel, is a

Richard Matheson

doppelgänger story with a TV-industry
background.

TV: *Amazing Stories*: 'Magic Saturday'/1986 *
Full Eclipse (+co-p)/1994

Mattei, Bruno (b. 1933)

Italian director. Beginning his career as an
editor in the late 50s, Mattei is guilty of per-
petrating some of the trashiest atrocities in
Italian genre cinema. Often aiming solely at
the export market, he has inflicted *Casa pri-
vata per le SS* (*SS Girls*, 1976), *K.Z9 lager di
stermini* (*Woman's Camp 119*, 1977), *Virus*
(*Zombie Creeping Flesh*, 1980), *L'altro inferno*
(*The Other Hell*, 1981) and *Rats, notte di terrore*
(*Rats: Night of Terror*, 1985) on the world.
Zombi 3 (1988), which Mattei took over from
an ailing **Fulci**, metamorphosised into an
even worse remake of *Virus*! Wisely, he
hides behind many pseudonyms, including
Stefan Oblowsky and Vincent Dawn, especially when venturing into **sex** sleaze (*Le
notti porno nel mondo*, 1977; *Caligola e
Messalina*, 1981). The height of his cheek is
the not-to-be-confused-with-anything-else
Terminator II (1991). MA

Gli occhi dentro [*Shocking Dark*]/1989

de Maupassant, Guy (1850–93)

French writer. A master of the short form,
Maupassant's work is threaded through with
cruelty and the weird. Films inspired by his
horror stories include: *Diary of a Madman*

(1963), from 'The Horla' (1887), *Le sang des
autres* (*Lips of Blood*, 1972), loosely from 'The
Hand' (1883), and *Golden Braid* (1990), from
the 1884 story.

Mayne, Ferdy [Ferdinand Mayer-
Boerckel] (b. 1916)

German-born actor, based in Britain. Often a
smooth villain, he is a spoof **vampire** in
Dance of the Vampires (1967) and **Dracula** in
Gebissen wird nur Nachts – Vampire Happening
[*The Vampire Happening*] (1971) and the
Czechoslovak/West German TV series *Frank-
enstein's Auntie* (1986). SJ

All Hallowe'en/1952 * *The Vampire Lovers*/
1970 * *The Horror Star*/1981 * *Conan the
Destroyer/Howling II Stirba – Werewolf Bitch*/
1984 * *Night Train to Terror*/1985 * *My Lovely
Monster*/1991 * *Knight Moves*/1993

TV: *One Step Beyond*: 'Nightmare'/1961 * *The
Avengers*: 'Legacy of Death'/1968 * *The New
Avengers*: 'Trap'/1977 * *Monsters*: 'Cell Mate'/
1990

Mediums

Spiritualism, a Victorian craze systematised
into something like a religion, popularised

Bruno Mattei's *Virus*

Ferdy Mayne

the figure of the medium, an otherwise ordinary person gifted with an ability to get in touch with the afterlife. Arthur Conan **Doyle**, one of the founding fathers of the movement, wrote *The Land of Mist* (1926), a serious novel in which Professor Challenger is converted to the cause and an attempt is made to deal with the professional life and legal problems of mediums.

Few films or novels use mediums as central characters, but they frequently pop up as plot-explaining or – moving devices, as in Vernon **Sewell**'s four versions of the same story (*The Medium*, 1934; *Latin Quarter*, 1945; *Ghost Ship*, 1953; *House of Mystery*, 1960), two passes at the murder-during-a-seance item *The Thirteenth Chair* (1929, 1937) and *Haunted* (1995). Scene-stealing mediums are Margaret Rutherford's Madame Arcati in *Blithe Spirit* (1945), Margaret Leighton in *From Beyond the Grave* (1973), Macha Meril in *Profondo rosso* (*Deep Red*, 1976) and Kathleen Wilhoite in *Witchboard* (1986).

Mainly fake mediums are played by Turhan **Bey** in *The Spiritualist* (1948), Marie Powers in *The Medium* (1951), Kenne Duncan (*Night of the Ghouls*, 1958) and Kim Stanley (*Seance on a Wet Afternoon*, 1964), while fraud Rosanna Arquette develops genuine powers in *Black Rainbow* (1989) and Pamela **Franklin** and Roddy **McDowall** in *The Legend of Hell House* (1973) use their talents in a haunted house. Spiritualism and s-f mix in *The Devil Commands* (1941), with **Karloff** going beyond conventional seances by using a mechanical device for contacting the afterlife. Especially evil mediums are *Count Yorga, Vampire* (1971) and *Dr. Death, Seeker of Souls* (1972). Table-rapping, ectoplasm, duplicity and voices from the beyond feature in many short stories and, therefore, TV episodes: 'The Borderland' (**The Outer Limits**, 1963), 'Zubrovnik's Ghost' (*Mission: Impossible*, 1966), 'The Indian Spirit Guide (**Journey to the Unknown**, 1968), 'The Dear Departed' (**Night Gallery**, 1971), 'A Case of Spirits' (*Cribb*, 1980).

Méliès, Georges (1861–1938)

French film-maker. Scion of a shoe dynasty, Méliès came to the cinema after a spell as a caricaturist and, more seriously, proprietor of the Théâtre Robert-Houdin, where he mounted elaborate stage shows as settings for his own conjuring. In 1895, he saw the films exhibited by the Brothers Lumière and petitioned them to sell him film-making apparatus. They turned him down, famously claiming there was no future in the gadget,

but he aquired British equipment and produced imitation Lumière films (*L'arroseur*, 1896) to add to the bill at the Robert-Houdin. Legend has it that a stalled camera prompted his invention of special effects as the projected film suggested an omnibus 'transforming' into a hearse, but it seems most likely that Méliès's tinkering ingenuity prompted him to segue from taking films to making them.

In later life, Méliès was rather embarrassed to be remembered for his 'trick films', claiming they were the only attractions that

Georges Méliès

would please his unlettered mass audience, and pointing out that his Star Film also made documentaries (*Exposition de 1900*, 1900), dramatic reconstructions (*Le sacré d'Edouard VII*, 1902), religious material (*Le Christ marchant sur les flots*, 1899), literary adaptations (*Hamlet*, 1907), historical epics (*Jeanne d'Arc*, 1900) and topical docu-drama (*L'affaire Dreyfus*, 1899). However, it is as the 'Jules Verne of the Cinema' or the founder of *film fantastique* that he remains important. His earliest fantasies are literal tricks, tiny narrative excuses for wonders, using double-exposure, animation and stage machinery to present *L'homme de têtes* (*The Man With Four Heads*, 1898) or *L'homme à la tête de caoutchouc* (*The Man With the Indiarubber Head*, 1902). He progressed to a series of Verne-like 'impossible voyages' which provided a quest theme upon which marvels could be hung: famously visiting the moon in *Voyage dans la lune* (*A Trip to the Moon*, 1901) but also head-

ing for the Sun in a train (*Voyage à travers l'impossible*, 1904), adapting Verne's submarine story (*Vingt mille lieues sous les mers*, 1907), tunneling the English Channel (*Le tunnel sous la manche*, 1907) and encountering giants at the North Pole (*A la conquête du pôle*, 1912).

Though capable of macabre callousness with exploding heads and bursting Selenites, Méliès was more interested in the marvellous than the horrific, setting out to surprise rather than shock. Devils and imps and malevolent fairies recur, but merely as conjurers who prompt magic transformations or play pranks on humankind. Nevertheless, he returned obsessively to **Faust** (*Le cabinet de Méphistophélès*, 1897; *Faust et Marguerite*, 1897; *damnation de Faust*, 1898; *Faust aux enfers*, 1903; *Damnation du docteur Faust*, 1904) and essayed early stabs at *She* (*La danse du feu*, 1899), Bluebeard (*Barbe-Bleue*, 1901) and the **Wandering Jew** (*Le juif errant*, 1904). Obsolete and bankrupt by World War I, he eked a living for some years selling toys at a railway station but was rediscovered and honoured in his last years. Georges **Franju**'s *Le grand Méliès* (1952) is a moving tribute.

*Le fakir, mystère indien/1896 * L'hallucination d'alchimiste/Le château hanté/1897 * Magie diabolique/La caverne maudite/1898 * Le spectre/Le diable au couvent/Le miroir de Cagliostro/L'ile du diable/1899 * Coppélia/1900 * Chez la sorcière/ Le temple de la magie/La fontaine sacrée/L'ecole infernale/1901 * Le diable géant/Les trésors de Satan/L'homme-mouche/1902 * Les filles du diable/Le cake-walk infernal/La statue animée/Le sorcier/Le monstre/Le royaume des fées/1903 * La dame fantôme/1904 * Le diable noir/Le baquet de Mesmer/Le peintre barbouillard et tableau diabolique/1905 * Le fantôme d'alger/Le 400 farces du diable/La fée Carabosse/1906 * Satan en prison/1907 * La cuisine de l'ogre/La poupée vivante/Le fakir de Singapour/1908 * Le locataire diabolique/1909*

Méndez, Fernando (1908–66)

Mexican director. Méndez helmed *Ladrón de cadávres* (*The Body Snatchers*, 1956), the first horror-**wrestling** movie, pitting Wolf **Ruvinskis** against a **mad scientist** who turns grapplers into monsters. He also directed *El vampiro* (*The Vampire*, 1956) and *El ataúd del vampiro* (*The Vampire's Coffin*, 1957), with German **Robles** as the **Dracula**-style Count Duval. His monochrome horrors combine the look of Universal and the energy of **Hammer** but their naïveté is most reminiscent of 40s American **serials**. Another notable credit is *La locura del rock and roll* (1958).

Las calaveras del terror/1944 * *Misterios de ultratumba* [*The Black Pit of Dr. M*]/1958 * *Los diablos del terror*/*El grito de la muerte*/1959

Menzies, William Cameron
(1896–1957)

American art director, director. Acclaimed for his contributions as designer and second-unit man to such epics as *The Thief of Bagdad* (1924) and *Gone With the Wind* (1939), Menzies' occasional directorial credits are remarkable for their use of impressive sets that represent intolerable social or psychological conditions. Though less sure with actors than his camera, Menzies consistently examines the human cost of living with oppressive architecture, whether in the utopia of *Things to Come* (1936), the Nazi Germany of *Address Unkown* (1944), the occupied America of *Invaders From Mars* (1953) or the cursed castle of *The Maze* (1953). *The Whip Hand* (1951), with its Nazi-Commie bioweapons, and *Invaders* are exercises in American paranoia, while the **3-D** *Maze*, with its human frog, is a remarkably sombre gothic which even makes its ridiculous monster touching.

The Bat/1926 * *The Spider* (d)/1931 * *Chandu the Magician* (d)/1932 * *Heartbeat* (d/s)/1949

Mephistopheles; Mephisto; Mephistophilis * See: Faust

Midi-Minuit Fantastique (1962–71)
Founded and edited by Eric Losfield, this French publication was as influential in Europe as **Famous Monsters of Filmland** was in the US. As passionate as *FM*, it was far more intellectual, cine-literate and erotically inclined, championing Barbara **Steele**, Riccardo **Freda** and **Hammer** well before it was fashionable so to do. Among its contributors were future film-makers Michel **Parry**, Christopher **Wicking** and Jean **Rollin** and important critics Raymond Durgnat and Jean-Claude Romer.

Mihalka, George (b. 1952)
Canadian director. Since the atmospheric but derivative **stalk-and-slash** *My Bloody Valentine* (1981), Mihalka has specialised in cheap thrills. *Eternal Evil* (1986), originally entitled *The Blue Man*, is his most ambitious effort.

Hostile Takeover/1988 * *Psychic*/1992 * *Relative Fear*/1994

TV: *The Hitchhiker*: 'Phantom Zone'/ 'Spinning Wheel'/1989

Mikels, Ted V. [Theodore Vincent Mikacevich] (b. 1929)
American director, writer, producer. A colourful no-budget indie, Mikels has directed a trio of horrors. *The Astro Zombies* (1968) and *The Corpse Grinders* (1971) take themselves less seriously than *Blood Orgy of the She Devils* (1972), but despite calculated kookiness all are hampered by a lack of exploitative energy. The producer of *The Worm Eaters* (1970), Mikels excised much gore before distributing David Graham's *The Undertaker and His Pals* (1966). *Dr. Sex* (1964) is a nudie with genre pretensions. DP

The Hostage (c)/1967 * *Children Shouldn't Play with Dead Things* (c)/1973 * *Dimension in Fear*/1995

The Military
Packed with evisceration and dismemberment, films about soldiers are as graphic as any conventional horror material. Brutal actuality – as restaged in the slaygrounds of *Nobi* (*Fires on the Plain*, 1959), *Soldier Blue* (1970), *Idi i smotri* (*Come and See*, 1985), *Platoon* (1986) or *Casualties of War* (1980) – confirms not only a continuing rejection of militarism in all its forms but also that the

William Cameron Menzies

challenging of authority in general has always been a crowd-pleaser.

Even prior to World War I, when the military presence was offered as a supposed comforter in the spate of Europhobic propa-

William Cameron Menzies's *The Maze*

ganda screened in Britain (*The Invaders*, 1909; *An Englishman's Home*, 1914; *If England Were Invaded*, 1914), the army was repeatedly downgraded to the minor role of nick-of-time rescue service, arriving only after civilian initiative had unmasked the infiltrators and struck the first blows of defence. The militia have seldom got it right ever since, whether mowing down giant apes, electrocuting rampant creatures from beneath the sea, picking off alien peacemakers, treating bioweapon-induced plague outbreaks with summary execution, or imposing quarantine on UFO landing sites. Erecting barriers and obscuring the truth are primary functions, while at top-brass level – as clumsy and bullheaded in *Stargate* (1994) as in *Dr. Strangelove* (1964) – treachery and brinkmanship habitually inspire scenarios of catastrophe.

On the ground, as usual, the grunt takes the brunt, suffering indoctrination (*The Manchurian Candidate*, 1962; *Body Snatchers*, 1993), dislocation (*The Philadelphia Experiment*, 1984; *Jacob's Ladder*, 1990), fatal entrapment (*The Keep*, 1984; *Aliens*, 1986), or bloody rearrangement (*Universal Soldier*, 1992; *Mind Ripper*, 1995). Still lurking behind the scenes in episodes of *Star Trek* (1966–9), *Babylon 5* (1993–), and *SeaQuest DSV* (1993–), a military stranglehold on the far future seems unavoidable. PS

Milland, Ray [Reginald Truscott-Jones] (1905–86)

Welsh-born actor, in Hollywood from the 30s. An Academy Award-winner as the hallucinating alcholic in *The Lost Weekend* (1945) and a director of some note (*Panic in Year Zero!*, 1962), he ended his career as a dependable character actor in TV movies and exploitation films. Satan in a slouch hat in *Alias Nick Beal* (1949). SJ

The Uninvited/1944 * *The Premature Burial*/ 1962 * *The Man with X-Ray Eyes*/1963 * *Frogs*/ *The Thing With Two Heads*/1972 * *Terror in the Wax Museum*/*The House in Nightmare Park*/ 1973 * *The Uncanny*/*La ragazza dal pigiama giallo*/1977 * *The Attic*/1980 * *Serpiente de mar*/1985

TV: *Alfred Hitchcock Hour*: 'A Home Away From Home'/1963 * *Daughter of the Mind*/ 1969 * *Night Gallery*: 'The Hand of Borgus Weems'/*Black Noon*/1971 * *The Dead Don't Die*/1975 * *Look What's Happened to Rosemary's Baby*/1976 * *The Hardy Boys*/*Nancy Drew Mysteries*: 'Voodoo Doll'/1978 * *Fantasy*

RIGHT Ray Milland, *Alias Nick Beal*

Island: 'Nightmare'/*Cruise into Terror*/1978 * *The Darker Side of Terror*/1979 * *The Masks of Death*/1984

Miller, Dick (b. 1928)

American actor; a regular in the films of Roger **Corman**, for whom he played the demented beatnik **artist** Walter Paisley in *A Bucket of Blood* (1959). He has subsequently recreated the character for a variety of directors paying homage to Corman's low-budget masterpiece. SJ

The Undead/1956 * *It Conquered the World*/ 1956 * *Not of This Earth*/1957 * *The Little Shop of Horrors*/1960 * *The Premature Burial*/1962 * *The Man With X-Ray Eyes*/*The Terror*/1963 * *Targets*/1967 * *Hollywood Boulevard*/1976 * *Piranha*/1978 * *Dr. Heckyl & Mr. Hype*/*The Howling*/1980 * *Twilight Zone: The Movie*/1983 * *Gremlins*/1984 * *Chopping Mall*/*Night of the Creeps*/1986 * *The 'Burbs*/*Far From Home*/ *Ghost Writer*/1989 * *Gremlins 2: The New Batch*/*Evil Toons*/1990 * *Amityville 1992: It's About Time*/1992 * *Matinee*/*Batman: Mask of the Phantasm*/*Quake*/1993 * *Tales From the Crypt: Demon Knight*/1994

TV: *Tales from the Darkside*: 'All a Clone by the Telephone'/1984 * *Amazing Stories*: 'The Greibble'/1986 * *Freddy's Nightmares*: 'Freddysomething'/1989 * *Eerie, Indiana*: 'The Losers'/1991 * *Batman: The Animated Series*: 'Harlequinade' (v)/1994

Milligan, Andy (1929–91)

American writer, director, cinematographer, editor. The tenacious but untalented Milligan's impoverished films are characterised by amateurish scripts, direction, and performances; anachronistic horror stereotypes; grating 'canned' music; and risible nudity and gore. *The Naked Witch* (1964), *The Ghastly Ones* (1968), *Torture Dungeon* (1969) and *Guru the Mad Monk* (1970), shot on Staten

Island, established his reputation on the drive-in circuit. *Bloodthirsty Butchers* (1970), the first **splatter** Sweeney **Todd**, *The Body Beneath* (1970), *The Rats Are Coming! The Werewolves Are Here!* (1971) and the **Jekyll and Hyde** revamp *The Man With Two Heads* (1971) were lensed in Britain, followed by *Blood* (1974), *Legacy of Blood* (1978), *Carnage* (1983), *Weirdo: The Beginning* (1990) and *Monstrosity* (1992).

Milligan's paucity of means and imagination inadvertently yielded memorably nasty images (a breast in a pie in *Bloodthirsty Butchers*, a writhing rat nailed to a window sill in *The Rats Are Coming!*) and a genuinely misanthropic universe, which may account for his enduring reputation. SB/DW

Mil Máscaras [Aaron Rodriguez] (b. 19??)

Mexican **wrestler**, actor; Man of a Thousand Masks, friendly rival of **Santo** and **Blue Demon**, frequent foe of murdering **mummies**.

Las vampiras/*Enigma de muerta*/1968 * *Las momias de Guanajuato*/1970 * *El robo de las momias de Guanajuato*/*El castillo de las momias de Guanajuato*/*Vuelven los campeones justicieros*/ 1972

The Mind Beyond (UK TV series, 1976)

Six original plays on the theme of **ESP**, produced for the BBC by Irene Shubik after the success of her productions of Daphne **du Maurier**'s 'The Breakthrough' (1975) and William Trevor's 'Mrs Acland's Ghosts' (1975). The first is David Halliwell's 'Meriel, the Ghost Girl', directed by Philip Saville, a *Rashomon* variant offering differing viewpoints on a seance shot in radically different styles, accommodating psychic investigator Donald **Pleasence**, private eye John Bluthal and *avant-la-lettre* video diarist Janet Street-Porter. The other plays deal with an autistic girl's uncanny rapport with her psychotherapist (Brian Hayles's 'Double Echo'), strange events at Stonehenge (Malcolm Christopher's 'Stones'), premonition (William Trevor's 'The Love of a Good Woman'), ghostly mathematics (Bruce Stewart's 'The Daedalus Equations') and second sight (Evan Jones's 'The Man With the Power'). Shubik edited a classy tie-in book from Penguin. TM

Minions

One of the most thankless roles in horror cinema is the villain's minion, usually played as a witless, abused, grotesque madman with dialogue limited to 'yes master' and 'please don't flog me again'. The originator of the type is Dwight **Frye**, fly-eating **Renfield** in *Dracula* (1930) and grave-robbing hunchback in *Frankenstein* (1931). Frye cringes again in *The Vampire Bat* (1933) and *Dead Men Walk* (1943).

Others to slobber through variations include Irving **Pichel** (*Dracula's Daughter*, 1936), Angelo **Rossitto** (*The Corpse Vanishes*, 1942), Victor Maddern (*Blood of the Vampire*, 1958), Oscar Quitak (*The Revenge of Frankenstein*, 1958), Riccardo Valle (*Gritos en la noche*, 1962), John Karlin (*Dark Shadows*, 1966–71), Terry Downes (*Dance of the Vampires*, 1967) and Patrick **Troughton** (*Scars of Dracula*, 1970). Marty Feldman (*Young Frankenstein*, 1974) and Richard **O'Brien** (*The Rocky Horror Picture Show*, 1975) parody the type, while Erich von **Stroheim** (*Sunset Blvd.*, 1950), Alida Valli (*Les yeux sans visage*, 1960) and James Mason (*Salem's Lot*, 1979) are less stereotyped but still minionous.

Mad scientists and **vampires** are usually content with a single slave, kept in line with an occasional spare nubile kidnappee or the promise of a new undeformed body, but master villains like **Fu Manchu** or **Mabuse** employ hordes of minions who mindlessly execute their will, often sacrificing themselves *en masse* for the cause of their evil master. A rare leading-man minion is Paul

Minion: Marty Feldman, *Young Frankenstein*

Naschy (*El jorobado del morgue*, 1972), though established characters like the **Mummy**, **Frankenstein**'s Monster or the **Hunchback of Notre Dame** could be considered marginally minionlike. Cliché, embodied by Charles Bronson (*House of Wax*, 1953) and Jack Mullaney (*Dr. Goldfoot and the Bikini Machine*, 1965), has it that all minions are called 'Igor'; Bela **Lugosi**'s 'Ygor' (*Son of Frankenstein*, 1939; *Ghost of Frankenstein*, 1942) is too self-interested and treacherous actually to work for anyone else.

Miner, Steve (b. 1951)

American director. Miner formed a working relationship with Sean **Cunningham** by editing *The Case of the Full Moon Murders* (1974) and associate producing **Friday the 13th** (1980). His first directing jobs, for Cunningham, were *Friday the 13th, Part 2* (1981) and *Friday the 13th, Part III in 3-D*, which cement the image of Jason Voorhees as an unstoppable hockey-masked **zombie**. AJ

House/1986 * *Warlock*/1989

Miranda, Soledad [Soledad Redon Bueno] (1943–71)

Sadly short-lived Spanish actress of Portuguese parentage, a striking fixture in Jesús **Franco** films: Lucy in *El conde Drácula* (*Count Dracula*, 1969), a blood-drinker in *Vampyros* *lesbos* (1970), a secret agent in *Der Teufel kam aus Akasawa* (1970). Billed as 'Susann Korda' in Franco's more explicit 1970 trio *Les cauchemars naissent la nuit*, *Sex Charade* and *Eugénie de Sade*.

Pyro/1963 * *El sonido prehistorico* [*Sound of Horror*]/1964 * *Vampir/Sie tötete in Ekstase* [*Mrs. Hyde*]/1970

Mirrors

The archetypal looking-glass ghost story is 'The Haunted Mirror' (*Dead of Night*, 1945), in which a murder committed in front of a mirror influences the antique's subsequent owners. Variations on the theme, with evil looking back at those whe peer too deeply into their own reflection, include 'The Mirror' (**The Twilight Zone**, 1961), 'The Gate-Crasher' (*From Beyond the Grave*, 1973), 'Guardian of the Abyss' (**Hammer House of Horror**, 1980), *The Boogey Man* (1980), 'Mirror, Mirror' (**Amazing Stories**, 1986), *Mirror of Death* (1987), 'Vanity Mirror' (**Friday the 13th**: *The Series*, 1988), *Mirror, Mirror* (1991), *Candyman* (1992), 'The Tale of the Captured Souls' (**Are You Afraid of the Dark?**, 1992) and 'The Eye of the Beholder' (**American Gothic**, 1995). Few of these are as eerie as *Orphée* (1949), with its liquid gateway to a reverse world, or even match the creepy mirror spirit of *Snow White and the Seven Dwarfs* (1937). Other Lewis Carroll-following through-the-looking-glass stories: 'The Painted Mirror' (**Night Gallery**, 1971), *House* (1986), *Dust Devil* (1992). **Vampires** traditionally cast no reflection, providing creepy moments: **Dracula** (1930), *Dance of the Vampires* (1967), *Vampire Circus* (1971), *Blood for Dracula* (1973).

Miserabilism

A movement within British horror writing, arising during the Thatcher years and prominent in the 90s, in which supernatural terror coexists with social realism. Influenced by precursors Ramsey **Campbell** and M. John Harrison, leading miserabilists are Nicholas Royle, Michael Marshall Smith, Joel Lane, Graham Joyce, Mark Morris and Conrad Williams. Royle's anthologies *Darklands* (1991) and *Darklands 2* (1992) are miserabilist primers. This is the horror of dole queues, bed-sits, relegated football teams, rainy British Sundays, loveless pick-ups and pub fights.

Mitchell, Cameron (1918–94)

American actor. Mitchell landed character and occasional lead roles through almost

Mirror: *Dead of Night*

fifty years of high, medium and low-budget features. His first genre roles are as every-man heroes in *Flight to Mars* (1951) and *Gorilla at Large* (1954), but he later made his mark as villains in international co-productions like Mario **Bava**'s *Sei donne per l'assassino* (*Blood and Black Lace*, 1964) and Mel **Welles**'s *Das Geheimnis der Todesinsel* (*Island of the Doomed*, 1967). Mitchell thereafter lent his stern masculine presence to countless exploitation films: Italian Viking actioners (Bava's *Gli invasori*/*Erik the Conqueror*, 1961; *I coltelli dei vendicatore*/*Knives of the Avenger*, 1965), spaghetti Westerns (Sergio Corbucci's *Minnesota Clay*, 1965), biker flicks (*Rebel Rousers*, 1970), blaxploitation (*Slaughter*, 1972).

Though too often saddled with embarrassing scripts, Mitchell was memorable in his many poverty-row shockers, whether ranting to shaky extras posing as mannequins in *Nightmare in Wax* (1969) or tunelessly droning 'Sometimes I Feel Like a Motherless Child' to a bound and gagged kidnap victim in *The Toolbox Murders* (1978). SB

Face of Fire/1959 * *Autopsia de una fantasma* [*Autopsy of a Ghost*]/1967 * *Medusa*/1974 *

Death: The Ultimate Journey (v)/1975 * *Haunts*/1977 * *The Swarm*/1978 * *Silent Scream*/*Without Warning*/1980 * *Screamers* (footage added to *L'isola degli uomini pesce*)/ *Cataclysm*/*The Demon*/1981 * *Raw Force*/ *Frankenstein's Island*/*Extrasensorial* [*The Link*]/ 1982 * *Night Train to Terror* (footage from *Cataclysm*)/1985 * *The Tomb*/1986 * *From a Whisper to a Scream*/*Deadly Prey*/1987 * *Memorial Valley Massacre*/1988 * *Trapped Alive*/1993

TV: *Studio One*: 'The Brotherhood of the Bell'/1958 * *Night Gallery*: 'Green Fingers'/ 'Finnegan's Flight'/1972 * *The Stranger*/1973 * *The Hanged Man*/1974

Moctezuma, Juan Lopez (1932–95)

Mexican director, actor, writer. Of his three colourful gothics, the **Poe**-based *La mansiòn de la locura* (*Dr. Tarr's Torture Dungeon*, 1972) and *Alucarda* (*Innocents From Hell*, 1975) are distinctive accomplishments. However, the **vampire** movie *Mary, Mary, Bloody Mary* (1974) is routine. Moctezuma was involved in the production of Alejandro Jodorowsky's *Fando and Lis* (1968) but not (as sometimes reported) *El topo* (1970). Jodorowsky maintains *La mansiòn de la locura* was covertly financed by money intended for *The Holy Mountain* (1973). SB

Moment of Fear (US TV series, 1960)

A short-lived colour mystery anthology, presented live by NBC Television. Notable sources include Cornell **Woolrich** ('Fire By Night', from 'The Night Reveals', 1936) and Fritz **Leiber** ('Conjure Wife', from the 1943 novel). Stars include Robert Redford, MacDonald Carey, Mark Richman, Inger Stevens, Leslie Nielsen, E.G. Marshall and Robert Lansing. The title was revived in 1964 and 1965 for reruns of selected episodes from other dramatic shows. TM

'The Monkey's Paw' (1902)

First published in the collection *The Lady of the Barge*, W.W. Jacobs' short story is one of the most reprinted, adapted and homaged of all horror stories. A couple are given a mummified monkey's paw which will grant three wishes: they wish for money, and their beloved but heavily insured son is killed in an industrial accident; they wish him alive, but he comes back mangled; the father wishes the son dead ... The story became a successful play by Louis N. Parker and was filmed in 1915, 1923, 1932, 1948, 1961 (as *Espiritismo*) and 1988. It has been adapted for television on *Suspense* (twice, 1949, 1950), *Great Ghost Tales* (1961), **The Alfred Hitchcock Hour** ('The Monkey's Paw: A Retelling', 1965), *The Monkees* ('The Monkees Paw', 1968) and *Orson Welles' Great Mysteries* (1973). Jacobs 'inspired' **EC comics**' 'Wish You Were Here' (*The Haunt of Fear*, 1953; filmed in *Tales From the Crypt*, 1972), the Vietnam **War** movie *Dead of Night* (1974),

Cameron Mitchell, *Nightmare in Wax*

Stephen **King**'s *Pet Sematary* (1983; filmed 1989), and 'The Tale of the Vulture's Claw' (***Are You Afraid of the Dark?***, 1992).

Monsters

The first plastic monster kits, providing glue-together copies of classic Universal Pictures characters like **Dracula**, the **Wolf Man** and the **Mummy**, went on sale in 1962. Later attractions were Bigfoot, Godzilla and Vampirella, with bits that glowed in the dark. The manufacturers explained to anxious parents that 'Movie Monsters actually perform a valuable service for the child' by reducing werewolves and the like to the level of playmates, thus rendering youngsters 'really far healthier emotionally' than if they indulged in 'anti-social behaviour in the real world'. More to the point, the monster-making process, modestly duplicating the anti-social endeavours of **Frankenstein**, served to perpetuate the fondly remembered iconic images of **Karloff**, **Lugosi**, **Chaney** and their clan (periodically resurrected wholesale, as in *The Monster Squad*, 1987) and to inspire a new generation of fantasists eager to model creatures of their own.

As a result, its fate sealed by *The Munsters* and *The Addams Family* (both launched as TV series in 1964 and still in demand thirty years later), the monster - old and new – is a regular component of the domestic unit. The **werewolf** goes to college (*Teen Wolf*, 1986), the bigfoot (or giant ape or Wookie) is a visiting relative (*Harry and the Hendersons*, 1987; converted into an interminable sitcom, 1992), and the artificial human has become gardener and hair-stylist (*Edward Scissorhands*, 1990). Continuing the Japanese menagerie tradition - Gamera, Mothra, Ebirah and their brood, now marooned in the wake of vastly superior special effects - the living dinosaurs of *Jurassic Park* (1993) have also become an irresistible attraction, big, extinct, bloodthirsty and playroom-friendly, the ideal safe threat. For many, in a time of fashionable recrimination between age-groups, the 'true' monster is seen as unruly child or overbearing parent, a two-way vendetta of abuse. In the suburban battlegrounds where kids are shrunk, blown up, or subjected to odious diets (as in the blood-boltered *Parents*, 1988), playthings are transformed into malignant entities, their strategies revealed in *Dolls* (1987), the infamous *Child's Play* series (1988, 1990, 1991), *Demonic Toys* (1991), *Dolly Dearest* (1991) and *Toys* (1992).

In the adult zone, too, monstrosities have

Elizabeth Montgomery, Agnes Moorehead, *Bewitched*

taken a more sinister turn, now that Tarantulas, Mantises, Scorpions and Fifty-Foot Women have long lost their bite. Though inheriting the Universal legacy of immortality, the new nightmare brigade is wildly less cherishable and considerably more unglued. The inventive savagery of Michael Myers (the **Halloween** series, launched 1978), Jason Voorhees (the ***Friday the 13th*** series, launched 1980) and Freddy Krueger (the ***Nightmare on Elm Street*** series, launched 1985) is fascinating for its almost crusading quality, its insistence on disfigurement and pain. Parallel, if possibly less prolific, sadism is to be found in Leatherface (***The Texas Chain Saw Massacre***, 1974), the Tall Man (*Phantasm*, 1979) and Hannibal Lecter (*The Silence of the Lambs*, 1991). And while armies of distorted beings, flayed and pinheaded, are superbly conceived for *The Evil Dead* (1982), **Hellraiser** (1986), or *Nightbreed* (1990), it is the monstrously mundane murderer of *Man Bites Dog* (1992) who scares us most. PS

Monsters (US TV series, 1988–91)

A cheap-ish offshoot of ***Tales From the Darkside*** (1984–8), featuring weekly gruesome effects creations manufactured under the supervision of consultant Dick **Smith**. Authors adapted include Robert **Bloch** ('Mannikins of Horror', 1989), Lisa Tuttle ('Bughouse', 1990) and Dan Simmons ('Shave and a Haircut, Two Bites', 1990). An

odd roster of directors includes make-up men Greg **Cannom** ('Fools' Gold', 1989) and Mark Shostrom ('Rouse Him Not', 1988), NY independents Lizzie Borden ('La Strega', 1989) and Bette Gordon ('The Mother Instinct', 1989), producer Debra Hill ('Far Below', 1990) and actor Tom Noonan ('The Bargain', 1990). TM

Montefiori, Luigi (b. 1942)

Italian actor, writer, director. Despite work for such notables as **Fellini**, Mario **Bava** (*Canni arrabbiati*, 1974), Pupi **Avati** and Lina Wertmüller, Montefiori – ideally cast as Goliath in *King David* (1985) – is fated to be remembered as the **cannibal** killer in the self-scripted *Antropophagus* (*The Anthropophagous Beast*, 1980) and his long association with Aristide **Massacesi**. Tall, dark and . . . er . . . imposing, he usually appears under the pseudonym George Eastman. After uncredited work on Massaccesi's *Anno 2020* (*2020: Texas Gladiators*, 1983), he made an official directorial debut as G.L. Eastman with the low-budget genetics shocker *DNA formula letale* (*Metamorphosis*, 1989). MA

Fellini Satyricon (a)/1969 * *Baba Yaga* [*Baba Yaga, Devil Witch*] (a)/1973 * *Emanuelle e Françoise, le sorelline* [*Blood Vengeance*]/1975 * *Quella strana voglia d'amare* (w)/1977 * *La ragazza del vagone letto* [*Terror Express*] (w)/1979 * *Il fiume del grande caimano* [*The Great Alligator*] (w)/1979 * *Notti erotiche dei morti* *viventi/Porno holocaust/1980 * Rosso sangue [Absurd]/1981 * Deliria [Stagefright] (w)/Le foto di Gioia [Delirium] (a)/1987*

Moorehead, Agnes (1906–74)

American character actress, originally on radio with Orson **Welles**'s Mercury Theatre and in the classic 'Sorry, Wrong Number' (1943) on *Suspense*. Often cast in films as matriarchs, she is Samantha's witchy mother Endora on **Bewitched** (1964–72). SJ

*Jane Eyre/1943 * Woman in White/1946 * The Lost Moment/1947 * The Story of Mankind/1957 * The Bat/1959 * Hush . . . Hush, Sweet Charlotte/1964 * What's the Matter With Helen?/1971 * Dear Dead Delilah/1972*

TV: *Matinee Theatre*: 'Greybeards and Witches'/1956 * *Shirley Temple Theatre*: 'The House of the Seven Gables'/1960 * *The Twilight Zone*: 'The Invaders'/1961 * *The Wild Wild West*: 'Night of the Vicious Valentine'/1967 * *Night Gallery*: 'Certain Shadows on the Wall'/1970; 'Witches' Feast'/1971 * *Frankenstein: The True Story*/1973

Mora, Philippe (b. 1949)

French-born Australian director. Painter and movie scholar Mora was a founder of Australia's influential *Cinema Papers* magazine. He first attracted attention with the documentary *Brother Can You Spare a Dime?*

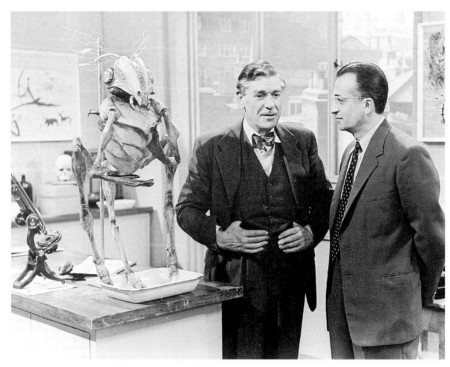

André Morell, Cec Linder, *Quatermass and the Pit* (1959)

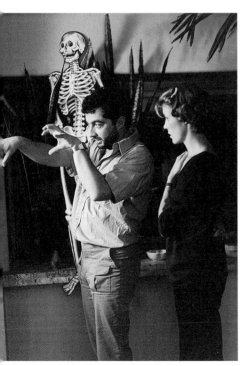

Philippe Mora, on the set of *Howling II: Stirba – Werewolf Bitch*

(1974). His work is unremarkable, notwithstanding an occasional streak of wild humour incorporated into blatantly ridiculous material, most especially in *The Marsupials: Howling III* (1987). Among his fringe credits are the superhero parody *The Return of Captain Invincible* (1983) and the film of Whitley **Strieber**'s *Communion* (1989). AJ

*The Beast Within/1982 * Howling III: Stirba – Werewolf Bitch/1986*

Moreland, Mantan (1901–73)

American actor. Invariably the frightened **comic relief** servant, he had a recurring role as 'Birmingham Brown', Charlie Chan's chauffeur (*Black Magic*, 1944; *The Scarlet Clue*, 1945). In *King of the Zombies* (1941), he transcends type-casting with bravura as he wisecracks among the living dead. He was top-billed in **black** neighbourhoods.

*Condemned Men/1940 * Dressed to Kill/1941 * The Strange Case of Dr.Rx/Professor Creeps/A-Haunting We Will Go/1942 * Revenge of the Zombies/1943 * Spider Baby/1965*

Morell, André [Cecil André Mesritz] (1909–78)

British actor. Watson in *The Hound of the Baskervilles* (1958), Quatermass in the TV *Quatermass and the Pit* (1959), a **Van Helsing** substitute in *The Plague of the Zombies* (1966).

He jovially tortures Peter **Cushing** on TV (*1984*, 1954) and film (*Cash on Demand*, 1961).

*So Long at the Fair/1950 * Seven Days to Noon/1951 * Stolen Face/1952 * Three Cases of Murder/1955 * Behemoth, the Sea Monster/1959 * The Shadow of the Cat/1961 * She/1965 * The Wrong Box/1966 * The Mummy's Shroud/The Vengeance of She/1967 * The Man and the Snake (s)/1972*

TV: *One Step Beyond*: 'The Avengers'/1961 * *Doctor Who*: 'The Massacre'/1966 * *The Avengers*: 'Death of a Batman'/1963; 'Death at Bargain Prices'/1966

Moriarty, Michael (b. 1941)

American actor. Simultaneously mild, forceful and eccentric, Moriarty has done serious work on Broadway and TV, winning a Tony (*Find Your Way Home*, 1974) and two Emmys (*The Glass Menagerie*, 1973; *Holocaust*, 1978). His film career is wayward, veering from *Bang the Drum Slowly* (1973) to *The Secret of the Ice Cave* (1989), with a scattering of international horror credits. After a remarkable performance as the hustler who holds the city to ransom in *Q* (1982), he reteamed with Larry **Cohen** for a run of equally off-beat heroes: *The Stuff* (1985), *A Return to Salem's Lot* (1987) and **It's Alive** III: Island of the Alive* (1987). In *Extrasensorial* (*The Link*,

221

1983), he is psychically linked separated Siamese twins, one a mad killer.

Reborn/1984 * *Pale Rider*/1985 * *Troll*/1986 * *Dark Tower*/1988

TV: *The Twilight Zone*: '20/20 Vision'/1988

Morricone, Ennio (b. 1928)

Italian composer. Though he came to international prominence with phenomenally popular scores for Sergio Leone's Spaghetti Westerns, Morricone has also worked extensively in the *giallo*, collaborating with Dario **Argento**. Originally an arranger (on over five hundred songs between 1959 and 1966), his first film work was orchestrating Mario Nascimbene's *Morte di un amico* (1959) and his first full score *Il federale* (1961). SL

I maniaci/1964 * *Gli amanti d'oltretomba* [*The Faceless Monster*]/1965 * *Le streghe* [*The Witches*]/1966 * *Un tranquillo posto di Campagna*/1968 * *L'uccello dalle piume di cristallo* [*The Bird With the Crystal Plumage*]/1969 * *Quattro mosche di velluto grigio* [*Four Flies on Grey Velvet*]/*Gli occhi freddi della paura*/*Giornata nera per l'ariete*/*La corta notte delle bambole di vetro* [*The Short Night of the Glass Dolls*]/*La tarantola dal ventre nero* [*Black Belly of the Tarantula*]/1971 * *Il gatto a nove code* [*Cat o' Nine Tails*]/*Bluebeard*/*Cosa avete fatto a Solange?*/*Il diavolo nel cervello*/1972 * *L'anticristo* [*The Antichrist*]/*Spasmo*/*Le trio infernal*/1974 * *L'ultimo treno della notte* [*Late Night Trains*]/*Macchie solari* [*Autopsy*]/*Salò*/1975 * *Exorcist II: The Heretic*/*Holocaust 2000*/*Il mostro*/1977 * *The Island*/1980 * *The Thing*/1982 * *Extrasensorial* [*The Link*]/1983 * *Rampage*/1987 * *Wolf*/1994 * *La sindrome di Stendahl* [*The Stendahl Syndrome*]/1996

Morrissey, Paul (b. 1938)

American writer, director. Andy Warhol's resident film-maker from 1965, Morrissey engineered a less contrary, more cinematic form of Factory movie that culminated in playful horrors, the **3-D** *Flesh for Frankenstein* (1973) and *Blood for Dracula* (1973). The bickeringly witty, exorbitantly **camp** and gory pair were made in Rome to satisfy Roman **Polanski**'s wish for a stereoscopic **Frankenstein**. Though often attributed to second-unit director Antonio **Margheriti**, they are provokingly informed by Morrissey's ambivalent interest in 60s libertinism. Deprived of virgins by a lascivious communist handyman, Udo **Kier**'s anachronistic Count is especially poignant. Urban horror-show *Bad* (1976) was written for Morrissey,

who instead escaped Warhol's orbit with *The Hound of the Baskervilles* (1977), a *Carry On* gothic damagingly co-authored by Peter Cook and Dudley Moore. DP

'The Most Dangerous Game' (1924)

Richard Connell's short story is perfectly structured suspense horror, pitting shipwrecked big-game hunter Rainsford against General Zaroff, an **island**-owning madman who has grown bored with lesser game and now stalks human beings. In Irving **Pichel** and Ernest B. **Schoedsack**'s faithful 1932 film (known in Britain as *The Hounds of Zaroff*), Count Zaroff is played by Leslie Banks, Rainsford by Joel McCrea and the prize by Fay **Wray**. Though one of the most imitated of all plots, only Robert **Wise**'s *A Game of Death* (1945), with Edgar Barrier as a **Nazi** manhunter and Noble **Johnson** repeating his sidekick role, is a close remake. Howard **Vernon** is Zaroff in Jesús **Franco**'s *La comtesse perverse* (1973), which makes Alice Arno's Countess Zaroff the woman-hunting villainess, and Michel Lemoine's *Les weekends du Comte Zaroff* (*Seven Women for Satan*, 1974). After Connell's story, the great suspense-horror manhunt tales are Geoffrey Household's *Rogue Male* (1939), filmed as *Man Hunt* (1941) and *Rogue Male* (1976), and Sarban's **Nazi** nightmare *The Sound of His Horn* (1952).

Paul Morrissey

Johnny Apollo/1948 * *Kill or Be Killed*/1950 * *The Black Forest*/1954 * *Run for the Sun*/1956 * *Bloodlust*/1963 * *The Naked Prey*/*Coplan sauve sa peau* [*The Devil's Garden*]/1966 * *Punishment Park*/1970 * *The Hunting Party*/1971 * *Woman Hunt*/1972 * *To Kill a Clown*/1973 * *Open Season*/*The Man With the Golden Gun*/1974 * *The Beast Must Die*/1974 * *Turkey Shoot*/1981 * *Bronx lotta finale* [*Endgame*]/*Le prix du danger* [*The Prize of Peril*]/1983 * *The Running Man*/1984 * *Predator*/*Slave Girls From Beyond Infinity*/1987 * *Death Ring*/*Final Round*/*Hard Target*/1993 * *Surviving the Game*/1994

TV: *The Man From U.N.C.L.E.*: 'The Deadly Quest Affair'/1967 * *Maneater*/1973 * *Savages*/1974 * *Hart to Hart*: 'Hunted Harts'/1983 * *Deadly Game*/1991

Moxey, John Llewellyn (b. 1920)

British director. Initially a British B-picture specialist, with the creepy *City of the Dead* (1960) to his credit, Moxey relocated to Hollywood and became a TV movie mainstay. *The Night Stalker* (1971), with Darren **McGavin** on the trail of a Vegas **vampire**, is a highlight. Though he has done his share of drearily conventional work, his two best horror credits are confident reworkings of familiar material, with a visual invention that complements their twisted scripts.

Strangler's Web/1965 * *Circus of Fear*/1967

TV: *The Avengers*: 'Who's Who???'/1967 * *The House That Wouldn't Die*/1970 * *A Taste of Evil*/1971 * *Ghost Story*: 'The New House'/1972 * *Home for the Holidays*/1972 * *A Strange and Deadly Occurrence*/1974 * *Conspiracy of Terror*/1975 * *I, Desire*/1982 * *The Cradle Will Fall*/1983 * *When Dreams Come True*/1985 * *Through Naked Eyes*/1987

Mulcahy, Russell (b. 1953)

Australian director. Mulcahy invented the rock video format which led to the start of the MTV network. His clips include 'Video Killed the Radio Star' by The Buggles, 'Bette Davis Eyes' by Kim Carnes and numerous Duran Duran songs. The latter's musical adaptation of William Burroughs's novel 'The Wild Boys' (1982) shows Mulcahy's epic talent for visual excess. He has not lived down the video promo tag in subsequent film work. AJ

Razorback/1984 * *Highlander*/1986 * *Highlander II: The Quickening*/1990 * *The Shadow*/1994 * *Algonquin Goodbye*/1996

Christopher Lee, *The Mummy* (1959)

Mummies

On 4th November 1922, Howard Carter uncovered the first stone step leading down to the tomb of the boy-pharaoh Tutankhamun in the Valley of the Kings near Luxor, Egypt. Three weeks later, accompanied by the sponsor of the expedition Lord Carnarvon, Carter made a small breach in the upper left-hand corner of the sealed doorway leading into the tomb and caught his first glimpse of the 'wonderful things' piled up inside. Something of a film buff himself, Carter described the most famous moment in the history of archeology in cine-matic terms: the 'details of the room within' suddenly came into focus as if on a stage, or through a camera lens, or on the screen of a cinema; the flickering candle, the blurred image of gold, the viewer's eyes gradually growing accustomed to the light in the total immersion of the tomb. For a second, Carter thought he was looking at wall paintings; then, as he adjusted focus, he realised they were three-dimensional things, 'everywhere the glint of gold'. The sight, he wrote in his notebook that same night, resembled 'the property-room of an opera of a vanished civilization'.

By the 30th of November, the first report of the find had appeared in the *Times*, leading eventually to a craze of 'Tutmania', which influenced everything from party frocks to bedside lights to the design of cine-mas themselves. Cecil B. DeMille ordered the Cairo offices of the Lasky Company to get hold of written and visual material on the discovery and took a lot of persuading not to make King Tut himself (rather than Ramses II) the pharaoh in *The Ten Commandments* (1923). But after the initial excitement had subsided, and after the newspapers discovered that the strictly historical significance of the find was less than dramatic – the excavators unearthed what they thought was a basketful of written records, but these manuscripts turned out, disappointingly, to be fragments of Tutankhamun's underwear – the story began to run out of steam.

Then, on the 5th of April 1923, Lord Carnarvon died of blood poisoning and pneumonia (following a mosquito bite) and,

Tom Tyler, Peggy Moran, *The Mummy's Hand*

new angle, and they turned to popular writers of the day to substantiate it. The writers were delighted to contribute to the hype.

Sax Rohmer, author of the **Fu Manchu** novels as well as numerous tales of nasty goings-on in the world of Egyptian archeology (*The Brood of the Witch Queen*, 1918) rushed his *Secret Egypt* on to the London stage, while Agatha **Christie** jumped on the bandwagon with her play *Akhnaton* – about the life and times of the 'heretic king' who may have been Tutankhamun's father as well as his father-in-law – and 'The Adventure of the Egyptian Tomb' (1924), a Poirot story about a curse which isn't really. The curse reached Hollywood with Karl **Freund**'s *The Mummy* (1932): Red Rock Canyon stands in for the Valley of the Kings, a well-wrapped **Karloff** shocks audiences by suddenly opening his dead eyes in the first reel, a blood-curdling curse ('Death, eternal punishment for anyone who opens this casket') is found by the British Museum archeologists, and the connection with events of ten years before is made explicit. 'Permit me', lisps Karloff as Im-Ho-Tep (a reincarnation, with a tarboosh on his head), 'to present you with the most sensational find since Tutankhamen.'

The Mummy is based on, but not credited to, Conan **Doyle**'s 'The Ring of Thoth' (1890). It lays down the ground rules for every mummy movie since that time. The association between ancient Egypt, dead things and magic spells had, of course, long been embedded within popular culture. The Egyptian Hall, housing a collection of spectacular, magical and bizarre sideshows (including a mummy in its case) and built in the Technicolor Nile style, opened in Piccadilly in 1812 – a spin-off from the Napoleonic phase of Egyptomania: a scaled-down facsimile still exists in Penzance. The first full-length mummy story, Jane Webb's triple-decker novel *The Mummy* (about exotic travels with a resurrected ancient Egyptian) was published in 1827. The genre really got into its jerky stride with Théophile Gautier's 'Le Pied de momie' ('The Mummy's Foot' or 'Princess Hermonthis', 1840), which later provided the idea for one of the earliest British trick-films, Walter Booth's *The Haunted Curiosity Shop* (1902), in which a **magician** conjures up a shapely Egyptian princess, who steps forward from within a cabinet of curiosities. **Poe**'s 'Some Words with a Mummy' (1845) fuses a galvanic experiment with a critique of the modern world from an ancient mummy's point of view.

as his sister Winifred wrote, a story that had opened 'like Aladdin's cave' turned overnight into 'a Greek myth of Nemesis'. It was reported in the popular press that the entire electricity supply of Cairo, all four grids, was blacked out for several minutes at the precise moment of his death, and that simultaneously – half a world away on the Carnarvon country estate of Highclere near Newbury – the family's favourite dog Susie, a three-legged terrier, let out a mournful howl and dropped down dead. Both events were attributed to the 'curse of Tutankhamun', which had apparently been busily energising itself since 1323 BC, waiting for someone to break in and desecrate the tomb.

Rumours began to circulate about strange artefacts which bore hieroglyphic messages protecting the tomb from intruders and which were deliberately 'suppressed' by the Egyptologists. The first of these concerned an 'ordinary clay tablet', said to have been found over the entrance to the tomb, which Carnarvon had the temerity to remove in order to substitute his own family's coat of arms. Loosely translated in the then-fashionable style of romantic novelist Marie Corelli, it read: 'Death shall come on swift wings to whoever touches the tomb of the Pharaoh.' There never was a clay tablet, there were no such artefacts bearing curses, but it didn't seem to matter. The newspapers had found a

By the turn of the century, short stories and novels (by the likes of Guy Boothby, Bram **Stoker** and Conan Doyle) associated ancient Egypt with various recurring stories: the artefact excavated from a tomb, brought back to England's green and pleasant land, endowed with magical (usually nasty) powers; the mummy in the British Museum, who comes back to life and wreaks havoc on its disturbers; the royal mummy deliberately reincarnated by a gang of initiates; and (preparing the ground for the newspaper coverage of 1923) the archeologist who lives to regret the day he had the temerity to open an ancient tomb (a displacement, perhaps, of public anxieties about the ethics of desecration).

Stoker's *The Jewel of Seven Stars* (1903) – which had such a disturbing final chapter that it was rewritten at the publisher's request for the second edition – has been adapted several times (*Blood from the Mummy's Tomb*, 1971; *The Awakening*, 1980) and Conan Doyle's other mummy tale 'Lot No. 249' (1892) was done on television (*Conan Doyle*, 1967) and film (*Tales From the Darkside: The Movie*, 1990). But there is no foundation mummy text, of the calibre and completeness of **Frankenstein**, **Dracula** and **Jekyll and Hyde**, and perhaps for this reason the mummy movie has always been the poor relation of other great horror stories. **Méliès** revived *Cléopatre* (1899) and a few other silents toy with Egyptian occult themes: *The Monster* (1903), *The Vengeance of Egypt* (1912), *The Egyptian Mummy* (1913), *The Avenging Hand* (1915), *Die Augen der Mumie Ma* (*Eyes of the Mummy*, 1918), *The Beetle* (1919). The last of this run of murky melodramas, made under the influence of *The Mummy* but predating the prevalence of the bandaged stalker, is *The Ghoul* (1933), with Karloff as another mad Egyptologist.

The Mummy (1932) begat *The Mummy's Hand* (1942), which produced a slew of Lon **Chaney Jr** sequels that got mixed into the original for the **Hammer** remake *The Mummy* (1959), which finally offers Christopher Lee as a lithe and athletic mummy. *Pharaoh's Curse* (1957), *The Curse of the Mummy's Tomb* (1964), *The Mummy's Shroud* (1967), *The Mummy and the Curse of the Jackals* (1969), *La venganza de la momia* (1973) and *The Mummy Lives* (1993) reshuffle the elements to little effect. *La momia azteca* (*The Aztec Mummy*, 1957) transplants the theme to Mexico, prompting imitations (*La casa del terror/Face of the Screaming Werewolf*, 1959; *La cabeza viviente/The Living Head*, 1961; *Las luchadoras contra la Momia/Wrestling Women vs. the Aztec Mummy*, 1962) and sequels (*La maldición de la momia azteca/Attack of the Mayan Mummy*, 1957; *El robot humano/The Robot vs. the Aztec Mummy*, 1957). A later cycle about different mummies (*Las momias de Guanjuato*, 1970; *El robo de las momias de Guanjanuato*, 1972; *El castillo de las momias de Guanjuanato*, 1972) revived the genre for *Las momias de San Angel* (1973) and *La mansión de las siete momias* (1975). The formula is recast with an ossified Pompeiian for *Curse of the Faceless Man* (1958), Brazil offers *O secredo da mumia* (1982) and there are even mummy elements in the Chinese *jiangshi* cycle.

Another possible reason for the sparsity of mummy variants is that a corpse which has been wrapped up for three thousand years lacks erotic possibilities, though *Le sang des autres* (*Lips of Blood*, 1972) offers a pharaonic **vampire** rapist, *The Cat Creature* (1973) has a seductive Egyptian vampire cat woman, and Anne **Rice** weighs in with *The Mummy; or: Rameses the Damned* (1989), which is novelettish in sentiment if not brevity. The mummy is reduced to a stooge in **monster** rallies from *El hombre que vino del Ummo* (*Dracula vs. Frankenstein*, 1970) and *The Monster Squad* (1986), in which one is unravelled entirely, to *Waxwork* (1988). Otherwise, the cycle only offers gimmicks like **zombie cannibal** mummies (*Dawn of*

André Morell, *The Mummy's Shroud*

the Mummy, 1981) and **alien** mummies (*Time Walker*, 1982). CF

The Mummy (Universal)

Karl **Freund**'s *The Mummy* (1932), with Boris **Karloff** as resurrected sorcerer Im-Ho-Tep searching for the **reincarnation** of his lost love, is a stand-alone reworking of *Dracula* (1930), but flashback footage from it was worked into Christy Cabanne's *The Mummy's Hand* (1940), which splits the villain role between Tom Tyler's **mummy** Kharis and George **Zucco**'s evil high priest. Kharis (Lon **Chaney**) returns in three programmers with fresh high priests: Harold **Young**'s *The Mummy's Tomb* (1942), with Turhan **Bey**; Reginald **LeBorg**'s *The Mummy's Ghost* (1944), with John **Carradine**; and Leslie Goodwins's *The Mummy's Curse* (1944), with Martin **Kosleck**. *Abbott and Costello Meet the Mummy* (1955), with Eddie Parker as 'Klaris', spoofs the series. Terence **Fisher**'s *The Mummy* (1959), with Christopher **Lee** as Kharis and Peter **Cushing** as an archaeologist, is Hammer's remake of the Universal cycle, using elements from all five films. Hammer's subsequent efforts (*The Curse of the Mummy's Tomb*, 1964; *The Mummy's Shroud*, 1967) are not sequels. *La momia azteca* (1957), which generated a series, is also a variation on Universal's formula, as is *The Mummy Lives* (1993).

Munro, Caroline (b. 1948)

British actress. A former 'Lamb's Navy Rum' pin-up and Bond Girl (*The Spy Who Loved Me*, 1977), the exotically suburban Munro became popular as a decorative corpse in *The Abominable Dr. Phibes* (1971) and *Dr. Phibes Rises Again* (1972), before secondary roles in *Dracula A.D. 1972* (1972), *Captain Kronos Vampire Hunter* (1972) and *I Don't Want To Be Born* (1975) and a **camp** lead as 'Stella Star' in *Scontri stellari oltre la terza dimensione* (*Starcrash*, 1979). Her turn in William **Lustig**'s gruelling *Maniac* (1980), replacing Daria **Nicolodi**, marked the beginning of a descent into tawdry **stalk-and-slash**.

Between stints as a TV quiz show hostess, she was reduced to the dizzying lows of *The Last Horror Film* (1981), *Don't Open Till Christmas* (1984) and *Slaughter High* (1987). MA

El aullido del diablo [*Howl of the Devil*]/1987 ∗ *Les prédateurs de la nuit* [*Faceless*]/1988 ∗ *Il gatto nero* [*Edgar Allan Poe's The Black Cat*]/1989 ∗ *Night Owl*/1993

TV: *The New Avengers*: 'Angels of Death'/1978

The Munsters (US TV series, 1964–6)

Created and produced by Joe Connelly and Bob Mosher, this **situation comedy** horror skit was produced by Universal TV, parodying the studio's copyright **Frankenstein** make-up. Fred **Gwynne** stars as Herman Munster, a seven-foot gentle giant afraid of his own (or anyone else's) shadow. Yvonne **De Carlo** is wife Lily, Al Lewis is the **vampire** Grandpa and Butch Patrick is the **werewolf** Eddie Munster. Pat Priest took over from Beverly Owen as the Munster niece Marilyn, the only normal member of the family. The feature *Munster Go Home!* (1966) stars most of the series cast, while Gwynne, De Carlo and Lewis return in the TV movie *The Munsters' Revenge* (1981). The format was revived for *The Munsters Today* (1988–91) – with John Shuck, Lee Meriwether and Howard Morton – which has none of the gentle humour of the original. *Here Come the Munsters* (1995), a revival TV special, casts Edward Herrmann, Veronica Hamel and Robert Morse. TM

John Peel, *The Addams Family and The Munsters Programme Guide* (1994)

'The Murders in the Rue Morgue' (1841)

Edgar Allan **Poe**'s story introduces dilettante sleuth C. Auguste Dupin, unmistakable forerunner of **Sherlock Holmes**, and has him deduce that an especially brutal locked-room murder is the work of a runaway ourang-outang. Dupin returns, in less macabre form, in 'The Mystery of Marie Roget' (1842–43) and 'The Purloined Letter' (1845), and is pastiched by Michael Harrison (*Murder in the Rue Royale*, 1972). Clive **Barker**, in 'The New Murders in the Rue Morgue' (1984), sides with the anarchic **ape** against the rational Dupin. *Sherlock Holmes in the Great Murder Mystery* (1908), the first screen version, omits Dupin and substitutes his most famous sucessor. Subsequent adaptations came in 1912 (in *The Raven*), 1914, 1932 (by Robert

Butch Patrick, Yvonne De Carlo, Fred Gwynne, Al Lewis, Pat Priest, *The Munsters*

Max Schreck, F.W. Murnau's *Nosferatu*

Florey with **Lugosi**), 1954 (Roy Del Ruth's *Phantom of the Rue Morgue*, with Karl Malden), 1972 (by Gordon **Hessler** with little Poe) and 1986 (by Jeannot **Szwarc** with George C. Scott). Patric Knowles is Dupin in the lone screen version of *The Mystery of Marie Roget* (1942).

Murnau, F.W. [Friedrich Wilhelm Plumpe] (1888–1931)

Though most of his films are lost and he died young, Murnau holds a secure place in world cinema with *Der letze Mann* (*The Last Laugh*, 1924), an exercise in sentimental **Expressionism**, and *Sunrise: A Story of Two Humans* (1927), a symbolic romance which won the soon-discontinued 'Best Artistic Achievement' Oscar. His major horror is *Nosferatu: Eine Symphonie des Grauens* (1922), an unauthorised *Dracula* with Max **Schreck** as a rat-faced **vampire**. Rather than **Caligarist** abstract sets, *Nosferatu* uses real locations for its shadowed shudders. Though eclipsed for decades by **Browning**'s *Dracula* (1931) and **Lugosi**'s sleek Count, the film has become influential through direct remakes (Werner **Herzog**'s *Nosferatu, Phan-*

tom der Nacht, 1979), borrowings of the Schreck look (*Salem's Lot*, 1979) and poaching of odd images (*Bram Stoker's Dracula*, 1992). Murnau's other surviving fantasy is **Faust** (1926), but tantalisingly lost is *Der Januskopf* (1919), a **Jekyll and Hyde** with

Conrad **Veidt** in the leads and Lugosi as his butler.

*Satanas/Der Bucklige und die Tänzerin/*1919 * *Schloss Vogelöd/*1921 * *Phantom/*1922

Lotte Eisner, *Murnau* (1964)

Musicals

The Incredibly Strange Creatures Who Stopped Living and Became Mixed-Up Zombies!!? (1964) advertised itself as 'the first monster musical', though the honour probably belongs to **Phantom of the Opera** (1943) and the list of even marginally successful horror-musicals stands at *Phantom of the Paradise* (1975) and *The Rocky Horror Picture Show* (1975). Odd musical numbers have cropped up in horror since the talkie re-release of *Phantom of the Opera* (1926) with a newly recorded soundtrack: most are as irritating as 'Faro-La, Faro-Li' (*Frankenstein Meets the Wolf Man*, 1943), 'Eeny Meenie Miney Moe' (*I Was a Teenage Werewolf*, 1957), 'You've Got to Have Ee-oo' (*How to Make a Monster*, 1958) and 'The Zombie Stomp' (*Horror of Party Beach*, 1963). However, Angela Lansbury's 'Good-Bye, Little Yellow Bird' in **The Picture of Dorian Gray** (1945) is quite affecting, and, in the **rock** field, there is camp value to the title songs of *The Blob* (1958), *The Green Slime* (1969), *Ben* (1972) and *Attack of the Killer Tomatoes* (1979).

A few mainstream musicals touch on horror, with devilish or ghostly presences between the production numbers: *The*

RIGHT Bela Lugosi, Leon Waycoff, *Murders in the Rue Morgue* (1932)

Musicals: *The Rocky Horror Picture Show*

Wizard of Oz (1939), *The 5,000 Fingers of Dr. T.* (1952), *Damn Yankees* (1958), *Chitty Chitty Bang Bang* (1968), *Scrooge* (1970). Following the success on stage and film of Richard **O'Brien**'s *The Rocky Horror Show* (1973), there have been several attempts at a horror movie musical: *Dr. Jekyll and Mr. Hyde* (1973), with a singing Kirk Douglas; *Son of Dracula* (1974), with Harry Nilsson as the Count and Ringo Starr as Merlin; *The Comeback* (1977), with Jack Jones; *The Monster Club* (1980); *Big Meat Eater* (1982); Lucio **Fulci**'s disco **stalk-and-slash** *Murderock uccide a passo di danza* (1983); *As sete vampiras* (1986); *Little Shop of Horrors* (1986), from Howard Ashman and Alan Menken's Broadway version of Roger **Corman**'s 1961 film; and *Rockula* (1990). On stage, musical treatment has been given to classic monsters (Larry Ferguson and David Davidson's **Dracula**, 1973; Dan Newmark's **Frankenstein**, 1977, Frank Wildhorn and Leslie Bricusse's *Jekyll & Hyde*, 1995) and associated characters (Ron Pember and Denis Marne's **Jack the Ripper**, 1974; Josh Alan's Ed **Wood** biography *The Worst!*, 1993). The

culmination of this trend is Andrew Lloyd Webber's hit *Phantom of the Opera* (1986), but the most successful combination of musical form and horror content is Stephen Sondheim's **Sweeney Todd** (1979).

Mutation

The process of change, while a fact of life, never fails to cause trouble. In horror the distorted human, whether altered for better or for worse, is invariably a threat. Misuse of scientific research is blamed for countless abominations, from *The Alligator People* (1959) to *The Slime People* (1963), from *The Fly* (1958, 1986) to the daftly homicidal flytrap of *The Mutations* (1973), and from **Swamp Thing** (1982) and *The Toxic Avenger* (1985) to the electronic **werewolf** of *Project Metalbeast* (1995). There is an interesting parallel concern about the fatal attractions of female mutants: *Cat Girl* (1957), *The Wasp Woman* (1960), *The Reptile* (1966), *Rabid* (1976), *Embryo* (1976), *Species* (1995).

An early unheeded warning against tampering with nature is *Island of Lost Souls* (1933; remade as **The Island of Dr. Moreau**

in 1977 and 1996). Irradiated and poisoned natures takes periodic revenge, as in *Them!* (1954), *Day of the Animals* (1977), *Kingdom of the Spiders* (1977), *Prophecy* (1979), *The Beast Within* (1982) and *Alligator II: The Mutation* (1991). Infections from space take a special toll, resulting in *The Hideous Sun Demon* (1959), *Monster of Terror* (1965), *The Incredible Melting Man* (1977), and the spectacle of Gil Gerard sprouting horns and a beard in a 1980 episode ('The Satyr') of *Buck Rogers in the 25th Century*. Among the most disturbing transformations are that of the luckless astronaut in *The Quatermass Experiment* (1955), while the fleshy excesses of *The Thing* (1982) heralded a fresh creativity in mutationary special effects.

Foremost in the wilder-the-better stakes are *Videodrome* (1982), *From Beyond* (1986), *Society* (1989), *Body Melt* (1993) and the extraordinary fusion of a man with writhing metal in *Tetsuo* (1989). Seemingly obsessed with cyborg evolution, the Japanese turn mutants into the action-men of the millennium in the shape of *Transformers* (1986), the Zoanoids from *The Guyver* (1991) and the *Mighty Morphin Power Rangers* (1995) who convert, between classes, from yucky teenagers to armoured superbeings. The runaway success of *Teenage Mutant Ninja Turtles* (1990) confirmed what the *X-Men* (animated series, 1993; *Generation X*, 1996) have been struggling to achieve since their first Marvel comics appearance in 1963: mutant respectability. Symbol of a new era, the hero (Kevin

Mutation: *Tetsuo*

Susannah York, 'The Fall of the House of Usher', *Mystery and Imagination*

ed during the series: Algernon **Blackwood**'s 'The Listener' (1967), James's 'Casting the Runes' (1968), Poe's **'The Tell-Tale Heart'** (1968), **'Sweeney Todd'** (1970). TM

N

Naish, J. Carrol (1897–1973)
Irish-American actor, often as evil or comic foreigners. He played the detective in the TV series *The New Adventures of Charlie Chan* (1957). SJ

The Return of the Terror/1934 *The Man in the Trunk*/*Dr. Renault's Secret*/1942 * *Calling Dr. Death*/*Batman*/1943 * *The Whistler*/*The Monster Maker*/*Jungle Woman*/*House of Frankenstein*/1944 * *Strange Confession*/1945 * *The Beast With Five Fingers*/1946 * *Dracula vs. Frankenstein*/1970

Nalder, Reggie [Alfred Reginald Natzick] (b. 1912–91)
Austrian character actor with distinctive scars on his lower face. Cast by **Hitchcock** as the assassin in *The Man Who Knew Too Much* (1955), he moved to Hollywood in the early 60s and began taking horror roles, including **Van Helsing** (under the alias Detlef Van Berg) in the hardcore *Dracula Sucks* (1979) and the Nosferatu-like **vampire** Barlow in *Salem's Lot* (1979). SJ

The Manchurian Candidate/1962 * *Hexen bis auf's blut gequält* [*Mark of the Devil*]/1969 *

J. Carroll Naish

Costner) of *Waterworld* (1995) has gills and webbed feet. PS

Myers, Michael * See: **Carpenter, John**; *Halloween*

My Partner the Ghost * See: *Randall and (Hopkirk, Deceased)*

Mystery and Imagination (UK TV series, 1966–70)
Initially produced by ABC TV, then Thames, this anthology drew on classic tales of terror during its irregular run. In its first season, David Buck appeared as storyteller Richard Beckett and stories came from **Stevenson** ('The Body Snatcher'), **Poe** (**'The Fall of the House of Usher'**, with Susannah York and Denholm **Elliott**), **Wilde** ('The Canterville Ghost', with Bruce Forsyth), M.R. **James** ('The Tractate Middith', 'Lost Hearts', 'Room 13') and **Le Fanu** (**'Carmilla'**, 'The Flying Dragon'). Later seasons offer ambitiously condensed novels: Ian Holm is Victor and the Monster in Robert Muller's adaptation of **'Frankenstein'** (1968), Denholm Elliott essays the Count in **'Dracula'** (1968) and Isobel Black is unwrapped in 'The Curse of the Mummy' (1970), from **Stoker**'s *Jewel of the Seven Stars* (1904). Other classics adapt-

L'uccello dalle piume di cristallo [*Bird With the Crystal Plumage*]/1970 * *Hexen – geschandet und zu Tode gequält* [*Mark of the Devil Part II*]/1972 * *Dracula's Dog*/1977 * *The Devil and Max Devlin*/1981

TV: *Thriller*: 'The Terror in Teakwood'/'The Return of Andrew Bentley'/1961 * *Wild Wild West*: 'The Night of the Gruesome Games'/1968 * *The Dead Don't Die*/1975 * *The Hardy Boys Mysteries*: 'The Mystery of the Haunted House'/*McCloud*: 'McCloud Meets Dracula'/1977

Napier, Alan [Alan Napier-Clavering] (1903–88)

British actor. Alfred the butler in *Batman* (1966–8). SJ

The Invisible Man Returns/*The House of the Seven Gables*/1940 * *Cat People*/1942 * *The Uninvited*/1944 * *Hangover Square*/*Isle of the Dead*/1945 * *House of Horrors*/1946 * *Master Minds*/1949 * *The Strange Door*/1951 * *Moonfleet*/1955 * *The Mole People*/1956 * *The Premature Burial*/1962 * *Batman*/1966

TV: *NBC Story Theater*: 'The Adventure of the Speckled Band'/1949 * *Front Row Center*: 'Outward Bound'/1955 * *Alfred Hitchcock Presents*: 'Into Thin Air'/1955; 'Whodunit'/1956; 'I Killed the Count'/1957; 'The Avon Emeralds'/1959 * *Thriller*: 'The Purple Room'/1960; 'Hay-Fork and Bill-Hook'/'Dark Legacy'/1961 * *Alfred Hitchcock Hour*: 'An Out for Oscar'/1963; 'Thou Still Unravished Bride'/1965 * *The Twilight Zone*: 'Passage on the Lady Ann'/1963 * *Night Gallery*: 'House – With Ghost'/1971; 'Fright Night'/1972

Naschy, Paul [Jacinto Molina Alvarez] (b. 1934)

Spanish actor, writer, director. Unarguably the kingpin of Spanish horror, Naschy claims with characteristic ego to have sparked the whole Iberian boom. A championship weightlifter and brawny bit-player, Naschy indulged a passion for Universal gothic by scripting *La marca del hombre lobo* (*Hell's Creatures*, 1967). Assuming the lead when Lon **Chaney Jr** proved unavailable, he has since limned Polish **werewolf** Waldemar Daninsky in eleven adventures; the fourth, *La noche del walpurgis* (*Shadow of the Werewolf*, 1970), was successful enough for him to play dress-up as a host of other horror types. *El espanto surge de la tumba* (*Horror Rises from the Tomb*, 1972), the first appearance of Naschy's Gilles de **Rais** character, marked the begin-

Reggie Nalder, *Dracula's Dog*

ning of a contract with the prolific Profilmes, the non-renewal of which led to his directorial debut, *Inquisición* (1976).

After a series of Japanese co-productions, Naschy typically takes ten different roles in his troubled Spanish comeback *El aullido del diablo* (1988). Deriving his pseudonym from Pope Paul VI, the well-fed, anxiously coiffured star finds it hard to resist imbuing the most vitiated role with heroic allure. The results are preening and unsatisfactory, but often also unwittingly perverse: both rapist and hero in *Los ojos azules de la muñeca rota* (*House of Psychotic Women*, 1973), Naschy beds the girl even as *El jorobado de la morgue* (*The Hunchback of the Morgue*, 1972). Denied the opportunity to mint an authentic Spanish horror tradition when John **Gilling** usurped the Gustavo Alfonso Becquer adaptation *La cruz del diablo* (1974), he is considered an anachronism by post-Franco film-makers. As Satan astounded at the world's corruption, he expresses his resentment in the heartfelt *El caminante* (1979). In *El carnaval de las bestias* (*Human Beasts*, 1980), Naschy is incredulous that he is simply being fattened for the pot. DP

Agonizando en el crimen/1967 * *Las noches del hombre lobo* (+w)/1968 * *Los monstruos del terror* (+w) [*Dracula vs. Frankenstein*]/1969 * *La furia del hombre lobo* (+w) [*Fury of the Wolf Man*]/1970 * *El doctor Jekyll y el hombre lobo* (+w) [*Dr. Jekyll and the Werewolf*]/*Jack el destripador de Londres* (+w)/1971 * *Los crimenes de Petiot* (+w)/*El gran amor del conde Drácula* (+w) [*Count Dracula's Great Love*]/*La rebelion de las muertas* (+w) [*Vengeance of the*

Zombies]/*La orgiá de los muertos* [*Brackula: Terror of the Living Dead*]/1972 * *El asesino está etre los trece* (+w)/*Una libelula para cada muerto* (+w) [*A Dragonfly for Each Corpse*]/*El retorno de walpurgis* (+w) [*Curse of the Devil*]/*La vengenza de la momia*/*Las ratas no duermen de noche*/1973 * *El mariscal del infierno* (+w)/*Todos los gritos del silencio* (+w)/*Los Pasajeros*/1974 * *Exorcismo* (+w) [*Exorcism*]/*La maldición de la bestia* (+w) [*The Werewolf and the Yeti*]/*Muerte de un quinqui* (+w)/1975 * *Secuestro* (+w)/*Ultimo deseo*/1976 * *El huerto del francés* (+w/d)/*Pecado mortal*/1977 * *Misterio en la isla de los monstruos* [*Mystery on Monster Island*]/*Los cantabros* (+w/d)/1980 * *El retorno del hombre lobo* (+w/d)/1981 * *Buenas noches señor monstruo*/1982 * *La bestia y la espada mágica* (+w/d)/*Latidos de panico* (+w/d)/1983 * *Pez* (s)/*Sssh* (s)/1986 * *Shadows of Blood*/1988 * *Horror en la museo de cera* (+w/d)/*Aqui huele a muerto . . . (¡Pues yo no he sido!)*/*La hija de Fu Manchu*/1990 * *La noche del ejecutor* (+w/d)/*State of Mind*/1992 * *Lycantropus*/1996

Native Americans * See: American Indians

Nazis

Nazis are such all-purpose villains (*Marathon Man*, 1976, *The Boys from Brazil*, 1978, and *Raiders of the Lost Ark*, 1981, are but three movies utilising the swastika as short-hand signifier for all that is vile and depraved) that it is hardly surprising they should feature as icons of the monstrous in horror.

In particular they surface in the **zombie** subgenre, as early as *King of the Zombies* (1941) and *Revenge of the Zombies* (1943), but also in the **Romero**-era *Le lac des morts vivants* (*Zombies' Lake*, 1980), *Shock Waves* (1977) and *Night of the Zombies* (1981). Other early attempts to give horror movies extra *frisson* by grafting on Nazi themes include such delirious stuff as *The Mysterious Doctor* (1943), *A Game of Death* (1945), *The Whip Hand* (1951), *She Demons* (1958), *They Saved Hitler's Brain* (1963) and *The Frozen Dead* (1967). Michael **Mann** confronts Nazis with a more ancient evil in *The Keep* (1984) and Lucio **Fulci** essays the Nazi theme in *I fantasmi di Sodoma* (*The Ghosts of Sodom*, 1988), in which kids visit a villa used for orgies by Nazis during the war and are possessed by their spirits (why didn't Pasolini think of that?).

Ever since Nazis first appeared in Hollywood films they have frequently been represented not as simple villains but the ultimate embodiment of evil. As such, like

LEFT Nazi: Dyanne Thorne,
Ilsa, She-Wolf of the SS

sinister grimoires of *Equinox* (1971) and *The Evil Dead* (1982). Jesús **Franco**'s *Necronomicon* (*Succubus*, 1967) merely uses the dread name. *H.R. Giger's Necronomicon* (1977) is a portfolio of **Giger**'s weird art; George Hay's *Necronomicon* (1978) is half literary spoof and half serious Lovecraft scholarship.

Neill, Roy William [Roland de Gostrie] (1886–1946)

Irish-born American director. Though he directed the barnstorming **Karloff** vehicle *The Black Room* (1935), the Universal monster rally *Frankenstein Meets the Wolf Man* and the Cornell **Woolrich** noir *Black Angel* (1946), Neill's major achievement is Universal's Basil **Rathbone**-Nigel **Bruce** **Sherlock Holmes** series. John Rawlins's *Sherlock Holmes and the Voice of Terror* (1942), established the contemporary setting foregrounded in Neill's first entries, which have Moriarty working for **Nazis** (*Sherlock Holmes and the Secret Weapon*, 1942) or Holmes foiling spies (*Sherlock Holmes in Washington*, 1943). With *Sherlock Holmes Faces Death* (1943), the series takes a detour into the macabre that Neill exploits with twisted plots, bizarre villains and perverse suspects. *The Scarlet Claw* (1944), a foggy mock **werewolf** film, is best of the run, but *The Spider Woman* (1944) has Gale **Sondergaard**'s villainy, *The Pearl of Death* (1944) a lumbering Rondo **Hatton**, and *The House of Fear* (1945) a very cunning plot. *The Woman in Green* (1945), *Pursuit to Algiers* (1945), *Terror by Night* (1946) and *Dressed to Kill* (1946) are

---

vampires, they exert a certain fascination, not least a sexual one, as Susan Sontag points out in 'Fascinating Fascism' (1975). The cinematic sexualisation of the Nazi monster is usually dated back to *Il portiere di notte* (*The Night Porter*) (1973), but it is clearly present in a number of wartime films, including Chaplin's *The Great Dictator* (1940), Fritz **Lang**'s *Hangmen Also Die!* (1943), Douglas Sirk's *Hitler's Madman* (1943), which has horror movie connotations since Heydrich is played by John **Carradine**, *Hitler's Children* (1943) and *Women in Bondage* (1943). Also predating *Il portiere di notte* was the still notorious *Love Camp 7* (1968), the first attempt to set a sexploitation film within an explicitly Nazi context, an extremely tacky equivalent of pulp novels then beginning to circulate (*Women in Terror, Two for Auschwitz*). Properly speaking, *Love Camp 7* and its (mostly Italian) successors – *Ilsa, She Wolf of the SS* (1974), *Lager SSadis kastrat kommandantur* (*SS Experiment Camp*, 1976), *Le lunghe notti della gestapo* (*Red Nights of the Gestapo*, 1976), *Le deportate della sezione speciale SS* (*Deported Women of the SS Special Section*, 1977), *L'ultima orgia del III Reich* (*The Gestapo's Last Orgy*, 1977) – belong in the Women in Prison genre, but their catalogues of **torture** and degradation, reminiscent of exercises like *Hexen bis auf's Blut gequält* (*Mark of the Devil*, 1970), bring them within the horror ambit, albeit tangentially.

From the perspective of the horror film proper, the most significant of this disreputable bunch is also the most grotesque and hysterically over-the-top: *SS Hell Camp* (*The Beast in Heat/Horrifing Experiments of SS Last Days*, 1976). Here, for no apparent reason, Nazis create a grotesque **Frankenstein** Monster with inordinate sexual powers. Unleashed on various female prisoners, the neanderthal proceeds to rape to death. Fans of the happy ending will be pleased to know he finally turns on his lesbian Nazi creator and gives her a dose of her own medicine. JP

The Necronomicon

The fabled tome of arcane secrets, originally the *Al Azif* of the 'Mad Arab' Abdul Alhazred, translated into Latin ('The Book of Dead Names') by Olaus Wormius. The invention of H.P. **Lovecraft**, inspired perhaps by the evil book of Robert W. Chambers' *The King in Yellow* (1895), the *Necronomicon* first appears in his 'The Nameless City' (1921). A cornerstone of Lovecraft's **Cthulhu Mythos** stories, it therefore reappears in many stories by his disciples: Fred Chappell's 'The Adder' (1989) is a rare story that uses the *Necronomicon* as more than a Macguffin, while Lin Carter's 'The Doom of Yakthoob' (1971) purports to be a passage from the book. It appears on screen in *The Haunted Palace* (1963) and *Necronomicon* (1993) and is imitated by the

RIGHT Roy William Neil

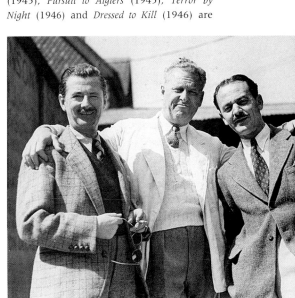

lesser efforts, with a bad-tempered Rathbone ceding ground to Bruce's comedy business, but all have their moments.

*Vanity's Price/1924 * The Ninth Guest/Black Moon/1934 * Destiny (p)/1944*

Newbrook, Peter (b. 1916)

British director. Having worked as a cinematographer and producer, Newbrook directed *The Disciple of Death* (1972) and *The Asphyx* (1972). The first is a lurid, mean-spirited attempt to make a horror star of reedy disc jockey Mike **Raven**. *The Asphyx* is Victorian weird science, comparable in its loony premise to *The Tingler* (1958), with Robert Stephens trapping the spirit of Death. While not exactly good, his films are interesting.

The Black Torment (c)/1964 * *Corruption* (p/c)/1968 * *Incense for the Damned* (p)/1970 * *Crucible of Terror* (c)/1971

Newfield, Sam (1899–1964)

American director. Brother of PRC head Sigmund Neufeld, Newfield ground out hundreds of quickies between 1919 and 1958, mostly three-day Westerns, using aliases (Sherman Scott, Peter Stewart) to disguise profligacy. His technique is so primitive that he can make a sixty-minute movie with George **Zucco**, a monster and five murders seem draggy.

*Ghost Patrol/1936 * The Mad Monster/Dead Men Walk/1942 * The Black Raven/Nabonga/ 1943 * The Monster Maker/1944 * The Flying Serpent/1945*

Newland, John (b. 1917)

American director. Originally a TV actor, Newland played **Frankenstein** and Dorian Gray on *Tales of Tomorrow* and was in two live versions of *The Man in Half Moon Street* (1949, 1953). Regular director and host of ***One Step Beyond*** (1959–61), a ***Twilight Zone*** competitor which offered half-hour dramatisations of 'actual' supernatural incidents, he did better by horror on ***Thriller***, especially with 'Pigeons From Hell' (1961). He handled Ray **Bradbury**'s play 'The Wonderful Ice Cream Suit' (*Rendezvous*, 1961) and horror/supernatural episodes of *Harry O* ('Second Sight', 1974) and *Wonder Woman* ('The Phantom of the Roller Coaster', 1979). Mostly active in TV, his notable theatrical credit is *The Legend of Hillbilly John* (1972), an unusual if scrappy adaptation of Manly Wade **Wellman**'s 'John the Balladeer' stories.

TV: *Lights Out* (a): 'The Strange Case of John Kingman'/'The Dark Corner'/1950; 'Grey Reminder'/1951; 'The Red Rose'/1952 * *Tales of Tomorrow* (a): 'Frankenstein'/1952; 'The Picture of Dorian Gray'/1953 * *Inner Sanctum* (a): 'The Sisters'/1954 * *Thriller*: 'The Return of Andrew Bentley' (+a)/ Portrait Without a Face' (+a)/1961; Man of Mystery/1962 * *Alfred Hitchcock Presents*: 'The Silk Petticoat'/'Bad Actor'/'Burglar Proof'/ 'The Twelve Hour Caper'/1962 * *Crawlspace*/ 1971 * *Night Gallery*: 'There Aren't Any More MacBanes'/1972 * *The Sixth Sense*: 'And Scream By the Light of the Moon, the Moon'/'Through a Flame Darkly'/'Dear Joan, We're Going to Scare You to Death'/ 1972 * *Don't Be Afraid of the Dark*/1973 * *The Next Step Beyond*/1978

Nicholson, James H. (1916–72)

American studio head. Nicholson and Samuel Z. **Arkoff** founded American Releasing Corporation, securing distribution rights to the Roger **Corman**-produced *Monster From the Ocean Floor* (1954). The company became American International Pictures in 1956, retaining Corman and others to turn out s-f, rock 'n' roll and action for the teenage drive-in market. Through the 60s, AIP presented **Poe** pictures, beach party musicals and biker-LSD youthsploitation films. Nicholson had a knack for coming up with catchy titles and lurid ad campaigns, then commissioning a film to fit the description. He left AIP in 1971 for a career as a hands-on producer, but made only *Legend of Hell House* (1972), scripted by Corman-Poe mainstay Richard **Matheson**, before his death.

Nicholson, Jack (b. 1937)

American actor, writer, director. An Academy Award winner for *One Flew Over the Cuckoo's Nest* (1975) and *Terms of Endearment* (1983), Nicholson became a star as the lawyer in *Easy Rider* (1969) and with strong roles in *Five Easy Pieces* (1970) and *The Last Detail* (1973). However, he began as a **Corman** psycho (*The Cry Baby Killer*, 1958) and spent the 60s knocking around exploitation: the masochist in *The Little Shop of*

LEFT Jack Nicholson, Joe Turkel, *The Shining*

Horrors (1960), a stooge in ***The Raven*** (1963), hero and one of many directors on *The Terror* (1963), writing *The Trip* (1967) and *Head* (1968), dropping out in *Hell's Angels on Wheels* (1967) and *Psych-Out* (1968). Much of his best work (*The King of Marvin Gardens*, 1972; *Chinatown*, 1974) is underplayed but following a remarkable sit-com out-of-control turn in *The Shining* (1980), he has taken an increasing number of horror or grotesque roles: the **Devil** (*The Witches of Eastwick*, 1987), the Joker (***Batman***, 1989), a **werewolf** (*Wolf*, 1994). Now so associated with bizarre make-up and comic-book mania that *Hoffa* (1992) makes his cube-headed Jimmy Hoffa seem like a Dick Tracy villain.

Mars Attacks!/1996

Nicolodi, Daria (b. 1950)

Italian actress, writer. An engaging, flirtatious heroine in *Profondo rosso* (*Deep Red*, 1975), Nicolodi became a fixture of Dario **Argento** films, co-writing *Suspiria* (1977) and again taking a lead in *Tenebre* (*Tenebrae*, 1982). Reflecting the disintegration of their offscreen relationship, she is slashed, abused, shot and killed in *Inferno* (1980), *Phenomena* (1985) and *Opera* (1987). Outstanding for Mario and Lamberto **Bava** as the madwoman of *Shock Transfert-Suspence-Hypnos* (*Shock*, 1977) and the automaton of *La venere d'ille* (1979).

Le foto di Gioia [*Delirium*]/1987 * *Il violino che uccide* [*Paganini Horror*] (+w)/1988 * *La fine è nota*/1992

Night Gallery (US TV series, 1970–73)

After the cancellation of **The Twilight Zone** (1959–64), Rod **Serling** scripted a pilot for a revival of the series. Before Universal backed the script as *Night Gallery* (1969), Serling turned the stories into prose for his collection *The Season to Be Wary* (1967). Directed by Boris Sagal, Steven **Spielberg** and Barry Shear, the **anthology** pilot resurrects the *TZ* formula of twist endings, magical interventions and **EC Comic** morality, though the emphasis is on the supernatural rather than s-f. In the subsequent series, Serling is seen loitering around the 'Night Gallery', a museum of the macabre. He introduces two or three stories, ranging from five to fifty minutes, each represented by a painting. It made its US TV debut under the title *Four In One: Night Gallery*, appearing on a monthly basis in rotation with three other shows; for a sec-

Rod Serling, *Night Gallery*

ond season, it ran as *Night Gallery* or *Rod Serling's Night Gallery*.

Though Serling provided some original material, notably award-winners 'They're Tearing Down Tim Riley's Bar' (1971) and 'The Messiah on Mott Street' (1971), the show adapted a wide range of contemporary and classic weird fiction, drawing on Joan Aiken ('Marmalade Wine', 1971), Algernon **Blackwood** ('The Doll', 1971), Basil Copper ('Camera Obscura', 1971), August **Derleth** ('House – With Ghost', 1971), David Ely ('The Academy', 1971), Fritz **Leiber** ('The Dead Man', 1970; 'The Girl With Hungry Eyes', 1972), H.P. **Lovecraft** ('Pickman's Model', 1971; 'Cool Air', 1971), Richard **Matheson** ('The Big Surprise', 1971; 'The Funeral', 1972), Seabury Quinn ('The Phantom Farmhouse', 1971), Clark Ashton **Smith** ('Return of The Sorcerer', 1972), Manly Wade **Wellman** ('The Devil is Not Mocked', 1971) and ***The Pan Book of Horror Stories*** ('The Sins of the Fathers', 1972; 'The Caterpillar', 1972). Blackout sketches involv-

ing vampires and blood banks ('A Matter of Semantics', 1971; 'A Midnight Visit to the Blood Bank', 1971) or twists on favourite characters ('The Phantom of What Opera?', 1971; 'With Apologies to Mr Hyde', 1971) allegedly lighten the tone.

The show's most prolific director was Jeannot **Szwarc**, who handled most of the creepier moments, but there were also detours into the macabre from Spielberg ('Make Me Laugh', 1971), Jeff Corey ('The Late Mr Peddington', 1971), John Badham ('The Boy Who Predicted Earthquakes', 1971; 'Camera Obscura'), John **Astin** ('A Fear of Spiders', 1971) and Leonard Nimoy ('Death on a Barge', 1972). The series was produced by Jack Laird, who also wrote many scripts. In syndication, re-edited and Serling-prefaced episodes of ***The Sixth Sense*** were added to the package and passed off as additional excursions into the Night Gallery. TM

Jean-Marc Lofficier, Randy Lofficier, *Into the*

Twilight Zone: The Rod Serling Programme Guide (1995)

A Nightmare on Elm Street (1984)

Wes **Craven**'s terror opus revitalised the moribund **stalk-and-slash** genre, introducing dream demon Freddy Krueger (Robert **Englund**) into monster culture. The razor-fingered, child-molesting 'bastard son of a hundred maniacs' who invades teenage nightmares became a shockingly popular icon, and Craven was finally acknowledged as the socially aware auteur he always thought himself to be. The exploitation of the id's collective fears and destructive desires continued in the most phenomenally successful fear film franchise of modern times.

Jack Sholder's *A Nightmare on Elm Street Part 2: Freddy's Revenge* (1985) unsuccessfully explores **homosexual** panic; Chuck Russell's *A Nightmare on Elm Street Part 3: Dream Warriors* (1987), co-written by Craven, is the most outlandishly surreal; Renny **Harlin**'s *A Nightmare on Elm Street 4: The Dream Master* (1988) features imaginative action set pieces

and remains the biggest box-office hit; Stephen Hopkins's *A Nightmare on Elm Street: The Dream Child* (1989) is unremarkable; and Rachel Talalay's *Freddy's Dead: The Final Nightmare* (1991) offers little but a **3-D** climax. Meanwhile, Englund introduced *Freddy's Nightmares* (1988–90), a syndicated anthology show set in Elm Street's Springwood. Craven cleverly redefines the Krueger universe in *Wes Craven's New Nightmare* (1994), a **recursive horror** which has the original cast play themselves and their characters, and features a canny acting turn from Craven as himself. While the sudden appearance of Freddy's gloved hand is the shock coda of *Jason Goes to Hell: The Final Friday* (1993), the anticipated Freddy vs Jason 'Battle of the Psychos' has yet to materialise. In addition to novelisations, the series has spun off Martin H. Greenberg's 'shared world' anthology *Nightmares on Elm Street* (1991) and a **young adult** series of novels commencing with Bruce Richards's *Freddy Krueger's Tales of Terror: Blind Date* (1994). AJ

Night of the Living Dead (1968)

Pittsburgh native George **Romero**'s cult classic about seven people barricaded in a remote farmhouse under sudden attack from **cannibal zombies** frightened unsuspecting audiences with its matter-of-fact horrors. Highly influential (Italian exploitation would have withered without it), Romero's crude black-and-white shocker was termed 'the best horror movie ever made', perhaps because it mirrors a 60s society coming apart at the seams. Far from the contemporary formulaic fright flicks of AIP/**Hammer**, *Night of the Living Dead* plumbed untouched depths of frantic despair, all-pervading hopelessness and nihilist terror while delivering visceral gross-out horror in the allegorical process.

Its growing Midnight Movie/Academic popularity led to two masterful Romero sequels, *Dawn of the Dead* (1979) and *Day of the Dead* (1985), and countless imitations including Lucio **Fulci**'s *Zombi 2* (*Zombie Flesh Eaters*, 1979) and the parodic *Return of the Living Dead* (1985) and sequels (after a legal battle over the property, Romero retained use of the word *Dead* in any future title

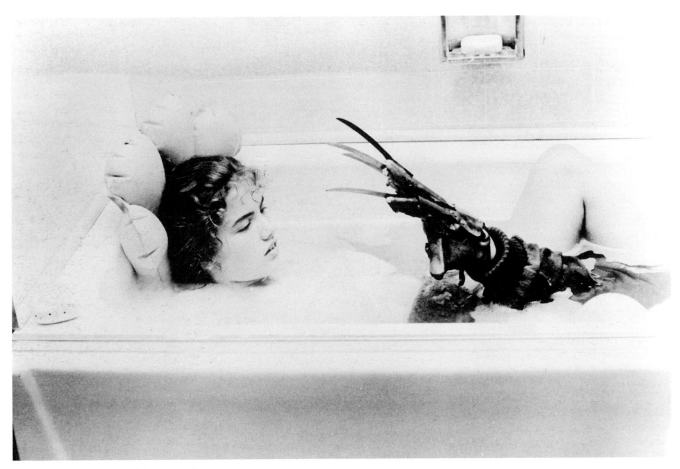

Heather Langenkamp, *A Nightmare on Elm Street*

Night of the Living Dead

while writer John **Russo** held on to *Living Dead*). Make-up effects man Tom **Savini**, a mainstay of the sequels, directed a noteworthy *Night of the Living Dead* remake (1990).

Russo novelised *Night* and Romero *Dawn*; John Skipp and Craig Spector edited *Book of the Dead* (1989) and *Still Dead: Book of the Dead 2* (1992), collecting stories set in the universe of the films; Philip Nutman expanded his *Book of the Dead* story into a novel *Wet Work* (1993), also highly derivative of the series; Nicholas Royle's *Saxophone Dreams* (1996), though similarly derived, takes a different approach. AJ

John Russo, *The Complete Night of the Living Dead Filmbook* (1985)

The Night Stalker (1972)

In 1970, Jeff Rice wrote *The Kolchak Papers*, a novel in which reporter Carl Kolchak investigates a series of murders in Las Vegas, penetrating a Watergate-style cover-up to confront a genuine **vampire**. The book, unpublished until 1973, was bought by producer Dan **Curtis** and turned into a *The Night Stalker*. An enormous ratings success, the TV movie benefits from Darren **McGavin**'s straw-hat and seedy-suit playing of Kolchak, Richard **Matheson**'s slick scripting and director John Llewellyn **Moxey**'s energetic action scenes as Janos Skorzeny (Barry

Atwater) tosses Las Vegas cops around like dummies.

Curtis produced and directed the Matheson-scripted *The Night Strangler* (1973), which Rice novelised: a riff on *The Man in Half-Moon Street* (1944), the sequel has McGavin's Kolchak in Seattle tackling **immortal** Richard Anderson. While the formula works twice, it is stretched somewhat in a series produced by and starring McGavin: *Kolchak: The Night Stalker* (1974–5). Set in Chicago, this has Kolchak, bossed by the irascible Tony Vincenzo (Simon Oakland, a holdover from the films), tangling with a different monster each week: a **werewolf**, a spin-off vampire, **aliens**, **Indian** curses, witches, dinosaurs, a robot, etc. Though well-played and written, the show suffers from repetition of the *Night Stalker* formula and fairly ropey monsters. Ersatz TV movies were created by combining episodes: *Demon and the Mummy* ('Demon in Lace', 'Legacy of Terror'), *Crackle of Death* ('Fire Fall', 'The Energy Eater'). Mark Dawidziak began writing new Kolchak novels with *The Kolchak Papers: Grave Secrets* (1994).

Mark Dawidziak, *Night Stalking: A 20th Anniversary Kolchak Companion* (1991)

Noir * See: **Film Noir**

Nostradamus [Michel de Nostredame] (1503–56)

French physician, seer. Nostradamus remains a tabloid perennial: his quatrains are more often interpreted as foretellings of war, assassination and disaster than, say, Elvis's appearance on the *Ed Sullivan Show* or the discovery of penicillin. *The Last Days of Planet Earth* (1974) and *The Man Who Saw Tomorrow* (1981) are spurious docu-dramas, while Tcheky Karyo stars in Roger Christian's earnest biopic *Nostradamus* (1994). The prophet's living **head** features in *Man Without a Body* (1957), his tomb in the film-within-a-film of *Demoni* (*Demons*, 1985). Germán **Robles** is Nostradamus's **vampire** son in a 1959 serial edited into four features: *La maldición de Nostradamus* (*The Curse of Nostradamus*), *Nostradamus y el destructor de monstruos* (*Monster Demolisher*), *Nostradamus, el genio de las tinieblas* (*Genii of Darkness*), *La sangre de Nostradamus* (*Blood of Nostradamus*).

Novelisations

Hit films (and plays before them) often spin off rapidly written and published novels, usually ground out by a hack who has seen only the screenplay and a few stills. In the early days of cinema, novelisations tended to come from name authors: Arthur B. Reeve scripted serials featuring his detective Craig Kennedy (*The Exploits of Elaine*, 1916) and simultaneously wrote prose versions of the stories; John Willard novelised his play ***The Cat and the Canary*** (1922) in 1927 to tie in with the film version. Robert **Bloch** (*The Couch*, 1962), Jimmy **Sangster** (*The Revenge*

Darren McGavin, *The Night Stalker*

of *Frankenstein*, 1958), Herschell Gordon **Lewis** (*Color Me Blood Red*, 1964), Edward D. **Wood** (*Orgy of the Dead*, 1966), John **Russo** (*Night of the Living Dead*, 1974), David Seltzer (*The Omen*, 1976) and Anthony Shaffer and Robin **Hardy** (*The Wicker Man*, 1978) have adapted their own screenplays, but many novelisations are the work of specialists like Dean Owen [Dudley Dean McGaughy] (*The Brides of Dracula*, 1960; *Konga*, 1960), John Burke (*Dr. Terror's House of Horrors*, 1965; *The Hammer Horror Omnibus*, 1966) and Alan Dean Foster (*Alien*, 1979; *The Thing*, 1982).

Notable authors to essay horror novelisations (frequently under pseudonyms) include Ellery Queen [Paul W. Fairman] (*A Study in Terror*, 1966), Michel **Parry** (*Countess Dracula*, 1970), Robert Black [Robert Holdstock] (*Legend of the Werewolf*, 1975), Guy N. Smith (*The Ghoul*, 1975), Carl Dreadstone [Ramsey **Campbell**, sometimes] (*The Wolf Man*, 1977), Jack Martin [Dennis **Etchison**] (*The Fog*, 1979; *Videodrome*, 1983), John Coyne (*The Legacy*, 1979), Chelsea Quinn Yarbro (*Nomads*, 1984), Owen West [Dean **Koontz**] (*The Funhouse*, 1980), Thomas Luke [Graham **Masterton**] (*Phobia*, 1980), Gary **Brandner** (*Cat People*, 1982), James Kahn (*Poltergeist*, 1982), John Skipp and Craig Spector (*Fright Night*, 1985), David Ferring [David Garnett] (*The Hills Have Eyes, Part 2*, 1984), Garry Douglas [Garry Kilworth] (*Highlander*, 1986), Ray Garton (*Warlock*, 1989), Craig Shaw Gardner (*The Lost Boys*, 1987) and Anne Billson (*Dream Demon*, 1989). An especially perfidious practice is the 're-novelising' of extant literary works to make them more like film adaptations: **The Island of Dr. Moreau** (1977) by Joseph Silva (Ron Goulart), *The Awakening* (1980) by R. **Chetwynd-Hayes** (from Bram **Stoker**'s *Jewel of the Seven Stars*, 1903), *Bram Stoker's Dracula* (1992) by Fred Saberhagen and James V. Hart.

O

O'Bannon, Dan (b. 1946)
American writer, director. O'Bannon's career is built on his much-rewritten original screenplay, *Alien* (1979). The unsustainedly goofy *Return of the Living Dead* (1985) is his writer-directorial debut. A semi-sequel to **Night of the Living Dead** (1968), it is the horror equivalent of his Kubrick retort *Dark

LEFT Old Dark House: Dorothy McGuire, *The Spiral Staircase* (1945)

Star* (1974). Though credited, O'Bannon denies co-writing *Dead and Buried* (1981) with frequent collaborator Ron Shusett. He is generally aggrieved at the fate of his scripts, which include *Blue Thunder* (1983), *Lifeforce* (1985), *Total Recall* (1990) and *Screamers* (1995). *The Resurrected* (1991), scripted by Brent Friedman from **Lovecraft**'s *The Case of Charles Dexter Ward* (1927), is, ironically, his most serious work to date.
DP

Oblowsky, Stefan * See: **Mattei, Bruno**

Oboler, Arch (1909–87)
American director, producer, writer. Oboler was a **radio** auteur, famous for horror work on **Lights Out** (1934–47). Stephen **King** notes he 'utilized two of radio's great strengths: the first is the mind's innate obedience, its willingness to try to see whatever someone suggests it see, no matter how absurd; the second is the fact that fear and horror are blinding emotions that knock our adult pins from beneath us and leave us groping in the dark like children who cannot find the light switch'. King cites 'The Chicken Heart That Ate the World' and 'A Day at the Dentist' as masterpieces.

A gimmick talent, Oboler's films mix makeshift production values with unusual subjects: *Bewitched* (1945), an early psycho film; *Strange Holiday* (1946), a vision of fascist America; *Five* (1951), the first after-the-Bomb drama. The success of *Bwana Devil* (1952) – 'a lion in your lap' – diverted him into **3-D**: *The Bubble* (1967), *The Stewardesses* (1969). He also made the uneasily comic *The Twonky* (1953), about a possessed TV set, and *1+1: Exploring the Kinsey Report* (1961).

O'Brien, Richard (b. 1942)
New Zealand-born British writer, actor. Creator of *The Rocky Horror Show* (1973). In *The Rocky Horror Picture Show* (1975), he recreates his stage role as Riff-Raff. Despite his witty score, the would-be follow-up *Shock Treatment* (1981) has failed to accrue a cult. A personality rather than a player, he is Dr John Dee in *Jubilee* (1977) and has introduced game shows (*The Crystal Maze*, 1991–4) and cult films on TV.

TV: *Robin of Sherwood*/1984–6

Ogilvy, Ian (b. 1943)
British actor, a trendy hero for Michael **Reeves**. SJ

Il lago di Satana [*The She Beast*]/1965 * *The Sorcerers*/1967 * *Matthew Hopkins Witchfinder General*/1968 * *Wuthering Heights*/1970 * *From Beyond the Grave*/– *And Now the Screaming Starts!*/1973 * *Death Becomes Her*/1992 * *Puppetmaster 5: The Final Chapter*/1995

TV: *The Liars*/1966 * *The Avengers*: 'They Keep Killing Steed'/1968 * *Wine of India*/1970 * Q.E.D.: 'Infernal Device'/1982 * *Robin of Sherwood*: 'Rutterkin'/1986

Old Dark Houses
This subgenre takes its name from James **Whale**'s seminal *The Old Dark House* (1932), a sophisticated example based on J.B. Priestley's novel *Benighted* (1927) and cast with such luminaries as Charles **Laughton**, Raymond **Massey** and Melvyn **Douglas** in addition to the more expected **Karloff** and a scene-stealing Ernest **Thesiger**. Actually the form dates back much farther, to frequently filmed plays like Mary Roberts Rinehart's *The Bat* (1920) and John Willard's **The Cat and the Canary** (1922). All feature a group of strangers drawn to a decrepit mansion where a murderous maniac lurks; sometimes the house is said to be haunted. Since the ghosts are frequently frauds and the murderers must be unmasked, many a mystery series includes relevant offerings, like *Charlie Chan's Secret* (1936) or the **Sherlock Holmesian** *The House of Fear* (1945).

This is a world of shadows and thunderstorms and sliding panels, and the cozy familiarity of long-established gothic conventions is most often played for laughs. Key silent films include D.W. Griffith's seminal *One Exciting Night* (1922) and Paul **Leni**'s influentially atmospheric version of *The Cat and the Canary* (1927). *The Terror* (1928) was the second all-talking feature ever made, and *The Bat Whispers* (1930) employs an early widescreen process. Star comedians visit old dark houses in the early days of shorts like Harold Lloyd's *Haunted Spooks* (1920) and *The Laurel-Hardy Murder Case* (1930). The pattern continues in features, with Hugh Herbert (*Sh! The Octopus*, 1937), Jack Oakie (*Super-Sleuth*, 1937) and Will Hay (*Oh Mr Porter*, 1937), then developed into a trend with the success of Bob Hope's joke-filled yet creepy *The Cat and the Canary* (1939) remake. After Hope, the deluge: the Ritz Brothers (*The Gorilla*, 1939), Red Skelton (*Whistling in the Dark*, 1941), **Abbott and Costello** (*Hold That Ghost*, 1941), the East Side Kids (*Spooks Run Wild*, 1941), Broderick Crawford (*The Black Cat*, 1941),

Old Dark House: Anthony Perkins, *Psycho*

Wayne Morris (*The Smiling Ghost*, 1941), Roland Young (*Topper Returns*, 1941), Jack Haley (*One Body Too Many*, 1944) and Wally Brown and Alan Carney (*Genius at Work*, 1946). There are even musical variations: bandleader Kay Kyser meets the terror triumvirate of **Lugosi**, Karloff, and **Lorre** (*You'll Find Out*, 1940), while the raucous Ole Olsen and Chick Johnson are stuck with a tap-dancing ghost and Lon **Chaney Jr** (*Ghost Catchers*, 1944). The spoofs of this era provided work for horror stalwarts from Lionel **Atwill** to George **Zucco**; Lugosi is in close to half of them, usually cast as a red herring.

Old dark houses of more serious mien are explored as well: *The Uninvited* (1944) portrays a haunted house with emphasis on the domestic side. *And Then There Were None* (1945), from Agatha **Christie**, features a rapidly dwindling cast of accomplished character actors, deftly put through their paces by director René Clair; a low-budget variant is *Fog Island* (1945). Robert **Siodmak** provides a quintessentially stylish spook house in *The Spiral Staircase* (1945), atmosphere abetted by cinematographer Nicholas Musuraca. Horror went temporarily out of fashion after World War II and the old dark house thriller, already anachronistic, never really recovered. There was one final flurry, however, with the genre revival of the late 50s. William **Castle**'s amusing *The House on*

Haunted Hill (1958) helped establish Vincent **Price** as the era's top American horror star; a sign of the times was Castle's decision to use exteriors of a modernistic Frank Lloyd Wright house rather than a Victorian mansion. Price also appears in a creaky remake of *The Bat* (1959), while Castle directed the calculatedly juvenile *13 Ghosts* (1960). Britain offered comedic entries including *What a Carve Up!* (1961) and *The Horror of It All* (1963), the latter a bizarre mismatch of Terence **Fisher** and Pat Boone. There is even a much maligned remake of *The Old Dark House* (1962), a collaboration between William Castle and **Hammer** featuring accomplished comedians Robert Morley and Joyce Grenfell. The film was shot in colour but released in America in black-and-white, a fading format that may have been essential to this subgenre.

Alfred **Hitchcock**'s *Psycho* (1960) and Robert **Wise**'s *The Haunting* (1963), two of the last major horror films made in monochrome, are set in old dark houses, yet in psychological intensity are almost the antithesis of the established form. The last gasp came in 1966 when hayseed comedian Don Knotts appeared in *The Ghost and Mr. Chicken*, a throwback that made money in rural America; the last nail in the coffin was *Hillbillys in a Haunted House* (1967), which marks Basil **Rathbone**'s final screen appearance. Attempts at revival have failed. Pete

Walker's *House of the Long Shadows* (1983) is a version of George Cohan and Earl Derr Biggers's play *Seven Keys to Baldpate* (1913), already filmed in 1917, 1926, 1929, 1935 and 1947; a cast of old troupers (Price, **Cushing**, **Lee**, **Carradine**) is given little to do. Writer-director-actor Gene Wilder's frankly nostalgic *Haunted Honeymoon* (1986) is truly terrifying when Dom DeLuise appears in drag but only fitfully entertaining. LD

The Ωmega Factor (UK TV series, 1979)

A ten-part series produced by BBC Scotland. Investigative reporter Tom Crane (James Hazeldine), a natural psychic, is recruited by Department 7, a special research department of MI5, to investigate cases of a paranormal nature. Louise Jameson co-stars as Dr Anne Reynolds, with John Carlisle as Roy Martindale and Brown Derby as Andrew Scott-Erskine. Written by Jack Gerson, Eric MacDonald and Nick McCarthy, produced by George Gallaccio, and directed by Paddy Russell, Norman Stewart, Kenny McBain, Eric Davidson, Gerald Blake and Peter Grimwade. The technical advisor in **parapsychology** was Professor Archie Roy of the University of Glasgow. TM

The Omen (1976)

Combining the Antichrist theme of *Rosemary's Baby* (1968) with the Satanic tone of *The Exorcist* (1974), plus oddments of Brian **Clemens**'s 'Nurse Will Make It Better' (*Thriller*, 1974), Richard **Donner**'s *The Omen* is blockbuster B horror, with respectable stars (Gregory Peck, Lee Remick) and flamboyant death scenes (David **Warner** beheaded, Patrick **Troughton** impaled) set to Jerry **Goldsmith**'s black mass. Producer Harvey Bernard followed his runaway hit with sequels, following Damien Thorn as he grows up between the freak accidents: Don Taylor's *Damien: Omen II* (1978), with William Holden and Lee Grant, and Graham Baker's *The Final Conflict* (1981), with Sam Neill as the adult Antichrist.

Writer David Seltzer novelised his own script and had a surprise best seller, which even generated non-film-related sequels (Gordon McGill's *Omen IV: Armageddon 2000*, 1983, *The Abomination: Omen V*, 1985). Jorge Montesi's tardy *Omen IV: The Awakening* (1991), a TV cheapie, introduces the Antichristine, Damien's similarly creepy lost daughter. *Holocaust 2000* (1978) and *The Servants of Twilight* (1991) are rip-offs; Neil Gaiman and Terry Pratchett's novel *Good*

Omens (1990) and *El dia de la bestia (Day of the Beast*, 1995) are parodies.

One Step Beyond (US TV series, 1959–61)

John **Newland** hosted this half hour supernatural anthology, presenting each week a tale supposedly based on a real life incident. The show (sometimes billed as *Alcoa Presents: One Step Beyond*) was created by Merwin Gerard, also the associate producer and main scriptwriter. In typical episodes, the spirit of a dead German soldier attends the birth of his son ('The Promise', 1960), and a midwestern town is terrified by a young girl's pet, a talking animal that can predict the future ('The Voice', 1960). Though an American series, some third season episodes were filmed in the UK with British casts.

'The Sorcerer' (1961), for instance, stars Christopher **Lee** and Martin Benson. The 'based on fact' tag limits the show's eerie quotient, imposing too many trite urban legend paraphenomena McGuffins. *The Next Step Beyond* (1978) is an updated version, with John Newland again as host and narrator. TM

O'Quinn, Terry (b. 1952)

American actor. Utility supporting player O'Quinn – Howard Hughes in *Rocketeer* (1991), a lawyer in *Young Guns* (1988) – is remarkable as the multi-identity serial killer of **The Stepfather** (1987), returning in *Stepfather II* (1989) but sitting out *Stepfather III* (1992). Most post-*Fatal Attraction* (1986) psycho films put up paranoid defense of American **family values**; O'Quinn's 'Jerry

Jack Lord, CeCe Whitney, 'Father Image', *One Step Beyond*

Blake' embodies them, killing only when new families fail to live up to his ideal. The performance landed him some decent horror roles: another creepy father in *Pin . . .* (1988), in love with a ghost in *The Forgotten One* (1989).

Silver Bullet/1985 * *The Jogger* (s)/1987 * *Black Widow*/1987 * *Amityville: A New Generation*/ *Visions of Murder*/1993

TV: *The Twilight Zone*: 'Chameleon'/1985 * *The X Files*: 'Aubrey'/1995

Orloff, Dr * See: Disfigurement and Plastic Surgery; Franco, Jesús; Vernon, Howard

Ormsby, Alan (b. 1944)

American writer. Though *Children Shouldn't Play With Dead Things* (1972) is directed by Bob **Clark**, Ormsby writes, provides **zombie** make-up and plays the lead, an obnoxious auteur called Alan. His most interesting scripts are *Dead of Night* (1974), again with Clark, and *Deranged* (1974), co-directed with *Children* co-star Jeff Gillen. Less happily, he is credited on **Cat People** (1982) and billed as 'Tod Hackett' on *Popcorn* (1991). He also worked with Clark on *Porky's II: The Next Day*

LEFT Asia Viera, *Omen IV: The Awakening*

RIGHT Bruce Dern, 'The Zanti Misfits',
The Outer Limits

(1983), and had a sleeper with *My Bodyguard* (1980).

Shock Waves (fx)/1977

TV: *Deadly Web*/1996

Orson Welles Great Mysteries (UK TV series, 1973–4)

A late-night anthology show, produced by John Jacobs for Anglia, lugubriously introduced by Orson **Welles**. Anglo-American casts feature in adaptations from famous authors: W.W. Jacobs (**'The Monkey's Paw'**), Stanley Ellin ('Death of an Old-Fashioned Girl'), O. Henry ('Compliments of the Season'), W. Somerset Maugham ('A Point of Law'), Wilkie Collins ('A Terribly Strange Bed') and Dorothy L. Sayers ('The Inspiration of Mr. Budd'). Moments of horror are provided by classic *contes cruels* with Peter **Cushing** (Balzac's 'La Grande Bretèche') and Christopher **Lee** (**Doyle**'s 'The Leather Funnel'). Other guest stars: Joan Collins, Victor **Buono**, Eli Wallach, Jose Ferrer, Patrick **Macnee**, Charles **Gray**, Claire Bloom, Susannah York, Patrick **Magee**, Hugh **Griffith**, Donald **Pleasence**. Directors include Peter **Sasdy**, Alan **Gibson**, Philip Saville and Peter **Sykes**. In the US, the show is known as *Great Mysteries*. TM

de Ossorio, Amando (b. 1926)

Spanish writer, director. De Ossorio contributed the sepulchral 'Blind Dead' series to Spain's pre-Juan Carlos horror boom: *La noche del terror ciego* (*Tombs of the Blind Dead*, 1971), *El ataque de los muertos sin ojos* (*Return of the Evil Dead*, 1973), *El buque maldito* (*Horror of the Zombies*, 1974), *La noche de las gaviotas* (*Night of the Seagulls*, 1975). Though often as clumsily 'with it' as most Iberian exploitation, the films succeed in presenting the past as a potent source of terror thanks to their impossibly skeletal Knights Templar **zombies**. The trick is not repeated elsewhere: *Malenka, la sobrina del vampiro* (*Malenka*, 1968) incoherently toys with the gothic, while *Las garras de Lorelei* (*The Lorelei's Grasp*, 1973) and *La noche de los brujos* (*Night of the Sorcerors*, 1973) garble mythic and imperialist texts. *La endemoniada* (*The Possessed*, 1974) is an at best unseemly *Exorcist* (1973) perm. DP

Serpiente de mar/1985

Nigel J. Burrell, *Knights of Terror: The Blind Dead Films of Amando de Ossorio* (1995)

Oswald, Gerd (1919–89)

German-born director; son of Richard **Oswald**. Though his early features (*A Kiss Before Dying*, 1956; *Fury at Showdown*, 1957; *Screaming Mimi*, 1958) are promising, Oswald became a TV director, working on everything from *Bonanza* ('Destiny's Child', 1966) through *The Fugitive* ('Joshua's Kingdom', 1966) to *Star Trek* ('The Conscience of the King', 1966). His major genre work is fifteen episodes of **The Outer Limits**, which are strikingly noirish with moments of real horror and the grotesque. 'The Forms of Things Unknown' (1964), an *Outer Limits* made as a pilot for another series, is one of the most surreal hours TV has ever done.

TV: *The Outer Limits*: 'O.B.I.T.'/'Corpus Earthling'/'It Crawled Out of the Wood-work'/1963; 'The Mice'/'Don't Open Til Doomsday'/'The Invisibles'/'Specimen: Unknown'/'Fun and Games'/'The Chameleon'/'Soldier'/'Expanding Human'/ 'The Duplicate Man'/'The Premonition'/ 1965 * *The Twilight Zone*: 'The Beacon'/'The Star'/1985

Oswald, Richard [Richard Ornstein] (1880–1963)

Austrian-born German director. More committed to literature than **expressionism**, Oswald took early stabs at **Poe**, **Stevenson**, **Wilde**, **Hoffmann** and **Doyle**, but also non-horror pop classics like Verne (*Die Reise um die Erde in 80 Tagen*, 1919). His other specialties were history (*Lucrezia Borgia*, 1922) and topical sensationalism (*Die Prostitution*, 1919). A refugee from the Nazis, he made a few films in France and the US (*Isle of Missing Men*, 1942).

Hoffmanns Erzählungen/Das Bildnis des Dorian Gray/1916 * *Der Lebende Leichnam*/1918 * *Unheimliche Geschichten*/1919 * *Nachtgestalten*/ 1920 * *Macbeth*/1921 * *Der Hund von Baskerville*/1929 * *Alraune*/1930 * *Unheimliche Geschichten*/1932

The Outer Limits (US TV series, 1963–5)

Created by executive producer Leslie Stevens, *The Outer Limits* was opened up the boundaries of TV s-f and fantasy. Its subjects range from spacemen on other worlds ('The Invisible Enemy', 1964) to experiments with the human **brain** ('The Sixth Finger, 1963), and from antlike creatures ('The Zanti Misfits', 1963) to time-travelling astronauts ('The Man Who Was Never Born', 1963). Joseph **Stefano** produced the first season of the show with Ben Brady taking over for the second; Stevens and Stefano wrote most first season teleplays, Harlan **Ellison** and Jerry Sohl worked on the second. The special effects were created by Jim Danforth and the team of Projects Unlimited, who created each episode's 'Bear', the monster of the week Stefano was required to include (in reality not every episode had one). Dominic Frontiere composed the eerie music used in the series, but the more melodic second season theme is by Harry Lubin.

In the pilot, 'The Galaxy Being' (1963), written and directed by Leslie Stevens, a radio engineer (Cliff Robertson) tunes into an **alien**'s waveband and brings him to Earth, accidentally causing havoc. Most subsequent episodes follow this pattern: morality plays with monsters who expose human weaknesses. But outstanding horror-themed episodes have genuinely frightening creatures like the alien McCarthyites of 'O.B.I.T.' (1963) and parasites of 'The Invisibles' (1964) and outstandingly strange effects like the time-twisting of 'The Forms of Things Unknown' (1964) and the allegorical noir conflict of 'Demon With a Glass Hand' (1964). An updated colour version of the series debuted with the feature-length 'Sandkings' (1994), but consistently misses the high-water mark of the original. TM

David J. Schow, Jeffrey Frentzen, *The Outer Limits: The Official Companion* (1986)

Out of Body Experiences

The ability to project one's spirit in astral form to do mischief appears in a few stories, most of which have the villain return to find himself a corpse. The plot originates in Davis Grubb's 'The Horsehair Trunk' (1948; adapted as 'The Last Laurel', **Night Gallery**, 1971) and imitated by *Psychic Killer* (1975), *The Invisible Strangler* (1976), *976 EVIL II* (1992) and 'I'll Be Watching You' (*Ghosts*, 1995). The comics sorcerer **Dr Strange** makes rare *ethical* use of astral projection. The commoner phenomenon of near-death, in which the subject's soul seems to leave the body only to return, is the McGuffin of Dennis Etchison's novel *Darkside* (1986) and the films *Flatliners* (1990), *Hideaway* (1995) and *The Frighteners* (1996).

Out of the Unknown (UK TV series, 1965–71)

Produced by Irene Shubik, this one-hour show was BBC2's attempt to produce a s-f series. It began with John Wyndham's 'No Place Like Earth' (1965), then turned to reliable but underfilmed authors Isaac Asimov ('The Dead Past,'), J.G. Ballard ('Thirteen to Centarus'), Frederik Pohl ('The Midas Plague', directed by Peter **Sasdy**), John Brunner ('The Last Lonely Man') and C.M. Kornbluth ('The Little Black Bag'). Serious enough to include s-f from E.M. Forster ('The Machine Stops') and J.B. Priestley (an adaptation of Mordecai Roshwald's 'Level 7'), the show mutated in its last season (1971), presenting a collection of mainly original **ghost stories**, notably Nigel **Kneale**'s 'The Chopper', with Patrick **Troughton** haunted by a dead Hells' Angel, and Michael J. Bird's chilling 'To Lay a Ghost', directed by Ken Hannam. TM

P

Palance, Jack [Vladimir Palanuik] (b. 1920)

American actor, known as the steely-eyed killer in *Shane* (1953). His subsequent career has been uneven, but includes **Jack the Ripper** in *Man in the Attic* (1953) and title roles in TV's *The Strange Case of Dr. Jekyll and Mr. Hyde* (1967) and **Dracula** (1973). An Oscar for *City Slickers* (1991) briefly revived his box-office value. SJ

Torture Garden/1967 * *Justine*/1968 * *Craze*/ 1974 * *Without Warning*/1980 * *Alone in the Dark*/1982 * *Batman*/1989

TV: *Lights Out*: 'The Man Who Couldn't Remember'/1950 * *Suspense*: 'The Kiss-Off'/ 'Cagliostro and the Chess Player'/1953 *

Tales of the Haunted: 'Evil Stalks This House'/ 1981 * *Twilight Zone: Rod Serling's Lost Classics*/ 1993

The Pan Book of Horror Stories

Between 1959 and 1989, Herbert van Thal (and, from 1985, Clarence Paget) edited an annual paperback anthology of original and reprint horror, noted for gruesome covers and **EC**-like *contes cruels*, which did much to shape the genre in Britain. Early volumes focus on established authors (**Wells**, **Bradbury**, **Stoker**), but van Thal, a literary agent scouting for fresh talent, moved to newer writers (M.S. Waddell, Adobe James, Alex Hamilton, William Sansom, R. **Chetwynd-Hayes**, John Burke, David Case, Conrad Hill). The series inspired imitations like *The Fontana Book of Great Horror Stories* (1966), and **Night Gallery** (1970–73) relied on stories published or republished by van Thal. The series deteriorated under Paget, propped up by Stephen **King** reprints, though early work appeared from Nicholas Royle and Christopher Fowler. *Dark Voices: The Best From the Pan Book of Horror Stories* (1990), by Stephen **Jones** and Paget, selects the pick of the thirty-year run. David Sutton and Jones edited *Dark Voices 2* (1994) through 6 (1994), drawing on new generations of writers (Ramsey **Campbell**, Brian **Lumley**, Michael Marshall Smith, Kathe Koja, Stephen Laws, David J. **Schow**, Graham Joyce). When Pan discontinued the series, Sutton and Jones's *Dark Voices 7* formed the basis of *Dark Terrors* (1995), published by Gollancz.

Jack Palance, *Man in the Attic*

Parapsychology: Ernie Hudson, Dan Aykroyd, Bill Murray, Harold Ramis, *Ghostbusters II*

Parapsychology

Scientific study of the supernatural, rooted in stalwart Victorian institutions like the Society for Psychical Research, has come to prominence in supernatural fiction since the50s, promoting sceptical researchers likeHolden (Dana Andrews) of *Night of the Demon* (1958) to roles once taken by scientific believers like **Van Helsing**.

Shirley **Jackson**'s influential *The Haunting of Hill House* (1959; filmed as *The Haunting*, 1963) has an investigator set up shop in a supposedly haunted house, a theme echoed by Richard **Matheson**'s *Hell House* (1971,; filmed as *The Legend of Hell House*, 1973). Nigel **Kneale**, whose rocket scientist dabbles in parapsychology in *Quatermass and the Pit* (1958), wrote two outstanding TV plays: *The Road* (1963), with eighteenth-century ghost-hunters finding a pre-echo of twentieth-century scientific horror in a haunted wood, and *The Stone Tape* (1972), a definitive reading of the modern science versus ancient haunting theme.

Oddly, the most substantial use in the cinema of parapsychology, complete with jargon and academic bickering, is the broadly comic but surprisingly committed *Ghostbusters* (1984), which spun off *Ghostbusters II* (1989) and a TV cartoon *The Real Ghostbusters* (1986–92). The discipline figures in films (*The Asphyx*, 1972; *Amityville 3-D*, 1983; *The Entity*, 1983; *Prince of Darkness*, 1987) and TV series (*The Sixth Sense*, 1972; *The Ωmega Factor*, 1979; *Shadow Chasers*, 1985–6; *Beyond Reality*, 1991–3; *The X Files*, 1993–).

Parker, Eddie (1900–1960)

American stuntman. For Universal, Parker did much leaping and fighting for **monster**-masked stars, doing more than officially billed **Lugosi** in *Frankenstein Meets the Wolf Man* (1943). He actually played **Hyde** (*Abbott and Costello Meet Dr. Jekyll and Mr. Hyde*, 1953), the **Mummy** (*Abbott and Costello Meet the Mummy*, 1955) and a Neanderthal Man (*Monster on Campus*, 1958). Contrary to *Ed Wood* (1994), Parker, doubling Lugosi again, grapples with a prop squid in *Bride of the Monster* (1956). He also racked up serial appearances in the role of 'henchman': *Flash Gordon* (1936), *Batman* (1943), *King of the Rocket Men* (1949).

The WereWolf of London/1935 * *Son of Frankenstein*/1939 * *The Mysterious Dr. Satan*/1940 * *Invisible Agent*/*The Mummy's Tomb*/*Ghost of Frankenstein*/1942 * *The Mummy's Ghost*/1943 * *Haunted Harbor*/*The Mummy's Curse*/1944 * *The Monster and the Ape*/1945 * *The Crimson Ghost*/1946 * *The Invisible Monster*/1950 * *The Strange Door*/1951 * *Tarantula*/1955 * *The Mole People*/1956 * *Curse of the Undead*/1959

Parry, Michel (b. 1947)

Belgian-born British writer. A critic and anthologist, Parry has scripted a few films. He novelised *Countess Dracula* (1970).

Hex (s)/1969 * *The Uncanny*/1977 * *The Evictors* (u)/1979 * *XTRO*/1983 * *The Zip* (s)/1988

TV: *Monsters*: 'Rouse Him Not'/1988

Parsons, Milton (1904–80)

American actor. A cadaverous red herring with a **Karloffian** lisp, often unbilled as a mortician. Perhaps his finest moment is as homicidal maniac John Channing in *The Hidden Hand* (1942). sj

Hold That Ghost/*Fingers at the Window*/*Dead Men Tell*/*Dressed to Kill*/*Castle in the Desert*/1941 * *Whispering Ghosts*/*The Man in the Trunk*/1942 * *Cry of the Werewolf*/1944 * *Dick Tracy, Detective*/1945 * *Dark Alibi*/*Dick Tracy vs. Cueball*/1946 * *Dick Tracy Meets Gruesome*/*The Secret Life of Walter Mitty*/1947 * *The Monster That Challenged the World*/1957 * *The Haunted Palace*/1963

TV: *The Twilight Zone*: 'The New Exhibit'/1963 * *Wild Wild West*: 'The Night of the Bars of Hell'/1966 * *Get Smart*: 'Shock It to Me'/1969 * *Night Gallery*: 'Camera Obscura'/1971 * *The Cat Creature*/1973 * *Kolchak: The Night Stalker*: 'Demon in Lace'/*The Dead Don't Die*/1975

Pataki, Michael (b. 1938)

American actor, director. Pataki, usually cast as cops and hoods, is interesting as an extremely unsympathetic **vampire** in *Grave of the Vampire* (1972). **Dracula** and a lookalike nice-guy descendant in *Dracula's Dog* (1977), a regular (a cop) on *The Amazing Spider-Man* (1977–9) and director of Charles **Band**'s first film, *Mansion of the Doomed* (1976).

The Return of Count Yorga/1971 * *The Bat People*/1974 * *Love at First Bite*/1979 * *Graduation Day*/*Dead and Buried*/1981 * *Sweet Sixteen*/1982 * *Halloween IV: The Return of Michael Myers*/1988

Michael Pate

TV: *The Twilight Zone*: 'A Quality of Mercy'/
1961 * *Mission: Impossible*: 'The Psychic'/1967
* *The Sixth Sense*: 'Face of Ice'/1972 * *Batman:
The Animated Series*: 'The Underdwellers' (v)/
1992

Pate, Michael (b. 1920)

Australian actor. Often seen as an Indian in
Westerns, wide-mouthed Pate did horror
service as a **minion**, with a striking role as a
vampire gunslinger in *Curse of the Undead*
(1959). Returning to Australia as a producer,
he is the US President in Philippe **Mora**'s
Return of Captain Invincible (1982) and *The
Marsupials: Howling III* (1987).

The Strange Door/1951 * *The Black Castle*/1952
* *The Maze*/1953 * *Beauty and the Beast*/1961 *
Tower of London/1962

TV: *Thriller*: 'Trio for Terror'/1961 * *Alfred
Hitchcock Hour*: 'The McGregor Affair'/1964;
'Thou Still Unravished Bride'/1965 * *Voyage
to the Bottom of the Sea*: 'Flaming Ice'/1968

Pearce, Jacqueline (b. 1943)

British actress. Remarkable as the **snake**
woman in *The Reptile* (1966) and a victim in
The Plague of the Zombies (1965), Pearce did
not fulfil early promise. A **camp** icon as
Servalan, villainess of *Blake's Seven* (1977–82).

How to Get Ahead in Advertising/1989

TV: *The Avengers*: 'A Sense of History'/1966 *
Leap in the Dark: 'The Ghost of Ardachie
Lodge'/1975 * *Doctor Who*: 'The Two
Doctors'/1985

Jacqueline Pearce

Peasants: Boris Karloff, Torch-bearing mob, *Bride of Frankenstein*

Peasants

A mob on the march, torches aloft, is a
familiar scene in horror films with a gothic
flavor; as they move to eradicate a monster,
these peasants may represent righteous rev-
olutionaries, or else just vigilantes looking
for a lynching. The metaphysical implications of membership in such a mob are
explored in Woody Allen's neglected spoof
of **expressionism**, *Shadows and Fog* (1992).
Early examples include Parisians rising up
against Lon **Chaney** in *The Hunchback of
Notre Dame* (1923) and *The Phantom of the
Opera* (1925); the studio involved, Universal, had a virtual patent after the peasant
parades in *Frankenstein* (1931), *The Ghost of
Frankenstein* (1942) and *House of Frankenstein*
(1944). However central European habits
look a bit questionable when transplanted to
small-town America for Universal's *The
Mummy's Tomb* (1942) and *The Mummy's
Ghost* (1944), complete with stock footage
from *Frankenstein*.

When the gothic style was revived, primarily in Europe, the people rose again.
Hammer Films in England staged periodic
revolts against the tyrannical undead in *Scars
of Dracula* (1970), *Lust for a Vampire* (1971),
Twins of Evil (1971) and *Vampire Circus*
(1972). Italian mobs burn Barbara **Steele** in
La maschera del demonio (*The Mask of Satan*,
1960) and incinerate Sara Bey in *La figlia di
Frankenstein* (*Lady Frankenstein*, 1971). And
when Burke and Hare are mobbed in John
Gilling's *The Flesh and the Fiends* (1959),

some of the crowd had originally been
filmed for David Lean's masterful *Oliver Twist*
(1948). A vampire of today is shown pursued by peasants via flashback in *Martin*
(1977), while offscreen sound effects suffice
for a similar scene in *Tale of a Vampire*
(1992), but the most significant modern
mobs appear in George **Romero**'s *Night of
the Living Dead* (1968) and *Dawn of the Dead*
(1979): gun-toting rednecks gleefully shooting everything in sight. LD

Peckinpah, Sam (1925–84)

American director, writer. Peckinpah started
as assistant, dialogue director and actor for
Don Siegel's ***Invasion of the Body Snatchers***

Sam Peckinpah, on the set of *Cross of Iron*

(1956) before establishing himself in television and feature films as a uniquely talented and visceral writer and director. His thematic obsession with **violence** cultimated in his masterpiece, *The Wild Bunch* (1969), an uncompromising portrait of the end of an era (and a genre) that marked a new threshold of screen **blood**shed, forever marking 'Bloody Sam' as America's most apocalyptic auteur. **Westerns** and action thrillers remained Peckinpah's forte, but two of his better features may be read as horror.

Straw Dogs (1971) melds the American Western with the British horror film, transplanting Fort Apache and the besieged household of *Night of the Living Dead* (1968) to the Cornish countryside, where vengeful, drunken villagers assault timid mathematician Dustin Hoffman, who ultimately defends home and hearth with devastating success. *Bring Me the Head of Alfredo Garcia* (1973) details a more personal apocalypse amid the ominous Mexican landscape of B. Traven and Malcolm Lowry. Peckinpah's only genuine gothic, *Alfredo Garcia* echoes his first feature, *The Deadly Companions* (1961), in which a loner redeems himself by transporting a body across hostile terrain, as Warren Oates's embittered quest for riches and redemption isolates with Garcia's fly-blown **head**, madness and death.

Peckinpah collaborated with Ray **Bradbury** in the early 70s in an effort to adapt *Something Wicked This Way Comes* (1963); alas, his only overt flirtation with the *fantastique* was doomed to limbo along with his many other unrealised projects. SB/DW

The Visitor (a)/1978

David Weddle, *'If They Move . . . Kill 'Em!': The Life and Times of Sam Peckinpah* (1994)

Perkins, Anthony (1932–92)

American actor, typecast as the homicidal Norman Bates of **Hitchcock**'s *Psycho* (1960) and its derivative sequels (one of which he directed). Capable of subtlety (as an innocent in *Pretty Poison*, 1968) and overripe dementia (as **Jekyll** and **Jack the Ripper** in *Edge of Sanity*, 1988). SJ

The Trial/1962 * *The Fool Killer*/1964 * *Psycho II*/1983 * *Crimes of Passion*/1984 * *Psycho III* (+d)/1986 * *Lucky Stiff* (d)/1988

TV: *How Awful About Allan*/1970 * *The Horror Show*/1979 * *The Sins of Dorian Gray*/1982 *

Anthony Perkins, *Crimes of Passion*

Daughter of Darkness/1989 * *I'm Dangerous Tonight*/1990 * *Ghost Writer*/1990–91 * *Psycho IV: The Beginning*/1991 * *A Demon in My View*/1992

The Phantom of the Opera

Le fantôme de l'Opéra, published in Paris 1911, is a mixture of fairytale (Beauty and the Beast), locked room mystery, haunted house story, theatrical superstition and paranoia about sitting in the stalls beneath the huge crystal chandeliers which had become a feature of mid- to late-nineteenth-century grand opera houses. In 1896, one of the counterweights holding up the chandelier in Charles Garnier's Paris Opéra had actually dropped on to the audience below.

Author Gaston **Leroux** was a qualified lawyer: the book is presented, like **Frankenstein** (1818) and **Dracula** (1897), as a series of documents – in this case 'ransacked from the archives of the National Academy of Music'. He was also an investigative journalist: he claimed the story originated in the testimony of a mysterious Persian who had actually met 'the Phantom' some thirty years before and the news story of some workmen unearthing a skeleton in the cellars of the Opéra. Leroux had studied Garnier's architectural plans and knew of the Opéra's labyrinth of tunnels, lakes and vaulted chambers, which – while still under construction – had been used as a political prison during the 1871 Commune.

Erik the Phantom is a master architect (son of a famous mason) who has designed a series of secret passageways, trapdoors and trick mirrors while the Opéra was being built. Erik is also known as 'the Angel of Music', and he wants singer Christine Daaé

RIGHT Lon Chaney, *The Phantom of the Opera* (1925)

244

Lon Chaney, *The Phantom of the Opera* (1925)

to be his protégée so she can create the female lead in his unperformed opera *Don Juan Triumphant*. He is born with a horrifying deformity (a face which has to be hidden by a **mask**, even in his cradle) and after spending his youth being exhibited in fairground freakshows is forced to use his great intellect – clandestinely – in mysterious ways. Leroux drops enough hints that Susan Kay was able to spin an entire (excellent) novel out of them, *Phantom* (1990). Less imaginatively, Nicholas Meyer's *The Canary Trainer* (1993) and Sam Siciliano's *The Angel of the Opera* (1994) confront **Sherlock Holmes** with the Phantom.

In most film versions, the Phantom is accidentally disfigured during a fight over the ownership of his composition. Instead of a crazed architect, he becomes escaped convict Lon **Chaney** (1925), shy violinist Claude **Rains** (1943), composer Herbert **Lom** (1962) or rock musician William **Finley**, who is unjustly imprisoned in Sing Sing and subsequently gets his face jammed in a disc-pressing machine (*The Phantom of the Paradise*, 1974). His motivation is revenge rather than disability. The key ingredients of the 1925 version, which came out of a meeting between Carl Laemmle and Leroux in Paris, are Chaney's seriously distorted face, the huge opera house set (upstairs designed by Charles D. **Hall**, downstairs by Ben Carré), a crowded masked ball in the Grand Foyer (where the Phantom appears as a heavily draped Red Death in a skull mask),

and a chase sequence at the end where Chaney revisits the sets for **The Hunchback of Notre Dame** (1923).

The 1943 version, a musical vehicle for Nelson Eddy and newcomer Susanna Foster (taking over from Jeanette MacDonald), has too much opera and not enough phantom: the opera house set is recycled, as is the music of Chopin and Tchaikovsky with the addition of saccharine lyrics. Terence **Fisher**'s **Hammer** film adds a dwarfish **minion** (school of Igor) – who does the dirty work for Lom's phantom and makes him seem even more sympathetic – and a scene where the composer finally gets to watch his protégée sing Joan of Arc and weeps through his mask. The less romantic *Phantom of the Paradise* reintroduces the **Faust** theme of the novel in the hard-nosed setting of the rock music industry – which paves the way for Andrew Lloyd Webber's 1986 **musical**, based partly on the 1925 film.

The most faithful adaptation is a 1967 feature-length TV cartoon, but there are further Phantoms from Leslie Nielsen ('The Phantom of What Opera?', *Night Gallery*, 1971), Conrad Phillips ('The Phantom', *Into the Labyrinth*, 1982), Maximilian Schell (1983), a statue (*Waxwork*, 1988), Robert **Englund** (1989) and Charles Dance (1990). Imitations include Lester Fletcher ('The Night of the Diva, *Wild Wild West*, 1969), Jack Cassidy (*The Phantom of Hollywood*, 1974), Joshua Sussmann (*Phantom of the Ritz*, 1988), Derek Rydall (*Phantom of the Mall: Eric's Revenge*, 1989) and Leslie Cheung (*The

Phantom Lover, 1996). The 'Duo-Vision' *Wicked, Wicked* (1973) reuses the entire organ score from the 1925 film and is thus also forced to borrow its plot structure. CF

The Philippines

The first Filipino horror movie was a gothic melodrama, *Tianak* (1926). Its success led to many similar productions, including *Ang Aswang* (1932), the first local sound movie, and *Dr. Kuba* (1933). Filmed cheaply in Tagalog, none of these pictures were distributed abroad, but after the success of *Terror is a Man* (1959), Filipino films found an overseas market. The film's two directors, Eddie **Romero** and Gerardo de **Leon**, became important figures. They co-directed *The Brides of Blood Island* (1965) and its sequel *The Mad Doctor of Blood Island* (1968). Romero, through his Hemisphere Films, directed US co-productions: *Beast of Blood* (1969), *Beast of the Yellow Night* (1970), *The Twilight People* (1971). De Leon made two interesting **vampire** films (*The Blood Drinkers*, 1966; *Creatures of Evil*, 1970). Romero also worked with Roger **Corman**'s New World on a series of women in prison exploiters (*Woman Hunt*, 1972; *Black Mama, White Mama*, 1974).

Many Filipino films are scattershot combinations of genres. *Men of Action Meet Women of Drakula* (1969) is a **wrestling**/sex/horror hybrid similar to the Mexican **Santo** series; *Raw Force* (1982) has kung fu-fighting **cannibal** monks. Snake films are another popular genre: *The Night of the Cobra Woman*

The Philppines: *Creatures of Evil*

Irving Pichel

(1972), *The Magic Curse* (1975), *Devil Woman* (1976). From the late 60s, 'bomba' films (violent sexploiters) began to dominate the market. Many (*Miss Leslie's Dolls*, 1972; *Kill Barbara with Panic*, 1973) have horror elements, a trend that continues with the later, more explicit, 'bold' movies such as *Silip* (1985). Comics are popular in the Philippines and provide the stories for many films, including *The Killing of Satan* (1979), *Zuma* (1985) and a long series featuring Mars Ravela's heroine, Darna. PT

Pichel, Irving (1891–1954)

American actor, director. A fine **minion** in *Murder by the Clock* (1931) and *Dracula's Daughter* (1936), Pichel has interesting credits as a director, mostly in collaboration. With Ernest B. **Schoedsack**, he made **The Most Dangerous Game** (1932), a compact masterpiece; with Lansing C. Holden, he guided Helen Gahagan through a lavish *She* (1935). On his own, he directed himself in *Before Dawn* (1933) and turned out *Destination Moon* (1950).

The Return of the Terror/1934 * *Topper Takes a Trip*/1938 * *Torture Ship*/1939

The Picture of Dorian Gray (1891)

Oscar **Wilde**'s novel is a deliciously decadent horror tale of a beautiful youth whose soul is captured on canvas by the **artist** Basil Hallward. Dorian retains beauty as he sinks into corruption, but sin makes monstrous his portrait. When, in despair, he stabs the painting, it is restored and he becomes a decrepit corpse. Though strangely moral, the

book allows Wilde to spout cynical epigrams in the person of Dorian's mentor, Sir Henry Wotton.

Some of the witty lines are lifted for the intertitles of *Dr. Jekyll and Mr. Hyde* (1920), but there are many faithful adaptations, most notably Albert **Lewin**'s 1945 film with Hurd Hatfield as Dorian, George **Sanders** as Sir Henry and Angela Lansbury as Dorian's first love-victim. Other versions are the Danish *Dorian Grays Portræt* (1910), with Wallace Reid (1913), with Harris Gordon (1915), the Russian *Portret Doriana Greja* (1915), with Henry Victor (1916), the

Hurd Hatfield, *The Picture of Dorian Gray* (1945)

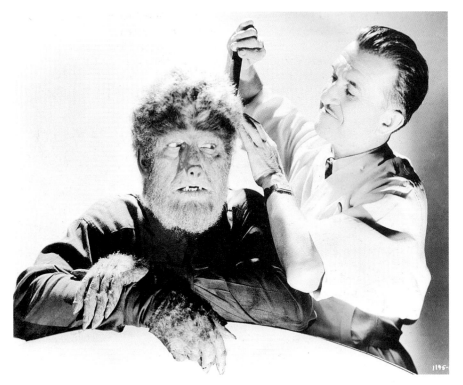

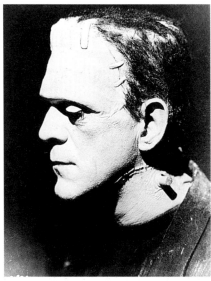

ABOVE Boris Karloff in Jack P. Pierce make-up, *Bride of Frankenstein*

LEFT Lon Chaney Jr, Jack P. Pierce

German *Das Bildnis Dorian Gray* (1916), the Hungarian *Az Élet Királya* (1916), an *Armchair Theatre* with John Fraser (1961), with Helmut Berger (*The Secret of Dorian Gray*, 1970), with Shane Briant (1973), on *Play of the Month* with Peter Firth (1976), Lina Romay as twin Dorianas for Jesus **Franco** (*Das Bildnis der Doriana Gray*, 1976), French (1977), the apt porno movies *Dorian Gay* (1981) and *Portrait of Dorian* (1992) and Belinda Bauer as another female Dorian in *The Sins of Dorian Gray* (1983).

Skits and variants, with unageing videotape or home movies, include *Phantom of the Paradise* (1975), *Take Off* (1978) and *Dinner With a Vampire* (1988). John Osborne adapted the book into a stage play and Amarantha Knight [Nancy Kilpatrick] added explicit sex in her renovelisation *The Darker Passions: The Picture of Dorian Gray* (1995).

Pierce, Jack (1889–1968)

American make-up artist. Universal's make-up man for twenty-two years, Pierce worked on the studio's horror classics of the 30s and '40s. Best known for creating the enduring image of the **Frankenstein** monster with the flat head and bolts through the neck, as portrayed by Boris **Karloff** in James **Whale**'s *Frankenstein* (1931), his contribution to **monster** culture cannot be underestimated. Also responsible for the look of *Dracula* (1930), *The Mummy* (1932), *Bride of Frankenstein* (1935) and *The Wolf Man* (1941). MS

*White Zombie/Murders in the Rue Morgue/*1932 * *The Black Cat/*1934 * *The WereWolf of London/Dracula's Daughter/The Raven/*1935 * *Son of Frankenstein/Tower of London/*1939 * *Black Friday/*1940 * *Man Made Monster/*1941 * *The Mummy's Tomb/The Ghost of Frankenstein/*1942 * *The Mummy's Ghost/Captive Wild Woman/Frankenstein Meets the Wolf Man/The Mad Ghoul/Calling Dr. Death/*1943 * *House of Frankenstein/The Climax/Jungle Captive/The Ghost Breakers/The Ghost Catchers/Dead Man's Eyes/*1944 * *House of Dracula/The Spider Woman Strikes Back/The Frozen Ghost/The Brute Man/The Cat Creeps/*1946 * *Master Minds/*1949 * *Teenage Monster/*1957 * *The Devil's Hand/*1958 * *Beyond the Time Barrier/*1960 * *Beauty and the Beast/Creation of the Humanoids/*1963

Pinhead * See: Atkins, Pete; Barker, Clive; Bradley, Doug; *Hellraiser*

Pirie, David (b. 1946)

British writer. Author of the seminal *A Heritage of Horror: The English Gothic Cinema, 1946–1972* (1973), Pirie also contributed to *Roger Corman: The Millenic Vision* (1970) and wrote *The Vampire Cinema* (1977). As a screenwriter, he did a first draft of *Dream Demon* (1987) and wrote the outstanding, creepy TV play *Rainy Day Women* (1984).

Pirro, Mark (b. 1956)

American director, writer, producer, actor. Auteur of near-home-made **camp** horrors, funnier in idea than execution. Typical is *Curse of the Queerwolf* (1987), in which a macho stud bitten on the bum by a gay **werewolf** turns **homosexual** under the full moon. His major influences are Forrest **Ackerman** and John **Waters**. A near-overground credit is the lame script of *My Mom's a Werewolf* (1989).

*A Polish Vampire in Burbank/*1983 * *Deathrow*

David Pirie

Gameshow/1987 * *Nudist Colony of the Dead*/ 1994

'The Pit and the Pendulum' (1843)

Edgar Allan **Poe**'s tale of the Spanish Inquisition is his strongest 'high concept' story, simply describing the protagonist's sufferings under **torture**. It was filmed in 1910 (*Le puits et le pendule*), 1913, 1961 (Roger **Corman**'s *Pit and the Pendulum*), 1962 (*The Pit*), 1983 (Jan **Švankmajer**'s *Kyvadlo, jáma a naděje*) and 1990 (by Stuart **Gordon**). Pendulum torture scenes feature in *The Raven* (1912), *The Avenging Conscience* (1914), *The Raven* (1935), *Drums of Fu Manchu* (1940), *Dr. Goldfoot and the Bikini Machine* (1965), *One Spy Too Many* (1966), *Die Schlangengrube und das Pendel* (1967), *An Evening of Edgar Allan Poe* (1971) and *The Uncanny* (1977). Švankmajer's first-person short, which stirs in Villiers de l'Isle Adam's 'Torture of Hope' (1883), is the most effective adaptation, but the Corman and Gordon films, with Inquisitors Vincent **Price** and Lance **Henriksen**, are the most lurid.

Pitt, Ingrid [Ingoushka Petrov] (b. 1944)

Polish actress, best remembered as Countess **Báthory** in *Countess Dracula* (1970). Her genre debut was the Spanish *El sonido prehistorico* (*Sound of Horror*, 1964) but she really made her mark as the sensuous **Carmilla** in **Hammer**'s steamy *The Vampire Lovers* (1970). Though she has a cameo in *The Wicker Man* (1974), the declining British film industry could not accommodate her predatory glamour and Pitt was consigned to the theatre and the *New Faces* judging panel. MA

The House That Dripped Blood/1970 * *El lobo*/ 1975 * *Underworld*/1985

TV: *Doctor Who*: 'The Time Monster'/1972; 'Warriors of the Deep'/1984 * *Thriller*: 'Where the Action Is'/1975 * *Artemis 81*/1981 * *The House*/1984

Plants

Fear of and fascination with killer plants stems from real-life plants that poison (ivies and nettles), strangle (convolvulus) and con-

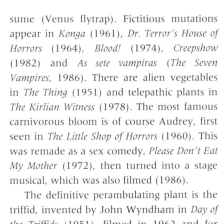

Ingrid Pitt, Kate O'Mara, *The Vampire Lovers*

sume (Venus flytrap). Fictitious mutations appear in *Konga* (1961), *Dr. Terror's House of Horrors* (1964), *Blood!* (1974), *Creepshow* (1982) and *As sete vampiras* (*The Seven Vampires*, 1986). There are alien vegetables in *The Thing* (1951) and telepathic plants in *The Kirlian Witness* (1978). The most famous carnivorous bloom is of course Audrey, first seen in *The Little Shop of Horrors* (1960). This was remade as a sex comedy, *Please Don't Eat My Mother* (1972), then turned into a stage musical, which was also filmed (1986).

The definitive perambulating plant is the triffid, invented by John Wyndham in *Day of the Triffids* (1951), filmed in 1962 and for television in 1981. But the cinema's favourite evil plant is none other than the tree, a reflection perhaps of childish fear of the dark wood, traceable further back to belief in tree demons. Trees become predators: *The Wizard of Oz* (1939), *From Hell It Came* (1957), *Womaneater* (1959), *The Navy vs. the Night Monsters* (1966), *Tales That Witness Madness* (1973), *Burnt Offerings* (1976), *Poltergeist* (1982), *The Evil Dead* (1983), *The Guardian* (1990). In *The Gardener* (1974), Joe Dallesandro turns into a tree. DM

Plastic Surgery * See: Disfigurement and Plastic Surgery

Playhouse: The Mind Beyond * See: The Mind Beyond

John Kerr, Vincent Price, *Pit and the Pendulum* (1961)

Pleasence, Donald (1919–95)

British actor. Having played the **Devil** in *The Greatest Story Ever Told* (1965), Pleasence could only, in terms of horrific character, go up or (depending on your religious proclivities) down. He chose, however, to go sideways, becoming a loose cannon on the decks of the genre, listed in the 80s by *Variety* as officially the busiest actor in the world. Nottinghamshire-born, he made a film debut in *The Beachcomber* (1954) and contributed bits to British films until reprising his stage success in Harold Pinter's *The Caretaker* (1963) gave him a career as a man with a dangerous cast of mind and an untrustworthy sort of face.

His role as the meekly murderous *Dr. Crippen* (1962) is an intriguing rehearsal for his unpredictability, as displayed by a run of bald bizarros including Hare (*The Flesh and the Fiends*, 1960), Blofeld (*You Only Live Twice*, 1967), a **vampire** (*Barry McKenzie Holds His Own*, 1975), the president (*Escape From New York*, 1981), a Scots entomologist (*Phenomena*, 1985) and another Devil (*Il violino che uccide/Paganini Horror*, 1988). In *From Beyond the Grave* (1973), he is partnered with daughter Angela as a fiercely moral angel disguised as a pavement match-seller; in *The Mutations* (1973), the story of twisted gene-therapy, he looks as bewildered as the audience.

He is on the side of the good in *The Devil's Men* (1977) as an Irish priest up against Peter **Cushing**'s coven of devil-worshippers on a Greek island and does a remarkable turn as

Donald Pleasence

the impish London copper of *Death Line* (1972), but it took director John **Carpenter** to see his risky persona as a counterbalance to the carefully weighted thrills of ***Halloween*** (1978), casting him as the psychiatrist, Sam Loomis. There was a brief spurt of heroic blood-letting as Dr Seward in *Dracula* (1979), but it added little to the valuation of a devious and unattractive typecasting which came not only from *The Caretaker*, but from the perverse, downcast husband in Roman **Polanski**'s *Cul-de-Sac* (1966). Polanski said: 'He was a tricky actor to work with, but he had an aura about him which was unmistakably his. I was privileged.' After all, it isn't everyone who can work with the Devil. TH

*Circus of Horrors/The Hands of Orlac/1960 * What a Carve Up!/1961 * Eye of the Devil/1967 * The Pied Piper/1972 * Tales That Witness Madness/I Don't Want to Be Born/1973 * The Uncanny/1977 * Out of the Darkness/1979 * The Monster Club/Halloween II/1981 * Alone in the Dark/The Devonsville Terror/1982 * Terror in the Aisles/1984 * Frankenstein's Great Aunt Tillie/Sotto il vestito niente [Nothing Underneath]/1986 * Spettri [Specters]/Prince of Darkness/Animali metropolitani/1987 * Un delitto poco comune [Phantom of Death]/ Nosferatu a Venezia [Vampire in Venice]/ Halloween 4: The Return of Michael Myers/1988 * Halloween 5/Ten Little Indians/Buried Alive/ The House of Usher/1989 * Shadows and Fog/ 1992 * Halloween: The Curse of Michael Myers/ Fotogrammi mortali [Fatal Frames]/1995*

TV: *One Step Beyond*: 'The Confession'/1961 * *The Twilight Zone*: 'The Changing of the

Plants: *Day of the Triffids*

Guard'/1962 * *The Outer Limits*/'The Man With the Power'/1963 * *Orson Welles' Great Mysteries*: 'Captain Rogers'/1973 * *Dr. Jekyll and Mr. Hyde*/1973 * *The Rivals of Sherlock Holmes*: 'The Horse of the Invisible'/1975 * *Playhouse: The Mind Beyond*: 'Meriel, The Ghost Girl'/1976 * *The Dark Secret of Harvest Home*/1978 * *The Final Eye*/1982 * *Ray Bradbury Theatre*: 'Punishment Without Crime'/1988

Edgar Allan Poe

Poe, Edgar Allan (1809–49)

American short-story writer, poet and critic. One of the first 'brand name' horror writers, his confrontational style, usually narrated by madman, **victim** or sensitive aesthete, helped define the genre and is still imitated. There is little supernatural in his work, and his rationalising of the apparently fantastic and impossible paved the way for the detective story (**'Murders in the Rue Morgue'**, 1841). His life was tragic: he was orphaned, disowned by his father, dismissed from the army for dereliction of duty, and watched his child bride die of tuberculosis. Given to bouts of depression, excessive drinking and suicide attempts, he disappeared on a three-day binge and was found dying in the street.

Most of his income was earned by editing periodicals and writing critical essays and much humorous material, but it was as a poet that he most wished to be recognised. Though a collection, *Tamerlane*, was pub-lished in 1827, he had to wait until **'The Raven'** (1845) before receiving any great recognition. His first short story, 'Metzengerstein' (1832) is full of the gothic trappings of the time, but he worked towards his own particular literary style, claiming 'terror is not of Germany, but the soul.' 'MS Found in a Bottle' (1833) won first prize in a short story competition; *Tales of the Grotesque and Arabesque*, his first collec-tion, was published in 1840. Among his most important works are 'Berenice' (1835), 'Ligeia' (1838), *The Narrative of Arthur Gordon Pym of Nantucket* (1838), 'William Wilson' (1839), **'The Fall of the House of Usher'** (1839), **'The Masque of the Red Death'** (1842), **'The Pit and the Pendulum'** (1843), **'The Tell-Tale Heart'** (1843), **'The Black Cat'** (1843), 'The Premature Burial' (1844), 'The Facts in the Case of M. Valdemar' (1845), 'The System of Dr. Tarr and Prof. Fether' (1845) and 'The Cask of Amontillado' (1846).

After death, his literary reputation was secured not in America but in France, where a collection translated by Baudelaire was an immense critical success. Word slowly fil-tered back to English-speaking countries and his importance was eventually realised. The now standard collection, *Tales of Mystery and Imagination* (1903), has never been out of print, and a *Complete Tales and Poems* was published in 1938. Incalculably influential on the fields of horror, mystery and s-f, Poe is evoked by many fictions: Julian Haw-thorne's 'My Adventure With Edgar Allan Poe' (1891), Manly Wade **Wellman**'s 'When It Was Moonlight' (1940), Robert **Bloch**'s 'The Man Who Collected Poe' (1951), Marc Olden's *Poe Must Die* (1978), David Madsen's *Black Plume* (1980), Peter Van Greenaway's *Edgar Allan Who?* (1981), Clive **Barker**'s 'The New Murders in the Rue Morgue' (1984), Robert **McCammon**'s *Usher's Passing* (1984), Timothy O'Neill's *Shades of Gray* (1987), Walter Jon Williams's 'No Spot of Ground' (1989), Rudy Rucker's *The Hollow Earth* (1990), William Hjortsberg's *Nevermore* (1995), Kim Newman's *The Bloody Red Baron* (1995), Stephen Marlowe's *The Lighthouse at the End of the World* (1995).

Film adaptations have appeared since a 'Murders in the Rue Morgue' which replaces detective Dupin with a famous successor *Sherlock Holmes in the Great Murder Mystery* (1908). The most familiar and popular Poe films remain a series from Roger **Corman**, mostly starring Vincent **Price**: *The Fall of the House of Usher* (1960), *Pit and the Pendulum* (1961), *Tales of Terror* (1962), *The Premature Burial* (1963), *Raven* (1963), *The Masque of the Red Death* (1964), *The Tomb of Ligeia* (1964). Even when only paying lip service to the original stories – *The Haunted Palace* (1963) takes its plot from H.P. **Lovecraft** – these capture the atmosphere of darkness, dread and complete absence of hope contained in Poe's work.

Among numberless other Poe-inspired film-makers: Henri Desfontaines (*Hop Frog*, 1910; *Le puits et le pendule*, 1910), Maurice Tourneur (*Le système du Docteur Gourdron et du Professeur Plume*, 1912), Alice Guy Blaché (*The Pit and the Pendulum*, 1913), D.W. Griffith (*The Avenging Conscience*, 1914), Richard **Oswald** (*Fünf unheimliche Geschichten*, 1919; remade 1931), Jean Epstein (*La chute de la Maison Usher*, 1929), Robert **Florey** (*Murders in the Rue Morgue*, 1932), Edgar G. **Ulmer** (*The Black Cat*, 1934), Dwayne Esper (*Maniac*, 1934), Louis **Friedlander** (*The Raven*, 1935), Jules Dassin (*The Tell-Tale Heart*, 1941), Curtis **Harrington** (*The Assignation*, 1952), William Cameron **Menzies** (*The Tell-Tale Heart*, 1954), Roy Del Ruth (*Phantom of the Rue Morgue*, 1954), W. Lee Wilder (*Manfish*, 1956), Federico **Fellini**, Roger **Vadim** and Louis Malle (*Histoires extraordinaires*, 1968), Howard Hawks (*El Dorado*, 1968), Gordon **Hessler** (*Murders in the Rue Morgue*, 1972), Juan Lopez Moctezuma (*Mansion de locura*/*House of Madness*, 1972), Lucio **Fulci** (*Il gatto nero*, 1980), Robert **Fuest** (*The Gold Bug*, 1980), Nicolas **Roeg** (*Eureka!*, 1981), Jan **Švank-majer** (*Zánik domu Usherů*/*The Fall of the House of Usher*, 1981; *Kyvadlo, jáma a naděje*/*The Pit, the Pendulum and Hope*, 1983), Jesús **Franco** (*El hundimento de la casa Usher*/*Revenge in the House of Usher*, 1983), Jeannot **Szwarc** (*Murders in the Rue Morgue*, 1986), Harry Allan **Towers** (*Masque of the Red Death*, 1989), George **Romero** and Dario **Argento** (*Due occhi diabolici*/*Two Evil Eyes*, 1990), Jim **Wynorski** (*The Haunting of Morella*, 1990), Stuart **Gordon** (*The Pit and the Pendulum*, 1990).

Poe appears as a character in the Abel Gance-scripted *Une vengeance d'Edgar Poe* (1912) and is played on screen by Henry B. Walthall (*The Raven*, 1915), Shepperd Strudwick (*The Loves of Edgar Allan Poe*, 1942), Joseph **Cotten** (*The Man With a Cloak*, 1951), Laurence Payne (*The Tell-Tale Heart*, 1960), Benito Stefanelli (*danza macabra*/*Castle of Blood*, 1963), Hedger Wallace ('The Man Who Collected Poe', *Torture Garden*, 1968), Bruce Karcher (*Gas-s-s-s*, 1970), Klaus

ABOVE Roman Polanski

Kinski (*Nella stretta morsa del ragno/Web of the Spider*, 1971), Marty Allen ('Quoth the Raven', **Night Gallery**, 1971), Robert Walker Jr (*The Spectre of Edgar Allan Poe*, 1972), Ben Kingsley ('The Need for Nightmare', *Omnibus*, 1974), John Cameron (*Lunatics: A Love Story*, 1991), Kenneth Cranham (*Tale of a Vampire*, 1992) and Clive Perrott (*The Black Cat*, 1993). MW

Marie Bonaparte, *Life and Work of Edgar Allan Poe* (1949); William Bittner, *Poe: A Biography* (1963); Kenneth Silverman, *Edgar A. Poe: Mournful and Never-Ending Remembrance* (1991)

Polanski, Roman [Raymond]
(b. 1933)

Expatriate French-born Polish director, writer, actor. Known for *Noz w wodzie* (*Knife in the Water*, 1962), *Cul-de-Sac* (1966), *Chinatown* (1974), *Tess* (1980) and *Death and the Maiden* (1995). His horror films express the paranoid fatalism of his work in its most intense form. *Repulsion* (1965) observes the mental degeneration of Carol (Catherine Deneuve), a repressed expatriate young woman left alone by her sister for a fortnight in a London flat. The directness with which the audience shares her hallucinations compensates for the detachment with which the character is scrutinised. As peripheral details prove to be seeds of Carol's terrors (for instance, the wall cracks open like a pavement seen earlier) the film renders her entire world liable to transformation.

The sense of apartment life as a source and reason for paranoia recurs in *Rosemary's*

Roman Polanski, Ferdy Mayne, *Dance of the Vampires*

Baby (1968), in which the pregnancy of Rosemary Woodhouse (Mia **Farrow**) becomes the psychological property of her neighbours, the unctuous Roman Castavet (Sidney Blackmer) and his wife Minnie – as portrayed by Ruth Gordon, both horribly funny and one of the cinema's enduring portraits of evil as banal. Like Ira **Levin**'s 1966 novel, which Polanski uses virtually as his script, the film makes the audience paranoid on Rosemary's behalf long before she realises anything is wrong. While Polanski's treatment of Satanism is as understated as **Lewton**'s in *The Seventh Victim* (1943), his third apartment nightmare, *Le locataire* (*The Tenant*, 1976) – *Repulsion* remade as a black **comedy** – lurches from horror to grotesque farce in the manner of, but more coherently

than, his **Hammer** parody *Dance of the Vampires* (1967), which was released cut and redubbed in America as *The Fearless Vampire Killers or Pardon Me But Your Teeth Are In My Neck*. In both films Polanski plays the terminally unlucky central character with a good deal of sympathy.

His most graphically violent and horrific film is *Macbeth* (1971), which ends with Donalbain riding to consult the witches in an image of the doomed recurrence which haunts Polanski's work. RC

The Magic Christian (a)/1969 * *Che?* [*What?*]/ 1973 * *Blood for Dracula* (a)/1974 * *Bitter Moon*/1992

Ivan Butler, *The Cinema of Roman Polanski* (1970); Barbara Leaming, *Roman Polanski*

(1982); Roman Polanski, *Roman* (1984); John Parker, *Polanski* (1993)

The Police

Not a happy lot, the legions of the law. On movie evidence, cop has become indistinguishable from quarry, equally armed, dangerous and self-destructive. Apart from the fetishistic trappings (helmets, shades, sirens, strobes, handcuffs) the lawman's main attraction is his outlaw status: at war with his own authority, he is avenger and victim in one. Capturing our sympathy, for example, behind the death-dealing exterior of *RoboCop* (1987; sequels 1990, 1992 and TV series 1994), the patrolman's mangled remains still dream of a 'real' life. On the strength of *RoboCop*, an archetypal armoured guardian on the brink of being beyond control, the Dirty Harry of the 70s is emulated and subverted in the likes of *Dead Heat* (1988), murdered officer reanimated to trace his killer, *Maniac Cop* (1988; sequels 1991, 1992), the TV series *Super Force* (1991), the inevitable *Cyborg Cop* (1993) and the definitive *Judge Dredd* (1995). Comparatively rare raincoated British plodders in horror include Alfred Marks in *Scream and Scream Again* (1969) and Donald **Pleasence** in *Death Line* (1972); more common are small-town Sheriffs, ineffectual (Charles Cyphers, **Halloween**, 1978), murderous (Farley Granger, *The Prowler*,

The Police: Hellcop (C.J. Graham), *Highway to Hell*

1981) or even demonic (Gary Cole, **American Gothic**, 1995–).

Derangement is common, from traffic-cop Sgt Bedlam in *Highway to Hell* (1991) to patrolman 666 in *Psycho Cop Returns* (1993) and from a squad of religious maniacs in *Street Asylum* (1991) to vigilante **werewolves** in *Full Eclipse* (1994). In the splendid *Scanner Cop* (1993; sequel 1994) townsfolk become killers at the sight of a uniform, while the mind-altering potency of police blues is assessed by *I Love a Man in Uniform* (1993). In *Magic Cop* (1990) the culprits are vampires, while in *Vampire Cop* (1990), *Midnight Kiss* (1993) and TV series **Forever Knight** (1995) the police are themselves the undead. And the restless futures of *Time Trax* (TV series, 1993), *Timecop* (1994), and the perennial *Trancers* (1984, 1990, 1992, 1993, 1994), along with the immeasurable consequences of virtual reality *(Virtuosity*, 1995), guarantee that copious and bizarre mayhem is yet to come. PS

Polidori, John (1795–1821)

British writer. Lord **Byron**'s physician and sidekick, he used the experience cattily in 'The Vampyre: A Tale' (*The New Monthly Magazine*, 1819), based partially on an 1818 Byron fragment. Polidori caricatures the poet as a blood-drinking rake, incidentally introducing the **vampire** to English letters. Originally thought to be *by* Byron, which must have irked and pleased its author in equal measure, 'The Vampyre' was adapted for the stage (Charles Nodier's *Le vampire*, 1820; James Plaché's *The Vampire*, 1820; Alexandre Dumas père's *Le vampire*, 1851) and as an opera (Heinrich Marschner's *Der Vampyr*, 1828).

The only film version is *The Vampire's Ghost* (1945), which shifts the action from Greece to Africa and replaces the Byronic Lord Ruthven with a pop-eyed bar-owner (John **Abbott**). The Marschner became a TV serial *The Vampyr: A Soap Opera* (1993), with Omar Ebrahim as Ruthven substitute Ripley. The tale was spun into a novel-length plagiarism, Berard's *Lord Ruthven ou les Vampires* (1820); Ruthven, undead at the end of the tale, reappears in Niel Straum's 'Vanishing Breed' (1970), Nancy Garden's *Prisoner of Vampires* (1984) and Kim Newman's *Anno Dracula* (1992) and *The Bloody Red Baron* (1995). Many **Draculas** are closer in character to Polidori's seducer than Bram **Stoker**'s brute.

Polidori's personal appearance in horror fiction is due to his presence at the Villa

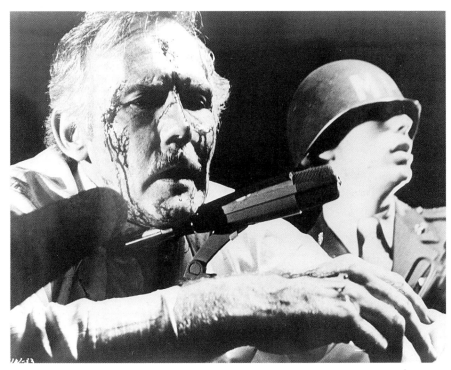

Politics: President Biff McGuire, *The Werewolf of Washington*

Diodati during the story contest which famously produced Mary **Shelley**'s *Frankenstein, or the Modern Prometheus* (1818). Though it is often, for neatness's sake, thought the great archetypes of modern horror come from that contest, Polidori's entry was not 'The Vampyre' but *Ernestus Berchtold, a Modern Oedipus* (1819). Nevertheless, Polidori appears in novels by Anne Edwards (*Haunted Summer*, 1972), Kathryn Ptacek (*In Silence Sealed*, 1988), Paul West (*Lord Byron's Doctor*, 1989), Tim Powers (*The Stress of Her Regard*, 1989) and Tom Holland (*The Vampyre*, 1995). His name is used for the James Mason character in *Frankenstein: The True Story* (1973) and he is portrayed by Tim Roth ('Frankenstein and Dracula', *The South Bank Show*, 1986), Timothy Spall (*Gothic*, 1987), Alex Winter (*Haunted Summer*, 1988) and José Luis Gómez (*Rowing with the Wind*, 1989).

Politics

Horror is popularly perceived as a reactionary form. Displaying disapproval by violent action, it routinely punishes the abnormality of both **monsters** and **victims**: illiberal torch-bearing **peasant** mobs pursue countless supernatural misfits; in murderthons like *Halloween* (1978), even promiscuity is considered an offence.

A propagandist tool in World War II America, horror possesses a misanthropy that even makes disturbing sense of **Lovecraft**'s fascism. Yet the turmoil that typifies the genre is also symptomatic of dissent. Famously intended to berate the Prussian war machine, *Das Cabinet des Dr. Caligari* (1919) points to an interest in issues of power that animates most horror myths: Count **Dracula** is only the most famous of a **vampire** group who abuse aristocratic status; the raging of a man against his negligent makers is the germ of the **Frankenstein** story. It is no coincidence that the macabre became a Hollywood staple during the Depression: crackling with factory-gauge machinery, James **Whale**'s *Frankenstein* (1931) is seminal and especially provocative, its hobo-like monster almost as untoward an underdog as *King Kong* (1933). Subsequent tragi-horror *The Wolf Man* (1941) stars Lon **Chaney Jr**, his previous high-point having been Lenny, the recessionary slow-wit of *Of Mice and Men* (1940).

Born from 50s s-f but free of the cold war metaphor that delimits much of the decade's fantasy, **Hammer**'s British horrors also benefit from a well-defined sense of class relations: developing the colonial themes of *The Mummy* (1958), John **Gilling**'s *The Plague of the Zombies* (1966) and *The Reptile* (1966) are important entries. Generated by English Empire building, their monsters pave the

way for *Matthew Hopkins Witchfinder General* (1968), which finds terror in the despotism of state arbiter Vincent **Price** rather than those he falsely accuses. With a Cromwell scene to stress the extent of its historical engagement, Michael **Reeves**'s film in turn enables such revisionist gothics as Gordon **Hessler**'s *The Oblong Box* (1969), Ken **Russell**'s *The Devils* (1971) and even Paul **Morrissey**'s **camp** politicisation *Blood for Dracula* (1973).

The US equivalent is *Night of the Living Dead* (1968): pitting not only man against his (**zombie**) fellows but also black against white, it depicts an apocalyptic civil struggle that correlates challengingly with the times. Undead allegories like *The Ωmega Man* (1971), hippy horrors like *I Drink Your Blood* (1972), **rape**-revengers like *I Spit on Your Grave* (1978) and numerous **black horror** perms all owe much to the agitatory drive of George **Romero**'s movie. Wes **Craven** has toyed with social critique since *Last House on the Left* (1972), going so far as to refer to the Kennedy assassination in the topography of his title *A Nightmare on Elm Street* (1985). Larry **Cohen** and David **Cronenberg** are among Craven's issue-led contemporaries; Dario **Argento**'s shockers place the bourgeois under unremitting siege.

A phenomenon of Generalissimo Franco's final years, the Spanish horror film has peculiar political opportunities. Paul **Naschy**, who originally intended Waldemar Daninsky to be an Iberian rather than Polish **werewolf**, claims a consistently anti-fascist intent to his genre entries. More convincingly applied are Jorge **Grau**'s Italian co-productions and Amando de **Ossorio**'s Blind Dead series. Vicente Aranda's *La novia ensangrentada* (*The Blood Spattered Bride*, 1972) is a **lesbian**-vampiric attack on Spanish machismo, Claudio Guerin Hill's *La campagna del infierno* (*The Bell of Hell*, 1973) passes corrosive judgement on Catholic familialism, and Narciso Ibañez Serrador's *¿Quién puede matar a un niño?* (*Would You Kill a Child?*, 1975) rends tourist images of the dictatorship. Communist Eloy de la Iglesia is responsible for a string of activist chillers: *El techo de cristal* (*The Glass Ceiling*, 1970), *La semana del asesino* (*The Cannibal Man*, 1972) and *Nadie oyó gritar* (1972) mire their dysfunctionals in the cities that were Franco's pride, while *Una gota de sangre para morir amando* (*Clockwork Terror*, 1973) makes complex use of *A Clockwork Orange* (1971), Stanley **Kubrick**'s momentous governmental irritant.

Poltergeist

Other politicos include Watergate **comedy** *The Werewolf of Washington* (1973), Reagan-era satires *The Texas Chainsaw Massacre, Part 2* (1986), *They Live* (1988) and *Society* (1989), Peter **Greenaway**'s anti-Thatcherite *The Cook the Thief his Wife & her Lover* (1989), HBO's McCarthyist skit *Witch Hunt* (1994) and the many Third World **zombie/cannibal** films brought on by Romero's parabolic *Dawn of the Dead* (1978). Siegfried Kracauer's post-war critique *From Caligari to Hitler: A Psychological History of German Film* (1947) has itself inspired *Jonathan* (1969), *The Keep* (1984) and Argento's putative version of *Frankenstein* (1818). Routinely politicised by **censorship**, horror films anyway practice a stark egalitarianism in their habit of reducing every player to dead meat. DP

Poltergeist (1982)

Steven **Spielberg**'s cinematic Ghost Train ride is a visually spectacular, sometimes cloyingly sentimental, spook-out about a possessed TV set. Rumoured to be more producer Spielberg than director Tobe **Hooper** (Spielberg took out damage-control trade ads complimenting Hooper), the fun frightener was a huge success. Sequels are Brian Gibson's pedestrian *Poltergeist II: The Other Side* (1986) and Gary **Sherman**'s ghastly *Poltergeist III* (1988). A supposed *Poltergeist* curse was blamed for teen actress Dominique Dunne's murder during the original film's release and the death of eleven-year-old actress Heather O'Rourke after the third's completion. Tangental to the trio is the TV series *Poltergeist: The Legacy* (1996–). AJ

Pornography

Though more concerned with the attractive surface of bodies than their messy insides, pornography is horror's twin by dint of obsession with flesh and oppositional involvement with **censorship**. As a post-40s genre, the **sex** film exerted a crucially libidinous influence on horror's new wave. While **Hitchcock** included *deshabillé* scenes in *Psycho* (1960) and naturist star Pamela Green posed for *Peeping Tom* (1960), David **Friedman** and H.G. **Lewis** invented **splatter** by substituting gore for the pulchritude of their earlier 'nudie cuties'; *Playboy* Playmate Connie Mason features in both *Blood Feast* (1963) and *Two Thousand Maniacs!* (1964).

Friedman and Lewis's *Scum of the Earth* (1963) takes a different route, conflating sex and **violence** to initiate the short-lived 'roughie' subgenre, which gets girls topless and then slaps them around. Examples are Sande Johnson's *The Beautiful, the Bloody and the Bare* (1964), R. Lee Frost's *The Defilers* (1965), Albert Zugsmith's *Psychopathia Sexualis* (1966) and William Rotsler's *Mantis in Lace* (1968). **Rape** horrors like *The Last House on the Left* (1972) and *I Spit on Your Grave* (1978) owe much to the trend. Roughie influences are found in a few overblown variants, involving fantastical or gothic elements: Russ Meyer's *Lorna* (1964), *Mud Honey* (1965) and *Motor Psycho* (1965), Koji Wakamatsu's *pinku eiga Okasareta Byakui* (*Violated Angels*, 1967), Barry Mahon's *Beast That Killed Women* (1965).

A European parallel offers pin-up girls in fetish underwear stalked through gothic settings by lecherous fiends: Fritz Böttger's *Ein Toter hing im Netz* (*The Horrors of Spider Island*, 1959), Piero Regnoli's *L'ultima preda del vampiro* (*Playgirls and the Vampire*, 1960), Massimo Pupillo's *Il boia scarlatto* (*Bloody Pit of Horror*, 1965). Considerably less charming are a run of unpleasant sex-and-death *gialli* which anerotically assail naked bodies with special effects violence: *Giallo a Venezia* (*Gore in Venice*, 1979), *Cannibal Ferox* (1981), *Lo squartatore di New York* (*The New York Ripper*, 1982) and pre-eminently *La casa sperduta nel parco* (*The House on the Edge of the Park*, 1981). In *Snuff* (1976), roughie veterans Michael and Roberta **Findlay** aspire to a pornographic confusion of *vérité* and fake.

Aristide **Massaccesi**'s *Emanuelle perché ... violenza alla donne?* (*Emanuelle in America*, 1976), and many other thrillers, feature snuff **film-making** as a plot device, mythologising a form of porno in which actual murder replaces actual sex as a titillating element. The censor's ultimate nightmare is depicted in Pedro Almodóvar's *Matador* (1986), where a serial killer masturbates while watching women murdered in Mario **Bava**'s *Sei donne per l'assassino* (*Blood and Black Lace*, 1964) and Jesús **Franco**'s *Die Säge des Todes* (*Bloody Moon*, 1981). The most mainstream surfacing of the roughie is Paul Verhoeven's *Basic Instinct* (1992), which opens with the bluntest imaginable sex-and-death zipless fuck/slasher murder.

Another strain of horror porno avoids the confrontational mingling of sex and violence but draws on the spooky **camp** of *Famous Monsters of Filmland* or Charles **Addams**. Among many topless gothics which mingle monsters, laughs and naked women are Bob Cresse's *House on Bare Mountain* (1962), Harry Novak's *Kiss Me Quick* (1964), Stephen C. Apostoloff's *Orgy of the Dead* (1965),

Emilio Vieyra's *La venganza del sexo* (*The Curious Dr. Humpp*, 1967) and William Edwards' *Dracula the Dirty Old Man* (1969). In the 70s, a serious (sometimes solemn) variant of the topless gothic came into being in the surreal softcore of Jean **Rollin**'s charades, **Hammer**'s 'Carmilla' series and Jesús Franco's monster orgies, which make explicit the sexualised undertones of almost all **vampire** movies. Rollin and Franco proceeded from soft to hardcore, often producing variant versions for different markets, and the vampire became a staple of mainstream porno.

Count Yorga, Vampire (1970) abandoned its original raincoat-oriented script to play as a straight horror, but suckers as thirsty for sex as blood appear in *Count Erotica, Vampire* (1971), Sean S. **Cunningham**'s *The Case of the Smiling Stiffs* (1973), the Jamie Gillis duo *Dracula Sucks* (1979) and *Dracula Exotica* (1981), *Trampire* (1987), *Out for Blood* (1990), *Bite* (1991), *Night Creatures* (1992), *Muffy the Vampire Layer* (1992), *Vampire's Kiss* (1993), *Interview With a Vamp* (1994) and *Intercourse With the Vampyre* (1994). The second most co-opted horror theme is **Jekyll and Hyde**, as evoked in his arty porno period by Walerian **Borowczyk**'s elegant *Dr. Jekyll et les femmes* (*The Blood of Dr. Jekyll*, 1981) and the considerably less interesting *Dr. Sexual and Mr. Hyde* (1971), *The Adult Version of Jekyll and Hide* (1971), *The Erotic Dr.*

Jekyll (1976), *The Lust Potion of Dr. F* (1986) and *Dr. Jeckel and Ms. Hide* (1990).

Hardcore pornography first achieved widespread currency with *Deep Throat* (1972), which collides documentary and fantasy via a circumspectly skittish plot involving Linda Lovelace's oesophageal clitoris. Director Gerard Damiano achieves more sophisticated, horror-inflected effects in *The Devil in Miss Jones* (1972), *Memories within Miss Aggie* (1973) and *The Story of Joanna* (1975). Miss Jones's vision of Hell as an orgasmless bunker is especially ambitious, though Damiano's 'straight' horror *Legacy of Satan* (1973) is a disappointment. For a while, it seemed as if hardcore would be of relevance not only to horror but to cinema in general, as the likes of Jim and Art Mitchell's *Beyond de Sade* (1973) and Jonas Middleton's *Through the Looking Glass* (1976) appeared alongside such porno-influenced miserabilism as *Last Tango in Paris* (1973), **The Exorcist** (1973), *Salò* (1975) and *Ai no Corrida* (1976).

The formularisation of hardcore has made crossover effects far rarer. John Leslie's *The Cat Woman* (1988) and *The Curse of the Cat Woman* (1990) ambitiously combine the self-criticism of Stephen Sayadian's nuclear anti-sex sex film *Cafe Flesh* (1982) with elements of Lewton's **Cat People** (1942). Other attempts to mix horror with hardcore include *Nightdreams* (1981), *Lust in the Fast*

Lane (1984), *The Other Side of Lianna* (1984), *Dream Lover* (1985), *The House of Strange Desires* (1985), *Phantom X* (1989), *Portrait of Dorian* (1992) and *The Witching Hour* (1992). Almost all of these are stymied by the limitations of the average porno performer, shaky production values and, most damagingly, the one-track expectations of their audiences.

The video porno industry of the 90s is wary of genuine mixes of sex and horror, preferring to update *Kiss Me Quick* in parodic monster rallies like *The Rocky Porno Video Show* (1986), *The Maddams Family* (1991) and *Frankenstein* (1994). A paradoxical wholesomeness, which excludes roughie elements even from vampire porno, means horror is only tolerated in joke terms: *Leena Meets Frankenstein* (1993) is even a remake of (**Abbott and Costello**) *Meet Frankenstein* (1948). Porno's relationship with the mainstream is demonstrated by the use of parody titles that add a dress-up-and-play skit level to the basic business of five or six fuck scenes in an hour and a half: *The Sperminator* (1984), *The Twilight Moan* (1986), *The Bitches of Westwood* (1987), *Whore of the Worlds* (1987), *Nightmare on Sex Street* (1988), *Beetlejism* (1991), *Erectnophobia* (1992), *Hannibal Lickter* (1992), *The Assford Wives* (1992), *Tailiens* (1992), *Jack the Stripper* (1992), *Juranal Park* (1993), *Tales From the Clit* (1993), *The XXX Files* (1995).

Porn stars to appear in horror include Marilyn Chambers (*Rabid*, 1977), Kelly Nichols (*The Toolbox Murders*, 1978), Brigitte Lahaie (*Fascination*, 1979), Sharon Mitchell (*Maniac*, 1980), Jamie Gillis (*Night of the Zombies*, 1981), Veronica Hart (*Bloodsucking Pharaohs in Pittsburgh*, 1990), Sylvia Kristel (*Dracula's Widow*, 1990) and Traci Lords (*Skinner*, 1992). DP

Linda Williams, *Hardcore* (1990); Cathal Tohill, Pete Tombs, *Immoral Tales: Sex and Horror Cinema in Europe 1956–1984* (1994)

Portraits * See: **Art**; *The Picture of Dorian Gray*

Possession

The idea that persons (or animals or inanimate objects) can be possessed by demons (or discarnate human spirits or space aliens) is ancient, famously demonstrated by Jesus's exorcism of the Gadarene swine. William Peter **Blatty**'s *The Exorcist* (1971; filmed 1973), based on the alleged possession and **exorcism** of thirteen-year-old Douglass Deen in 1949, popularised possession in literature and the cinema.

Possession: Linda Blair, Max Von Sydow, *The Exorcist*

Michael Powell

Frederick Ashton, Powell and Pressburger's *Tales of Hoffmann*

Shloimeh Ansky's play *The Dybbuk* (1921; filmed 1937, 1969) and less-remembered items like *The Haunted Palace* (1963), *Devil Doll* (1964), *The Mephisto Waltz* (1971), *Nothing But the Night* (1972), *The Possession of Joel Delaney* (1972) and *Burnt Offerings* (1976) offer different, less Catholic readings of the concept, but *Exorcist* imitations proliferated: *Abby* (1974), *Anticristo* (*The Tempter*, 1974), *Chi sei?* (*The Devil Within Her*, 1974), *Exorcismo* (*Exorcism*, 1974), *L'ossessa* (*The Sexorcist*, 1974), *Un urlo nelle tenebre* (*Naked Exorcism*, 1975), *The Possession* (1977), *I Don't Want to Be Born* (1977), *Jadu Tona* (1979).

Subsequent *Exorcist*-influenced films often mix in **reincarnation**: *Mausoleum* (1982), *The Evil Dead* (1982), *Demoni* (*Demons*, 1985), *Ninja III: The Domination* (1984), *Retribution* (1987), *Witchboard* (1987), *Rabid Grannies* (1989). The comic possibilities are addressed in *All of Me* (1983), *The Duxorcist* (1987) and *Repossessed* (1990). Curt **Siodmak**'s oft-filmed **Donovan's Brain** (1943) deals with possession by a disembodied **brain** and *Trancers* (1985) has modern-day folks possessed by time-travelling descendents, while possession by **aliens** is the theme of *Invaders From Mars* (1954), *Quatermass 2* (1958), *The Brain Eaters* (1959), *They Came From Beyond Space* (1967), *Night Slaves* (1970) and *The Puppet Masters* (1994).

Post, Don (1902–79)

American make-up artist, **mask**-maker. Though his credits are few and (**Invasion of the Body Snatchers**, 1956, apart) minor, Post influenced the field with commercially available monster masks, which still turn up in low-budget pictures eager to cut make-up costs. A Post 'William Shatner' mask is worn by Michael in **Halloween** (1978) and *Halloween III: Season of the Witch* (1983) not only uses Post masks but his factory. A killer in *Strange Behavior* (1981) wears a popular Post 'Tor **Johnson**' mask.

Space Master X-7/1958 * *The Haunted Palace*/*The Comedy of Terrors*/1963

Potter, Dennis (1934–94)

British writer. Active mainly in TV, Potter is a major *fantasiste*, passionately involved with the insanities of his country and of human relationships, committed to examination of popular culture and given to structural innovation. *Pennies From Heaven* (1978) and *The Singing Detective* (1986), Potter's master-pieces, use musical fantasy interludes to counterpoint the grimness of their protagonists' lives, which are haunted by the promise and the failure implicit in double-edged nostalgia. Potter touches on genre horror in the Satanic *Brimstone & Treacle* (1976) and the **Aldrich**ian *Midnight Movie* (1994), but more frequently stirs moments of horror and craziness into apparently mainstream fare.

Brimstone & Treacle/1982 * *DreamChild*/1984 * *Track 29*/1987 * *James and the Giant Peach* (u)/*Mesmer*/1996

TV: *A Beast With Two Backs*/1968 * *Angels Are So Few*/1970 * *Follow the Yellow Brick Road*/1972 * *Only Make Believe*/1973 * *Schmoedipus*/1974 * *Double Dare*/1976 * *Karaoke*/*Cold Lazarus*/1996

Powell, Michael (1905–90)

British director. Auteur-in-tandem with Emeric Pressburger of an unparalleled series of British masterpieces, Powell's most significant contribution to horror, *sans* Emeric, is *Peeping Tom* (1959), a still-shocking, groundbreaking psycho sleaze item conceived as a deliberate (and successful) insult to the film industry, British popular and high culture and a voyeuristic audience. Yet, mixed with its savagery and cruel dissection of the processes of watching and **film-making** is an almost wistful tenderness, suggesting Powell's enduring love for cinema itself.

An apprentice of Rex Ingram, Powell worked on *The Magician* (1926), and entered the industry with quota quickies, including the haunted-lighthouse melodrama *The Phantom Light* (1935), first showing distinction with *The Edge of the World* (1937) and as one of many directors on *The Thief of Bagdad* (1940). He first teamed with Pressburger on the wartime Conrad **Veidt** vehicles *The Spy in Black* (1939) and *Contraband* (1940), and, billed as 'The Archers', turned out a run of thoughtful, exciting, strangely magical films on war-related themes: *49th Parallel* (1941), *The Life and Death of Colonel Blimp* (1943), *I Know Where I'm Going!* (1945), *Ill Met By Moonlight* (1957).

The Archers find terror and wonder in contemporary Britain, touching on horror in the glue-man attacks of *A Canterbury Tale* (1944), the bureaucratic afterlife of *A Matter of Life and Death* (*Stairway to Heaven*, 1946), the erotic dementia of nun Kathleen Byron in *Black Narcissus* (1947) and the manifest drink demons of bomb disposal man David Farrar in *The Small Back Room* (1949). Even more fantastical are *The Red Shoes* (1948), a ballet fairytale with a dark ending, and the remarkable Offenbach adaptation *Tales of Hoffmann* (1951), in which Moira Shearer dances herself to death again.

The Night of the Party/1934 * *The Man Behind the Mask*/1936 * *The Sorcerer's Apprentice*/1955 * *Bluebeard's Castle*/1964

Ian Christie, *Powell, Pressburger and Others* (1978), *Arrows of Desire* (1985); Michael Powell, *A Life in Movies* (1986), *Million-Dollar Movie* (1992); Kevin Macdonald, *Emeric Pressburger: The Life and Death of a Screenwriter* (1994).

Powell, Robert (b. 1944)

British actor. A *Doomwatch* (1970) regular, departing the series in an atomic explosion, Powell's sensitivity won him the role of *Jesus of Nazareth* (1977) and suits offbeat characters, often psychic or psychotic.

Asylum/*The Asphyx*/1972 * *Tommy*/1975 * *Harlequin*/1980 * *The Survivor*/1981 * *The Mystery of Edwin Drood*/1993

TV: *Thriller*: 'Murder is a One-Act Play'/ 1972; 'The Death Policy'/1973 * *Zodiac*: 'Sting, Sting Scorpio'/1974 * *The Hunchback of Notre Dame*/1982 * *Frankenstein*/1984 * *Classic Ghost Stories*/1986

Power Tools

The frail human frame has been violated by everything from the sawmill blades of the silent serials to the wood-chipper of *Fargo* (1996), but portable power tools became lethal icons of the horror films of the 70s and 80s. The chainsaw replaced the knife as the phallic weapon of choice (*Last House on the Left*, 1972; *Motel Hell*, 1980; *The Evil Dead*, 1982), along with power drills (*Frightmare*, 1974; *The Incredible Torture Show*, 1977; *The Driller Killer*, 1979), jackhammers (*Rabid*, 1978), outboard motors (*The Deep*, 1977; *Zombi holocaust*, 1979), stationary woodshop tools (*The Wizard of Gore*, 1970; *Cutting Class*, 1989) and the imaginative airborne driller-spheres of the *Phantasm* series.

The Texas Chain Saw Massacre (1974) elevated power tools to box-office prominence, revving up three sequels to date and a hardware store inventory of horrors: *The Toolbox Murders* (1978), *Nail Gun Massacre* (1985), *Hollywood Chainsaw Hookers* (1988), *The Carpenter* (1989). A co-ed lopping off an outsized power drill bit in *Slumber Party Massacre* (1982) effectively emasculates the movement, reducing it to the stuff of satire, while Brian **De Palma** legitimises the handyman's arsenal in *Scarface* (1983) and *Body Double* (1984). By the 90s, the like of nailguns are *de rigueur* in mainstream thrillers (*Pacific Heights*, 1990; *The Color of Night*, 1994), and a chainsaw is worth a chuckle in *Pulp Fiction* (1994). SB/DW

Preiss, Wolfgang (b. 1910)

German actor. A Rudolf **Klein-Rogge** lookalike, Preiss took over the villainy (also billed as 'Lupo Prezzi' in disguise) in Fritz **Lang**'s *Die tausend Augen des Dr. Mabuse* (*The Thousand Eyes of Dr. Mabuse*, 1960) and a string of *krimi* sequels. His is a **mad scientist** transplanting hearts in *Arzt ohne Gewissen* (*Doctor Without a Conscience*, 1959) and exsanguinating girls in *Il mulino delle donne di pietra* (*Mill of the Stone Women*, 1960), and a **vampire** in *Der fluch der grünen augen* (*Cave of the Living Dead*, 1964). He cameos in Claude Chabrol's **Mabuse** tribute *Dr. M* (1989).

Im Stahlnetz des Dr. Mabuse [*The Return of Dr. Mabuse*]/*Die unsichtbaren Krallen des Dr. Mabuse* [*The Invisible Dr. Mabuse*]/1961 * *Das Testament des Dr. Mabuse* [*The Testament of Dr. Mabuse*]/1962 * *Scotland Yard jagt Dr. Mabuse*/*Der Henker von London*/1963 * *Die Todesstrahlen des Dr. Mabuse*/1964 * *The Boys From Brazil*/1978

Pressburger, Emeric (1902–88) * See: Powell, Michael

Price, Dennis [Dennistoun Franklyn John Rose-Price] (1915–73)

Urbane British actor. An inventive serial killer in Ealing's *Kind Hearts and Coronets* (1949), his career hit the skids in the 70s. SJ

A Place of One's Own/1944 * *Helter Skelter*/ 1949 * *What a Carve Up!*/1961 * *The Horror of it All*/1963 * *The Curse of Simba*/*The Earth Dies Screaming*/1964 * *Ten Little Indians*/1965 * *The Magic Christian*/*Venus in Furs*/*The Haunted House of Horror*/1969 * *Horror of Frankenstein*/ 1970 * *Twins of Evil*/1971 * *Go For a Take*/ *Tower of Evil*/*Dracula, prisonnier de*

Dennis Price, *Horror of Frankenstein*

ABOVE Vincent Price

BELOW Boris Karloff, Basil Rathbone, Vincent Price, *Tower of London* (1939)

Frankenstein [*Dracula, Prisoner of Franken-stein*]/*La maldición de Frankenstein* [*The Erotic Rites of Frankenstein*]/1972 * *Theatre of Blood/ Horror Hospital*/1973 * *Son of Dracula/* 1974

TV: *The Cases of Sherlock Holmes*: 'The Greek Interpreter'/1968 * *The Avengers*: 'Whoever Shot Poor George Oblique Stroke XR40'/ 1968

Price, Vincent (1911–93)

American actor. He pitched camp in charnel houses. One of the most confident-looking, and sounding, actors in the cinema of alarm and dismay, Price's illustrious beginnings – Missouri-born scion of the National Candy Company – created a self-possession which helped prop up a reputation as the doomed, yet quizzical, aristocrat of many horror movies. Educated at such benign institutions as Yale to relish art and cookery (about both of which he wrote books), he found the fancy and flavour of gore more to his dramatic taste.

After a medium-grade stage career – working with Orson **Welles**'s Mercury Theatre in the 30s and a 1941 Broadway run in *Angel Street*, the retitled **Gas Light** (1938) - he achieved a medium-grade career in Hollywood, which stretched neither his menace nor his ability. He took over from Claude **Rains** in *The Invisible Man Returns* (1940), but *Tower of London* (1939), with Boris **Karloff** and Basil **Rathbone**, gave some inkling he might be suited to the horrific. Karloff loved his rolling Rs and sibilant hisses: Price had a voice like decayed plush, and his slight sneer ensured horror was not long in enfolding his talent. He embraced it back in a spasm of mutual attraction.

After a run of **film noir** weaklings from *Laura* (1944) to *While the City Sleeps* (1956) and a few starring semi-psychos like *Dragon-wyck* (1946) and *Shock* (1946), he was cast as the wildly scarred proprietor of *House of Wax* (1953), reprising the act in the imitative **3-D** *The Mad Magician* (1954). In the nonsensical

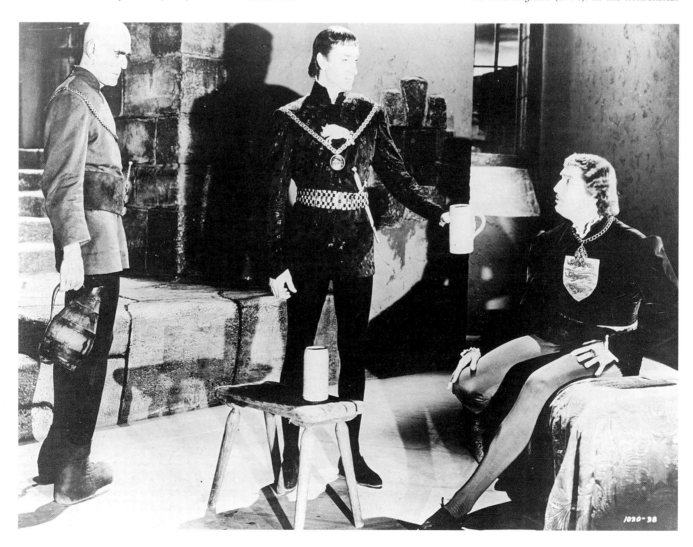

The Fly (1958), he hums with realistic bemusement, also continuing into its quickie sequel, *The Return of the Fly* (1959). He joined producer-director William **Castle** to give audiences cheap thrills at expensive prices with *The House on Haunted Hill* (1958) and *The Tingler* (1959). If they were a decline, then followed a slide into Albert Zugsmith's *Confessions of an Opium Eater* (1962) in which Price, as the seaman de Quincey (!), falls in with a Chinese tong. Gasped the *Monthly Film Bulletin*: 'It has to be seen to be believed – starved girls captive in cages, secret panels, sliding doors, sewer escape routes, opium dens and opium nightmares.' *Diary of a Madman* (1965), in which a killer explains his actions by saying he has been possessed by a devil, only compounds the offence done to Price's talent.

Alongside these mediocrities, Price moved up in horror's otherworld via schlockmeister Roger **Corman**, whose low-budget adaptations of Edgar Allan **Poe** are notably in accord with Poe's description of his work as 'bizarre and arabesque'. Not being best served by back-up actors proves a kind of advantage, spotlighting Price as he cuts to the case of Poe's obsessions, while Floyd Crosby's bloodshot camerawork waves the filigree in which he is usually enmeshed. The first of Corman's necrology is **The Fall of the House of Usher** (1960) in which Price is mightily phobic about being **buried alive** (along with **incest**, Poe's principal obsession), followed by **Pit and the Pendulum** (1961), *Tales of Terror* (1961), **The Raven** (1962) and *The Haunted Palace* (1963). *The Tomb of Ligeia* (1964) has moments of visual poetry as Price seeks in other creatures the spirit of his dead wife, but **The Masque of the Red Death** (1964) is an astonishingly rich mood-piece, with Price's plague-defying Italian nobleman hosting devil-worship orgies but finding slyboots Death has gate-crashed the proceedings.

Balderdash was to follow after Corman's departure into other realms of film-making: Price commented on the kind of movie he took on at that time as 'indescribable', contenting himself with the thought that *Dr. Goldfoot and the Bikini Machine* (1965), in which he is a mad scientist programming girl androids to lure wealthy men into his clutches, was really a spoof. That is not how it comes across. He was available as a TV master-villain, guesting on *The Man From U.N.C.L.E.* ('The Foxes and Hounds Affair', 1965) and as Egghead on *Batman* ('An Egg Grows in Gotham'/'The Yegg Foes in

Gotham', 1966). *The Oblong Box* (1969) has pervasive and persuasive shudders, while in the intriguingly fractured *Scream and Scream Again* (1969) he is yet another mad scientist creating superbeings.

However, *Matthew Hopkins Witchfinder General* (1968), directed by the tragically short-lived Michael **Reeves**, provides better uplift for a flagging career with the role of a Judge Jeffreys-like roving Inquisitor seeking out so-called witches to demand their execution. It is a seriously sadistic role to which Price gives life and meaning beyond the **cliché** contrivance of character. Black humour creeps into *The Abominable Dr. Phibes* (1971) and *Dr. Phibes Rises Again* (1973), made with the young Robert **Fuest**, whose sense of decoration is as illuminating as his narrative impetus; in the first, 'a disfigured musical genius' lays down a series of Pharaoh-curse revenges on the surgeons who failed to save his wife from death; the superior sequel has the same abominable medico risen from the dead and seeking an Egyptian elixir to keep him and his wife from going under. These twin black pearls were followed by the bloodier, but deeply satisfying, ruby of *Theatre of Blood* (1973), in which an actor visits Shakespearian deaths upon theatre critics: it gives enormous scope to Price's tongue-in-cheek bravura.

Tim **Burton** had him narrate *Vincent* (1983), a touching short tribute, then game him his final cameo in the fable *Edward Scissorhands* (1990). It was a triumph to go out on: the story of a boy with radical hands aligned well with Price's confession, 'I have never been realistic, but I hope that I have been stylish.' It was a style expressed in terms of a flourish. Sometimes, because of the exigencies of making a living, the flourish might seem an empty gesture. But at his commanding best, Vincent Price could turn that brandish into a magician's command for us to suspend disbelief. Like his friend Orson Welles, magic had always been a hobby with him. TH

Green Hell/The House of Seven Gables/1940 * *Meet Frankenstein* (u)/1948 * *The Story of Mankind*/1957 * *The Bat*/1959 * *Tower of London*/1962 * *Twice Told Tales/The Comedy of Terrors*/1963 * *The Last Man on Earth*/1964 * *City in the Sea*/1965 * *Dr. Goldfoot and the Bikini Machine*/1966 * *Das Haus der tausend Freuden* [*House of 1,000 Dolls*]/1967 * *Histoires extraordinaires* [narrator of export version, *Spirits of the Dead*]/1968 * *Cry of the Banshee*/ 1970 * *Madhouse*/1974 * *The Monster Club*/

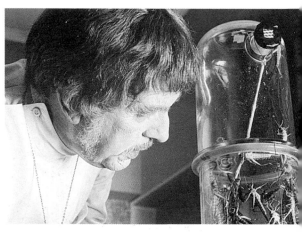

Vincent Price, *The Abminable Dr. Phibes*

1980 * *House of the Long Shadows*/1983 * *Blood Bath at the House of Death*/1984 * *Dracula: The Great Undead/The Sorcerer's Apprentice* (s)/ 1985 * *The Great Mouse Detective* (v)/*Escapes*/ 1986 * *From a Whisper to a Scream/America Screams*/1987 * *Dead Heat*/1988

TV: *Lights Out*: 'The Third Door'/1952 * *Playhouse 90*: 'Forbidden Area'/1956 * *Alfred Hitchcock Presents*: 'The Perfect Crime'/1957 * *Studio 57*: 'Secret Darkness'/1957 * *Matinee Theatre*: 'Angel Street'/1958 * *Mystery Show*: 'Run-Around'/1960 * *F Troop*: 'V is for Vampire'/1966 * *Voyage to the Bottom of the Sea*: 'The Deadly Dolls'/1967 * *Night Gallery*: 'The Class of '99'/1971; 'The Return of the Sorcerer'/1972 * *An Evening With Edgar Allan Poe*/1973 * *The Snoop Sisters*: 'Bad Day for Bluebeard'/1974 * *The Hilarious House of Frightenstein*/1974 * *The Bionic Woman*: 'Black Magic'/1976 * *CBS Library*: 'Once Upon a Midnight Scary'/1979 * *Faerie Tale Theatre*: 'The Boy Who Left Home to Find Out About the Shivers'/1981 * *Ruddigore/The 13 Ghosts of Scooby-Doo* (v)/1985 * *Blacke's Magic*: 'Wax Poetic'/1986

James Robert Parish, Steven Whitney, *Vincent Price Unmasked* (1974); Lucy Chase Williams, *The Complete Films of Vincent Price* (1996).

Prine, Andrew (b. 1936)

American actor. A specialist in 'hey man' paisley-shirt parts, Prine has fun with the title role of *Simon, King of Witches* (1971), which he followed up by playing hero in *La tumba de la isla maldita* (*Hannah, Queen of the Vampires*, 1972). He is a degenerate in *Barn of the Naked Dead* (1973), *The Centerfold Girls* (1974) and *Mind Over Murder* (1979).

The Town That Dreaded Sundown/Grizzly/1976 * *The Evil/1978* * *Amityville II: The Possession/1982* * *They're Playing With Fire/1984* * *Serial Killer/1995*

TV: *One Step Beyond*: 'The Peter Hurkos Story'/1960 * *Alfred Hitchcock Presents*: 'The Faith of Aaron Menefee' * *The Alfred Hitchcock Hour*: 'The McGregor Affair'/1964 * *Kolchak: The Night Stalker*: 'Demon in Lace'/1975 * *Darkroom*: 'Lost in Translation'/1982 * *Freddy's Nightmares*: 'The End of the World'/'Memory Overload'

Prisons

In the late 80s, Renny **Harlin**'s *Prison* (1987) was merely most effective of a run of prison-set supernatural horror movies: *Force of Darkness* (1986), *Slaughterhouse Rock* (1987),

David Prowse, *Horror of Frankenstein*

Terror on Alcatraz (1987), *Death Row Diner* (1988), *The Chair* (1987), *Death House* (1989). The theme was prefigured by Clive **Barker**'s stories 'Pig Blood Blues' (1984) and 'In the Flesh' (1985). Convicts use psychic powers to make mischief in *Das Testament des Dr. Mabuse* (1932), *Psychic Killer* (1975), *The Invisible Strangler* (1976) and 'I'll Be Watching You' (*Ghosts*, 1995), while *Tombs of the Undead* (1972) is a **zombie** movie set on a prison farm. Executions in the electric chair (which fail to 'take') feature in *The Walking Dead* (1936), *The Monster and the Girl* (1941), *Man-Made Monster* (1941) and *Shocker* (1989). Regular prison movies often verge on *grand guignol*: the most horrific are Jules Dassin's *Brute Force* (1948), with Hume Cronyn listening to Wagner as he uses his rubber hose, and *Ghosts . . . of the Civil Dead*

ABOVE Prostitution: Kathleen Turner, *Crimes of Passion*

(1988), with its convincing depiction of a system out of control. For concentration camp horror, see **Nazis**.

Prostitutes

Members of the oldest profession figure in horror mainly as **victims** in **stalk-and-slash**: the drabs slaughtered by **Jack the Ripper**, also the disposable starlets who get naked and die in *Night After Night After Night* (1970), *Don't Answer the Phone* (1979) and *Angel* (1984). A few working-girl monsters prey on customers: *Vampire Hookers* (1979), *I, Desire* (1982), *Cannibal Hookers* (1987), *Hollywood Chainsaw Hookers* (1987), *Beverly Hills Vamp* (1989), *Frankenhooker* (1989). *The Nesting* (1981), *Sex Dreams on Maple Street* (1985) and *Blood Sisters* (1986) are set in former brothels haunted by dead prostitutes. Call girls Nancy **Allen** and Kathleen Turner are resourceful heroines in *Dressed to Kill* (1980) and *Crimes of Passion* (1984).

Prowse, David (b. 1935)

British weightlifter, actor. Cast as the **Frankenstein** Monster in *Casino Royale* (1967), he recreated the role for **Hammer** in *Horror of Frankenstein* (1970) and *Frankenstein and the Monster from Hell* (1973) and on TV in 'The Need for Nightmare' (*Omnibus*,

1974). The body (but not the voice) of Darth Vader in the *Star Wars* films. SJ

*Vampire Circus/A Clockwork Orange/1971 * Blacksnake!/1973 * Jabberwocky/1977*

TV: *Doctor Who*: 'The Time Monster'/1972

Psychiatry

Cinema's contemporary, modern psychiatry is an important influence on the horror film. An impetus to **expressionism** before its persecution by Hitler as a Jewish science, it had a considerable effect on Hollywood's classier 40s entries, responsible for the guilt narrative of even *Devil Bat's Daughter* (1946). Deliriously expressed in *The Spiral Staircase* (1946), *Secret Beyond the Door . . .* (1947) and *El hombre sin rostro* (*The Man Without a Face*, 1950), it sowed the seeds for a whole new strain of realist shocker to boot.

Notwithstanding, horror psychiatrists are a consistently crummy lot. Lascivious obsessives in *Cat People* (1942) and *Screaming Mimi* (1958) and duplicitous killers in *Fingers at the Window* (1942) and *Un gatto nel cervello* (*Nightmare Concert,* 1991), they are literal monsters in *House of Dracula* (1945) and *Hellbound: Hellraiser II* (1988). *Das Cabinet des Dr. Caligari* (1919) targets institutional shrinks and the mesmerists that preceded them. *The Undead* (1956), *I Was a Teenage Werewolf* (1957), *Dressed to Kill* (1980) and *The Silence of the Lambs* (1991) detail couch abuses that include cannibalism, cross-dressing and fourth-dimensional devil worship.

Distrustful of the power relations involved in analysis and unwilling to have its fantasies interpreted away, horror at best presents psychiatrists as impotent: confounded by supernature in *Dracula's Daughter* (1936) and *Night of the Demon* (1957), by the mad in *Don't Look in the Basement* (1973) and *Frightmare* (1974), and by both in *Asylum* (1971) and **Halloween** (1978). **Asylum** films from *The Monster* (1925) through *Spellbound* (1948) to *Disturbed* (1990) feature mad shrinks. Like *Häxan* (1921) and *L'uccello dalle piume di cristallo* (*The Bird With the Crystal Plumage*, 1970), **Psycho** (1960) mockingly closes with a therapist's rationalisation of the scenes that have gone before. A rare effective shrink is the Crime Doctor (Warner Baxter), who analyses away apparent hauntings (*Shadows in the Night*, 1944), **vampires** (*Crime Doctor's Courage*, 1945) and homicidal undertakers (*Just Before Dawn*, 1946). DP

Psycho

Alfred **Hitchcock**'s 1960 black **comedy**, based on Robert **Bloch**'s 1959 novel (and loosely the exploits of 50s Wisconsin serial killer Ed **Gein**), is one of the most influential movies ever made and remains a potent shocker. A pivotal masterwork, and founder of a durable genre, every plot point (notably the groundbreaking early slaughter of 'heroine' Janet **Leigh**), striking imagery (the shower murder), camera angle (detective Martin Balsam's attack and stairway fall) and music cue (composed by Bernard Herrmann) has been copied, parodied or stolen by countless imitations. Anthony **Perkins** was typecast forever by his performance as cross-dressing maniac Norman Bates.

Self-confessed Hitch groupie Richard **Franklin** directed the belated sequel *Psycho II* (1983), a clever embroidering of the original theme. Perkins directed *Psycho III* (1986), reducing the Bates Motel saga to **Friday the 13th** schlock level. Mick Garris's formula *Psycho IV: The Beginning* (1990) has Henry Thomas as young Norman and Olivia Hussey as his mother, Norma. Bloch's own sequels, *Psycho II* (1982) and *Psycho House* (1990), are less noteworthy, as is a TV pilot, *Bates Motel* (1987). *Psycho* is the most analysed film in the genre. AJ

Stephen Rebello, *Alfred Hitchcock and the Making of Psycho* (1990); Janet Leigh, Christopher Nickens, *Psycho: Behind the Scenes of the Classic Thriller* (1995).

Psychopaths

In common parlance, a psychopath is a raving madman, bent on multiple murder and usually armed with something sharp. Actually a psychopath (now often called a sociopath) appears normal but is deficient in ethics and empathy. The bloodthirsty figure on view in so many horror films is properly termed a psychotic; the confusion may result from the title Robert **Bloch** chose for the novel that became Alfred **Hitchcock**'s classic shocker, *Psycho* (1960).

Once called lunatics, maniacs, thrill killers, or sex murderers, such characters are now rather dully described as **serial killers**, and are probably the most numerous menaces in the sinister cinema. Real psychos were comparatively rare in silent films; the protagonist of Hitchcock's **The Lodger** (1926) turns out not to be **Jack the Ripper** after all and the vaunted maniac in *The Cat and the Canary* (1927) is a sane man in disguise. That tricky tradition continues in early talkies like *Night of Terror* (1933) and is still on view in Mario **Bava**'s stylistically influential *giallo* *Sei donne per l'assassino* (*Blood and Black Lace*, 1964). On the other hand, madmen are sometimes to blame for killings attributed to the supernatural (*The Beast with Five Fingers*, 1946) or even animals (*The Leopard Man*, 1943).

Talkies of the black-and-white era range from Fritz **Lang**'s sordid *M* (1931) to Robert **Siodmak**'s stylised *The Spiral Staircase* (1946); such atmospheric films were considered more upscale than mere monster movies, and attracted different audiences. Especially common were stories about women with homicidal husbands, like *The Two Mrs. Carrolls* (1947) with Barbara Stanwyck and Humphrey Bogart, and many variations on **Gas Light** (1939). Noteworthy psychos of the period appear in **The Most Dangerous Game** (1932), *Murders in the Zoo* (1933), *Night Must Fall* (1937), *The Stranger on the Third Floor* (1940), *Bluebeard* (1944), *Hangover Square* (1945) and Charles **Laughton**'s brilliantly eccentric *The Night of the Hunter* (1955).

The films gradually grew more violent and film makers playfully accused themselves by finding killers among crime writers (*Grip of the Strangler*, 1958; *Horrors of the Black Museum*, 1959) or makeup artists (*How to Make a Monster*, 1958). In Michael **Powell**'s

Anthony Perkins, *Psycho*

Peeping Tom (1960), a cinematographer 'shoots' his victims while killing them; the film was reviled on release but is now acclaimed for its reflexive theme. *Psycho* was similarly savaged by critics but won huge audiences with a setpiece that conjured up complex emotions by presenting an unprecedentedly unclad leading lady (Janet **Leigh**) stabbed to death in a style strongly suggesting sexual intercourse. Box-office returns inspired a flood of imitators, devoid of similar resonance but burdened with increasingly improbable twist endings: *Homicidal* (1961), *Paranoiac* (1963), *Maniac* (1963), Francis **Coppola**'s *Dementia 13* (1963), *Nightmare* (1963), *Strait-Jacket* (1964), *Hysteria* (1965) and *The Psychopath* (1966).

The level of **violence** is increased, in colour, by crude films like Herschell Gordon **Lewis**' *Blood Feast* (1963) and Wes **Craven**'s *The Last House on the Left* (1972), while finer moments are provided by Patrick O'Neal's barnstorming performance in *Chamber of Horrors* (1966), Peter Bogdanovich's meditation on genre in *Targets* (1968) and Hitchcock's simultaneously witty and distressing *Frenzy* (1972). Meanwhile, Dario **Argento** became a master of the subgenre with a string of visually dazzling exercises including *L'ucello dalle piume di cristallo* (*The Bird with the Crystal Plumage*, 1970), *Profondo rosso* (*Deep Red*, 1976) and *Opera* (1987).

Tobe **Hooper**'s *The Texas Chain Saw Massacre* (1974), less bloody than expected, anticipated a trend by pitting teens against a brutal and unstoppable psycho; the breakthrough came with John Carpenter's *Halloween* (1978), a stripped-down scare machine. Immensely profitable, it was followed by Sean **Cunningham**'s *Friday the 13th* (1980), enlivened by the bloody pyrotechnics of make-up man Tom **Savini**. Cheap imitations came in unprecedented numbers even for the trend-following horror field: just the idea of special days, for instance, produced such titles as *Mother's Day* (1980), *Prom Night* (1980), *Bloody Birthday* (1980), *Graduation Day* (1981), *Hell Night* (1981), *Happy Birthday to Me* (1981), *My Bloody Valentine* (1981), *New Year's Evil* (1981), *April Fool's Day* (1986) and *Pledge Night* (1988). There are five sequels to *Halloween*, seven to *Friday the 13th* and five to Wes **Craven**'s latecomer *A Nightmare on Elm Street* (1984), plus over a hundred less famous films cut from the same cloth.

Critics grew ever more indignant, as films like *Maniac* (1980), *Nightmare* (1981), *Lo squartatore di New York* (*The New York Ripper*, 1982), and *Mil gritos tiene la noche* (*Pieces*, 1983) grew ever more gruesome. In less than a decade, the public interest in inexpensive horror films seemed all but exhausted. Yet psychos endured, as the bloody murders of modest quickies inspired expensive hits like Brian **De Palma**'s *Dressed to Kill* (1980), David **Lynch**'s *Blue Velvet* (1986) and Jonathan **Demme**'s Oscar winner *The Silence of the Lambs* (1991). In a misguided attempt to placate feminists, Hollywood unleashed female psychos in *Fatal Attraction* (1987), *Basic Instinct* (1992), *The Hand That Rocks the Cradle* (1992) and *Single White Female* (1992). Complaints continued but money was made and Kathy Bates got an Academy Award for *Misery* (1990). The occasional low-budget gem is still a possibility, as shown by John **McNaughton**'s convincing *Henry: Portrait of a Serial Killer* (1986), but for most fans of what was now called **stalk-and-slash**, there was only the awful warning provided by entertainments like *He Knows You're Alone* (1980), *Anguish* (1987) and *Popcorn* (1991), in which people are butchered while watching horror movies. LD

Pulp Magazines

Periodicals printed on cheap, brittle pulpwood paper began to appear in the USA at the end of the 19th century. Offering at least 120 large pages of fiction and ads, wrapped in colour covers and selling for a dime, they grew steadily in popularity, reaching a golden age between world wars. *Argosy*, *All Story* and *Adventure*, the original pulps, adopted a something-for-everyone policy, mingling **Western**, romance, adventure and detective, with the occasional **fantasy** or horror story thrown in for variety. Single category titles began around the time of World War I. *Detective Story* and *Western Story* were rapidly followed by *The Thrill Book*, a first attempt at a horror pulp, which advised potential contributors it was looking for 'strange, bizarre, occult, mysterious tales . . . the unusual, the harrowing', but soon expanded its interests to include mainstream **jungle** and adventure yarns. Rumours that editor Harvey Hersey and his mother wrote much of the magazine under pseudonyms cannot have helped, and it folded after sixteen issues.

Weird Tales began in 1923: though plagued continually with financial woes and frequently unable to pay writers until months after publication, this Chicago-based magazine lasted for almost thirty years. Mixing reprints and new stories, *WT* offered **Doyle** and **Poe** shoulder to shoulder with E. Hoffman Price, Frank Owen, C.M. Eddy and other masters of the pulp form. H.P. **Lovecraft** and Clark Ashton **Smith** found the little reputation they enjoyed in their lifetimes there, while the magazine encouraged such fantasists as Robert **Bloch**, Ray **Bradbury**, Fritz **Leiber** and Theodore Sturgeon. The most popular and typical *WT* writer was, however, Seabury Quinn, with lurid stories of occult detective Jules de Grandin. With the 30s and the interest in horror films came serious competition.

Popular Publications brought out a slew of similar-minded titles: *Dime Mystery*, *Terror Tales*, *Horror Stories*. Other publishers tried *Uncanny Tales*, *Mystery Tales*, *Thrilling Mystery* and *Ace Mystery*. Though *Weird Tales* was famous for titillating covers (many by Margaret Brundage), the contents were almost invariably 'wholesome'. Not so the competition, who spiced up stories with what was, for the time, kinky nastiness: decades before **Troma**, pulps offered impossible-to-parody titles like 'Lash of the Living Dead', 'Goddess of the Half-World Brood' and 'The Pain Master's Bride'. Wartime paper shortages hurt the field, but competition from paperbacks and TV, along with a campaign to have pulps banned, killed them off. *WT* soldiered on alone for a time, finally ceasing publication in 1954. For good or bad, the influence of *WT* and the other pulps in developing and popularising horror as a separate category, was immense.

Many pulp writers, then just establishing themselves, have become among the most famous names in the field. *Weird Tales* itself, king of the horror pulps, has been revived to some of its former glory. Though *Pulp Fiction* (1994) repopularised the term, few horror films attempt the particular blend of the lurid and the naive that characterised 'the tale of weird menace'. The odd B (*The Walking Dead*, 1936; *Bowery at Midnight*, 1942) delivers a pulp feel echoed by such tongue-in-cheek items as *The Dead Don't Die* (1974) and *Re-Animator* (1985). MW

Peter Haining, *Terror!* (1976); Lee Server, *Danger is My Business* (1993)

Q

Quarry, Robert (b. 1923)

American actor who made his debut in a bit cut from *Shadow of a Doubt* (1943). After a fluke hit in and as *Count Yorga, Vampire* (1970), Samuel **Arkoff** put him under contract and groomed him to be AIP's new hor-

The Quay Brothers

ror star. A serious car accident kept him off screen for nearly a decade. Now trapped in low-budget trash from Fred Olen **Ray** or Jim **Wynorski**. SJ

The Return of Count Yorga/1971 * *Dr. Phibes Rises Again*/*The Deathmaster*/1972 * *Sugar Hill*/*Madhouse*/1974 * *Moon in Scorpio*/*The Phantom Empire*/1987 * *Beverly Hills Vamp*/1988 * *Alienator*/*Sexbomb*/1989 * *Spirits*/1990 * *Evil Spirits*/1991 * *Teenage Exorcist*/1994

Quasimodo * See: **Chaney, Lon**; *The Hunchback of Notre Dame*; **Laughton, Charles**

Quatermass, Professor Bernard * See: **Keir, Andrew**; **Kneale, Nigel**; **Morell, André**

Quay, The Brothers [Stephen, Timothy] (b. 1947)
American-born animators, based in Britain. Adept at creating stifling hermetic worlds populated by figures as morose as they are grotesque, Brothers Quay **animations** are final refuges for the morbid detritus of modernism: surrealism (particularly Ernst) and **expressionism** (**Caligarism**) jostle with the spectres of Beckett and **Kafka**. Out of this terminal region of ossified psychic malaise emerge sorrowful, absurdly moving figures, haunted by life but possessing only motion.

After paying homage (with co-director Keith Griffiths) to the disturbing Czech animator Jan **Švankmajer** (*The Cabinet of Jan Švankmajer: Prague's Alchemist of Film*, 1984),

the Quays stepped into a nursery-rhyme world of swift, compelling horror with the very weird *Little Songs of the Chief Officer of Hunar Louse, or This Unnameable Little Broom (Being Largely a Disguised Reduction of the Epic of Gilgamesh) Tableau II* (1985). Their most accomplished work is *Street of Crocodiles* (1986): plagued with existential dread, it depicts a shabby puppet of a man exploring a desolate yet teeming microworld, where rusty screws unscrew themselves from miniature factory floors and hollow-headed dolls examine slices of glistening red meat or

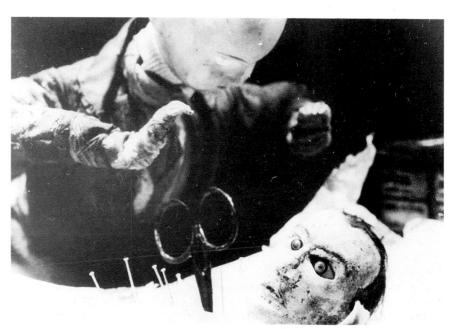

The Quay Brothers' *Street of Crocodiles*

apply forensic attention to hairy spiders. This accumulated arcana, with its tattered figurines and animistic automata, is brilliantly photographed via constantly moving focal planes and precision camera tracking. Response to their work is almost doomed to the adjectival: like David **Lynch**'s *Eraserhead* (1977), their best films make a monkey of psychoanalytic interpretation.

Sadly, *The Institute Benjamenta: or This Dream People Call Human Life* (1995), their first foray into feature-length live-action is simultaneously masochistic and peevish in its evocation of powerlessness, overstretching the fine detail of the animated work into repetitive longueur. ST

The Falls (s)/1980 * *Ein Brudermord* (s)/*The Eternal Day of Michel De Ghelderode, 1898–1962* (s)/1981 * *Igor – The Paris Years Chez Pleyel* (s)/ *Leos Janácek: Intimate Excursions* (s)/1983 * *Rehearsals for Extinct Anatomies*/1988 * *The Comb*/1990

'The Queen of Spades' (1834)
Alexander Pushkin's 'Pikovaia Dama' is one of the most anthologised **ghost stories**: a German officer in St Petersburg seeks the secret of the three cards that will ensure a winning streak at faro and pesters an ancient countess to death only to learn the secret from her spectre and suffer madness and punishment when he tries to make his fortune with the trick. Tchaikovsky turned the tale into an 1890 opera, and it is often done on stage, screen and radio. Thorold Dickin-

son's *The Queen of Spades* (1949), with Anton Walbrook and Edith Evans, is a faithful, impressive version. Other adaptations (*Pikovaia Dama, Pique dame, La dama di picche*) came in 1910 (German and Russian), 1913 (Italian and American), 1916 (Russian), 1921 (Hungarian), 1927 (French, German), 1937 (French), 1954 (American short and an *Inner Sanctum*), 1960 (Russian, from the opera) and 1965 (French).

Quigley, Linnea (b. 1959)

American actress. Overexposed starlet: a nude punkette **zombie** in *Return of the Living Dead* (1985), more often cast as a perky blonde in the Goldie Hawn mold. Her breasts are in more bad films than the boom microphone.

Psycho From Texas/1974 * *Don't Go Near the Park*/*Stone Cold Dead*/1979 * *Graduation Day*/ *The Black Room*/1981 * *Fatal Games*/1982 * *Silent Night, Deadly Night*/1984 * *Silent Night, Deadly Night, Part 2* (footage from *Silent Night, Deadly Night*)/1986 * *Creepozoids*/*Sorority Babes in the Slime-Ball Bowl-a-Rama*/*Hollywood Chainsaw Hookers*/*Nightmare Sisters*/1987 * *A Nightmare on Elm Street IV: The Dream Master*/ *Night of the Demons*/1988 * *Witchtrap*/*Sexbomb*/ *Murder Weapon*/*Robot Ninja*/1989 * *Linnea Quigley's Horror Workout*/1990 * *The Guyver*/ *Freddy's Dead: The Final Nightmare*/*Scream Queen Hot Tub Party*/1991 * *Innocent Blood*/ *Blood Church*/*Blood Nasty*/1992 * *Pumpkinhead II: Blood Wings*/1994 * *Jack-O*/1995 * *Fotogrammi mortali* [*Fatal Frames*]/1996

TV: *The Burial of the Rats*/1995

R

Radcliffe, Ann (1764–1823)

British novelist. Horace Walpole's *The Castle of Otranto* (1764) is the first English **gothic novel**, but Mrs Radcliffe's sentimental romances popularised the form: *The Romance of the Forest* (1791), *The Mysteries of Udolpho* (1794), *The Italian; or: The Confession of the Black Penitents* (1797). She favours virginal heroines, foreign villains, historical settings, extensively described **castles** in exotic landscapes, and inevitably employs **rationalised supernatural** machinery: skeleton horsemen turn out to be banditti in disguise.

Radio

The 'Theatre of the Mind' established itself as a medium for horror in the 30s. Orson **Welles** and his Mercury Theatre of the Air's *The War of the Worlds* (1938), from H.G. **Wells**, is nominally science fiction, but the pseudo-documentary play went out on Halloween. The same players presented a *Dracula* (1938) which, though it didn't panic America, remains one of the best adaptations of the novel in any medium. *The Shadow* (1930–54) began as a mere announcer who introduced mystery stories; by 1937, he was a caped and macabre crime fighter voiced by the busy Welles. Ensuing series became more fantastic and horrific, not to say silly. *I Love a Mystery* (1939–52) was similar pulp, with two-fisted adventurers tackling weird menaces.

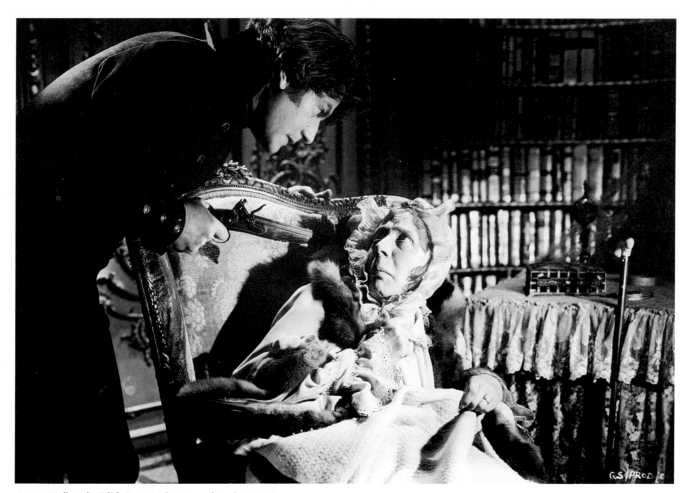

Anton Walbrook, Edith Evans, *The Queen of Spades* (1949)

Sam Raimi's *The Evil Dead*

effects and unabashed deployment of horror **clichés**. The **zombie** meltdowns, in particular, touch on hitherto unseen extremes of sizzling liquefaction.

Evil Dead II (1987) is virtually a remake, though Raimi plays more for **comedy** with a carefully choreographed riot of flying eyeballs and severed limbs. In a classic piece of gruesome slapstick, producer-star Bruce **Campbell**, reprising his role as 'Ash', is forced to hack off his own demon-possessed **hand** and imprison it beneath a copy of *A Farewell to Arms*. The ending is a radical departure: Ash and the demons are sucked through a vortex and dumped in the middle ages, setting for *Army of Darkness* (1992). The blend of horror and slapstick is not quite as seamless as before (the underbudgeted skeleton army, in particular, is ropey) but the novel setting and some ideas (Ash under assault from evil miniatures of himself or face-to-face with his own decaying **doppelgänger**) are inspired.

Outside this signature series, Raimi has directed the cartoonish *Crimewave* (1985),

Lights Out (1934–47), initially a fifteen-minute filler, expanded to a half-hour famous for bloodcurdling sound effects: the crunch of a broken neck, the splat of a victim hitting a sidewalk after a fall, the beat of a giant chicken heart crushing the world. *Inner Sanctum* (1941–52), another anthology of creepy stories, was popular enough to spin-off books and movies. It was foremost among a stream of similar mystery and supernatural shows which were repeated into the 60s, even heard in Europe on the American Forces Network: *The Witch's Tale* (1931–8), *The Hermit's Cave* (1940–43), *Suspense* (1942–62), *The Mysterious Traveller* (1943–52), *The Black Castle* (1943–4), *Stay Tuned for Terror* (1944–5, written by Robert **Bloch**), *Quiet Please* (1947–8), *Escape* (1950–53). *Lights Out*, *Inner Sanctum* and *Suspense* transferred, like such favourites as *Dragnet* and *Gunsmoke* though without their lasting success, to television.

Britain's *Appointment with Fear* (1943–55), created for the BBC by John Dickson Carr, made a star of its storyteller, the Man in Black (Valentine **Dyall**), who had a cinema outing in **Hammer**'s *The Man in Black* (1949). The studio retained Dyall for the radio-derived creepies *Dr. Morelle: The Case of*

the *Missing Heiress* (1949) and *Room to Let* (1950) and has periodically announced an as-yet unmade film version of Brian Hayles's radio play *Prince Dracula* (1972). In the 80s, the Man in Black (Edward de Souza) returned to the BBC to host *Fear on Four*. Less given to anthologies than American radio, British airwaves have supported adaptions of classic horrors, especially the **ghost stories** of Algernon **Blackwood** (who read his own work) and M.R. **James**. Authors who have specialised in radio horror include Americans Arch **Oboler** and Willis Cooper and Britons A.A. Fair and J.C.W. Brook. MW

Raimi, Sam (b. 1959)

American director, writer, actor. Raimi's feature debut is a triumph of DIY exploitation: the young writer-director screened a teaser trailer (*Within the Woods*) to an assortment of white-collar professionals he then persuaded to provide him with financial backing to finish the film. *The Evil Dead* (1982), in which five young people holed up for the weekend in an isolated cabin in Tennessee are systematically menaced and ultimately possessed by ancient Sumerian demons, is an **EC comic** come to life, courtesy of Raimi's gleeful use of **subjective camera**, gross-out **splatter**

Sam Raimi's *Evil Dead II*

the horror-superhero crossover *Darkman* (1990) and the **Western** *The Quick and the Dead* (1995), demonstrating quirky strengths but failing to establish a commercial identity. He has become a successful TV producer with *Hercules: The Legendary Journeys* (1994–) and **American Gothic** (1995–). AB

Thou Shalt Not Kill . . . Except (a)/1987 * *Maniac Cop* (a)/1988 * *The Dead Next Door* (p)/ *Intruder* (a)/1989 * *Maniac Cop 2* (a)/1990 * *Lunatics: A Love Story* (p)/1991 * *Innocent Blood* (a)/1992 * *Hard Target* (p)/1993 * *The Hudsucker Proxy* (w/a)/1994

TV: *Body Bags* (a)/1993 * *The Stand* (a)/1994 * *Darkman II: The Return of Durant* (p)/*Darkman III: Die, Darkman, Die* (p)/1995

Rains, Claude (1889–1967)

British actor who made his career in Hollywood, often as suave villains. Except for the last scene, only his voice is heard in his debut, *The Invisible Man* (1933). Despite starring in **The Wolf Man** (1941) and playing the **Phantom of the Opera** (1943), his horror appearances are inferior to other work. Wonderful for Michael **Curtiz** as Prince John in *The Adventures of Robin Hood* (1938), Inspector Renault of *Casablanca* (1944) and a sly murderer in *The Unsuspected* (1947), and one of **Hitchcock**'s most complex villains in *Notorious* (1946). SJ

The Man Who Reclaimed His Head/*The Mystery of Edwin Drood*/*The Clairvoyant*/1935 * *Angel on My Shoulder*/1946 * *The Lost World*/1960

TV: *Alfred Hitchcock Presents*: 'And So Died Riabouchinska'/1956; 'The Cream of the

Claude Rains

Jest'/1957; 'The Diamond Necklace'/1959; 'The Horse Player'/1961; 'The Door Without a Key'/1962 * *Hallmark Hall of Fame*: 'On Borrowed Time'/1957

de Rais, Gilles (1404–40)

French mass murderer. A soldier and follower of Joan of Arc, the aristocrat de Rais tortured, raped and killed over 140 peasant children, mostly boys. Executed by hanging and burning, he remains one of history's great bogeymen, often conflated with the fairytale figure of Bluebeard. He figures in novels: J.K. Huysmans's *Là-bas* (1891), Philip José Farmer's *The Image of the Beast* (1968), Michel Tournier's *Gilles et Jeanne* (1983), S.P. Somtow's *Vampire Junction* (1984), Robert Nye's *The Life and Death of My Lord Gilles de Rais* (1990), James Havoc and Mark Philbin's *Raism: The Songs of Gilles de Rais* (1998). Paul **Naschy** plays Rais-inspired characters in *El espanto surge de la tumba* (*Horror Rises From the Tomb*, 1972) and *El mariscal del infierno* (*The Marshal of Hell*, 1974); Bruno Wolkowitch takes the role in *Jeanne la Pucelle* (1994).

Eugène Bossard, *Gilles de Rais, Maréchal de France dit Barbe Bleu* (1886); Georges Bataille, *Le Procès de Gilles de Rais* (1965)

Ramsay Films Combine

Tulsi (b. 1944) and Shyam Ramsay (b. 1952), **India**'s horror pioneers, have been joined by brothers Kumar, Keshu, Gangu,

Kenneth Cope, Edina Ronay, Mike Pratt, 'Never Trust a Ghost', *Randall and Hopkirk (Deceased)*

Reshma and Kiran to make Ramsay Films Combine a horror factory. Their early productions, *Do Gaz Zameen ke Neeche* (1972), *Andhera* (1975) and *Darwaza* (1978) are energetic, crude, highly enjoyable ventures into unknown territory. Ramsay films, like most Indian horror movies, feature jaw-dropping scenes of pure terror interspersed with comic interludes and sexy dance numbers, all underlined by the insistent music of Bappi Lahiri or the Anand-Milind duo.

In *Gunghroo ki Awaaz* (1981) they turn down the volume and produce a highly effective, low-key ghost story with nods to **Les diaboliques** (1955) and *Vertigo* (1958). *Saamri* (1985) is a rare experiment in **3-D**. The brothers' most effective film is probably *Dak Bangla* (1987), directed by Keshu, with its telepathic monster made of sewn-up body parts. *Bandh Darwaza* (1989) brings **Dracula** to India for the first time, and *Mahakaal* (1993) features an Indian Freddy Krueger. When not making horrors, the Ramsays turn out stylish thrillers, like the hit *Inspector Danush* (1992). They moved into TV with *Zee Horror Show* (1993–5). PT

Aur Kaun/1979 * *Saboot*/1980 * *Hotel*/ *Sannatta Dahshat*/*Guest House*/1981 * *Purana Mandir*/1984 * *Taikhana*/1986 * *Khoj* (Keshu)/*Om*/1988 * *Purani Haveli*/*Saaya* (Keshu)/*Veerana*/*Mahal* (Keshu)/1989 * *Shaitani Ilaaka* (Kiran)/1990 * *Aakhri Cheekh* (Kiran)/*Ajooba Kudrat Ka*/1991

Randall and Hopkirk (Deceased)
(UK TV series, 1969–70)

Private eyes Jeff Randall (Mike Pratt) and Marty Hopkirk (Kenneth Cope) make a more unusual team when Marty is killed working on a case and manifests as a white-suited ghost who can only be seen by his partner. Because he fails to return to his grave by midnight in the first episode ('My Late, Lamented Friend and Partner'), Marty must walk the Earth for a century. With Marty's widow Jean (Annette Andre) as a puzzled observer, the team investigate cases of the bizarre, supernatural and downright unusual. Created by Dennis Spooner, this offbeat but rather staid detective series is known as *My Partner the Ghost* in the US. ™

Geoff Tibballs, *Randall and Hopkirk (Deceased)* (1994)

Randel, Tony (b. 1956)

American director, producer, writer. A New World functionary who handled special effects on *Escape From New York* (1981) and *Galaxy of Terror* (1983), Randel rose to supervisory duties on *Godzilla 1985* (1985) and **Hellraiser** (1986). He made a directorial debut with *Hellbound: Hellraiser II* (1988) and became a manufacturer of competent scary movies.

Children of the Night/1991 * *Amityville 1992: It's About Time*/1992 * *Ticks*/1993 * *Fist of the North Star*/*Rattled*/1995

Rape

Though rape has been represented on screen since the birth of cinema (or at least – notoriously – since D.W. Griffith's *The Birth of a Nation*, 1915), representations of sexual **violence** have become increasingly problematic, for viewers and censors, as codes governing what can be seen have responded first to sexual permissiveness in the 60s and 70s, and then to the rise of feminism.

Horror cinema has courted the criticism of some feminists in its fetishisation of women as **victims** or as punishable vamps, and the unfortunate history of cinematic rape has formed one focus for this. Rape has constituted the prime moment of horror in films which might be better classed as thrillers, fantasy or action films: notorious sequences feature in *Straw Dogs* (1971), *A Clockwork Orange* (1971), *Frenzy* (1972), *Death Wish II* (1981) and *Sudden Impact* (1983). However, critics in the 80s and 90s, looking both at alternative images of men in cinema, and turning to other possible ways

Rasputin: Alexei Petrenko, *Agonia*

of reading rape scenarios from women's point of view, have cast a different light on these issues. Carol J. Clover has seen the victimised female protagonists of *Lipstick* (1976), *I Spit on Your Grave* (1977) and *Ms .45* (1981) as ultimately triumphant 'final girls', so that rape scenarios (victimising women) become rape-revenge narratives (women take control).

John Boorman's *Deliverance* (1972) might be read as a male rape-revenge narrative (parodied in Tarantino's *Pulp Fiction*, 1994), while similar sentiments run through *Act of Vengeance* (1974), *Death Weekend* (1976), *Jackson County Jail* (1976), *Savage Streets* (1984), *Extremities* (1986), *Dirty Weekend* (1993), *La sindrome di Stendhal* (*The Stendhal Syndrome*, 1996), Ingmar **Bergman**'s *Jungfrukällan* (*The Virgin Spring*, 1959) and its exploitation descendant, Wes **Craven**'s *Last House on the Left* (1972), even *Thelma & Louise* (1991) and *An Eye for an Eye* (1995). The aftermath of rape is also tackled in *Shame* (1987) and *The Accused* (1988). Genre horror tends to allegorise violation and penetration as **vampire** attacks or **torture**, but Peter **Cushing** commits a ground-breaking rape in

some versions of *Frankenstein Must Be Destroyed* (1969) and monster rapists appear in *Grave of the Vampire* (1972), *Humanoids From the Deep* (1980), *The Entity* (1983), *Incubus* (1983) and *Urotsukidoji* (*Legend of the Overfiend*, 1989). LRW

Carol J. Clover, *Men, Women and Chain Saws: Gender in the Modern Horror Film* (1992)

Rasputin, Gregory Yefimovich
(1872–1916)

Mystic and libertine who gained influence in pre-Revolutionary Russia through an apparent ability to assuage the Tsarevich's haemophilia (not, as Boney M have it, as 'lover of the Russian queen'). He showed remarkable resistance to shooting and poisoning during a protracted assassination by Prince Yusopoff. Widely believed to have supernatural powers, he is inevitably simplified in films as a malevolent fiend with horror movie trimmings like glowing **hypnotic eyes**.

The role affords hams the opportunity to leer through beard: Edward Connolly (*The Fall of the Romanoffs*, 1917), Max Neufeld

(*Rasputin*, 1917), Montagu Love (*Rasputin, the Black Monk*, 1917), Gregor Chmara (*Rasputin*, 1929), Nikolai Malikoff (*Rasputins Liebesabenteuer*, 1930), Conrad **Veidt** (*Rasputin*, 1932), Lionel **Barrymore** (*Rasputin and the Empress*, 1932), Harry Baur (*Rasputin*, 1939), Pierre Brasseur (*Raspoutine*, 1953), Boris **Karloff** ('The Black Prophet', *Suspense*, 1953), Edmond Purdom (*L'ultimo Zar*, 1962), Christopher **Lee** (*Rasputin the Mad Monk*, 1966), Gert Fröbe (*J'ai tué Raspoutine*, 1967), Tom Baker (*Nicholas and Alexandra*, 1971), Robert **Powell** (*Harlequin*, 1980), Alexei Petrenko (*Agonia*, 1981), Alexander Conte (*Rasputin*, 1986), Alan Rickman (*Rasputin*, 1996). Alberto De Mendoza is a lookalike in *Pánico en el Transiberiano* (*Horror Express*, 1972).

Sir David Napley, *Rasputin in Hollywood* (1989)

Rathbone, Basil (1892–1967)

South African-born British actor, in America from 1922. An urbane villain in *The Mad Doctor* (1940) and *Fingers at the Window* (1941), a swashbuckling dastard in *The Adventures of Robin Hood* (1938) and *The Mark of Zorro* (1940), and a definitive **Sherlock Holmes** on stage, screen and radio. A 30s Universal horror star with a **Frankenstein** descendant and Richard III to his credit, he seems somewhat bad-tempered in later entries, which are mostly humiliating comedies, though he rises with relish to the Shakespearean cataleptic ('What place is this?') of *The Comedy of Terrors* (1963). SJ

Love from a Stranger/1936 * *The Hound of the Baskervilles*/*The Adventures of Sherlock Holmes*/*Son of Frankenstein*/*Tower of London*/1939 * *The Black Cat*/1941 * *Sherlock Holmes and the Voice of Terror*/*Sherlock Holmes and the Secret Weapon*/*Sherlock Holmes in Washington*/1942 * *Sherlock Holmes Faces Death*/*Crazy House*/1943 * *The Spider Woman*/*The Scarlet Claw*/*The Pearl of Death*/*The House of Fear*/1944 * *The Woman in Green*/*Pursuit to Algiers*/1945 * *Terror by Night*/*Dressed to Kill*/1946 * *The Black Sleep*/1956 * *The Magic Sword*/1961 * *Tales of Terror*/1962 * *The Ghost in the Invisible Bikini*/*Queen of Blood*/1966 * *Hillbillys in a Haunted House*/*Autopsia de un fantasma*/1967 * *Madhouse*/1974 * *The Great Mouse Detective* (v)/1986

TV: *NBC Showcase*: 'Sherlock Holmes'/1950 * *Suspense*: 'Dr. Jekyll and Mr. Hyde'/1951 * *Lights Out*: 'Dead Man's Coat'/1951; 'The Adventure of the Black Baronet'/1953 * *Shower of Stars*: 'A Christmas Carol'/1954 *

Alcoa Hour: 'The Stingiest Man in Town'/1956

Basil Rathbone, *In and Out of Character* (1962); Michael B. Druxman, *Basil Rathbone: His Life and His Films* (1975)

Basil Rathbone

Rationalised Supernatural

From Mrs **Radcliffe** and **'The Legend of Sleepy Hollow'** (1819–20), a teasing strain of horror summons the trappings of the ghostly only to dispel them by revealing human trickery behind the weird phenomena. It is a rule of the detective story (effectively broken on occasion by John Dickson Carr) that nothing genuinely supernatural should mar the puzzle: a locked-room murder may not be committed by a culprit who can dematerialise. Even Arthur Conan **Doyle**, a committed (not to say credulous) believer in spirits, observes the rule in the most famous 'rationalised supernatural' story, *The Hound of the Baskervilles* (1901), where a phantom hound is faked in order to cover a scheme to gain an unmerited inheritance.

The '**Scooby-Doo** ending' (cf: *Wayne's World*, 1992) in which a spectre is captured and unmasked as a smuggler or spy is a commonplace of **Old Dark House** mysteries. *London After Midnight* (1927) and its remake *Mark of the Vampire* (1935) unusually reverse the convention by making **vampire** goings-on a plot on the part of the detective to unmask a murderer. The formula is troublesome: contrivances required to simulate the supernatural often seem more unbelievable than an actual unearthly explanation. Lonely hold-outs *Scream of the Wolf* (1974) and *Vampire at Midnight* (1988) more or less convincingly set up and then explain **werewolf**

and vampire scenarios. An occasional variant, used by William Hope **Hodgson** in 'The Horse of the Invisible' (*Carnacki the Ghost-Finder*, 1913), is to explain a haunting as trickery but have genuine ghostliness intrude in the finale.

Rats

Reacting through primitive fear of the animal as a plague-carrier, an audience tends to squirm at a cutaway of a rat gnawing or scurrying. Virtually no dark house, prison cell and sewer is complete without one. Ironically, however, films in which rats are central characters tend to fail because the rodents can be recognised as the nervous, inquisitive creatures they are. *Willard* (1970) works because of its spooky Hollywood mansion rather than its (notably clean) rats. Its sequel, *Ben* (1972), is remembered only for young Michael Jackson's title song. Irrelevant rat sequences were added at a late stage to *The Rats Are Coming! The Werewolves Are Here!* (1972) and there is an attack by rats in *Inferno* (1980). The silly *Graveyard Shift* (1990), set in a rat-infested mill, features a maniacal exterminator (Brad **Dourif**).

Giant rats, along with other giant animals, are seen in *Village of the Giants* (1965), remade as *Food of the Gods* (1976) and are the sole monsters in an unconnected sequel, *Food of the Gods II* (1989). Super-rats, popularised by James **Herbert**'s novels (*The Rats*, 1974; *Lair*, 1979; *Domain*, 1984), figure in 'Tomorrow, the Rat' (*Doomwatch*, 1970), 'During Barty's Party' (*Beasts*, 1976), *Deadly Eyes* (from *The Rats*, 1982), *Of Unknown Origin* (1983), *Nightmares* (1983) and *Rats, notte di terrore* (*Rats: Night of Terror*, 1984). Dead rats are served as food in *What Ever Happened to Baby Jane?* (1962) and *I Drink Your Blood* (1971) and a live one is chomped by a monster baby in *Species* (1995). DM

'The Raven' (1845)

Edgar Allan **Poe**'s poem of a grieving narrator tormented by a raven's bleat of 'nevermore' was one of his most successful works, and he often fell back on reciting it at lecture appearances. The title was used for Poe-related films in 1912, 1915, 1935 and 1963, but a 1940 cartoon is the only literal adaptation. The 1935 film (with **Karloff** and **Lugosi**) and Roger **Corman**'s 1963 **comedy** (with **Price** and **Karloff**) feature readings of the poem. Corman casts Hazel **Court** as 'lost Lenore' and Peter **Lorre** as a sorcerer transformed into a raven.

Raven, Mike [Austin Fairman]
(b. 1924)
Disc jockey Raven made an unsuccessful attempt to turn himself into a horror star in the early 70s. Despite looking like a combination of Vincent **Price** and Christopher **Lee**, his career fizzled when it became obvious that he couldn't act. SJ

Lust for a Vampire/1970 * *I, Monster*/*Crucible of Terror*/1971 * *Disciple of Death*/1972

Ray, Aldo [Aldo DaRe] (1926–91)
American actor. Ray was briefly an A-list player (*Miss Sadie Thompson*, 1953; *We're No Angels*, 1954), then more suitably a thick-ear crime or services character (*Nightfall*, 1956; *Men in War*, 1957). Potently cast as the Bad Man From Bodie, Western villain cum force of nature, in *Welcome to Hard Times* (1967), he slipped into exploitation (*Angel Unchained*, 1970) and even porno (*Sweet Savage*, 1979). His horror credits mostly date from a lengthy career slide. His son is actor Eric DaRe (*Silent Night, Deadly Night III: Better Watch Out*, 1989; *Twin Peaks*, 1990–91).

The Power/1967 * *The Centerfold Girls*/1974 * *Psychic Killer*/1976 * *Haunts*/1977 * *The Lucifer Complex*/*Bog*/1978 * *Don't Go Near the Park*/ *The Glove*/1979 * *Human Experiments*/1980 * *Mongrel*/1982 * *Evils of the Night*/*Dark Sanity*/ 1983 * *Biohazard*/1984 * *Frankenstein's Great Aunt Tillie*/1985 * *Terror on Alcatraz*/1986 * *Night Shadow*/*Shock 'Em Dead*/1990

Ray, Fred Olen (b. 1954)
American writer, producer, director. Ray is an entrepreneurial independent whose films prove the persistent market for low-budget exploitation; unfortunately, they do so with a beer 'n' bimbos purview he himself is quick to disdain. Fanatical film knowledge informs his many gimmick castings. DP

Shock Waves (production assistant)/1977 * *The Brain Leeches*/1978 * *The Alien Dead*/1979 * *Scalps*/1983 * *Biohazard*/1985 * *The Tomb*/ *Moon in Scorpio* (p)/1986 * *Evil Spawn* (w/u)/ *Demented Death Farm Massacre . . . the Movie* (additional d)/*Deep Space*/*The Phantom Empire*/1987 * *Hollywood Chainsaw Hookers*/ *Beverly Hills Vamp*/1988 * *Alienator*/*The Haunting Fear*/1989 * *Bad Girls from Mars*/*Evil Toons*/*Spirits*/*Death House* (additional d)/ *Millennium Countdown* (additional d)/1990 * *Inner Sanctum*/*Little Devils*/*Witch Academy*/ *Teenage Exorcist* (p)/*Ghost Wars* (additional d)/ 1991 * *Sex Bomb* (p)/*Mind Twister*/*Dark Universe* (p)/1992 * *Scream Queen Hot Tub*

Party/*Possessed By the Night*/*Inner Sanctum II*/*Dinosaur Island* (co-d)/*Stepmonster* (p)/1993 * *Bikini Drive-In*/*Biohazard II* (p)/*Haunter of the Dark* (p)/*Sorceress*/(p)/1994 * *Attack of the 60 Foot Centrefold*/*Jack-O* (p/w)/1995

TV: *Halloween Planet*/1980

Fred Olen Ray, *The New Poverty Row: Independent Film-makers as Distributors* (1991), *Grind Show: Weirdness as Entertainment* (1993); J.R. Bookwalter, *B-Movies in the 90s and Beyond* (1992)

Ray, Jean [Jean Raymond Marie de Kremer] (1887–1964)
Belgian writer, also published under the name of John Flanders. His many short stories and one novel are widely admired throughout Europe but unknown to the English-speaking world. Jean Pierre Mocky's *La cité de l'indicible peur* (*La grande Frousse*, 1964) is a brave attempt to put Ray's vision onto film, but Harry **Kümel**'s *Malpertuis* (1972) comes closer. To describe him as a combination of **Poe**, **Lovecraft** and Joseph Conrad only shows how indescribable he really is. Walerian **Borowczyk**, Jean **Rollin** and Alain **Resnais** have failed to film his weird detective stories featuring series character Harry Dickson. PT

La maison des cicognes (s)/1966 * *Ultra je t'aime* (s)/*Le gardien* (s)/1967 * *Trois etranges histoires*/1968

Rebane, Bill (b. 1938)
American producer, director. *Terror at Halfday*, Wisconsin-based DIY film-maker Rebane's first feature, was abandoned but shoddily completed by H.G. **Lewis** as *Monster a-Go-Go* (1965). Most Rebane films are simply terrible, but *The Giant Spider Invasion* (1975) is 50s-style schlock with odd stars and ridiculous modelwork, and *The Demons of Ludlow* (1983), a puritan devil movie, has moments of interest.

The Devil's Express/1975 * *The Alpha Incident*/ 1976 * *Invasion From Inner Earth*/*Maggots*/ 1977 * *The Capture of Bigfoot*/1979 * *Rana: The Legend of Shadow Lake*/1980 * *Blood Harvest*/ 1987

Recursive Horror
Biopics of horror writers like **Poe** (*The Loves of Edgar Allan Poe*, 1942) and Mary **Shelley** (*Gothic*, 1986; *Haunted Summer*, 1987) probe personal histories for neuroses and traumas that 'explain' their works. More fantastical efforts about Poe (Manly Wade **Wellman**'s

'When It Was Moonlight', 1937; *The Spectre of Edgar Allan Poe*, 1971), **Doyle** (Mark Frost's *The List of Seven*, 1993; William Hjortsberg's *Nevermore*, 1995), **Stoker** (*Burial of the Rats*, 1995) and **Lovecraft** (*Necronomicon*, 1993) suppose they wrote about supernatural horrors from experience, which serves subtly to downgrade their imaginative achievements by depicting them as mere fictionalisers of their diaries.

The use of horror **film-making** as a background to a horror movie (*How to Make a Monster*, 1957; *Frankenstein 1970*, 1958; *House of the Seven Corpses*, 1972; *Return to Horror High*, 1987) allows for a shifting of focus between levels of reality: in *Targets* (1968), the old-fashioned, polite screen horror of **Karloff** is contrasted with the modern, more disturbing psychosis of an all-American sniper, and *Fright Night* (1986) confronts a broken-down actor (Roddy **McDowall**) who specialised in **Van Helsing** roles with a real-life **vampire**. Besides *Targets*, several films bring real horror to cinemas, usually in the middle of horror films: *The Blob* (1958), *Drive-In Massacre* (1976), *The Meat Eater* (1989), *He Knows You're Alone* (1980), *Midnight Movie Massacre* (1986), *Angustia* (*Anguish*, 1987), *Phantom of the Ritz* (1988), *Popcorn* (1991), *Matinee* (1992).

A few films even concentrate on **Grand Guignol** horror theatre: *Mad Love* (1935), *Theatre of Death* (1967), **Murders in the Rue Morgue** (1971). It is fashionable (Peter **Straub**'s *Ghost Story*, 1979; Stephen **King**'s *It*, 1986; Mark Morris's *The Immaculate*, 1992) to make horror writers heroes of horror novels, which saves research time. By contrast, films (*Seizure*, 1974; *Deadline*, 1980, *House*, 1986; *In the Mouth of Madness*, 1994) have horror writers turn to their craft in futile attempts to exorcise horrors for which they feel partially responsible and suffering as their imagined horrors are exceeded by reality. In revenge, novels (Jonathan Carroll's *A Child Across the Sky*, 1989; Theodore Roszak's *Flicker*, 1991; Geoff Ryman's *Was . . .*, 1992) make horror film-makers in part culpable for real-life horrors, a theme elaborated by *Wes Craven's New Nightmare* (1994), which argues evil can be caged in *good* horror but is released into the real world by bad sequels.

Redgrave, Michael (1908–85)
British actor. In a long career, Redgrave naturally brushed the macabre, effectively as the **ventriloquist** who loses his identity to his own dummy in *Dead of Night* (1945). His

dynasty have all detoured into genre: Vanessa (*The Devils*, 1971), Lynn (*Midnight*, 1989), Corin ('**Dracula**', *Mystery and Imagination*, 1970) and Jemma (*Dream Demon*, 1988), not to mention Natasha (*Gothic*, 1986) and Joely (*Drowning By Numbers*, 1987) Richardson.

Secret Beyond the Door . . ./1947 * *The Night My Number Came Up*/1955 * *The Innocents*/1961 * *Goodbye Gemini*/1970

TV: *ABC Stage '67*: 'The Canterville Ghost'/1966 * *Dr. Jekyll and Mr. Hyde*/1973

Reed, Joel M. (b. 1933)

American director, producer, writer. Reed's notoriety derives from mugging 16mm **sex**-gore atrocity *The Incredible Torture Show* (1978). Re-released by **Troma** in 1981 as *Bloodsucking Freaks*, the film is an unacknowledged influence on their own bad-taste **comedy** *The Toxic Avenger* (1985). Reed has less flagrant horror credits: *Blood Bath* (1975), a threadbare **anthology**, and *Night of the Zombies* (1981), which features **Nazis** and Jamie Gillis. DP

Reed, Oliver (b. 1938)

British actor, who began his film career at **Hammer** as handsome rakes or twitchy psychos. Later cast as unruly rebels, he has subsequently lived out his life as one.Surprisingly understated as the brooding youth suffering *The Curse of the Werewolf* (1960). Many recent performances border on caricature. SJ

The Two Faces of Dr. Jekyll/1960 * *The Damned/ Captain Clegg*/1962 * *Paranoiac*/1963 * *The Shuttered Room*/1966 * *The Assassination Bureau, Limited*/1970 * *The Devils*/1971 * *Blue Blood*/1973 * *And Then There Were None*/1974 * *Burnt Offerings*/1976 * *The Brood*/1979 * *Dr. Heckyl & Mr. Hype*/1980 * *Spasms*/1981 * *The House of Usher*/1989 * *The Pit and the Pendulum*/1990 * *Severed Ties*/1992 * *Funny Bones*/1994

Reeves, Michael (1944–69)

British director. Reeves, who died of a drug overdose after completing only three features, was the first to articulate a youthful viewpoint in British horror, challenging in an aggressive and systematic way the paternalism of the tradition. Others (Peter **Sasdy**, Peter **Sykes**, Christopher **Wicking**) followed, but Reeves's films remain the most intense and disturbing expressions of this moment of change.

His brief career began with largely uncredited work on the Italian *Il castello dei morti vivi* (*Castle of the Living Dead*, 1964), on which he was notionally assistant director. This led to a solo project, *Il lago di Satana*

(*Revenge of the Blood Beast*, 1965), produced in Italy, written by Reeves himself under the name Michael Byron, starring Barbara **Steele** and Ian **Ogilvy**. While extreme budgetary restraints often show, this is nevertheless an impressive debut. Disturbing and unrestrainedly violent scenes involving the torture and killing of a **witch** by a mob of **peasants** demonstrate that Reeves at this stage was closer to the delirious excess of Italian masters Mario **Bava** and Riccardo **Freda** than the altogether sterner world of Britain's **Hammer**.

His final films were made in Britain and deal with generational conflict. In *The Sorcerers* (1967), an aged couple played by Boris **Karloff** and Catherine **Lacey** telepathically possess and control the mind of a young man (**Ogilvy**) to gain access to the world of sensation and experience from which they have been excluded. In *Matthew Hopkins Witchfinder General* (1968), Hopkins (one of Vincent **Price**'s best performances) drives to the point of insanity the young couple who provide the moral centre of the film. Reeves portrays scenes of extreme **violence** with an intensity that is unique in British horror: his despairing conclusions, in which both victims and victimisers are destroyed, derive from an obvious lack of faith in the ability of young characters to resist the depredations of an older, repressive generation.

Despite his relatively small output, Reeves represented an undoubted cinematic presence: British horror cinema could ill afford his loss. PH

Reference Books

Since the pioneering checklists published by *Castle of Frankenstein* magazine and the filmography in Carlos **Clarens**'s *An Illustrated History of the Horror Film* (1967), many researchers have set out to map the parameters of horror and related genres by collating credits. Walt Lee (*Reference Guide to Fantastic Films*; three volumes, 1972, 1973, 1974) and Don Willis (*Horror and Science Fiction Films*; three volumes, 1972, 1982, 1984) did the groundwork, but essential work has been added by Phil Hardy (*The Aurum Film Encyclopedia: Science Fiction*, 1984, 1995; *The Aurum Film Encyclopedia: Horror*, 1985, 1993), Michael Weldon (*The Psychotronic Encyclopedia of Film*, 1983, 1996), Harris M. Lentz (*Science Fiction, Horror & Fantasy Film and Television Credits*; four volumes, 1983, 1989, 1994) and Stephen **Jones** (*The Illustrated Vampire Movie Guide*, 1993; *The Illustrated Dinosaur Movie*

Michael Redgrave, *Dead of Night*

Oliver Reed, *The Devils*

Guide, 1993; *The Illustrated Frankenstein Movie Guide*, 1994; *The Illustrated Werewolf Movie Guide*, 1996). There are now many checklist volumes, covering the field as a whole or concentrating on subgenres or the work of a particular creator. Paramount among magazines as devoted to reference as **criticism** are *The Monthly Film Bulletin* (*Sight & Sound*), *Psychotronic Video* and *Video Watchdog*.

Donald F. Glut, *The Frankenstein Legend* (1973), *The Dracula Book* (1975), *Classic Movie Monsters* (1978), *The Frankenstein Catalog* (1984); Gary Gerani, Paul H. Schulman, *Fantastic Television* (1977); John Stanley, *Creature Features Movie Guide* (1981–); Alan Frank, *The Horror Film Handbook* (1982); James J. Mulay, *The Horror Film* (1989); The Phantom of the Movies, *The Phantom's Ultimate Video Guide* (1989); John McCarty, *The Official Splatter Movie Guide* (1989, 1992); Dennis Fischer, *Horror Film Directors, 1931–1990* (1991); *Hoffman's Guide to SF, Horror and Fantasy Movies 1991–92* (1991); Bryan Senn, John Johnson, *Fantastic Cinema Subject Guide* (1992); James O'Neill, *Terror on Tape* (1994); Roger Fulton, *The Encyclopedia of TV Science Fiction* (1995); Roy Kinnard, *Horror in Silent Films: A Filmography, 1896–1929* (1995)

Reicher, Frank (1875–1964)

German-born character actor who emigrated to America in 1899 and enjoyed a long career in Hollywood, originally as a silents director and later as a dependable, often uncredited, supporting player. The stolid Captain Englehorn from **King Kong** (1933), his last known credit was *Superman and the Mole Men* (1951). SJ

*Black Waters/1929 * Rasputin and the Empress/ The Crooked Circle/1932 * Before Dawn/The Son of Kong/1933 * The Return of the Terror/1934 * Life Returns/The Florentine Dagger/The Great Impersonation/1935 * The Invisible Ray/1936 * Night Key/1937 * Devil's Island/Dr Cyclops/ 1939 * The Face Behind the Mask/1941 * Mystery of Marie Roget/Night Monster/The Mummy's Tomb/1942 * Gildersleeve's Ghost/The Canterville Ghost/1943 * Phantoms Inc (s)/The Mummy's Ghost/House of Frankenstein/Captain America/1944 * The Strange Mr Gregory/1945*

Reincarnation

A belief that souls are reused is central to major religions: in *Audrey Rose* (1977), Anthony **Hopkins** claims 'more people in this world believe in reincarnation than don't'. One of the most tedious horror clichés, perhaps derived from *She* (1887), is the monster's search for a modern incarnation of a lost love: *The Mummy* (1932, 1959), *Curse of the Faceless Man* (1958), *Blacula* (1972), **Dracula** (1973), *Bram Stoker's Dracula* (1992), *Embrace of the Vampire* (1995).

The Bridey Murphy case, in which a modern woman 'remembered' an earlier life under **hypnosis**, spun off *The Search for Bridey Murphy* (1956) and lurid variants: woman remembers she was a prehistoric sea monster (*The She-Creature*, 1956), woman remembers she was burned as a **witch** (*The Undead*, 1956), woman remembers she was an **ape** (*The Bride and the Beast*, 1958). More sober, less entertaining regression movies are *I've Lived Before* (1956), *Fright* (1957) and *On a Clear Day You Can See Forever* (1970). *Audrey Rose*, from Frank **De Felitta**'s 1976 novel, has Marsha Mason persuaded her child is a reincarnate; *Little Buddha* (1993) has the same plot as Bridget Fonda is convinced her son is a recycled lama.

Reincarnation allows victims to avenge their own murders in *You Never Can Tell* (1951), *The Reincarnation of Peter Proud* (1975), *Dead Again* (1991) and 'Born Again' (**The X Files**, 1994). Reincarnate romance features in *Made in Heaven* (1987) and *Chances Are* (1989), people return as dogs (*Let's Live Again*, 1948; *Fluke*, 1995) and cars (*My Mother the Car*, 1965–6), and men come back as women (*Goodbye Charlie*, 1964; *Angel on Fire*, 1979; *Switch*, 1991). *The Reincarnate* (1971) – like *The Haunted Palace* (1963), *The Mephisto Waltz* (1971), *Nothing But the Night* (1972) and *All of Me* (1984) – is not about reincarnation proper but soul transference.

Frank Reicher

Religion: Peter Cushing *Brides of Dracula*

Reinl, Harald (1908–86)

Austrian-born German director. He continued Dr **Mabuse** after Fritz **Lang** revived the franchise and handled the big-budget *Nibelungen* remake (1964) originally announced for Lang. His work on German-Yugoslav Karl May Westerns (*Winnetou*, 1963) prefigures the spaghetti cycle. He also made Edgar **Wallace** krimis. *Die Schlangengrube und das Pendel* (*Blood Demon*, 1967), a **Poe**-derived **vampire** movie casts Christopher **Lee**, Lex Barker and Reinl's frequent leading lady and wife, Karin Dor.

*Der Frosch mit der Maske/1959 * Die Bande des Schreckens/1960 * Im Stahlnetz des Dr. Mabuse [The Return of Dr. Mabuse]/Die unsichtbaren Krallen des Dr. Mabuse [The Invisible Dr. Mabuse]/1961 * Der Würger von Schloss Blackmoor/1963 * Der unheimliche Mönch/ 1965*

Reitman, Ivan (b. 1946)

Czech-born Canadian director, producer. The Hollywood family entertainer of *Kindergarten Cop* (1990) and *Junior* (1994) began as a Canadian exploitation producer: the mild porno *Columbus of Sex* (1970), **Cronenberg**'s *Shivers* (1976) and *Rabid*

(1977), the grim *Death Weekend* (1977), the breakthrough hit *National Lampoon's Animal House* (1978). He directed the amusing improv *Cannibal Girls* (1972), returning to horror comedy with *Ghostbusters* (1984) and *Ghostbusters II* (1989), wreaking supernatural havoc 'of biblical proportions'.

Religion

Much horror replays a classic Christian conflict between divinely inspired Good and diabolic Evil. The victory of God is represented by the power of the crucifix to repel **Dracula** or, more literally, Jesus's triumph over Damien Thorn in *The Final Conflict* (1981). There are comparatively few ordained **vampire** killers in the genre: Andrew **Keir**'s stake-toting monk in *Dracula, Prince of Darkness* (1965) is a rare priest hero, but an era of doubt that has Jewish vampire Alfie Bass shrugging off a cross in *Dance of the Vampires* (1967) produced more tormented divines like Ewan Hooper in *Dracula Has Risen From the Grave* (1968), Harvey Keitel in *From Dusk Till Dawn* (1996), Alex Angulo in *El dia de la bestia* (*Day of the Beast*, 1995) and even Jason Miller in *The Exorcist* (1974).

The **Devil** cycle that began with *Rosemary's Baby* (1968) and *The Exorcist* relies on Catholic theology but tends gloomily to depict clergy as impotent and doomed: *The Omen* (1976), *Exorcist II: The Heretic* (1977), *The Sentinel* (1977), *The Seventh Sign* (1988). Meanwhile, following *Matthew Hopkins Witchfinder General* (1968) and *The Devils* (1971), **witch hunt** films depict righteous **Van Helsings** as intolerant or self-seeking sadists. This theme is represented in modern-set horror by the evil evangelists of Robert **McCammon**'s *Mystery Walk* (1983), Stephen **King** and Peter **Straub**'s *The Talisman* (1984) and Lucius Shepard's *Green Eyes* (1986). King is unparalleled at creating frightening born-again Christians like Carrie's mother, played by Piper Laurie in the 1976 film.

Of course, *non-Christian* religions – like **voodoo** (*White Zombie*, 1932; *The Believers*, 1987), paganism (*The Wicker Man*, 1974), the beliefs of ancient Egypt (all **Mummy** films) – suffer ambiguous treatment in horror: for the sake of the plot, old gods must have real power to raise the dead or make high priests **immortal**; but for the sake of Christian morality, they must be seen as an Evil on a par with Devil worship. However, in *The Legend of the 7 Golden Vampires* (1973), Peter **Cushing** allows that a statue of Buddha is as potent against an Eastern undead as a crucifix is against a Western fiend, while *Rawhead Rex* (1986) is defeated by a pagan fertility venus.

Religion: Barbara Yu Ling, *The Satanic Rites of Dracula*

Renfield

The fly-eating madman of Bram **Stoker**'s *Dracula* (1897) is one of the great **minion** characters in horror. With a complex interplay of sympathy and fiendishness, he is the showiest role in many adaptations. Screen Renfields: Alexander Granach (*Nosferatu*, 1922), Dwight **Frye** (*Dracula*, 1930), Pablo Alvarez Rubio (the Spanish *Drácula*, 1930), Thorley **Walters** (as 'Ludwig', *Dracula, Prince of Darkness*, 1965), Corin Redgrave (as 'Jonathan Harker' but with Renfield's character, 'Dracula', *Mystery and Imagination*, 1970), Klaus **Kinski** (*El conde Drácula*, 1971), Jack Shepherd (*Count Dracula*, 1977), Richard Bulik (*Dracula Sucks*, 1979), Roland Topor (*Nosferatu, Phantom der Nacht*, 1979), Tony Haygarth (*Dracula*, 1979), Arte Johnson (*Love at First Bite*, 1979), Tom Waits (*Bram Stoker's Dracula*, 1992), Karl Geary (*Nadja*, 1995), Peter MacNichol (*Dracula: Dead and Loving It*, 1996).

Reptiles * See: **Snakes and Reptiles**.

Rice, Anne [O'Brien] (b. 1941)

American writer. *Interview With the Vampire* (1976), supposedly written as grief therapy after the death of a daughter, is the most influential **vampire** novel since *Dracula* (1897). Louis, the vampire, discusses his long life and explains at length his philosophical and emotional dilemmas. It is a rich (intermittently overripe), potent novel, with memorable characters (Claudia, the vampire child) and set-pieces. *The Vampire Lestat* (1985), a sequel, takes the point of view of Lestat, the more flamboyant vampire who is villain of the first novel but superheroic in subsequent, increasingly terrible, books: *Queen of the Damned* (1992), *Tale of the Body Thief* (1992), *Memnoch: The Devil* (1995).

Though she once wrote historicals (*The Feast of All Saints*, 1979; *Cry to Heaven*, 1982) and erotica (*Belinda*, 1986; *Exit to Eden*, 1986), she now concentrates on horror, commencing fresh series with *The Mummy; or: Rameses the Damned* (1989), *The Witching Hour* (1990) and *Servant of the Bones* (1996). After lengthy development, *Interview* was filmed in 1994 by Neil **Jordan**, with Brad Pitt and Tom Cruise as Louis and Lestat. Rice publically criticised the casting of Cruise and more publically retracted the complaint, but did not protest the casting of Dan Aykroyd and Rosie O'Donnell as the heroes of her sex fantasy *Exit to Eden* (1995). Given her interest in erotica, Rice was probably disappoint-

ABOVE Renfield: Roland Topor, *Nosferatu Phantom der Nacht*.

BELOW Renfield: Thorley Walters, *Dracula Prince of Darkness*

ed by *Interview With a Vamp* (1994) and *Intercourse With the Vampyre* (1994).

Katherine Ramsland, *Prism of the Night: A Biography of Anne Rice* (1991), *The Vampire Companion* (1993); Michael Riley, *Interview With Anne Rice*

Richardson, Sir Ralph (1902–83)

British actor. His range of eccentrics includes **EC**'s Crypt Keeper in *Tales from the Crypt* (1972), the blind hermit in *Frankenstein: The True Story* (1973) and The Supreme Being in *Time Bandits* (1980). SJ

*The Ghoul/1933 * Things to Come/The Man*

273

Ralph Richardson, *Dragonslayer*

Who Could Work Miracles/1936 * *The Wrong Box*/1966 * *The Bed Sitting Room*/1969 * *Whoever Slew Auntie Roo?*/1971 * *O Lucky Man!*/1973 * *Dragonslayer*/1981

TV: *Fireside Theatre*: 'A Christmas Carol'/1951

Ripper, Michael (b. 1913)

British character actor, one of a band who throughout the 50s and '60s were as much a part of the scenery of **Hammer** horror as the sets and costumes. He was the most ver-satile (and widely cast) of this group, ranging from relatively straightforward supporting roles (the innkeeper in *The Reptile*, 1966) to the grotesque (the cabbie in *The Phantom of the Opera*, 1962) with diversions into the downright bizarre (a Japanese officer in *Secret of Blood Island*, 1965). Best as the grov-elling but strangely endearing Longbarrow in *The Mummy's Shroud* (1967). PH

Quatermass 2/X – The Unknown/1957 * *The Revenge of Frankenstein*/1958 * *The Ugly Duckling*/*The Mummy*/*The Man Who Could Cheat Death*/1959 * *The Curse of the Werewolf*/*The Brides of Dracula*/1960 * *The Anatomist*/1961 * *The Curse of the Mummy's Tomb*/1964 * *The Plague of the Zombies*/*The Deadly Bees*/1966 * *Dracula Has Risen From The Grave*/*The Lost Continent*/1968 * *Taste the Blood of Dracula*/*Mumsy, Nanny, Sonny and Girly*/1969 * *Scars of Dracula*/1970 * *The Creeping Flesh*/1973 * *Legend of the Werewolf*/1974 * *The Revenge of Billy the Kid*/1991

TV: *Quatermass and the Pit*/1959 * *Journey to the Unknown*: 'Paper Dolls'/1968 * *Randall and Hopkirk (Deceased)*: 'It's Supposed to Be Thicker Than Water'/1970 * *Tales of the Unexpected*: 'The Man at the Top'/1980

Roald Dahl's Tales of the Unexpected
(UK TV series, 1979–88)

Produced by Sir John Woolf for Anglia Television, this run of *contes cruels* began with Ronald Harwood adaptations of Roald **Dahl** stories. Many episodes were remakes of sto-ries already seen on **Alfred Hitchcock Presents** (1955–62) and other anthology shows. The most gruesome are 'William and Mary' (1979), with Elaine Stritch and a **brain**, 'Lamb to the Slaughter' (1979), with Susan George murdering with a leg of lamb, and 'Royal Jelly' (1979), with beekeeper Timothy West mutating his own baby. From the second season on, with the show renamed *Tales of the Unexpected*, stories came from other authors, including Robert **Bloch** ('Fat Chance', 1980), John Collier ('Back For Christmas', 1980), Stanley Ellin ('The Best of Everything', 1981), Ruth Rendell ('A Glow-ing Future', 1981), Patricia Highsmith ('Sauce for the Goose', 1984) and Henry Slesar ('The Dirty Detail', 1984). Though widely ridiculed as *Tales of the Blatantly Obvious*, the series proved popular and racked up over 100 episodes. Trading mostly in criminal irony, the series touches occasionally on the macabre and the supernatural. TM

Robinson, Bernard
(1912–70)

British production designer. His first genre credits are *Crimes at the Dark House* (1940) and *Mother Riley Meets the Vampire* (1952), but he is known for a long association with **Hammer**. Robinson worked on nearly all the classic Hammer horrors made before the mid-60s and was a major contributor to their look. His inventive deployment of the limit-ed resources provided by Bray Studios and constant recycling of sets and props did much to disguise low budgets. Arguably Hammer's departure from Bray in 1967 and shortly thereafter Robinson's departure from Hammer did significant damage to the stu-dio. PH

The Abominable Snowman/*The Curse of Frankenstein*/1957 * *Dracula*/*The Revenge of Frankenstein*/*Quatermass 2*/*X-The Unknown*/1958 * *The Mummy*/*The Man Who Could Cheat Death*/*The Ugly Duckling*/*The Hound of the Baskervilles*/1959 * *The Stranglers of Bombay*/*The Two Faces of Dr. Jekyll*/*The Brides of Dracula*/*Never Take Sweets From a Stranger*/1960 * *The Terror of the Tongs*/*Taste of Fear*/*The Curse of the Werewolf*/*The Shadow of the Cat*/1961 * *Phantom of the Opera*/*Captain Clegg*/1962 * *The Old Dark House*/*The Damned*/*Paranoiac*/*Kiss of the Vampire*/1963 * *Nightmare*/*Curse of the Mummy's Tomb*/*The Gorgon*/1964 * *The Plague of Zombies*/*The*

Rod Taylor, Cyril Cusack, 'The Hitchhiker', *Roald Dahl's Tales of the Unexpected*

Mark Robson

*Reptile/Dracula – Prince of Darkness/Rasputin the Mad Monk/1965 * Frankenstein Created Woman/The Witches/1966 * The Mummy's Shroud/Quatermass and the Pit/1967 * The Devil Rides Out/Dracula Has Risen From the Grave/1968 * Frankenstein Must Be Destroyed/1969*

Robinson, George (1895?–1958)

American cinematographer. After the Spanish *Drácula* (1931), widely regarded as better work than Karl **Freund**'s on the **Browning** version, Robinson became cameraman of choice for Universal horror. His work on super-productions like *Son of Frankenstein* (1939) is strong, but he also achieves weird effects in modest Bs, bringing **fog** and hallucination to *Son of Dracula* (1943), *The Scarlet Claw* (1944) and *The Creeper* (1948).

*The Invisible Ray/1935 * Dracula's Daughter/1936 * Tower of London/1939 * The Mummy's Tomb/1942 * Frankenstein Meets the Wolf Man/Captive Wild Woman/1943 * House of Frankenstein/Murder in the Blue Room/Destiny/1944 * House of Dracula/1945 * Abbott and Costello Meet Dr. Jekyll and Mr. Hyde/1953 * Abbott and Costello Meet the Mummy/Tarantula/1955 * Francis in the Haunted House/1956*

Robles, Germán (b. 19??–)

Mexican actor, a specialist in **vampire** roles, with series characters 'Count Duval' (*El vampiro*, 1956; *El ataúd del vampiro*, 1957) and

the undead **Nostradamus**. So identified with vampires that he wears a cape and fangs in the **Abbott and Costello**-style spoof *El castillo de los monstruos* (1957).

*El vampiro acecha/La maldición de Nostradamus/Nostradamus y el destructor de monstruos/Nostradamus, el genio de las tinieblas/La sangre de Nostradamus/1959 * La cabeza viviente/El barón del terror/1961 * Il cuarto chino/1966 * Las vampiras de Coyoacán/1974*

Robson, Mark (1913–78)

American director. An editor on the **Welles** unit, Robson joined Val **Lewton** in that capacity. After cutting **Cat People** (1942), *I Walked With a Zombie* (1943) and *The Leopard Man* (1943), he was promoted to director for *The Seventh Victim* (1943), *The Ghost Ship* (1943), *Isle of the Dead* (1945) and *Bedlam* (1946). These are remarkable, stretching the genre in unusual ways, full of real suspense and eeriness, with an eye for character and insight. He also handled *Youth Runs Wild* (1944), Lewton's juvenile delinquency drama and went on to critical and popular success with *Champion* (1949), *The Bridges at Toko-Ri* (1955) and *Peyton Place* (1957). His somewhat stuffy A-features now seem much lesser works than his Bs.

Daddy's Gone a-Hunting/1969

Rock Music

Popular music and horror borrow from and support each other because music is directly

Rock Music: Tony Fields, Marc Price, *Trick or Treat*

affecting and thus able immediately to convey mood and character, providing a further level for the stratagems adopted by artists to unsettle and scare their audiences. Generally, this also means music is cast in a supportive role. Those who mounted Roman popular spectacles in the 15th century, including the sculptor Bernini, were as concerned to create (briefly) fear in their audiences as amazement and the pleasures of looking at objects signifying untold wealth. To this effect, they used music as well as theatrically contrived visual effects. Even closer to horror were the near operas staged in Venice's many theatres in the 17th century: often with a supernatural theme, they meshed well-oiled stage machines with lengthy arias.

Another example of the melding of popular music and horror took place in England: early nineteenth-century London audiences leaving sensationally staged adaptations of such **gothic novels** as *The Monk* (1796) and *Frankenstein* (1818) were pestered by street sellers hawking murder ballads. Though based on fact, these were essentially works of fiction, often as sensational as they were mournful. With the notable exception of this form, evoked by Nick Cave in *Murder Ballads* (1995), which draws on horror themes, music is usually the servant of horror, applied as an intensifying agent for spectacles, plays and finally film. Moreover, it is when operating in this manner that musicians achieve the best effects: Bernard **Herrmann**'s several scores for **Hitchcock** films are rare in succeeding as scores and in their own right.

Some rock groups attempt horror-themed songs: The Damned, **KISS**, the UK Goth subgenre of punk in the late 80s, numerous heavy metal bands, GWAR, even Led Zeppelin. However, the Rolling Stones' 'Sympathy for the Devil' (1968) aside, the Satanism and occultism of these efforts is generally more theatrical and generalised (like the Alice **Cooper** stage routines in which he 'killed' chickens and **dolls**) than malevolent. A classic example is Ozzy Osbourne's *volte face*: after the **werewolf**-inspired album *Barking at the Moon* (1983), he released 'The Ultimate Sin' (1986) which led the family of an American teenager who committed suicide reportedly as a result of listening to it unsuccessfully to sue. Osbourne claimed the song had no malevolent message and subsequently appeared in *Trick or Treat* (1986) as a fundamentalist preacher campaigning against the evils of rock.

When popular music appropriates horror themes for its own purposes, it is generally as parody. The first, mould-setting example of this is Len Spencer's 'The Transformation Scene from "Dr Jekyll and Mr Hyde"' (1905), recorded for Columbia and Edison (and later Victor). The son of the American educator who developed the Spencerian method of penmanship, Leonard Garfield Spencer was probably the first nationally known American recording star: originally a ballad singer, he switched after 1900 to dramatic and comic monologues (often with Ada Jones). 'The Transformation' is one such: probably drawing on the stage version of **Stevenson**'s classic tale mounted in New York in 1898, the recording parodies the stage transformation of **Jekyll** into Hyde, rather in the manner Stan Freberg and Peter Sellers would parody rock'n'roll in the 50s, simply by using different voices.

If 'The Transformation' points the way, it is the congruence of rock'n'roll, late-night television horror shows and the emergence of the teenager as a cash-rich, emotionally limited consumer half a century later that set the tone of the parodic relationship between music and horror. The year 1956 offered run-ins with **aliens** in Buchanan & Goodman's 'Flying Saucer Rock'n'Roll' (a No. 7 hit that inspired three charting sequels) and the comic notion of a drunk driver in need of blood after a car crash in Nervous Norvus's jive-talking 'Transfusion'. Far more substantial is Screamin' Jay Hawkins's 'I Put a Spell on You' (1956): replete with maniacal laughter, the powerful recording, virtually a parody of horror film conventions, anticipates Dr John's Ju-Ju Man Night-tripper histrionics of two decades later.

But 1958 was the *annus mirabilis* of monster rock. Along with **Hammer**'s *Dracula*, AIP's *I Was a Teenage Frankenstein*, Screen Gems' syndicated *Shock Theatre* package of Universal horror films and **Famous Monsters of Filmland**, this was the year of Sheb Wooley's 'Purple People Eater' and David Seville's 'Witch Doctor', No. 1 hits that inspired Joe South's 'The Purple People Eater Meets The Witch Doctor', which actually reached No. 71 in the US charts. Also in the charts were the Five Blobs, who made No. 33 with 'The Blob' (co-written by Burt Bacharach, theme song to the film), and the 'Cool Ghoul' **horror host** John **Zacherle**, who reached No. 6 with 'Dinner With Drac'. Subsequently Bobby Boris Pickett and the Crypt Kickers had a US and UK-chart-top-

Nicolas Roeg

ping and million-selling success with the perfectly targeted 'Monster Mash' (1962), covered by Vincent **Price** and the Bonzo Dog Doo-Dah Band, and heard in the film *Frankenstein Sings* (1995).

In the UK Screaming Lord Sutch, who aped Hawkins in being carried on stage in a coffin, attempted to launch a career with the almost-hit '**Jack the Ripper**' (1963). In parallel with his conversion into a Grand Old British institution as a perpetually deposit-losing parliamentary candidate for the (horror-inflected) Monster Raving Loony Party, he cut at least two more explicit horror outings, the albums *Hands of Jack the Ripper* (1972) and *Rock and Horror* (1982). KISS founder Edgar Winter had a No. 1 in 1973 with 'Frankenstein', and funkster George Clinton adapted **Frankenstein** into his (increasingly) private universe with Parliament's *Clones of Doctor Funkenstein* (1976), which led to further name checks (notably the Clinton offshoot The Brides of Funkenstein). Similarly, DJ Cool essays the machismo 'Jack the Rapper' (a minor UK hit in 1988) while **splatter movie** imagery infects the lyrics and videos of The Gravediggaz.

However, as the years roll on, it became apparent that the 50s defined the meeting of popular music and horror, as witness the retro-trappings of Brian **De Palma**'s *The Phantom of the Paradise* (1974) and Michael Jackson's 'Thriller' (1983). The culmination of this retro-admiration is Richard **O'Brien**'s *The Rocky Horror (Picture) Show*, a successful stage and film (1975) **musical** which perfectly captures the melding of music, sci-fi (as it was known in the 50s) and horror with a story that cleverly articulates memories of the experience of the 50s through its horror and s-f borrowings. PHa

Alan Clayson, *Death Discs: Ashes to Smashes – An Account of Fatality in the Popular Song* (1992)

Rod Serling's Night Gallery * See: *Night Gallery*

Roeg, Nicolas (b. 1928)

British director, cinematographer. Roeg began his career at seventeen, dubbing French films into English, then got a job as a clapperboy and worked his way up to lighting cameraman. His credits as cinematographer include second unit on David Lean's *Lawrence of Arabia* (1962), **Corman**'s ravishing *The Masque of the Red Death* (1964), François Truffaut's *Fahrenheit 451* (1966) and Richard Lester's *Petulia* (1968). Roeg made his directing debut with the wildly reviled *Performance* (1968), co-directed with Donald Cammell.

Driven by a firm belief in the cinema as art – he claims to love filming and hate the film *business* – his work is distinguished by disturbing eroticism and an eerie sense of the mysteries that lie just beyond the surface of the everyday world. Roeg often employs convoluted and sometimes non-linear narratives, focusing his attention on theme and atmosphere rather than story and character. In his best films, the effect is haunting, striking a precarious balance between the mundane and the transcendental: *Walkabout* (1971), the story of two children lost in the outback and their relationship with an aboriginal youth; *Don't Look Now* (1973), in which a couple devastated by the death of their daughter is visited by troubling premonitions; *The Man Who Fell to Earth* (1976), about an **alien** corrupted by contact with human beings; and *Bad Timing* (1980), the chronicle of an obsessive love affair that culminates in near madness and death. His less successful films seem muddled and deliberately obscure, but *The Witches* (1990), a grim-

ly witty fairytale about witches who turn children into mice, is one of the best adaptations of Roald **Dahl** ever committed to screen. MM

Doctor Blood's Coffin (camera operator)/1960 * *Casino Royale* (c)/1967 * *Eureka*/1983 * *Insignificance*/1985 * *Castaway*/1986 * *Aria*: 'Un ballo in mascera'/*Track 29*/1987 * *Cold Heaven*/1992 * *Two Deaths*/1995 * *Delilah*/1996

TV: *Heart of Darkness*/1994

Neil Sinyard, *The Films of Nicolas Roeg* (1991)

Rohmer, Sax * See: **Fu Manchu**

Rolfe, Guy (b. 1915)

Gaunt British actor, formerly a professional boxer and racing driver. Notable for his ear-to-ear grin as the cursed *Mr. Sardonicus* (1961), he is a regular in Charles **Band**'s direct-to-video *Puppetmaster* series. SJ

Uncle Silas/1947 * *The Stranglers of Bombay*/1959 * *–And Now the Screaming Starts!*/1973 * *The Bride*/1985 * *Dolls*/1986 * *Puppet Master III Toulon's Revenge*/1990 * *Puppetmaster IV*/1994 * *Puppetmaster 5: The Final Chapter*/1995

TV: *Thriller*: 'The Terror in Teakwood'/1961 * *The Avengers*: 'Fog'/1969

Rollin, Jean [Jean-Michel Rollin le Gentil] (b. 1938)

French director, writer. France's sole horror auteur, Rollin prefers the label *'fantastique'* to describe his erotic, rhyming, manifestly personal work. Typified by wistful lesbian **vampires** and a narcotic narrative drive, his films use gothic paraphernalia to ponder the paired mysteries of death and desire and are very much 60s products. Notwithstanding their limited native impact, they are also thoroughly Gallic, blending the melancholy romance of the poetic realists with the generic play of the *nouvelle vague*. Meagre budgets accentuate a surreal sensibility, with fetishistically attired players sighted amid derelict locations.

His freeform monochrome debut *Le viol du vampire* (1968) attracted fluke attention by opening in Paris at the height of *les evenements*. Originally intended as a short, it boasts a second half that oneirically resurrects a cast killed at the end of the first. Subsequent colour experiments are supplemented by a series of hardcore entries 1973–80: excepting *Phantasmes* (*Once Upon a Virgin*, 1975), all are signed pseudonymous-

ly, though some adumbrate Rollin's horror themes. Gory compromises *Les raisins de la mort* (*Pesticide*, 1978) and *La morte vivante* (*The Living Dead Girl*, 1983) failed to gain backing for several 80s ideas. The one-time comics artist turned novelist with *Une petite fille magique* (1988). Rollin's low-point remains *Le lac des morts vivants* (*Zombies' Lake*, 1980), an aquatic effort slated for Jesús **Franco**. A feature comeback, *Les deux orphelines vampires* (1995) may also be his tuneful swansong. DP

Les pays loin (s)/1965 * *La vampire nue* [*The Nude Vampire*]/1969 * *Le frisson des vampires* [*Sex and the Vampire*]/1970 * *Requiem pour un vampire* [*Requiem for a Vampire*]/1972 * *La rose de fer*/1973 * *Les démoniaques*/*Tout le monde il y en a deux*/1974 * *Lèvres de sang*/1976 * *Fascination*/1979 * *La nuit des traquées*/1980 * *La griffe d'Horus* (s)/1990 * *La femme dangereuse*/1993

TV: *Perdues dans New York* (s)/1989

Role-Playing * See: **Gaming**

Romay, Lina [Rosa Maria Almirall] (b. 1954?)

Spanish actress, muse of Jesús **Franco**. From *La maldición de Frankenstein* (*The Erotic Rites of Frankenstein*, 1972), Romay has appeared in dozens of Franco films, often in multiple versions of the same title with less or more sexual content. Most striking as the mute **Carmilla** clone of *La comtesse noire* (*Female Vampire*, 1973). Named after a minor Hollywood starlet who features in Tex

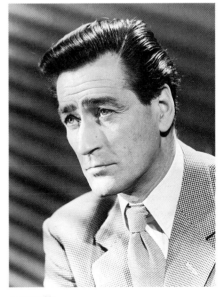

Guy Rolfe

LEFT George A. Romero, on the set of *Day of the Dead*

Avery's cartoon *Señor Droopy* (1949), she is sometimes billed as Candy Coster or Line Castel. As Rosa Almirall, she works as an assitant director on Franco films in which she does not appear, like *Die Säge des Todes* (*Bloody Moon*, 1980), *Il cacciatore di uomini* (*The Devil Hunter*, 1980 and *Killer Barbys*, 1996); as Lulú Laverne, she directs hardcore.

Los ojos siniestros del Doctor Orloff/Plaisir à trois [*How to Seduce a Virgin*]/*La comtesse perverse/Al otro lado del espejo* [French version only, *Beyond the Grave*]/*Les exploits érotiques de Maciste dans l'Atlantide/Maciste contre la reine des Amazones/La noche de los asesinos/Mais qui donc a violé Linda?*/1973 * *Exorcisme/Lorna, l'exorciste*/1974 * *Shining Sex/De Sade's Juliette*/1975 * *Jack the Ripper/Das Bildnis der Doriana Gray*/1976 * *Greta, Haus ohne Männer* [*Greta the Torturer*]/1977 * *Sinfonia erótica/Le sadique de Notre-Dame*/1979 * *Mondo cannibale* [*The Cannibals*]/*Eugenia, historia di una perversion*/1980 * *La tumba de los muertos vivientes* (Spanish version only)/*Macumba sexual*/1981 * *Gemidos de placer/Mil sexos tiene la noche/La casa de las mujeres perdidas/La mansión de los muertos vivientes*/1982 * *Sola ante el terror/El hundimiento de la Casa Usher* [*Revenge in the House of Usher*]/1983 * *Voces de muerte*/1984 * *Les prédateurs de la nuit* [*Faceless*]/1988

Romero, Eddie (b. 1924)

Filipino director, producer. Romero is behind the 'Blood Island' series, often with John Ashley and a continuing monster, the 'Chlorophyll Man'. *Terror is a Man* (1959), co-directed with Gerardo de **Leon**, is a fairly sober Moreau knock-off, but the rest of the run are demented. DeLeon was involved in *The Brides of Blood Island* (1965) and *The Mad Doctor of Blood Island* (1968), but Romero handled *Beast of Blood* (1969) and *Twilight People* (1971) by himself. These made enough impact on the drive-ins to prompt a Filipino imitation (*Superbeast*, 1972) and even a Stateside cash-in (Al **Adamson**'s *Brain of Blood*, 1971). Romero has worked as liaison on American films shot in the Philippines, from *The Big Doll House* (1971) to *Apocalypse Now* (1979).

The Beast of the Yellow Night/1970 * *Woman Hunt*/1972 * *Beyond Atlantis*/1973

Romero, George A. (b. 1940)

American writer, director. Perhaps because he is best known for movies about flesh-eating **zombies**, Romero is one of the most underrated film-makers currently working in America.

His debut feature, **Night of the Living Dead** (1968), changed the course of cinema history, standing alongside *The Wild Bunch* (1968) and *Easy Rider* (1969) as a sign that the era of peace and love was giving way to a pessimism more in tune with a generation sceptical of authority and opposed to continued American involvement in Vietnam.

Made for peanuts, in black-and-white, with an inexperienced cast (including co-writer John **Russo** in two different bits, and producers Russell Streiner and Karl Hardman in prominent speaking roles), *Night of the Living Dead* swept away horror movie conventions. When the dead come back to life and try to eat the living, there are no comic interludes and no let-up from the very first scene, in which a **Karloff**-lookalike turns out to be one of the living dead and causes the death of the character who had looked all set to become the **hero**. His sister escapes to meet up with other survivors in an isolated farmhouse, but remains stupefied with shock for the rest of the film. The sick little girl doesn't get better but turns into a zombie and tucks into her own mother, the young romantic couple end up barbecued, and Duane **Jones** takes over the hero role (not only is he **black** – unusual enough in the 60s – but the colour of his skin is never an issue) only to succeed in getting everyone killed. *Night of the Living Dead* spawned many imitators, but Romero showed class with his realisation that though the zombies provide the external threat, as much tension is generated by the protagonists as, barricaded within their farmhouse, they do nothing but bicker. It is a masterly, all too credible portrait of human beings torn apart (sometimes literally) under intolerable circumstances, and years ahead of its time in its examination of the questionable role played by the media in times of crisis.

In subsequent films, Romero continues to turn convention upside-down and invest what might otherwise be stock horror situations with acute insight into the darker side of human nature: *Jack's Wife* (1973) is not just about a dissatisfied housewife who joins a coven but also a Bergmanesque study of a woman undergoing a mid-life crisis; *The Crazies* (1973) is not just about the **military**'s attempts to contain a deadly virus within the town where it has been accidently released but also about the collapse of social order and the impossibility of distinguishing between those who have been driven mad by the virus and those whose seemingly insane behaviour is understandable under the circumstances; *Martin* (1978) is not just an updating of the **vampire** myth but also a study of a dysfunctional young outsider in a recessed steel town.

Romero returned to zombies in *Dawn of*

the Dead (1979), which continues to document the breakdown of society overrun by the ever-increasing undead hordes. Apart from a devastating sequence in which a SWAT team descends on a tenement building where the Hispanic inhabitants are refusing to surrender their dead, the film is less grim and more action-orientated than *Night of the Living Dead*, eventually turning into the ultimate satire on consumerism. The four protagonists (again including a black hero and a woman) escape by helicopter and hole up in a shopping mall, where they live the ultimate materialist lifestyle before their idyll is rudely interrupted by a gang of marauding bikers (one played by Tom **Savini**, who devised the innovative and bloody effects), whose violent behaviour makes the zombies look almost civilised. Italian horror maestro Dario **Argento**, whose brother was an executive producer, was script consultant and contributed to the score, and *Dawn of the Dead* became a huge international hit, despite a high **splatter** content which led to release in the US without a rating (normally a kiss of commercial death).

Romero next collaborated with Stephen **King** on *Creepshow* (1982), an **anthology** homage to **EC Comics**, though all five segments are disappointingly lightweight and reproduce the trademarked EC gruesomeness rather less effectively than the zombie films. Romero concluded the living dead 'trilogy' with *Day of the Dead* (1985): having originally envisaged a scenario in which battalions of zombies are trained for combat, budgetary restraints forced him to lower his sights, and he ended up with just one zom

bie ('Bub') put through obedience training by a **mad scientist** in an underground bunker, while other scientists maintain an uneasy stand-off with a military unit led by a megalomaniac. Leading roles are once again filled by a woman and a black actor, and this time inter-survivor bickering reaches new extremes of viciousness before being cut short in a spectacularly gory climax.

Monkey Shines (1988) is an effective version of the **Jekyll and Hyde** story in which a quadraplegic's monkey begins to act out his subconscious wishes; it also depicts the everyday actualities of disability with a candour which leaves mainstream efforts such as *My Left Foot* (1989) standing. Romero marked time with 'The Facts in the Case of Mr Valdemar', his segment of Argento's *Due occhi diabolici* (*Two Evil Eyes*, 1989), which is more like daytime soap opera than Edgar Allan **Poe**. *The Dark Half* (1993), another Jekyll and Hyde scenario, is Romero's own adaptation of a Stephen King novel in which a novelist's pseudonym is incarnated as a sort of murderous id. The story is sillier and less coherent than King's other novelist's nightmare, *Misery* (1986), and the result is one of the director's least personal films. AB

Knightriders/1981 * *Creepshow 2* (w)/1987 * *Tales from the Darkside: The Movie* (co-w, 'Cat From Hell')/*Night of the Living Dead* (p/w)/1990 * *The Silence of the Lambs* (a)/1991

TV: *Tales from the Darkside* (p)/1984–6: 'Trick or Treat' (w)/1984; 'The Devil's Advocate' (w)/1985; 'Baker's Dozen' (w)/'Circus' (w)/1986

George A. Romero's *Monkey Shines*

Paul R. Gagne, *The Zombies That Ate Pittsburgh: The Films of George A. Romero* (1987)

Rose, Bernard (b. 1960)
British director, writer. *Paperhouse* (1988), Rose's debut after pop videos, is impressive **young adult** horror, exploring the dreams of a disaffected girl, skilfully segueing from horror to insight as the heroine comes to understand herself. *Chicago Joe and the Showgirl* (1989), a World War II true-crime piece, is a disaster, but *Candyman* (1992), Rose's first American project, is the best screen adaptation of Clive **Barker** yet, again entering a heroine's nightmares to confront her with an ambiguous monster father. *Immortal Beloved* (1994), a Beethoven biopic, is patchy, but has a transcendent 'Ode to Joy' as the young composer seems to bathe in stars.

Army of Darkness (a)/1992

Rosenberg, Max J. * See: **Amicus**; **Subotsky, Milton**

Rossitto, Angelo (1901–91)
Dwarf newspaper seller in Los Angeles who occasionally took in acting roles. Discovered by John **Barrymore**, he features as a character in Nathanael West's novel *Day of the Locust* (1939). His career spanned an incredible six decades in films of wildly varying quality. SJ

Seven Footprints to Satan/1929 * *Freaks*/1932 * *Spooks Run Wild*/1941 * *The Corpse Vanishes*/1942 * *The Spider Woman*/1944 * *Scared to Death*/1947 * *Mesa of Lost Women*/1952 * *Invasion of the Saucer Men*/1957 * *The Magic Sword*/1961 * *Dracula vs. Frankenstein*/1970 * *From a Whisper to a Scream*/1986

Rothman, Stephanie (b. 1936)
American director. The first woman regularly to work as an exploitation director, Rothman began a career taking over *Blood Bath* (1966) from Jack **Hill** and ended it taking over *Ruby* (1977) from Curtis **Harrington**. Her most achieved works are a sunstruck California gothic (*The Velvet Vampire*, 1971) and a philosophical future **prison** movie (*Terminal Island*, 1973) but her commercial successes are sexploitation: *It's a Bikini World* (1967), *The Student Nurses* (1970), *Group Marriage* (1973), *The Working Girls* (1977).

Ruben, Joseph (b. 1951)
American director, writer. After teen sex-

ploitation (*The Pom-Pom Girls*, 1976; *Joyride*, 1977), Ruben wrote and directed the s-f/horror *Dreamscape* (1984) in which psychic Dennis Quaid enters President Eddie Albert's recurrent post-nuke nightmares to save him from a paranormal assassin. Wes **Craven** has commented on its similarities with the concurrent *A Nightmare on Elm Street*. Since *The Stepfather* (1986), a sardonic shocker with suburban **family values** as a suspenseful backdrop, Ruben has 'Gone Hollywood' with lacklustre results. AJ

Sleeping With the Enemy/1990 * *The Good Son*/1994

Rural Horror

The countryside is a regular antechamber to the unknown, isolating **Dracula**'s castle, **Frankenstein**'s lab and countless **Old Dark Houses**. Woods and jungles are invariably hunting grounds: the moors equip *The Hound of The Baskervilles* (1902) with its treacherous terrain, while deserts distinguish *Them!* (1954), *The Velvet Vampire* (1971) and *Dust Devil* (1991). The dissoluble atmosphere and deus ex machinas of numerous genre entries derive from their swampland settings. In *Fährmann Maria* (*Death and the Maiden*, 1936) and its remake *Strangler of the Swamp* (1946), the groves themselves are the monsters; forestry fulfils a similar function in *The Wizard of Oz* (1939), *The Evil Dead* (1982) and even *Night of the Demon* (1957) and *Suspiria* (1976).

An issue of **The Wolf Man** (1941), *Legend of Hillbilly John* (1972) and *Pumpkinhead* (1988), rural magic is also explored in hippy-inflected items *Blood on Satan's Claw* (1970), *The Wicker Man* (1973), *The Guardian* (1990) and *La setta* (*The Sect*, 1991). The degenerates found off the beaten track in **The Old Dark House** (1932) and **Psycho** (1960) are likewise given new emphasis in the later 60s. Using town/country tensions to suggest an America at war with itself, **Night of the Living Dead** (1968) sets the tone for such meat movies as **The Texas Chain Saw Massacre** (1974) and *The Hills Have Eyes* (1977), and in turn rural **stalk-and-slash** like **Friday the 13th** (1980) and *Mother's Day* (1980). *Let's Scare Jessica to Death* (1971) and *I Drink Your Blood* (1971) are particularly pointed post-Aquarian horrors. *Two Thousand Maniacs!* (1964) and *The Shuttered Room* (1966) are in some ways prescient. Mainstream equivalents include *The Beguiled* (1971), *Straw Dogs* (1971) and *Deliverance* (1972); Lucio **Fulci**'s *Non si sevizia un paperino* (*Don't Torture a Duckling*, 1972) is a creditable European backwoodster. Extrapolating Stephen **King**'s 1977 short story, the *Children of the Corn* series (1984–) attempts an agrarian franchise. DP

Ruric, Peter [George Sims] (1902–66)

American writer. Though he used the name

Rural Horror: Ray Bolger, Judy Garland, Angry Tree, *The Wizard of Oz* (1939)

Ken Russell, Blair Brown, William Hurt, on the set of *Altered States*

sexually insane nuns. He drifted towards the American semi-mainstream in the early 80s, following up the visionary **Jekyll and Hyde** rethink *Altered States* (1980) with *Crimes of Passion* (1984), which has committed performances from Anthony **Perkins** and Kathleen Turner and benefits from Barry Sandler's strong script. Too easy to caricature and too often given to stodge, Russell remains at once endearing and essential.

Tommy/1975 * *Salome's Last Dance*/1988

John Baxter, *Ken Russell: An Appalling Talent* (1973); Ken Russell, *A British Picture* (1989), *Fire Over England* (1994)

Russell, Ray (b. 1924)
American writer. Best known for short fiction, Russell became a screenwriter with *Mr. Sardonicus* (1961), based on his own 'Sardonicus' (1960). His novels include *The Case Against Satan* (1963), which prefigures **The Exorcist** (1971), and *Incubus* (1976), a small-town demon rape saga filmed in 1983.

The Premature Burial/1961 * *Zotz!*/1962 * *The Man With X-Ray Eyes*/1963 * *The Horror of It All*/1964

Russo, John (b. 1939)
American writer, director. Russo co-scripted **Night of the Living Dead** (1968) and novelised it (1974), then turned out a novel sequel *Return of the Living Dead* (1978), loosely adapted into the 1983 film, which he then re-novelised. He produces near-simultaneous novels and low-budget films: *The Majorettes* (1979; filmed as *One by One*, 1986), *Midnight* (1980; filmed 1980), *Bloodsisters* (1982), *The Awakening* (1983; filmed as *Heartstopper*, 1989), *Day Care* (1985), *Voodoo Dawn* (1987; filmed 1990). Russo directed *Midnight*, *Heartstopper* and a shot-on-video sequel *Midnight 2: Sex, Death and Videotape* (1993).

The Booby Hatch (d)/1975 * *Night of the Living Dead* (p)/1990

John Russo, *The Complete Night of the Living Dead Filmbook* (1985), *Making Movies* (1989), *Scare Tactics* (1992)

Ruthven, Lord * See: **Byron, Lord; Polidori, John**

'Paul Cain' on *Black Mask* stories and his one novel (*Fast One*, 1933), Sims used 'Peter Ruric' as a regular by-line on his screen work, which included Edgar G. **Ulmer**'s *The Black Cat* (1934) and Val **Lewton** and Robert **Wise**'s *Mademoiselle Fifi* (1944).

Russell, Elizabeth (b. 1916)
American actress. Unforgettable as the chic werecat who recognises Simone **Simon** as a 'suestra' in *Cat People* (1942), Russell was a **Lewton** regular, often in lesbian or neurotic roles. **Lugosi**'s undead wife in *The Corpse Vanishes* (1942) and the barely glimpsed but recognisable-in-a-portrait ghost of *The Uninvited* (1944).

The Seventh Victim/1943 * *Curse of the Cat People*/*Weird Woman*/1944 * *Bedlam*/1946

Russell, Ken (b. 1927)
British director. Russell flirts with the macabre but is more drawn to the absurd, finding insane comedy even in the **witch hunt** atrocities of *The Devils* (1971). *The Lair of the White Worm* (1988), his only outright horror, is a **camp** homage to **Stoker** and **Hammer**, as Amanda Donohoe's **snake** woman writhes through a deal of pantomime ridiculousness. Were he not obsessed with the lives of composers and poets, he would have made an ideal director for *The Rocky Horror Picture Show* (1975): instead, he

makes do with a **vampire**-fanged Wagner (*Lisztomania*, 1975) and cranking up the hysteria in the Byron-Shelley-**Frankenstein** menage to shrieking heights (*Gothic*, 1987).

With a filmography that veers from *Women in Love* (1969) and *The Music Lovers* (1970), once greeted as exciting, to *Mahler* (1974) and *The Rainbow* (1989), reviled as self-imitation, Russell is a wild presence in cinema, delighting in mock crucifixions and

Elizabeth Russell

S

Sacchetti, Dardano (b. 1944)

Italian writer. The prolific Sacchetti has worked with many Italo-auteurs and is thus skilled with outbursts of the irrational. His credit is on *Spettri* (*Specters*, 1987) and *Il camping del terror* (*Body Count*, 1987), which he didn't write. Sometimes billed as 'David Parker, Jr'.

Il gatto a nove code [*Cat o' Nine Tails*]/*Ecologia del delitto* [*Bay of Blood*]/1971 * *Il terrore con gli occhi storti*/*Perché quelle strane gocce di sangue sul corpo di Jennifer?*/*Sette orchidee macchiate di rosso*/1972 * *L'ultimo mondo cannibale* [*Cannibal*]/*Shock Transfert-Suspence-Hypnos* [*Shock*]/*Sette notte in nero* [*The Psychic*]/1977 * *Zombi 2* [*Zombie Flesh Eaters*]/1979 * *Paura nella città dei morti viventi* [*City of the Living Dead*]/*Inferno*/*Apocalypse domani* [*Cannibal Apocalypse*]/*Il cacciatore di uomini* [*The Man Hunter*]/*L'ultimo squalo* [*Great White*]/1980 * *L'aldilà* [*The Beyond*]/*Quella villa accanto il cimitero* [*The House by the Cemetary*]/1981 * *Lo squartatore di New York* [*The New York Ripper*]/*Manhattan Baby* [*Possessed*]/*Assassinio al cimitero etrusco*/*Amityville II: The Possession*/1982 * *La casa con la scala nel buio* [*A Blade in the Dark*]/1983 * *Shark, rosso nell'oceano* [*Devouring Waves*]/1984 * *Demoni* [*Demons*]/*Inferno in diretta* [*Cut and Run*]/1985 * *Vendetta dal futuro* [*Fists of Steel*]/*Morirai a mezzanotte* [*Carol Will Die at Midnight*]/*Demoni 2* [*Demons 2*]/1986 * *Quella villa in fondo al parco* [*Ratman*]/1987 * *Killer Crocodile*/1988 * *Killer Crocodile 2*/1989 * *Alibi perfetto* [*Circle of Fear*] 1993

TV: *Giallo*/1987 * *Telefono giallo*/1988–90 * *Brivido caldo*: 'Per sempre, fini alla morte' [*Changeling 2*]/'Una notte nel cimitero' [*Graveyard Disturbance*]/'La casa dell'orco' [*Demons 3: The Ogre*]/'A cena con il vampiro' [*Dinner With the Vampire*]/1987 * *Alta tensione*: 'Il maestro del terrore'/'Il gioko'/1990

The Marquis de Sade

de Sade, Donatien-Alphonse-François (1740–1814)

French writer, philosopher. Though his enthusiasm for excess tends to the infantile, the Marquis de Sade remains important and influential, often evoked by those who wish to shock. *Les 120 journées de Sodome* (1785), his most notorious novel, is unfinished and abandoned, perhaps intended not for publication but to exercise fantasies during a lengthy incarceration: it dwells at onanist length on the **torture** and murder of young people. *Justine, ou les malheurs de la vertu* (1791), *La philosophie dans le boudoir* (1795) and *Juliette, ou les prosperités du vice* (1797), which are extreme but more restrained than *Les 120 journées*, veer between misanthropy, sentiment and **pornography**.

It should be noted that, despite a personal fondness for flagellation and sodomy, the cruel world of de Sade's fiction, shaped by the last days of the Bourbons and the blood orgy of the Terror, purports to represent the universe as he saw it not as he thought it should be. While he admired Mrs **Radcliffe** and M.G. **Lewis** and laced his work with borrowed gothic furniture, he eschewed supernatural horror. Writing in 1800, de Sade commented 'there was not a single person who had not experienced greater misfortune in four or five years than the most famous novelist in literature could paint in a century. So it was necessary to call upon the assistance of Hell in order to compound the interest and to find in the realm of fantasy those things which we know only too well by investigating the everyday life of mankind in this age of steel.'

Among those who find use in de Sade are the writers Roland Barthes (*Sade, Fourier, Loyola*, 1971) and Angela Carter (*The Sadeian Woman*, 1979) and film-makers Luis **Buñuel** (*L'age d'or*, 1930) and Pier Paolo Pasolini (*Salò o le 120 giornate di Sodoma*, 1975). He pops up in novels like Guy **Endore**'s *Satan's Saint* (1965) and Les **Daniels**'s *Citizen Vampire* (1981), and Peter Weiss's play *The Persecution and Assassination of Marat as Performed by the Inmates of the Asylum of Charenton under the Direction of the Marquis de Sade* (1965). He maintains a presence in horror mainly on the scandalous reputation of his name. Film adaptations of *Justine* range from softcore picaresque (*Cruel Passions*, 1979) to deconstruction (*Justine*, 1976), while his name and those of his works remain evocative in several types of pornography, from Jesús **Franco**'s *De Sade 70* (*Eugenie: The Story of Her Journey into Perversion*, 1969) to wretched hardcore like the German *Excesse De Sade* (n.d.) and the French *De Sade* series.

George Sanders

Movie Sades include Patrick **Magee** (the film of *Marat/Sade*, 1966), Klaus **Kinski** (*Justine*, 1968), Keir Dullea (*De Sade*, 1969), J. Kenneth Campbell (*Waxwork*, 1988), a puppet-masked Philippe Bizot (*Marquis*, 1989) and Robert **Englund** (*Night Terrors*, 1993). He figures in Abel Gance's script for *Napoléon* (1927) but not any version of the film. Robert **Bloch**'s 'The Skull of the Marquis de Sade' (1945), filmed as *The Skull* (1965), elaborates from the historical fact that the Marquis's skull was stolen by phrenologists and features the floating, biting skull of Sade.

Guillaume Apollinaire, *Oeuvre du marquis de Sade* (1907); Montague Summers, *The Marquis de Sade: A Study in Algolania* (1920); Donald Thomas, *The Marquis de Sade* (1990); Maurice Lever, *Donatien Alphonse François, marquis de Sade* (1991)

Salazar, Abel (1917–95)

Mexican actor, producer. **Cushing** to Germán **Robles**'s **Lee**, Salazar (who produced most of the team's vehicles) specialised in fearless **vampire**-hunters. A break from type-casting is *El barón del terror* (*The Brainiac*, 1962) in which he is a remarkable, long-tongued monster. He produced but did not appear in *El mundo de los vampiros* (1960) and *El espejo de las brujas* (1960).

Las cinco advertencias de Satansas/1945 * *Ella, Lucifer y Yo*/*El fantasma se enamora*/1952 * *El vampiro* [*The Vampire*]/1956 * *El ataúd del vampiro* [*The Vampire's Coffin*]/1957 * *El hombre y el monstruo*/1958 * *El vampiro acecha*/1959 * *La cabeza viviente* [*The Living Head*]/*La maldición de la llorona*/1961

Salter, Hans J. (1896–1994)

Austrian-born composer. A prolific scorer for Universal, Salter handled many horror films, though his most significant work is in film noir: *Phantom Lady* (1944), *Scarlet Street* (1945), *The Reckless Moment* (1949). He was still around to work on 50s s-f, though it's hard to sort out which elements come from Salter and which from Joseph Gershenson or Henry Mancini in the scores of *The Creature From the Black Lagoon* (1954), *This Island Earth* (1955) and *The Incredible Shrinking Man* (1957).

Tower of London/1939 * *The Invisible Man Returns*/*Black Friday*/*The Mummy's Hand*/1940 * *The Wolf Man*/*Man Made Monster*/*The Black Cat*/*Horror Island*/*The Strange Case of Dr. Rx*/*Hold That Ghost*/1941 * *The Ghost of*

Frankenstein/*Invisible Agent*/*The Mad Doctor of Market Street*/*The Mystery of Marie Roget*/*The Mummy's Tomb*/*Calling Dr. Death*/*Night Monster*/1944 * *Frankenstein Meets the Wolf Man*/*Son of Dracula*/*The Mad Ghoul*/*The Mummy's Ghost*/*Captive Wild Woman*/1943 * *House of Frankenstein*/*The Spider Woman*/*The Invisible Man's Revenge*/*Weird Woman*/*House of Fear*/*Jungle Captive*/*Jungle Woman*/1944 * *House of Dracula*/*The Frozen Ghost*/*House of Horrors*/1945 * *The Brute Man*/1946 * *The Black Castle*/*Abbott and Costello Meet Dr. Jekyll and Mr. Hyde*/1952 * *Abbott and Costello Meet the Mummy*/1955 * *The Mole People*/*The Creature Walks Among Us*/1956 * *The Land Unknown*/1957

Sanders, George (1906–72)

Russian-born British actor, known for scoundrels, bounders and cads. His most committed genre work is a finely decadent turn as Sir Henry in *The Picture of Dorian Gray* (1945). SJ

Things to Come/*The Man Who Could Work Miracles*/1936 * *The House of the Seven Gables*/*Rebecca*/1940 * *The Lodger*/1944 * *Hangover Square*/1945 * *The Ghost and Mrs. Muir*/1947 * *Moonfleet*/1955 * *Bluebeard's Ten Honeymoons*/*Village of the Damned*/1960 * *Die sieben Männer der Sumuru* [*Rio 70*]/1968 * *The Body Stealers*/*The Candy Man*/1969 * *Endless Night*/1971 * *Doomwatch*/*Psychomania*/1972

TV: *George Sanders Mystery Theatre*/1958 * *Voyage to the Bottom of the Sea*: 'The Traitor'/1965

George Sanders, *Memoirs of a Professional Cad* (1960)

Sangster, Jimmy (b. 1924)

British writer, producer, director. Sangster began work for **Hammer** in a minor production capacity in the late 40s (as assistant director on *Room to Let*, 1950) but quickly graduated to scriptwriting. *The Curse of Frankenstein* (1957), *Dracula* (1958), *The Revenge of Frankenstein* (1958), *The Mummy* (1959) and *The Man Who Could Cheat Death* (1959) are brisk, lively affairs with a streak of black humour, setting the tone for Hammer horror in this formative period. As a producer for the studio, he worked on a series of psychological thrillers inspired by the success of **Psycho** (1960) and *Les diaboliques* (1955): only *Taste of Fear* (1961) and *The Nanny* (1965) are wholly successful in transplanting the format to a British context.

Sangster moved briefly into direction

with the disastrous *The Horror of Frankenstein* (1970), Hammer's leaden attempt to redo the **Frankenstein** story with Ralph **Bates** taking over from Peter **Cushing**. His next film, *Lust for a Vampire* (1970), second in Hammer's **'Carmilla'** trilogy, is slightly better, though marred by uneven performances and clumsy shifts in tone. Sangster spent much of the 70s working as a writer-producer for American television where he was associated with projects by John Llewellyn **Moxey** (*A Taste of Evil*, 1971) and Gordon **Hessler** (*Scream Pretty Peggy*, 1973). PH

X-The Unknown/1956 * *Blood of the Vampire/ The Trollenberg Terror*/1958 * *Jack the Ripper/ 1959 * The Brides of Dracula*/1960 * *Taste of Fear* (+p)/1961 * *Paranoiac*/1962 * *Maniac* (+p)/*Nightmare* (+p)/1963 * *Hysteria* (+p)/1964 * *The Nanny* (+p)/1965 * *The Anniversary*/1968 * *Crescendo*/ 1969 * *Whoever Slew Auntie Roo?*/1971 * *Fear in the Night* (+p/d)/1972 * *Good Against Evil*/ 1977 * *The Legacy*/1978 * *Phobia*/1980

TV: *Ghost Story*: 'The Concrete Captain'/'Time of Terror'/1972 * *Circle of Fear*: 'Doorway to Death'/'Spare Parts'/'The Phantom of Herald Square'/1973 * *Kolchak: The Night Stalker*: 'Horror in the Heights'/1974 * *A Man Called Sloane*: 'Demon's Triangle'/1979

Jimmy Sangster

Chris Sarandon, *Fright Night*

Santa Claus * See: **Christmas**

Santo [Rodolfo Guzmán Huerta] (1915–84)

The most popular of Mexico's masked **wrestling** heroes, Santo el Enmascarado de Plata was created and essentially played by Huerta. He became a star of the ring after World War II and, as Santo, never appeared without his silver mask. His first movie was *Cerebro del mal* [*Santo contra el cerebro del mal*] (1958), filmed in Cuba just before the revolution and co-starring another masked hero, El Incógnito (Fernando Osés). It was shot back-to-back with *Cargamento blanco* [*Santo contra hombres infernales*] (1958), which uses footage from the previous film. However, neither was released until 1961, after the success of a weekly *Santo* comic-book had furthered the character's popularity and led to a series of low-budget movies. Whether in the persona of a simple wrestler, superscientist or secret agent, Santo battled **vampires**, **werewolves**, **zombies**, **mad scientists**, **aliens** and other outlandish monstrosities. In his final brief appearances in *Chanoc y el hijo del Santo contra los vampiros asesinos* (1981) and *El hijo del Santo en frontera sin ley* (1982), he passed the baton and some words of wisdom on to his superhero son. SJ

Santo contra los zombies [*Invasion of the Zombies*]/*Santo contra el cerebro diabolico*/*El rey de crimen* [*Santo contra el rey de crimen*]/*Santo*

en el hotel de la muerte/*Santo contra las mujeres vampiro* [*Samson vs. the Vampire Women*]/1961 * *Santo en el museo de cera* [*Samson in the Wax Museum*]/*Santo contra el estrangulador* [*Santo contra el espectro del estrangulador*]/1963 * *Blue Demon contra el poder satanico*/*Atacan las brujas*/*El hacha diabolica*/1964 * *Profanadores de tumbas*/*El barón Brakola*/1965 * *La invasion de los marcianos*/*Santo contra los villanos del ring*/*Operacion 67*/*Santo y el tesoro de Moctezuma*/1966 * *Santo y el tesoro de Dracula*/ 1967 * *Santo contra Capulina*/*Santo y Blue Demon contra los monstruos*/1968 * *Santo y Blue Demon en el mundo de los muertos*/*Santo contra Blue Demon en la Atlantida*/*Santo contra los cazadores de cabezas*/*Santo contra los asesinos de la mafia*/*Mision secreta en la Caribe*/*La venganza de las mujeres vampiro*/*Santo contra las diabolicas* (unfinished)/1969 * *Santo contra los jinetes del terror*/*Santo en la venganza de la momia*/ *Santo contra la mafia del vicio*/*Las momias de Guanajuato*/1970 * *Santo contra la hija de Frankenstein*/*Santo contra los asesinos de otros mundos*/*Mision suicida*/*Santo y Blue Demon contra Dracula y el hombre lobo*/*Santo y el aguila real*/*Santo frente a la muerte*/1971 * *¡Las bestias del terror!*/*Santo contra la magia negra*/*Santo contra los secuestradores*/*Santo contra el Doctor Muerte*/1972 * *Santo y Blue Demon contra el Dr Frankenstein*/1973 * *Santo y Mantequilla Napoles en la venganza de la llorona*/*Santo contra el anonimo mortal*/*Santo en el mistererio de la perla negra*/*Santo contra las lobas*/*Santo en oro negro*/1974 * *Santo y Blue Demon en el misterio* de las Bermudas/1977 * *Santo en la frontera del terror*/1978 * *Santo contra el asesino de la television*/1980 * *Santo en la furia de los Karatecas*/1981

Sapphire and Steel (UK TV series, 1979–82)

David McCallum and Joanna Lumley star as Sapphire and Steel, mysterious time-travelling agents sent by an unknown benevolent force to correct anomalies in the space-and-time corridor and battle the forces of evil. P.J. Hammond created this off-beat series and wrote most of the serialised stories, which manage to be intricate on a low budget but too often pad out eerie ideas with repetition and waffle. Following Nigel **Kneale**'s format, most serials present a supernatural situation (a disused railway station haunted by a soldier from World War I, Edwardian children escaped from an old photograph) but provide nebulous s-f rationale for the phenomena. The show was produced by Shaun O'Riordan (who also directed the bulk of it), the theme music was created by Cyril Ornadel. TM

Sarandon, Chris (b. 1942)

American actor, former husband of Susan Sarandon. Oscar-nominated as Best Supporting Actor for his drag queen debut in *Dog Day Afternoon* (1975). Subsequent performances, apart from the **vampire** in *Fright Night* (1985), are colourless and unremarkable. AJ

Lipstick/1976 * *The Sentinel*/1977 * *Child's Play*/1988 * *Whispers*/1990 * *The Resurrected*/1992 * *Dark Tide*/1993 * *Dark Goddess/The Nightmare Before Christmas* (v)/*Temptress*/1994 * *Terminal Justice/Tales From the Crypt: Bordello of Blood*/1996

TV: *The Satan Murders*/1974 * *The Stranger Within*/1990 * *The Outer Limits*: 'Corner of the Eye'/1995 * *When the Dark Man Calls*/1995

Sasdy, Peter (b. 1934)

Hungarian-born British director. One of the most promising of the group of film-makers who started in British horror in the late 60s when experimentation was, within limits, welcome within the genre. Sasdy's first film was for **Hammer** and turned out to be the studio's last good **Dracula**; *Taste the Blood of Dracula* (1969) convincingly portrays a world of Victorian sexual hypocrisy, providing a powerful critique of those patriarchal figures who in earlier Hammers had been the source of moral authority, here revealed as little

Peter Sasdy

more than domestic bullies terrorising their defenceless children.

Sasdy's next two Hammer films take further this notion of monstrous parents: Ingrid **Pitt** is the devouring mother in *Countess Dracula* (1970), the only British film about Elizabeth **Báthory**, and, most successfully, **Jack the Ripper** is a tyrannical father in *Hands of the Ripper* (1971). The Ripper's daughter (Angharad Rees) finds herself surrounded by male authority figures who seek to deny her autonomy, probably the closest Hammer ever gets to an overtly feminist statement. Sasdy's films away from Hammer are uneven. The interesting *Nothing But the Night* (1972) deals again with old people possessing the bodies of the young but is hampered by an overly complicated thriller structure. Sasdy also directed Nigel **Kneale**'s *The Stone Tape* (1972), arguably the scariest TV production of the 70s. PH

Doomwatch/1972 * *I Don't Want to Be Born*/1975

TV: *Sherlock Holmes*: 'The Illustrious Client'/1965 * *Out of the Unknown*: 'The Eye'/1966 * *Wuthering Heights*/1967 * *Journey to the Unknown*: 'The New People'/'Girl of My Dreams'/1969 * *Orson Welles' Great Mysteries*: 'The Inspiration of Mr. Budd'/'Come Into My Parlour'/1973; 'The Ingenious Reporter'/ 'In the Confessional'/'The Power of Fear'/ 'Under Suspicion'/1974 * *Supernatural*: 'Viktoria'/1977 * *Hammer House of Horror*: 'The Thirteenth Reunion'/'Rude Awakening'/'Visitor from the Grave'/1980 * *Hammer House of Mystery and Suspense*: 'The Sweet

Scent of Death'/'The Late Nancy Irving'/'Last Video and Testament'/1984 * *Sherlock Holmes and the Leading Lady/ Witchcraft*/1992

Savini, Tom (b. 1947)

American make-up effects artist, director, actor, stuntman, author. Though associated with **stalk and slash** through work on *Friday the 13th* (1980) and *Maniac* (1980), Savini's major contribution to **splatter movies** comes though a long-standing collaboration with George **Romero**. In addition to effects on *Martin* (1976), *Dawn of the Dead* (1979), *Creepshow* (1982), *Day of the Dead* (1985), *Monkey Shines* (1988) and *Due occhi diabolici* (*Two Evil Eyes*, 1990), he directed the remake of *Night of the Living Dead* (1990) and acts in *Knightriders* (1981). MS

Dead of Night/Deranged/1974 * *Effects* (+a)/ *Midnight*/1980 * *Eyes of a Stranger/The Burning/The Prowler*/1981 * *Friday the 13th: The Final Chapter*/1984 * *The Ripper* (a)/*The Texas Chainsaw Massacre, Part 2*/1986 * *Creepshow 2* (a)/1987 * *Bloodsucking Pharaohs in Pittsburgh*/1988 * *Heartstopper* (a)/1989 * *Innocent Blood* (a)/1992 * *Trauma/ Necronomicon*/1993 * *From Dusk Till Dawn* (a)/*The Demolitionist* (a)/1996

TV: *Tales From the Darkside*: 'Inside the Closet' (d)/1984 * 'Halloween Candy'/1985; 'The

Tom Savini, *Creepshow 2*

Angus Scrimm, *Phantasm*

Family Reunion'/1988 * *Mr Stitch*/1996

Tom Savini, *Grande Illusions* (1983)

Saxon, John [Carmen Orrico] (b. 1935)

American actor. He began his career in the mid-50s playing teenage rebels and has ended up usually cast as a cop (as in his horror hit *A Nightmare on Elm Street*, 1984) or other authority figure. SJ

La ragazza che sapeva troppo [*The Evil Eye*]/ 1962 * *The Night Caller*/1965 * *Queen of Blood*/ 1966 * *Black Christmas*/1975 * *Un Magnum Special per Tony Saitta* [*Blazing Magnum*]/1976 * *The Bees*/*The Glove*/1978 * *Beyond Evil*/ *Apocalypse Domani* [*Cannibal Apocalypse*]/*Blood Beach*/1980 * *Assassinio al cimitero etrusco*/1982 * *Tenebre* [*Tenebrae*]/1983 * *Vendetta dal futuro* [*Fists of Steel*]/1985 * *A Nightmare on Elm Street Part 3: Dream Warriors*/1987 * *My Mom's a Werewolf*/1988 * *Death House* (+d)/ *Nightmare Beach: La spiaggia del terrore* [*Welcome to Spring Break*]/1989 * *Blood Salvage*/*The Arrival*/*Hellmaster*/1990 * *Wes Craven's New Nightmare*/1994 * *From Dusk Till Dawn*/1996

TV: *The Sixth Sense*: 'Lady, Lady, Take My Life'/*Night Gallery*: 'I'll Never Leave You, Ever'/1972 * *Alfred Hitchcock Presents*: 'The Specialty of the House'/1987 * *Ray Bradbury Theatre*: 'The Wonderful Death of Dudley Stone'/1989 * *Monsters*: 'The Waiting Room'/ 1991

Schlingensief, Christoph (b. 1960)

German director, writer. Auteur of home-made politico-gore Euro-charades, usually with Udo **Kier** as Hitler. Influenced by Fassbinder and John Waters, he is only just more interesting than Jörg **Buttgereit**.

100 Jahre Adolf Hitler [*100 Years of Adolf Hitler*]/*Das deutsche Kettensägenmassaker* [*The German Chainsaw Massacre*]/1991 * *Terror 2000*/1993 * *Die Spalte* [*The Slit*]/1995

Schmoeller, David (b. 1947)

American director, often for Charles **Band**. *Tourist Trap* (1979), Schmoeller's debut, is not good but has an interesting telekinetic riff on its Ed **Gein** set-up. *Crawlspace* (1986), with Klaus **Kinski** as a **Nazi** voyeur, is merely nasty, but the competent *Puppet Master* (1989) kicked off a series and *Catacombs* (1988), his best to date, is a decent ghost story which transposes the plot of *Prison* (1987) into an Italian monastary.

The Seduction/1981 * *Ghost Town* (w)/1988 * *The Arrival*/1990 * *Netherworld*/1991

Schoedsack, Ernest B. * See: Cooper, Merian C.

Schow, David J. (b. 1955)

German-born American writer. At once inheritor of the Californian weird tradition of Richard **Matheson** and Dennis **Etchison** and leading light of the **splatterpunk** movement, Schow's powerful, sometimes witty, sometimes strangely sentimental stories are collected in *Seeing Red* (1990), *Lost Angels* (1990) and *Black Leather Required* (1994). In addition to the novels *The Kill Riff* (1990) and *The Shaft* (1990), he is co-author with Jeffrey Frentzen of *The Outer Limits: The Official Companion* (1986) and editor of *Silver Scream* (1988). As yet, his screen work has not approached his prose fiction in quality.

A Nightmare on Elm Street, Part IV: The Dream Child (u)/1988 * *Leatherface: The Texas Chainsaw Massacre III*/1989 * *Critters 3*/1991 * *Critters 4*/1992 * *The Crow*/1994

TV: *Freddy's Nightmares*: 'Safe Sex'/1989 * *Tales From the Crypt*: 'Oil's Well That Ends Well'/1994 * *The Outer Limits*: 'Corner of the Eye'/1995 * *Perversions of Science*/1996

Schreck, Max (1879–1936)

German actor. A genre immortal for a single role: the bald, ratlike, scuttling Graf von Orlok – the screen's first **Dracula** – in **Murnau**'s *Nosferatu: Eine Symphonie des Grauens* (1922). Imitated by Reggie **Nalder** in *Salem's Lot* (1979) and Klaus **Kinski** in *Nosferatu, Phantom der Nacht* (1979), Orlok's face is indelible.

Ramper – der Tiermensch/1927 * *Rasputins Liebesabenteuer*/1928

Scooby-Doo

One of Hanna-Barbera's most enduring cartoon characters, dumb dog Scooby Doo has been running away from ghosts for over twenty-five years. He first appeared in the half-hour *Scooby Doo Where Are You!* (1969–70), partnered by perennial beatnik Shaggy Rogers, plump but smart Velma Dinkley, and 'normal' teenagers Daphne Blake and Freddy Jones. Each week, the gang come across a supernatural mystery (with songs!) ultimately revealed as the work of a human criminal – typically the least likely (but only) suspect. The basic formula is repeated, with increasing reliance on real hauntings, in subsequent variations.

The New Scooby-Doo Movies (1972) are forty-minute shows in which the gang travel around in their van The Mystery Machine, meeting other Hanna-Barbera characters (**The Addams Family**, The Three Stooges, Laurel and Hardy) and celebrity guest stars (**Batman**, Don Knotts, Jonathan Winters, Phyllis Diller, Sonny and Cher). The usual gang return in *The Scooby-Doo Show* (1976), and Scooby's over-confident nephew Scrappy-Doo joins the team for *Scooby-Doo and Scrappy-Doo* (1979–82). Scrappy teams with his other uncle Yabba-Doo and Deputy Dusty in *Scrappy-Doo and Yabba-Doo* (1982), a spin-off series of wild west adventures, co-produced by Ruby-Spears Enterprises. When Velma becomes an apprentice at NASA and Freddy turns into a mystery writer, Scooby, Shaggy, Scrappy and Daphne solve *The New Scooby-Doo Mysteries* (1984). In *The 13 Ghosts of Scooby-Doo* (1985), Scooby and Shaggy are tricked by phantoms into opening an ancient demon chest; with sorcerer Vincent Van Ghoul (voiced by Vincent **Price**), Flim-Flam and Daphne, they must return thirteen ghosts to the chest. This mini-series was followed by two full-length TV movies, *Scooby-Doo Meets the Boo Brothers* (1987) and *Scooby-Doo and the Reluctant Werewolf* (1988). *A Pup Named Scooby-Doo* (1988–9), aimed at very small children, features the characters as infants.

Rhona Cameron (as 'Thelma Fudd') parodies Velma in *Funny Man* (1994); a live action movie was announced in 1996. Casey Kasem and Don Messick created the roles of Shaggy and Scooby; other regular voices include Joe Baker, Daws Butler, Hamilton Camp, Darryl Hickman, Arte Johnson, Ted Knight, Kenneth Mars, Alan Oppenheimer, Jean Vander Pyl, Avery Schrieber, Les Tremayne and Frank Welker. The format

proved so successful that Hanna-Barbera recreated it (with minor variations) in *The Funky Phantom* (1971) and *Goober and the Ghost Chasers* (1973), and it was copied by rivals Ruby-Spears Enterprises (*Fangface*, 1978) and Filmation (*Ghostbusters*, 1986). SJ

Screaming Mad George [Joji Tani] (b. 1956)

Japanese-born American special make-up effects artist, director. 'Surrealistic make-up effects by Screaming Mad George' runs the credit on *Society* (1989), aptly signalling the interests of a man more interested in the bizarre than the splattery. With fellow make-up man Steve Wang, George turned director on *The Guyver* (1991).

*Hide and Go Shriek/Don't Panic/1987 * A Nightmare on Elm Street, Part 4: The Dream Master/1988 * Curse II: The Bite/1989 * Silent Night, Deadly Night 4: Initiation/1990 * Bride of Re-Animator/Silent Night, Deadly Night 5: The Toy Maker/1991 * Necronomicon/Freaked/1993 * Children of the Corn III: Urban Harvest/1994 * Tales From the Hood/1995 * Jack Frost/1996*

Scrimm, Angus [Lawrence Rory Guy] (b. 1938)

American actor. As 'the Tall Man', an old-style movie monster, in the *Phantasm* films, Scrimm has become a minor horror icon. He parodies the silver ball-throwing in *Transylvania Twist* (1989).

*Sweet Kill/1970 * Phantasm/1979 * The Lost Empire/1983 * Phantasm II/1988 * Subspecies/1991 * Mindwarp/Munchie/1992 * Phantasm III/1994 * Fotogrammi mortali [Fatal Frames]/1995 * Munchy Strikes Back/Vampirella/1996*

Sculpture * See: Art

Serial Murder

A phrase coined to describe the protracted 70s crimes of thrill-killers like Ted Bundy, John Wayne Gacy and Ed Kemper. Though exponents include Elizabeth **Báthory** and **Jack the Ripper**, serial murder is often taken as evidence of twentieth-century decline. It is also the favoured activity of every horror movie protagonist from **Dracula** down.

Early, non-fantastic genre killers tend to be financially motivated, but as evidenced by the lip-smacking Tod **Slaughter**, there is always a compulsive delight in homicide. Celebrations of the serial urge like **Halloween** (1978) and **Friday the 13th** (1980) represent the *reductio ad absurdum* of horror film plotting; *Mystery of the Wax Museum* (1933), *Color Me Blood Red* (1965) and their ilk erroneously suggest the close connection between **art** and murder. *The Silence of the Lambs* (1991) climaxes an interest in serial slaying that runs to comics, collectors cards and Ed **Gein** statuary. Fielding two villains, the film cleverly portrays the repeat killer both as pathetic fantasist and charismatic superior being. Jonathan **Demme**'s Oscar triumph is merely the most prominent of a run of cop-on-the-case serial killer thrillers: *Cruising* (1980), *Still of the Night* (1982), **The Stepfather** (1986), *Manhunter* (1986), *The January Man* (1989), *Copycat* (1995), *Se7en* (1995).

Real-life serial killers have inspired many films: Albert De Salvo, *The Boston Strangler* (1968); Reginald Christie, *10 Rillington Place* (1970); Ray Fernandez and Martha Beck, *The Honeymoon Killers* (1970); Dennis Nilsen, *The Cold Light of Day* (1991); Marcel Petiot, *Los crimenes de Petiot* (1972), *Docteur Petiot* (1990); Charles Starkweather and Carol Ann Fugate, *Badlands* (1973), *Natural Born Killers* (1994); Ted Bundy, *The Dark Ride* (1984); Jeffrey Dahmer, *The Secret Life – Jeffrey Dahmer* (1993). Henri Desire Landru is treated directly in Claude Chabrol's *Landru* (1963) and less so in *Bluebeard* (1944), *Monsieur Verdoux* (1947), *Bluebeard's Ten Honeymoons* (1960) and the Gilles de **Rais** cross *Bluebeard* (1972). The troubling *M* (1930, remade 1951) is based on Düsseldorf

Serial Murder: Anthony Hopkins, Jodie Foster, *The Silence of the Lambs*

Serials

Vampire Peter Kürten, with a bit of Fritz Haarman of *Die Zärtlichkeit der Wölfe* (*The Tenderness of Wolves*, 1973) and *Der Totmacher* (*The Deathmaker*, 1995) thrown in. Italy's Ludwig murders are one of the elements behind Dario **Argento**'s *Tenebre* (*Tenebrae*, 1982). Alexandro Jodorowsky claims a chance meeting with Mexican mass murderer Gojo Cardinas resulted in *Santa Sangre* (1989). The unapprehended Zodiac Killer is speculated on in *Dirty Harry* (1971), *The Zodiac Killer* (1971) and *Exorcist III* (1990), while the unsolved Moonlight Murders of Texarkana inform Charles B. Pierce's oddly atonal *The Town That Dreaded Sundown* (1977). *Il mostro di Firenze* (1985) and *L'assassino á ancora tra noi* (1986) were both spawned by Pietro Pacciani prior to his arrest in 1994.

Television contrastingly details the capture of Bundy (*The Deliberate Stranger*, 1986), Gacy (*To Catch a Killer*, 1992), Kenneth Bianchi (*The Hillside Stranglers*, 1989), Richard Ramirez (*Manhunt: The Search for the Nightstalker*, 1991) and Andrei Chikatilo (*Citizen X*, 1995). Like *Confessions of a Serial Killer* (1987), the scrupulous acme of multicide movies *Henry: Portrait of a Serial Killer* (1987) takes as its basis Henry Lee Lucas. Encouraged to confess to hundreds of slayings from his prison cell, Lucas perhaps best encapsulates society's ambiguous obsession with serial murder. An act of terrifying, Old Testament arbitrariness, it nevertheless offers perverse reassurance by suggesting that killing is the province of a monstrous few. DP

Elliott Leyton, *Hunting Humans: The Rise of the Modern Multiple Murderer* (1986)

Serial Murder: Michael Rooker, *Henry Portrait of a Serial Killer*

Serials: Clayton Moore, Mystery Man, Stanley Price, *The Crimson Ghost*

Serials

A logical extension of the popular series stories of the Victorian periodical press, the film serial emerged during the 10s, epitomised in France by Louis Feuillade's *Fantômas* (1913) and *Les vampires* (1916) and in America by Pearl White vehicles, *The Perils of Pauline* (1914) and *The Exploits of Elaine* (1915). Though *What Happened to Mary?* (1912) is the first serial, it consists (like Feuillade's films) of self-contained episodes; *The Adventures of Kathlyn* (1913) invents the cliff-hanger, leaving heroine in peril and audience in suspense until the next episode. From the first, serials specialised in sensational adventure with the odd macabre touch: invariably, colourfully costumed or deformed master villains are behind the heroine's troubles. Sax Rohmer's **Fu Manchu** stories were obvious serial stuff and were swiftly turned into a British series *The Mysteries of Dr. Fu Manchu* (1923).

Silent serials were intended for adult audiences, often including sexual or sadistic titillation that prefigure the Bond films: it could be argued that Fritz **Lang**'s two-part **Mabuse** epic is essentially a serial, down to its criminal mastermind. The German *Homunculus* (1916) is a rare serious serial, though its artificial man-turned-dictator is perhaps a variation on the master villain stereotype. In the talkie era, the Hollywood serial downgraded into rapidly-produced episodes exhibited at children's matinees, often adapting familiar comic strip or pulp stories: *Flash Gordon* (1935), *Dick Tracy* (1937), *The Shadow* (1940), *The Adventures of Captain Marvel* (1941), **Batman** (1943), *Superman* (1948). Serials provided a refuge for the villainy of horror star Bela **Lugosi** (*The Whispering Shadow*, 1933; *The Return of Chandu*, 1934; *S.O.S. Coastguard*, 1937; *Shadow of Chinatown*, 1937; *The Phantom Creeps*, 1939) and adventure serials feature **torture** (the pit and the pendulum of *Drums of Fu Manchu*, 1940), **zombies** (the deracinated native giants of *The Lost City*, 1935), a fake monster (the sea creature of *Haunted Harbor*, 1944), a killer robot (the ambulatory dustbin of *The Mysterious Dr. Satan*, 1940) and hooded fiends (the 'Lightning' of *Fighting Devil Dogs*, 1938; *The Iron Claw*, 1941; *The Crimson Ghost*, 1946).

Though Hollywood ceased serial production in 1956, the form continued in Mexico: *El maldición de Nostradamus* (1959) and *Orlak, el infierno de Frankenstein* (1960) were shot as serials to circumvent union rules and promptly re-edited into features. The form currently survives as the Original Release Video of Japanese *anime*, with the combining of several chapters into features also common, as in *Urotsukidoji* (*Legend of the Overfiend*, 1989). Some film series, like the **Friday the 13th** or **Nightmare on Elm Street** sagas, take on a serial-like feel, which is deliberately exploited, down to 'coming soon' previews and cliffhangers, by Charles **Band** in the *Subspecies* or *Puppet Master* sequels. In *Star Wars* (1977) and *Raiders of the*

Lost Ark (1981), Hollywood children George Lucas and Steven **Spielberg** began to revive the conventions of the chapterplays of their childhood in A-ticket big-budget movies, prompting remakes of serial properties: *Superman* (1978), *Flash Gordon* (1980), *Batman* (1988), *Dick Tracy* (1990), *The Shadow* (1994), *The Phantom* (1996).

Serling, Rod (1924–75)

American writer. Serling made a name in TV in the 50s, specialising in intense, earnest, relevant drama: 'Patterns' (*Kraft Television Theatre*, 1955), 'The Rack' (*The United States Steel Hour*, 1955), 'Requiem for a Heavyweight' (*Playhouse 90*, 1956), 'The Comedian' (*Playhouse 90*, 1957). He attained a genre profile as creator, frequent writer, executive producer and host of **The Twilight Zone** (1959–64), an anthology series that often uses s-f, fantasy or horror to grind axes Serling had worked in his 'realist' work.

Flawed by overwriting and occasional cliché concepts that would have been rejected by any pulp, *The Twilight Zone* is nevertheless an important, often outstanding series. Serling wrote many fine episodes, though the horror-oriented shows tend to come from Richard **Matheson** or Charles **Beaumont**. Serling revived the format, with a horror slant, in **Night Gallery** (pilot, 1969; series, 1970–73), which has a certain 70s paisley feel but draws interestingly on **Weird Tales** and **The Pan Book of Horror Stories** for source material. Serling also wrote screenplays (*Seven Days in May*, 1964; *Planet of the Apes*, 1968) and prose adaptations of his teleplays (*Stories From the Twilight Zone*, 1960).

Rod Serling

Sex: Veronica Carlson, Christopher Lee, *Dracula Has Risen From the Grave*

His clipped, much-imitated tones won him narrator jobs on documentaries (*Encounter With the Unknown*, 1975) and features (*Phantom of the Paradise*, 1974), and he appears, with Jodie Foster as a teenage witch, in 'Bubble, Bubble, Toil and Murder' (*Ironside*, 1972).

Marc Scott Zicree, *The Twilight Zone Companion* (1982); Joel Engel, *Rod Serling: The Dreams and Nightmares of Life in the Twilight Zone* (1989); Geoffrey F. Sander, *Serling: The Rise and Twilight of Television's Last Angry Man* (1992); Jean-Marc Lofficier, Randy Lofficier, *Into the Twilight Zone* (1995)

Sewell, Vernon (b. 1903)

British director. A prolific film-maker whose career stretched from the 30s through to the early 70s, Sewell's output included two early **Hammer** films, *The Dark Light* (1951) and *Black Widow* (1951). He adapted Pierre Mills and Celia de Vylar's play *L'Angoisse* (19??) on four occasions – as *The Medium* (1934), *Latin Quarter* (1945), *Ghost Ship* (1952) and *House of Mystery* (1961). In all of these, a sexually motivated crime committed in the past reaches out to the present and can only be dispelled by a psychic uncovering the crime and locating the victims. In *Latin Quarter*, the bodies are concealed, most strikingly, inside a statue, though one wonders why the murderer of *Ghost Ship* bothered to stash the corpses in the ballast rather than throw them overboard. *House of Mystery* is the most accomplished version: Sewell gives this modestly budgeted B movie structural complexity (with flashbacks within flashbacks) and a genuine sense of menace as a bland young househunting couple stumble into a story of sadistic cruelty. Sewell's later films are something of a disappointment, though *The Curse of the Crimson Altar* (1968), with its half-hearted psychedelia, has a certain period charm. PH

The Ghosts of Berkeley Square/1947 * *The Man in the Back Seat*/1961 * *The Blood Beast Terror*/1967 * *Burke & Hare*/1971

TV: *The Avengers*: 'Homicide and Old Lace' (u/co-d)/1967

Sex

A focus for physical anxiety and psychological obsession as well as a life-affirming act, sex is an integral component of horror. Many of the genre's most obviously modernising entries lay bare the carnal: between Fritz **Lang**'s fatalistic sex-death equations and the s&m revenants of *Hellraiser* (1987) come *The Unknown* (1927), *Cat People* (1942), *La frusta e il corpo* (*The Whip and the Flesh*, 1963), **Hammer** and David **Cronenberg**. The lascivious imperative of Hollywood horror prior to the strict enforcement of the Hays Code is obvious from *Dr. Jekyll and Mr. Hyde* (1931), **Murders in the Rue Morgue** (1932), *Mad Love* (1935) and even **King Kong** (1933), while latterday Europeans like **Borowczyk**, **Franco** and **Rollin** spend much energy switching between and mingling horror film and **pornography**. **Vampire** movies routinely detail seduction, but there is in contrast something masturbatory about Colin **Clive**'s cry of 'with my own hands!' in *Frankenstein* (1931). As spoofed in the lusty advances of Oddbod Jr in *Carry On Screaming* (1968), sex is central to horror's **teenage** appeal, putting monsters among starlets to excite frissons of fear and desire.

Sex as **violence**, **rape** is an inevitable horror subject in the candour of post-50s film. Sublimated in *Peeping Tom* (1960) and **Psycho** (1960) and graphically portrayed from *Rosemary's Baby* (1968) on, it is even committed by the monsters of *Humanoids from the Deep* (1980), *Inseminoid* (1980), *Incubus* (1981), *The Entity* (1982) and *Xtro* (1982). **Alien** (1979) and sequels consistently mine fears of impregnation while 'have sex and die' is the narrative rule of countless sub-**Halloween** (1978) **stalk-and-slash** epics. Exploited since at least **The Black Cat** (1934), the more passive infringement of necrophilia makes an AIDS-conscious comeback in *Lucker* (1986), *Nekromantik* (1988) and *Living Doll* (1989). DP

Trevor Eve, *Shadow Chasers*

Gustav von Seyffertitz

von Seyffertitz, Gustav (1863–1943)

Austrian actor. A long-faced player, at his peak as a silent villain: Moriarty in *Sherlock Holmes* (1922) and the **mad scientist** of *The Wizard* (1927). He conducts a seance in James **Whale**'s mystery *Remember Last Night?* (1935).

The Devil-Stone/1917 * *Unknown Treasures*/*The Bells*/*Sparrows*/1926 * *Seven Faces*/1929 * *The Bat Whispers*/1929 * *Rasputin and the Empress*/1932 * *Mystery Liner*/1934 * *The Moonstone*/1934 * *She*/1935 * *Son of Frankenstein*/1939

Shadow Chasers (US TV series, 1985–6)

Tabloid reporter 'Benny' Benedick (Dennis Dugan) teams up with anthropologist Jonathon Mackenzie (Trevor Eve) to investigate unexplained phenomena. Nina Foch costars as Dr Moorhouse, Jonathon's boss. In the pilot movie, directed by creator Kenneth Johnson, the duo investigate abnormal happenings in a small-town, tracking an evil spirit. Later episodes deal with the curse of King Tut ('Spirit of St Louis', 1985), **out-of-body experiences** ('Amazing Grace', 1985), **zombies** ('Parts Unknown', 1985), **vampires** ('Blood and Magnolias', 1986) and **werewolves** ('Curse of the Full Moon', 1986). Not dissimilar to **The X Files** (1993-) in subject, this light-hearted, short-lived adventure series never clicked. TM

Sharks

Sea creatures in horror are generally fictitious mutations. The object of native superstition in films such as *White Death* (1936)

and *Death Curse of Tartu* (1967), sharks were not perceived as monsters until Steven **Spielberg**'s *Jaws* (1975). This film, in its day the most financially successful of all time, was so influential that, as Stephen Sondheim observed, it is hard to hear its theme without experiencing nervousness. *Jaws* begat sequels (*Jaws 2*, 1978; *Jaws 3-D*, 1982; *Jaws: The Revenge*, 1987), a trend for fish films (*Killer Fish*, 1978; *Piranha*, 1978; *Barracuda*, 1978), a buzzword appropriated by unrelated B movies (*Jaws of Satan*, 1979) and is the name of an adversary of James Bond (Richard Kiel). Only the original film has merit and even this sags between the shark attacks: in its its wake are *Mako: The Jaws of Death* (1976), *Tentacles* (1976), *Tintorera* (1977), *Orca* (1977), *Bermude, la fossa maledetta* (*The Sharks' Cave*, 1978) and *Up from the Depths* (1979). *L'ultimo squalo* (1981), shown in the US as *Great White* and the UK as *Shark*, follows *Jaws* so closely that Universal applied for an injunction. A particularly audacious **3-D** rip-off, *A*P*E* (1976), pitted a **King Kong**-sized gorilla against a giant shark. After that, the only thing left was the shark-vs-**zombie** scene of *Zombi 2* (*Zombie Flesh Eaters*, 1979). DM

Sharp, Don (b. 1922)

Australian director. Sharp came to Britain as an actor and stayed to write for Group 3,

Sharks: *Jaws*

Barbara Shelley, Suzan Farmer, *Dracula, Prince of Darkness*

then direct for the Children's Film Foundation. Avowedly unfamiliar with horror, he coupled period insight with a careful sense of decadence in *Kiss of the Vampire* (1962), his **Hammer** debut. *Witchcraft* (1964), a Lon **Chaney Jr** vehicle made for Lippert, is almost as well-regarded for its cheaply realised revisionism. Though significant compromises were imposed by a new Hammer regime, the dynamic historical horror *Rasputin the Mad Monk* (1966) represents a further gothic experiment. Sharp's background in juvenilia and action-oriented second-unit work boosted Harry Alan **Towers**'s *The Face of Fu Manchu* (1965), but had less of an effect on its set-bound sequel, *The Brides of Fu Manchu* (1966).

Passing unambitiously into the mainstream, he managed one more worthwhile horror, the witty, ridiculous biker eccentricity *Psychomania* (1972). Christopher **Lee** reteaming *Dark Places* (1974) is at least better

Don Sharp

than the infantile *Secrets of the Phantom Caverns* (1983). Sharp turned down *To the Devil a Daughter* (1975) and retired in 1989. Excepting Hammer holiday romp *Devil-Ship Pirates* (1964) and psychological thriller *A Taste of Excitement* (1968), his only other pertinent feature is the underrated Lippert freak-fest *Curse of the Fly* (1965). DP

TV: *The Avengers*: 'Invasion of the Earthmen'/ 'The Curious Case of the Countless Clues'/ 'Get-a-Way'/1968 * *Hammer House of Horror*: 'Guardian of the Abyss'/1980 * *Q.E.D.*: 'Target: London'/'The Great Motor Race'/'To Catch a Ghost'/1982

Shelley, Barbara (b. 1933)

British actress. A former model, Shelley made her genre debut as the mousy neurotic turned feline predator in *Cat Girl* (1957). Long associated with **Hammer**, she is particularly effective as the repressed Victorian wife turned lustful **vampire** in *Dracula, Prince of Darkness* (1965). Her sensitive beauty is used hauntingly in *The Gorgon* (1964). MA

Blood of the Vampire/1958 * *Village of the Damned*/1960 * *The Shadow of the Cat*/1961 * *Rasputin the Mad Monk*/1965 * *Quatermass and the Pit*/1967 * *Ghost Story*/1974

TV: *The Avengers*: 'Dragonsfield'/1961; 'From Venus With Love'/1967 * *Doctor Who*: 'Planet of Fire'/1984 * *The Dark Angel*/1991

Shelley, Mary Wollstonecraft

[Godwin] (1797–1851)
British writer. Daughter of novelist and freethinker William Godwin and feminist Mary Wollstonecraft, Mary Shelley was the second wife of Percy Bysshe Shelley and half-sister of Claire Clairmont, Lord **Byron**'s sometime mistress. Her lasting fame rests on *Frankenstein; or: The Modern Prometheus* (1818), purportedly composed as part of a contest proposed by Byron. Subsequently, she wrote an end-of-the-world novel, *The Last Man* (1826). The **Frankenstein** theme is so central to horror that Mary Shelley figures in much fiction and meta-fiction: Guy Bolton's *The Olympians* (1961), Anne Edwards's *Haunted Summer* (1972), Brian Aldiss's *Frankenstein Unbound* (1973), Barbara Lynn Devlin's *I Am Mary Shelley* (1977), Kathryn Ptacek's *In Silence Sealed* (1988), Tim Powers's *The Stress of Her Regard* (1989), Paul West's *Lord Byron's Doctor* (1989), Walter Jon Williams's *Wall Stone Craft* (1992), Tom Holland's *The Vampyre* (1995). Film and TV Marys: Elsa **Lanchester** (*Bride of Frankenstein*, 1935), Vickery Turner ('The Need for Nightmare', *Omnibus*, 1974), Miranda Richardson ('Frankenstein and Dracula', *The South Bank Show*, 1986), Sylvestra le Touzel ('The True Story of Frankenstein', *Everyman*, 1986), Natasha Richardson (*Gothic*, 1986), Alice Krige (*Haunted Summer*, 1988), Lizzy McInnerny (*Rowing With the Wind*, 1989), Bridget Fonda (*Frankenstein Unbound*, 1990), Gwyneth Strong ('Mary Shelley', *Writing on the Line*, 1994).

Christopher Small, *Ariel Like a Harpy: Shelley, Mary and Frankenstein* (1972); Martin Tropp, *Mary Shelley's Monster: The Story of Frankenstein* (1976); Jane Dunn, *Moon in Eclipse: A Life of Mary Shelley* (1985); Anne K. Mellor, *Mary Shelley: Her Life, Her Fiction, Her Monsters* (1989)

Shepard, Paty (b. 1945)

American actress. In Spain from age eighteen, Shepard gained fame through TV com-

Natasha Richardson as Mary Shelley, *Gothic*

mercials. She appears alongside Paul **Naschy** in *Los monstruos del terror* (*Dracula vs. Frankenstein*, 1969), and plays the **Báthory**-inspired Countess Wandessa in *La noche de Walpurgis* (*Shadow of the Werewolf*, 1970) and *El retorno de Walpurgis* (*Curse of the Devil*, 1972). Vaguely resembling Barbara **Steele**, Shepard shows some flair for genre. Dissatisfaction with the parts offered – including *Mio caro assassino* (*My Dear Killer*, 1972) in which she is horribly mutilated by a

buzz saw – drove her into semi-retirement during the 80s, but she returned with cameos in such choice items as *Slugs, muerte viscosa* (*Slugs: The Movie*, 1987), *Descanse en peizas* (*Rest In Pieces*, 1987) and *Filo del hacha* (*Edge of the Axe*, 1987). MA

Escalofrio diabolico [*Diabolical Shudder*]/1971 * *El monte de las brujas* [*Witches Mountain*]/1972 * *La tumba de la isla maldita* [*Hannah, Queen of the Vampires*]/*El refugio del miedo* [*Refuge of*

Fear]/1973 * *Los diablos del mar* [*Sea Devils*]/ 1981

Sherlock Holmes and *The Hound of the Baskervilles*

Sherlock Holmes, the world's first consulting detective, died at the Reichenbach Falls – after a hand-to-hand fight with Professor Moriarty, 'the Napoleon of crime' – in 'The Final Problem' (1893). After novels (*A Study in Scarlet*, 1887; *The Sign of the Four*, 1890), a book of short stories (*The Adventures of Sherlock Holmes*, 1892) and several more *Strand* magazine stories, Arthur Conan **Doyle** was, he said, 'weary of his name' because 'he takes my mind from better things'. Black armbands were worn by usually sensible City of London businessmen; Doyle, meanwhile, wrote in his diary with evident relish 'killed Holmes'. Like his friend Arthur Sullivan, he had the sneaking suspicion that the work he was best at, which made his name a household word, was in some sense unworthy of an eminent Victorian. He preferred to write heavy-going historical novels.

Seven years later, in March 1901, while on a golfing holiday in Cromer, Doyle was told the legend of a phantom black dog. It was probably the story of the huge, shaggy Black Shuck (Shuck or Scucca meaning 'the demon' in Anglo-Saxon), a creature which appears at dusk and causes death to whoever catches sight of him. Doyle was beginning to flirt with spiritualism, and the legend appealed to his imagination. A couple of weeks later, he stayed at Park Hill House, Ipplepen on the edge of Dartmoor – where the coachman and groom was one Henry (or Harry) Baskerville. There, he seems to have heard another legend of a black dog (the folklore of the British Isles is littered with them), this time concerning a nasty squire called Richard Cabell (or Capel) who died on old midsummer's eve in 1672 near Buckfastleigh having been chased across Dartmoor by a pack of 'Whisht' hounds. The story of the phantom boar-hound of Hergest in the Welsh border-country, belonging to a family which intermarried with the Baskerville family of Clyro near Hay-on-Wye, may also have been an influence.

Doyle must also have read Sabine Baring Gould's *A Book of Dartmoor* (1900), which contains a wealth of material on the mists, mires, bogs, stone huts, tors and legends of the moor. For Baring Gould, as for Doyle, Dartmoor was an untamed wilderness rather than a living, working landscape. Basing himself – with journalist friend Bertram Fletcher Robinson – at Rowe's Duchy Hotel Princetown, just down the road from Dartmoor prison, Doyle explored the moor itself – including Fox Tor Mire (which became Grimpen Mire) and the neolithic huts of Grimspound, which had recently been excavated by archeologists. At this stage he decided to turn the novel he was planning from 'a real creeper' into a Holmes story, and he wrote it – as usual – at great speed, with very little revision: to confront the evil of the legend and provide a **rationalised supernatural** explanation, Doyle required a suitably larger-than-life master of destinies who could credibly stand up to it.

The Hound of the Baskervilles was published in *The Strand* magazine as an adventure which predated 'The Final Problem', in August 1901 – much to the relief of the shareholders. Two years before the golfing holiday, an American actor-manager had opened '*Sherlock Holmes* by Arthur Conan Doyle and William Gillette' – to great box-office – in New York. Mainly based on 'The Final Problem', it pitted Holmes against the Moriarty gang – with the big difference that the detective falls in love, not off a waterfall. This play, which opened at the Lyceum in September 1901 (one month after the first instalment of *Hound*) had already caused a strong revival of interest in Sherlock Holmes. It created the popular image of the great detective, complete with

Peter Cushing, *The Hound of the Baskervilles* (1958)

aquiline features, deerstalker hat and pipe (from Sidney Paget's illustrations rather than the text), and catch-phrase 'Elementary, my dear Watson' (which first appeared in an early acting version). Gillette's *Sherlock Holmes* may have contributed to Doyle's decision to write another Holmes novel, when he had vowed never to do so again.

One more novel (*The Valley of Fear*, 1915) and three further collections followed. In 'The Adventure of the Empty House' (1903), it was revealed to Dr Watson that Holmes had never actually died, and he was at liberty to pursue evil-doers in the narrative present, though Doyle specified that Holmes retired to keep bees in the year he returned to life and, with the exception of the World War I exploit 'His Last Bow' (1917), his adventures remained in the gaslit and fog-bound era rather than part of the 20th cen-

Arthur Conan Doyle

tury. Though *Hound* is the most concentratedly horrific of the canon, Doyle (elsewhere a writer of much supernatural or fantastical fiction) frequently confronts his detective with the gruesome or the apparently impossible – as in 'The Devil's Foot' (1910), 'The Creeping Man' (1923) and 'The Sussex Vampire' (1924). This gothic side of the stories has gained equal prominence with the deduction in the ensuing years, and Holmes has been pitted in film against real fiends like **Jack the Ripper** (*A Study in Terror*, 1965; *Murder By Decree*, 1979) and in books against imaginary ones like **Dracula** (Fred Saberhagen's *The Holmes/Dracula File*, 1978; Loren D. Estleman's *Sherlock Holmes vs. Dracula*, 1978), **Jekyll and Hyde** (Estleman's *Dr. Jekyll and Mr. Holmes*, 1979) and the **Phantom of the Opera** (Nicholas Meyer's *The Canary Trainer*, 1993;, Sam Siciliano's *The Angel of the Opera*, 1994).

The Hound of the Baskervilles is the most-filmed Sherlock Holmes story – partly because (unlike the other novels featuring the detective) it doesn't read like a fleshed-out short story with flashbacks, partly because of the atmosphere of the moor and its legend which contrasts so effectively with the cosiness and eccentricity of 221b Baker Street. P.D. James has called the novel an 'atavistic study of violence and evil in the mists of Dartmoor', while Watson reckoned that life itself was 'like that great Grimpen Mire . . . with no guide to point the track'. The conflict between civilised rationality (Holmes) and the uncivilised moor (the black dog) – a conflict which seems to have been part of Doyle's own psyche – was first filmed in Denmark as *Den graa dame* (*The Gray Dame*, 1903), in which the dog is rewritten as a spectral lady.

Alwin Neuss, cast in support to Viggo Larsen's Holmes in *Den graa dame*, donned the deerstalker for the first faithful version *Der hund von Baskerville* (1914), which inspired six sequels in which Holmes thwarts further schemes by the evil Stapleton. Subsequent film and TV versions star Eille Norwood (1921), Carlyle Blackwell (1929), Basil **Rathbone** (1939), Peter **Cushing** (1959, and a TV remake in 1968), Stewart Granger (1972), Peter Cook (1978, by far the worst version), Vasilly Livanov (1982), Tom Baker (1982), Ian Richardson (1983), **Scooby-Doo** ('The Hound of the Scooby-villes', *The New Scooby and Scrappy Doo Show*, 1983), Peter O'Toole (*Sherlock Holmes: The Baskerville Curse*, animated, 1984) and Jeremy Brett (1988). *Silver Blaze* (1936),

with Arthur Wontner, rejigs the story to make it a sequel set at Baskerville Hall, and even throws in Moriarty (Lynn Harding).

The 1938 film, with Rathbone and Nigel **Bruce**, produced a genuine sequel in *The Adventures of Sherlock Holmes* (1939), with George **Zucco** as Moriarty. Two years later, Rathbone and Bruce began a series of new-minted adventures with *Sherlock Holmes and the Voice of Terror* (1942), which brings the heroes up to date and sets them against the Nazis. Masterminded by Roy William **Neill**, later films play as much for horror as deduction, with especially creepy moments distinguishing *Sherlock Holmes Faces Death* (1943), *The Scarlet Claw* (1944), *The Spider Woman* (1944), *The Pearl of Death* (1944) and *The House of Fear* (1945). These Holmesian horrors were prefigured by *The Speckled Band* (1931), with Raymond Massey, and *A Study in Scarlet* (1933), with Reginald Owen, and echoed by such pulp adventures as *Young Sherlock Holmes* (1985). **Hammer**'s *Hound* stirred spirited scariness back into the mix, with an increased emphasis on Victorian **sex** and **violence**, influencing television versions with Douglas Wilmer (*Sherlock Holmes*, 1965) and Cushing (*The Cases of Sherlock Holmes*, 1968; *The Masks of Death*, 1984), and even some of Jeremy Brett's more extreme adventures (*The Last Vampyre*, 1993). CF

William S. Baring-Gould, *The Annotated Sherlock Holmes* (1967); Robert W. Pohle, Douglas C. Hart, *Sherlock Holmes on the Screen* (1977); Chris Steinburnner, Norman Michaels, *The Films of Sherlock Holmes* (1978); Peter Haining, *The Television Sherlock Holmes* (1991); Gordon E. Kelly, *Sherlock Holmes: Screen and Sound Guide* (1994)

Sherman, Gary (b. 1945)

American director. A former animator, Sherman made multivalent **cannibal** feature *Death Line* (1972) during his time in UK commercials; the film is a unique merging of classic British and modern American sensibilities. *Dead and Buried* (1981) also attempts an unusual currency, addressing the supremacy of the make-up artist through its necromantic mortician narrative. Ironically, gore reshoots were required. Sherman furnished the story for what became *Phobia* (1980), and, after TV and action sojourns, returned with milksop tower-block horror *Poltergeist III* (1988). DP

Lisa/1991

TV: *Murderous Vision*/1991

She-Wolf of London (US TV series, 1990–91)

Though it takes its title from Universal's *She-Wolf of London* (1946), this show, created by Mick **Garris** and Tom **McLoughlin**, owes more to *An American Werewolf in London* (1981). Randi Wallace (Kate Hodge), an American student in London, is attacked by a gypsy **werewolf** out of *The Wolf Man* (1941) and has to live with her monthly transformations into a rather cute monster (Diane Youdale). Professor Ian Matheson (Neil Dickson) helps Randi seek a cure, and they run into sundry ghosts and monsters. With 'Curiosity Killed the Cravitz', the fourteenth episode, the show changed its title to *Love and Curses* and relocated to California, limping along for five further episodes until cancellation. Despite likeable leads, never more than negligible.

Silva, Henry (b. 1928)

American character actor of Italian-Basque descent. Usually swarthy villains or sadistic megalomaniacs. SJ

The Manchurian Candidate/1962 * *Thirst*/1979 * *Alligator*/1980 * *Trapped*/1982 * *Vendetta dal futuro* [*Fists of Steel*]/*Amazon Women on the Moon*/1986 * *Dick Tracy*/1990 * *The Silence of the Hams*/1993

TV: *Alfred Hitchcock Presents*: 'A Better

Henry Silva, *Code of Silence*

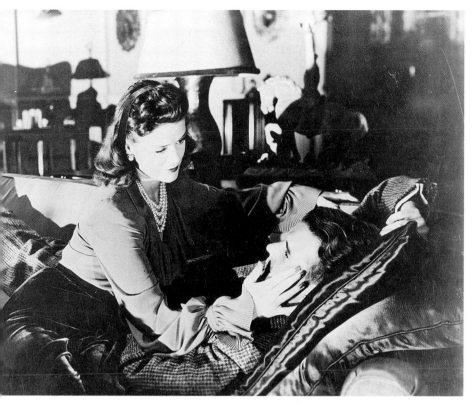

Simone Simon, Kent Smith, *Cat People*

Man (1941), for which he made up much now-standard **werewolf** lore. As a director, he helmed lurid B pictures which don't bear comparison with the work of his brother: *Bride of the Gorilla* (1951), *The Magnetic Monster* (1953), *Curucu, Beast of the Amazon* (1956), *Love Slaves of the Amazon* (1957), *The Devil's Messenger* (1962).

Black Friday/The Ape/The Invisible Man Returns/1940 * *Invisible Agent*/1942 * *I Walked With a Zombie/Son of Dracula/Frankenstein Meets the Wolf Man*/1943 * *House of Frankenstein/The Climax*/1944 * *The Beast With Five Fingers*/1946 * *Earth vs. the Flying Saucers*/1956 * *Sherlock Holmes und das Halsband des Todes* [*Sherlock Holmes and the Deadly Necklace*]/1962

TV: *Tales of Frankenstein*: 'The Face in the Tombstone Mirror' (d)/1958

Siodmak, Robert (1900–1973)

American-born German director, brother of Curt **Siodmak**. After establishing a reputation by co-directing *Menschen am Sonntag* (1929) with Edgar G. **Ulmer**, Siodmak had a career as a commercial director of thrillers in Germany (*Der Mann der seinen Mörder sucht*, 1931) and France (*Pièges*, 1939) before coming to Hollywood as a wartime refugee. He displayed visual flair and an eerie touch with *Son of Dracula* (1943), based on a story by his brother Curt, and did his B picture duty by *Cobra Woman* (1944), with Maria Montez

Bargain'/1956 * *Thriller*: 'Dark Legacy'/1961 * *Alfred Hitchcock Hour*: 'An Out for Oscar'/1963 * *The Outer Limits*: 'Tourist Attraction'/1963; 'The Mice'/1964 * *Voyage to the Bottom of the Sea*: 'The Enemies'/1965 * *Night Gallery*: 'The Doll'/1971 * *Black Noon*/1971 * *The Sixth Sense*: 'Shadow in the Well'/1972

Simon, Simone (b. 1911)

French actress. As 'Irena Dubrovna' in the **Lewton-Tourneur** *Cat People* (1942), a frigid Serbian exile afraid she will turn into a panther if sexually aroused, Simon is sexy and scary, innocent and dangerous. Her horror as she examines the claw-scratches she has accidentally left in the upholstery is a marvellous moment. She reprises Irena as a benevolent ghost in *Curse of the Cat People* (1944) and otherwise is striking as the wife in *La bête humaine* (1936), the **Devil**'s temptress in *All That Money Can Buy* (1941) and the noble prostitute in *Mademoiselle Fifi* (1944).

Johnny Doesn't Live Here Any More/1944

Siodmak, Curt (b. 1902)

German writer, director, brother of Robert **Siodmak**. A s-f writer and scenarist in Germany (the book and film of *F.P.1 antwortet nicht*, 1932) and America (the much-filmed **Donovan's Brain**, 1943), Siodmak has an impressive number of 40s horror credits though most are in collaboration or limited to original stories. An exception is **The Wolf**

Robert Siodmak's *Son of Dracula*

Robert Siodmak

Dorothy McGuire, Robert Siodmak's *The Spiral Staircase* (1945)

and Lon **Chaney Jr**, before launching on a series of impressive, fatalist **films noirs**. *Phantom Lady* (1943), from a Cornell **Woolrich** story, is at once a descent into urban nightmare and an early psycho movie, while *The Spiral Staircase* (1945) is a Victorian lady-in-peril story with mute Dorothy McGuire stalked by a maniac who murders the disabled. A similar mix of romantic fatalism, hardboiled Americana and psychotic violence informs *Christmas Holiday* (1944), *The Suspect* (1945), *The Killers* (1946), *The Dark Mirror* (1946), *Cry of the City* (1948), *Criss Cross* (1949) and *The File on Thelma Jordon* (1950).

Situation Comedy

The TV **comedy/fantasy** genre began with *Topper* (1953–6), a series based on the popular 1937 movie, starring Leo G. Carroll as Cosmo Topper, a mild bank clerk who buys a house haunted by the ghosts of the recently departed George and Marion Kirby (Robert Stirling and Ann Jeffreys). Most episodes depict the Kirbys' attempts to bring 'life' into the staid Topper household. *Topper* was popular, which is why it is surprising that no other comedy fantasy show appeared until 1963 and the landing of *My Favorite Martian* (1963–6). The genre's best year was 1964, with three hit shows and one flop: **The Munsters** (1964–6)), **Bewitched** (1964–72) and **The Addams Family** (1966) made it; the failure was *My Living Doll* (1964–5), with Bob Cummings as a psychiatrist in charge of the training of a female robot (Julie Newmar).

The next year brought *I Dream of Jeannie* (1965–70), *The Smothers Brothers Shows* (1965–6) and the legendary 'turkey' *My Mother the Car* (1965–6).

In the following years every possible aspect of the fantasy genre has been covered: spacemen and cavemen (*It's About Time*, 1966–7), superheroes (*Captain Nice*, 1967; *Mr. Terrific*, 1967), miracles (*The Flying Nun*, 1967–70), ghosts (*The Ghost and Mrs. Muir*, 1968–70), a Mary Poppins-style magical helpmeet (*Nanny and the Professor*, 1970–71), ESP (*The Girl with Something Extra*, 1973–4), a robot cop (*Holmes and Yoyo*, 1976), an angel (*Good Heavens*, 1976), a teen-witch (*Tabitha*, 1977–8), more aliens (*Mork and Mindy*, 1978–82; *ALF*, 1986–90), **Frankenstein** (*Struck by Lightning*, 1979), body-swapping

(*Turnabout*, 1979), **Dracula** (*Mr. & Mrs. Dracula*, 1980), weird small towns (**Eerie, Indiana**, 1991–2). Most 'straight' sit-coms, from 'Bilko's Vampire' (*The Phil Silvers Show*, 1958) on, manage a Halloween episode.
TM

The Sixth Sense (US TV series, 1972)

A one-hour dramatic show with Gary Collins as **parapsychologist** Dr Michael Rhodes investigating psychic phenomena. Robert Collins, Don Dingalls and John W. Bloch provided the teleplays that take Rhodes into the bizarre worlds of Satanism ('Whisper of Evil'), **witchcraft** ('Witch, Witch, Burning Bright'), past-life regression ('With Affection, Jack the Ripper') and cryonics ('Once Upon a Chilling'). Created by Anthony Lawrence, the flop series was rerun under the *Night Gallery* banner, with new introductions by Rod **Serling**. TM

Skal, David J. (b. 1952)

American critic. Author of important non-fiction studies: *Hollywood Gothic: The Tangled Web of 'Dracula' from Novel to Stage to Screen* (1990), *The Monster Show: A Cultural History of Horror* (1993), *Dracula: The Ultimate Illustrated Edition of the World-Famous Vampire Play* (editor, 1993), *Dark Carnival: The Secret World of Tod Browning, Hollywood's Master of the Macabre* (with Elias Savada, 1995), *V is for Vampire: The A-to-Z Guide to Everything Undead* (1996), *Screams of Reason: Mad Science and Modern Culture* (1996). His novels include *Scavengers* (1980) and *Antibodies* (1989).

Slasher Movies * See: Stalk and Slash

Slaughter, Tod [Norman Carter Slaughter] (1885–1956)

Barnstorming British actor, known for his revivals of melodramas which he preserved on film. He portrayed lecherous scoundrels and sadistic murderers, most memorably 'polishing 'em off' as **Sweeney Todd** in *Sweeney Todd the Demon Barber of Fleet Street* (1936). In the first scene of *Crimes at the Dark House* (1940), Slaughter laughs hysterically as he drives a tent-peg through his best

Gary Collins, *The Sixth Sense*

friend's head. William **Everson** noted 'Slaughter relished his villainy to the utmost, chuckling with delight at his own horrendous crimes, making a determined assault on the virginity of every young lady he met, and never letting slip any chance of making a dishonest pound.' SJ

Maria Marten, or the Murder in the Red Barn/ 1935 * *The Crimes of Stephen Hawke*/1936 * *It's Never Too Late to Mend*/*The Ticket of Leave Man*/ 1937 * *Sexton Blake and the Hooded Terror*/ 1938 * *The Face at the Window*/1939 * *The Curse of the Wraydons*/*Bothered By a Beard* (s)/ 1946 * *The Greed of William Hart*/1948 * *King of the Underworld*/*Murder at Scotland Yard*/ *Murder at the Grange*/*A Ghost for Sale*/1952

Smith, Clark Ashton (1893–1961)

American writer. A *Weird Tales* contributor and associate of the **Lovecraft** circle, Smith blends pulp material and an overripe decadent style, piling the verbiage sometimes to effect, sometimes prompting ridicule. He favours evocative fantasy settings (Atlantis, Zothique, Averoigne, Xiccarph), but often tells wry little horror stories. His collections include *Out of Space and Time* (1942), *Lost Worlds* (194) and *Genius Loci* (1948). Even more than Lovecraft, he has resisted adaptation, though 'Return of the Sorcerer' (1931) became a 1972 *Night Gallery* and *The Book of Eibon*, his answer to the **Necronomicon**, features in *L'aldilà* (*The Beyond*, 1981).

Smith, Cheryl 'Rainbeaux' (b. 1955)

American actress. A baby-doll blonde who appeared as 'Rainbeaux' in sexploitation (*The Other Cinderella*, 1977), Smith has a starring role in *The Legendary Curse of Lemora* (1973) and is unnervingly effective as a runaway choirgirl seduced by an ambiguous **vampire** lady. Among many trash credits, she is in Jonathan **Demme**'s *Caged Heat* (1974), Cheech and Chong's *Up in Smoke* (1978) and the *Heathers* (1988) like *Massacre at Central High* (1976). Typically cast as a nymphomaniac Southern belle (*Drum*, 1976) or a groupie (*The Phantom of the Paradise*, 1975).

The Incredible Melting Man/*Laserblast*/1977 * *Parasite*/1982

Smith, Dick (b. 1922)

American make-up artist, considered the godfather of special make-up effects. His *Monster Make-Up Handbook* (1965), sold through *Famous Monsters of Filmland*, inspired many subsequent artists. Smith

Madeline Smith

joined NBC on a six-month contract in 1945 as TV's first staff make-up artist and stayed fourteen years, before making his feature debut with *Misty* (1959). Though known for mainstream work *Midnight Cowboy* (1969), *Little Big Man* (1970), *The Godfather* (1973) and *Amadeus* (1984), his work on *The Exorcist* (1973) – transforming a cherubic Linda **Blair** into a vomit-spewing, head-spinning demon – revolutionised the horror field, essentially inventing the role of the special make-up effects artist. MS

House of Dark Shadows/1970 * *The Stepford Wives*/1974 * *Burnt Offerings*/1976 * *The Sentinel*/*Exorcist II: The Heretic*/1977 * *The Fury*/1978 * *Altered States*/1980 * *Ghost Story*/ *Scanners*/*The Fan*/1981 * *Spasms*/1982 * *The Hunger*/1983 * *Videodrome*/1984 * *Poltergeist 3*/1988 * *Tales From the Darkside: The Movie*/ 1990 * *Death Becomes Her*/1992

TV: *The Devil and Daniel Webster*/1960 * *Way Out*: 'False Face'/'Side Show'/'Soft Focus'/ 1961 * *Armchair Theatre*: 'The Picture of Dorian Gray'/1961 * *Dark Shadows*/1966-71 * *The Strange Case of Dr. Jekyll and Mr. Hyde*/ 1968 * *Drama Special*: 'Arsenic and Old Lace'/ 1969

Smith, Madeline (b. 1949)

British actress. Enormous of bust, tiny of voice, Smith was an early 70s starlet, typically cast as 'Erotica' in *Up Pompeii* (1971) and Roger Moore's first Bond girl in *Live and Let Die* (1973). For **Hammer**, she was cuddled and bitten by Ingrid **Pitt** in *The Vampire Lovers* (1970) and the mute assistant of

Snakes and Reptiles: Richard Crane, Beverly Garland, *The Alligator People*

Frankenstein and the Monster From Hell (1973).

Goodbye Gemini/1967 * *Taste the Blood of Dracula*/*Tam Lin*/1970 * *The Amazing Mr. Blunden*/1972 * *Theatre of Blood*/1973 * *Bloodbath at the House of Death*/1983

Smith, William (b. 1932)

Steely-eyed American actor. Cast as bikers in the 60s, he graduated to interesting character roles. SJ

Atlantis, The Lost Continent/1960 * *Grave of the Vampire*/1972 * *Invasion of the Bee Girls*/1973 * *Conan the Barbarian*/1982 * *Red Dawn*/1984 * *Moon in Scorpio*/*Hell Comes to Frogtown*/*Evil Altar*/1987 * *Maniac Cop*/*Memorial Day Massacre*/*B.O.R.N.*/1988 * *Deadly Breed*/1989

TV: *Alfred Hitchcock Hour*: 'The McGregor Affair'/1964 * *The Man Hunter*/1969 * *Crowhaven Farm*/1970 * *Kolchak The Night Stalker*: 'The Energy Eater'/1974 * *Fantasy Island*: 'The Lady and the Monster'/1981 * *The Twilight Zone*: 'Shadow Play'/1986

Smithee, Alan

Directors' Guild of America pseudonym (sometimes 'Allen'), used when an actual director (or directors) wishes his name removed from the credits. Collaborator Peter **Atkins** remarked on 'the stylistic touches a cineaste has learned to recognise as this auteur's signature: narrative incoherence, apalling performances, mismatched shots, and an overall dullness – all adding up, as they have done in nearly all his work, to the meta-textual *cri-de-coeur* "what's the fucking point, mate?"' Since inception in 1967 (for *Death of a Gunfighter*, directed by Don Siegel and Robert Totten), the Smithee name has been on a number of genre projects, replacing Michael Ritchie (a rare producer credit, *Student Bodies*, 1981), David **Lynch** (the TV extended version of *Dune*, 1984), Gilbert Cates ('Paladin of the Lost Hour', *The Twilight Zone*, 1985), Ramzi Thomas (*Appointment With Fear*, 1987), Lee Madden (*Ghost Fever*, 1987), Dean Tschetter (*Bloodsuckeing Pharaohs in Pittsburgh*, 1989), Fritz Kiersch (*Fatal Charm*, 1992), Rick Rosenthal (*The Birds II: Land's End*, 1994), Kevin **Yagher** and Joe Chapelle (*Hellraiser: Bloodline*, 1996) and ??????? (*Raging Angels*, 1996).

Snakes and Reptiles

Horror films with venomous snakes as their chief predators came into vogue in the 70s: *Stanley* (1972), *Jennifer* (1978), *King Cobra* (1979), *Venom* (1981), *Spasms* (1982), *Serpent Warriors* (1986), *Fair Game* (1988). A python crushes Christopher **Lee** in *The Two Faces of Dr. Jekyll* (1960), but the forthcoming *Anaconda* will mark the first time that a plot has been constructed around a constrictor. Despite ugliness, other reptiles feature only sporadically in horror: big lizards appear in *The Giant Gila Monster* (1959) and *Space Avenger* (1989); Neville Brand feeds victims to his crocodile in *Death Trap* (1976) and a rogue croc terrorises the outback in the Australian *Crocodile* (1977); the highly enjoy-

Snakes and Reptiles: Amanda Donohoe, *Lair of the White Worm*

Gale Sondergaard

RIGHT *The Spectre* (DC Comics). Artist: Tom Mandrake

able *Alligator* (1980), written by John Sayles, inspired a mundane 1991 sequel.

Frogs (1972), in which the massed creatures of the swamplands turn on their human aggressors, is an early example of **eco-horror**. The Bermuda Triangle conceals a giant turtle in *The Bermuda Depths* (1978); the eponymous creature of *Gamera* (*Gamera the Invincible*, 1966) and many sequels is also a turtle. Human-reptile transformation, the result of either native ritual or scientific experiment, occurs in *Cult of the Cobra* (1955), *The Alligator People* (1959), *The Snake Woman* (1961), *The Curse of the Swamp Creature* (1966), *The Reptile* (1966), *La muerte viviente* (*The Snake People*, 1968), *SSSSSSS* (1973), *Lair of the White Worm* (1988) and *Curse II: The Bite* (1989). DM

Snuff Movies * See: **Film-making**

Sociopaths * See: **Psychopaths**

Soavi, Michele (b. 1957)
Italian director, actor. Originally monster food in *Alien 2 sulla terra* (*Alien Terror*, 1980) and *Paura nella città dei morti viventi* (*City of the Living Dead*, 1980), Soavi gravitated to assisting Dario **Argento** and Aristide **Massaccesi**. He directed pop videos and the documentary *Il mondo di Dario Argento* (*Dario Argento's World of Horror*, 1986) before debuting with the stylish **stalk-and-slash** *Deliria* (*Stagefright*, 1987). Subsequent features have won some admirers, though he consistently plumps for elaborate visuals over coherence or emotional effects.

Il gatto nero [*The Black Cat*] (a)/*Rosso sangue* [*Absurd*] (a)/1981 * *La casa con la scala nel buio* [*A Blade in the Dark*] (a)/*Tenebre* [*Tenebrae*] (2nd assist d)/1983 * *Demoni* (a)/*Phenomena* (assist d/a)/1985 * *Opera* (2nd unit d)/1987 * *La maschera del demonio* (a)/*La chiesa* [*The Church*] (d)/1989 * *La setta* [*The Sect*] (d)/1991 * *Dellamorte Dellamore* [*Cemetery Man*] (d)/1994

Sole, Alfred (b. 1943)
American director, writer. His horror high is *Communion* (1976): coruscating Catholic **stalk-and-slash**, it was made to answer those who precipitated his prosecution over debut feature *Deep Sleep* (1972), a skittish no-budget porno. *Tanya's Island* (1981) and *Pandemonium* (1982) are regressive journeyman efforts that led to Sole's retirement from direction. Author (with Paul Monette) of two **Friday the 13th: The Series** episodes ('Tales of the Undead', 1988; 'Bedazzled', 1988), he has latterly worked as a production designer. DP

Soles, P.J. (b. 1956)
American actress. A high-school icon as Nancy **Allen**'s baseball cap-wearing sidekick in *Carrie* (1976), the most promiscuous victim ('totally') in **Halloween** (1978) and the Ramones' greatest fan in *Rock 'n' Roll High School* (1979).

Blood Bath/1975 * *Alienator*/*B.O.R.N.*/1989 * *Little Bigfoot*/*Uncle Sam*/1996

TV: *The Possessed*/1977 * *Out There*/1995

Sondergaard, Gale [Edith Sondergaard] (1899–1985)
Sinister but rather sexy American actress, often a menacing housekeeper. She is capable of delivering lines like 'It won't really be dying because you'll live on in this plant' (*The Spider Woman Strikes Back*) but also of subtle dramatics (*The Letter*, 1940). Married to Communist director Herbert Biberman, her career never recovered from 50s blacklisting-by-association. SJ

Maid of Salem/1937 * *The Cat and the Canary*/1939 * *The Black Cat*/1941 * *The Spider Woman*/*The Climax*/*The Invisible Man's Revenge*/1944 * *The Time of Their Lives*/1946 * *The Savage Intruder*/1973 * *Echoes*/1983

TV: *Get Smart*: 'Rebecca of Funny-Folk Farm'/1970 * *Night Gallery*: 'The Dark Boy'/1971 * *The Cat Creature*/1973

Southern Gothic
Recognised as a genre of twentieth-century American letters (e.g., William Faulkner, Flannery O'Connor, Tennessee Williams), 'Southern Gothic' has haunted cinema since as early as *The Birth of a Nation* (1915). Defined through the likes of the Mary Pickford vehicle *Sparrows* (1926), the cinema of Southern Gothic found its seminal entries in *To Kill a Mockingbird* (1962) and *Cape Fear* (1962). Its essential films portray an American South whose faux aristocracy, locked away in dilapidated mansions and misty plantations, must confront the death of Dixie Romanticism and its perverse dream of racial (and class) coexistence through servitude.

Though the gothic impulse survives in Robert **Aldrich**'s *Hush . . . Hush, Sweet Charlotte* (1964), Don Siegel's *The Beguiled* (1971), Richard Fleischer's *Mandingo* (1975) and Bill Condon's *Sister, Sister* (1988), *Cape Fear* signals a recurrent vision of the South as a backward and barbarous landscape that welcomes only violence and death. The myth of Southern hospitality is undone in blood-drenched predation and degradation in films as diverse as H.G. **Lewis**'s *Two Thousand Maniacs!* (1964), *Lemora: A Child's Tale of the Supernatural* (1973), Tobe **Hooper**'s **The Texas Chain Saw Massacre** (1974) and *Death Trap* (1977), and, in particular, *Deliverance* (1972) and the aptly titled *Southern Comfort* (1981). DW

The Spectre

Created by writer Jerry Siegel and artist Bernard Baily, the Spectre (murdered cop Jim Corrigan returned to Earth as a cloaked ghost) made his debut in *More Fun Comics* (1940). Most important of DC's early supernatural superheroes, who included Dr Occult and Dr Fate, the Spectre's original series petered out in 1945 but he is often revived. After a spell as an ultra-violent vigilante and an increase in powers which brought him close to godhood, the Spectre has in the 90s been taken back to street level by writer John Ostrander and artist Tom Mandrake.

Spiders * See: Insects and Arachnids

Steven Spielberg

Spielberg, Steven (b. 1947)

American director who has made some of the most successful films of all time. A keen film-maker since childhood (his mother once cooked cherries jubilee in a pressure cooker so he could film the explosion for an amateur horror movie), he accrued experience bluffing his way into studios and watching directors like **Hitchcock** working on set. He made his critical reputation with the TV movie *Duel* (1971), theatrically released in Europe to great success. It remains his best and least sentimental effort. He cemented his audience-pleasing reputation with *Jaws* (1975), his brand-name image with *Raiders of the Lost Ark* (1981), his blockbuster status with *ET: The Extra-Terrestrial* (1982), his monster movie aptitude with *Jurassic Park* (1993) and his Oscar credentials with *Schindler's List* (1993).

Spielberg is the Peter Pan of popular cinema – he even directed a version, *Hook* (1992) – and his 'gift' is the enviable ability he has to instil a sense of wonder in children and

adults alike. Detractors feel he is the bland face of modern fantasy cinema, reducing everything to comic-strip safeness. As producer, his horrid streak shows in *Poltergeist* (1982), *Gremlins* (1984), *Arachnophobia* (1990) and *Gremlins II: The New Batch* (1990). AJ

Twilight Zone: The Movie (co-d)/1982 * *Indiana Jones and the Temple of Doom*/1984 * *Indiana Jones and the Last Crusade*/1989 * *The Lost World*/1997

TV: *Night Gallery*: pilot/1969; 'Make Me Laugh'/1970 * *Something Evil*/1972 * *Amazing Stories* (p)/1985–87

Tony Crawley, *The Steven Spielberg Story* (1983); John Baxter, *Steven Spielberg* (1996)

Spinell, Joe [Joseph Spagnuolo] (1936–89)

American actor; specialist in thugs, sleazeballs and psychos. A chance encounter with Sam **Peckinpah** in a taxi led to an introduction to Francis **Coppola**, who cast him in *The Godfather* (1972). He starred in, and executive produced, William **Lustig**'s *Maniac* (1980), a graphic gore exploiter often cited as the most sickening of the **stalk-and-slash** cycle. He died during pre-production on the unmade *Maniac II*. AJ

The Exorcist/1973 * *Taxi Driver*/1976 * *The Ninth Configuration*/1979 * *Cruising*/1980 * *The Last Horror Film*/1982 * *Eureka*/1985

TV: *Vampire*/1979

Splatter Movies

The term seems to have been coined by George A. **Romero** and has replaced the more staid 'gore movies' or the more repulsive 'meat movies' just as the kinetic, Tom **Savini**-created exploding **heads** and dismembered **zombies** of **Romero**'s films have eclipsed the slow-moving, stagey eviscerations of H.G. **Lewis**. Popularised by John **McCarty**'s *Splatter Movies* (1981, revised 1984), the expression refers to those films in which gory make-up effects are prominent, whether integrated into the overall tone as in *Dawn of the Dead* (1979) or *The Evil Dead* (1982) or merely set-pieces as in *Friday the 13th* (1980) and *Maniac* (1980). The heyday of pure splatter was quite brief in the late 70s and early 80s, eclipsed somewhat by the fashion for more fantastical transformation effects in *An American Werewolf in London* (1980) or *The Thing* (1982). See also: **Cannibalism**, *Fangoria*, **Stalk-and-Slash**, **Video Nasties**.

Splatterpunk

An unwieldy coinage in imitation of the successful 'cyberpunk' s-f movement, 'splatterpunk' was first used in the late 80s to describe a loose group of mostly American writers who littered stories with explicit and flashy descriptions of ultra-**violence** just as the makers of **splatter movies** litter their films with gory special effects. Leading lights of splatterpunk, most of whom have tried to dissociate themselves from it, are Clive **Barker**, David **Schow**, John Skipp and Craig Spector, Joe Lansdale and Richard Christian **Matheson**. While coattail-riders have written much that is objectionable and trite, the best work of these writers, who are too varied in approach and style to feel like a movement, has considerable subtlety and merit. Paul M. Sammon's anthology *Splatterpunks* (1990) is less useful a summation of the subgenre than Skipp and Spector's *Book of the Dead* (1989), which pays homage to filmic roots with stories that play riffs on George A. **Romero**'s Living Dead films. The term achieved mainstream currency when applied, not inaptly, to Bret Easton Ellis's *American Psycho* (1991).

Stalk-and-Slash

Closely related both to the psychological horror film and to the **splatter** movie, the stalk-and-slash film was conceived by **Hitchcock**'s *Psycho* (1960), nurtured by **Hooper**'s *The Texas Chain Saw Massacre* (1974) and came of age with **Carpenter**'s *Halloween* (1978). Here the **psychopath**, supernatural or all-too-natural, figures as central menace to a string of (usually) women-in-peril, though any vaguely promiscuous teenager is a natural target. Countless examples litter cinema in the 70s and 80s, ranging from exploitation schlock to 'classier' big-budget offerings: *He Knows You're Alone* (1980), *Dressed to Kill* (1980), *The Boogeyman* (1980), *Hell Night* (1981) and *Jagged Edge* (1985), as well as the *Halloween* and *Friday the 13th* films.

Black satires include *The Slumber Party Massacre* (1982) and *Motel Hell* (1980). While the stalk-and-slash movie is itself a hybrid of thriller and horror narratives, elements of it are present in 'purer' works of surreal or body-horror (eg. the *Alien* trilogy or the *Nightmare on Elm Street* films). Alongside *Psycho*, a worthy co-ancestor which mixes psychotic slashing with liberal doses of self-reflexive voyeurism is **Powell**'s *Peeping Tom* (1960), itself spawning an energetic tradition of voyeuristically hooked slashers in

The Eyes of Laura Mars (1978), *Manhunter* (1986) and *Strange Days* (1995). LRW

Vera Diker, *Games of Terror* (1990); Carol Clover, *Men, Women and Chain Saws: Gender in the Modern Horror Film* (1992)

Star Trek (US TV series, 1966–9)

Created by Gene Roddenberry, *Star Trek* has grown to be such a phenomenon that its devotees outnumber those of the science fiction genre from which it emerged. Initially a marginally popular show following the adventures of Captain Kirk (William Shatner) and Mr Spock (Leonard Nimoy) of the starship *Enterprise*, the franchise has spun off novelisations, original novels, a film series commencing with *Star Trek: The Motion Picture* (1979) and sequel or tributary TV series: the cartoon *Star Trek* (1973–4), *Star Trek: The Next Generation* (1987–94), *Star Trek: Deep Space 9* (1993–), *Star Trek: Voyager* (1995–). The original show has an inclination to gothic horror, aided by scripts from Richard **Matheson** and Robert **Bloch**, with Kirk and Company facing alien salt **vampires** ('The Man Trap', 1966), **Frankenstein**ian androids ('What Are Little Girls Made Of?, 1966), castle-dwelling minigods ('The Squire of Gothos', 1966), sorcerers ('Catspaw', 1967) and a body-hopping **Jack the Ripper** ('Wolf in the Fold', 1967). The spin-off shows tend to play up soap and politics at the expense of the horrific, but *The Next Generation*'s 'Sub Rosa' (1994) is a ghostly romance.

Barara Steele, *Lo spettro*

Steckler, Ray Dennis (b. 1939)

American writer, producer, director, actor. Abler and more eccentric than Z-movie fellows Ted **Mikels** and H.G. **Lewis**, Steckler worked on Timothy Carey's Messianic cult item *The World's Greatest Sinner* (1962) before his own directorial debut, *Wild Guitar* (1962). A goofily extempore, horror-related quartet followed: *The Incredibly Strange Creatures Who Stopped Living and Became Mixed-Up Zombies!!?* (1963), *The Thrill Killers* (1964), *Rat Pfink a Boo Boo* (1965) and shorts aggregate *The Lemon Grove Kids Meet the Monsters* (1966). Billed as 'the first monster **musical**', *Creatures* had shock-masked ghouls raid the audience at many engagements; the more concerted *Killers* repeated the gimmick, and again stars Steckler under his Cash Flagg pseudonym.

His last watchable relevancy is *Sinthia, the Devil's Doll* (1970), a surreal psychosexual effort attributed to Sven Christian because Texan financiers thought it 'too European'. As Wolfgang Schmidt, he has since managed a smattering of bowed no-budget **stalk-and-slash**: *The Chooper* (1971), *The Hollywood Strangler Meets the Skid Row Slasher* (1979), *The Las Vegas Serial Killer* (1985), *The Las Vegas Thrill Killers* (1993). Also a porn director and cinematographer, Steckler appears in *Eegah!* (1962) and is divorced from frequent heroine Carolyn Brandt. DP

Steele, Barbara (b. 1938)

British actress. Virtually uncastable in Rank's constipated 50s output, Steele escaped the clutches of the Charm School to become unquestionably the ultimate baroque horror starlet. From her astonishing genre debut as **vampire** and victim in Mario **Bava**'s superlative *La maschera del demonio* (*The Mask of Satan*, 1960), the 'only girl whose eyelids can snarl' (*pace* Raymond Durgnat) became a popular fixture in Italian gothics.

Turbulent sexual undertones and obsessive attention to decorative detail perfectly compliment her otherworldly glamour. Adept at both persecuted **heroines** and lethal *femmes fatales*, she is the fetishist focus of outrageously lurid plotlines, notably Riccardo **Freda**'s kinky classic (*L'orribile segreto del dr. Hichcock* (*The Terror of Dr. Hichcock*, 1962). Mario Caiano's *Gli amanti d'oltretomba* (*Night of the Doomed*, 1965) is a rare incidence of Steele using her actual voice. One of her best films, *5 tombe per un medium* (*Cemetery of the Living Dead*, 1965), unfortunately provides her most thankless role. *Lo spettro* (*The Ghost*, 1963), *Danza macabra* (*Castle of Blood*,

301

1963) and *I lunghi capelli della morte* (*The Long Hair of Death*, 1964) allow her ornately eerie presence to dominate the proceedings.

After the subtler *Un angelo per Satana* (*An Angel for Satan*, 1966), her career began to come adrift; she expressed concern at not being known for upmarket projects like **Fellini**'s *8½* (1963). Resurfacing Stateside, she took excellent supporting roles in *Caged Heat* (1974), *Shivers* (1974), *Piranha* (1978) and *Silent Scream* (1980) but eventually gravitated to production. Unable to escape her macabre roots, she was involved in the revival of *Dark Shadows* (1990–1). Pleasingly, Steele's attitude to her 60s output has recently softened, and the only actress to truly deserve the title 'Queen of Horror' has come forward to reclaim her crown. MA

Pit and The Pendulum/1961 * *Il lago di Satana* [*The She Beast*]/1965 * *The Curse of the Crimson Altar*/1968 * *The Island of Dr. Moreau* (role deleted)/1996

TV: *Honeymoon with a Stranger*/1969 * *Night Gallery*: 'The Sins of the Father'/1972

Stefano, Joseph (b. 1922)

American writer, producer. After collaborating with **Hitchcock** in adapting Robert **Bloch**'s 1959 novel into *Psycho* (1960), Stefano gained a horror reputation that won him a producing-writing deal on *The Outer Limits* (1963–5), to which he contributed dark episodes. The credits have haunted him: he scripted the interesting *Psycho IV: The Beginning* (1990) and is an associate on the *Outer Limits* revival (1995–).

The Eye of the Cat/1969 * *The Kindred*/1986 * *Blackout*/1988

TV: *The Outer Limits*: 'Nightmare'/'It Crawled Out of the Woodwork'/'The Zanti Misfits'/ 1963; 'The Mice'/'Don't Open Till Doomsday'/'The Invisibles'/'The Bellero Shield'/ 'Fun and Games'/'The Special One'/'A Feasability Study'/'The Chameleon'/'The Forms of Things Unknown' * *Revenge*/1971 * *Home for the Holidays*/1972 * *Snowbeast*/1977

Steiner, Max (1888–1971)

Austrian composer. Responsible for an amazing 307 scores in Hollywood's Golden Age, Steiner won three Academy Awards and a further twenty-three nominations. More than any other composer, he was responsible for championing the full symphonic score at a time when Hollywood favoured 'source' music. Though his best-remembered score is *Gone With the Wind*

(1939), his thrilling and uniquely theatrical style is heard at its best in **King Kong** (1932). SL

The Monkey's Paw/*The Phantom of Crestwood*/ *The Most Dangerous Game*/*Bird of Paradise*/ 1932 * *The Son of Kong*/1933 * *She*/1935 * *Arsenic and Old Lace*/1944 * *The Beast With Five Fingers*/1948 * *Two on a Guillotine*/1966

The Stepfather (1987)

Directed by Joseph **Ruben** from a script by Donald E. Westlake, this features a remarkable performance from Terry **O'Quinn** as a **serial killer** who believes so heavily in **family values** that he murders his new families when they let him down. A theatrical flop, it was one of the first films to generate a series on the strength of video rentals. O'Quinn returns in Jeff **Burr**'s *Stepfather II* (1989) but is replaced via plastic surgery by Robert Wightman in Guy Magar's *Stepfather III* (1992).

Though *The Stepfather* is interesting for its vicious dissection of the 80s values embodied by such rivals as *Fatal Attraction* (1987), a run of imitative minor chillers have tended to demonise powerless outsiders rather than blame an unrealistic sit-com suburban ideal: *The Perfect Bride* (1991), *The Hand That Rocks the Cradle* (1992), *Unlawful Entry* (1992), *Single White Female* (1992), *The Good Son* (1993), *The Substitute* (1993), *The Temp* (1993), *The Crush* (1993), *The Paperboy* (1994), *The Nurse* (1995), *The Cable Guy* (1996.

Steven Spielberg's Amazing Stories * See: *Amazing Stories*

Stevens, Brinke [Charlene Brinkeman] (b. 1954)

American actress. A leading light of the posse of starlets known as 'Scream Queens', Stevens appears in forgettable films but is second only to Linnea **Quigley** in tireless self-publicity. Typical early roles: 'girl in bathroom no. 3' (*Body Double*, 1984), 'girl in shower' (*Fatal Games*, 1984), 'body double for Diana Scarwid' (*Psycho III*, 1986). She scripted *Teenage Exorcist* (1993).

The Slumber Party Massacre/*Sole Survivor*/1982 * *The Witching* (footage added to *Necromancy*, 1971)/1983 * *Dark Romances*/1986 * *Nightmare Sisters*/*Slave Girls From Beyond Infinity*/*Sorority Babes in the Slime-Ball Bowl-a-Rama*/1987 * *The Jigsaw Murders*/*Phantom of the Mall: Eric's Revenge*/*Attack of the B Movie Monster*/1988 * *Transylvania Twist*/ *Grandmother's House*/1989 * *Spirits*/*Haunting*

Fear/1990 * *Shadows in the City*/*Roots of Evil*/ 1991 * *Munchie*/1992 * *Scream Queen Hot Tub Party*/1993 * *Mommy*/*Jack-O*/1995

TV: *Tales From the Darkside*: 'Basher Malone'/ 1988

Stevens, Onslow [Onslow Ford Stevenson] (1902–77)

American actor. Notable as **mad scientist** Franz Edelmann, infected with the Count's blood in *House of Dracula* (1945). SJ

Secret of the Blue Room/1933 * *The Vanishing Shadow*/1934 * *Life Returns*/1935 * *The Monster and the Girl*/1941 * *Angel on My Shoulder*/1946 * *The Night Has a Thousand Eyes*/*The Creeper*/1948 * *Mark of the Gorilla*/ 1950 * *Them!*/1954

Stevenson, Robert Louis (1850–94)

Scots writer. *Treasure Island* (1883) and *Strange Case of Dr. Jekyll and Mr. Hyde* (1886) are permanent additions to the shelf of popular classic literature. Aside from **Jekyll and Hyde**, one of the key properties of the horror genre, Stevenson wrote a few other oft-anthologised horror stories: 'The Body Snatcher' (1884), filmed in 1945 and on *Mystery and Imagination* (1966) and 'Markheim' (1887), made for TV in 1952, 1974 and 1990. *The Suicide Club* (1878), about a bizarre secret society, was filmed in 1909, 1910 (*The American Suicide Club*), 1913 (*Simple Simon and the Suicide Club*), 1914, 1919 (*Unheimliche Geschichten*), 1931 (*Unheimliche Geschichten*), 1936 (*Trouble for Two*), 1946 (*La dama en el muerte*), 1958 (on *Matinee Theatre*), 1960 (on *The Mystery Show*), 1968 (on *Mystery*

Onslow Stevens

Robert Louis Stevenson

Glenn Strange

and Imagination), 1971, 1973 and 1988. Other Stevenson-derived horrors: *The Strange Door* (1951), *The Wrong Box* (1966). Laurence Carter and Wayne Brooks play Stevenson in 'The Need for Nightmare' (*Omnibus*, 1974).

Stoker, Bram (1847–1912)

Anglo-Irish writer. Besides ***Dracula*** (1987), Stoker produced lesser novels and a handful of fine stories collected in *Dracula's Guest* (1914). *The Jewel of the Seven Stars* (1903) deals with the resurrection of an Egyptian **mummy** and has been frequently adapted or imitated: *The Wraith of the Tomb* (1915), *La cabeza viviente* (*The Living Head*, 1959), 'Curse of the Mummy' (*Mystery and Imagination*, 1970), *Blood From the Mummy's Tomb* (1971), *The Awakening* (1980). Ken **Russell**'s *Lair of the White Worm* (1988) is from the 1911 novel. Stoker features in novels, often juxtaposed with actual **vampires**: Nicholas Meyer's *The West End Horror* (1976), Arabella Randolphe's *The Vampire Tapes* (1977), Simon Hawke's *The Dracula Caper* (1988), Brian Aldiss's *Dracula Unbound* (1991), Kim Newman's *Anno Dracula* (1992), Mark Frost's *The List of Seven* (1993). Screen Stokers: Dominic Allan ('The Need for Nightmare', *Omnibus*, 1974), Kevin Bundy ('The Baron's

Bride', ***Friday the 13th***, 1988), Kevin Alber (*Burial of the Rats*, 1995).

Harry Ludlam, *A Biography of Dracula* (1962); Leonard Wolf, *The Annotated Dracula* (1975); Daniel Farson, *Bram Stoker: The Man Who Wrote Dracula* (1975); Christopher Frayling, *Vampyres: Lord Byron to Count Dracula* (1990); David Skal, *Hollywood Gothic: The Tangled Web of 'Dracula' from Novel to Stage to Screen* (1990); Barbara Belford, *Bram Stoker: A Biography of the Author of Dracula* (1996)

Stone, Oliver (b. 1946)

American director, writer, producer. Oscar-centrically suppressed, Stone's debut features are not *Midnight Express* (1978) and *Platoon* (1986), but overwrought horrors *Seizure* (1973) and *The Hand* (1981). The first has a novelist at war with his latest characters; the second pits a comics artist against his severed tool-of-trade: both dramatise the frustrations Stone experienced on graduating from NYU in 1971. Though often horror inflected, his acknowledged works harness the autobiographic in a more politicised fashion by recalling Vietnam brutalities. Stone has latterly renewed his interest in the genre. *JFK* (1991) makes rousingly mondo-ish use of the Zapruder assasination footage, while complex, frenzied hate film *Natural Born Killers* (1994) employs a vogue pair of psychos to critique the US; in between, the director oversaw the conspiratorial TV fantasy *Wild Palms* (1993). New York sex-horror *Sugar Cookies* (1972) credits Stone as associate producer. DP

Conan the Barbarian (w)/1982 * *Talk Radio*/1988 * *Blue Steel* (p)/1989 * *The Doors*/1991

Strange, Glenn [George Glenn Strange] (1899–1973)

American actor. Formerly a fiddle player, heavyweight boxer and rodeo rider, he appears as a villain in cowboy films. Coached by **Karloff** to play the **Frankenstein** Monster in *House of Frankenstein* (1944), he recreated the role in *House of Dracula* (1945) and *Meet Frankenstein* (1948), also on TV's *Colgate Comedy Hour* with **Abbott and Costello** in 1953 and the amateur short *The Adventures of the Spirit* (1963). He unsuccessfully tested for the roles of *Tarzan the Ape Man* (1932) and the *Creature from the Black Lagoon* (1954), and in later years played Sam the bartender on *Gunsmoke* (1960-73). SJ

Flash Gordon/1936 * *The Mad Monster*/*The Mummy's Tomb*/1942 * *The Black Raven*/1943

* *The Monster Maker*/1944 * *Master Minds*/1949

TV: *Thriller*: 'A Good Imagination'/1961

Strange Case of Dr. Jekyll and Mr. Hyde * See: **Jekyll and Hyde**

Straub, Peter (b. 1943)

American writer. Originally a poet and mainstream novelist (*Marriages*, 1973), Straub turned to horror with *Julia* (1975), filmed as *Full Circle* (*The Haunting of Julia*, 1976), and a run of subtle, creepy, best sellers: *If You Could See Me Now* (1977), *Ghost Story* (1979, filmed 1981), *Shadowland* (1980), *Floating Dragon* (1983), *The Talisman* (with Stephen **King**, 1984). Recently, he has forsaken outright supernatural for macabre mysteries: *Koko* (1988), *Mystery* (1989), *The Throat* (1993), *The Hellfire Club* (1996). His short fiction is collected in *Houses Without Doors* (1990).

Strayer, Frank (1891–1964)

American director. Poverty-row hack Strayer turned out the interesting **vampire** variants *The Vampire Bat* (1933) and *Condemned to Live* (1935). Influenced by, but not slavishly imitative of, the Universal horrors, these are strange pictures with wild ideas. *The Vampire Bat* has fine ham performances from Lionel **Atwill** ('Mad? I who have discovered the secret of life, you call me mad?') and Dwight **Frye** ('You give Hermann apple, Hermann give you nice soft bat').

The Monster Walks/1932 * *The Ghost Walks*/1935

Erich von Stroheim

Strieber, Whitley (b. 1945)

American writer. *The Wolfen* (1978; filmed 1981) and *The Hunger* (1981; filmed 1983) reinterpret **werewolf** and **vampire** themes with more ingenuity than style, but Strieber is best known for *Communion* (1987; filmed 1989 with Christopher **Walken** as Strieber), an account of a bizarre personal experience which could be interpreted as an alien abduction. *War Day* (1984), with James Kunetka, is an impressive novel of nuclear war, in which Strieber appears as a fictional character. His other novels are more conventional fictions: *Black Magic* (1982), *The Night Church* (1983), *Cat Magic* (1986), *Billy* (1990), *The Wild* (1991), *Unholy Fire* (1992).

Strock, Herbert L. (b. 1918)

American director. A former editor, Strock went into staid s-f for *Riders to the Stars* (1953), which he produced, *Gog* (1954) and many episodes of *Science Fiction Theatre* (1955–7). He hooked up with Herman **Cohen** and handled *I Was a Teenage Frankenstein* (1957), *Blood of Dracula* (1957) and *How to Make a Monster* (1958). Less well-directed than Gene Fowler Jr's *I Was a Teenage Werewolf* (1957), first in the series, this trio

are still enjoyably demented exercises in drive-in mad science, and the third is an amusingly self-promotional summation of the cycle, set in a studio during production of *Teenage Werewolf Meets Teenage Frankenstein*. Strock's other work is at best marginal, though *The Crawling Hand* (1963) has moments. He assisted the credited Curt **Siodmak** in the direction of *The Magnetic Monster* (1953), to which *Gog* is a semi-sequel, and *The Devil's Messenger* (1962).

Donovan's Brain (e)/1953 * *Psycho Sisters* (e)/ 1972 * *Monster*/1978

TV: *The Veil*/1958

von Stroheim, Erich (1885–1957)

Austrian director, actor. A major figure in silent cinema, known for the martyrdom of many of his projects, Stroheim is the director of *Blind Husbands* (1919), *Foolish Wives* (1922), *Greed* (1923), *The Merry Widow* (1925) and *The Wedding March* (1928). Unable to work as a director, he fell back on acting, appearing in classics like Jean Renoir's *La grande illusion* (1935) and Billy Wilder's *Sunset Blvd.* (1950), but also as B movie psychos and mad doctors.

(a) *The Great Gabbo*/1929 * *The Crime of Dr. Crespi*/1935 * *Pièges*/1939 * *The Lady and the Monster*/1944 * *The Mask of Dijon*/1945 * *Alraune*/1952

Subjective Camera

The replacement of a character by a camera position enabled intimate, hallucinogenic scares (*Vampyr*, 1930; *Repulsion*, 1965) but is chiefly associated with horror as a means to obscure the identity of assailants. *Fantasies* (1982) unprecedentedly has the subjective camera voyeur turn out to be a red herring character and not the actual killer, while *The Man With Two Brains* (1983) caps several **cliché** sequences in which victims turn with smiling recognition to the subjective camera before they are murdered by revealing that the culprit is not someone important to the plot but universally recognisable celebrity Merv Griffin. Employed by the voyeuristic *Psycho* (1960) and boosted by developments in hand-held technology, the device cut monster make-up bills and became a suspenseful **stalk-and-slash** given following its attention-grabbing use in *Halloween* (1978).

Detractors made much of the audience identifications encouraged by such point-of-view work. In Dario **Argento**'s movies, the fallibility of eye witnesses is a theme

enlarged upon by bravura camera movements that draw attention to the film-making process. The split-screen of *The Boston Strangler* (1968), *Sisters* (1972) and *Wicked Wicked* (1973) likewise toys with viewing positions. Riffing on the **3-D** craze, *13 Ghosts* (1960) furnished 'ghost-viewers' to enable patrons to see as a haunted character does; the same year's *Peeping Tom* most famously queried the division between subjective and objective horror via its camera-mirror contraption. In the opening to *Dr. Jekyll and Mr. Hyde* (1931), the subjective technique suggests the ego of Fredric March's character, and tricky distortions suggest monstrous viewpoints in *It Came From Outer Space* (1953) and *Cult of the Cobra* (1955), which fog the screen edges to indicate monocular vision in the former and a desire to reuse the effect in the latter, and *The Fly* (1958), which uses a kaleidoscope of the screaming Patricia Owens to convey insectile compound eyesight. The low-angle, red-filtered tracking shots of *Legend of the Werewolf* (1975) gave way to the more sophisticated, semi-psychedelic beastly vision of *Wolfen* (1981) and *Cat People* (1982). When Alex jumps from the window in *A Clockwork Orange* (1971), **Kubrick** literally defenestrates his camera. DP

Subotsky, Milton (1921–91)

American producer, writer, long resident in Britain. Subotsky's first horror credit was as co-writer on John Llewellyn **Moxey**'s splendid *City of the Dead* (1960), an unrepeated experiment in **expressionism**. Shortly thereafter Subotsky joined forces with fellow American Max J. Rosenberg (with whom he had worked in the States) to form **Amicus**, a company which quickly became the Avis of British horror. As a writer Subotsky was a skilful adapter of other people's source material (**EC Comics**, Robert **Bloch**) rather than an originator of ideas. His main contribution was development of the **anthology** format first used in the genre by Ealing with *Dead of Night* (1945). In the 70s, Subotsky switched to Edgar Rice Burroughs (*The Land That Time Forgot*, 1974) but made an ill-advised return to portmanteau horror with *The Monster Club* in 1980. Having acquired and resold some horror properties, notably a clutch of early Stephen King stories, Subotsky has earned token credits, some posthumous: *Cat People* (1982), *Cat's Eye* (1984), *Maximum Overdrive* (1986), *Sometimes They Come Back* (1991), *The Lawnmower Man* (1992), *Sometimes They Come Back . . . Again* (1996). PH

Jeremy Brett, 'Mr. Nightingale', *Supernatural*

Dr. Terror's House of Horrors (+w)/1964 * *The Skull* (+w)/*The Psychopath*/1965 * *The Deadly Bees*/1966 * *Torture Garden*/1967 * *Scream and Scream Again*/*The House That Dripped Blood*/*I, Monster* (+w)/1970 * *Tales From the Crypt* (+w)/ *Asylum*/1972 * *–And Now the Screaming Starts!*/*Vault of Horror* (+w)/*From Beyond the Grave*/1973 * *Madhouse*/*The Beast Must Die*/ 1974 * *The Uncanny*/1977 * *Dominique*/1978

Supernatural (UK TV series, 1977)

Created by Robert Muller and produced for BBC TV by Pieter Rogers, this taped anthology series is set in The Club of the Damned, a Victorian institution that admits only those who can recount genuine stories of personal supernatural experience. The eight episodes, mostly written by Muller, cover the basic gothic horror themes: ghosts ('Ghost of Venice', with Robert Hardy), **werewolves** (the two-part 'Countess Ilona'/'The Werewolf Reunion', with Billie Whitelaw and Ian **Hendry**), *doppelgängers* ('Mr. Nightingale', with Jeremy Brett), **Jekyll and Hyde** ('Lady Sybil', with Denholm **Elliott** and John Osborne), the evil **child** ('Viktoria'), **Frankenstein** ('Night of the Marionettes', with Gordon Jackson) and **vampires** ('Dorabella'). Directors working on the series included Simon Langton and Peter **Sasdy**. TM

Sutherland, Donald (b. 1935)

Canadian actor. After establishing himself in European horror films, he briefly became a fashionable leading man in the late 60s and early 70s and has now settled down as a superior character actor. SJ

Il castello dei morti vivi [*The Castle of the Living Dead*]/1964 * *Fanatic*/*Dr. Terror's House of Horrors*/1965 * *Don't Look Now*/1973 *Fellini's Casanova*/1976 * *Invasion of the Body Snatchers*/ *Murder By Decree*/1978 * *The Rosary Murders*/ 1987 * *Apprentice to Murder*/1988 * *Buffy the Vampire Slayer*/1992 * *Benefit of the Doubt*/ 1993 * *The Puppet Masters*/1994 * *Outbreak*/ 1995

TV: *The Avengers*: 'The Superlative Seven'/ 1967 * *The Champions*: 'Shadow of the Panther'/1969 * *Citizen X*/1995 * *The Lifeforce Experiment*/1996

Švankmajer, Jan (b. 1934)

Czech director, animator, surrealist. A Prague native, Švankmajer trained at the Institute of Applied Arts (1950–54) and Prague Academy of Performing Arts (Department of Puppetry) prior to involvement in the Theatre of Masks, the Black Theatre and the Laterna Magika Puppet Theatre. The duelling wooden-headed performers of *Poslední trik pana Schwarcewalldea a pana Edgara* (*The Last Trick*, 1964) anticipate his subsequent use of any and every single frame and live action film technique to create an absurdist universe. Impossibly huge pebbles emerge from taps in *Spiel mit Steinen*

(*A Game With Stones*, 1965), a somersaulting penknife closes its blade to gush **blood** in *Žvahlav* (*Jabberwocky*, 1971) and greasy food is delivered from below via lift shafts inside immobilised people in *Jídlo* (*Food*, 1992).

When unauthorised footage in the edit of *Leonardův deník* (*Leonardo's Diary*, 1973) earned him a seven-year film production ban, Švankmajer shifted to 'tactile experiments' in other media which fed back in to **Poe**-inspired *Zánik domu Usherů* (*The Fall of the House of Usher*, 1981), uniquely terrifying **subjective camera** exercise *Kyvadlo, jáma a naděje* (*The Pit, the Pendulum and Hope*, 1983) and plasticine lovers pulverising each other in *Možnosti dialogu* (*Dimensions of Dialogue*, 1982). His features *Něco z Alenky* (*Alice*, 1987), after Lewis Carroll, and *Lekce Faust* (***Faust***, 1994) play liberally with, while remaining true to, the spirit of their source texts. Major influence on Andrew McEwan's short *Toxic* (1990) and the **Quay** brothers. JC

Johann Sebastian Bach: Fantasia G-Mol/1965 * *Rakvičkárna* [*Punch and Judy*]/*Et Cetera*/1966 * *Historia naturae (suita)*/1967 * *Zahrada* [*The Garden*]/*Byt* [*The Flat*]/*Picknick mit Weissmann* [*Picnic With Weissman*]/1968 * *Tichý týden uv domě* [*A Quiet Week in a House*]/1969 * *Don Šajn* [*Don Juan*]/*Kostnice* [*The Ossuary*]/1970 * *Otranský zámek* [*The Castle of Otranto*]/1973–7 * *Do pivnice* [*Down to the Cellar*]/1983 * *Mužné hry* [*Virile Games*]/1988 * *Tma-Světlo-Tma* [*Darkness Light Darkness*]/1989 * *Flora*/1989 * *Konec stalinismu v Čechach* [*The Death of Stalinism in Bohemia*]/1990

Peter Hames, *Dark Alchemy: The Films of Jan Švankmajer* (1995)

Donald Sutherland

RIGHT Jab Švankmajer's *Možnosti dialogu*

Svengali * See: *Trilby*

Swamp Thing

Introduced by writer Len Wein and artist Bernie Wrightson in a singleton story in DC Comics' *House of Secrets* (1971), Swamp Thing (whose precursors include the Heap and near-rival Man-Thing) was one of the most successful new comic characters of the 70s. From 1972 to 1974, Wein and Wrightson produced a *Swamp Thing* comic, which reincarnates the nineteenth-century creature of the original as Dr Alec Holland, a biochemist whose mind is rehoused in a vegetable-and-muck swamp giant and who encounters sundry sorcerous or mad science creations. The monster seemed at first to exist independently of DC's ongoing continuity, but an encounter with a maniacal **Batman** yoked him into the company's universe.

Wes **Craven**'s *Swamp Thing* (1982) – with Ray Wise as Holland, Dick Durock as Swamp Thing and Louis **Jourdan** as master villain Arcane – encouraged DC to revive the comic. Written by Alan Moore and drawn by John Totelben, Steve Bissette and Rick Veitch, *Swamp Thing* went through a strong patch in the mid-80s, retackling basic horror themes sometimes with some fresh insights. One of Moore's innovations was the character of John Constantine, a trenchcoated cockney occultist who spun off into his own

book, *Hellblazer* (1989–). Jim **Wynorski**'s *Return of the Swamp Thing* (1989), with Durock and Jourdan, is as unimpressive as the half-hour TV series *Swamp Thing* (1990-92) with Durock pursued by Mark Lindsay Chapman's Arcane. After Moore's departure, the comic has been written by many hands (including Nancy Anne Collins) and sometimes floundered.

Sweeney Todd

According to the story, 'The Demon Barber of Fleet Street' cut the throats of selected clients and tumbled their bodies into the cellar beneath his establishment. Mrs Lovett, his neighbour, would turn the corpses into meat pies, and sell them in her pie shop. The tale gained wide prominence in England during the latter half of the 19th century, initially popularised by playwright George Dibdin Pitt (1799–1853) in his play *The String of Pearls; or the Fiend of Fleet Street* (1847), and an unknown author of penny-dreadfuls, posssibly Thomas Pecket Prest. *The String of Pearls; or the Sailor's Gift. A Romance of Peculiar Interest* (1846–7), the first penny-dreadful, written or not by Prest, appeared as part-work over eighteen issues.

Sweeney Todd (who soon took his place above the title) became a staple of the Victorian Penny Theatres. Frederick Hazleton's *Sweeney Todd, the Barber of Fleet Street; or The String of Pearls* (1862), while based on Dibdin Pitt's play, introduces a number of new elements. Hazleton himself novelised his play; published in 1862 by George Vickers, 'For Sale in Bookshops, Newsagents and Theatres', it was priced at one penny. In the 1880s a new penny-dreadful appeared, far longer than the original, published by Charles Fox and Co: *Sweeney Todd, the Demon Barber of Fleet Street*. It took elements from the plays and the original dreadful, extensively plagiarised the Hazleton novelisation, and expanded the whole out to almost half a million occasionally rather desperate words.

Sweeney Todd was filmed twice in the silent era: as a burlesque comedy with G.A. Baughan (1926) and as a bloody thriller with Moore Marriott (1928). *Sweeney Todd, the Demon Barber of Fleet Street* (1936) is not uninteresting, if only for its view of Victorian stage techniques. Star Tod **Slaughter** toured for many years in a stage version of the tale and reprised the role in the short *Bothered By a Beard* (1948). Andy Milligan's *Bloodthirsty*

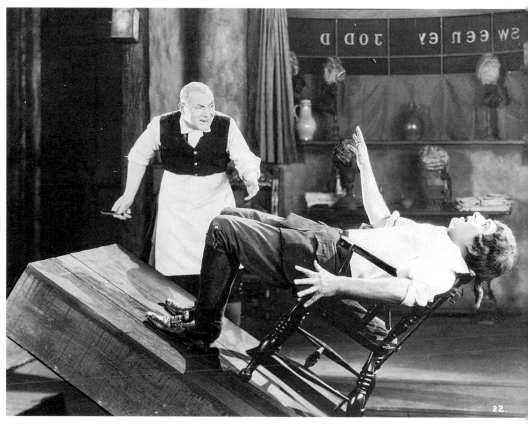

Moore Marriott, *Sweeney Todd* (1926)

Butchers (1969) is memorable only for the rubber-breast-in-the-pie scene. On television, the role was taken by Freddie **Jones** ('Sweeney Todd', ***Mystery and Imagination***, 1970). There have been many retellings of the tale over the last 150 years in plays, pulps, even a ballet: Robert **Aickman**'s subtle take is 'Mark Ingestre: The Customer's Tale' (1980).

English playwright Christopher Bond crafted a new *Sweeney Todd, the Demon Barber of Fleet Street* (1968) based on elements of the Dibdin Pitt play, introducing a far more sympathetic interpretation of Sweeney; this was adapted into a 1979 Broadway **musical** by Stephen Sondheim (music and lyrics) and Hugh Wheeler (book). The lead roles were originated by Len Cariou and Angela Lansbury; George Hearn and Lansbury appear in a 1984 television recording of the show; Denis Quilley and Sheila Hancock lead the 1980 London company. NG

von Sydow, Max (b. 1929)

Swedish actor. Von Sydow was thought fit for the title role of Father Merrin in ***The Exorcist*** (1973) because of the spiritual agonies he had endured in Ingmar **Bergman**

films and on the cross in *The Greatest Story Ever Told* (1965). Many of his Bergman movies verge on the horrific and mystic: *Det sjunde inseglet* (*The Seventh Seal*, 1957), *Ansiktet* (*The Face*, 1958), *Jungfrukällan* (*The*

RIGHT Max von Sydow, *Needful Things*

Virgin Spring, 1960), *Vargtimmen* (*Hour of the Wolf*, 1968), *Skammen* (*Shame*, 1968), *En Passion* (*L182: A Passion*, 1969). In international films, he does sly villains (Ming in *Flash Gordon*, 1980; Blofeld in *Never Say Never Again*, 1983) or father figures (*Conan the Barbarian*, 1982; *Judge Dredd*, 1995). Playing the **Devil** in *Needful Things* (1993), he joined the exclusive ranks of those who have served Heaven and Hell equally in the cinema.

The Night Visitor/1971 * *Warum Belt Herr Bobikow?*/1976 * *Exorcist II: The Heretic*/*Gran Bolitto*/1977 * *Strange Brew*/1983 * *Dreamscape*/1984

TV: *Citizen X*/1995

Sykes, Peter (b. 1939)

Australian-born British director. With collaborator Christopher **Wicking**, Sykes was one of a group in the early 70s who sought to revise and update the increasingly stale conventions of **Hammer** horror. *Demons of the Mind* (1971) is a spirited, if confused, attack on patriarchal attitudes endorsed by earlier Hammers. *To the Devil a Daughter* (1976) is a superior **possession** movie which improves on Dennis **Wheatley**'s 1953 novel but is let down by a feeble conclusion. Away from Hammer, Sykes directed the Frankie Howerd horror-comedy *The House in Nightmare Park* (1973). PH

Venom/1971

TV: *Orson Welles' Great Mysteries*: 'Farewell to the Faulkners'/'For Sale – Silence'/1973; 'Trial for Murder'/1974

Sylvester, William (1922–96)

American actor, in British films from 1949. A resident Yank in low-budget horror movies in the 60s, his career highlight is Dr Floyd in *2001: A Space Odyssey* (1968). Returning to America, he was a regular on the TV series *Gemini Man* (1976–7). SJ

Gorgo/1961 * *Devil Doll*/1963 * *Devils of Darkness*/1964 * *Hand of Night*/1966

TV: *Don't Be Afraid of the Dark*/1973

Szwarc, Jeannot (b. 1939)

French-born American director. Known for standing jokes like *Jaws 2* (1978), *Supergirl* (1984) and *Santa Claus* (1985), Szwarc has the strange *Bug* (1975) and the romantic *Somewhere in Time* (1980) to his credit. His TV work includes decent, gruesome **Night Gallery** episodes: Laurence Harvey's **brain**

William Sylvester

eaten by an earwig ('The Caterpillar', 1972), Barbara **Steele** presiding at a Welsh sin-eating ceremony ('The Sins of the Father', 1972), Sondra Locke drained by a brooch that turns into a giant vole ('A Feast of Blood', 1972). 'Red Snow' (*The Twilight Zone*, 1986), scripted by Michael Cassutt, is an unusual **vampire** story set in Siberia.

TV: *Night Gallery*: 'The Little Black Bag'/1970; 'The Class of '99'/'A Death in the Family'/'The Merciful'/'With Apologies to Mr Hyde'/'The Phantom Farmhouse'/'Midnight Never Ends'/'The Big Surprise'/'Cool Air'/1971; 'The Funeral'/'The Waiting Room'/'Stop Killing Me'/'The Sins of the Father'/'Satisfaction Guaranteed'/'Room for One Less'/'Return of the Sorcerer'/'Rare Objects'/'Spectre in Tap Shoes'/'The Ring With the Red Velvet Ropes'/1972; 'Whisper'/1973 * *The Devil's Daughter*/1972 * *Night of Terror*/1972 * *You'll Never See Me Again*/1973 * *The Murders in the Rue Morgue*/1986 * *The Twilight Zone*: 'The Last Defender of Camelot' /1986

T

Takacs, Tibor (b. 1954)

Hungarian-born director. Toronto-based Takacs helmed sprightly teeny horror *The Gate* (1986) to good effect. *I, Madman* (1989) is a writer-from-the-grave movie that once more manages to include a forced-perspective demon. DP

Bloody Wednesday (assistant d)/1987 * *Gate II*/1990

TV: *The Tomorrow Man*/1979 * *The Outer Limits*: 'Outbreak'/'White Light Fever'/1995

Talbot, Lawrence Stewart * See: Chaney Jr, Lon; Werewolves; *The Wolf Man*

Talbott, Gloria (b. 1932)

American actress. Statuesque but hard-faced, Talbott was an interesting heroine in *I Married a Monster From Outer Space* (1958). Her other horrors are inferior: she takes the title role in Edgar G. **Ulmer**'s shoddy *Daughter of Dr. Jekyll* (1957) without having to turn into a monster.

The Cyclops/1957 * *The Leech Woman*/1960 * *Attack of the B Movie Monster*/1988

Tales From the Crypt * See: **EC Comics**.

Tales From the Darkside (US TV series, 1984–6)

George **Romero**'s half-hour anthology horror poses that 'man lives in the sunlit world of what he believes to be reality, but there is another world just as real . . . the Darkside'. The pilot, 'Trick or Treat' (1984), written by Romero and directed by Bob **Balaban**, has mean storekeeper Barnard Hughes discover the realities of Halloween. Typical episodes, mainly black-humorous, include an adaptation of Robert **Bloch**'s 'A Case of the Stubborns' (1984) with Eddie Bracken as a grandfather who refuses to admit that he is dead, Harlan **Ellison**'s 'D'Jinn, No Chaser' (1984), with Kareem Abdul Jabbar as an evil Genie, and Clive **Barker**'s 'The Yattering and Jack' (1987), with Phil Fondacaro as a petty demon. More serious are episodes from Stephen **King** ('Word Processor of the Gods', 1984) and Michael **McDowell** ('Inside the Closet', 1984). Directors include Armand **Mastroianni**, Tom **Savini**, John **Hayes** and Jodie **Foster**. John Harrison directed a spin-off, *Tales From the Darkside: The Movie* (1989). TM

Taylor, Bernard (b. 1936)

British writer. After writing the outstanding **ghost stories** *The Godsend* (1976) and *Sweetheart, Sweetheart* (1977), Taylor diversified into true crime (*Cruelly Murdered*, 1979) and psychological suspense (*Mother's Boys*, 1988). He is unfortunate in the cinema: *The Godsend* (1980) and *Mother's Boys* (1994), from his novels, are terrible.

Taylor, Eric (1897–1952)

American writer. A *Black Mask* boy, Taylor worked on the Ellery Queen, Crime Doctor and Dick Tracy series and 40s Universal monsters.

Black Friday/1940 * *The Black Cat*/1941 * *Ghost of Frankenstein*/1942 * *Phantom of the Opera/Son of Dracula*/1943 * *The Whistler/ Shadows in the Night*/1944 * *The Crime Doctor's Courage*/1945 * *The Spider Woman Strikes Back/The Crime Doctor's Manhunt*/1946

Taylor, Jack [George Brown Randall] (b. 19??)

American actor. Known as 'Grek Martin' for the Mexican *Neutron contra Dr. Caronte* (1960), he adopted his preferred pseudonym after moving to Spain. Most appreciated because of work for Jesús **Franco**, his atypical looks made him a staple player in European sex-horrors of the 60s and 70s. Not to be confused with the English Jack Taylor, TV's 'Captain Bird's Eye'. MA

Necronomicon [*Succubus*]/1967 * *El proceso de*

Gloria Talbott

las brujas [*The Bloody Judge*]/1969 * *El conde Drácula* [*Count Dracula*]/*De Sade '70* (*Eugenie, Story of Her Journey into Perversion*]/*La venganza del dr. Mabuse*/1970 * *El doctor Jekyll y el hombre lobo* [*Dr. Jekyll and the Werewolf*]/ *Vampir*/1971 * *La orgia nocturna de los vampiros* [*The Vampire's Night Orgy*]/*La venganza de la momia/La comtesse noire* [*Female Vampire*]/*La noche de los brujas* [*The Night of the Sorcerers*]/*Autopsia* [*Autopsy*]/1973 * *El buque maldito* [*Horror of the Zombies*]/1974 * *Enigma rosso* [*Rings of Fear*]/1978 * *Mil gritos tiene la noche* [*Pieces*]/1980 * *Conan the Barbarian*/1982 * *Serpiente de mar* [*Sea Serpent*]/1985 * *Descanse en piezas* [*Rest In Pieces*]/*Filo del hacha* [*Edge of the Axe*]/1987

Teenagers

The emergence of the teenage market force is vital to the development of the post-World War II horror film: Herman **Cohen**'s AIP *I*

ABOVE AND BELOW Tibor Takacs's *The Gate*

ABOVE Barnard Highes, 'Trick or Treat', *Tales From the Darkside*

Teenagers: Michael Landon, Whit Bissell, *I Was a Teenage Werewolf*

Michael **Reeves** emanates from the same dissenting mindset, while Nigel **Kneale**'s defiantly fogyish *Quatermass* (1978) dismisses the teenager as a product of **alien** interference.

Showcasing masturbation and menstruation, high-profile 70s titles ***The Exorcist*** (1973) and *Carrie* (1976) have a pubertal charge shared by numerous 80s transformationers, notably *The Beast Within* (1982), while school is a snake-pit of ritual and murder in *Massacre at Central High* (1976) and *Heathers* (1989). Perhaps reflecting the dubious state of youth culture, 90s teens are an infantilising rather than edgy horror influence: *Teenage Exorcist* (1990) and the *Elm Street* sequels are emblematic, as perhaps is the boom in **young adult** horror fiction. DP

Telekinesis * See: **ESP**

'The Tell-Tale Heart' (1843)
In one of Edgar Allan **Poe**'s simplest stories, a murderer is driven mad by the apparent

Was a Teenage Werewolf (1957) is as directional an entry as anything from Terence **Fisher**, Riccardo **Freda** or Georges **Franju**. *I Was a Teenage Frankenstein* (1957), *Teenage Monster* (1957), *Teenage Zombies* (1960), *Teenagers from Outer Space* (1959) and *Teenage Strangler* (1964) target an impertinent, sensation-seeking audience also exaggeratedly provided for by *Blood of Dracula* (1957), *Invasion of the Saucermen* (1957), *Frankenstein's Daughter* (1958), *Ghost of Dragstrip Hollow* (1959) and *Konga* (1960). A youthful, beatnik energy is central to **Corman**'s pre-gothics, and recurs in *The Wild Angels* (1967), which inspired such biker horrors as *Psychomania* (1971) and *Werewolves on Wheels* (1971).

Attempting to cash in on the generation-gap sleeper *Village of the Damned* (1960), *The Damned* (1961) is **Hammer**'s most explicit teen pic, mixing j.d.s Oliver **Reed** and Shirley Anne Field with radioactive **children**, though the studio later offered thirty-ish swinging teens up to the Count in *Dracula A.D. 1972* (1972). The newly politicised divide between adults and teenagers that came in the latter 60s inspired a series of internecine US shockers which began with ***Night of the Living Dead*** (1968) and culminated in such teeny-kill items as ***Friday the 13th*** (1980) and ***A Nightmare on Elm Street*** (1985). The British revisionism of

RIGHT Teenagers: Sisy Spacek, William Katt, *Carrie*

beating heart of a victim stashed under the floorboards. Similar in concept to 'The Black Cat' (1843), the vignette is more acute in its analysis of guilt and mania. It is often adapted as short films, anthology segments, subplots or TV episodes in 1914 (*The Avenging Conscience*), 1927, 1928, 1934, 1941, 1947, 1949 (*Histoires extraordinaires*), 1949 (*Actor's Studio*), 1950 (William Cameron Menzies's *Heartbeat*), 1953 (a **3-D** cartoon), 1953 (with Stanley Baker), 1953 (*Mono Drama Theatre*), 1956 (*Manfish*), 1956 (*Matinee Theatre*), 1960 (*Obras maestras del terror*), 1966, 1967, 1968 (*Das verräterische Herz*), 1968 (**Mystery and Imagination**), 1971 (*An Evening of Edgar Allan Poe*), 1972 (*Legend of Horror*), 1996 (*The Suspect*). A rare feature-length version was shot by Ernest Morris in 1960.

Tenney, Del (b. 19??)

American director. Connecticut-based schlockpiler, remembered uneasily for *The Horror of Party Beach* (1963). He only produced *Psychomania* (1963), his best credit, and *I Eat Your Skin* (1964).

Curse of the Living Corpse/1963

Tenney, Kevin S. (b. 1955)

American director, writer. *Witchboard* (1987), Tenney's ouija debut, was a sleeper, earning a direct-to-video career: it has unusually solid characterisation but is let down by acting from the likes of Tawny Kitaen. More fun, if unimportant, are *Night of the Demons* (1988) and *Peacemaker* (1990), imitations of *The Evil Dead* (1982) and *The Hidden* (1987).

Witchtrap/1989 * *The Cellar*/1990 * *Witchboard: The Return*/1993 * *Witchboard: The Possession* (w)/1995 * *Pinocchio*/*Night of the Demons 3* (w)/1996

The Texas Chain Saw Massacre (1974)

In common with *Psycho* (1960) and *Deranged* (1974), Tobe **Hooper**'s low-budget shocker was inspired by the crimes of Wisconsin **serial killer** Ed **Gein**. Though the chainsaw made its genre debut in Wes **Craven**'s *Last House on the Left* (1972), Hooper crystallised the potent **censor**-riling iconographic qualities of **power tools** in this cult flesh-crawler. Hooper and co-scripter Kim Henkel offer a nightmare slice of American **grand guignol** as five young Texans encounter a **cannibal** family who kill passersby and use human meat to stuff their sausages. Emphasising claustrophobic terror and oppressive charnel-house atmosphere by

Gunnar Hansen, *The Texas Chain Saw Massacre*

filming everything with bloodless docudrama reality, Hooper established new levels of jaw-dropping macabre horror, forcing viewers to identify with **victims** as they're slaughtered, hung on meathooks and **tortured**. Marilyn Burns sets a screaming record as she is relentlessly pursued by Leatherface (Gunnar **Hansen**), the most demented family member.

Hooper ups the sick comedy in his admirably satiric **splatter** sequel *The Texas Chainsaw Massacre 2* (1986) which shows in gory detail everything only suggested in the first outing. L.M. Kit Carson's script surfs the sociological subtext with a surreal sense of farce exemplified by two chainsaws strapped to hero Dennis Hopper's gun belt. Jeff **Burr**'s *Leatherface: The Texas Chainsaw Massacre III* (1989), written by **splatterpunk** David J. **Schow**, is a virtual remake of the original, its mutilations heavily cut before release. Kim Henkel's creditable *The Return of The Texas Chainsaw Massacre* (1995) reveals a ludicrous *Westworld* (1973) connection. Parodies include *John Boy Meets the Texas Chainsaw Killer* (1977) and *Das deutsche Kettensägenmassaker* (*The German Chainsaw Massacre*, 1991). The original is known in

Italy as *Non aprite quella porta*, prompting Claudio Fragasso to make a spurious *Non aprite quella porta 3* (1990). AJ

Theodore, Brother [Gottlieb] (b. 19??)

American performer. A macabre beat poet, Theodore narrates the multi-titled *Horror of the Blood Monsters* (1970) and is the voice of Gollum in *The Hobbit* (1977) and *The Return of the King* (1980). He appears as himself in *Nocturna* (1978) and lurks evilly in *The 'Burbs* (1989).

So Dark the Night/1946 * *The Black Widow*/1947 * *The Tell-Tale Heart* (s)/1966 * *Gums*/1976

Thesiger, Ernest (1879–1961)

Prissy, emaciated British actor. For James **Whale**, the cowardly Horace Femm in *The Old Dark House* (1932) and Dr Pretorius, toasting 'a new world of gods and monsters', in *Bride of Frankenstein* (1935). His most underrated performance is as the sleazy psycho in *They Drive By Night* (1938). An exhibited artist and accomplished petit point expert. SJ

Ernest Thesiger

The Real Thing at Last/1916 * *The Ghoul*/1933 * *The Man Who Could Work Miracles*/1936 * *My Learned Friend*/1943 * *Don't Take it to Heart!*/*A Place of One's Own*/1944 * *The Ghosts of Berkeley Square*/1947 * *A Christmas Carol*/1951 * *Meet Mr. Lucifer*/1953

Ernest Thesiger, *Practically True* (1927)

3-D

Stereoscopic experiments were conducted in the cinema's infancy, and there were 3-D horror shorts as early as a silent French *Faust* (1922) and the **Frankenstein** parody *Third Dimensional Murder* (1941). The Hollywood 3-D boom began with Arch **Oboler**'s 'lion in your lap' *Bwana Devil* (1952), whose success meant the process was applied to a flurry of Westerns (*The Charge at Feather River*, 1953; *Fort Ti*, 1953) and s-f films (*It Came From Outer Space*, 1953; *The Creature From the Black Lagoon*, 1954). *House of Wax* (1953), a 3-D remake of *Mystery of the Wax Museum* (1932), made Vincent **Price** a horror star and allowed for a blip of period gothics midway between the end of the Universal cycle and the commencement of **Hammer**'s revival. *House of Wax*, as memorable for a rubber ball

bounced into the audience as its horrors, was imitated by *Phantom of the Rue Morgue* (1954) and *The Mad Magician* (1954). The fad passed after *The Maze* (1953), *Robot Monster* (1953), *The Tell-Tale Heart* (1953), *Gorilla at Large* (1954), *Cat Women of the Moon* (1954), *Gog* (1954) and *Revenge of the Creature* (1955).

3-D horror was relegated to gimmick sequences in *The Mask* (*Eyes of Hell*, 1961), *Asylum of the Insane* (1971; an 'augmented' re-release of *She Freak*, 1967) and *The Flesh and Blood Show* (1974). From Europe came the lavish *La marca del hombre lobo* (1969), a 70mm roadshow horror cropped and flattened for US release as *Frankenstein's Bloody Terror*; *I, Monster* (1973), shot in 3-D but released flat; and *Flesh for Frankenstein* (1974), which one-ups *Bwana Devil*'s lion with 'a liver in your lap'. Another mini-boom yielded *Rottweiler* (1981), *Parasite* (1982), *Jaws 3-D* (1983), **Friday the 13th** *Part III in 3-D* (1983), with its shooting eyeball, **Amityville** *3-D* (1983), *Tales of the Third Dimension* (1984) and *Silent Madness* (1984). The polarised glasses went back into storage until the gimmick finale of *Freddy's Dead: The Final Nightmare* (1991).

R.M. Hayes, *3-D Movies: A History and Filmography of Stereoscopic Cinema* (1989)

Thriller (US TV series, 1960–62)

The host and occasional star of this mystery horror anthology frequently concluded introductions with 'as sure as my name is Boris **Karloff**, it's a *thriller*!'. The series started out with basic crime thrillers, but ventured into gothic horror. In 'The Cheaters' (1960), directed by John **Brahm**, an innocent pair of spectacles become a weapon of terror and death. In 'The Hungry Glass' (1961), directed and written by Douglas Heyes, a young couple's new home has a strange attic room with wall to wall mirrors, the room is haunted by the spectre of a young woman. In 'The Terror in Teakwood' (1961), directed by Paul Henreid, a pianist (Guy **Rolfe**) steals the hands of his dead rival, in an attempt to regain his former glory. Robert **Bloch**, Charles **Beaumont** and Richard **Matheson** wrote for the series; directors included Arthur Hiller, Ida Lupino, Ray **Milland**, John **Newland**, Herschel Daugherty and Robert **Florey**. Pulpier and less moralistic than its rival **The Twilight Zone** (1959–65), *Thriller* offers some of the most gruesome, bizarre horror on television, with **vampires**, **witches** and axe murderers lurking in the favoured haunted house set.

Not to be confused with Brian **Clemens**'s UK *Thriller* (1973–5). TM

Todd, Sweeney * See: Sweeney Todd

Todd, Tony (b. 19??)

American actor. Having played the Duane **Jones** role in **Night of the Living Dead** (1990), Todd won a franchise as the hook-handed urban legend of *Candyman* (1992).

Voodoo Dawn/1990 * *The Crow*/1993 * *Candyman: Farewell to the Flesh*/1995

TV: *Werewolf*: 'The Unicorn'/1987 * *The X Files*: 'Sleepless'/1994 * *Beastmaster: The Eye of Braxus*/1995

Torch-Bearing Mobs * See: Peasants

Torture

Torture is central to a few major horror stories (**'The Pit and the Pendulum'**) and subgenres like the **Witch Hunt** film or the **Nazi** camp cycle, but features as a main attraction in **grand guignol** like *The Raven* (1935), *Tower of London* (1939), *Terror of the Tongs* (1961), *Two Thousand Maniacs!* (1964) and *Torture Dungeon* (1969). Especially chilling is the bureaucratic torturer played by

Boris Karloff, *Thriller*

whose extravagant pain-inflicting devices are usually deployed purposefully to extract information from **victims** rather than just for fun.

Tourneur, Jacques (1894–77)

French-born American director. Son of stylist Maurice Tourneur (*Le système du Docteur Gourdron et du Professeur Plume*, 1912; *La main du diable*, 1943), Tourneur made films in France and a few MGM Bs (*Nick Carter, Master Detective*, 1939) before joining Val **Lewton**'s RKO unit as in-house director for *Cat People* (1942), *I Walked With a Zombie* (1943) and *The Leopard Man* (1943). Along with the British-shot *Night of the Demon* (1958), a conscious attempt to return to his roots, the Lewton films establish Tourneur as a major horror director. Blessed with scripts that take care with characterisation and the problem of credibility, the films deal with people whose rationality is eaten away by supernatural encounters. In suspense and horror set-pieces, characters are stalked by night, isolated in the city or countryside. The screen is plunged into darkness illuminated by the occasional pool of suggestive light, while the soundtrack provides night-sounds that hiss and nudge an audience to fear.

Unquestionably a better director than

Torture: LEFT *The Face of Fu Manchu*.
BELOW Bela Lugosi, Arlene Francis, *Murders in the Rue Morgue* (1932)

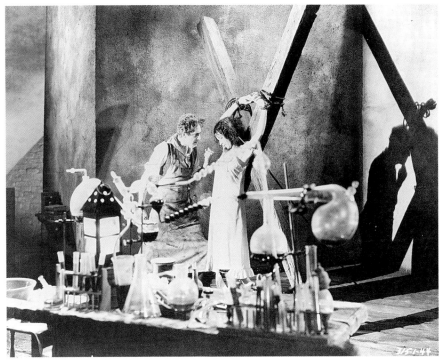

Michael Palin in *Brazil* (1984), blunt instrument of an oppressive state. An Italian craze features hooded torturers, usually haunting a castle in imitation of a distant ancestor: *La vergine di Norimberga* (*Horror Castle*, 1963), *Gli amanti d'oltretomba* (*The Faceless Monster*, 1965), *Il boia scarlatto* (*Bloody Pit of Horror*, 1965), a demented subgenre masterpiece with Mickey Hargitay oiled as 'the Crimson Executioner', and *Gli orrori del castello di Norimberga* (*Baron Blood*, 1971).

Horror films are more concerned with murder than torture, though some victims suffer discomfort that might legally be defined as torture: the girls abducted, abused and raped in *Last House on the Left* (1972); Marilyn Burns battered and prodded in **The Texas Chain Saw Massacre** (1974); James Caan drugged and hobbled in *Misery* (1990). Among recurrent characters with a predilection for torture are the Marquis de **Sade**, for whom fantasies of torture were entertainment and in whose name a many sado-porno movies are made, and **Fu Manchu**,

Robert **Wise** or Mark **Robson**, he did not win as many major projects during his post-Lewton career, though he made a **film noir** classic, *Out of the Past* (*Build My Gallows High*, 1947), tough little thrillers (*Circle of Danger*, 1951; *Nightfall*, 1956; *The Fearmakers*, 1958) and offbeat Westerns (*Canyon Passage*, 1946; *Stars in My Crown*, 1950; *Wichita*, 1955). His Burt Lancaster swashbuckler *The Flame and the Arrow* (1950) won him the Steve Reeves spectacle *La battaglia di Maratona* (*The Giant of Marathon*, 1960), co-directed by Mario **Bava**.

Experiment Perilous/1944 * *The Comedy of Terrors*/1963 * *City in the Sea*/1965

TV: *The Twilight Zone*: 'Night Call'/1964

Towers, Harry Alan (b. 1920)
British producer, writer (as 'Peter Welbeck'). An international adventurer with a penchant for out-of-copyright properties, Towers, the sleazehound's Dan **Curtis**, has tackled Sax Rohmer, **Wells**, Haggard, **Stoker**, Verne, de **Sade**, **Wilde**, **Stevenson**, **Poe** and **Doyle**, and has filmed in Ireland, Spain, Hong Kong, Brazil, Turkey, Iran, Liechtenstein, the UK, Hungary, Israel, Canada, Russia, South Africa, Germany and

Jacques Tourneur's *Night of the Demon*:
ABOVE The Demon
LEFT Dana Andrews

Italy. His best is Don **Sharp**'s spirited *The Face of Fu Manchu* (1965) and he had a period as the favoured producer of the remarkable if rarely interesting Jesús **Franco**. He has done Agatha **Christie**'s *Ten Little Niggers* (1939) in three countries (*Ten Little Indians*, 1966; *And Then There Were None*, 1975; *Ten Little Indians*, 1989). Originally in radio, Towers produced a *Sherlock Holmes* (1954) with John Gielgud and Ralph **Richardson** as Holmes and Watson, reprising the act in the TV series *Sherlock Holmes: The Golden Years* (1992), with Christopher **Lee** (a Towers regular) and Patrick **Macnee**.

The Brides of Fu Manchu/*Circus of Fear*/1966 * *Vengeance of Fu Manchu*/*The Million Eyes of Su-Muru*/1967 * *Castle of Fu Manchu*/*Blood of Fu Manchu*/1968 * *Die sieben Männer der Sumuru* [*Rio 70*]/*Dorian Gray*/*El conde Drácula* [*Count Dracula*]/1970 * *Howling IV: The Original Nightmare*/*The Phantom of the Opera*/*Edge of Sanity*/1989 * *The House of Usher*/*Masque of the Red Death*/*Buried Alive*/1990 * *Dance Macabre*/1991 * *Night Terrors*/*The Mummy Lives*/1993 * *The Mangler*/1995

Transvestitism * See: **Homosexuality**
Transsexuality * See: **Homosexuality**

Transylvania
With the popularity of **Stoker**'s **Dracula** (1897), the region became a favoured locale for folkloric horror. Historically part of

Hungary, Transylvania was in 1897 (as now) a province of Romania. Seen in many Dracula movies and *Howling II: Stirba – Werewolf Bitch* (1986), Transylvania is jokily a setting for *Dance of the Vampires* (1967), *Transylvania 6-5000* (1985) and *Transylvania Twist* (1989).

Trees * See: **Plants**

Trilby (1894)

Gerald du Maurier's melodramatic best seller touches on horror in the relationship between Svengali, a Jewish **hypnotist**, and Trilby O'Ferral, a captivated protégée who is only a great singer while under his influence. From *Ella Lola, à la Trilby* (1898), the novel has beem much-adapted: as *Trilby* in 1908, 1912 (twice), 1913, 1914 with Herbert Beerbohm-Tree and Vira Birkett, 1915, 1922, 1923 and 1976 with Alan Badel and Sinead Cusack; and as *Svengali* in 1914 (an Austrian film also known as *Der Hypnotiseur*), 1927 with Paul **Wegener** and Anita Dorris, 1931 with John **Barrymore** and Marian Marsh, 1954 with Donald Wolfit and Hildegarde Neff, and 1983 (an updated version) with Peter O'Toole and Jodie Foster. Parodies: *Adventures of Pimple: Trilby* (1914), *Miss Trillie's Big Feet* (1915), *Frilby Frilled* (1916), *Mighty Mouse in Svengali's Cat* (1946).

Troma

A New York-based production/distribution outfit founded in 1974 by Yale alumni Lloyd **Kaufman** and Michael Herz. Troma firmed its horror connections following the success of bad-taste gore **comedy** *The Toxic Avenger* (1985). Allegedly made to contradict *Variety*'s pronouncement that horror was dead, the film resites the crude jock humour of earlier Troma ventures in a cheesy world of punks and eco-apocalypse. *Class of Nuke 'Em High* (1986), *Surf Nazis Must Die* (1987), *Troma's War* (1988), *Fortress of Amerikkka* (1989), *The Toxic Avenger Part II* (1989), *The Toxic Avenger Part III: The Last Temptation of Toxie* (1990), *Class of Nuke 'Em High Part 2: Subhumanoid Meltdown* (1991), *Sgt. Kabukiman, NYPD* (1992), *Class of Nuke 'Em High 3: The Good, the Bad and the Subhumanoid* (1995) and *Tromeo and Juliet* (1996) occupy the same splatstick terrain, several as Japanese co-productions. Troma's flagship mutant has latterly served as children's entertainment, with a Marvel comic, the *Toxic Crusaders* cartoon show and attendant action figures.

Some Troma pick-ups (*Redneck Zombies*, 1986; *Rabid Grannies*, 1989) consciously ape the house style; others (*Stuff Stephanie in the Incinerator*, 1990; *Chopper Chicks in Zombie Town*, 1991) are, more watchably, merely titled in imitation. Rufus Seder's *Screamplay* (1986) and Buddy Giovinazzo's *Combat Shock*

Troma: Rick Collins, Lisa Gaye, *The Toxic Avenger, Part III: The Last Temptation of Toxie*

(1987) are untypically distinguished purchases; *The Incredible Torture Show* (1976) is the most notorious. Involved with the Oliver **Stone**-related *Sugar Cookies* (1972), the company deserves credit for financing **black horror** reprise *Def by Temptation* (1990). Boastfully moribund, Troma can nevertheless also be praised for constant sniping at corporate Hollywood. DP

Troughton, Patrick (1926–91)

British actor, often supporting proles in **Hammer** films. The second *Doctor Who* (1966–9). SJ

The Curse of Frankenstein/1957 * *The Phantom of the Opera*/1962 * *The Gorgon*/*The Black Torment*/1964 * *The Scars of Dracula*/1970 * *Frankenstein and the Monster from Hell*/1973 * *The Omen*/1976

TV: *Sherlock Holmes: 'The Devil's Foot'*/1965 * *Adam Adamant Lives!: 'D for Destruction'*/1966 * *Out of the Unknown: 'The Chopper'*/1971 * *Thriller: 'Nurse Will Make It Better'*/1974 * *The Box of Delights*/1984

Trilby (1923)

Thomas Tryon

Tryon, Thomas (1926–91)

American writer, actor. A stiffly handsome leading man, memorable as an impotent **alien** in *I Married a Monster From Outer Space* (1958), Tryon was evidently so bullied by Otto Preminger on *The Cardinal* (1963) that he gave up acting to became an important writer of popular fiction. *The Other* (1971) and *Harvest Home* (1973) blend supernatural and macabre themes with Americana, clearing territory for the best selling horror of Stephen **King** and Peter **Straub**. Tryon scripted *The Other* (1972), while *Harvest Home* was turned into a mini-series (*The Dark Secret of Harvest Home*, 1978) and a story from *Crowned Heads* (1976) became Billy Wilder's *Fedora* (1978). More literary than King, who is especially influenced by *Harvest Home*, Tryon wrote relatively little in the 80s (*The Night of the Moonbow*, 1989) and left an unfinished novel, completed by Valerie Martin and John Cullen (*Night Magic*, 1995).

TV: *Matinee Theatre*: 'The Fall of the House of Usher' (a)/1956

Tsui Hark [Tsui Man-kwong] (b. 1951)

Vietnamese-born Chinese director, producer. Since the early 80s, Tsui has been one of the most influential film-makers in Hong Kong. After education in America and work for television, Tsui directed the strange and gory horror movie *Dap Bin* (*Butterfly Murders*, 1979), the **cannibal comedy** *Deiyuk Mou Mum* (*We Are Going to Eat You*, 1980) and the revolutionary **fantasy** *San Susan Gimgap* (*Zu Warriors from the Magic Mountain*, 1983),

which mixes many of Hong Kong's ingratiating stars, Western effects techniques and classic Chinese legend.

With wife Nansun Shi, Tsui created his own company, Films Workshop, in the mid 80s and backed many of Hong Kong's most interesting directors: John Woo (*Yingxiong Bense*/*A Better Tomorrow*, 1986), Kirk Wong (*Tianluo Diwang*/*Gunmen*, 1988), King Hu and Ann Hui (*Xiao Ao Jiang Hu*/*Swordsman*, 1990), **Ching** Siu-Tung (*Qian Nu Youhoun*/*A Chinese Ghost Story*, 1987), Mak Tai-Kit (*Yaoshou Dushi*/*The Wicked City*, 1993). His authoritarian attitude to directors working for his studio is reminiscent of old Hollywood and has caused many fights with creative protégés like Woo and Wong, but there is no doubt that he has set new standards for Hong Kong film-making. Often credited or uncredited co-director or action director on his productions, he even plays a **comic relief** co-starring role in the s-f actioner *Tiejia Wudi Maliya* (*I Love Maria*, 1988). CV

Kaixin Guizhonggui [*Happy Ghost 3*]/1984 * *Yangan Dou* [*A Chinese Ghost Story II*] (p)/1990 * *Qiannu Youhun III Dao Dao Dao* [*A Chinese Ghost Story III*] (p)/1991

'The Turn of the Screw' (1898)

Henry James's novella is one of the greatest of all classic **ghost stories**, opening with a typical clubland frame but plunging deeper into unhealthy psychology via the narrative

Tsui Hark

of a nameless governess sent to the remote Bly House to care for children Miles and Flora. The heroine comes to believe her charges are affected by the ghosts of groom Peter Quint and his mistress Miss Jessell, and her attempts to end the haunting have tragic consequences. William Archibald adapted the story into a play, *The Innocents* (1950), which became Jack **Clayton**'s 1961 film with Deborah Kerr, while Benjamin Britten composed a 1954 opera. Other adaptations appeared in 1955 (*Omnibus*, with Geraldine Page), 1957 (*The Others*), 1959 (*Ford Startime*, with Ingrid Bergman), 1974 (with Lynn Redgrave), 1989 (*Nightmare Classics*, with Amy Irving) and 1992 (with Patsy Kensit). Michael Hastings, in his screenplay for Michael Winner's *The Nightcomers* (1971, with Marlon Brando and Stephanie Beacham as Quint and Miss Jessell), and Joyce Carol Oates, in 'Accursed Inhabitants of the House of Bly' (1992), take the point of view of the ghosts.

The Twilight Zone (US TV series, 1959–64)

Created and narrated by Rod **Serling** and produced by Buck Houghton, *The Twilight Zone* remains American TV's premier science fiction-fantasy anthology. Serling's imaginative stories ranged from standard s-f to Western, from period drama to futuristic tales, though excellent episodes were contributed by Richard **Matheson**, Charles **Beaumont** and George Clayton Johnson.

In the pilot, 'Where is Everybody?' (1959), directed by Robert Stevens, an Air force pilot awakes to find himself alone in a small deserted town. In the classic 'Walking Distance' (1959), a disillusioned business man (Gig Young) returns to his childhood to discover 'you can go home, but not for long'. In 'The Monsters Are Due On Maple Street' (1960), a small town's paranoia regarding Martians leads the way to an **alien** invasion. In 'The Eye of the Beholder' (1960), a young woman discovers beauty is not to everyone's liking. Among the more horrific episodes, in which ordinary people step into a world of threatening shadows, are 'Perchance to Dream' (1959), 'The Hitch-Hiker' (1960), 'The Howling Man' (1960), 'It's a *Good* Life' (1961), 'The Dummy' (1962) and 'Nightmare at 20,000 Feet' (1963). The show expanded to an hour for its fourth season, but was best suited to the thirty-minute format to which it reverted in its fifth and last season. The recognisable, much-parodied theme was created by Marius Constant.

the development that Laura's murderer, eventually revealed as her father Leland (Ray Wise), is ambiguously possessed by an extra-dimensional fiend, Bob (Frank Silva).

Though the show is variable, losing its way after the resolution of the initial story-line, it takes interesting, bizarre turns with **Lovecraftian** hints of malevolent forces in the outer darkness and hold-overs from a UFO project which point the route, taken by *TP* regulars David Duchovny and Don Davis, to **The X-Files** (1993–). The cast includes Joan Chen, Piper Laurie, Sherilyn Fenn, Jack Nance, Peggy Lipton, Richard Beymer, Madchen Amick, Eric DaRe, Lara Flynn Boyle, Michael Horse, James Marshall, Russ Tamblyn, Harry Goaz, Everett McGill, Wendy Robie, Miguel Ferrer, Kimmy Robertson, Grace Zabriskie, Catherine Coulson ('the Log Lady') and Lynch himself. The show was cancelled on a cliff-hanger, with Cooper possessed by Bob.

Lynch's film *Twin Peaks Fire Walk With Me* (1992) is a disturbing prequel, partially adapted from Jennifer Lynch's tie-in book *The Secret Diary of Laura Palmer* (1990). A fad on its way to being a cult, *TP* was subtly influential on mainstream horror – Stephen **King**'s *Needful Things* (1991) is an extended

'The Turn of the Screw': Deborah Kerr, *The Innocents*

Twilight Zone: The Movie (1983) was a feature film revival, while the TV movie *The Twilight Zone: Rod Serling's Lost Classics* (1994) filmed leftover scripts. From 1985 to 1988, an updated colour version was produced: overall it lacks the magic, but one or two episodes capture the flavour of the original series. In 'The Once and Future King' (1986), directed by Jim McBride, a twist of fate turns a young man into 'the king of rock 'n' roll'. In the special 'A Day in Beaumont' (1986), directed by Phillip DeGuire the s-f movie world of the 50s is revisited with affection. *The Twilight Zone* (1981-9) was a fiction magazine, and there have been collections under the name, either Serling's adapted scripts, material adapted for the

shows or original stories in the TZ style. TM Marc Scott Zicree, *The Twilight Zone Companion* (1982); Jean-Marc Lofficier, Randy Lofficier, *Into the Twilight Zone* (1995)

Twin Peaks (US TV series, 1990–91)

Created by David **Lynch** and Mark Frost, *Twin Peaks* crept onto network television disguised as a small-town soap/murder mystery. In the pilot, quixotic FBI agent Dale Cooper (Kyle MacLachlan) joins Sheriff Harry Truman (Michael Ontkean) to investigate the murder of 'prom queen from Hell' Laura Palmer (Sheryl Lee). Though much of the series was offbeat comedy or police procedural, a strain of weirdness immediately surfaced in Cooper's prophetic dreams and

H.M. Wynant, Robin Hughes, John Carradine, 'The Howling Man', *The Twilight Zone*

tribute – with images and performers from the show turning up in conventional horrors from *The People Under the Stairs* (1991) to *Howling VI: The Freaks* (1990). Looser spin-offs are the pornos *Twin Peeks* (1991), *Twin Cheeks* (1991) and *Twin Freaks* (1992).

Twins * See: **Doppelgängers, Family Values**

U

Ulmer, Edgar G. (1904–72)

Austrian-born director. A camera assistant on *Der Golem* (1920) and collaborator with Billy Wilder and Robert **Siodmak** on *Menschen am Sonntag* (1929), Ulmer emigrated to become the archetypal Hollywood marginal, eking out a career on the sidelines, making films in Yiddish or for such despised outfits as PRC. However, his most significant horror is *The Black Cat* (1934), a well-mounted Universal top-lining **Lugosi** and **Karloff**, remarkable for perversity, the sly ham of its stars and art deco gothicism. In his PRC period, Ulmer mounted the quite elaborate *Bluebeard* (1944), a stuffy, overrated John **Carradine** vehicle that strains hard for respectability, and the justly celebrated *Detour* (1946), a dead end **film noir** that touches truly horrific American roadside fatalism.

The Man From Planet X (1951) is an interesting anomaly: made hurriedly to get into theatres before *The Thing From Another World* (1951), it is an **alien**-on-Earth film in the **expressionist** tradition of Universal, with a torch-bearing Scots mob and a ruined castle, rather than the semi-documentary, conversationally militarist s-f style that predominated after Howard Hawks's production was released. Ulmer devotees have a hard time, though, with *Daughter of Dr. Jekyll* (1957), *The Amazing Transparent Man* (1960) and *Beyond the Time Barrier* (1960).

Universities

Campus settings are common in horror, affording a chance to bring together repositories of arcane wisdom, fatherly or fiendish professors of folklore or **mad science**, and nubile, screaming co-eds. Academic politics are central to Fritz **Leiber**'s *Conjure Wife* (1943), filmed as *Weird Woman* (1944) and *Night of the Eagle* (1962), and secret or Satanic societies flourish on campus in *City of the Dead* (1960), with Christopher **Lee** as a Devil-worshipping professor, *The Brotherhood*

Urban Horror: The shadow of Peter Lorre, *M* (1932)

of the Bell (1970), *Zombie High* (1987) and *Voodoo* (1995).

Otherwise, **vampires** study (*Incense for the Damned*, 1970; *The Addiction*, 1995) or teach (*Grave of the Vampire*, 1972); **mummies** stalk study halls (*Time Walker*, 1982; *Tales From the Darkside: the Movie*, 1990); science creates creatures which run amok in dorms (*Monster on the Campus*, 1958; *Primal Rage*, 1990); sorority pledges are possessed by angry ghosts (*Killer Party*, 1986); **stalk-and-slash** killers prey on students (*Pranks*, 1981; *Student Bodies*, 1981; *Hell Night*, 1982; *The House on Sorority Row*, 1983; *T.A.G.: The Assassination Game*, 1983; *Rush Week*, 1989); and a fanged ape is used to get rid of uppity faculty wife Adrienne **Barbeau** (*Creepshow*, 1982).

The most famous college in horror is H.P. **Lovecraft**'s Miskatonic University in Arkham, Massachusetts, seen in *The Dunwich Horror* (1970), *Re-Animator* (1986), *The Unnameable* (1988) and *The Unnameable Returns* (1992). Horror novels with campus settings: Simon Raven's *Doctors Wear Scarlet* (1959), Marc Brendel's *The Lizard's Tail* (1979), Suzy McKee Charnas's *The Vampire Tapestry* (1980), Jack Yeovil's *Orgy of the Blood Parasites* (1994), R.L. Stine's *Superstitious* (1995).

Urban Horror

The city is a formative site for horror: its rooftops leer in **Das Cabinet des Dr. Caligari** (1919), its passageways haunt the post-*Metropolis* (1926) *M* (1930), its catacombs house **The Phantom of the Opera** (1925). In nascent Iberian entry *La torre de los siete jorobados* (*The Tower of the Seven Hunchbacks*, 1944), a subterranean city is the habitation of freaks. *Die Pest in Florenz* (*The Plague in Florence*, 1919) makes much of its architecture, as does *Der Golem* (*The Golem*, 1920). Fashioned to defend Prague's Jewish ghetto, Paul **Wegener**'s clay-man is a specifically urban monster.

The anonymity and isolation of city life throws up both killers and victims: *Taxi Driver* (1976), *Henry: Portrait of a Serial Killer* (1987), Dario **Argento**'s frigid *gialli* and Abel **Ferrara**'s New York films are thoroughly urban horrors. Eloy de la Iglesia provocatively locates genre items in Franco's city sprawls; Edinburgh keeps **Burke and Hare** in business; Paris is responsible for *El sadico de Notre Dame* (*The Sadist of Notre Dame*, 1974); London is a sleazy site for **Jack the Ripper** and Edgar **Wallace**. In George **Romero**'s *Day of the Dead* (1985), the city-

as-necropolis is vividly realised. *The Penalty* (1920), *Simon, King of the Witches* (1973), *Street Trash* (1986), *Prince of Darkness* (1987) and *The Vagrant* (1992) teem with the city dispossessed. *Death Line* (1972), *Alligator* (1981) and *Candyman* (1992) make clever use of urban myths, while **black horror** reprise *Tales from the Hood* (1995) trades heavily on inner-city credentials. Conurbations are regularly stomped by *King Kong* (1933) and his clones; Tokyo is particularly hard done by in Japan's *kaiju eiga*. DP

Urecal, Minerva (1896–1966)

American actress. Poverty-row harridan, usually a leering housekeeper or insane relation.

The Ghost Creeps/1940 * *Murder By Invitation*/1941 * *The Living Ghost*/*The Corpse Vanishes*/1942 * *Ghosts on the Loose*/*The Ape Man*/1943 * *The Lost Moment*/1947 * *Master Minds*/1949 * *The Seven Faces of Dr. Lao*/1964

V

Vadim, Roger (b. 1928)

French director. Known for exposing his sex-goddess wives Brigitte Bardot (*Et Dieu . . . créa la femme*, 1956) and Jane Fonda (*Barbarella*, 1968), Vadim ventures into horror with the delicate **'Carmilla'** variation . . . *et mourir de plaisir* (*Blood and Roses*, 1960), the overblown 'Metzengerstein' of *Histoires extraordinaires* (*Spirits of the Dead*, 1968) and the unusual Californian Rock Hudson-as-psycho-stud picture *Pretty Maids All in a Row* (1971).

TV: *The Hitchhiker*: 'Dead Man's Curve'/1986

Vampira [Maila Nurmi] (b. 1921)

Finnish-born American actress. From 1954 to 1955, Vampira was the first **horror host**, introducing creaky movies on Los Angeles' KABC-TV, dressed like Charles **Addams**'s Ghoul Lady. After a brief burst of popularity, she had a spotty film career, lowlighted by a

Urban Horror: Robert De Niro, *Taxi Driver*

Vampira, *Plan 9 From Outer Space*

silent bit in **Wood**'s *Plan 9 From Outer Space* (1956). She appears in Albert Zugsmith's *The Big Operator* (1959), *The Beat Generation* (1959) and *Sex Kittens Go to College* (1960). Lisa Marie plays her in *Ed Wood* (1994).

The Magic Sword/1962 * *Bungalow Invader* (s)/ 1981

Vampirella

Both a **vampire** and an **alien**, Vampirella, created by Forrest J. **Ackerman**, appeared in her own black-and-white **comic** (1969–88) from Warren. Officially a magazine, *Vampirella* avoided the post-**EC** censorship that kept vampires out of comics through the 60s, but the sophisticated girlie art of Frank Frazetta and José Gonzalez is accompanied by infantile scripting (Vampi hails from Planet Drakulon). **Hammer** announced a film in the 70s, casting Barbara Leigh, but the project was abandoned. The character returned to comics in the 90s and Roger **Corman** produced *Vampirella* (1996), a TV movie with Talisa Soto.

Vampirism (Before *Dracula*)

References to vampires of various descriptions go right back to Classical times, but the literary vampire really took off at the famous **ghost story** session in a villa on the shore of Lake Geneva, summer 1816. After Mary Godwin had spun *Frankenstein*, Lord **Byron**

began a tale about a blue-blooded aristocrat of ancient family called Darvell who accompanies a young man on a trip to Turkey and dies in a graveyard there – having promised to return from the dead a month later. Some of the participants in the session had been reading about the folkloric vampire, and they also knew of the German romantics such as Goethe, who had written of the vampiric 'Bride of Corinth'.

The folkloric vampire is more often than not a ruddy-faced agricultural labourer from Eastern Europe, Greece or Turkey – complete with bellowing voice, wide-open mouth, three-day growth of beard and serious breath problem – and just as likely to attack sheep and cows as his own relatives. This vampire was much debated by the philosophers and glitterati of eighteenth-century Paris and London. Most concluded this 'primitive superstition' (subscribed to by them not us) was really about the spread of contagious **diseases**, the natural growth of hair and nails after death, rabies, the funerary customs of preliterate societies or a satirical reversal of the communion service. Rousseau was not so sure; he met enough vampires at fashionable Parisian salons to give credence at least to a metaphorical version. In writing about the folkloric vampire – even if only to dismiss him (and it was usually *him*) – Voltaire and the Encyclopedists

made him visible for the first time among the chattering classes; launched him, so to speak, into the literary bloodstream.

The literary vampire, more often than not a fashionably pallid aristocrat – complete with seductive voice, pouting lips, and a mean, moody and magnificent personality – was born in prose at the Villa Diodati with Byron's unfinished tale. It was resurrected in London by Dr John **Polidori**, Byron's ex-physician. Without permission, Polidori rewrote and expanded the fragment during 'two or three idle mornings' and published it under the title *The Vampyre* (1819). The poetic Darvell turned into the villainous Lord Ruthven with his 'dead grey eye' and 'the deadly hue of his face', a satire on Byron himself (who retaliated by shouting 'Damn the vampyre!'); and Ruthven returned from Turkey to bite his way through London society during the season. Some editions bore the initials 'L.B.' on the title page, and Goethe reckoned it 'the English poet's finest work'.

For the first thirty years of its literary life, from 1820 to round about 1850, the vampire was indelibly associated with the public image of Byron as Satanic Milord who exercised his *droit de seigneur* by leading young debutants and debutantes to their doom, usually while on a Grand Tour. This tended seriously to limit the possibilities of character development within the genre. A novel, several plays and burlesques and an opera were written in England, France and Germany to cash in on the Ruthven craze, and, by a process of product differentiation, new elements were added: a happy ending (not in the original) that upholds the sanctity of marriage; the villainous aristocrat who debauches peasant girls (rather than travelling companions and debs); even the vampire as 'a Wallachian Boyar' (in the English version of a German *Vampyr* opera).

The *genus vampiricus* entered the bloodstream of mass culture with ex-civil engineer James Malcolm Rymer's marathon penny-dreadful of 868 double-column pages, *Varney the Vampire; or: The Feast of Blood* (1847) – starring Sir Francis Varney of Radford Hall, Yorkshire, a Restoration decadent who haunts the charnel houses of mid-Victorian England. Varney combines the traditional folkloric vampire with his Byronic descendent. Several aspects of his comic-book saga found their way, half a century later, into *Dracula*: a vigil by a vampire's tomb, the arrival of a deserted ship and a chase to the villain's resting-place. Bram **Stoker** was in fact born in the year Varney finally leapt into Mount Vesuvius. The success of Rymer's masterpiece led to the authors of pious moral tracts exploiting the vampire myth as an aid to popular education: there were, from the late 1840s onwards, pamphlets on temperance (in which the Vampyre Inn sucks unwary alcoholics to their doom), on the evils of gambling (by 'The Spectre') and on the advantages of avoiding solitary vices (*Modern Vampirism: Its Dangers and How to Avoid Them*).

Meanwhile, French writers, more obsessed than their British counterparts with the female of the species, busily transformed the vampire from melodramatic villain into a more personalised kind of sexy predator. Théophile Gautier's 'Clarimonde' (1836) has 'sea-green eyes and teeth of purest Orient pearl' with which she easily manages to seduce a young country priest; Charles Baudelaire's 'woman with the strawberry mouth' (1857) sucks the pith from the bones of a young poet, until he wakes up and sees 'an old leather bottle with sticky sides and full of pus'. Female vampires made a few tentative appearances during the Ruthven craze, but came into their own during 1840–90, a period of fascination (among male authors) with the exotic, the aesthetic and the decadent: part of the bourgeois century when, as historian Peter Gay has put it, 'man's fear of women . . . became a prominent theme in popular novels and medical treatises'. Walter Pater even saw a hint of the toothsome in the best-known portrait of a woman in Western art, Leonardo's *Mona Lisa*: 'Like a vampire, she has been dead many times, and learned the secrets of the grave.' Which perhaps explains that enigmatic smile.

The finest of the *belles dames sans merci* in this period appears in Sheridan **Le Fanu**'s dreamy novella **'Carmilla'** (1871), which recounts a rich and strange **lesbian** relationship between Carmilla Karnstein and the young female narrator which eventually destroys them both. 'Think me not cruel', says the seductive Styrian Countess, 'because I obey the irresistible law of my strength and weakness . . . I cannot help it.' 'Carmilla' undoubtedly influenced *Dracula*, not just thematically but biographically: Stoker and Le Fanu came shared a similar Anglo-Irish background, the cultural and administrative elite of Dublin society.

Dracula is in effect a synthesis of the various vampire themes and motifs which had been resurrected, interred and resurrected again over a seventy-five year period: one of the very first examples of the concerns of 'high culture' (Goethe, Byron, Shelley) being transmitted – through novels, stories, poems, comics, woodcuts and music-hall songs – into the culture of the increasingly crowded inner cities. Stoker's novel not only features a Satanic Milord accompanied by three *belles dames sans merci* (and more to come), the novel is also infested with legions of wolves, black **dogs**, **bats**, **rats** and all the paraphernalia of the vampires of folklore: indeed, the Count himself – who, when the story begins, has been deceased for all of 421 years – is himself as much folkloric as Byronic, and his behaviour proves it.

The only literary tradition which Stoker felt unable to assimilate was the camp vampire – epitomised by Count Stenbock's 'A True Story of a Vampire' (1894), in which the narrator is an elderly Polish woman who, in memory of her long-dead brother (the vampire's victim and a vegetarian), sets up an asylum for stray cats and dogs in Westbourne Park. 'A True Story' begins provocatively 'Vampire stories are generally located in Styria; mine is also. Styria is . . . a flat, uninteresting country, only celebrated for its turkeys, its capons and the stupidity of its inhabitants.'

By the time *Dracula* was published in 1897, the 'rules' of the genre were firmly established – and most variations had been tried out. An article in *The Bookman* magazine suggested that it was high time that authors of vampire stories did away with forests and gypsies and ancient folklore altogether: 'We need horrors that survive modern plumbing and the brilliance of electric light.' The stage was set for the entrance of the cinematic vampire. Despite the changes of detail, setting and atmosphere horror movies have contributed to the myth since *Nosferatu: Eine Symphonie des Grauens* (1922) – and despite numerous parodies, postmodern citations, porno versions and the democratisation of the **blood**-sucker – the nineteenth-century literary vampire (male and female) remains immortal, still able to get under the skin. CF

Dudley Wright, *Vampires and Vampirism* (1914); Montague Summers, *The Vampire: His Kith and Kin* (1928), *The Vampire in Europe* (1929); Tony Faivre, *Les Vampires* (1962); Ornella Volta, *Il Vampiro* (1962); Margaret L. Carter, *The Vampire in Literature* (1989); Christopher Frayling, *Vampires: Lord Byron to Count Dracula* (1991)

Vampirism (After *Dracula*)

Given the instant popularity of **Dracula** (1897), it is surprising that imitative vampire stories emerged at such a slight trickle thereafter. Bram **Stoker**'s own belated follow-up *The Lady of the Shroud* (1909), like Conan **Doyle**'s **Holmes** tale 'The Adventure of the Sussex Vampire' (1924) and the films *London After Midnight* (1927), *Mark of the Vampire* (1935) and *The Crime Doctor's Courage* (1945), introduces apparent vampires into a mystery plot, then banishes them with frankly unlikely exercises in **rationalised supernatural**.

A run of well-regarded, often-anthologised vampire stories – F.G. Loring's 'The Tomb of Sarah' (1900), F. Marion Crawford's 'For the Blood is the Life' (1911), E.F. Benson's 'Mrs. Amworth' (1920) – seem now somewhat slight, content with the revelation that, yes, the predatory female is indeed a vampire. In this period also, the non-traditional vampire emerged in stories about **blood**-sucking **plants** (H.G. **Wells**'s 'The Flowering of the Strange Orchid', 1894), human 'psychic sponges' (Mary E. Wilkins Freeman's 'Luella Miller', 1902; George Sylvester Viereck's *The House of the Vampire*, 1907; Algernon **Blackwood**'s 'The Transfer', 1912), even the first of many **alien** blood-drinkers (Wells's *The War of the Worlds*, 1898).

In the 10s, the expression 'vampire' or 'vamp' was most commonly used in application to predatory women of the Theda Bara or, later, Louise Brooks type. Louis Feuillade's **serial** *Les vampires* (1915–6) features Musidora in a black body-stocking as slinky super-criminal Irma Vep, and semi-supernatural business crops up in *The Vampire of the Desert* (1913), *The Vampire* (1913) and *The Vampire* (1914). The vampire proper did not appear in film until *Nosferatu: Eine Symphonie des Grauens* (1922) and then disappeared – *London After Midnight* excepted – until **Dracula** (1930), in which Bela **Lugosi** set a precedent for the standard screen depiction of the vampire that has lasted ever since.

Oddly, as with the novel, *Dracula* yielded few direct imitations – the closest is not a vampire film at all, but **The Mummy** (1932). Other 30s screen vampires, with the exception of Gloria Holden's incarnation of a feminine version of Lugosi in *Dracula's Daughter* (1936), are unstereotyped: the hag of **Dreyer**'s *Vampyr* (1932), the blob-like creature of *The Vampire Bat* (1933), the semi-**werewolf** of *Condemned to Live* (1935), the

mad scientist of *The Return of Dr. X* (1939). In the 40s, the rules became more established, with Dracula types stalking through *Dead Men Walk* (1943), *The Return of the Vampire* (1943), *Son of Dracula* (1943) and *The Vampire's Ghost* (1945), though there was still room for the odd electrically-enlarged **bat** (*The Devil Bat*, 1940), haemovorous plant (*The Spider Woman Strikes Back*, 1945) and folkloric plague (*Isle of the Dead*, 1945).

Though there were many **pulp** magazine vampires – Everill Worrell's 'The Canal' (1927), Robert E. Howard's 'The Horror From the Mound' (1932), Carl Jacobi's 'Revelations' in Black (1933), Robert **Bloch**'s 'The Cloak' (1939), Cornell **Woolrich**'s 'Vampire's Honeymoon' (1939) – few vampire novels appeared in the first half of the century, most as undistinguished as Sydney Horler's *The Vampire* (1935). Fritz **Leiber**'s non-traditional 'The Girl with the Hungry Eyes' (1949) signalled the beginning of a revival, with writers finally discovering that summoning up and staking vampires was not enough for a story. The 50s and 60s brought s-f or psychology-tinged takes on the theme, stretching beyond weird melodrama. In Richard **Matheson**'s *I Am Legend* (1954), scientifically explained vampires take over a ruined world. Also fine are C.M. Kornbluth's 'The Mindworm' (1950), Simon Raven's *Doctors Wear Scarlet* (1960), Theodore Sturgeon's *Some of Your Blood* (1961) and Leslie H. Whitten's *Progeny of the Adder* (1965).

While **Hammer** revived the fortunes of the traditional vampire with *Dracula* (1958), the cinema made tentative experiments: the alien blood-drinkers of *The Thing From Another World* (1951), *Not of This Earth* (1957) and *It! The Terror From Beyond Space* (1958); the **mutant** human monsters of *The Vampire* (1957) and *Blood of the Vampire* (1958); the **Western** *Curse of the Undead* (1959); the **Báthory**-inspired *I vampiri* (1956); and the supernatural but matter-of-fact *Blood of Dracula* (1957) and *The Return of Dracula* (1958). Though the bloodthirsty Counts of Mexico's *El vampiro* (1957) and the **Nostradamus** series are simply Dracula in disguise, Mario **Bava**'s Italian contributions diverge from the cape and fang image to present a sensually **witch**-like Barbara **Steele** (*La maschera del demonio*/*The Mask of Satan*, 1960) and folkloric peasant predator Boris **Karloff** (*I tre volti della paura*/*Black Sabbath*, 1963).

Subsequently, distinct vampire movie traditions – often cross-breeding the Dracula or

Vampires: Gloria Holden, *Dracula's Daughter*

Carmilla types with local styles and legends – emerged in France (the surreal erotica of *. . . et mourir de plaisir*/*Blood and Roses*, 1960, and Jean **Rollin**), Italy (titillating charades like *L'ultima preda del vampiro*/*Playgirls and the Vampire*, 1960, and *La strage dei vampiri*/*Slaughter of the Vampires*, 1962), Spain (the sex-and-blood pulp of Paul **Naschy**, Jesús **Franco** and *La orgia nocturna de los vampiros*/*The Vampires' Night Orgy*, 1972), the **Philippines** (the heavily Catholic *The Blood Drinkers*, 1966; *Creatures of Evil*, 1970), **Japan** (from the traditional *Onna Kyuketsuki*, 1959, to the Westernised *Chi o Suu Bara*/*Evil of Dracula*, 1975), Germany (the lumpen echt-Hammer of *Der Fluch der grünen Augen*/*Cave of the Living Dead*, 1964, and *Die Schlangengrube und das Pendel*/*Blood Demon*, 1967), China (the **Jiangshi** cycle) and Korea (*Ahkea Khots*, 1961). This diversity even influenced British cinema: oddities like the Moroccan-set *The Hand of Night* (1966) sit alongside Dracula knock-offs like *Devils of Darkness* (1964) and ironic, pulpish vampire anecdotes feature in the **anthologies** *Dr. Terror's House of Horrors* (1964), *The House that Dripped Blood* (1970) and *Vault of Horror* (1973).

While Hammer's cycle ran its course – taking in such non-Dracula items as *The Brides of Dracula* (1960), *Kiss of the Vampire* (1964), *The Vampire Lovers* (1970), and sequels, *Vampire Circus* (1971) and *Captain Kronos, Vampire Hunter* (1974) – the swash-

buckling period vampire became less common outside Windsor Great Park. *Count Yorga, Vampire* (1970) and *The Return of Count Yorga* (1971) star Robert **Quarry** as a Dracula-ish cloaked aristo, but exchange **Transylvania** for hip, modern Californian settings. These films – instantly imitated by the likes of *Blacula* (1972), *Grave of the Vampire* (1972) and even **The Night Stalker** (1972) – synthesise two strands of horror. Originally, *Count Yorga* was to be called *The Loves of Count Iorga* and would have joined the steady stream of **pornography** that includes *Count Erotica, Vampire* (1971), *Bite!* (1991) and *Intercourse With the Vampyre* (1994). Rewritten before production as 'straight' horror, it draws on the ferocity, contemporary feel and counterculture buzz of **Night of the Living Dead** (1968), surrounding its King Vampire with female acolytes who are at once blatantly sexual and mindlessly **zombie**-like.

Even Hammer, in *Dracula A.D. 1972* (1972), took note, and the 70s were overrun by vampires trying to get away from their roots, casting off their capes to prance naked, and craving blood less with the decadent hauteur of Lugosi or Christopher **Lee** than a junkie-like need. Especially striking are the shuffling ghouls of *Let's Scare Jessica to Death* (1971) and *Messiah of Evil* (1973), the blood-drinking cults of *Bloedverwanten* (*Blood Relations*, 1977) and *Thirst* (1979), the **psychopaths** of *Martin* (1977) and *Vampire's*

Kiss (1989) and the philosophical blood-junkies of *The Addiction* (1995). A sado-sensuality, derived from the likes of Rollin, is expressed in the the **lesbian** chic and bat fetishism of *Le rouge aux lèvres* (*Daughters of Darkness*, 1971) and *The Velvet Vampire* (1971) and romanticised in the gothic soap of ***Dark Shadows*** (1966–71).

The ghoulishness and sexual adventure combine in *Lemora: A Child's Tale of the Supernatural* (1973) and *Alucarda* (*Sisters of Satan*, 1975) and figure heavily in the blockbuster novels that made vampirism again a best selling as well as a box-office theme. Stephen **King**'s *'Salem's Lot* (1975; filmed 1979) is in the Yorga tradition, bringing a Dracula-type to an American small town, where his corrupt contagion runs through the population, while Anne **Rice**'s *Interview With the Vampire* (1976; filmed 1994) echoes *Dark Shadows* with its romanticised, decadent first-person vampire and a supporting cast of flamboyant night creatures who shuffle through increasingly turgid sequels. To King can be traced such film exercises as *Fright Night* (1985), *The Lost Boys* (1987), *A Return to Salem's Lot* (1987) and *From Dusk Till Dawn* (1996), which rework old themes with energy and effects, often playing for cynical laughs. Rice's heirs tend to follow heroic or at least tormented vampire protagonists in a blurry night-time world: *Graveyard Shift*

(1986), *Near Dark* (1987), *Dance of the Damned* (1988), *Nick Knight* (1989), *Tale of a Vampire* (1992), *Innocent Blood* (1993).

Further major vampire novels (or even vampire series) have come from Chelsea Quinn Yarbro (*Hôtel Transylvania*, 1977), Les Daniels (*The Black Castle*, 1978), Suzy McKee **Charnas** (*The Vampire Tapestry*, 1980), Whitley **Strieber** (*The Hunger*, 1981; filmed 1983), Robert McCammon (*They Thirst*, 1981), George R.R. Martin (*Fevre Dream*, 1982), John Skipp and Craig Spector (*The Light at the End*, 1986), Brian **Lumley** (*Necroscope*, 1986), Brian Stableford (*The Empire of Fear*, 1988), Dan Simmons (*Carrion Comfort*, 1989), Nancy Anne Collins (*Sunglasses After Dark*, 1989), Kim Newman (*Anno Dracula*, 1992), Poppy Z. Brite (*Lost Souls*, 1992), Anne Billson (*Suckers*, 1993), Lucius Shepard (*The Golden*, 1993), Michael Conner (*Archangel*, 1995) and Michael Cadnum (*The Judas Glass*, 1996). With the proliferation of vampire role-play **gaming** – which has spun off a deal of disposable fiction and a TV series (*The Kindred*, 1995–) – and Goth fashions, the vampire remains central to horror's pantheon, whether in the eternally revived forms of Dracula (resurrected with a Rice-ish romance in *Bram Stoker's Dracula*, 1992) or the new breed of leather-and-eyeliner party boys and girls.

Barrie Pattison, *The Seal of Dracula* (1975); Alain Silver, James Ursini, *The Vampire Film* (1975); David Pirie, *The Vampire Cinema* (1977); Stephen Jones, *The Illustrated Vampire Movie Guide* (1993); Greg Cox, *The Transylvanian Library* (1993); Matthew Bunson, *Vampire: The Encyclopedia* (1993); J. Gordon Melton, *The Vampire Book* (1994); David J. Skal, *V is for Vampire: The A-to-Z Guide to Everything Undead* (1996)

Van Helsing

Professor or Doctor Abraham Van Helsing is the original Fearless **Vampire** Killer, the master of arcane lore who turns up in Bram **Stoker**'s *Dracula* (1897) to explain vampirism and carry the fight to the undead villain with cross, stake and consecrated wafer. Edward **Van Sloan** (*Dracula*, 1930; *Dracula's Daughter*, 1936) was identified with the role in the 30s, but Peter **Cushing**, whose Holmesian English fanatic is very different from the novel's funny Dutchman, became the definitive Van Helsing: *Dracula* (1958), *The Brides of Dracula* (1960), *Dracula A.D. 1972* (1972), *The Satanic Rites of Dracula* (1973), *The Legend of the 7 Golden Vampires* (1974).

Other Van Helsings: John Gottow (*Nosferatu*, 1922), Eduardo Arozamena (*Drácula*, 1930), John Karlson (*Il lago di Satana*, 1965), Otto Schlesinger (*A Taste of Blood*, 1967), Bernard Archard ('Dracula', *Mystery and Imagination*, 1970), Herbert **Lom** (*El conde Drácula*, 1970), Oskar von Schab (*Jonathan*, 1970), Nehemiah Persoff ('Dracula', *Purple Playhouse*, 1973), Nigel Davenport (*Dracula*, 1974), Dennis **Price** (*Son of Dracula*, 1974), Frank Finlay (*Count Dracula*, 1977), Detlef Van Berg [Reggie **Nalder**] (*Dracula Sucks*, 1979), Walter Ladengast (*Nosferatu, Phantom der Nacht*, 1979), Laurence Olivier (*Dracula*, 1979), Richard Benjamin (*Love at First Bite*, 1979), Stephen Johnson ('The Curse of Dracula', *Cliffhangers*, 1979), Severn Darden (*Saturday the 14th*, 1981), Stefan Schnabel (*Dracula's Widow*, 1987), Jack Gwillim (*The Monster Squad*, 1987), Bruce **Campbell** (*Sundown: The Vampire in Retreat*, 1988), Ace Mask (*Transylvania Twist*, 1989), Bernard Behrens (*Dracula, the Series*, 1990–91), Michael **Berryman** ('The Reluctant Vampire', *Tales From the Crypt*, 1991), Anthony **Hopkins** (*Bram Stoker's Dracula*, 1992), Randy Spears (*Leena Meets Frankenstein*, 1993), Peter Fonda (*Nadja*, 1995), Mel Brooks (*Dracula: Dead and Loving It*, 1996).

The need for strong opposition to the undead has meant the creation of pseudo-

Vampires: Douglas Wilmer, Kirsten Betts, *The Vampire Lovers*

Van Helsings to combat incarnations of Dracula: Lionel **Barrymore** (*Mark of the Vampire*, 1935), J. Edward Bromberg (*Son of Dracula*, 1943), Frieda Inescourt (*Return of the Vampire*, 1943), Abel **Salazar** (*El vampiro*, 1956), Darren **McGavin** (*The Night Stalker*, 1971), Roddy **McDowall** (*Fright Night*, 1985), Sam Fuller (*A Return to Salem's Lot*, 1987), Christopher Plummer (*Nosferatu a Venezia*, 1988), Kirsty Swanson (*Buffy the Vampire Slayer*, 1992). Following Jack Mac-Gowran's Van Helsing parody as the dotty Professor Abronsius in *Dance of the Vampires* (1967), fearless vampire killers have become buffoonish, mad or even malevolent.

Van Sloan, Edward [Edward Van Sloun] (1882–1964)

American actor of Dutch origins. As **Van Helsing**, he confronted *Dracula* (1930) and (as 'von' Helsing) *Dracula's Daughter* (1936). He retired in 1946. SJ

Frankenstein/1931 * *The Mummy*/*The Death Kiss*/*Behind the Mask*/1932 * *Deluge*/1933 * *Death Takes a Holiday*/1934 * *The Black Room*/

The Man Who Reclaimed His Head/1935 * *The Phantom Creeps*/1939 * *Before I Hang*/1940 * *The Monster and the Girl*/1941 * *Captain America*/1944 * *The Mask of Dijon*/1945

Conrad Veidt

Veidt, Conrad (1893–1943)

German actor. Like Lon **Chaney** (to whom he was briefly a rival), Veidt specialised in the weird before horror coalesced as a genre, escaping the typecasting that afflicts subsequent horror stars. His range includes Cesare the Somnambulist (***Das Cabinet des Dr. Caligari***, 1919), the **Devil** (*Satanas*, 1919; *Kurfürstendamm*, 1920), Phileas Fogg (*Die Reise um die Erde in 80 Tagen*, 1919), Death

(*Unheimliche Geschichten*, 1919), the **Jekyll and Hyde** team of Dr Warren and Mr O'Connor (*Der Januskopf*, 1920), *Der Graf von Cagliostro* (1920), Nelson (*Lady Hamilton*, 1921), Cesare Borgia (*Lucrezia Borgia*, 1922), *Paganini* (which he produced, 1922), Ivan the Terrible (*Das Wachsfigurenkabinett*, 1924), the pianist with the murderer's hands (*Orlacs Hände*, 1925), **Faust**-cum-William Wilson (*Der Student von Prag*, 1926), a proto-Joker grinning freak (*The Man Who Laughs*, 1927), ***Rasputin*** (1930), ***The Wandering Jew*** (1938), Jesus (*The Passing of the Third Floor Back*, 1935) and the sorcerer Jaffar (*The Thief of Bagdad*, 1940). An exile from Germany, he had a period in Britain as a romantic hero with a terrifying grin (*Under the Red Robe*, 1937; *The Spy in Black*, 1939), ending his days in Hollywood, typecast at last, as a Nazi villain (*All Through the Night*, 1942; *Casablanca*, 1943).

Das indische Grabmal/1920 * *The Last Performance*/1927 * *Joueur d'echecs*/1937 * *Whistling in the Dark*/1941

Ventriloquism

In real life nothing more than the wines and spirits on a variety bill, the vent act is (since Charles Brockden Brown's *Weiland*, 1798) in horror a hellish partnership of crazed manipulator and possessed dummy. Ironically, the

Van Helsing: LEFT Laurence Olivier, *Dracula* (1979). ABOVE Peter Cushing, *Dracula* (1958)

Ventriloquism: Michael Redgrave, Hugo the Dummy, *Dead of Night*

screen's first evil ventriloquist is Lon **Chaney** in *The Unholy Three* (1925), a silent film; he reprised the role more logically in a 1930 talkie remake. In *The Great Gabbo* (1929), Erich von **Stroheim** establishes a precedent as the eccentric ventriloquist who talks to his dummy (Otto) off stage as well as on and finally tries to 'kill' it. In *The Dummy Talks* (1943), the murderer of ventriloquist Manning Whiley confesses when accused by the dummy. In the most frightening episode of the **anthology** *Dead of Night* (1945), Michael **Redgrave** plays an insane ventriloquist who believes his dummy, Hugo, is controlling him.

The theme is given an uneasy comic twist in *Knock on Wood* (1954), which is almost a kinder, gentler *Psycho* (1960): meek ventril-

oquist Danny Kaye, through a deep-seated fear of commitment, cuts loose in the alternate personality of his dummy, insulting women he is attracted to. In *Nur tote Zeugen schweigen* (*Dummy of Death*, 1962), ventriloquist-murderer Jean Sorel is again entrapped by a 'living' dummy. Obviously influenced by *Dead of Night*, *Devil Doll* (1963) even features a dummy called Hugo. *Magic* (1978), from William Goldman's 1976 novel, has Anthony **Hopkins** committing murders under the supposed influence of his dummy Fats, while the psycho of *When a Stranger Calls Back* (1993) performs an especially disturbing vent act. TV variations: *Alfred Hitchcock Presents* ('The Glass Eye', 1957), *The Twilight Zone* ('The Dummy', 1962; 'Caesar and Me', 1964), *Doctor Who* ('The

Talons of Weng-Chiang', 1977), *Mrs Columbo* ('A Riddle for Puppets', 1979), *Friday the 13th: The Series* ('Read My Lips', 1988), *Tales From the Crypt* ('The Ventriloquist's Dummy', 1990), *Batman: The Animated Series* ('Read My Lips', 1993). DM

Vernon, Howard [Mario Lippert] (b. 1914)

Swiss-American actor. The cultured Vernon has worked with many greats (a hit-man for Fritz **Lang** in *Die tausend Augen des Dr. Mabuse*/*The Thousand Eyes of Dr Mabuse*, 1960; Professor Nosferatu for Jean-Luc Godard in *Alphaville*, 1965), but is best known as Jesús **Franco**'s most enduring associate (over 35 films). He created the 'Dr Orloff' role in Franco's *Gritos en la noche* (*The Awful Dr.*

Orlof, 1961), sat out *El secreto del Dr Orloff* (1964) and *Los ojos siniestros del Doctor Orloff* (1973), but reprises the **mad scientist** for *Solo un ataúd* (*Only a Coffin*, 1966), *Orloff y el hombre invisible* (*The Invisible Dead*, 1970), *El Siniestro Dr. Orloff* (1982) and *Les prédateurs de la nuit* (*Faceless*, 1988). Though one of the worst screen Draculas (*Dracula, prisonnier de Frankenstein/Dracula, Prisoner of Frankenstein*, 1971), Vernon's maverick stance and unique screen presence make him worthy of his growing reputation as one of European cinema's treasures. MA

La mano de un hombre muerto [*Hand of a Dead Man*]/1963 * *Miss Muerte* [*The Diabolical Dr. Z*]/1965 * *Necronomicon: Geträumte Sünden* [*Succubus*]/*Im Schloss der blutigen Begierde* [*Castle of Lust*]/*L'Inconnu de Shandigor*/1967 * *Justine*/1968 * *El proceso de las brujas* [*Night of the Blood Monsters*]/*La rose ecorchée* [*Ravaged*]/1969 * *Sie tötete in Ekstase* [*Mrs. Hyde*]/1970 * *Una vergine tra i morti viventi* [*A Virgin Among the Living Dead*]/*La fille de Dracula*/1971 * *La maldición de Frankenstein* [*The Erotic Rites of Frankenstein*]/*Os demonios* [*The Demons*]/1972 * *Al otro lado del espejo* [*Beyond the Grave*]/*Plaisir à trois* [*How to Seduce a Virgin*]/*La comtesse perverse*/1973 * *Les possédées du diable/Les weekends du comte Zaroff* [*Seven Women for Satan*]/1974 * *Le lac des morts vivants* [*Zombies Lake*]/1980 * *Dr. Jekyll et les femmes* [*Blood of Dr. Jekyll*]/1981 * *El hundimiento de la Casa Usher* [*Revenge in the House of Usher*/1983 * *El aullido del diablo* [*Howl of the Devil*]/1988 * *Le champignon des Carpathes*/1990 * *Delicatessen*/1991

Victims

Characters whose deaths serve merely to advance the plot or illustrate the monstrousness of the monster, victims are the footsoldiers of horror. Archetypal is Lucy Westenra of *Dracula* (1897), drained by the Count as an appetiser before his assault on **heroine** Mina, then staked and beheaded in **vampire** form by a cadre of staunch ex-boyfriends.

Horrors on the pattern of *Dracula* (1931) are content with one Lucy figure (eg: Fay Helm in *The Wolf Man*, 1941) but *The Man They Could Not Hang* (1939) and *The Devil Bat* (1941), adapting a subplot from *Son of Frankenstein* (1939), are early incidences of 'body count', structuring a plot around the deaths of sundry characters who have angered the monster or **mad scientist**. Typical ninepins are the dismembered girls of *Blood Feast* (1963), the curse-defying

Egyptologists of *Blood From the Mummy's Tomb* (1971), the doctors of *The Abominable Dr. Phibes* (1971), the critics of *Theatre of Blood* (1972), the apostate Satanists of **The Omen** (1975) and the punks of *The Toxic Avenger* (1984). These have somehow earned their deaths: the spies of *Black Dragons* (1942) and the Victorian hypocrites of *Taste the Blood of Dracula* (1969) are so unpleasant that the villains almost become sympathetic.

Victims are more often poignantly wasted, like the youthful sacrifices paraded by the **stalk-and-slash** cycle. Just as Lucy is marked for doom because she flirts more than Mina, these often single out the surviving heroine (Jamie Lee **Curtis**, *Halloween*, 1977) by having her adopt a more serious, perhaps repressed attitude to sexuality. While the 'have sex and die' cliché is frequently valid, the overall effect of hundreds of slashers is of a frightening randomness that marks everybody as a potential victim: little distinguishes survivor Adrienne King of **Friday the 13th** (1980) from her butchered friends and she is slaughtered off-hand in the prologue of *Friday the 13th, Part 2* (1981).

Video Games * See: **Interactive**

Video Nasties

The expression 'nasty' was first used in the book trade to describe the early novels of James **Herbert**, but the dispiriting catch-all phrase 'video nasty' was coined by the British tabloid press to discredit a disparate slew of uncertificated horror movies released in the UK during the unregulated video boom of the early 80s. Key titles like *I Spit on Your Grave* (1978), *The Driller Killer* (1979) and *Cannibal holocaust* (1979) were considered potentially obscene by the Department of Public Prosecution, whose actionable 'hit list' – focusing on **splatter movies, stalk-and-slash, rape, cannibalism, Nazis**, general **violence** and Lucio **Fulci** – became affectionately known to fans and collectors as 'The Big Sixty'. Regulated only by the notoriously unreliable Obscene Publications Act, 'video nasties' were blamed by the media for inattentiveness at school, muggings, rape etc. In a *coup de grace*, the Tory government rushed through the 1984 Video Recordings Act (formerly Graham Bright's private member's bill), imposing a **censorship** which outlawed any video lacking a government approved certificate.

Along with the few genuinely *outré* 'nasties' to which UK audiences were unaccustomed, the VRA banned a number of main-

stream 'problem titles'. *The Evil Dead* (1982) and **The Exorcist** (1973) were considered unacceptable on video, though approved for cinema audiences by the British Board of Film Classification (*né* Censors): *The Evil Dead* was finally passed with severe cuts in 1990, while *The Exorcist* remains banned on video. In 1993, the spectre of the 'video nasty' was resurrected when Justice Morland spuriously linked the murder by two Liverpool youths of toddler James Bulger to the relatively innocuous *Child's Play 3* (1991). An ensuing media panic led directly to further tightening of VRA regulations via the 1994 Criminal Justice Act. A sad testament to Britain's long-standing demonisation of horror, the myth of the 'video nasty' remains a source of much hilarity in Europe and America. MK

Martin Barker, *The Video Nasties* (1984); John Martin, *The Seduction of the Gullible* (1993)

Violence

Violence is the subject of much art, and the basis for many forms of cinema. It is indeed bound up with the earliest moments of the moving image: the approaching train of Louis Lumière's *L'arrivée d'un train en gare de la Ciotat* (1895) carries with it a physical threat that also informs much of the sensationalist fantasy of Georges **Méliès**, as well as such British entries as George Harrison & Co.'s *Fight with Sledge Hammers* (1902) and William Haggar's *True as Steel* (1902). The transgressive final shot of Edwin S. Porter's *The Great Train Robbery* (1903) has a felon firing point-blank into the camera.

A precondition of war movies and the disturbing means by which America is shaped in the Western, violence is, notwithstanding, primarily associated with horror – perhaps because horror is a genre in which death itself is the subject of enquiry. As the motive force of Hollywood macabre, Lon **Chaney** was fêted not only for starring in films of often forthright thuggishness but also for submitting to masochistic regimes in the course of their production. The talkies that succeeded him are underratedly egregious: *Frankenstein* (1931) includes casual infanticide; *Island of Lost Souls* (1932), vivisection; **Murders in the Rue Morgue** (1932), surgical rape; **The Black Cat** (1934), a climactic flaying. *Mystery of the Wax Museum* (1933) contrives a noteworthy explicitness by rending Lionel **Atwill**'s wax face to reveal the fleshy mess beneath. A similar stategy is employed in *Son of Frankenstein* (1939) when, as Inspector Krogh, Atwill is disarticulated by **Karloff**'s ripping off of his false arm. An early example of penetrative violence occurs in *The Ghost Ship* (1943); though lionised for his implicit horrors, Val Lewton also uses **grand guignol** imagery in *The Leopard Man* (1943), as Jacques Tourneur quotes the blood-beneath-the-door image from his father Maurice's *Le système du Docteur Goudron et du Professeur Plume* (*The Lunatics*, 1912).

Moulded by the political demands of the time, lesser programmers exhibited a briskness that had its own brutality. World War II's most radical effects however came in its aftermath, as the institutional sadism of **Nazi** Germany began to impact on European cinema. *Les diaboliques* (1955) offers an innovatively assaultive, misanthropic, vastly influential concept of screen terror. Made by Henri-Georges **Clouzot** (whose *Le corbeau*, 1943, was not irrelevantly embroiled in arguments about French war guilt), the film shares writers Boileau and Narcejac with Georges **Franju**'s *Les yeux sans visage* (*Eyes Without a Face*, 1959), which boasts surgical scenes emblematic of an unflinching new kind of horror. Other directionally gruesome moments include the smearing of Eastmancolor **blood** across Peter **Cushing**'s lapel in **Hammer**'s *The Curse of Frankenstein* (1957) and the application of the eponymous mask to Barbara **Steele** in the opening of Mario **Bava**'s *La maschera del demonio* (*The Mask of Satan*, 1960).

Enlarging on the self-reflexive nastiness of *Peeping Tom* (1960), *Psycho* (1960) famously suggests the radical formal potential of this viciousness by dispatching heroine Janet **Leigh** forty-five minutes in; soon after, H.G. **Lewis** would construct a film (*Blood Feast*, 1963) in which narrative does little more than wad a collection of hyperbolic kills. The *gialli* spawned by Bava's *La ragazza che sapeva troppo* (*The Evil Eye*, 1963) and *Sei donne per l'assassino* (*Blood and Black Lace*, 1964) bring about a comparable deconstruction of the detective thriller through a favouring of visceral set-pieces. The 70s sees film at its most feral. While Dario **Argento** turned **splatter** into an increasingly abstract art, an interrogative strain of low-budget American shocker emerged courtesy of *Night of the Living Dead* (1968), besieging establishment values and harrying audiences into thinking they saw worse than was actually shown. Less is left to the imagination in a series of Italian **cannibal** films whose excruciating intemperance best codifies a decade where *A Clockwork Orange* (1971), *The Exorcist* (1973) and *The Omen* (1976) are considered mainstream prospects.

The 'snuff' rumour – fed by New York distributor Allan Shackleton in 1976 to promote a repackaged version of Michael and Roberta **Findlay**'s *Slaughter* (1971) and current as late as *Mute Witness* (1995) – is an almost inevitable by-blow of the period. More legitimate offspring comprise the

stalk-and-slash cycle and such body-racking transformationers as John **Carpenter**'s *The Thing* (1982). Making idols of special efects artistes, *Fangoria* magazine (1979–) has grown out of the persistent importance of gore to the horror fan. As cinema relented in the 80s, video generated a nostalgia for excess, enshrining the work of pathological Catholics like Lucio **Fulci** and encouraging the discovery of unfettered Asian and South American horror traditions. *Violent Shit* (1988) and *Gorgasm* (1992) are representative of the amateur efforts energised by home-viewing; *Bad Taste* (1988) and *Reservoir Dogs* (1993) are overground equivalents. With *The Silence of the Lambs* (1991) and *Se7en* (1995), a millenarian interest in **serial murder** once more returned violence to studio agendas. DP

von Seyffertitz, Gustav * See: Seyffertitz

von Stroheim, Erich * See: Stroheim

Von Sydow, Max * See: Sydow

Volk, Stephen (b. 1954)

British writer. Though his theatrical projects range from the **camp** *Gothic* (1986) to the disastrous *The Guardian* (1990), Volk's television play *Ghostwatch* (1992) manages to pull off the difficult mock-documentary form and climaxes with a genuine moment of terror.

The Kiss/1988

TV: *Ghosts*: 'I'll Be Watching You'/'Massage'/ 1994

Voodoo

A **religion**, practised in Haiti and certain regions of Latin America, which arose in the 18th century among transported slaves, cross-breeding of Catholic ritual with elements of African beliefs. William Seabrook's *The Magic Island* (1929) popularised the image of voodoo, notably the supposed practice of raising the dead (as **zombies**) to work as slaves and, to a lesser extent, the use of pin-pierced **dolls** to cast curses. Seabrook influenced a run of films about Caribbean voodoo: *White Zombie* (1932), *Black Noon* (1934), *Drums O'Voodoo* (1934), *Ouanga* (1935), *Condemned Men* (1940), *The Ghost Breakers* (1940), *King of the Zombies* (1941), *I Walked With a Zombie* (1943), *Voodoo Man* (1944), *Zombies on Broadway* (1945), *Voodoo Island* (1957), *I Eat Your Skin* (1964), *The Plague of the Zombies* (1966), *Voodoo Dawn*

Violence: Véra Clouzot, *Les diaboliques*

Voodoo: John Carson, *The Plague of the Zombies*

(1989). A parallel strain favours African settings: *Voodoo Woman* (1957), *The Disembodied* (1957), *Zombies of Mora Tau* (1957), *Curse of the Voodoo* (1965).

With **blaxploitation** in the 70s, voodoo made a comeback in *Live and Let Die* (1973) and *Sugar Hill* (1974), which feature the top-hatted god Baron Samedi, and *Scream, Blacula, Scream* (1973) and *Lord Shango* (1975). The post-*Night of the Living Dead* (1968) zombie movie eschews voodoo as an explanation for the walking dead, but it creeps back via *Zombi 2* (1980) and even, through undertones, *Dawn of the Dead* (1979) and *Day of the Dead* (1985). There are films on related beliefs like Macumba (*Macumba Love*, 1960) and Santeria (*The Believers*, 1987) and recent serious (*The Serpent and the Rainbow*, 1987) and spurious (*Child's Play*, 1988; *Voodoo*, 1995) attempts to make less

stereotyped voodoo horror films. New Orleans voodoo features in *Angel Heart* (1987) and *The Big Easy* (1987), voodoo is merely a plot device in *Black Magic Woman* (1990) and *Scared Stiff* (1987) and there are even voodoo comedies: *Dead Men Don't Die* (1990), *Weekend at Bernie's II* (1993), *Shrunken Heads* (1994). Cornell **Woolrich**'s 'Dark Melody of Madness' (1935), about a jazz musician cursed when he steals a chant for a hit tune, was done as a *Thriller* episode ('Papa Benjamin', 1961) and lifted for *Dr. Terror's House of Horrors* (1964), prefiguring the discovery of voodoo by world music in the 90s.

Voorhees, Jason * See: **Cunnigham, Sean S.**; *Friday the 13th*; **Hodder, Kane**

Voyage to the Bottom of the Sea (US TV series, 1964–8)
Created and produced by Irwin Allen, based on his 1961 movie, this s-f adventure series stars Richard Basehart as Admiral Nelson and David Hedison as Captain Lee Crane, commanding officers of the first atomic powered submarine, the *Seaview*. First season black-and-white episodes find the crew battling menaces from tidal waves to foreign secret agents. As the series progressed in colour, plots became more fantastic, involving a giant monster in a giant cardigan ('Leviathan', 1965), a ghostly U-Boat captain ('The Phantom Strikes', 1966), **werewolves** ('Werewolf', 1966; 'The Brand of the Beast', 1966), screaming underwater plants ('The Plant Man', 1966), *doppelgängers* ('The Wax Men', 1967), **mad scientists** (Vincent **Price** in 'The Deadly Dolls', 1967), the Flying

Dutchman ('Cave of the Dead', 1967) and alien crustaceans ('The Lobster Man', 1968).

William Welch and the team of William Read Woodfield and Allan Balter provided most of the scripts; Harlan **Ellison** contributed just one, 'The Price of Doom' (1964), rewritten seventeen times and signed 'Cord Wainer Bird'. Despite Basehart's intensity and sometimes amiably loony plots, the show was mostly notable for its **clichés** (the only lower-ranks crewman was an all-purpose swab called Kowalski), its low-rent effects and stock footage from Irwin Allen's films. TM

W

Waggner, George [Waggoner] (1894–1984)

American producer, director. Waggner's directorial work ranges from the reasonable *Man Made Monster* (1941) to the dull *The Climax* (1944). However, **The Wolf Man** is a pop classic: Waggner surrounds the amiably cursed Lon **Chaney Jr** with pro hams (Claude **Rains**, **Lugosi**, Maria Ouspenskaya) who make something of Curt **Siodmak**'s ominous script. He went to TV, sometimes billed as WaGGner, and introduced Vincent **Price**'s Egghead on *Batman* ('An Egg Grows in Gotham/The Yegg Foes in Gotham', 1966).

Horror Island (+d)/1940 * *Ghost of Frankenstein*/1942 * *Phantom of the Opera/Frankenstein Meets the Wolf Man*/1943

Walas, Chris (b. 1957)

American special make-up effects artist, director. His first major breaks were fishmen for *Screamers* (1981) – an Americanised recut of *L'isola degli uomini pesce* (*Island of the Mutations*, 1978) – and melting **heads** for *Raiders of the Lost Ark* (1980). He supervised creature effects for *Gremlins* (1984) and *Arachnophobia* (1990) and won an Oscar for transforming Jeff **Goldblum** into *The Fly* (1986). He turned director with *The Fly II* (1989). MS

The Golden Child/1986 * *House II: The Second Story*/1987 * *The Kiss*/1988 * *Naked Lunch*/1991 * *The Vagrant* (d)/1992

TV: *Tales From the Crypt*: ''Til Death' (d)/1990

Walken, Christopher [Ronald Walken] (b. 1943)

American actor. Despite high-profile weirdo roles in *The Deer Hunter* (1978), *Heaven's Gate*

Tom Skerritt, Christopher Walken, *The Dead Zone*

(1980), *The Dogs of War* (1981), *Pennies From Heaven* (1981) and *Brainstorm* (1983), Walken was too unpredictable to remain an A-list star. He now rotates big-budget bad guys (*A View to a Kill*, 1985; *Batman Returns*, 1992), exploitation enlivened by his presence (*All-American Murder*, 1991) and bizarro cameos (*True Romance*, 1993; *Pulp Fiction*, 1994). Stephen **King**'s psychic Everyman in *The Dead Zone* (1983), the abducted Whitley **Strieber** in *Communion* (1989), Abel **Ferrara**'s hyperactive druglord in *King of New York* (1990), a killer angel in *The Prophecy* (1995) and a **vampire** in Ferrara's *The Addiction* (1995). He is a cop in *Ripper* (1995), a futuristic slasher on CD-ROM as an '**interactive** movie'.

The Happiness Cage/1972 * *The Sentinel*/1977 * *The Funeral*/1995

Walker, Peter (b. 1935)

British producer and director. Like Norman **Warren**, Walker began his career in **sex** comedies (*Cool It, Carol*, 1970) before switching to gruesome, low-budget horror. His most effective films conjure extremely bleak worlds in which the forces of repression have crushed all that is potentially life-enhancing. They are a quintessentially British take on themes and issues occupying American horror in the 1970s, breaking similar taboos and refusing the reassurance of the happy ending. *Frightmare* (1974) features a **cannibal** old lady (played with terrifying intensity by Sheila **Keith**, a Walker favourite) whose sickness is indulged by her family and who escapes punishment at the conclusion. Master of what collaborator David **McGillivray** calls 'suburban menace', Walker's work represents the fullest expression of the nihilistic element that entered British horror with Michael **Reeves** in the late 1960s. After a period of inactivity, his unsuccessful comeback was the **Old Dark House** mystery *House of the Long Shadows* (1983). PH

Die Screaming, Marianne/1970 * *The Flesh and Blood Show*/1972 * *House of Whipcord*/1974 * *House of Mortal Sin*/1975 * *Schizo*/1976 * *The Comeback*/1977

Wallace, Edgar [Richard Horatio Edgar Wallace] (1875–1932)

British writer. A briskly flamboyant thrillerist

Edgar Wallace

who followed the self-published *The Four Just Men* (1905) with more than a thousand novels, short stories and plays, Wallace is of recurrent cinematic significance. As a living legend, he furnished sources for horror's first talkie, *The Terror* (1928), and Britain's first full sound entry, *The Clue of the New Pin* (1929), before leaving **King Kong** (1933) as an epitaph. Posthumous adaptations include the first British film to merit an 'H' certificate (*Dark Eyes of London*, 1939), and a formally self-conscious run of West German *krimis* that commenced with Rialto's *Der Frosch mit der Maske* (*Fellowship of the Frog*, 1959) and proved a fundamental influence on the Italian *giallo*.

Anglo-Amalgamated's thirty-nine featurettes (1960–4) and the two items directed by the author as chairman of British Lion (*Red Aces*, 1929; *The Squeaker*, 1930) are lesser examples of the 170-plus movies that claim Wallace's paternity, and which terminate in Jesús **Franco**'s *Viaje a Bangkok, ataúd incluido* (1985). Co-scripted by Wallace, *The Hound of the Baskervilles* (1931) is a rare adaptation of others' work. DP

Wallace, Tommy Lee (b. 1949)

American director. For schoolfriend John **Carpenter**, Wallace worked as production designer/editor on *Dark Star* (1974), *Assault on Precinct 13* (1976), **Halloween** (1978) and *The Fog* (1980). He scripted the awkward

Amityville II: – The Possession (1982) and passed on *Halloween II* (1981) to tackle the more ingeniously original *Halloween III: Season of the Witch* (1983). After the dues-paying of *Fright Night, Part 2* (1988), he handled the Stephen **King** mini-series *It* (1990). AJ

The Baby (extra)/1971

TV: *The Twilight Zone*: 'Dreams for Sale'/ 'Little Boy Lost'/1985; 'The Leprechaun-Artist' (+w)/1986 * *Danger Island*/1992

Walters, Thorley (1913–91)

British actor. In roles for **Hammer**, Walters projects an appealing gentleness and vulnerability. He is Ludwig, the **Renfield** character in *Dracula, Prince of Darkness* (1965). As Frankenstein's assistant in *Frankenstein Created Woman* (1966), some of his niceness appears to rub off on **Frankenstein** himself, who is at his most benign. Like many jobbing actors associated with Hammer, Walters thought little of his performances and was somewhat embarrassed by attention received from horror fans. Dr Watson in several **Holmes** projects: *Sherlock Holmes und das Halsband des Todes* (*Sherlock Holmes and the Deadly Necklace*, 1962), *The Adventure of Sherlock Holmes' Smarter Brother* (1975) and 'Silver Blaze' (1980). PH

The Phantom of the Opera/1962 * *The Earth*

Dies Screaming/1964 * *The Psychopath*/1965 * *The Wrong Box*/1966 * *Frankenstein Must Be Destroyed*/1969 * *The Man Who Haunted Himself/Trog*/1970 * *Vampire Circus*/1972

TV: *The Avengers*: 'What the Butler Saw'/ 1966 * *Thriller*: 'Death in Small Doses'/1973 * *Orson Welles' Great Mysteries*: 'Ice Storm'/ 1974 * *Beasts*: 'The Dummy'/1975 * *The Sign of Four*/1983 * *Tales of the Unexpected*: 'The Surgeon'/1988

Walton, Fred (b. 19??)

American director. Creator of the seminal **stalk-and-slash** *When a Stranger Calls* (1979), an expansion of his short *The Sitter* (1977), which uses the urban legend of a babysitter in peril from a psycho already in the same house. He effectively reprises it for TV sequel *When a Stranger Calls Back* (1994). *April Fools Day* (1986), inspired by Agatha **Christie** and **Friday the 13th** (1980), and *The Rosary Murders* (1987), a neat twist on **Hitchcock**'s *I Confess* (1953), prove Walton's quiet talent for disarmingly individual flourishes. AJ

TV: *Alfred Hitchcock Presents*: 'An Unlocked Window'/1985 * *I Saw What You Did*/1988 * *Homewrecker*/1992

The Wandering Jew

Like Cain and the Flying Dutchman, the Wandering Jew is a cursed **immortal**. The story, first written down in 1223, goes that a Jew, usually named Cartaphilius or Ahaseurus, abuses Jesus on his way to the cross, and Christ confers immortality upon him, declaring 'I go but thou shall tarry 'til I come again'. He wanders the centuries, worn by guilt and the sorrows of the world. The legend was popular in the middle ages,

Tony Beckley, Colleen Dewhurst, Fred Walton's *When a Stranger Calls*

War: *Apocalypse Now*

when various individuals claimed to be the Wandering Jew, and is touched upon by many novels, poems, plays and stories: M.G. **Lewis**'s *The Monk* (1796), Franz Horn's *Der ewige Jude* (1814), August Klingemann's *Ahasver* (1827), Edgar Quinet's *Ahasvérus* (1833), Eugène Sue's *Le Juif errant* (1844–5), George Macdonald's *Thomas Wingfield, Curate* (1876), Alexandre Dumas's *Isaac Laquedem* (1853), George Viereck and Paul Eldridge's *My First Two Thousand Years* (1928), Pär Lagerkvist's *Ahasverus Död* (1959), Walter M. Miller Jr's *A Canticle for Leibowitz* (1960), Tom Holland's *The Vampyre* (1995).

For a mythic archetype, the Wandering Jew has been underrepresented in the cinema: he is played by Matheson Lang and Conrad **Veidt** in 1923 and 1933 films of E. Temple Thurston's play *The Wandering Jew* (1920), and Peter Friedman in *The Seventh Sign* (1988). Georges **Méliès** made *Le juif errant* (1904), Italian versions came in 1913 (*L'ebreo errante*), 1917 (*Morok*) and 1948 (*L'ebreo errante*) and there is a Yiddish American film called *The Wandering Jew* (1933).

George Y. Anderson, *The Legend of the Wandering Jew* (1965); Brian Stableford, *Tales of the Wandering Jew* (1991)

War

Filled with mortality and coercion, horror is a genre in which characters are habitually in a state of war; its cinema is much influenced by the century's conflicts. World War I stimulated the **expressionist** experimentation vital to horror as much by depriving Germany of foreign product as by its unprecedented death-dealing. ***Das Cabinet des Dr. Caligari*** (1919) was written to attack Prussian militarism. Fritz **Lang** turned to film as a war-wounded ex-lieutenant. In Hollywood, James **Whale** employed trench

humour; his are among the many American entries whose European settings/monsters make implicit reference to the Great War. Edgar **Ulmer**'s ***The Black Cat*** (1934) takes place atop a military grave. Indirectly responsible for the **psychiatric** subgenre, World War II nevertheless made damaging, propagandistic demands of horror.

While Britain discouraged the terror film, America produced simplistic right-versus-might knockabouts in which bogeys are despatched with encouraging ease. A dynamited dam is the tellingly martial climax to *Frankenstein Meets the Wolf Man* (1943), the first in a series of Universal team-ups which so cartoon its demons they can eventually be dealt with by Abbott and Costello. Explicit **Nazis** are found behind surgical (*Black Dragons*, 1942) and supernatural (*The Mysterious Doctor*, 1943) disguises, and, after *Revolt of the Zombies* (1936), attempting monster armies (*Revenge of the Zombies*, 1943). **Lewton**'s *Isle of the Dead* (1945) is an untypically depressive war-themed entry.

Korea proved the world was still a warzone: an anti-Communist action in which germ weaponry was rumoured, it moved the US to reformulate horror in newly paranoid s-f terms. *Gojira* (*Godzilla, King of the Monsters*, 1954) signalled a series of Japanese nuclear-age monster movies that rehearse Hiroshima-Nagasaki devastation. In the guilt-riven narratives and Sadean tableaux of European

War: Martin Sheen, *Apocalypse Now*

ground-breakers like *Les yeux sans visage* (*Eyes without a Face*, 1959), World War II's most apocalyptic legacy – the holocaust – seems also addressed. US soul-searching over Vietnam helped politicise horror. One of a clutch of engaged independents, *Last House on the Left* (1972) was intended as a protest against war brutalities. Upfront allegory *Dead of Night* (1972) features effects from Nam veteran Tom **Savini**. Vietnam supplies psychos for *Stanley* (1973), *Poor White Trash Part II* (1976), *Don't Answer the Phone* (1980), *Street Trash* (1986), *The Texas Chainsaw Massacre Part 2* (1986) and *Combat Shock* (1987), and revenants for *House* (1986) and *Jacob's Ladder* (1990). It has also made horror-hybrids of war movies (*Platoon*, 1986; *Full Metal Jacket*, 1987) and given new twists to Spanish (*Autopsia*, 1973) and Italian (*Apocalypse domani*, 1980) exploiters.

Other horrors featuring the **military**: *King of the Zombies* (1941), *The Return of the Vampire* (1944), *The Beast in the Cellar* (1970), *The Prowler* (1981), *The Lost Platoon* (1989), *Bride of Re-Animator* (1991), *Hellraiser III: Hell on Earth* (1992). The English Civil War provides the backdrop to *Matthew Hopkins Witchfinder General* (1968); the American Civil War, *Two Thousand Maniacs!* (1964), *The Supernaturals* (1986) and *The Killing Box* (1993). *Dream Demon* (1988) and Welsh short *Home Front* (1992) make use of the Falklands War as 'The Walk' (*The X-Files*, 1995) and *Uncle Sam* (1996) do of the Gulf; Balkan strife informs *Bram Stoker's Dracula* (1992); a plethora of dystopian s-f suggests

David Warner, *Morgan – A Suitable Case for Treatment*

the many similar opportunities to come. DP

Warbeck, David (b. 1942)

New Zealand-born British actor. Likable leading man in British and Italian horrors.

Trog/1969 * *Tam Lin*/1970 * *Twins of Evil*/ 1971 * *Blacksnake!*/1972 * *Craze*/*Voices*/1973 * *Il gatto nero* [*The Black Cat*]/*L'aldilà* [*The Beyond*]/1980 * *Panic*/1981 * *7 Hyden Park* [*Formula for a Murder*]/*Miami Golem*/1985 * *Ratman*/1986 * *Domino*/1988 * *Breakfast With Dracula*/1993 * *Fotogrammi mortali* [*Fatal Frames*]/1995

TV: *Journey to the Unknown*: 'Do Me a Favour and Kill Me'/1968 * *Thriller*: 'Only a Scream Away'/1974

Warner, David (b. 1941)

British actor. Warner made an impression in *Tom Jones* (1963), *Morgan, a Suitable Case for Treatment* (1966) and *The Bofors Gun* (1968), but now does more exploitation than art. He was a **Peckinpah** regular (*The Ballad of Cable Hogue*, 1970; *Straw Dogs*, 1971; *Cross of Iron*, 1977). Between arch-villains (*Time Bandits*, 1981; *Tron*, 1982), scientists (*Teenage Mutant Ninja Turtles II: The Secret of the Ooze*, 1991) and Klingons (*Star Trek VI: The Undiscovered Country*, 1991), Warner is beheaded spectacularly in **The Omen** (1976), an occasional **werewolf** for Alain Resnais in *Providence* (1977), a well-intentioned but unsuccessful TV monster in **Frankenstein** (1982) and the voice of R'as al Ghul on **Batman**: *The Animated Series* ('The Demon's Quest', 1993;

'Showdown', 1994). His best genre role is a definitive **Jack the Ripper** in *Time After Time* (1979).

From Beyond the Grave/1973 * *Nightwing*/1979 * *The Island*/1980 * *The Man With Two Brains*/ 1983 * *The Company of Wolves*/1984 * *Pulse Pounders* (unfinished)/*My Best Friend is a Vampire*/1987 * *Waxwork*/1988 * *Grave Secrets*/*S.P.O.O.K.S.*/1989 * *The Unnameable II*/ 1992 * *Necronomicon*/1993 * *In the Mouth of Madness*/1994 * *The Ice Cream Man*/*Final Equinox*/*Naked Souls*/1995

TV: *Twin Peaks*/1990–91 * *Cast a Deadly Spell*/ 1991 * *Body Bags*/1993 * *Gargoyles* (v)/1994– * *The Outer Limits*: 'Virtual Future'/1995 * *Beastmaster: The Eye of Braxus*/1995 * *Perversions of Science*/1996

Warren, Norman J. (b. 1942)

British director. Warren worked in the same low-budget exploitation horror genre as Peter **Walker** in the 1970s: there are obvious links between the two, notably shared screenwriter David **McGillivray** and a reliance on generally gratuitous gore and nudity. While Walker's films relentlessly convey a grim sense of a society falling apart, Warren's work tends to be more high-spirited, skipping cheerfully from **witches**' curses (*Satan's Slave*, 1976; *Terror*, 1978) to **Alien**-derived s-f/horror (*Inseminoid*, 1980). In Warren's films, effective and imaginative scenes are interrupted by longueurs and uninteresting violence. In *Prey* (1977), an **alien** comes to earth and eats two lesbians (arguably the most irresistibly schlocky storyline in British cinema) but more time is spent on character relationships than on anthropophagy and the film's most effective sequence has the male alien bizarrely don drag. PH

Bloody New Year/1986

Warren, Jerry (1923–88)

American director, producer. Far more than Ed **Wood**, Warren deserves the title of the world's worst film-maker, padding footage poached from Mexican films with acres of dreary dialogue observed from locked-down camera positions: *Face of the Screaming Werewolf* (1959), *Curse of the Stone Hand* (1959), *Attack of the Mayan Mummy* (1963). He turned Virgil Vogel's *Terror in the Midnight Sun* (1958) into the shorter, duller *Invasion of the Animal People* (1960). *Teenage Zombies* (1958) and *The Incredible Petrified World* (1959), his 'originals', are even worse, unrelieved by well-photographed scenes from

Waxworks: Phillis Kirk, Charles Bronson, *House of Wax*

foreign films. Scenes are done entirely in static master shot, as amateur actors awkwardly stand around. While Wood displays bizarre enthusiasm, Warren gives the impression that he never cared about his films or his audiences. Audiences reciprocated. *Frankenstein Island* (1982), a partial remake of *Teenage Zombies*, is in colour but otherwise shows not a jot of development.

Man Beast/1955 * *Creature of the Walking Dead* (p)/1965 * *The Wild World of Batwoman*/1966

Waxworks

What are now taken for granted as the sinister aspects of the wax museum were not exploited in films until the 1930s, though Paul **Leni**'s *Das Wachsfigurenkabinett* (*Waxworks*, 1924) concludes with a brief sequence in which the hero dreams he is being pursued by an animated statue of **Jack the Ripper**. The cliché of the wax museum owned by a madman, occupied by a killer, or both, figures in *While Paris Sleeps* (1923), but was popularised by *Mystery of the Wax Museum* (1933), remade as *House of Wax* (1953). It is perpetuated by *Midnight at Madame Tussaud's* (1936), *The Frozen Ghost* (1945), 'Waxworks' (**Thriller**, 1962), *Santo en el museo de cera* (*Samson in the Wax Museum*, 1963), 'The New Exhibit' (**The Twilight Zone**, 1963), *Chamber of Horrors* (1966), *Nightmare in Wax* (1969), 'Chamber of Fear' (*Land of the Giants*, 1969), *The House That Dripped Blood* (1970), *Terror in the Wax Museum* (1973), 'Wax Magic' (*Friday the 13th: The Series*, 1988), 'In His Own Image' (*Something is Out There*, 1988), *Waxwork* (1988), 'The Works . . . in Wax' (*Tales From the Cryptkeeper*, 1993) and *La maschera di cera* (*Wax Mask*, 1996). In many of these, human victims are embalmed in wax: the theme of corpses displayed as works of **art** is taken up by *A Bucket of Blood* (1959), *Il mostro di Venezia* (1965), *Blood Bath* (1966), *El collecionista de cadavres* (*Cauldron of Blood*, 1967) and *Crucible of Terror* (1971). In *Mad Love* (1935), Peter **Lorre** is obsessed by a wax effigy of Frances Drake. In *Torture Garden* (1967), Burgess Meredith uses a waxwork to illustrate what fate holds for the visitors to his sideshow. In too many cases, film waxworks are played by actors who have trouble remaining motionless. DM

Way Out (US TV series, 1961)

A short-lived horror anthology produced as a summer replacement for CBS. Roald **Dahl**

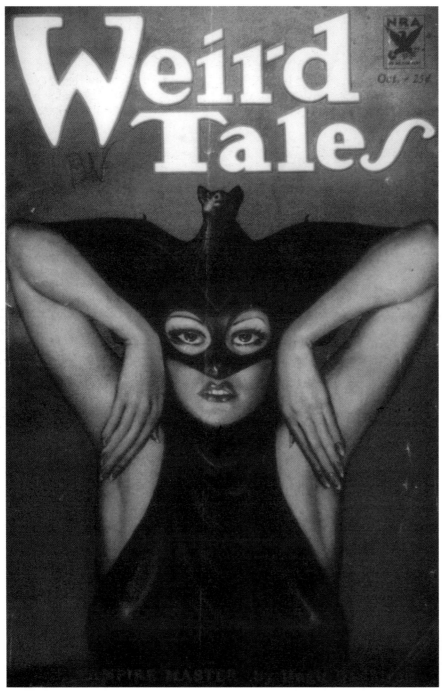

Weird Tales

hosted contemporary tales of mystery and the macabre. The first episode was an adaptation of Dahl's 'William and Mary', directed by Marc Daniels. In 'False Face', teleplay by Larry **Cohen** and directed by Paul Bogart, actor Alfred Ryder prepares to play the part of **The Hunchback of Notre Dame** but suffers a bizarre trick of fate. In 'Soft Focus', photographer Barry Morse discovers an extraordinary chemical which, when used on a portrait, has the power to change the actual person's face. Both episodes wind up with spectacular Dick **Smith** mutilations for the protagonist. TM

Weeks, Stephen (b. 1948)

British director. Starting out in British horror just as it entered a period of commercial decline, his career has been troubled by production difficulties. *I, Monster* (1970), a

Jekyll and Hyde for **Amicus**, is fatally damaged by an abortive **3-D** process. *Ghost Story* (1974), set in England but made in India, is more interesting in its attempt, not entirely successful, to do something different with a period setting. PH

Wegener, Paul (1874–1948)

German actor, director. An enormous presence, Wegener went to Prague as producer and actor to make the **Faustian** *Der Student von Prag* (1913) and stayed to film a local legend. He not only played the first continuing monster character in *Der Golem* (1914), *Der Golem und die Tänzerin* (1917) and *Der Golem, wie er in die Welt kam* (1920) but directed and co-wrote the films. In the parodic middle entry, he plays himself, impressing a dancer in his hulking **golem** suit. He plays mad genius roles in *Svengali* (1927), *Alraune* (1928) and *The Magician* (1928). Though his golem makes sympathetic use of Jewish lore, he became an Actor of State under Hitler and appeared in Nazi propaganda (*Hans Westmar*, 1932).

Rübezahls Hochzeit (+d)/1915 * *Der Yoghi* (+d)/1916 * *Der Rattenfänger* (+d)/1918 * *Sumurun*/1920 * *Der verlorene Schatten* (+d)/1921 * *Ramper der Tiermensch*/1927 * *Unheimliche Geschichten*/1932

Weir, Peter (b. 1944)

Australian director, writer. His first three features reveal a striking voice. *The Cars That Ate Paris* (1974) is a blackly comic variation on the cautionary tale about what goes on in rural wastelands of **The Texas Chain Saw Massacre** (1974), while *Picnic at Hanging Rock* (1975) and the **apocalyptic** *The Last Wave* (1977) are shimmering explorations of the limitations of the rational world, suffused by a delicately terrifying sense of foreboding. After *Gallipoli* (1981) and *The Year of Living Dangerously* (1982), Weir abandoned *cinefantastique* to make polished, critically acclaimed American films (*Witness*, 1985; *The Mosquito Coast*, 1986; *Dead Poets Society*, 1989; *Green Card*, 1990), though he returned tentatively to earlier concerns with *Fearless* (1993). MM

TV: *The Plumber*/1980

Don Shiach, *The Films of Peter Weir* (1993)

Weird Tales

Published from 1923 to 1954, discounting various relaunches, *Weird Tales* was the most important horror and supernatural **pulp**. Though it popularised **Lovecraft**, Clark

Ashton **Smith**, Robert E. Howard, **Leiber**, **Bradbury**, **Bloch** and **Wellman**, its mainstays were more lurid offerings from the likes of Seabury Quinn, hailed by readers of the 'Unique Magazine' as its most popular writer. In 1995, it was announced that a *Weird Tales* TV series would be produced.

Welles, Mel (b. 1924)

American actor, director. A **Corman** regular, memorably as the grasping Mushnik in *The Little Shop of Horrors* (1960), Welles also directed loony Euro-horrors: *Das Geheimnis der Todesinsel* (*Island of the Doomed*, 1966), *La figlia de Frankenstein* (*Lady Frankenstein*, 1971).

Abbott and Costello Meet the Mummy/1955 * *The Undead*/1956 * *Attack of the Crab Monsters*/1957 * *Il lago di Satana* [*The She Beast*]/1966 * *Dr. Heckyl and Mr. Hype*/1980 * *Wolfen*/1981 * *Chopping Mall*/1986

TV: *The Adventures of Dr. Fu Manchu*: 'Dr. Fu Manchu's Raid'/1956 * *Alfred Hitchcock Presents*: 'Flight to the East'/1958

Welles, Orson (1915–85)

American actor, director, **magician**. Welles's interest in horror is evident in the **Caligarism** of his experimental film short *The Hearts of Age* (1934), the **voodoo** of his famous stage *Macbeth* (1936) and several **radio** adaptations (*Dracula*, 1938; *The War of the Worlds*, 1938). Too huge to be encompassed by genre, Welles nevertheless inhabited a gothic cinema: both *Citizen Kane* (1941) and *The Magnificent Ambersons* (1942) explore houses that merely await the deaths of their occupants to become properly haunted (a ghost sequence was pruned from *Ambersons* by the studio). Personnel (Mark **Robson**, Robert **Wise**) and sets from his RKO unit were passed down to Val **Lewton** for use in his arty shockers.

Various forms of horror overshadow his **films noirs** (*The Stranger*, 1946; *Lady From Shanghai*, 1948; *Mr Arkadin*, 1955; *Touch of Evil*, 1958), his 'archaeologically correct' *Macbeth* (1948) and, most of all, his paranoid-eccentric take on **Kafka**, *Le Procès* (*The Trial*, 1962). As an actor, he often took bizarre roles, frequently sporting a waxy false nose to suggest contempt for shoddy surroundings: Rochester in *Jane Eyre* (1944), Cagliostro in *Black Magic* (1948), a cult leader in *Necromancy* (1971), the dying sorcerer of *Malpertuis* (1972). He lent his imitably ripe voice to radio's *The Shadow* (1937–8), the narration of a *Night Gallery* ('Silent Snow,

Orson Welles, *Black Magic*

Secret Snow', 1971) and, not inaptly, the role of a planet in *Transformers: The Movie* (1986). He hosted a TV series, ***Orson Welles' Great Mysteries*** (1973–4).

Return to Glennascaul (s/a)/1951 * *Three Cases of Murder* (a)/1955 * *A Safe Place* (a)/1971

TV: *The Orson Welles Show*: 'The Fountain of Youth' (d/w/a)/1958

Barbara Leaming, *Orson Welles: A Biography* (1985); Simon Callow, *Orson Welles: The Road to Xanadu* (1995)

Wellman, Manly Wade (1905–86)

Angola-born American writer, a **pulp** mainstay who wrote series about such enemies of supernatural evil as Judge Pursuivant, John Thunstone and John the Balladeer. The latter series, collected in *Who Fears the Devil?* (1963), are his best work; John **Newland**'s *The Legend of Hillbilly John* (1972) has Hedge Capers bland as John, with the supporting players more in tone with Wellman's folkloric strangeness. Collections: *Worse Things Waiting* (1973), *Lonely Vigils* (1981) and *The Valley So Low* (1987).

TV: *The Twilight Zone*: 'The Still Valley' (st)/1961 * *Night Gallery*: 'The Devil is Not Mocked' (st)/1971 * *Monsters*: 'Rouse Him Not' (st)/1988

Wells, H.G. [Herbert George] (1866–1945)

British author. Cornerstone, of course, of science fiction, Wells is also a significant horror writer. ***The Island of Dr Moreau*** (1896) and ***The Invisible Man*** (1897) are influential modifications of the **Faust-Frankenstein** figure of the **mad scientist**, while *The War of the Worlds* (1898), with **vampire** squid from Mars, establishes the terror-by-**alien** genre that straddles s-f and horror. Among his underrated short fiction are remarkable horror items: 'The Cone' (1895), 'The Sea Raiders' (1896), 'Pollock and the Porroh Man' (1897), 'The Door in the Wall' (1906). The golfing anecdote of *Dead of Night* (1945) is from 'The Story of the Inexperienced Ghost' (1902), and Wells sources are turned to catchpenny use by Bert I. **Gordon** in *Village of the Giants* (1965), *Food of the Gods* (1974) and *Empire of the Ants* (1977). Malcolm **McDowell** plays Wells in *Time*

After Time (1979), using the eponymous device of *The Time Machine* (1895) to pursue **Jack the Ripper** into the future.

Alan Wykes, *H.G. Wells in the Cinema* (1977); Norman Mackenzie, Jeanne Mackenzie, *The Life of H.G. Wells: The Time Traveller* (1987); Thomas C. Renzi, *H.G. Wells: Six Scientific Romances Adapted for Film* (1992)

Wendkos, Paul (b. 1922)

American director. In a B-picture career, Wendkos alternated very unusual (*The Burglar*, 1957; *Angel Baby*, 1961) and very ordinary (*Gidget Goes to Rome*, 1963; *Guns of the Magnificent Seven*, 1969). *The Mephisto Waltz* (1970), a Satanic conspiracy theory with Alan Alda possessed by Curt Jurgens, is his most elaborate film, but he has done much TV, including the psychic sleuth pilot *Fear No Evil* (1969), the paranoid classic *Brotherhood of the Bell* (1970) and the specu-

H. G. Wells

H.G. Wells

latory *The Legend of Lizzie Borden* (1975). *Haunts of the Very Rich* (1973) unnervingly suggests **Hell** is a 1970s TV movie with Lloyd Bridges, Cloris Leachman, Tony Bill, Ed Asner and Anne Francis in paisley isolation by the swimming-pool.

TV: *Wild Wild West*: 'The Night of the Howling Light'/1965 * *The Invaders*: 'The Mutation'/'The Leeches'/'Vikor'/'Nightmare'/ 'Doomsday Minus One'/'Storm'/ 'Moonshot'/'The Believers'/1967; 'The Life Seekers'/1968 * *Terror on the Beach*/1973 * *Good Against Evil*/1977 * *The Bad Seed*/1987 * *From the Dead of Night*/1989

Werewolf (US TV series, 1987–8)

In the pilot movie, directed by David **Hemmings** from a script by Frank Lupo, young Eric Cord (John J. York) is bitten by a **werewolf**. Eric's double quest, modelled like many American shows on *The Fugitive*

Henry Hull, *The WereWolf of London*

Steven Ritch, *The Werewolf*

(1963–7), is to find a cure and also track down Janos Skorzeny (Chuck Connors), head of the werewolf clan (the name is a nod to **The Night Stalker**, 1972). Meanwhile, Eric is hunted by Alamo Joe (Lance LeGault), whose high powered rifle is loaded with silver bullets. Executive producers were Frank Lupo and John Ashley, **monster** make-up was by Rick **Baker**. TM

Werewolves

The belief that men may turn into wolves or wolflike creatures dates back to antiquity. Similar traditions involving other predators like leopards or bears exist in most cultures. In fiction, the werewolf appears as early as the 13th century (Marie de France's *Lay of the Bisclavaret*) and features in late gothics like Frederick Marryat's *The Phantom Ship* (1839), Erckmann-Chatrian's *Hugues-le-Loup* (1869) and G.W. Reynolds's penny-dreadful *Wagner: The Wehr-Wolf* (1846). Though *Strange Case of Dr Jekyll and Mr Hyde* (1886) is an influential variant, with a man becoming a brutish but still human creature, the popular culture werewolf suffers the lack of a cornerstone text like *Frankenstein* (1818) or *Dracula* (1887), which has promoted the film *The Wolf Man* (1941) to the position of most-imitated and elaborated-upon werewolf story.

The most notable werewolf novel remains Guy **Endore**'s *The Werewolf of Paris* (1933), filmed as *The Curse of the Werewolf*

(1960), but interesting attempts include Jessie Douglas Kerruish's *The Undying Monster* (1936; filmed 1942), Jack Williamson's *Darker Than You Think* (1948), Denise Danvers' *Wilderness* (1991), S.P. Somtow's *Moon Dance* (1991) and Michael Cadnum's *Saint Peter's Wolf* (1991). Anthologies of werewolf fiction include Brian J. Frost's *Book of the Werewolf* (1973) and Stephen **Jones**'s *The Mammoth Book of Werewolves* (1994).

Shapeshifters appear frequently in silent cinema, often associated with vengeful native witchery, whether the **American Indian** sorcery of *The Werewolf* (1913) and *The White Wolf* (1914) or **snake** women of colonial India in *The Vampire* (1913) and South America in *Heba the Snake Woman* (1915). Though **Lugosi** turns offscreen into a wolf in *Dracula* (1930) and is a scientifically created Wolf Man in *Island of Lost Souls* (1932), the familiar movie werewolf (bipedal, fanged, furred, tormented, afflicted by the full moon) did not debut until Universal's *The WereWolf of London* (1935), with Henry Hull cursed in Tibet by the bite of another werewolf, trying to cure himself with an extract from a rare plant. Indebted to **Jekyll and Hyde**, this seems now a rough draft for George **Waggner**'s *The Wolf Man*, scripted by Curt **Siodmak** with Lon **Chaney Jr** under definitive Jack **Pierce** make-up as the accursed Larry Talbot. The film's success prompted sequels (from *Frankenstein Meets the Wolf Man*, 1944, to

(**Abbott and Costello**) *Meet Frankenstein*, 1948), imitations with Talbot-style make-ups (*The Mad Monster*, 1942; *The Return of the Vampire*, 1944) and reverse imitations which reuse the plot but take different approaches to monsters and curses (**Cat People**, 1942; *Cry of the Werewolf*, 1944).

From the fake werewolves of *The Scarlet Claw* (1944) and *She-Wolf of London* (1946) into the 1950s, shapeshifting fell out of fashion, only to be revived in s-f terms by *The Werewolf* (1956) and *I Was a Teenage Werewolf* (1957), in which lycanthropes are created by experiments designed to help mankind transcend atomic warfare, and by the more supernatural efforts of *Daughter of Dr. Jekyll* (1957) and *Cat Girl* (1957). **Hammer**'s *The Curse of the Werewolf*, with a traumatised Oliver Reed despatched by a silver bullet, borrows as much from *The Wolf Man* as from Endore's source novel, but notably fails to imprint on the werewolf theme the studio's brand of revisionism. Post-1950s screen versions of Frankenstein and Dracula are influenced by Hammer, but most werewolf films still stubbornly follow *The Wolf Man*. *The Reptile* (1966), Hammer's only subsequent effort harks back interestingly to the silents with its colonial curse and snake woman.

Writer-star Paul **Naschy**'s *La marca del hombre lobo* (1967) introduces the character of Waldemar Daninsky, as featured in films from *Las noches del hombre lobo* (1968) to *Lycantropus* (1966), and is patterned explicitly on the Talbot films, with added sex and gore. Perhaps inspired by *The Undying Monster*, *The Catman of Paris* (1946) or *Daughter of Dr. Jekyll*, a minor strain of whodunit uses the theme, with characters revealed in the climax as behind the werewolf killings: *Lycanthropus* (*Werewolf in a Girls' Dormitory*, 1961), *Cry of the Banshee* (1970), *Moon of the Wolf* (1972), *The Beast Must Die* (1973), *The Incubus* (1982), *Silver Bullet* (1985). Though *Legend of the Werewolf* (1974) tries to recreate the feel of *The Curse of the Werewolf* and odd directions are taken by *Werewolves on Wheels* (1971) and *The Boy Who Cried Werewolf* (1973), the theme became so formularised that it was open to the silliness of *The Werewolf of Washington* (1973), *The Werewolf of Woodstock* (1975) and even *Curse of the Queerwolf* (1987).

When Rick **Baker** and Rob **Bottin** replaced the lap dissolves and yak hair of Pierce with impressively physical shapeshifting effects, there was a major werewolf revival spearheaded by *The Howling* (1980) and *An American Werewolf in London* (1981).

David Naughton, *An American Werewolf in London*

In their wake have come remakes (a new *Cat People*, 1982), *Howling* sequels, arty folklorics (*The Company of Wolves*, 1984), an **insect** boy (*The Beast Within*, 1982), shapeshifting **vampires** (*Fright Night*, 1985), Michael Jackson's freak-out ('Thriller', 1983), comedies (*Full Moon High*, 1981; *Teen Wolf*, 1985), quickies (*Lone Wolf*, 1988; *Night Shadow*, 1990), TV series (**Werewolf**, 1987–8; **She-Wolf of London**, 1990), werewolf cops (*Full Eclipse*, 1993) and a return to the Henry Hull look for Jack **Nicholson** (*Wolf*, 1994). Because transformations require sophisticated effects rather than mere make-up, werewolves feature less frequently on TV than vampires or ghosts. Series episodes include 'Werewolf' (**Voyage to the Bottom of the Sea**, 1966), 'The Werewolf' (**Kolchak: The Night Stalker**, 1974), 'What Big Eyes' (*Beasts*, 1975), 'Countess Ilona'/'The Werewolf Reunion' (**Supernatural**, 1977), 'Children of the Full Moon' (**Hammer House of Horror**, 1980), 'The Boogeyman Will Get You' (**Darkroom**, 1981), 'One Wolf's Family' (**Monsters**, 1990), 'Moon of the Wolf' (**Batman: The Animated Series**, 1992), 'The Werewolf Concerto' (*Tales From the Crypt*, 1992) and 'Shapes' (**The X Files**, 1994). Though the metamorphosis of man into raging beast offers many thematic possibilities, the werewolf is less frequent a fiend than the vampire or the **mad scientist**. There seem to be a very limited number of approaches: werewolves are either tragic Talbots or defiant savages like the back-to-nature creatures of *The Howling*,

in which John **Carradine** resists Patrick **MacNee**'s civilising influences with 'You can't tame what's wild, doc'.

Sabine Baring-Gould, *The Book of Were-Wolves* (1865); Elliott O'Donnell, *Werwolves* (1912); Riccardo Esposito, *Il cinema dei licantropi* (1987); Stephen Jones, *The Illustrated Werewolf Movie Guide* (1996)

West, Roland [Van Ziemer] (1887–1952)

American director. West made interesting

Roland West

silent melodramas with a **camp** sensibility that prefigures James **Whale**: *The Monster* (1925) and *The Bat* (1926) are **Old Dark House** parodies, the former with Lon **Chaney** as a mad surgeon. In the talkie era, he effectively remade *The Bat* in experimental widescreen (*The Bat Whispers*, 1929) and went into the restaurant business. Posthumously nominated as a suspect in the 1935 murder of starlet Thelma Todd.

The Unknown Purple/1923

The Western

So resolutely secular is the Western genre that most attempts to graft on elements of the horror film have all the awkwardness of a **Frankenstein** transplant. The most determined effort is William **Beaudine**'s mid-1960s pair *Billy the Kid vs. Dracula* (1965) and *Jesse James Meets Frankenstein's Daughter* (1966): these manage to preserve a surprising amount of generic Western elements (for instance, the Kid's traditional jailbreak), but the desperate **camp**, epitomised by the unrestrained ham of John **Carradine**'s **Dracula**, defeats any possibility of real horror. The early John Wayne vehicle *Haunted Gold* (1932) is a Western **Old Dark House** variation but rarely do the ghosts, even in ghost towns, turn out to be genuinely supernatural. However, Clint Eastwood's *High Plains Drifter* (1972) and *Pale Rider* (1985) return from the dead, while *Ghost Town* (1988) and *Ghostriders* (1988) feature spectral outlaws.

American Indian religion can be used to propel the Western into a spiritual sphere, but *The Manitou* (1978), in which The Exorcist Goes West, produced no sequels, unless we count *Shadow Hunter* (1993), in which cop Scott Glenn finds his mind being taken over by Navajo magic. Yet the clash of the genres continues to exert a fascination: *Curse of the Undead* (1959), with Michael **Pate** as a **vampire** gunslinger, may have failed to inject fresh blood into the genre, but Kathryn Bigelow's modern-day *Near Dark* (1987) shows what can be done by transporting **Transylvania** to the desert, and *Grim Prairie Tales* (1990) manages an agreeable combination of the weird and the uncanny. EB

Whale, James (1889–1957)

British director. Whale is responsible for the most impishly stylish, brittly intelligent horror films of Universal's talkie period: *Frankenstein* (1931), **The Old Dark House**

Westerns: John Carradine, *Billy the Kid vs. Dracula*

(1932), *The Invisible Man* (1933), *Bride of Frankenstein* (1935). The hugely influential first provides the definitive image of **monster**-as-victim. The remainder give vent to a darkening absurdism and culminate in perhaps the most outrageous and liberty-taking of all sequels.

The former factory worker's pre-film career is distinguished by self-invention. World War I allowed him to realise both social and artistic ambitions: as a commissioned officer, his first involvement in theatre came while in prison camp. *Sans* Dudley accent, he continued as an actor/designer/ stage manager, appearing in the 1928 adaptation of Hugh Walpole's Sadean *Portrait of a Man with Red Hair* and London **grand guignol** *The Old Firm's Awakening* and *After Death* before directing R.C. Sherriff's *Journey's End* (1928). The first successful war play, it catapulted him to Hollywood on its Broadway transference. Three off-centre war movies followed that demonstrated a quick mastery of sound and spectacle, making Whale a prestige name: *Hell's Angels* (1930, dialogue inserts), *Journey's End* (1930), *Waterloo Bridge* (1931).

Frankenstein was a means to escape pigeon-holing. Rejecting original director Robert **Florey**'s conception, Whale complicated both creature and creator by shoring a new screenplay with crucial castings. The anxious, spiky Colin **Clive** was chosen over

Leslie Howard for Henry Frankenstein; Boris **Karloff** filled his opposite after a suggestion from Whale's lover, David Lewis. Whale insisted on the two most censurable moments of his morbid **expressionist** nightmare (Clive's self-comparison to God

and Karloff's uncomprehending murder of a little girl), but finally sanctioned a 'semi-happy' ending. The next four years were spent trying to avoid a sequel to the resultant smash.

A tenebrous tour-de-force, *The Old Dark House* answered studio requests for a further Karloff vehicle. Somewhat resentful of the rising star, Whale employed him as a hulking counterpoint to comic monsters Ernest **Thesiger** and Eva Moore, whose epicene grotesquerie is integral. Delighting in atheistic barbs and a dubious atmosphere that extends to bedridden patriarch Roderick Femm being played by a woman, the film shares the jocular cynicism of Melvyn **Douglas**'s war-wearied hero. In a change from J.B. Priestley's pedantic source-novel (*Benighted*, 1927), Douglas is allowed to survive his tangle with the house psycho – who, notwithstanding, is a far more perverse creature than originally written.

Once also intended as a star-builder for Karloff, *The Invisible Man* (from H.G. **Wells**'s 1897 novel) is a remarkable exercise in integrated special effectsery and the director's most shocking and obviously misanthropic work. Made after the bizarre adultery drama *The Kiss Before the Mirror* (1933), the movie viciously confuses homicide with slapstick while rejecting the romantic conclusion that ameliorates Whale's other horrors. Its Home

Boris Karloff, James Whale, on the set of *Bride of Frankenstein*

Counties setting expands upon *House*'s Welsh onslaught, with both villagers and **police** ruthlessly satirised. Usurping the conventional position of hero, Claude **Rains**' 'Invisible One' is a notably class-ridden fiend. Pure voice, he is almost as perturbingly human a monster as Frankenstein's.

Bride of Frankenstein replaced the scrapped *A Trip to Mars* as Whale's final Karloff assignment. Resolved to make a 'hoot', he commissioned a script again loaded with sexual and religious caprice, and with vital provision for Thesiger, Dwight **Frye** and Invisible Man functionaries Una **O'Connor** and E.E. **Clive**. Undiminished by post-production trims, the **camp** of the piece is established by a prologue in which **Byron** recounts the action not of Mary **Shelley**'s book, but of the first film. A Production Code climax where Frankenstein is spared only exaggerates a caustic Christ allegory that has the sad, raging monster betrayed by both maker and man. Karloff objected to the creature's dialogue, but his suicidal 'we belong dead' is, daringly, the movie's most noble moment.

Briefly associated with *Dracula's Daughter* (1936), Whale more aptly closed his horror career with the murderous screwball of *Remember Last Night?* (1936). After the hit *Showboat* (1936), Whale fell foul of a new Universal regime and retired to paint in 1941, killing himself after a minor stroke. Waning features include *The Man in the Iron Mask* (1939), with Peter **Cushing** twinning for Louis Hayward. The temple from *Green Hell* (1940, with Vincent **Price**) reappears in *The Mummy's Hand* (1940). DP

James Curtis, *James Whale* (1982); Mark Gatiss, *James Whale: A Biography* (1995); Christopher Bram, *Father of Frankenstein* (1995)

Wheatley, Dennis (1897–1977)

British writer. Though he wrote thrillers, spy stories, historical adventures and lost-world s-f, Wheatley was best known for black magic: *The Devil Rides Out* (1934), *The Haunting of Toby Jugg* (1948), *To the Devil a Daughter* (1953), *The Ka of Gifford Hillary* (1956), *The Satanist* (1960), *They Used Dark Forces* (1964). A rare British specialist in novel-length horror from the 1930s through to the '60s, he has more in common with Edgar **Wallace** or Dornford Yates than James **Herbert**, his successor as Britain's best selling horror writer, or Ramsey **Campbell**. **Hammer** made three Wheatley adaptations: Terence **Fisher**'s spirited *The*

Devil Rides Out (1968), with Christopher **Lee** as Wheatley's witch-buster hero the Duc de Richleau, Michael **Carreras**'s *The Lost Continent* (1968; from *Uncharted Seas*, 1938) and Peter **Sykes**'s *To the Devil a Daughter* (1975). Enormously popular in his day, enormously unfashionable now.

White, Robb (b. 1909)

American writer. William **Castle**'s collaborator on a run of bizarre films whose gimmick releases tend to obscure their twisted **EC** cynicism. The seat-buzzers and floating skeletons may be jokey, but White's scripts are full of grasping characters plotting casually to torture their spouses to death and left field concepts like the killer bug created in the spine by fear.

Macabre/1958 * *The House on Haunted Hill*/*The Tingler*/1959 * *13 Ghosts*/1960 * *Homicidal*/1961

Wicking, Christopher (b. 1943)

British writer. Originally a critic, Wicking collaborated interestingly with directors Gordon **Hessler** and Peter **Sykes** on a run of unconventional, structurally daring, genre-conscious horrors for AIP and **Hammer**. Among his unfilmed Hammer projects are *Nessie*, **Vampirella** and *Kali, Devil Bride of Dracula*.

The Oblong Box/*Scream and Scream Again*/1969 * *Cry of the Banshee*/1970 * *Murders in the Rue Morgue*/*Blood From the Mummy's Tomb*/*Demons of the Mind*/*Venom*/1971 * *Medusa*/1974 * *To the Devil a Daughter*/1976 * *Dream Demon*/1988

TV: *Jemima Shaw Investigates*: 'Dr Ziegler's Casebook'/1983

Wiene, Robert (1881–1938)

German director. A last-minute replacement for Fritz **Lang** on ***Das Cabinet des Dr. Caligari*** (1919), Wiene became a leading exponent of **expressionist** cinema. His Caligarism is notably stagey and few of his follow-ups are more than curiosities. *Orlacs Hände* (1925) is the screen debut of the oft-told ***Les Mains d'Orlac***, and *Raskolnikow* (1923), a competent stab at Dostoevsky.

Der Andere/1930

Uli Jung, Walter Schatzberg, *Robert Weine: Der Caligari Regisseur* (1995)

Wild Wild West (US TV series, 1865–70)

Created by Michael Garrison, this transposes

Joseph Campanella, 'The Night of the Wolf', *Wild Wild West*

the feel of *The Man From U.N.C.L.E.* (1964–8) or *I Spy* (1965–8) into the **Western** setting of *Have Gun, Will Travel* (1957–63) or *Maverick* (1957–62). Action man James T. West (Robert Conrad) and disguise master Artemus Gordon (Ross Martin) are secret servicemen in the employ of President Grant, tackling threats to the nation in the West. The show is strong on proto-steampunk Victorian gadgetry and flamboyant villains, notably Michael **Dunn**'s recurring fiend Dr Miguelito Loveless, and many episodes deal with apparent supernatural phenomena: *Terminator*-ish robots ('The Night of the Steel Assassin, 1966), bottled **brains** ('The Night of the Druid's Blood', 1966), **zombies** ('The Night of the Returning Dead', 1966), UFOs ('The Night of the Flying Pie Plate, 1966), time warps ('The Night of the Lord of Limbo, 1966), **werewolves** ('The Night of the Wolf', 1967), **voodoo** ('The Night of the Undead', 1968) and a **Phantom of the Opera** ('The Night of the Diva, 1969). Reunion TV movies: *The Wild Wild West Revisited* (1979) and *More Wild Wild West* (1980).

Susan E. Kesler, *The Wild Wild West: The Series* (1988)

Wilde, Oscar (1854–1900)

Irish author. Besides ***The Picture of Dorian***

Gray (1891), Wilde wrote a handful of acidic supernatural comedies, notably 'Lord Arthur Savile's Crime' (1891), adapted as *Le crime de Lord Arthur Savile* (1921) and in *Flesh and Fantasy* (1943), and 'The Canterville Ghost' (1891), filmed or televised with Charles **Laughton** (1944), Monty Woolley (1954), Bruce Forsyth (*Mystery and Imagination*, 1966), David Niven (1975), Richard Kiley (*Wonderworks*, 1985), John Gielgud (1986) and Patrick Stewart (1996). An associate of Bram **Stoker**, Wilde appears in horror-related fictions: Nicholas Meyer's *The West End Horror* (1976), Kim Newman's *Anno Dracula* (1992), Peter Ackroyd's *Dan Leno and the Limehouse Golem* (1994), Brian Stableford's 'The Hunger and Ecstasy of Vampires' (1995) and Joe R. Lansdale's 'Jonah Hex' comic *Riders of the Worm and Such* (1995).

Richard Ellmann, *Oscar Wilde* (1987)

Willard, John * See: *The Cat and the Canary*

Willman, Noel (1918–88)

British actor. Slyly sinister for **Hammer** in *Kiss of the Vampire* (1963) and *The Reptile* (1966).

The Vengance of She/1967

Wilson, F. Paul (b. 1946)

American writer. With the World War II-set *The Keep* (1981), Wilson began a horror cycle that blends nods to the **pulps** with analyses of the nature of evil. *The Tomb* (1984) and *The Touch* (1986) seem steps away from *The Keep*, but *Reborn* (1990), *Reprisal* (1991) and *Nightworld* (1991) pull the strands together. Michael **Mann**'s *The Keep* (1993) prompted Wilson to write 'Cuts' (1988), a story in which an author puts a **voodoo** curse on 'Milo Gherl', the director who butchered his novel.

Winston, Stan (b. 19??)

American special make-up effects artist, director. Winston's excursions into horror (*Blacula*, 1972; *Dracula's Dog*, 1977; *Parasite*, 1982) were mostly forgettable until he joined forces with writer-director James Cameron to produce robotic effects for *The Terminator* (1984), an association which has since spawned *Aliens* (1986) and *Terminator 2: Judgment Day* (1991). The Stan Winston Studio has become *the* make-up effects company in Hollywood, responsible for *Predator* (1987) and *Predator 2* (1990), full-size dinosaurs in *Jurassic Park* (1993) and *Interview With the Vampire* (1995). His directorial debut *Pumpkinhead* (1988), is a competent **rural horror** with a good monster, but *Upworld* (1991), his sophomore effort, is a dumb fantasy/comedy. MS

The Bat People/1974 * *Dead and Buried*/1981 * *The Thing*/1982 * *The Entity*/*Something Wicked This Way Comes*/1983 * *Invaders From Mars*/*The Vindicator*/1986 * *The Monster Squad*/1987 * *Leviathan*/1989 * *Edward Scissorhands*/1990 * *Batman Returns*/1992 * *Congo*/1995 * *The Relic*/1996

TV: *Gargoyles*/1972 * *Manimal*/1983

Wisbar, Frank [Frank Wysbar] (1899–1967)

German director. A wartime exile, Wisbar won a few admirers with *Strangler of the Swamp* (1945), an eerily ramshackle PRC remake of his allegorical *Fährmann Maria* (*Death and the Maiden*, 1935). He won no admirers with *Devil Bat's Daughter* (1946), the draggiest sequel on poverty row.

Wise, Robert (b. 1914)

American director, editor. A cutter on *The Hunchback of Notre Dame* (1939), *All That Money Can Buy* (1941) and *Citizen Kane* (1941), Wise replaced Gunther von Fritsch as director of Val **Lewton**'s *Curse of the Cat People* (1944), a fairytale of troubled childhood with more terror than many outright horrors. Wise was rewarded with two more period-set Lewtons, the underrated **Maupassant** adaptation *Mademoiselle Fifi* (*The Silent Bell*, 1944) and the justly regarded **Stevenson** horror *The Body Snatcher* (1945), with great work from **Karloff** and Henry **Daniell** and a powerful out-of-control climax.

After remaking *The Most Dangerous Game* (1932) as *A Game of Death* (1945) and handling the amazingly embittered **film noir** *Born to Kill* (1947), Wise advanced through interesting sleepers (*The Set-Up*, 1949; *The Day the Earth Stood Still*, 1951) to varied, professional, respectable A features: *The Desert Rats* (1953), *Executive Suite* (1954), *West Side Story* (1961), *The Sound of Music* (1965), *Star Trek: The Motion Picture* (1979). He returned to horror with *The Haunting* (1963), from Shirley **Jackson**'s *The Haunting of Hill House* (1963), which strains slightly to provide psychological rationale for truly terrifying manifestations. Also interesting and sincere are the high-tech viral drama *The Andromeda Strain* (1971) and the earnest **reincarnation** movie *Audrey Rose* (1977).

Witchcraft

Horror movie **monsters** are predominantly male, but the witch is usually a woman, generating various representations of female monstrousness: hag, evil mother, resurrected avenger, *femme fatale*. This is not necessarily progressive: often the focus is on a male witchfinder or leader of a coven or cult. Nevertheless, this female monster is the most widely feared in the horror family.

Historically, though witches are credited with practising both good and evil magic, they are the most persecuted of all supernatural creatures. Witchcraft was deemed a heresy by the Catholic Church in the 14h century and there is no comparable document in other traditions (such as **vampirism**) to the treatise against witchcraft, *Malleus maleficarum* (1486). The development of the witch as a film icon also differs from that of other horror figures. Though witchcraft paraphernalia has featured at least since **Méliès**'s *Chez la sorcière* (1901), few films – the pseudo-documentary *Häxan* (*Witchcraft Through the Ages*, 1921) excepted – treat the subject seriously. Until the late 1950s, film witches tend to figure in **comedy** (*I Married a Witch*, 1942; *Bell, Book and Candle*, 1958) or a historical context (*Joan of Arc*, 1948; *Saint Joan*, 1957).

Frightening witches first appear in children's films, *Snow White and the Seven Dwarfs* (1937) and *The Wizard of Oz* (1939), then creep into adult horror via *The Seventh Victim* (1943) and *Weird Woman* (1944), but the witch did not become a regular figure of terror until films like *La maschera del demonio* (*Mask of Satan*, 1960) and *Witchcraft* (1964) combined witchiness with vampirism to create a crossbred icon. Unfortunately, the witch motif is only rarely used to explore post-modern concerns such as the breakdown of the family, as in *Rosemary's Baby* (1968), *Jack's Wife* (1972) and *The Rapture* (1991). Most witch films have more conservative concerns, such as preventing the likes of a layabout Raymond Lovelock from indulging in free love in *Le regine* (*Queens of Evil*, 1970).

The stereotype of the witch is historically linked to fears about female sexuality: during the **witch hunts**, the most commonly cited witch crimes were intercourse with the **Devil** and causing male impotence. Witches in film express similar fears about female sexuality by being inexplicably linked to female beauty. The witch theme incorporates the desire to be/find the ideal woman

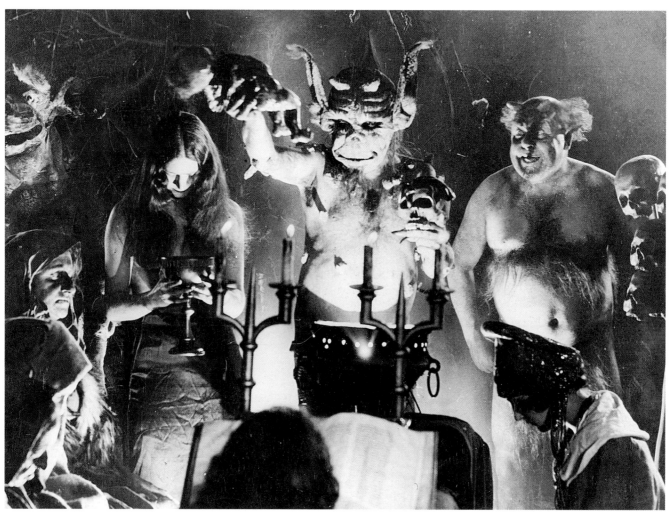

Witchcraft: *Häxen*

while also expressing fears about the sexual power of such creatures, through exploration of narcissism, paranoia and revenge. Ever since *The Seventh Victim*'s tragically neurotic Jacqueline, beauty has been a main *raison d'être* for witchcraft. Many films tap into gothic notions of *la belle dame sans merci* by presenting a beautiful woman as a figure of guile and suspicion. The loss of beauty or youth is a popular motivating factor for the practice of witchcraft (presumably in order to be attractive to the opposite sex) as in *Valerie a tyden divu* (*Valerie and Her Week of Wonders*, 1970), *The Kiss* (1988) and *The Craft* (1996). Desirable women tend to be temporary fronts for evil hags as (*Damn Yankees*, 1958; *Something Weird*, 1966; *Wicked Stepmother*, 1989) or bait to lure new sacrifices to a coven (*Spellbinder*, 1988). The apparent celebration of fertility and nubile flesh in *The Wicker Man* (1973) is only a foil to reveal their terrible pagan nature.

Rare films have the emotional honesty of Philip Ridley's *Passion of Darkly Noon* (1995), in which a girl is hounded by her neighbours because of her self-assured sexuality. Some films exploit more erotic elements of Satanism, progressing from the tongue in cheek of *The Undead* (1956) to the blatant sexuality of *Blood Orgy of the She-Devils* (1973). The theme takes a misogynistic twist when girls-next-door are shown to be more assertive and difficult when possessed: *Mark of the Witch* (1970), *Witchboard* (1985). *Silent Night, Deadly Night 4: Initiation* (1990), *Witchboard II: The Return* (1993). Even more extreme are the oral sadistic monster mothers of **Argento**'s trilogy in two films, *Suspiria* (1976) and *Inferno* (1980). Other films which present the female as abject include *Burnt Offerings* (1976), *Il gatto nero* (*The Black Cat*, 1981), *The Evil Dead* (1982), *Tales From the Darkside: The Movie* (1990) and *The Witches* (1990), where the witchy presence is associated with darkness, death, maggots and other unpleasantness.

The image of the witch is such an effective stereotype that associations can be indirectly invoked by discreet references (red shoes, candles, disfigurement) in *Blue Velvet* (1986) and *After Hours* (1987). Hollywood refreshingly sends up some of these sterotypes in *The Witches of Eastwick* (1987) and *Death Becomes Her* (1992). Films featuring the male witch equivalent (warlock) are less popular, but include *The Devil's Partner* (1958), *City of the Dead* (1960), *The Haunted Palace* (1963), *The Witchmaker* (1969), *El espanto surge de la tumba* (*Horror Rises From the Tomb*, 1972), *The Devil's Rain* (1975), *Ghoulies* (1984) and *Warlock* (1991). MP

Witch Hunts

As Arthur Miller proved in 'The Crucible' (1953), the Puritan witch hunts of colonial America and their European forerunners are

WItchcraft: Ingrid Pitt, *The Wicker Man*

accounts: *Maid of Salem* (1937), *Les sorcières de Salem* (*The Crucible*, 1957), *Three Sovereigns for Sarah* (1985), *The Crucible* (1996). Paul Schrader's *Witch Hunt* (1994), like Kim Newman's 'The McCarthy Witch Hunt' (1994), depicts the anti-Communist purge of the 1950s as an actual witch hunt.

The Wolf Man

Stuart Walker's *The WereWolf of London* (1935) was Universal's first attempt at adding a **werewolf** to their monster pantheon, but it was not until *The Wolf Man* (1941), produced and directed by George **Waggner** from a script by Curt **Siodmak**, that the creature caught on, partially due to the horror star presence of Lon **Chaney Jr** as Lawrence Stewart Talbot. The amiable American returns to his ancestral Wales, is bitten by gypsy lycanthrope Bela **Lugosi** and turns periodically into a hirsute beast until killed by a silver walking stick wielded by 'the hand of one who loves him', his father (Claude **Rains**). Siodmak added much lore and cliché to the werewolf genre: the full moon, silver bullets, the incantatory rhyme, the man-shaped monster.

The Wolf Man is the only Universal mon-

exemplars of species of intolerance, paranoia and persecution that persist to the present. Presumably, witch-hunters think themselves **Van Helsings**, righteously destroying the **Devil**'s minions, but horror films offer few heroic witchfinders like Patrick **Wymark** (*Blood on Satan's Claw*, 1971) or Richard E. Grant (*Warlock*, 1989). As far back as **Christensen**'s *Häxan* (1921) and **Dreyer**'s *Vredens dag* (*Day of Wrath*, 1943), movie Inquisitors have been self-seeking, hypocritical bigots. The epitome is Vincent **Price** as the historical *Matthew Hopkins Witchfinder General* (*The Conqueror Worm*, 1968). Michael **Reeves**'s film prompted a spate of similar items, offering sinister actors as **torturing** and burning dastards: Christopher **Lee** (*El proceso de las brujas*, 1969), Herbert **Lom** and Reggie **Nalder** (*Hexen bis auf's Blut gequält/ Mark of the Devil*, 1970), Howard **Vernon** (*Os demonios*, 1971), Michael Gothard (*The Devils*, 1971), Price again (*Cry of the Banshee*, 1971), Anton **Diffring** (*Hexen – geschändet und zu Tode gequält*, 1972), Paul **Naschy** (*Inquisicion*, 1976), Lance **Henriksen** (*The Pit and the Pendulum*, 1990).

European cinema is prepared to admit the witch hunts were a hideous injustice, but American films tend to get burnings out of the way in pre-credits scenes to set up modern-day tales of evil witches avenging themselves on the descendants of right-thinking persecutors: *Witchcraft* (1964), *Mark of the Witch* (1972), *Superstition* (1982), *The Coming* (1983), *The Devonsville Terror* (1983), *The Demons of Ludlow* (1983), *Necropolis* (1987).

Even the silly *Hocus Pocus* (1993) assumes audiences will accept the women executed in Salem for **witchcraft** deserved to die, though the sillier *Love at Stake* (1988) exposes the trials as arrant injustice. More sober

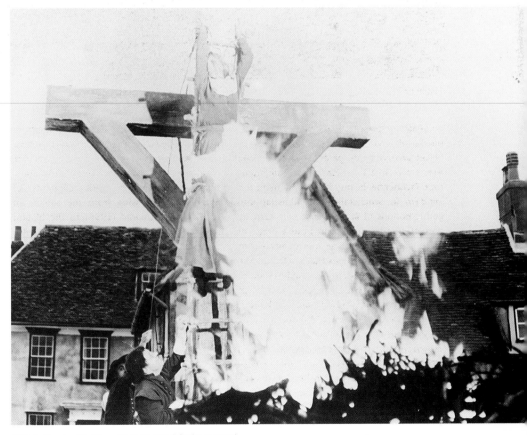

Witch Hunts: *Matthew Hopkins Witchfinder General*

ster never to have been played by anyone but the star who originated the role; Chaney called Talbot 'my baby' and stirred a bit of Lennie from *Of Mice and Men* (1939) into the part. The tormented Talbot, a crybaby between yak-hair episodes, returns in *Frankenstein Meets the Wolf Man* (1943), *House of Frankenstein* (1944), *House of Dracula* (1945), in which he is cured, and (**Abbott and Costello**) *Meet Frankenstein* (1948). He has filtered into horror lore, serving as the template for hobby kits and masks: Andy **Milligan**'s *Blood* (1973) features Talbot's son, though it is set in the 1890s and the Universal films have notional contemporary settings, and the character features in Gene Wolfe's 'A Method Bit in "B"' (1970), Harlan **Ellison**'s 'Adrift Just Off the Islets of Langerhans: Latitude 38° 54'N, Longitude 77° 00113'W' (1975), David **Schow**'s 'Last Call for the Sons of Shock' (1991), Roger Zelazny's *A Night in the Lonesome October* (1993) and Neil Gaiman's 'Only the End of the World Again' (1994). In 'Scarlet Cinema' (**Friday the 13th**: *The Series*, 1989), the film obsesses a student who wishes to become a werewolf.

A chubbier Chaney returned to the make-up in *La casa del terror* (*Face of the Screaming Werewolf*, 1959) and 'Lizard's Leg and Owlet's Wing' (*Route 66*, 1962). The *Wolf Man* plot (an innocent protagonist is afflicted and struggles with the curse) became the standard werewolf film format for decades (**Cat People**, 1942; *The Werewolf*, 1957; *The Curse of the Werewolf*, 1961; *La marca nel hombre lobo*, 1968) and is parodied in *The Werewolf of Washington* (1973), *An American Werewolf in London* (1981) and *Curse of the Queerwolf* (1987). *Leena Meets Frankenstein* (1993), a remake of *Meet Frankenstein* (1948), not only features Tony Tedeschi as the Wolf Man but is directed by 'L.S. Talbot'.

Wolfe, Ian (1896–1992)

American actor. He made over 200 films in a career spanning seven decades, often as officious little men. SJ

The Raven/*Mad Love*/1935 * *On Borrowed Time*/*The Return of Dr. X*/1939 * *Earthbound*/1940 * *Sherlock Holmes Faces Death*/*Flesh and Fantasy*/1943 * *Murder in the Blue Room*/*The Pearl of Death*/*The Scarlet Claw*/*The Invisible Man's Revenge*/1944 * *The Brighton Strangler*/*Zombies on Broadway*/1945 * *Bedlam*/1946 * *The Lost World*/1960 * *Diary of a Madman*/1962 * *Games*/1967 * *Homebodies*/1973 * *The Terminal Man*/1974 * *Mr. Sycamore*/1975 * *Creator*/1985 * *Dick Tracy*/1990

Lon Chaney Jr, *The Wolf Man*

TV: *One Step Beyond*: 'Father Image'/1959 * *The Twilight Zone*: 'Uncle Simon'/1963 * *The Green Hornet*: 'Alias the Scarf'/1967 * *The Invaders*: 'The Summit Meeting'/1967 * *Night Gallery*: 'Deliveries in the Rear'/1972 * *The Devil's Daughter*/1972

Wood Jr, Edward D. [Davis] (1924–1978)

American director, writer, often cited as the world's worst (for which read entertainingly inept) commercial film-maker. A fan of Bela **Lugosi**, whom he cast as a symbolic puppeteer in *Glen or Glenda* (1953): Wood plays the angora-sporting title character; Lugosi rants about 'the big green dragon who eats little boys' and much else of surreal relevance. In *Bride of the Monster* (1955) Lugosi plays Dr Eric Vornoff, who plots to create a race of supermen with the help of mute Tor **Johnson** but is eventually killed by a stubbornly stationary octopus borrowed from Republic's *Wake of the Red Witch* (1948). *Plan 9 from Outer Space* (1956) is Wood's most famous film, with new rewards for the attentive audience on every viewing. Any incompetent can switch from day to night and back again in the course of a single scene, but it takes an Ed Wood to switch police cars between shots as well.

Night of the Ghouls (1958) addresses the wellnigh impossible problem of making a fake seance look more spurious than Wood's usual effects. The last two films are introduced by Criswell, a newscaster turned television psychic, who stars as the Emperor in

Orgy of the Dead (1965) and calls up topless women from the dead to dance for him. This is only written by Wood, as is *The Bride and the Beast* (1958) in which an explorer's wife turns out to be the **reincarnation** of the mate of the gorilla he keeps in his cellar. Tim **Burton**'s *Ed Wood* (1994) shows Wood's career up to 1956 and adds a happy ending; the rest of the tale is in Rudolph Grey's book *Nightmare of Ecstasy: the Life and Art of Edward D. Wood, Jr.* (1992). RC

Woodbridge, George (1907–73)

British character actor. The fat man of British horror, fondly remembered by **Hammer** fans as the innkeeper in *Dracula* (1958) and *Dracula, Prince of Darkness* (1965) and a surly villager in *The Curse of the Werewolf* (1960) and *The Reptile* (1966). Less versatile (and cast less often) than Michael **Ripper**, Woodbridge's most memorable moment comes in *The Revenge of Frankenstein* (1958) as the sweaty and brutal janitor who sadistically beats Michael **Gwynn**. PH

Tower of Terror/1941 * *Queen of Spades*/1948 * *Jack the Ripper*/1959 * *The Flesh and the Fiends*/1960 * *What a Carve Up!*/1961

TV: *Mystery and Imagination*: 'Room 13'/1966 * *Omnibus*: 'Whistle and I'll Come to You'/1968

Woolrich, Cornell (1903–68)

American writer, sometimes under the pseudonyms William Irish or George Hopley. Of the hard-boiled or *noir* writers of the 1930s and '40s, Woolrich is closest to horror. He often uses the supernatural or malign chance and frequently suggests an almost **Lovecraftian** cosmic terror in the predicaments of doomed characters. After early failure as a Fitzgerald-like mainstream author, Woolrich had a spell in Hollywood – almost certainly contributing as William Irish to Benjamin **Christensen**'s *The Haunted House* (1928), *The House of Horror* (1929) and *Seven Footprints to Satan* (1929) – and became a recluse.

Living in New York hotels with his mother, he loathed his homosexuality, sickliness and status as a **pulp** fictioneer, yet turned out an unmatched run of suspense novels: *The Bride Wore Black* (1940), *The Black Curtain* (1941), *Black Alibi* (1942), *Phantom Lady* (1942), *The Black Angel* (1943), *Deadline at Dawn* (1944), *The Black Path of Fear* (1944), *Waltz into Darkness* (1947), *Rendezvous in Black* (1948), *I Married a Dead Man* (1950). Below these peaks are overt supernatural novels

(*Savage Bride*, 1950; *Death is My Dancing Partner*, 1959; *The Doom Stone*, 1960), but *Night Has a Thousand Eyes* (1949), which turns on prophetic visions, is a masterpiece. Among his weird short fiction are the fine novelettes 'Dark Melody of Madness' ('Papa Benjamin', 1935), 'I'm Dangerous Tonight' (1937) and 'Graves for the Living' (1937), but there is real horror in suspense classics like 'Three O'Clock' (1938), 'Guillotine' ('Men Must Die', 'Steps Going Up', 1939) and 'It Had to Be Murder' ('Rear Window', 1942).

Woolrich was a mainstay of 1940s **film noir**, of **radio** suspense shows and of TV anthologies but, aside from the early Irish credits and a few disputed radio scripts, seems never to have been personally involved in other media. The most notable film adaptations are **Lewton** and **Tourneur**'s *The Leopard Man* (from *Black Alibi*, 1943), Robert **Siodmak**'s *Phantom Lady* (1944), Roy William **Neill**'s *Black Angel* (1946), John Farrow's *Night Has a Thousand Eyes* (1948), **Hitchcock**'s *Rear Window* (1954), François Truffaut's *La marée était en noir* (*The Bride Wore Black*, 1968) and *La sirène du Mississipi* (*Mississippi Mermaid*, from *Waltz into Darkness*, 1969) and Rainer Werner Fassbinder's *Martha* (1973). The **voodoo** episode of *Dr. Terror's House of Horrors* (1964) is one of many unauthorised adaptations, a riff on 'Dark Melody of Madness'.

Convicted/1938 * *Street of Chance*/1942 * *The Mark of the Whistler*/1944 * *The Chase*/1946 *

Bela Lugosi, Tony McCoy, Ed Wood's *Bride of the Monster*

Fall Guy/The Guilty/Fear in the Night/1947 ∗ The Return of the Whistler/I Wouldn't Be in Your Shoes/Han matado a Tongele/1948 ∗ The Window/1949 ∗ No Man of Her Own/1950 ∗ El pendiente/1951 ∗ Si muero antes de despertar/No abras nunca esa puerta/1952 ∗ Obsession/1954 ∗ Nightmare/1956 ∗ El Vampiro aecheca/1962 ∗ The Boy Cried Murder/1966 ∗ Yoru no eana/1967 ∗ Union City/1979 ∗ J'ai epousé une ombre/1983 ∗ Cloak & Dagger/1984 ∗ Mrs. Winterbourne/1996

TV: Suspense: 'Revenge'/'The Man Upstairs'/'After-Dinner Story'/'Post Mortem'/1949; 'Nightmare'/1951 ∗ The Actor's Studio: 'Three O'Clock'/1949 ∗ Silver Theater: 'Silent as the Grave'/1949 ∗ Mystery Playhouse: 'Three O'Clock'/'The Night Reveals'/1949 ∗ Robert Montgomery Presents: 'Phantom Lady'/1950; 'Three O'Clock'/'I Wouldn't Be in Your Shoes'/1951 ∗ Video Theatre: 'Change of Murder'/1950 ∗ Nash Airflyte Theater: 'I Won't Take a Minute'/1950 ∗ Assignment Manhunt: 'Through a Dead Man's Eye'/1951 ∗ Revlon Mirror Theatre: 'Lullaby'/'Summer Dance'/1953 ∗ Pepsi-Cola Playhouse: 'Wait for Me Downstairs'/1953 ∗ The Mask: 'The Loophole'/1954 ∗ Lux Video Theatre: 'The Chase'/1954; 'The Guilty'/1956; 'Black Angel'/1957 ∗ Stage 7: 'Debt of Honor'/1955 ∗ Fireside Theatre: 'Once Upon a Nightmare'/1956 ∗ Alfred Hitchcock Presents: 'The Big Switch'/'Momentum'/1956; 'Post Mortem'/1958 ∗ Four Star Playhouse: 'The Listener'/1956 ∗ Climax!: 'Sit Down With

Death'/1956 ∗ Playhouse 90: 'Rendezvous in Black'/1956 ∗ General Electric Theater: 'The Earring'/1957 ∗ George Sanders Mystery Theatre: 'The Night I Died'/1957 ∗ Suspicion: 'Four O'Clock'/1957 ∗ Schlitz Playhouse of Stars: 'Bluebeard's Seventh Wife'/1958 ∗ Armchair Summer Theatre: 'You'll Never See Me Again'/1959 ∗ Moment of Fear: 'Fire by Night'/1960 ∗ Thriller: 'Papa Benjamin'/Late Date'/'Guillotine'/1961 ∗ The Alfred Hitchcock Hour: 'The Black Curtain'/1962 ∗ Journey to the Unknown: 'Jane Brown's Body'/1968 ∗ You'll Never See Me Again/1973 ∗ Darkroom: 'Guillotine'/1982 ∗ Alfred Hitchcock Presents: 'Four O'Clock'/1986 ∗ I'm Dangerous Tonight/1990

Francis M. Nevins Jr, Cornell Woolrich: First You Dream, Then You Die (1988)

Woronov, Mary (b. 1946)

American actress. Initially a Warhol Factory superstar (Chelsea Girls, 1966), Woronov became a regular in Paul **Bartel** movies. Outstanding as Calamity Jane in Death Race 2000 (1975) and Mary Bland in Eating Raoul (1982), she is also fun for Roger **Corman** as the killer B movie diva of Hollywood Boulevard (1976) and the mad principal of Rock 'n' Roll High School (1979).

Kemek/1970 ∗ Silent Night, Bloody Night/1972 ∗ Seizure/1974 ∗ Movie House Massacre/Night of the Comet/1984 ∗ Hellhole/Nomads/1985 ∗ Chopping Mall/TerrorVision/1986 ∗ Black

LEFT Cornell Woolrich's Black Alibi, filmed as The Leopard Man

Widow/1987 ∗ Mortuary Academy/1988 ∗ Warlock/1989 ∗ Watchers II/1990 ∗ Here Come the Munsters/1995
TV: Amazing Stories: 'Secret Cinema'/1986 ∗ Monsters: 'Pillow Talk'/1988

Wray, Fay (b. 1907)

Canadian-born American actress. Immortal as the blonde screamer of **King Kong** (1933), Wray was actually a brunette. In Mystery of the Wax Museum (1932), her Technicolor loveliness is outclassed by wisecracking Glenda Farrell, but she shows spunk slogging through the jungle in **The Most Dangerous Game** (1932) and is attractively winsome in Doctor X (1932) and The Vampire Bat (1934).

Black Moon/1934 ∗ The Clairvoyant/1935

Fay Wray, On the Other Hand: A Life Story (1989)

Wrestling

Tor **Johnson**, Eddie Carmel (The Brain That Wouldn't Die, 1959) and the grapple-happy Roddy Piper (They Live, 1988) all hail from the square ring, but wrestling's full horrific potential has been realised only in Mexico – where bemasked, barrel-chested luchadores fought all manner of evil-in-tights in a prolific film series that foundered mid-1970s. The reason for this unlikely genre lies in the

Fay Wray

Laurence Olivier, *Wuthering Heights* (1939)

erosion of foreign markets two decades before. New profits were glimpsed in the Mexican passion for wrestling; the sport's theatricality (together with the fierce identification of practitioners with their heroic or villainous personae) suggested films of a fantastic bent.

Fernando **Mendez**'s seminal *El ladron de cadaveres* (1956) combines wrestling with the ripe melancholy of previous Latino horrors. Subsequent features generally and more jovially opt for the fighter-as-superhero, with **Blue Demon**, **Mil Mascaras** and fake female team Las Luchadoras aping the success of Neutron and crashmat king El **Santo**. To avoid union complications, América studios entries were shot as TV serials, a ruse which also upped the comic-strip feel. Never attaining the sinewy grace of kung fu cinema, horror-wrestling boasts instead an innocence stinted neither by the introduction of sex nor shoddy colour. In the improbable person of La Santa, *Santa Sangre* (1989) homages the form's surreal heroics. DP

Wuthering Heights (1847)

Emily Brontë's novel is remembered as a romance but is also, as demonstrated by Kate Bush's eerie 1978 single, a **ghost story**, with Heathcliff tormented by the spectre of dead Cathy. The lovers are played on film by Laurence Olivier and Merle Oberon (1939),

Jorge Mistral and Irasema Dilian (Luis **Buñuel**'s Mexican *Abismos de pasión*, 1954), Timothy Dalton and Anna Calder-Marshall (1970) and Ralph Fiennes and Juliette Binoche (1991). BBC-TV adapts it every decade or so: with Kieron Moore and Katharine Blake (1948), Richard Todd and Yvonne Mitchell (1953), Keith Michell and Claire Bloom (1962), Ian McShane and Angela Scoular (1967, directed by Peter **Sasdy**) and Ken Hutchinson and Kay Adshead (1978). Bernard **Herrmann** composed an operatic version (1950).

Wymark, Patrick [Patrick Cheesman] (1926–70)

British actor. Solid character man in authoritarian roles: Cromwell in *Matthew Hopkins Witchfinder General* (1968), a **witch-hunting** judge in *Blood on Satan's Claw* (1970).

The Psychopath/Repulsion/The Skull/1965

Wyngarde, Peter [Cyril Goldbert] (b. 1928)

French-born British actor. A 1970s icon as the flamboyantly dressed and moustached detective on *Department S* (1969–70) and *Jason King* (1971–2), Wyngarde had signature roles as a charismatic Peter Quint in *The Innocents* (1961) and the sceptic **hero** of *Night of the Eagle* (1962). He often guested on

cult TV: running the Hellfire Club on *The Avengers* ('A Touch of Brimstone', 1966), a Number Two on *The Prisoner* ('Checkmate', 1968). He disappeared in the later '70s but returned, masked, as a villain in *Flash Gordon* (1980).

TV: *One Step Beyond*: 'Nightmare'/1961 ∗ *Sherlock Holmes*: 'The Illustrious Client'/1965 ∗ *The Avengers*: 'Epic'/1967 ∗ *Doctor Who*: 'Planet of Fire'/1983 ∗ *Hammer House of Mystery and Suspense*: 'And the Wall Came Tumbling Down'/1984 ∗ *The Memoirs of Sherlock Holmes*: 'The Three Gables'/1995

Wynorski, Jim [Jim Wnorski] (b. 1950)

American director, writer, producer. *Fangoria* contributor then Roger **Corman** publicist, Wynorski helms derivatives and sequels. He shot a trailer for *Screamers* (1981), an Americanised recut of *L'isola degli uomini pesce* (*Island of the Mutations*, 1978), that was spliced into some prints. Fred Olen **Ray** team-ups *Dinosaur Island* (1993), *Scream Queen Hot Tub Party* (1993) and *Haunter of the Dark* (1994) are the natural outcome of his smirking, starlet-bound style. *The Lost Empire* (1983) remains his best attempt. DP

Forbidden World (w)/1982 ∗ *Chopping Mall/ 1985 ∗ Not of This Earth/1988 ∗ The Return of Swamp Thing/Transylvania Twist/1989 ∗ The Haunting of Morella/Sorority House Massacre II/ 1990 ∗ 976-EVIL II/Hard to Die/House IV* (w)/ *1991 ∗ Munchie* (+w)/*1992 ∗ Munchie Strikes Back/Ghoulies 4/1993 ∗ Sorceress/Biohazard II* (p)/*Dark Universe* (p)/*1994 ∗ Attack of the 60 Foot Centrefold* (a)/*1995 ∗ Munchy Strikes Back/ 1996*

TV: *Heartstoppers/1992 ∗ The Wasp Woman/ 1995 ∗ Vampirella/1996*

X Y Z

The X Files (US TV series, 1993–)

A cross between Jack Webb's *Project: UFO* (1978) and **Kolchak: The Night Stalker** (1974–5), with elements, and star David Duchovny, borrowed from **Twin Peaks** (1990–1). Created by Chris Carter, the show has agents Fox Mulder (Duchovny) and Dana Scully (Gillian Anderson) assigned to the X Files, the FBI's repository for inexplicable phenomena. Though many episodes deal with UFO encounters (a backstory is that Mulder's sister was abducted by aliens), there are stories of **werewolves**, **vampires**, **mutations**, **witchcraft**, **eco-horror**, **pos-**

Young Adult: Charlotte Burke, *Paperhouse*

session and reincarnation. Stirred in with paranormal elements are overlapping government conspiracies and subtle sexual tension between the leads.

Some episodes are modelled on films ('Ice', 1993, on *The Thing*, 1982; 'Beyond the Sea', 1993, on *Exorcist III*, 1990), but the high-points are originals: 'Squeeze' (1993), 'Eve' (1993), 'Miracle Man' (1994), 'Duane Barry' (1994), 'Irresistible' (1995), 'Humbug' (1995). The most popular horror-themed TV series to come out of the US (though shot in Canada, which is why X Files often involve bland urban locales and heavily wooded rural areas), the show has spun off novels (Charles **Grant**'s *Goblins*, 1994, *Whirlwind*, 1995), fanzines and comics.

Jane Goldman, *The X Files Book of the Unexplained* (1995); Brian Lowry, *The Truth Is Out There: The Official Guide to The X Files* (1995); N.E. Genge, *The Unofficial X Files Companion* (1995)

Yagher, Kevin (b. 1962)

American make-up artist, director. Having supervised creature effects for Chucky and Freddy, Yagher took to directing the Crypt Keeper wraparounds of *Tales From the Crypt* (1989–). His feature debut *Hellraiser: Bloodline* (1996) was troubled enough to emerge with an Allan **Smithee** credit.

*Trick or Treat/A Nightmare on Elm Street, Part 2: Freddy's Revenge/1986 * Retribution/A Nightmare on Elm Street, Part 3: The Dream Warriors/1987 * Child's Play/The Hidden/1988 * 976-EVIL/The Phantom of the Opera/1989 * Child's Play 2/The Borrower/Meet the Apple-gates/1990 * Child's Play 3/1991 Man's Best Friend/1993 * Children of the Corn III: Urban Harvest/ Rumplestiltskin/1994 * Tales From the Crypt: Demon Knight/1995 * Starship Troopers/1996*

TV: *Freddy's Nightmares*/1988–90 * *Tales From the Crypt*: 'Lower Berth' (d)/1990; 'Strung Along' (d)/1992

Yarbrough, Jean (1900–75)

American director. Yarbrough's Bs are degrees more perverse and imaginative than those of his contemporaries. At PRC and Monogram, he made *The Devil Bat* (1941), with **Lugosi** and enlarged bats, and *King of the Zombies* (1941), a creepy comedy with Mantan **Moreland**. At Universal, he was mainly given **Abbott and Costello** and musicals until slipping to the B unit for *House of Horrors* (1946) and *The Brute Man* (1946), twisted vehicles for the malformed Rondo **Hatton**. *The Creeper* (1948), his oddest film, is torn between 1940s **mad scientist** conventions and the bizarro style of *The Outer Limits* (1963–5). His saddest is a final theatrical credit, *Hillbillys in a Haunted House* (1967), with **Rathbone**, **Carradine** and **Chaney Jr** mixing with country stars.

She-Wolf of London/1946

Yarnell, Celeste (b. 1946)

American actress, a low-rent vamp effective as 'Diane Le Fanu', *The Velvet Vampire* (1971).

The Nutty Professor/1962 * *Beast of Blood*/1970

TV: *Wild Wild West*: 'The Night of a Thousand Eyes'/1965

The Yellow Peril * See: **Fu Manchu**

Young, Harold (1897–1959)

American director. Characterless Universal hack.

The Mummy's Tomb/1943 * *Jungle Captive*/*The Frozen Ghost*/1945

Young Adult

One of the most extraordinary growth areas in publishing from the mid-1980s onwards has been the rise in the category of Young Adult Horror. Not a new phenomenon, it is the natural successor to the teenage-skewed **EC comics** and drive-in movies of the '50s. These, in turn, owed their genesis not to the **pulp magazines** of the '20, which were aimed at a slightly older audience, but to the penny dreadfuls and Boys Papers of the 19th century. Magazines like the *The Boy's Own Paper* (1879–1967) were jingoistic in tone and relied heavily on what would now be considered s-f, but also included elements of horror. They drew the general opprobrium of parents, educators and even Parliament, but not, it would seem, the audience. Following both World Wars, many magazines fell by the wayside, and those which remained dropped the horror elements.

It was left to American comics to re-introduce blatant horror for teenagers. With Fredric Wertham's *The Seduction of the Innocent* (1954), a study of the corrupting influences of comic books, the tide turned against horror fiction for young readers. With the foundation of the Comics Code, overt horror disappeared from comic books and young adult fiction for more than two decades. But in the mid-1980s, publishers discovered that a significant number of readers of Stephen **King**, Dean **Koontz**, James **Herbert** and Shaun Hutson were teenagers. Given the existence of this market, many publishers launched lines explicitly aimed at satisfying teenage horror fans. While publishers and booksellers have enjoyed enormous success with some titles, many parents and teachers still find the concept distasteful.

The field is dominated by Christopher Pike and R.L. Stine. Pike's work is darker, more adult oriented and most certainly written to the older teenage market, often dealing with overtly sexual and violent themes. In *Die Softly* (1993), a young man who installs a hidden camera in the girl's showers witnesses a murder, while *Monster* (1993) opens with a teenager shooting two people with a shotgun during a party. Robert Lawrence Stine, 'the Stephen King for kids', has been undoubted master of the genre since the success of his first book, *Blind Date* (1986). In addition to 'young adult' titles, Stine has created, in the *Goosebumps* series, a horror line for readers aged from eight to ten. Though *The Amazing Mr. Blunden* (1971) and *Paperhouse* (1988) are effective and creepy adaptations of British supernatural novels written for children, *A Nightmare on Elm Street* (1984) is closer in feel to the American high-school world of Pike and Stine.

In America, horror films have always been thought of as teenage entertainment, and are so rated by **censorship** and classification bodies. It is unsurprising that many American films share themes, plot devices, characterisations and overall tone with young adult horror novels, even if they predate the trend: *Phantasm* (1979), *Silver Bullet* (1985), *The Monster Squad* (1987). Inevitably, there have been television series aimed at the market, *Are You Afraid of the Dark?* (1993–5) and the Stine spin-off *Goosebumps* (1995–). MSc

Younger, Henry * See: **Michael Carreras**

Yuzna, Brian (b. 1949)

Philippines-born American producer, director. Yuzna's inner auteur may wince at the

fact that his best known films are ones he produced, but his directing career seems to be on a solid trajectory. Since his shaky debut, *Bride of Re-Animator* (1988), both *Society* (1989), a nightmarish social satire disguised as a horror movie, and *Return of the Living Dead III* (1993) have earned praise. Yuzna made an entrance into the film industry with a bang as producer of the gleefully ghoulish *Re-Animator* (1985). Yuzna and director Stuart **Gordon** immediately made two more films together (*Dolls*, 1986; *From Beyond*, 1987) and cooked up the hugely successful Disney fantasy *Honey, I Shrunk the Kids* (1987) at a backyard barbecue. MM

Silent Night, Deadly Night 4: Initiation (+d)/ *Silent Night, Deadly Night 5: The Toymaker* (+w)/1990 * *The Guyver*/1991 * *Ticks*/1993 * *Necronomicon* (+co-d)/1994 * *Crying Freeman*/ *The Dentist*/1996

Zacherley [John Zacherle] (b. 19??)

American **horror host**. Originally 'Roland' (on Philadelphia's WCAU-TV, 1957–8) and then 'Zacherley' (on New York's WABC-TV and WOR-TV, 1958–63), 'the Cool Ghoul' hosted Universal horrors, chuckling in grey face-paint and frock coat. During a screening of *The Black Cat* (1934), he invented the idea of splicing himself into (and arguably ruining) the film. Popular enough for spin-off Top Ten singles ('Dinner With Drac', 1958) and a joke 1960 presidential campaign ('Put a Vampire in the White House'), he hosts *Geek Maggot Bingo* (1983) and the compilation *Horrible Horror* (1986). The voice of Elmer the Parasite in *Brain Damage* (1988).

Frankenhooker/1990 * *Niagravation*/1996

Zemeckis, Robert (b. 1951)

American director, writer, producer. In the wake of such enthused cross-genre blockbusters as the *Back to the Future* triptych (1985, 1989, 1990) and *Who Framed Roger Rabbit* (1988), Zemeckis fulfilled his wish to work in horror by executive-producing HBO's *Tales From the Crypt* (1989–). The spin-off feature *Tales From the Crypt: Bordello of Blood* (1996) is from the first script Zemeckis ever wrote with regular partner Bob Gale. *Death Becomes Her* (1992) is an unexpectedly brittle swipe at Hollywood manners in **zombie**-comic form. DP

Tales From the Crypt: Demon Knight (exec p)/ 1994 * *The Frighteners* (p)/1996

LEFT Robert Zemeckis

349

Zombies: *The Plague of the Zombies*

TV: *Kolchak: The Night Stalker*: 'Chopper'
(s)/1975 * *Amazing Stories*: 'Go To the Head
of the Class'/1986 * *Tales From the Crypt*: 'And
All Through the House'/'Yellow'/1989; 'You,
Murderer'/1995

Zito, Joe (b. 1946)

American director. Zito corrals Tom **Savini**
splatter effects in murderthons *The Prowler*
(1981) and *Friday the 13th: The Final Chapter*
(1984). Retrograde actioners include the
paranoid Chuck Norris peroration *Invasion
USA* (1985), which also uses Savini
violence. DP

Bloodrage (p)/1979

Zombies

Unlike those other horror staples **Dracula**,
Frankenstein and the **werewolf**, the zombie was a movie monster from the beginning. Horror literature was bereft of zombie
tales until well after they appeared in the
cinema.

The word 'zombie' entered the English
language with its appearance in William
Seabrook's study of **voodoo**, *The Magic Island*
(1929). *White Zombie* (1932), with Bela
Lugosi as a voodoo master enslaving the
Haitian dead, is a lurid extrapolation from
Seabrook's study. *Revolt of the Zombies* (1936),
drawing on another French colonial culture,
revives Cambodian corpses to fight in the
trenches. The delicate 'chiller' *I Walked With
a Zombie* (1943), the comedy *The Ghost
Breakers* (1940) and the late-coming *I Eat
Your Skin* (1964) offer more Caribbean
voodoo. *King of the Zombies* (1941) and
Revenge of the Zombies (1943), which have

voodoo trappings, actually involve **mad scientists** creating a **Nazi** super-race, a theme
which persists as late as *Shock Waves* (1977)
and *Le lac des morts vivants* (*Zombies' Lake*,
1980). Often mixing magical mumbo-jumbo
with mad science, and unsure whether its
hollow-eyed extras are revivified corpses or
hypnotised goons, none of these make it
exactly clear what the ontological status of a
zombie might be.

Only in the '60s did 'things' really start to
move. John **Gilling**'s *Plague of the Zombies*
(1966) dispenses with the bamboozling
blinds of exoticism. These **Hammer** zombies
are slaves of a local squire (and voodoo master) put to work down a Cornish tin mine,
and their status is explicitly clarified once
and for all – they are definitely reanimated
cadavers. *Plague* boasts a brilliant resurrec-

tion scene as the dead emerge from soily graves. They cut a much more alarming appearance than before, too, bearing expressions of ghastly, leering malice in place of the traditional blank look. The pure voodoo strain of zombie recurs in the **blaxploitation** *Sugar Hill* (1974) and the island-set *Zombi 2* (*Zombie Flesh Eaters*, 1980), and Wes **Craven**'s 'anthropological thriller' *The Serpent and the Rainbow* (1987) revolves around the mystery of how exactly zombie slaves are made (a drug called 'teteradotoxin' is involved).

Invasion of the Body Snatchers (1956) and other invasions offer unfeeling **doppelgängers** sometimes (as in *Quatermass 2*, 1958) explicitly called 'zombies', while other **aliens** stoop to possessing the dead *en masse* (*Invisible Invaders*, 1959) or reanimating them in ones and twos (*Plan 9 From Outer Space*, 1956). Richard Matheson's *I Am Legend* (1953) and the film version *The Last Man on Earth* (1964) offer vampires who act like zombies but can pass on their contagion with a bite. While the vampire creates a sort of perversely desirable club status for his undead victims, as they join him in nocturnal limbo, zombies (at best) reflect instead the fear of depersonalisation and alienation. The zombies, presented without even a whisper of eroticism, is far more than the vampire, the monster figure of the **apocalypse**.

This radical strain of zombie lore found an apotheosis in George **Romero**'s ferocious *Night of the Living Dead* (1968), a radical reworking of zombie lore that changed everything. The risen dead, called 'ghouls' rather than 'zombies', have a new purpose, albeit a hideously mindless one. Their one aim, propelling them into terrifying attacks, is to eat the flesh of the living. At a stroke they became not just scary-looking but horribly dangerous. The trappings of voodoo are gone; *Night* shows an almost total disinterest in cause-and-effect explanations. Instead, Romero's film exemplifies the horror of senseless, unmotivated attack. The characters' hysteria, panic and ultimate despair are generated by a pervading air of meaninglessness. The studied absence of real answers gave the film its shattering impact as much as the emergence of a new level of visceral horror. *Dawn of the Dead* (1978) and *Day of the Dead* (1985), Romero's sequels, usher in a further escalation of graphic violence, along with allegorical conceits about consumer society that upholster their raging pessimism.

Though *Let's Scare Jessica to Death* (1971) and *Messiah of Evil* (1973), with their senile vampire villagers, manage to build on the influence of *Night of the Living Dead*, most American imitations concentrate on gutmunching and slow-moving chases: *Children Shouldn't Play With Dead Things* (1972), *The Child* (1977), *The Children* (1980), *Raiders of the Living Dead* (1985), *Bloodsuckers From Outer Space* (1987), *Chopper Chicks in Zombie Town* (1989). More personal are those **'Monkey's Paw'** items that deal with the consequences not of mass zombification but of living with a single living dead person: *The Walking Dead* (1936), *Neither the Sea nor the Sand* (1972), *Dead of Night* (1974), *Kiss Daddy Goodbye* (1981), *La morte vivante* (*The Living Dead Girl*, 1983), *Dead Heat* (1988), *Pet Sematary* (1989), *My Boyfriend's Back* (1993).

Zombies embody a slippage of representation, where death has failed to contain the dead because it has been defined in terms inferior to the imagination. It's hardly surprising then that Catholic Italy should produce the most dedicated and compulsive volume of zombie films. Italian zombies carry an iconoclastic connotation by showing the implacable presence of something supernatural yet stubbornly corporeal, parading the flesh without the much-vaunted spirit. To Christians, the body is a mere waste-product, excreted by the passage of the soul into Heaven. Lucio **Fulci** explores this contiguence between the body as 'surplus of the soul' and as 'excretion' in his zombie films *Zombi 2* (1979), *Paura nella città dei morti viventi* (*City of the Living Dead*, 1980) and *L'aldilà* (*The Beyond*, 1981).

Stumbling along in Fulci's tracks came *Zombi holocaust* (1980), *Virus* (*Zombie Creeping Flesh*, 1980), *La notte erotiche dei morti viventi* (1980), *La notti del terrore* (*Zombi 3*, 1980), *Incubo sulla città contaminata* (*Nightmare City*, 1980) and *Zombi 3* (1988). From Spain, Jorge **Grau**'s **eco-horror** tale *No profanar el sueño de los muertos* (*Living Dead at the Manchester Morgue*, 1974) anticipated the glorious carnage of Fulci's zombie epics, and Amando de **Ossorio**'s *La noche del terror ciego* (*Tombs of the Blind Dead*, 1971) provided a classically creepy ambience with its withered, skeletal zombies on horseback. Jean **Rollin** diverted

Zombies: Frances Dee, the shadow of Darby Jones, *I Walked with a Zombie*

himself from vampires to essay a few zombie films, including the Grau imitation *Les raisins de la mort* (*Pesticide*, 1978). And Jesús **Franco** arrived at the blood feast with *Una vergine tra i morti viventi* (*Virgin Among the Living Dead*, 1970), *La tumba de los muertos vivientes* (*Oasis of the Living Dead*, 1981) and *La mansión de los muertos vivientes* (1982).

In the wake of *Dawn of the Dead*'s intermittent slapstick, American films began to play the living dead for **comedy**. *Return of the Living Dead* (1985), an unofficial sequel to Romero's debut, spurred the trend, showing American punks slaughtered by shambling comic-strip ghouls. Like *Re-Animator* (1985), it manages to combine thrills with the tacky humour, but the approach led downhill; first into a series of bungling sequels and crass heavy-metal horror items (*Night Life*, 1989), then to total burn-out in New Zealander Peter **Jackson**'s *Braindead* (1992) – wall-to-wall comedy **splatter** in an ear-to-ear vacuum. The social criticism of Romero's trilogy is rendered absurd by gore fans' gormless desire to *be* zombies; and film-makers now find it hard to resurrect the dead as figures of

George Zucco

terror. Perhaps the only harrowing zombies of the 1990s are the dazed heroin addicts in Abel **Ferrara**'s *Bad Lieutenant* (1992). ST

Rose London, *Zombie: The Living Dead* (1976)

Zucco, George (1886–1960)
British actor, the poor man's **mad scientist**. Despite Hollywood success as a supporting player in major films, he starred in numerous poverty-row productions, often alongside poor old **Lugosi** and **Carradine**. A first-rate Moriarty in *The Adventures of Sherlock Holmes* (1939), even he had the career sense to pull out of *Return of the Ape Man* (1944), though he still shared star billing and can be glimpsed in a few scenes as the thawed-out caveman. SJ

The Man Who Could Work Miracles/1936 * *Charlie Chan in Honolulu*/1938 * *The Cat and the Canary*/*The Hunchback of Notre Dame*/1939 * *The Mummy's Hand*/1940 * *The Monster and the Girl*/*Topper Returns*/1941 * *Dr Renault's Secret*/*The Mummy's Tomb*/*The Mad Monster*/1942 * *Dead Men Walk*/*The Mad Ghoul*/*The Black Raven*/1943 * *The Mummy's Ghost*/*Shadows in the Night*/*Voodoo Man*/*One Body Too Many*/*House of Frankenstein*/1944 * *Fog Island*/*The Flying Serpent*/1945 * *Moss Rose*/*Lured*/*Scared to Death*/1947 * *Who Killed 'Doc' Robbin?*/1948 * *The Secret Garden*/1949